Finding The Right Pitch

A Guide To The Study Of Music Fundamentals

OR

An Introduction To Music Theory

David Nivans

California State University Dominguez Hills

World Bet Books

Copyright © 2012 David Nivans

All rights reserved. No part of this publication may be reproduced, transmitted, stored in a retrieval system or a database in any form or by any means, be it graphic, electronic, or mechanical, including but not limited to photocopying, recording, scanning, digitizing, or otherwise, without prior written permission of the publisher.

World Bet Books
www.worldbetbooks.com
worldbetbooks@gmail.com

ISBN 978-1-937214-00-5

Library of Congress Control Number: 2011928530

This book is printed on acid-free paper.

To the Memory of

Wally Bower

1929–2008

About the Author

David Nivans holds a Ph.D. in historical musicology from University of California Los Angeles. He has taught courses in music fundamentals, harmony, counterpoint, musicianship, world music, music appreciation, music and art appreciation, music history, and surveys of popular music, jazz, rock, and film music. Dr. Nivans is also the author of *Introduction To Music Fundamentals And Lead-Sheet Terminology* and *Finding The Right Pitch: A Guide To The Study Of Basic Harmony*.

TABLE OF CONTENTS

Preface xi

Chapter 1 Time and Performance 1

    Ties and Dots 3

    Meter and Beat 4

    Divisions of Beats 5

    Time Signatures 5

    Counting Note Values 7

    Rhythm 9

    Syncopation 9

    Displacement 10

    Hemiola 11

    Repeat Signs 12

    First and Second Endings 13

    Da Capo al Fine, Dal Segno al Fine, Da Capo al Coda, and *Dal Segno al Coda* 14

    Performance Marks 16

    Tempo 16

    Dynamics 17

    Rarely-Used Note Values 17

Chapter 2 Pitch 19

    Accidentals and Enharmonic Equivalency 20

    Chromatic and Diatonic Half Steps 22

    The Great Staff and Clefs 23

    Octave Registers 25

    Octave Signs 29

Chapter 3   The Major Scale 31

Moving the Major Scale to Octaves Other Than C with the Addition of Sharps 33

Moving the Major Scale to Octaves Other Than C with the Addition of Flats 41

Singing the Major Scale 48

Articulation Marks 49

Singing the Chromatic Scale 50

Chapter 4   Major Key Signatures 51

The Circle of 5ths 53

Identifying Major Key Signatures 55

Diatonicism, Chromaticism, Tonality, and Atonality 55

Chapter 5   Intervals 57

The Essential Diatonic Intervals of Major 58

Two Principles for Recognizing and Constructing the Qualities of Intervals 59

When the Bottom Pitch of the Interval Is Not Scale Degree 1 of C Major 62

When the Bottom Pitch Does Not Correspond to One
of the Fourteen Transpositions of C Major 65

The Principle of Like Inflection 66

Compound Intervals 67

Interval Inversion 68

Constructing Intervals Below a Given Tone: the Practical Application of Interval Inversion 69

Consonance and Dissonance 72

Chapter 6 The Minor Mode 75

The Natural Minor Mode 75

The Relative Minor 76

The Parallel Minor and the Parallel Major 77

The Relative Major 78

The Circle of 5ths for Minor 79

The Harmonic Minor Mode 81

The Melodic Minor Mode 82

The Ascending Form of the Melodic Minor 82

The Descending Form of the Melodic Minor 83

Finding the Variable Scale Degrees in the Minor Mode 84

Comparing the Three Forms of Minor 84

Singing the Three Forms of Minor 86

Chapter 7 Advanced Concepts in Meter 87

Section 1: Simple and Compound Meter Exchange 87

    Triplets 87

    Duplets 91

    Alternative Notation 95

    Fitting an Irregular Group into the Meter at the Level
        of the Beat or the Division of the Beat 95

Section 2: Other Irregular Groupings of Notes Occurring within the Span of a Single Beat 98

Section 3: Other Irregular Groupings of Notes Extending Across Two or More Beats 101

Section 4: Asymmetrical Meter 105

Chapter 8 Triads 107

    Triad Quality 109

    Triad Qualities in Major 111

    Inverting the Major Triad 114

    Inverting the Minor Triad 116

    Inverting the Diminished Triad 116

    Inverting the Augmented Triad 117

    Identifying Triad Position 119

    Identifying Triad Quality in Root Position 119

    Applying the Principle of Like Inflection to Triads 120

    When the Root of the Triad Does Not Represent
        One of the Fourteen Transpositions of C Major 121

    Identifying Triad Quality in $\frac{6}{3}$ and $\frac{6}{4}$ Positions 123

    Constructing the Four Triad Qualities in Root Position 126

    Option 1: Using the Major Triad as a Prototype for Root-Position Constructions 126

    Option 2: Measuring the Intervallic Content of the Triad for Root-Position Constructions 130

    Constructing the Four Triad Qualities in $\frac{6}{3}$ and $\frac{6}{4}$ Positions 133

    Enharmonic Respelling of Triads 137

    Triad Qualities in Minor 138

    Roman Numeral Chord Symbols 140

    Contextualization of Triads 142

    Triads in $\frac{5}{3}$ Position 142

    Triads in $\frac{6}{3}$ and $\frac{6}{4}$ Positions 151

    Four-Part Texture 154

    Triad Voicing 154

    Vocal Range 155

    Close and Open Structure 156

    Spacing Between Adjacent Voices 156

Stem Direction 157
The Doubling of Chord Tones in Four-Voice Texture 157
Tonality and the Names of the Scale Degrees 159
The Harmonic Series 161
Omitting the Fifth in Four-Voice Texture 162
Singing the Four Triad Qualities in All Chord Positions 162

Appendix A   **Rhythmic Exercises** **167**

Appendix B   **Rhythmic Exercises: Two Hands** **195**

Appendix C   **The Church Modes** **217**

Appendix D   **The Cadential Six-Four Chord** **235**

Appendix E   **The Dominant Seventh Chord** **239**

Appendix F   **The Cadence** **243**

Appendix G   **Nonharmonic Tones** **253**

Glossary **265**

Index **279**

Worksheets **287**

Preface

A few years ago, I told a senior colleague about my plans to write a music fundamentals text, to which he responded: "Oh great, just what the world needs, another music fundamentals book." He considered all fundamentals books to be virtually interchangeable, simplistic, and useless. Although I was surprised by his comment, I soon realized that my colleague was probably right; music education hardly needs another fundamentals book. There ought to be a good reason for the present volume, and there is.

Making the Transition from Music Fundamentals to Basic Harmony

Today, primary and secondary education provides very little formal instruction in music, leaving many college students who would identify music as their degree objective ill-prepared to meet the challenges that await them. As a consequence, students begin the study of fundamentals with vastly different levels of musical knowledge and experience.

In most colleges and universities, the music theory sequence spans about two years (or less). Many institutions have one fundamentals class and two or three harmony courses. Some schools separate music majors from non-music majors and offer a different fundamentals course to each group. At other schools, music fundamentals is split into two consecutive courses. The sequence begins with a class containing both music majors and non-music majors; however, the students in the latter group rarely continue their music education beyond the first course in fundamentals.

Ostensibly, the second course prepares music majors for a successful outcome in harmony. But sometimes, such preparation is ineffective; and for students who had difficulty with music fundamentals, the struggle continues. Despite the good intentions of authors and educators, having different pedagogies for music fundamentals and basic harmony often produces a disconnect, indeed a chasm, between the two courses. Some students who complete music fundamentals and who subsequently enroll in a harmony class find their second course in music to be considerably more challenging than their first.

Making the transition from music fundamentals to harmony can be problematic. One obvious solution would be to offer a fundamentals book that meets the needs of both music majors and non-music majors. Unfortunately, the vast majority of music fundamentals books are designed for the general student population rather than for those majoring in music.

Finding The Right Pitch: A Guide To The Study Of Music Fundamentals is intended for both groups. Students who are not pursuing a career in music should confine their reading to selected topics according to personal preferences or the priorities of an instructor. However, students who want to continue learning about music after completing fundamentals should conduct a more thorough inspection of the text, including all of the appendices and worksheets.

The Worksheets

The worksheets, which follow the index, may serve as either practice exercises, homework assignments, or test materials. Since metric and rhythmic skills are acquired over time through a continuous study of music's temporal framework, exercises for meter and rhythm accompany each chapter of worksheets. Thus, the student learns about pitch, scale, the major mode, key signatures, intervals, the minor mode, and triads while also exploring the properties of meter and rhythm. At this writing, the worksheets are available as free downloads at www.worldbetbooks.com.

The Appendices

The metric and rhythmic exercises in Appendix A should be used with Chapters 1–8. For those who would focus solely on meter and rhythm, Chapters 1 and 7, Appendices A and B, and appropriate exercises from the worksheets form a separate course of study. The exercises in Appendix B promote bilateral hand-to-hand coordination, a skill usually reserved for drummers.

Appendices C, D, E, F, and G contain excerpts from my *Finding The Right Pitch: A Guide To The Study Of Basic Harmony*. I have included them in this text to provide both instructors and students with some additional options for the study of music fundamentals. Accordingly, the appendices present concise treatments of the dominant seventh chord, the church modes, cadences, the cadential six-four chord, and nonharmonic tones.

Guide To The Study Of Basic Harmony focuses on voice leading, a process that controls the linear succession of tones in each voice (i.e., melodic line), optimizing how each voice moves through time in relation to the rest of the musical texture. *Basic Harmony* covers

(1) the formation and construction of triads within the church mode system;
(2) singing, transposing, and identifying the church modes;
(3) the different types of six-four chords;
(4) cadence formation;
(5) harmonic and contrapuntal progressions;
(6) the properties of seventh chords;
(7) the formation of seventh chords within the church modes and the major-minor tonal system;
(8) using the interval of the 7th to improve voice leading;
(9) real and apparent seventh chords;
(10) interlocking seventh chords;
(11) harmonic and contrapuntal sequences;
(12) the two-progression framework;
(13) singing seventh chords in all positions from a common bass pitch;
(14) the utility of nonharmonic tones for correcting faulty motion between chords;
(15) the application of voice-leading principles and chord progression to the piano keyboard.

Ninety worksheets complete the study of basic harmony.

Acknowledgments

I extend my lasting gratitude to the following people for giving generously of their time to review portions of the manuscript: Marius Sapkus; Tommy Harrison, Jacksonville University; Alyson McLamore, Cal Poly San Luis Obispo; Tom Owens, El Camino College; Ted Stern, Glendale College; and David Bradfield, California State University Dominguez Hills.

Wally Bower

Finally, this work is a tribute to my teacher, the late Wallace Henry Bower, Jr., professor of music theory at El Camino College in Torrance, California. Wally was a gifted pianist, brilliant composer, and an excellent teacher with a wonderful sense of humor that served him well throughout his distinguished career.

David Nivans

Chapter 1 Time and Performance

The creation of music involves the organization of two complementary elements: sound and silence. An aural art that depends on the unfolding of time for its performance and appreciation, music is produced from fixed units of duration called notes and rests. Notes represent musical sound, while rests represent musical silence. Musical sound and silence are signified in written form by the shapes of the notes and rests that exist on a set of five parallel lines and four spaces called a **staff**.

Example 1–1 illustrates the differences in the shapes of the various musical sounds on the staff. Both whole notes and half notes appear as oval hollowed-out structures. This structure is called the **note head**. Quarter notes, eighth notes, sixteenth notes, thirty-second notes, and sixty-fourth notes all have filled-in note heads.

All notes smaller than the whole note contain a **stem** (1–1). Eighth notes, sixteenth notes, thirty-second notes, and sixty-fourth notes also carry a **flag**, an additional component that is always attached to the right side of the stem. Eighth notes have one flag, sixteenth notes two, thirty-second notes three, and sixty-fourth notes four. As we shall soon see, any two notes with flags may be joined together with a thick horizontal line called a **beam**. Since half notes and quarter notes do not have flags, neither can they have beams.

Example 1–1: note values on the staff

Another significant aspect of a note's musical shape involves its location on the staff and the position of its stem (1–1). If a stemmed note in a single vocal or instrumental part occurs above the center line, then the stem proceeds downwards from the left side of the note head. If a stemmed note in a single vocal or instrumental part occurs below the center line, then the stem proceeds upwards from the right of the note head. If a stemmed note is located on the center line, then the stem may point in either direction according to the musical context. In most cases, however, the stem of a note on the center line points down.

The staff is also the means by which **pitches** (see Chapter 2) can be distinguished from one another in written form. The relative highness or lowness of any pitch corresponds to the highness or lowness of the line or space of the staff on which the pitch is located. In 1–1 above, the notes with downward stems are higher in pitch than those with upward stems. (Although the highness or lowness of a pitch is best represented with a staff, musical durations can be indicated without a staff.)

Example 1–2 displays the shapes of the corresponding rests for each of the notes discussed above. Both the whole rest and half rest resemble a black rectangular box. Counting the lines from the bottom of the staff, the whole rest hangs on the fourth line, while the half rest stands on the center line. Unlike the notes on the staff, which can appear on any space or line, the rests are always located in the same position.

Example 1–2: rest values on the staff

The design for the quarter rest, consisting of diagonal and curved lines, is dissimilar to all the other rests, resembling a bird flying sideways at a 90-degree angle to the earth. The remaining eighth, sixteenth, thirty-second, and sixty-fourth rests have one, two, three, and four hooks respectively, with each hook pointing towards the left. The eighth-note rest, with its single hook, resembles the number 7; while the sixteenth, thirty-second, and sixty-fourth rests add to this number one hook for each shorter rest value. (Though rarely used, both the double whole note and the one hundred and twenty-eighth note, as well as their respective rests, are discussed at the end of this chapter and shown in examples 1–24, 25, and 26.)

As indicated in example 1–3, half notes, quarter notes, eighth notes, sixteenth notes, thirty-second notes, and sixty-fourth notes have a mathematical relationship to each other and to the whole note. Assuming that the duration of the whole note carries a relative value of "one," two halves, four quarters, eight eighths, sixteen sixteenths, thirty-two thirty-seconds, and sixty-four sixty-fourths will all fill the span of a single whole note. Further, two quarters fill the duration of a single half note, two eighths equal a single quarter, two sixteenths equal a single eighth, two thirty-seconds equal a single sixteenth, and two sixty-fourths equal a single thirty-second. Thus, smaller note divisions in relation to the whole note exhibit the following equivalent durations:

Example 1–3: mathematical relationships between note values

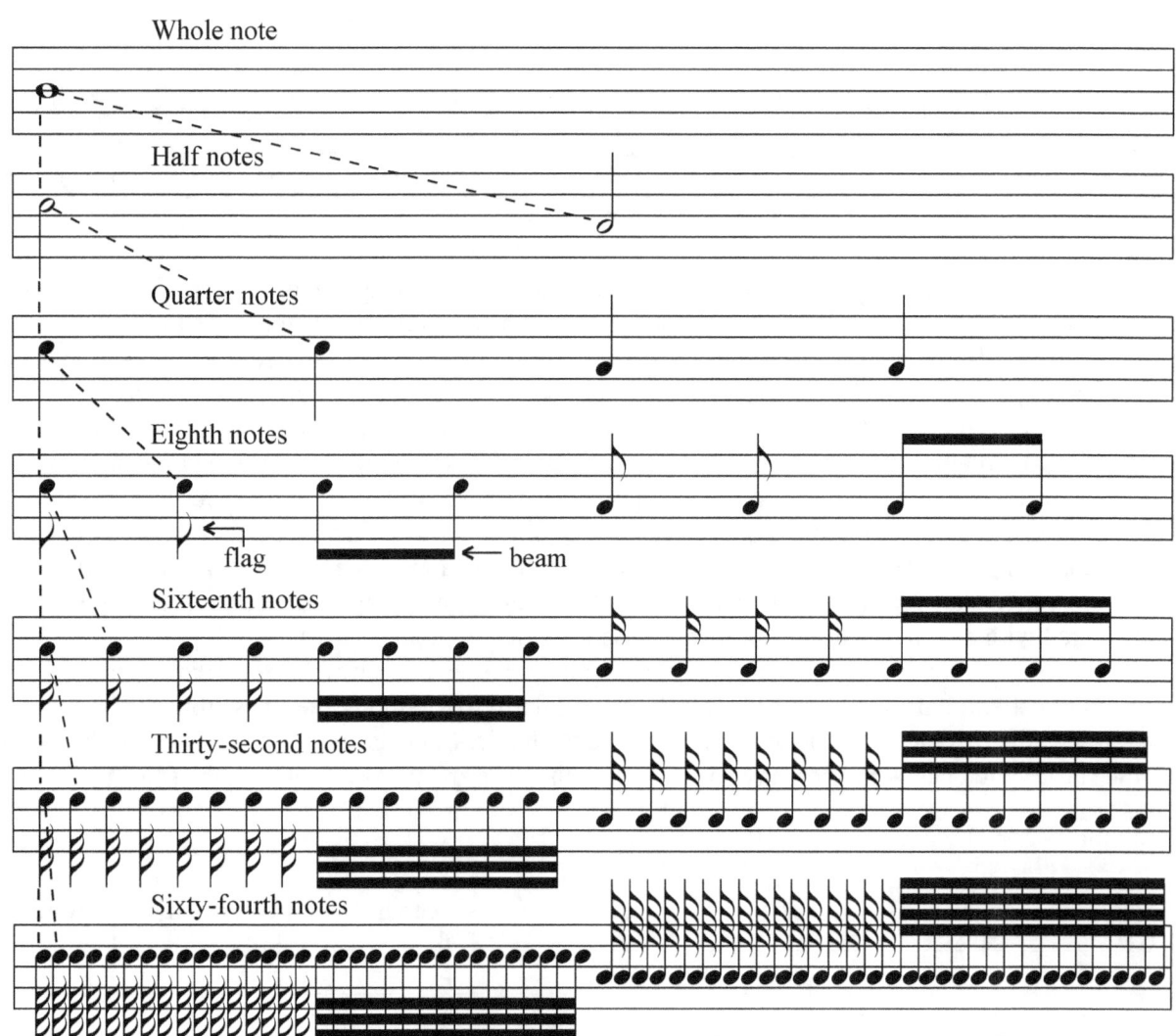

Example 1–3 above demonstrates how two or more notes with flags may be joined together with a corresponding number of beams. Eighth notes may have one beam, sixteenth notes two, thirty-second notes three, and sixty-fourth notes four. The common practice in music today is to use beams rather than flags whenever both options are available, as beamed notes are easier to read than flagged notes. In vocal music, however, the former practice was to assign one or more flags to any duration smaller than a quarter note that carried a single syllable of text.

It is also possible to group different note values together with beams. Moreover, in certain cases, the use of beams may appear to contradict the principle of stem position. For example, if most of the notes of a group take upward stems, then all of the notes will be stemmed up and beamed above the notes. Conversely, if most of the notes of a group take downward stems, then all of the notes will be stemmed down and beamed below the notes (see the dotted lines and circled notes in example 1–4).

Example 1–4: stem direction

Ties and Dots

There are two different ways to extend the duration of any note: with a **tie** or a **dot**. A tie, as shown in example 1–5, is a curved line that connects two or more notes together; however, only the first note of any tied pair or group of notes is articulated. The second note of the tied pair (or group of notes) is sustained for the duration of the note values presented. Tied notes are particularly useful for extending the duration of a note across the **bar line** (we shall discuss the bar line in the next section).

The second way to extend the duration of a note is to add a dot to it, as shown in example 1–6. The addition of a dot extends the duration of a note (or rest) by *one half its original value*. The tied notes in 1–5 correspond to the dotted note and rest values in 1–6. Thus, the whole note tied to the half note on the center line of 1–5 corresponds to the dotted whole note on the center line of 1–6. The same holds true for the other tied and dotted values on each of the lines and spaces in both examples.

Adding a second dot extends the duration of a note (or rest) by *one half the value of the first dot*. Therefore, if a single dot extends the duration of a quarter note by one eighth, a second dot extends the duration by one sixteenth. If a single dot extends the duration of a half note by one quarter note, a second dot extends the duration by one eighth.

Meter and Beat

In music, notes and rests are organized into a series of pulses, or beats. Some of these beats are theoretically stronger and receive more emphasis than others. The stronger beats, or stressed beats, are called **primary accents**. Indicated in example 1–7 with the uppercase letter P, they are the first accents we perceive when hearing a stream of accents unfold in time as a piece of music is being performed. The weaker beats, or unstressed beats, are called **secondary accents**, indicated in 1–7 with the letter s.

Usually, the notes and rests that signify both the primary and secondary accents of a musical composition are arranged in various configurations that produce a larger temporal framework called **meter**. As demonstrated in 1–7, it is the distance between primary accents that determines the meter (see the brackets in the example), a distance measured by the number of intervening secondary accents that both precede and follow the primary accents.

At least two basic types of meter, namely, duple and triple, arise from the distances that span any two primary accents. Duple meter (1–7a) has one intervening secondary accent between primary accents: P s P s. Quadruple meter (1–7b), a subcategory of duple meter, has three intervening secondary accents: P s S s P s S s, the second of which receives more stress than the first or third (notice the uppercase S). The other main type of meter, triple meter (1–7c), has two intervening secondary accents: P s s P s s. Duple, quadruple, and triple meters are all considered to be **symmetrical meters** because they can be divided evenly by either 2 or 3.

The distance between two primary accents, in addition to producing meter, constitutes a unit of measured musical space. And each unit so measured is marked off by vertical lines called bar lines, or measure lines. The spaces these lines enclose are called **measures**, or **bars**.

The value of the beat for the measures of duple, quadruple, and triple meters displayed in 1–7 is the quarter note. To count primary and secondary accents within duple, quadruple, and triple meters, we use the numbers: 1-2, 1-2-3-4, and 1-2-3 respectively.

Example 1–7: the distance between primary accents in duple, quadruple, and triple meters

a. duple meter (two beats per measure, one secondary accent between primary accents)

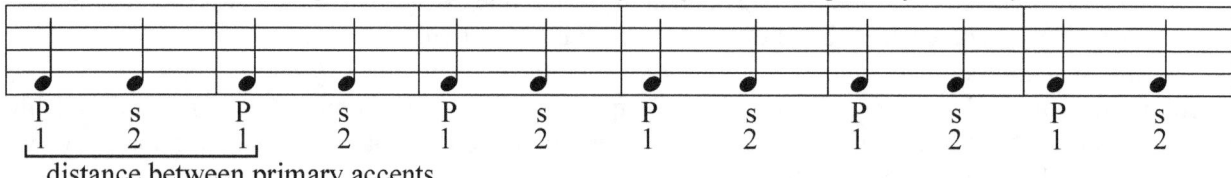

b. quadruple meter (four beats per measure, three secondary accents between primary accents)

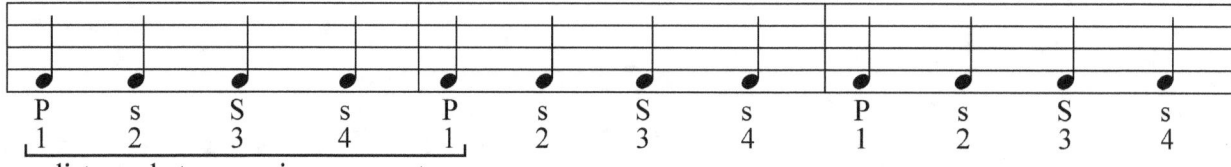

c. triple meter (three beats per measure, two secondary accents between primary accents)

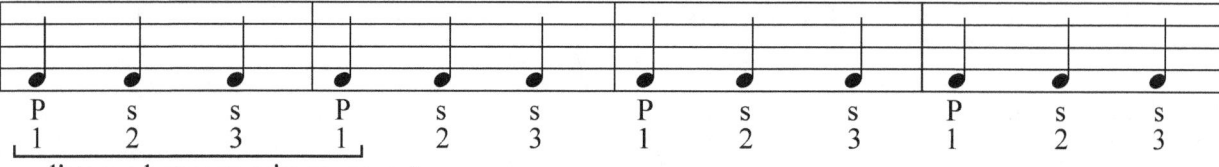

Divisions of Beats

There are two basic ways to divide the beat of any meter. If each of the beats is divided into two equal parts (or multiples of two), then the meter is classified as **simple**. If, however, each of the beats is divided into three equal parts (or multiples of three), then the meter is classified as **compound**. Therefore, any duple, quadruple, or triple meter may have either a simple division or compound division of the beat.

As shown in example 1–8, the first simple division of the quarter-note beat is the eighth note while the second division is the sixteenth note (on beat 2 of the first measure, a quarter rest is used instead of a quarter note). *A plus sign indicates the location of where the second half of each quarter-note beat falls.*

Example 1–8: simple duple meter

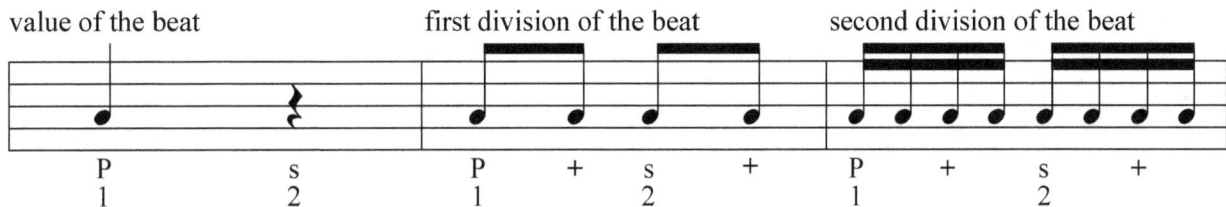

The next example illustrates the difference between a duple meter with a *simple* division of the beat and a duple meter with a *compound* division of the beat. In the latter (example 1–9b), the value of the beat is a dotted quarter note (on beat 2 of the first measure, a dotted quarter rest is used instead of a dotted quarter note). As we have said, the beat of a compound meter is divided into three equal parts or multiples of three. A dotted quarter can be divided into either three eighth notes (the first compound division) or six sixteenth notes (the second division).

Example 1–9: simple and compound duple meter

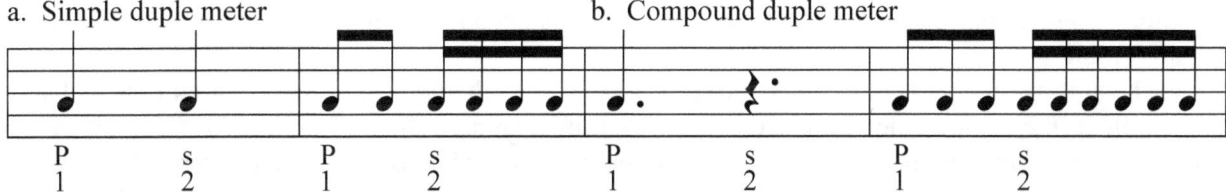

Time Signatures

Examples 1–8 and 9 demonstrate how some of the most basic configurations of notes and rests may occur within simple and compound meters. It is not difficult to see where these configurations of notes and rests coincide with the primary and secondary accents because they are clearly marked. Since the primary and secondary accents are not so identified in actual music, it would be helpful to have a sign or symbol that could tell us the value of the beat and how many beats are distributed across each measure.

The **time signature**, or **meter signature**, provides this valuable information. Consisting of two components, the time signature appears as a pair of Arabic numbers, one located directly above the other. If the meter is simple, then the top number designates the number of beats per measure and the bottom number reveals the value of each beat. All simple meters are read in this way.

If, therefore, the bottom number is 4 in a simple meter, then the value of the beat is the quarter note. There are two quarter-note beats per measure in example 1–10a, four quarter-note beats per measure in 1–10b, and three quarter-note beats per measure in 1–10c. Had the bottom number in examples 1–10a, 10b, and 10c been 16, the value of the beat would have been a sixteenth note. Had the bottom number been 32, the value of the beat would have been a thirty-second note.

Example 1–10: simple meters

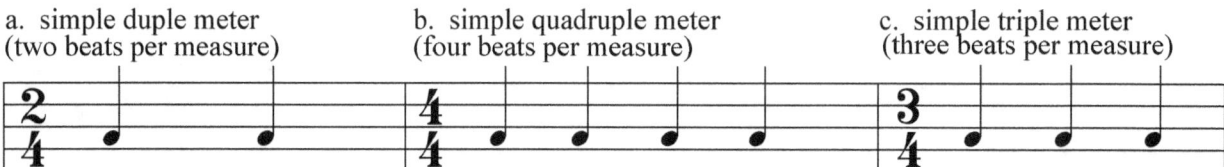

The reading of compound time signatures is somewhat more complicated. If we attempt to read the meters represented in example 1–11 according to the method for reading simple meters described above, then 1–11a would have six eighth-note beats per measure, 1–11b would have twelve eighth-note beats per measure, and 1–11c would have nine eighth-note beats per measure. But as we shall see presently, this is usually not the way to interpret compound signatures, unless the meter is performed very slowly (see below, p. 8).

In order to identify, read, and classify compound meters accurately, it is necessary to perform a basic arithmetic operation. If dividing the number 3 into the top number of the time signature results in a quotient is 2, 3, or 4, then the number of beats per measure is 2, 3, or 4 (for an example of a time signature with a quotient greater than 4, see Chapter 7, p. 106). To determine the value of the beat, take the note value that the bottom number represents, proceed to the note value that is one denomination higher, and add a dot to that note value.

If the bottom number is 8, which signifies an eighth note, then proceed to the quarter note and add a dot; therefore, the value of the beat is a dotted quarter. In examples 1–11a, 11b, and 11c, the value of the beat is the dotted quarter note with two, four, and three beats distributed across each respective measure. Had the bottom number in examples 1–11a, 11b, and 11c been 16, the value of the beat would have been a dotted eighth. Had the bottom number been 32, the value of the beat would have been a dotted sixteenth.

Example 1–11: compound meters

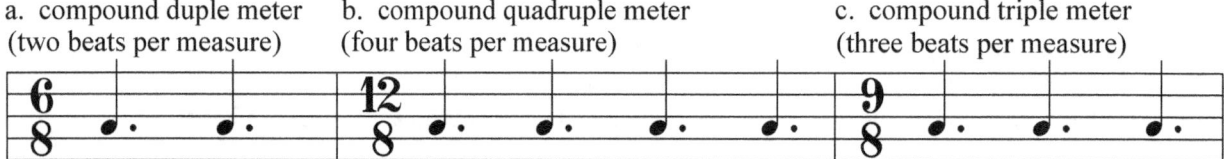

Nearly all time signatures resemble those shown above: pairs of Arabic numbers with one number located directly above the other. There are, however, two principal exceptions to this practice, each of which involves a symbol that looks somewhat like the letter C. The first symbol (example 1–12a), often referred to as "common time," is the equivalent of $\frac{4}{4}$ time. The second symbol (1–12b), often referred to as either "cut time" or *alla breve*, is the same as $\frac{2}{2}$ time. Here, the value of the beat is the half note while the first division of that beat is the quarter note.

At this point, we will dispense with marking primary and secondary accents with P and s and instead use numbers to represent each beat. The first division of the beat is indicated with a plus sign on the second half of each beat. Counting beats and half beats will be explained in more detail in the following section.

Example 1–12: common time and cut time

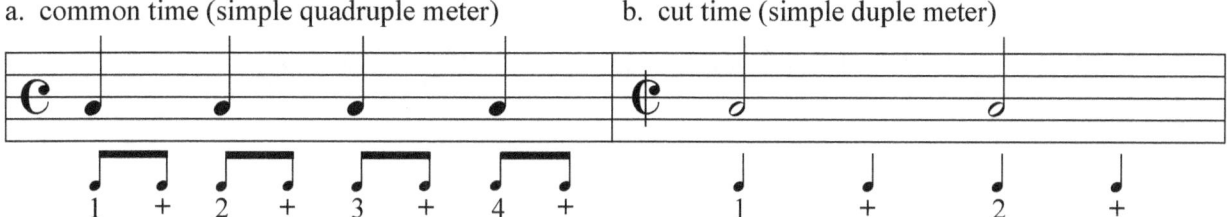

Counting Note Values

When performing or reading note values such as those put forward in examples 1–8 and 12b, musicians vocalize or internalize the numbers and plus signs. Usually, musicians counting aloud replace the plus sign with the word "and." Accordingly, both the beat and the first division of the beat in, say, 1–12b would be expressed as: "one and two and." If we include the second and third divisions of the beat, as in example 1–13, then additional syllables may be used.

With the quarter note as the value of the beat, the second division brings us to the level of the sixteenth note—four sixteenth notes fill the duration of one quarter. For each group of four sixteenths, the syllables "e" (pronounced ee) and "a" (pronounced uh or ah) are applied to the second and fourth sixteenth notes respectively. Counting at the level of the third division requires no additional syllables beyond those already employed for the second division.

We shall avoid adding syllables beyond the second division of the beat in simple meter because vocalizing or internalizing syllables and words becomes unwieldy if the note values are performed at a very quick pace. In any event, it can be seen that the note values in 1–13 all have a mathematical relationship to each other: a single quarter note can be divided into two eighths, four sixteenths, or eight thirty-seconds (the "in 2" designation in the example means that there are two beats to each measure).

Example 1–13: counting the first, second, and third divisions of the beat in simple duple meter (in 2)

Earlier, we said that the reading of time signatures for compound meter is more complicated than reading those for simple meter. Two different methods for counting aid the performance and reading of note values in compound meter. Example 1–14 illustrates the first method. The value of the beat is the dotted quarter note. The first division of the beat would be counted as: 1 + a 2 + a ("one and uh two and uh").

Notice that for the second division of the beat, each intervening sixteenth note does not receive a syllable. For the third division of the beat, only six of twenty-four thirty-second notes are counted. As in example 1–13, the note values in 1–14 all have a mathematical relationship to each other: a dotted quarter note can be divided into three eighths, six sixteenths, or twelve thirty-seconds.

Example 1–14: counting the first, second, and third divisions of the beat in compound duple meter (in 2)

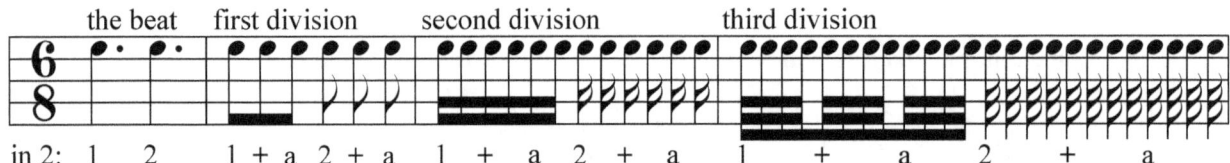

The second method for performing and reading compound meter appears to contradict the process of classifying time signatures by dividing three into the top number and by adding a dot to the note value that is one denomination higher than the bottom number (see above, p. 6). That compound meters are sometimes performed very slowly accounts for the apparent contradiction. When a compound meter such as $\frac{6}{8}$ is performed slowly, we hear the first division rather than the dotted quarter note as the value of the beat. Thus, the meter in 1–14 above would be interpreted as having not *two* beats per measure but *six* and the value of the beat would be the eighth note, not the dotted quarter.

Example 1–15 demonstrates how the preceding example would be counted if the notes were played slowly. When interpreting the first division of a compound meter as the value of the beat, the note values are counted with the syllables used in simple meter. According to this method, the second division of compound meter is counted as if it were in simple meter with every note receiving a syllable.

Example 1–15: counting compound duple meter with six beats to the measure

Showing the two methods of counting together, the numbers and syllables for both the beats and first divisions of beats in $\frac{6}{8}$ meter should coincide according to the pattern indicated in example 1–16.

Example 1–16: counting compound duple meter (in 2 and in 6)

Example 1–17 illustrates the coincidence of numbers and syllables for both the second and third divisions of the beat in $\frac{6}{8}$ meter.

Example 1–17: counting compound duple meter (in 2 and in 6)

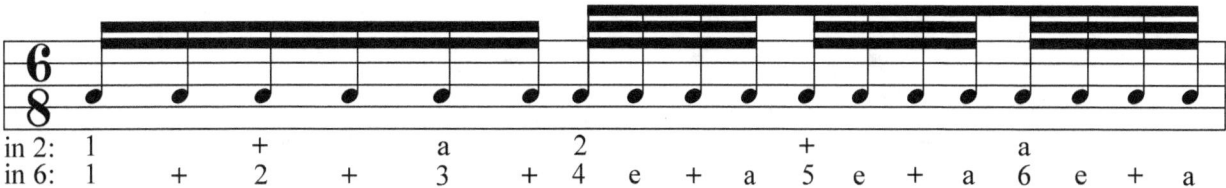

Rhythm

If meter is the distance between two primary accents, then **rhythm** is the measurement of both the primary and secondary accents within that meter. Rhythm involves how the accents are organized, or configured. In the preceding exercises and examples, we have seen various types of rhythmic configurations. Some of the rhythms presented in this chapter are quite simple to read, count, and interpret, while others are more challenging for the beginning music student.

It would be instructive to tap out the rhythm to the song "Jingle Bells" to see if your friends can identify the music without actually hearing the words or the tune. Not surprisingly, most listeners recognize the music from hearing only the rhythm. To be sure, the song has a very distinctive rhythmic profile. But in any case, we can take from this exercise the following lesson: *rhythm is that particular arrangement of notes and rests within each measure that ultimately helps to inform the individuality of a musical composition.*

Syncopation

Under normal musical conditions, we expect notes of longer duration to fall on primary accents and those of shorter duration to occur on secondary accents. When divisions of beats are emphasized and/or when the strongest part of the primary accent is left either unarticulated or weakened in some way, it disrupts the regular distribution of note values and creates an effect known as **syncopation**. *Syncopation makes strong that which is otherwise weak.*

Musicians produce syncopations by using ties, rests, or shorter notes followed by longer ones. The syncopated figure in example 1–18a shifts the focus to the first division of the quarter-note beat by introducing an eighth note on the strongest part of the primary accent and following it with a quarter, a note value that is twice as long as the preceding eighth.

Example 1–18: four types of syncopation

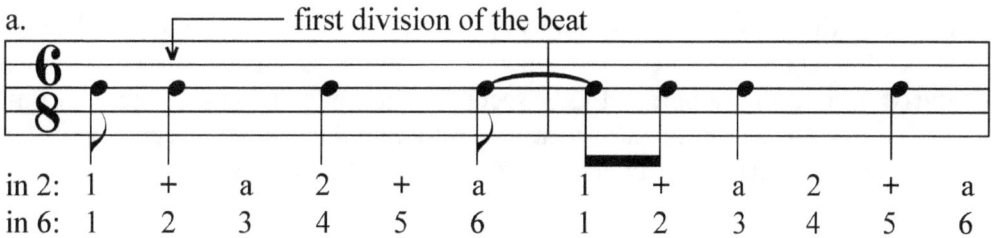

Example 1–18b shows syncopation within the second division of the beat at the level of the sixteenth note. The rhythmic syllables in parentheses indicate that their inclusion here adds nothing to the basic count and that their absence would not obscure the recognition of any of the beats or first divisions of beats.

An eighth rest produces the syncopation in the first measure of 1–18c. The second measure of 1–18c weakens the first part of the primary accent with the placement of two sixteenth notes followed by an eighth tied to a sixteenth.

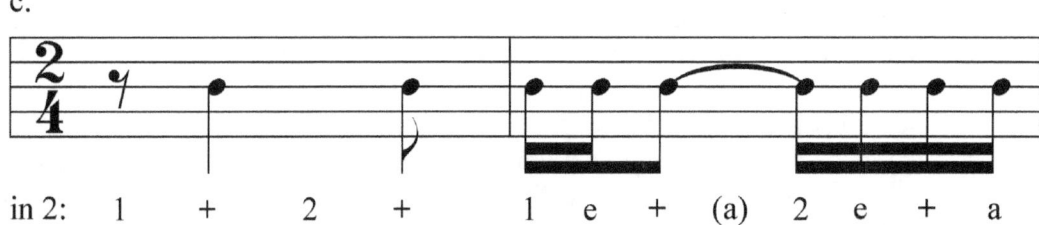

The first measure of 1–18d exhibits the same kind of syncopation as the first measure of 1–18a and even uses identical notes values. Notice, however, that the meter and therefore the counting in both examples is completely different, which underscores the importance of knowing the value of the beat and whether the meter is simple or compound.

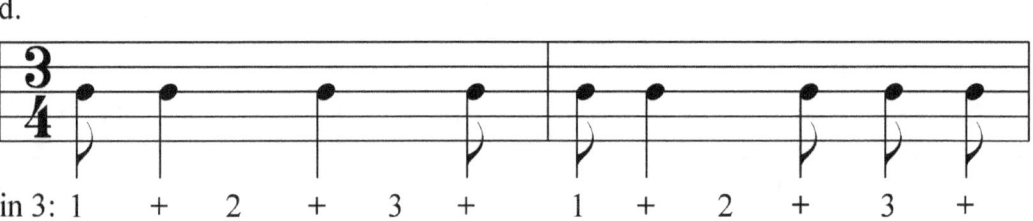

Displacement

If the normal rhythmic flow has been disrupted at the level of the beat rather than the division of the beat, this procedure is distinguished from syncopation and is usually referred to as either a **cross accent** or a **displaced accent**. In example 1–19, the secondary accent carries the longer note value, which is then tied into the primary accent of the next measure. Although the primary accent appears to be weakened, it has been shifted, or displaced, to another part of the measure (see brackets).

Example 1–19: the displaced accent (cross accent)

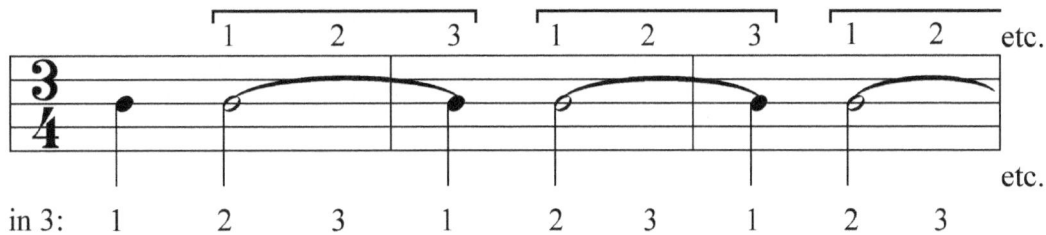

Hemiola

Hemiola is a process by which a composer may displace the accents in such a way that it transforms either a duple meter into what sounds like a triple meter or a triple meter into what sounds like a duple meter. It may occur within the measure, as in examples 1–20a and 20b, or across measures, as in 1–20c and 20d (see brackets).

In 1–20a, a measure of $\frac{3}{4}$ is placed within the metric context of $\frac{6}{8}$. Example 1–20b shows the opposite process: the transformation of $\frac{3}{4}$ into $\frac{6}{8}$. Three measures of $\frac{2}{4}$ span two measures of $\frac{3}{4}$ in 1–20c. Grouping three quarter notes of duration together by dots and ties transforms three measures of quadruple meter (a subcategory of duple) into four measures of triple meter in 1–20d.

Example 1–20: types of hemiola

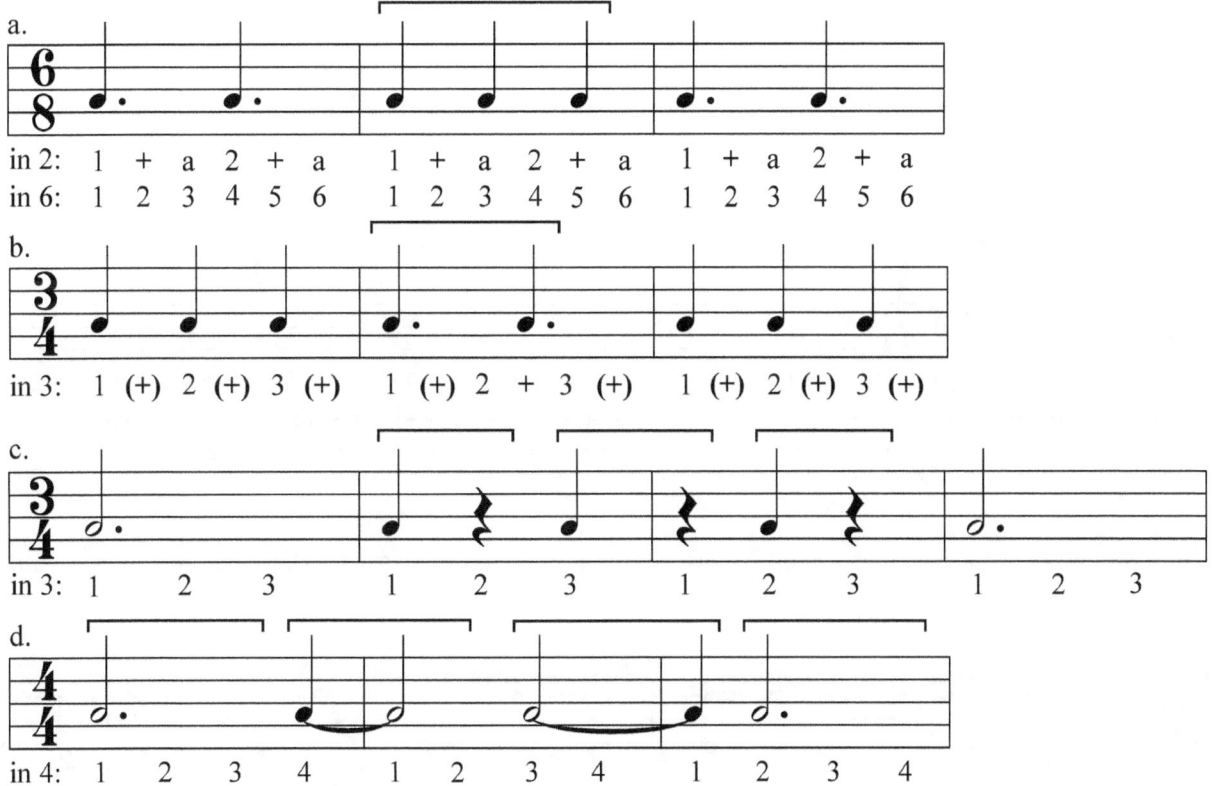

12   Chapter 1 Time and Performance

Repeat Signs

It is possible to repeat sections or passages of music without actually writing the notes out twice. Composers use various signs to indicate where such repetitions should occur. A **repeat sign** consisting of two dots on the second and third spaces of the staff followed by a **double bar** tells the performer that everything before the sign should be played again from the beginning.

The double bar itself has one narrow bar line and one thicker bar line. Upon reaching the double bar, as shown in step 2 of example 1–21a, the performer starts over from the beginning (step 3) and then continues with the rest of the music, passing through the first double bar until a second double bar, one without dots, indicates the conclusion of the composition. As we shall see in example 1–23, another common type of double bar, consisting of two narrow bar lines of the same thickness, is used to close off a section of music *before the end*.

Example 1–21: types of repeat signs

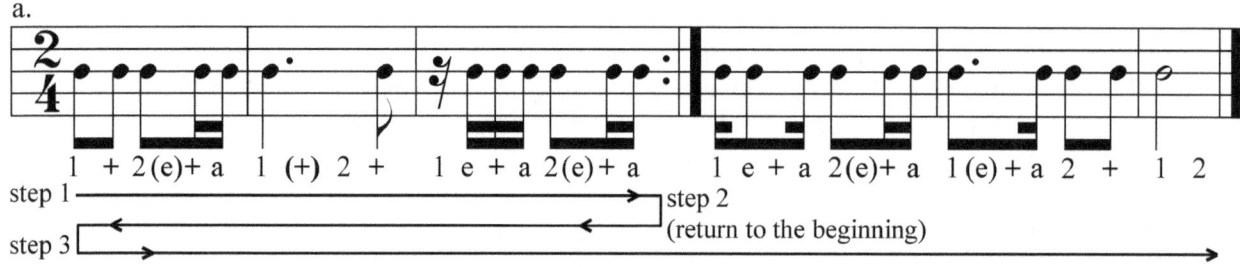

An additional double bar with dots placed after the beginning of the composition, but before the double bar shown in the foregoing example, may be used to limit the amount of repetition; here, the performer is directed to execute a single repetition of the music within the two double bars before continuing with the rest of composition (1–21b).

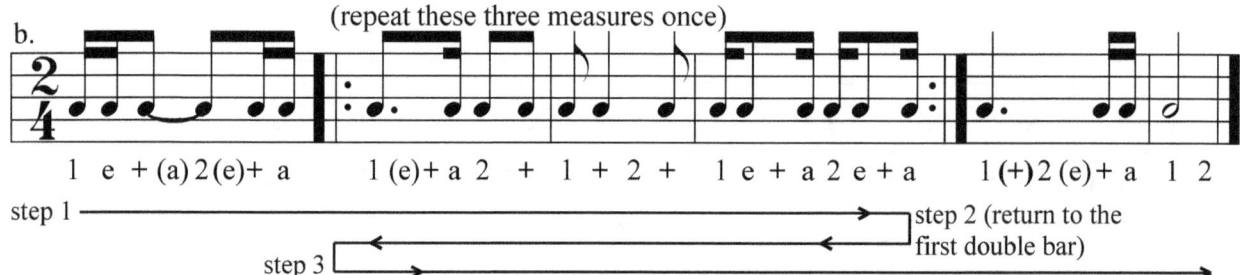

If the repeat involves just a single measure, then the sign consists of a diagonal slash and two dots (1–21c).

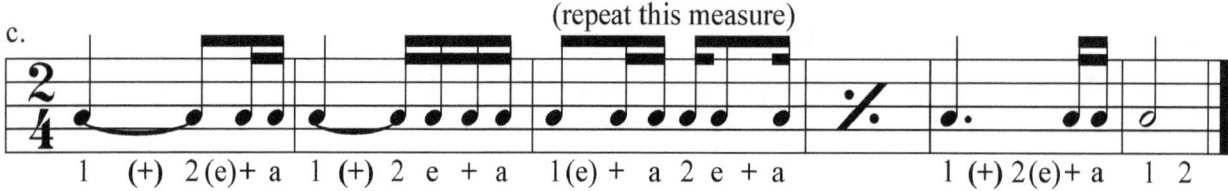

Chapter 1 Time and Performance   13

A sign resembling the single-measure repeat but crossing over the bar line instructs the performer to repeat the previous two measures, rather than just one. Sometimes the sign includes the number 2 above the bar line to clarify that the repetition should include only two measures (1–21d).

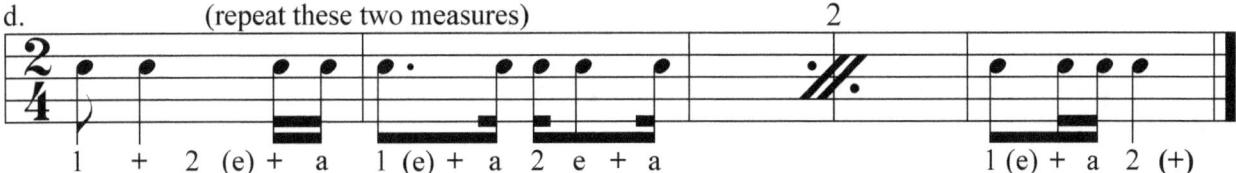

The Latin word *bis* (which means twice) may also be used to indicate a two-measure repeat (1–21e). According to this practice, *bis* is enclosed in a bracket and appears directly over the bar line.

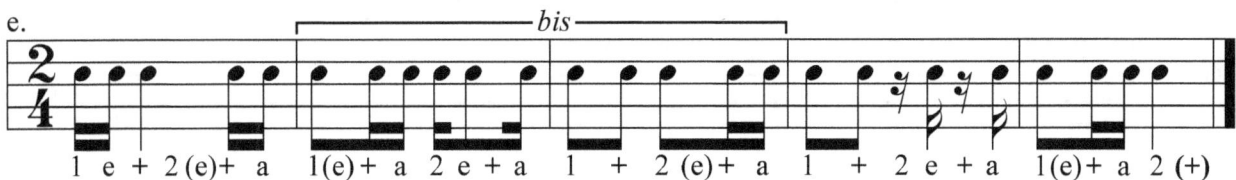

First and Second Endings

Alternate endings for compositions or musical passages can be indicated with first and second endings (numbered 1 and 2 respectively in example 1–22). The **first ending** directs the performer to return either to the beginning of the composition (1–22a) or to an earlier repeat sign (1–22b). After the music has been repeated, the performer takes the **second ending** rather than the first.

Example 1–22: first and second endings

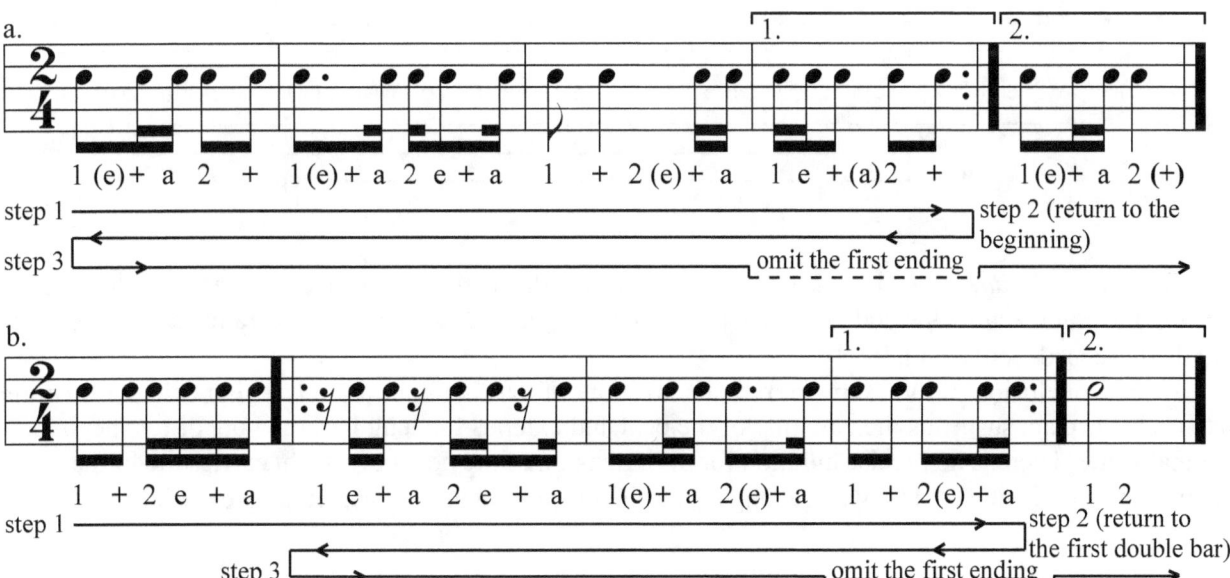

14   Chapter 1 Time and Performance

Da Capo al Fine, Dal Segno al Fine, Da Capo al Coda,* and *Dal Segno al Coda

Other repeat signs include the following Italian expressions: *Da Capo al Fine, Dal Segno al Fine, Da Capo al Coda,* and *Dal Segno al Coda*. The abbreviation *D.C.*, shown in example 1–23a, stands for *Da Capo*, which means "from the head," or in this context "from the beginning." The English word for *Fine* is end; therefore, the expression *D.C. al Fine* directs the performer to repeat the music "from the beginning to the end." Notice that the final double bar coincides with the single word *Fine* rather than with the last measure of the example.

Example 1–23: *Da Capo al Fine, Dal Segno al Fine, Da Capo al Coda,* and *Dal Segno al Coda*

The words *Dal Segno*, abbreviated as *D.S.* in 1–23b, means "from the sign." The expression *Dal Segno al Fine*, which translates as "from the sign to the end," indicates that the music repeats back to the point where the sign (𝄋) first appears and then stops at the word *Fine*. In the second measure of the example, the note values include two thirty-seconds; representing the third division of the beat, the second of the two thirty-second notes does not receive a syllable (*).

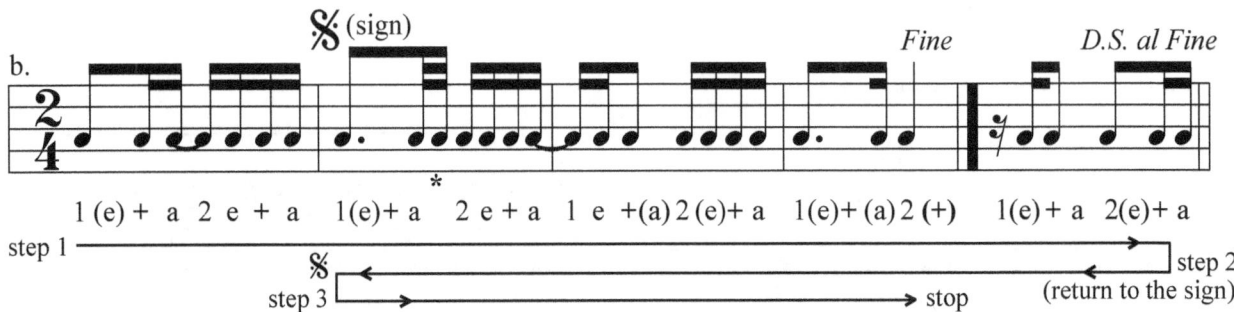

Da Capo al Coda, shown in 1–23c, denotes a return to the beginning and a continuation up to the coda sign (⊕). Upon reaching the coda sign, the performer skips ahead to the next appearance of the coda sign and then proceeds to the end.

At the conclusion of the example over the last note of the final bar, there is a sign called a **fermata** (⌢). The fermata suspends the counting of the beat and extends the length of the note or rest beyond its original value. There is no precise duration for the extension of the note or rest that carries the fermata, but usually, the suspension of time will be longer in a slow **tempo** than in a fast tempo (see below, p. 16).

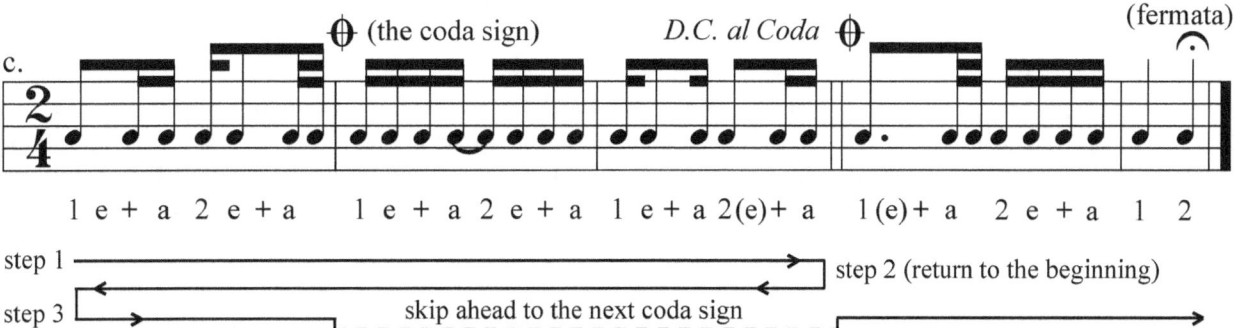

As demonstrated in 1–23d, the expression *Dal Segno al Coda* directs the performer to repeat the music from where the sign first appears (𝄋) until reaching the first coda sign (𝄌); after arriving at the first coda sign, the performer skips ahead to the appearance of the second coda sign. From the second coda sign forward, the performer proceeds to the end of the composition.

The example below begins with a measure that does not contain all of the note values required to constitute a complete measure according to the given time signature. Indeed, not all compositions begin with the primary accent of the first measure. In such cases, the first measure is incomplete; the traditional practice is to complete the measure at the end of the composition, that is, to include the missing note values in the final measure of the work.

The incomplete measure at the beginning is known variously as the anacrusis, the upbeat, or the pickup; it is considered to be the upbeat for the following downbeat of the first complete measure. The downbeat is always the first primary accent of the composition.

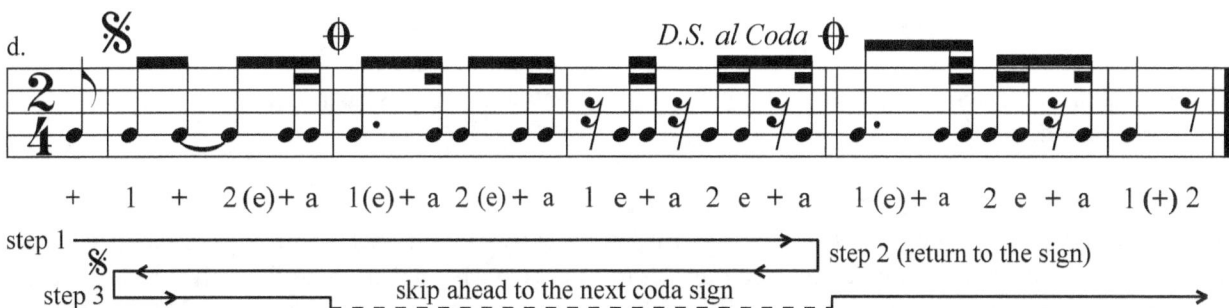

Performance Marks

If the performance of a musical score consisted only of written durations and pitches without any other elements of expression, the result would be little more than a mechanical rendering that could just as easily be produced by a machine or a computer. A musical score, however, contains a variety of words and symbols to help supplement, shape, and refine the performance of a composition. These words and symbols help the performer to understand the composer's intentions so that a more faithful interpretation of those intentions can be presented.

Two of the most important indications for shaping the expression of a composition involve both the speed and the volume of the performance. These indications are known as tempo and **dynamics**. A third category of performance directions, called articulation marks, is discussed at the conclusion of Chapter 3 (see below, pp. 49–50).

Tempo

Tempo is the rate of speed at which the beat in a music composition is performed. Earlier in this chapter, we referred to fast and slow performances of note values. The traditional language of choice for words such as fast and slow is Italian, however, one might encounter descriptions of tempo in other languages as well, most notably, German and French.

Words signifying tempo are usually placed above the staff. Below is a list of some of the Italian words used to indicate the relative speed of the music, progressing from slower to faster tempos:

largo	very slow	*moderato*	moderate (faster than *andante*)
grave	slow, serious	*allegretto*	moderately fast
lento	slow	*allegro*	fast
larghetto	slow (not as slow as *largo*)	*vivace*	fast
adagio	slow	*presto*	very fast
adagietto	slow (faster than *adagio*)	*prestissimo*	as fast as possible
andante	moderately slow		

The tempo signs shown above are general and imprecise. Any two musicians will probably have a slightly different feeling for what is very slow, slow, moderately slow, moderate, moderately fast, fast, very fast, and so on. Since the early nineteenth century, composers have been using a device called a **metronome** to provide more precise tempo indications. The metronome produces a steady and repeated click that helps the musician to know exactly how fast or slow to play a composition. Usually, a metronome marking appears at the beginning of a composition in one of two ways: M.M. ♩ = 60 or ♩ = 60.

The M.M. abbreviation stands for Maelzel's metronome, after Johann Maelzel (1772–1838), the first person to mass produce and popularize the device. The note value preceding the equal sign designates the value of the beat, or pulse. The number of clicks the metronome generates ranges from 40 to about 208 beats per minute. In the present instance, the number 60 indicates 60 clicks per minute. Although a quarter note was given here, any note value may be used as part of the metronome marking.

Sometimes, the musical score may contain an instruction directing the performer to change the prevailing tempo. The two most common instructions for changing the tempo are represented by the Italian words **ritardando** and **accelerando**. *Ritardando* directs the performer to gradually slow down, while *accelerando* means to gradually increase the speed of a musical passage.

Dynamics

The term dynamics refers to marks in the musical score that instruct the performer to play within a wide range of volume levels, from a barely audible whisper to an excruciating roar. Relative degrees of loudness and softness are expressed most commonly with Italian words, although one might encounter dynamics in other languages as well, particularly German and French.

The following list of Italian words presents the most prevalent dynamics, progressing from softer to louder volume levels. The abbreviation for each word is also indicated, as dynamic marks are usually abbreviated in musical scores and placed below the staff.

Italian	Abbreviation	English
pianissimo	*pp*	very soft
piano	*p*	soft
mezzo piano	*mp*	moderately soft
mezzo forte	*mf*	moderately loud
forte	*f*	loud
fortissimo	*ff*	very loud

Another dynamic instruction to the performer may involve playing certain notes louder than others; this type of mark is called a **dynamic accent**. The most common symbol for a dynamic accent is $>$. For examples of the dynamic accent, see the rhythmic exercises in Appendix B.

Directions for gradual increases or decreases in volume are represented by the Italian words ***crescendo*** and ***decrescendo***; both terms are signified by elongated wedges (also called "hairpins"), as shown below. (The sign for the *decrescendo* symbol should not be confused with the symbol for the dynamic accent. The *decrescendo* is more elongated in appearance than the latter and may be used in conjunction with a large number of notes, whereas each dynamic accent mark occurs with a single note, is placed directly adjacent to the note head, and is much smaller in appearance.)

Italian	Abbreviation	English	Sign
crescendo	*cresc.*	getting louder	$<$
decrescendo	*decresc.*	getting softer	$>$

Rarely-Used Note Values

This excursion into time and performance concludes with a brief look at two additional note and rest values, one that is longer than the whole note and one that is shorter than the sixty-fourth note: namely, the double whole note and the one hundred and twenty-eighth note. Though rarely used in modern music literature, both can be found occasionally.

The double whole note, sometimes referred to as the breve, is twice as long as the more common whole note. Modern music notation usually represents the double whole note as either a whole note with one or two vertical lines on each side of the note head (example 1–24a) or as a hollowed-out rectangular box with a vertical line on each side of the note box (1–24b). While the double whole note may appear on any line or space of the five-line staff, the double whole rest is confined to the third space on the staff, between the center line and the fourth line from the bottom (1–24c).

Example 1–24: the double whole note and its rest

The double whole note (or its silent equivalent) appears in meters that contain at least two whole notes of duration per measure, such as $\frac{4}{2}$ time which has four beats per measure with the half note constituting the value of the beat (four half notes may occupy the space of either two whole notes or one double whole note).

As with the double whole note, the one hundred and twenty-eighth note and its corresponding rest are rarely seen in music literature. The one hundred and twenty-eighth note may be expressed with either five flags (example 1–25a) or five beams (1–25b). The one hundred and twenty-eighth rest has five hooks that point to the left, the lowest of which stands below the lowest line of the five-line staff (1–25c).

Example 1–25: the one hundred and twenty-eighth note and its rest

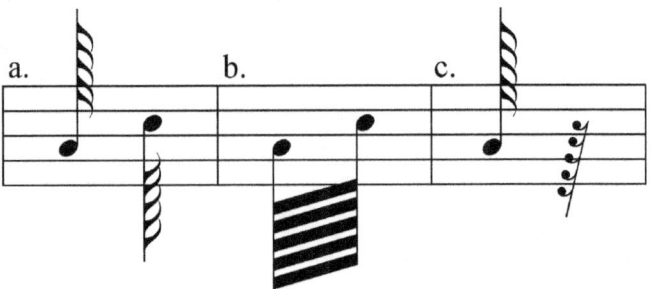

Two one hundred and twenty-eighth notes fill the duration of a single sixty-fourth note (example 1–26a), just as two six-fourth notes fill the duration of one thirty-second note (1–26b).

Example 1–26: note equivalencies

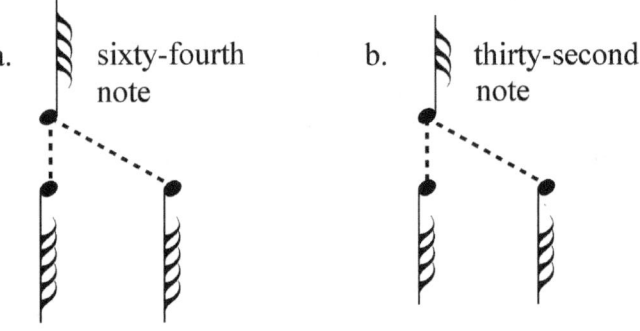

Chapter 2 Pitch

An object moved by force produces vibrations that in turn create displacements throughout the surrounding area. The displaced area, which can be a liquid, a solid, or a gas, serves as a medium of transmission that carries the vibrations to the human ear. Functioning as a receptor, the ear perceives the vibrations as sound. The number of sound vibrations completed in one second of time is called **frequency**.

If the vibrating object produces a regular number of frequencies at a steady rate, then the sound will be heard as a musical tone. Such tones are referred to as pitches. The relative lowness or highness of any pitch corresponds to the rate of the vibrating frequency of the sound-producing object. Slower vibrating frequencies result in lower pitches, while faster vibrating frequencies produce higher pitches.

An inspection of the piano keyboard demonstrates the difference between lower and higher pitches. The standard 88-key piano, as represented in example 2–1, has 52 white keys and 36 black keys. Moving from the extreme left to the extreme right of the keyboard, each key produces a pitch that is incrementally higher and its equivalent frequency faster. From the lowest to the highest pitch, the frequencies range from 27.5 to 4186 vibrations per second. All of the pitches on the keyboard have names that correspond to the first seven letters of the alphabet, letters A through G. Every eighth pitch and letter repeats the first; this repetition is called an **octave**. Any two pitches of the same letter name that are one octave apart have a frequency ratio of 2:1. For example, the lowest A on the piano produces 27.5 vibrations per second; one octave above that A produces twice as many frequencies: 55 vibrations per second.

Musicians interpret the numerical relationship between pitches in spatial terms, using the word **interval** to describe the distance from one pitch to any other pitch. On the keyboard, the distance between any two immediately adjacent piano keys constitutes an increment in pitch called a **half step**, **semitone**, or **minor 2nd**. The half step is the smallest possible interval on the piano keyboard and in our Western tradition of music. There are twelve half steps within any single octave.

Example 2–1: the standard 88-key piano

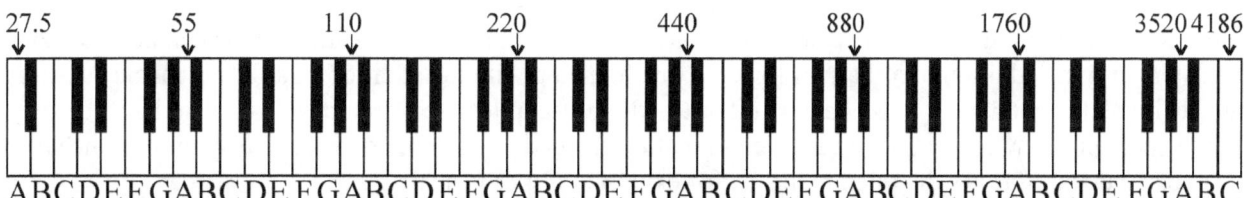

Study example 2–2 and notice the intervallic distances between both the white and black keys of the piano keyboard. The black keys are arranged in alternating groups of two and three with one intervening black key between each white key except in two places: from E to F and from B to C. Since the distance between any two immediately adjacent piano keys is a half step, E to F and B to C constitute the only two places within the octave where there are half steps between two adjacent white keys.

Example 2–2

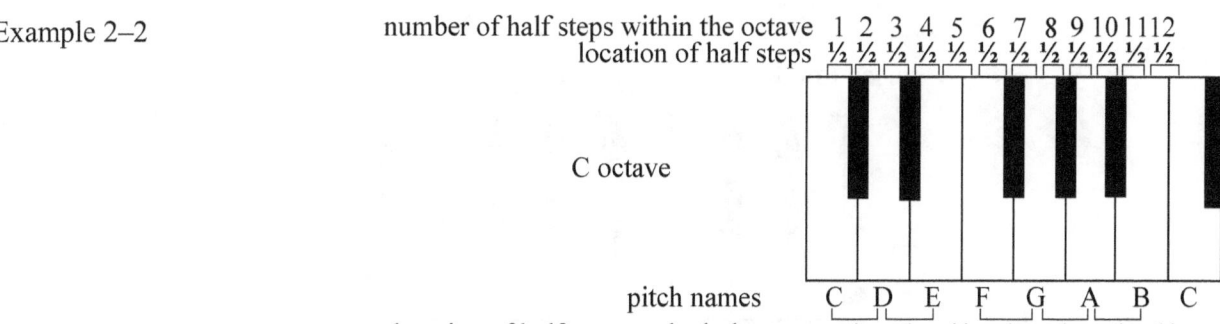

In all other places, two adjacent white keys produce two half steps because a black key separates each pair. Two consecutive half steps between any two piano keys comprise the interval of a **whole step** (sometimes referred to as a "step"). Thus, with the exception of E to F and B to C, the distance between white keys is always a whole step, also known as a **major 2nd**. With respect to the alternating groups of two and three black keys that extend across the piano keyboard, three half steps separate each group while the distance between black keys within each group is a whole step (example 2–3).

Example 2–3

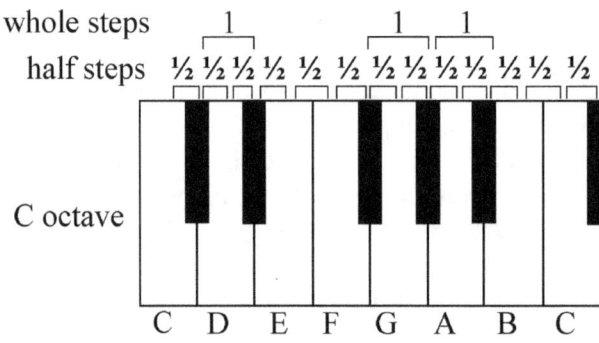

Accidentals and Enharmonic Equivalency

A conflict arises from the fact that twelve half steps fill the span of any octave but only seven alphabet letters are available to designate pitches. The conflict is more apparent than real because each of the seven pitch names can have more than one spelling of itself; that is to say, the seven pitch names can be modified with additional symbols called **accidentals**.

Accidentals raise or lower any of the seven pitch names. The names and the shapes of the accidentals are as follows: sharp (♯), flat (♭), double flat (♭♭), double sharp (𝄪), and natural (♮). The natural sign cancels any accidental used to raise or lower a pitch. Each pitch and its associated name can be raised one half step with the addition of a sharp or lowered one half step with the addition of a flat. In music notation, the accidental immediately *precedes* the pitch to which it applies (see examples 2–23b and 23d below). When speaking or writing about an accidental that is attached to a pitch, however, the symbol or the word for the accidental *follows* the pitch name, as for example: C♯ or C sharp.

Example 2–4 shows how the pitch C can be raised one half step on the piano keyboard with the addition of a sharp to become C♯ (pronounced C sharp). The pitch B can be lowered one half step with the addition of a flat to become B♭ (pronounced B flat). Raising the pitch from C to C♯ requires a move from the left to the right of the keyboard, whereas lowering the pitch from B to B♭ necessitates a move from right to left. In both cases, the move to C♯ and B♭ ends on one of the black keys. We shall soon see, however, that raising and lowering a pitch does not always involve using one of the black keys.

Example 2–4

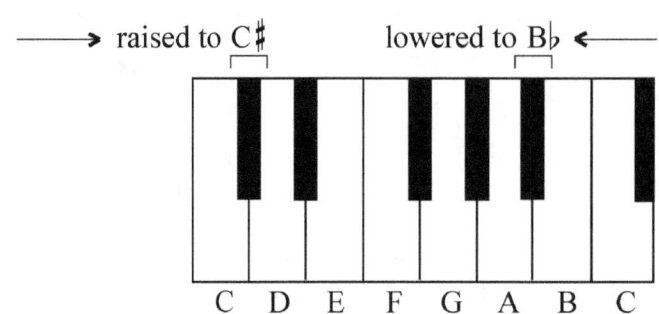

It is also possible to raise a pitch (and its name) two half steps with the addition of a double sharp and to lower it two half steps with the addition of a double flat. As illustrated in example 2–5, a move from C to C× (pronounced C double sharp) can be accomplished by raising the pitch from C to C♯ and then from C♯ to C× (example 2–5). Similarly, the move to B♭♭ (pronounced B double flat) can be made by lowering the pitch from B to B♭ and then from B♭ to B♭♭.

Raising C to C× takes us to the equivalent white key and pitch of D. If we lower B two half steps, the operation changes the white key and pitch of A into B♭♭. By using sharps, flats, double sharps, and double flats, at least two different letter names may be assigned to any single pitch. In fact, every pitch can have three different letter names except for G♯ and A♭ (see example 2–7 below). When we apply different letter names to the same pitch, the names are called **enharmonic equivalents**.

Example 2–5

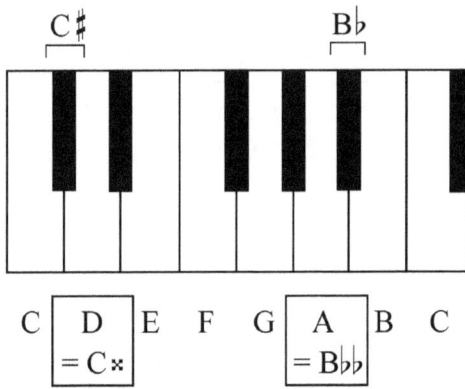

Example 2–6 demonstrates how the black piano key of C♯ can also be reinterpreted as D♭ if we lower D one half step. Hence, C♯ and D♭ are enharmonic equivalents. If F is lowered one half step to F♭, it falls on the white key of E. Raising D to D× brings us again to the white key of E, thereby producing three names for the same pitch: F♭, E, and D×.

Example 2–6

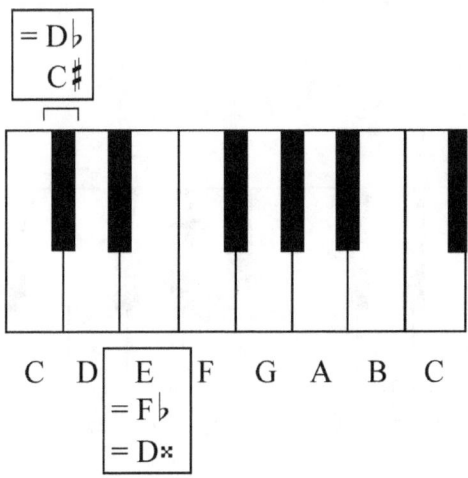

Example 2–7 locates all of the possible enharmonic equivalents within the C octave; the names of these pitches remain the same regardless of the octave in which they occur. Again, every pitch can have at least three different letter names except for G♯ and A♭.

Example 2–7

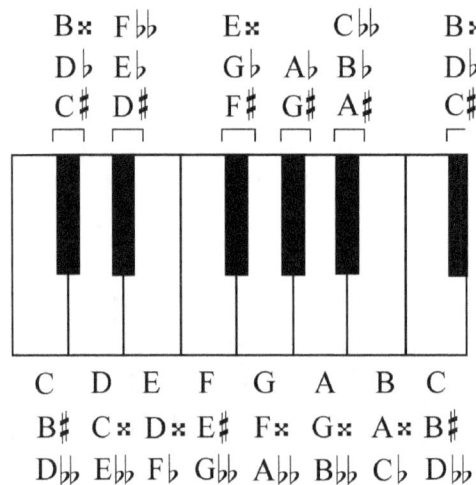

Chromatic and Diatonic Half Steps

In example 2–4, we saw how the pitch C could be raised one half step with the addition of a sharp. Raising C one half step requires a move to the immediate right on the keyboard from the white key of C to the adjacent black key of C♯ (example 2–8). When there is a half step between two different versions of the same letter name, the intervallic relationship between the two pitches is termed chromatic. In other words, the pitches C and C♯ constitute a **chromatic half step**. C♯ and C𝑥 is also a chromatic half step. The distance from B to B♭ is a chromatic half step, as is the distance from B♭ to B♭♭.

Chromatic half steps may be formed between all of the black and white keys of the piano and in two places where there are no intervening black keys, two white-key areas: from E to F and from B to C. However, in order to produce chromatic half steps without using black keys, we must respell F, E, C, and B enharmonically: F becomes E♯, E becomes F♭, C becomes B♯, and B becomes C♭. Thus, enharmonic respelling creates chromatic half steps from E to E♯, F to F♭, B to B♯, and C to C♭.

Example 2–8

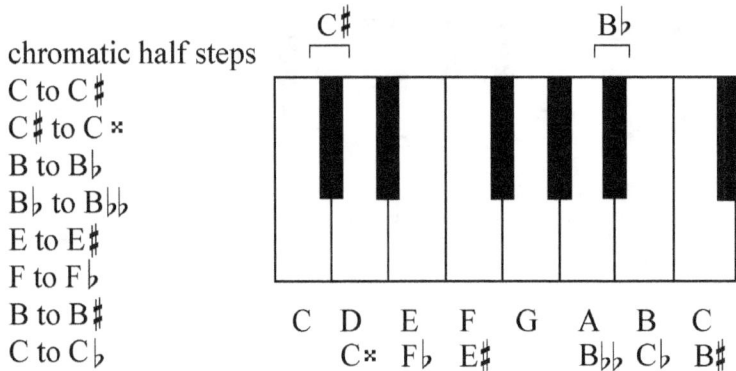

When there is a half step between two different letter names, the intervallic relationship between the two pitches is termed diatonic. If we respell C♯ enharmonically as D♭, then the pitches C and D♭ constitute a **diatonic half step** (example 2–9). Re-evaluating B♭ as A♯ produces a diatonic half step between A♯ and B. The only two places within the octave where diatonic half steps may occur without an enharmonic respelling to produce two different letter names are from E to F and from B to C.

Example 2–9

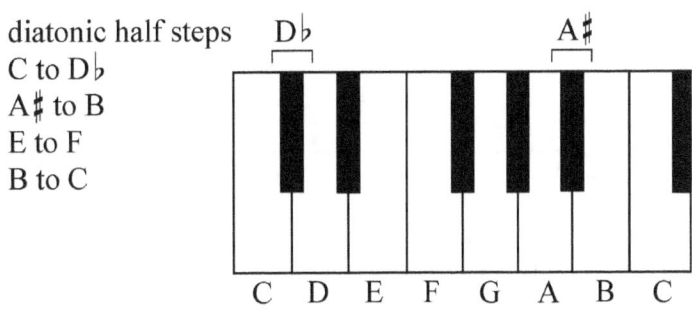

The Great Staff and Clefs

As mentioned in Chapter 1, the staff consists of five lines and four spaces and is an integral component of most music notation. Example 2–10 displays two staffs, or staves (an alternate plural for staff), joined together by a bracket in the left margin known as a brace. This apparent two-staff ten-line configuration is referred to variously as the **great staff**, the **grand staff**, or the **piano staff**. The staff alone cannot represent pitches, however. Any set or range of pitches requires the use of a symbol called a clef sign. The two most common clefs are the **F clef** and the **G clef**.

Example 2–10 shows the location and appearance of both the F clef and the G clef on the great staff. The F clef is so named because the sign's two dots surround the line on which the pitch F is fixed. Another name for the F clef is the **bass clef**. The G clef takes its name from the swirl around the second line from the bottom, the line on which the pitch G is designated. Another name for the G clef is the **treble clef**.

Between the two staves of the great staff is an additional line called a **ledger line**. Here, the line designates a pitch called "middle C." Musicians use ledger lines to retain within a single clef pitches that exceed the limits of any single staff (see examples 2–18, 19 and 20 below).

Example 2–10

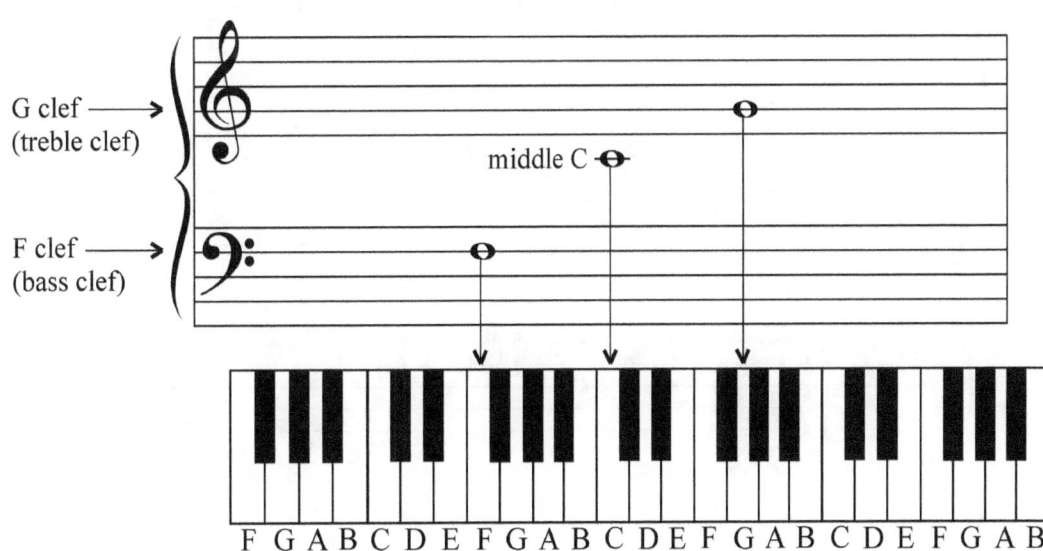

With F and G located on the staff by their respective clefs, it is possible to find the other pitches on the lines and spaces according to the letters of the alphabet (example 2–11).

Example 2–11

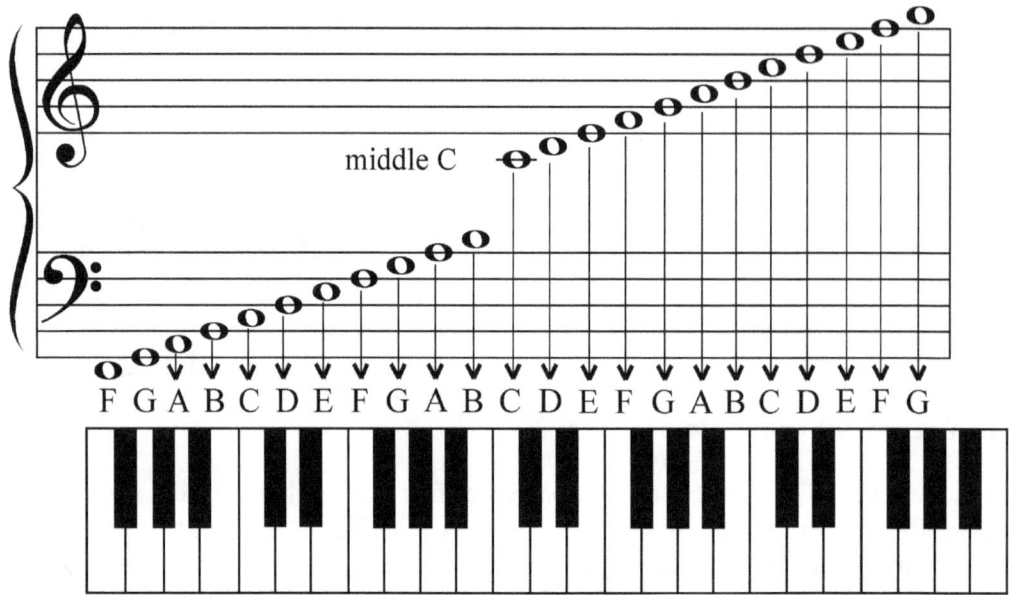

Traditionally, when learning the names of the lines and spaces on the F and G clefs, music teachers have provided students with helpful ways for remembering the location of the various pitches. For the five lines of the G clef, from the bottom to top, the pitch names are as follows: E, G, B, D, and F (example 2–12). An easy way to recall the names of these five lines is to associate them respectively with the first letter of each word of the sentence "every good boy does fine." The four spaces of the G clef, from bottom to top, spell the word "face."

For the lines of the F clef, from bottom to top, the pitch names are as follows: G, B, D, F, and A. These lines would read "good boys do fine always." The four spaces of the F clef, from bottom to top, read "all cows eat grass" for the pitches A, C, E, and G (or perhaps "all cars eat gas").

Example 2–12

Other clefs use middle C to fix the location of the seven pitch names. Such clefs are called **C clefs** because they locate middle C with a design that encircles the line on which middle C is to be read. C clefs can be placed on any of the five lines of the staff and therefore are considered to be movable clefs. More than two hundred years ago, C clefs were widely used; however, today, only two C clefs are commonly found, namely, the alto and tenor clefs. The alto clef is used for the viola and the alto trombone and the tenor clef often serves the upper register of the trombone, bassoon, and cello.

Example 2–13 presents all five C clefs on each of the five lines of the staff along with their respective names. As with the F and G clefs, the other pitches of the C clef precede and follow middle C according to the order of the alphabet.

Example 2–13

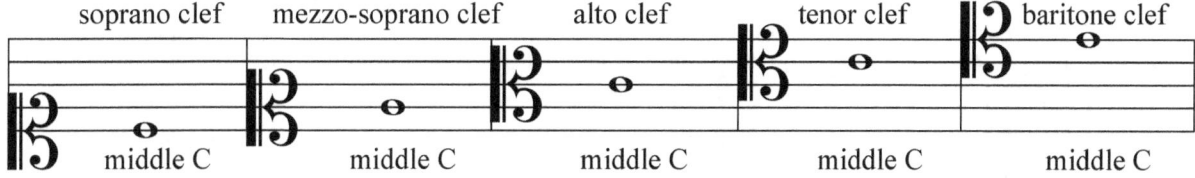

In vocal music, when the tenor part is written on its own staff, the G clef is often used with the number 8 attached to bottom loop of the sign (example 2–14). The eight indicates that the tenor voice will sound one octave lower than the written pitch.

Example 2–14

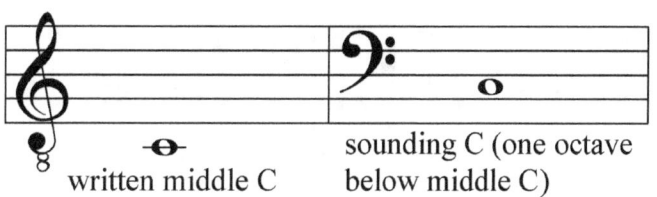

Octave registers

In the previous sections of this chapter, we located the seven basic pitch names on the standard 88-key piano, introduced the five types of accidental signs, explained the concept of enharmonic equivalency, distinguished between chromatic and diatonic half steps, explored the range of the great staff within the general context of the F and G clefs, and discussed the principal characteristics of the various C clefs.

Initially, we used uppercase letters to represent the seven pitch names that span the seven octaves of the keyboard. Middle C, which is expressed on the great staff with the use of a single ledger line, is the fourth C from the extreme left of the keyboard. Below the first C are the two lowest pitches on the keyboard, A and B. As can be seen in example 2–15, the pitches A, B, and C occur eight times across the keyboard; D, E, F, and G appear seven times.

Example 2–15

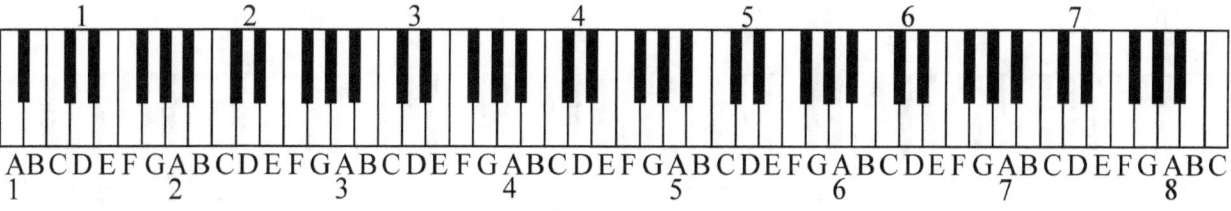

If we are referring to pitches in general terms, then there is no need to identify any given pitch within a specific octave register. But if we want to identify a pitch that occurs within a particular octave, then the problem of precise pitch location, or pitch register, arises—a problem for which a couple of different solutions have been put forward.

One solution for identifying a pitch within a specific octave register, shown in examples 2–16 and 18, divides the keyboard into seven segments of pitches with each segment beginning on C and ending on B. The first of the seven segments is preceded by the pitches A and B while the seventh segment is followed by the seventh repetition of C. All of the segments as well as the additional pitches at both extremes of the keyboard are given names to identify the exact register of any given pitch.

The designations for the various registers (and segments) are sub-contra, contra, great, small, one-line or prime, two-line or double prime, three-line or triple prime, four-line or quadruple prime, and five-line or quintuple prime. Pitches occurring in the prime registers use lowercase letters and carry either superscripts or vertical slashes. For example, middle C appears as either c^1 or c'. In the double prime register, C is written as either c^2 or c". (Example 2–18 shows all of the pitches on the great staff in relation to their location on the keyboard.)

Both the sub-contra and contra registers take uppercase letters and use subscript numbers. A_2 and B_2 of the sub-contra register are pronounced as "double A" and "double B." In the great and small registers, pitches are represented with uppercase and lowercase lettering respectively. The alternative to describing the sub-contra and contra registers with uppercase letters followed by subscripts is to use three uppercase letters for the sub-contra register and two uppercase letters for the contra register (2–18).

Example 2–16

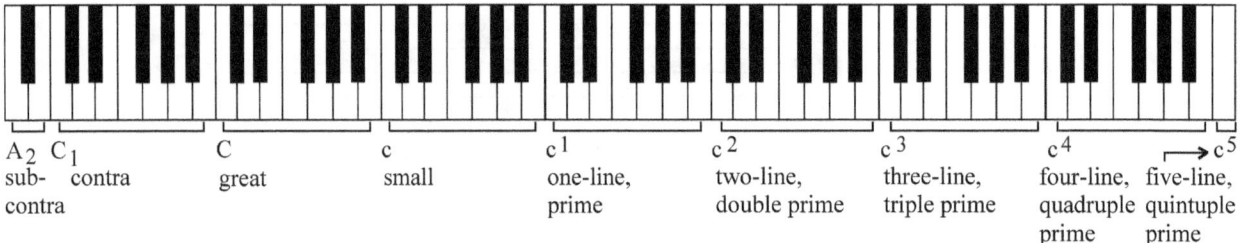

A less complicated system for identifying any pitch within a specific octave register is shown in examples 2–17 and 19. The first C to the extreme left of the keyboard is designated as C1. Thus, the first D and G would be D1 and G1 respectively. The second C is C2. Middle C is C4. The highest C on the keyboard would be C8. The two lowest pitches on the keyboard, A and B, are sometimes referred to as A0 and B0. (Example 2–19 shows all of the pitches on the great staff in relation to their location on the keyboard.)

Obviously, the learning curve for the second system of octave identification (2–17) is less steep than that of the first approach (2–16). Therefore, the remainder of this chapter will focus more on the first method than on the second so that you will have a better understanding of how to use it.

Example 2–17

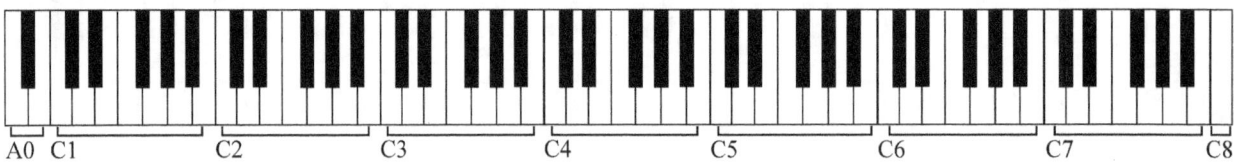

Example 2-18

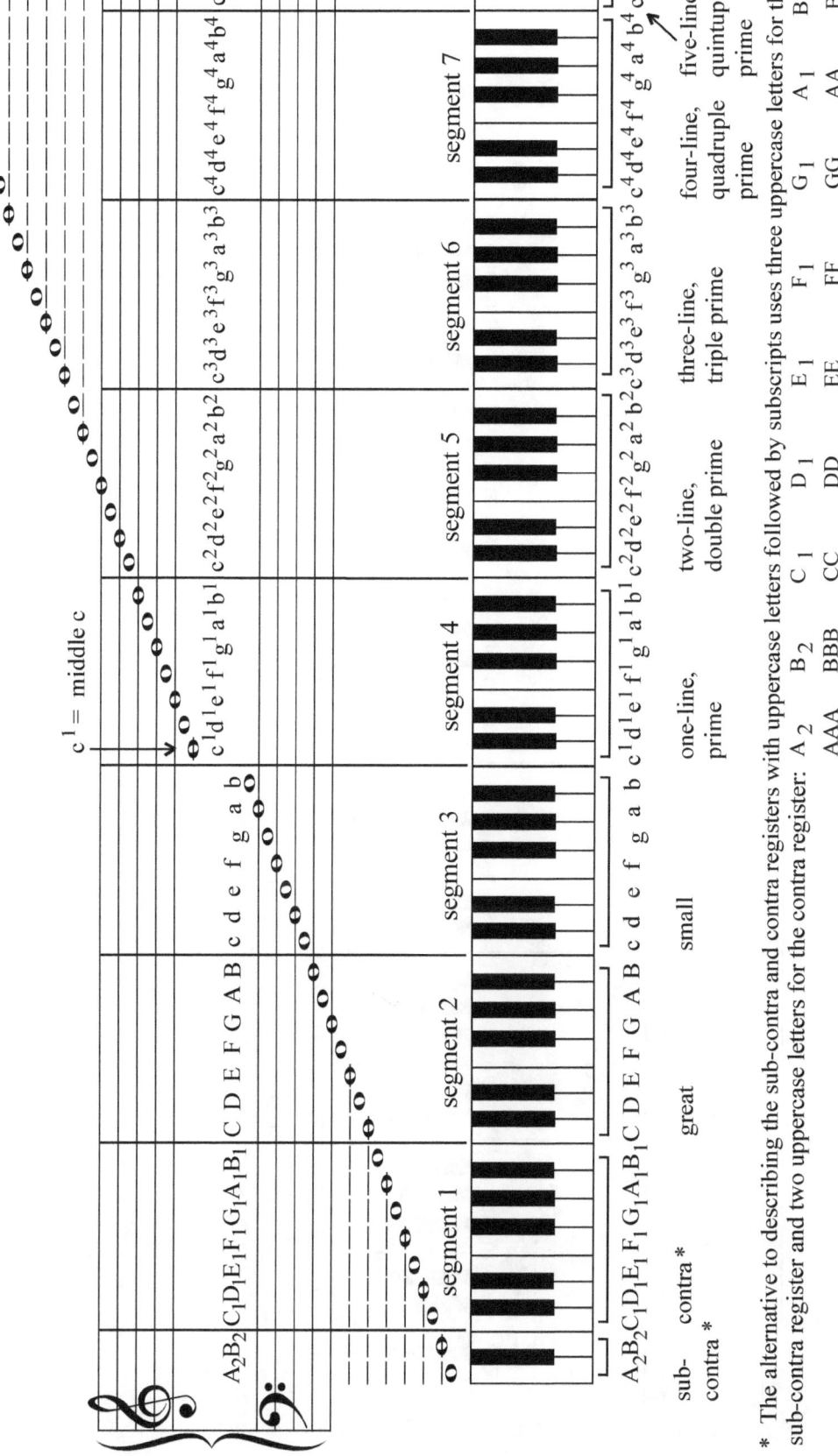

* The alternative to describing the sub-contra and contra registers with uppercase letters followed by subscripts uses three uppercase letters for the sub-contra register and two uppercase letters for the contra register.

28 Chapter 2 Pitch

Example 2–19

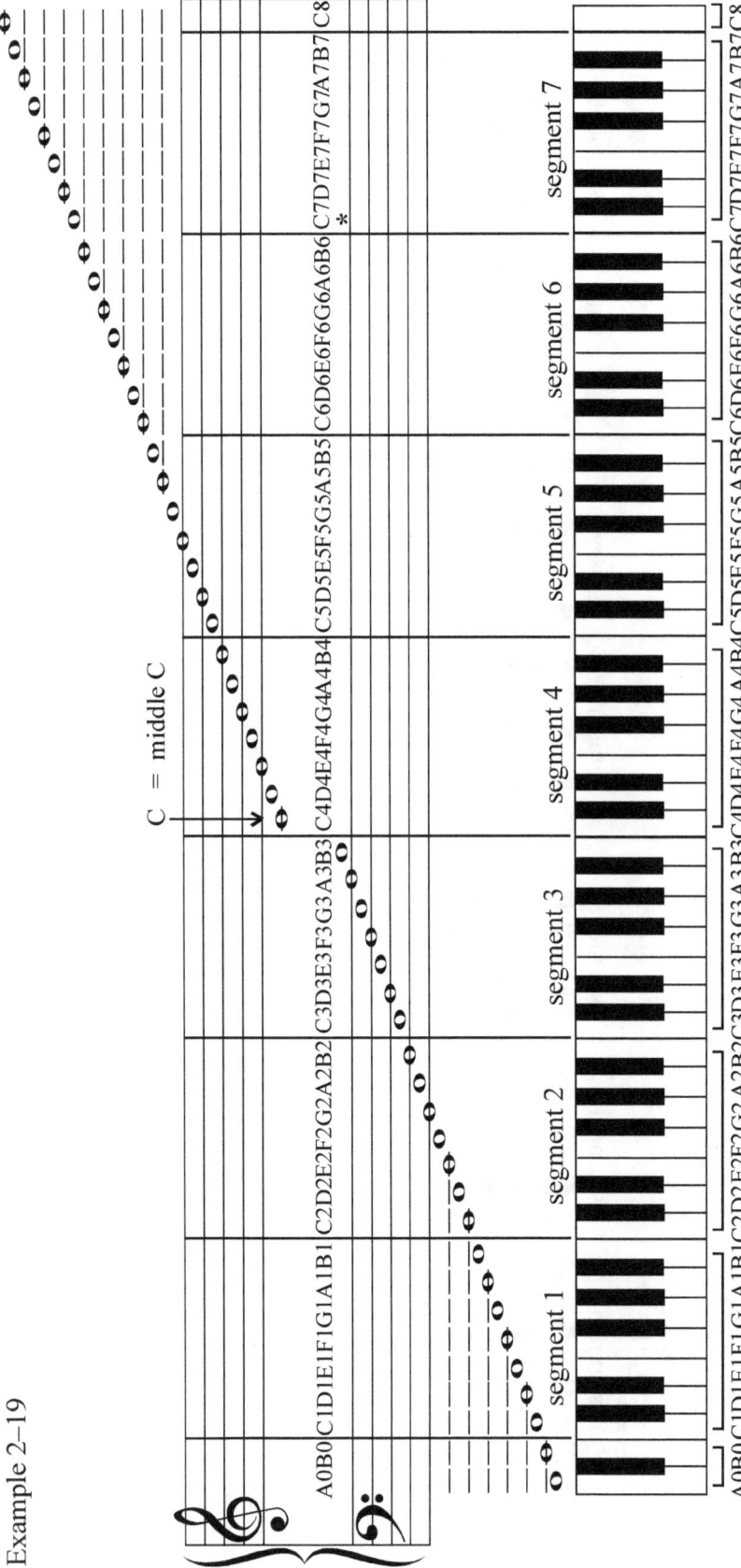

* This method of octave identification presents certain problems for those students who have a background in commercial music and/or jazz; for descriptions of the highest octave, such as C7, D7, E7, etc., also refer to a particular type of four-note chord called the dominant seventh chord.

Example 2–20, which illustrates how the same octave on G can be written in three different clefs using ledger lines. The eight pitches of the G-octave span both the small and prime registers. The G in the small register would be *spoken* of as "small G" and *written* in text form as lowercase g. Thus, we would speak of the outer pitches of this octave as "small G" to "G prime" or "small G" to "one-line G." In text, this octave register would be written as g–g¹.

Example 2–20

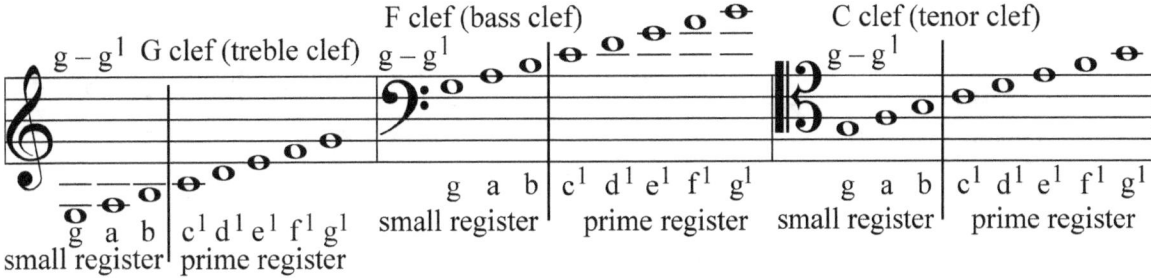

Octave Signs

In both examples 2–18 and 19 above, notice that it is possible to use up to six ledger lines in the F clef and nine ledger lines in the G clef to represent pitches that extend beyond the limits of the staves on which these clefs appear. However, reading music with too many ledger lines is very difficult. Fortunately, there is a sign that makes it possible to avoid or minimize some of the difficulties of reading ledger lines.

The sign, shown in example 2–21, is an abbreviation of the Italian expression *all'ottava* ("at the octave") and consists of the Arabic number 8 (or *8va*) followed by a dotted bracket. The *all'ottava* sign instructs the performer to play the pitches one octave higher than written when appearing in the G clef or one octave lower than written when appearing in the F clef. When used with the G clef, the sign usually appears above the staff and when used with the F clef, below the staff. In 2–21a, the octave sign indicates that the span of pitches in the F clef sounds one octave below the great and small registers. In 2–21b, the octave sign indicates that the span of pitches sounds one octave above the double and triple prime (two-line and three-line) registers.

Occasionally, the sign *8 bassa* or *8va bassa* is found in musical scores (often followed by a dotted bracket) instead of the *all'ottava* sign. The *8 bassa* sign means "at the octave below."

Example 2–21: the sign for *all'ottava*

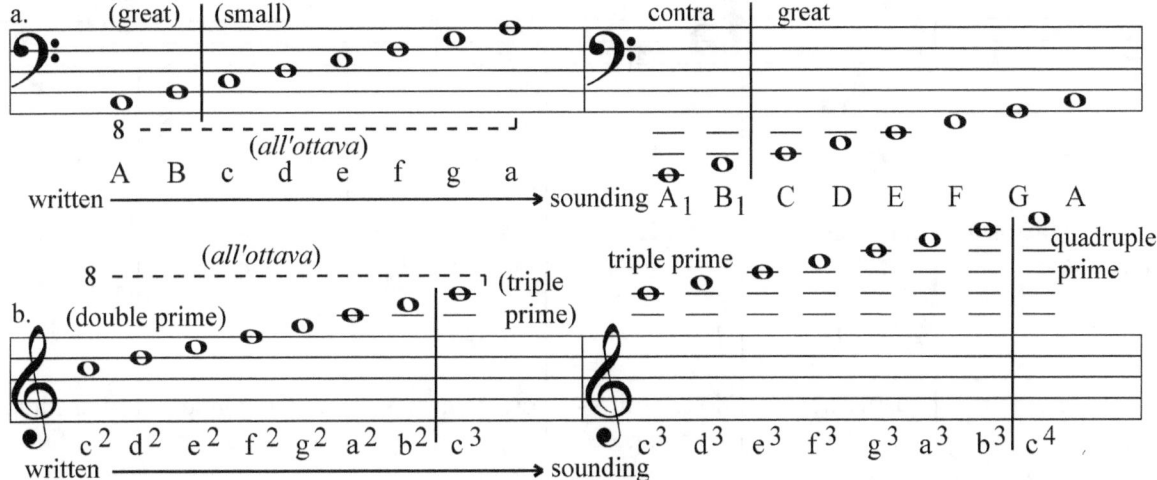

The octave sign for indicating pitches to be played two octaves higher than written consists of the Arabic number 15 (or *15ma*) followed by a dotted bracket. The sign is an abbreviation for the Italian expression *a la quindicesima*, which means "at the fifteenth." It should be recognized that the span of two octaves consists of fifteen pitches rather than sixteen because the top pitch of the first octave duplicates the bottom pitch and therefore should not be counted twice. In example 2–22, the *a la quindicesima* places the pitches in the G clef two octaves higher than the small and prime registers in which they are written.

Example 2–22: the sign for *a la quindicesima*

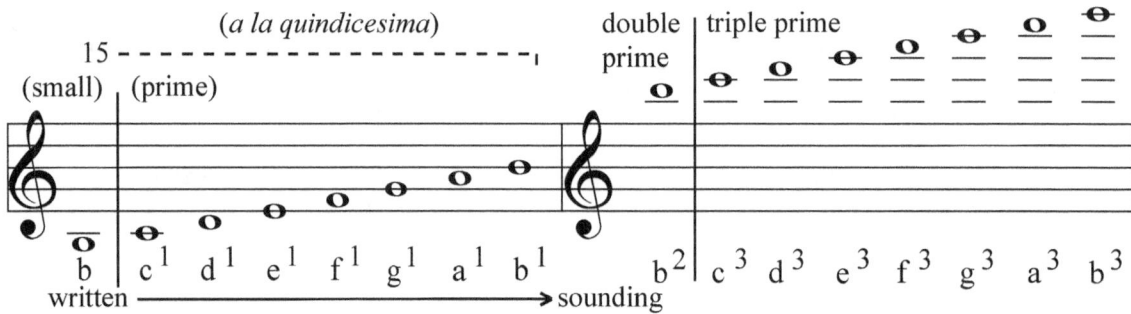

Study example 2–23, which shows various pitches and registers in the G, F, and C clefs. Notice the duration of each pitch as well as the use of ledger lines and octave signs. The exact names and registers are given using both methods for octave identification, one or two options for verbal description provided, and the rhythmic values of each note identified. (Worksheets 2–5 and 2–6 follow the format of example 2–23.)

Examples 2–23b and 23d merit additional comment. In 2–23b, $C\flat_1$ is the first pitch of the contra register; however, we should be careful not to look at $C\flat_1$ and conclude that since its enharmonic equivalent is B_2 that its real register falls within the sub-contra range. The written pitch name is $C\flat_1$ not B_2; therefore, $C\flat_1$ constitutes the first note of the contra register rather than the last note of the sub-contra register. Similarly, the $b\sharp^3$ in 2–23d should not be interpreted as c^4, the first note of the quadruple prime register.

Example 2–23

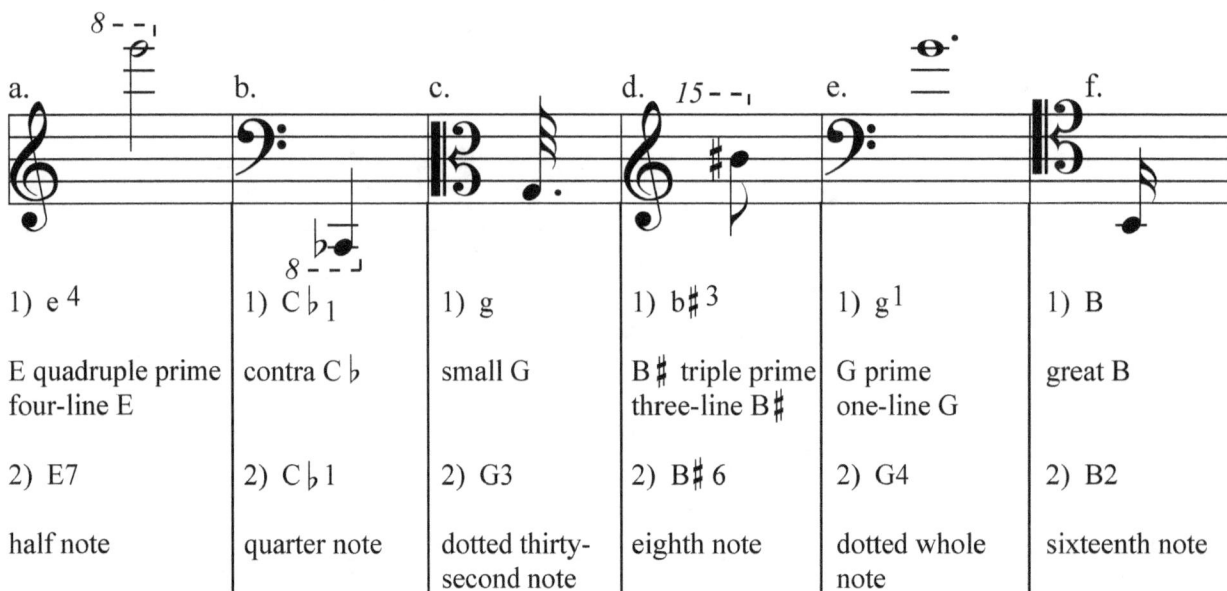

Chapter 3 The Major Scale

In Chapter 2, example 2–21 displayed octave spans on A and C in which eight pitches were arranged alphabetically in an ascending stepwise pattern. These octave configurations bring us to the concept of **scale**. The term scale derives from the Italian word *scala*, which means ladder. A scale is a ladder of tones: a representation of stepwise pitches running upwards or downwards. The tones of the scale are identified by the letter names of the alphabet.

The **chromatic scale**, as presented in example 3–1, divides the octave into twelve half steps. Sharps are generally used when the scale is notated in its ascending form, flats in its descending form. The chromatic scale contains pairs of pitches that involve two different versions of the same letter name: in the ascending form, C–C♯, D–D♯, F–F♯, G–G♯, and A–A♯ (3–1a); and in the descending form, B–B♭, A–A♭, G–G♭, E–E♭, and D–D♭ (3–1b).

Two exceptional areas of the chromatic scale have diatonic half steps, that is, two consecutive pitches with different letter names: E to F and B to C. In the examples below, the tones of the chromatic scale occur within the span of a single octave; however, the chromatic scale may be expressed in any register, starting on any of the seven alphabet names.

Example 3–1: the chromatic scale on C

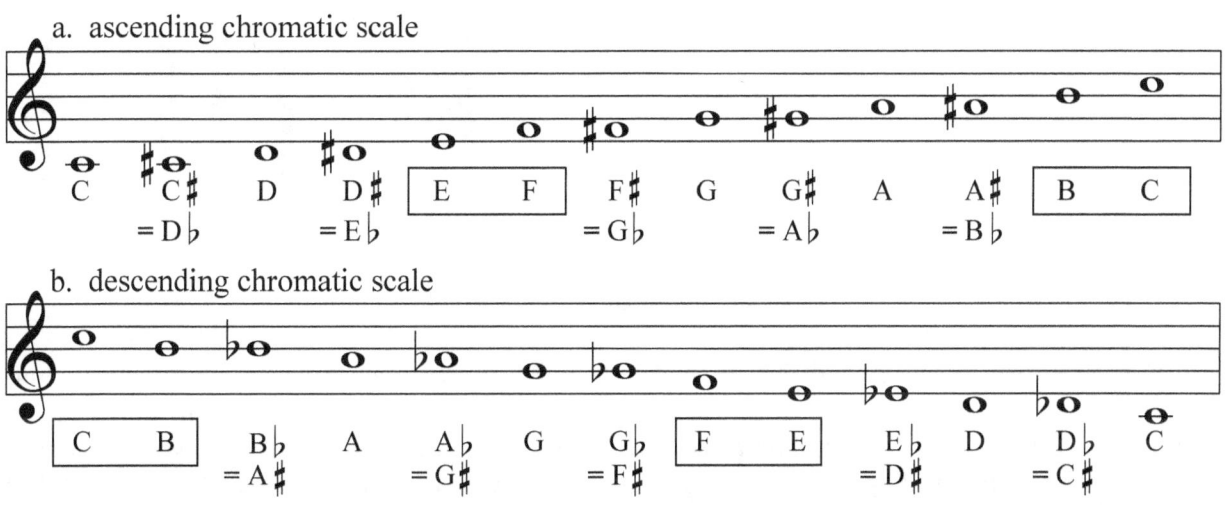

A scale having only one letter name for each of its seven pitches, spanning a single octave, and comprising five whole steps and two half steps is called a **diatonic scale**. The distribution of whole steps and half steps across the seven pitches of a diatonic scale can be found by examining the white keys of the piano within any octave of the keyboard. Example 3–2 shows a diatonic scale within the C octave.

Example 3–2

32   Chapter 3   The Major Scale

Each of the seven pitches of the diatonic scale is called a scale degree and assigned a number according to its relationship to the first pitch of the scale. Example 3–3 identifies C as scale degree 1 and D, E, F, G, A, and B as scale degrees 2, 3, 4, 5, 6, and 7 respectively. The octave duplication of C is 8, which is equivalent to scale degree 1. All diatonic scales can be divided into two four-note segments: from scale degrees 1 to 4 and 5 to 8. These segments are called **tetrachords**; they are usually separated by a whole step between scale degrees 4 and 5 (example 3–3).

The **major scale** on C occurs naturally on the white keys of the piano. The combined distribution of whole steps and half steps across the C-major octave creates, in this case, two matching tetrachords (whole step, whole step, half step from scale degrees 1 to 4 and whole step, whole step, half step from scale degrees 5 to 8). The *profile* of the complete scale consists of half steps between scale degrees 3 and 4 and scale degrees 7 and 8, with all other adjacent notes being whole steps.

Example 3–3

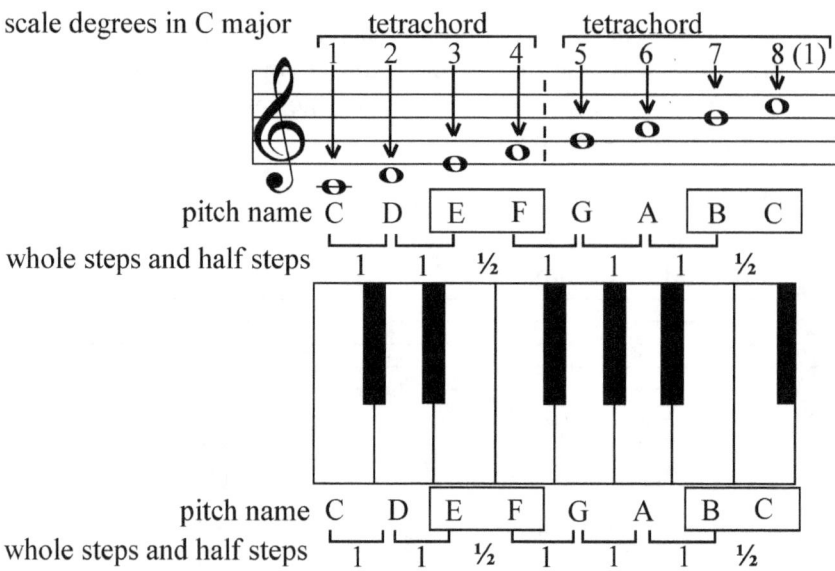

The pattern of half steps and whole steps in the major scale reflects two things, namely, **key** and **mode**. Key, which is also known variously as the **keynote** or **tonal center**, is that pitch to which all other pitches are related and toward which they ultimately move. If we play every pitch of the C-major scale in the numerical order of its scale degrees, starting with C as scale degree 1, the arrival of scale degree 7 confirms the strength of the key; for here, there is a compelling drive to complete the upward succession of pitches by ending on scale degree 8.

In addition to having an assigned number, each scale degree has a name. Scale degree 1 (or 8) is called the **tonic**, scale degree 2 the **supertonic**, 3 the **mediant**, 4 the **subdominant**, 5 the **dominant**, 6 the **submediant**, and 7 the **leading tone**. Later in this text, we shall add the term **subtonic** to our list of scale degrees (Chapter 6) and then discuss the reasons for all of the names (Chapter 8). For now, suffice it to say that the leading tone is so named because of its compelling drive to move upwards by a half step to the tonic.

The mode of a composition has a more direct relationship to the actual music than does the concept of scale, which is merely an alphabetical inventory of pitches derived from the music. Expressing certain characteristic patterns and configurations of pitches, the mode confirms and establishes the key of a musical work. Among the most important characteristic patterns of any mode is the arrangement of linear half steps and whole steps such as the one shown above in 3–3, which illustrates the C-major scale and mode. Indeed, its profile of half steps between scale degrees 3 and 4 and scale degrees 7 and 8 distinguishes the major mode from the profiles of other diatonic modes (see Chapter 6 and Appendix C).

Moving the Major Scale to Octaves Other Than C with the Addition of Sharps

Since there are twelve half steps and pitches within any octave, each pitch may have its own major mode and scale. It is therefore possible to move the C-major scale to any of the remaining eleven pitches within the octave. However, when moving the major scale to octaves other than C, its profile of half steps can be maintained only with the inclusion of one or more black keys of the piano.

Let us begin with the G octave. The first step is to start on C, scale degree 1 of C major, and go up to G, scale degree 5 of C major (example 3–4). Note carefully that the distance from C to G is 3½ steps (3½ steps is an abbreviation for three whole steps and one half step). Later, in Chapter 5, we shall refer to this distance as a **perfect 5th**.

Example 3–4

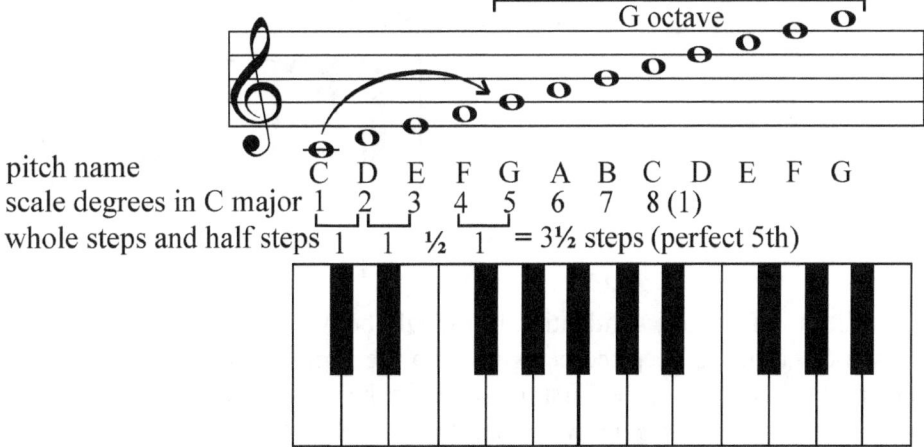

Once the G octave has been identified, C major's profile of half steps and whole steps must be preserved in G major. In order for the half steps to remain between scale degrees 3 and 4 and scale degrees 7 and 8, the tetrachord structure of the major mode has to be maintained (each tetrachord contains within its four-note span the following pattern: whole step, whole step, half step).

In example 3–5, we can see that the **lower tetrachord**, scale degrees 1 to 4, does not require the addition of black keys to preserve the four-note pattern of whole steps and half steps; however, the **upper tetrachord**, scale degrees 5 to 8, does. In order to establish a half step between scale degrees 7 and 8 and to maintain the tetrachord structure, it is necessary to raise the F one half step to F♯.

Example 3–5

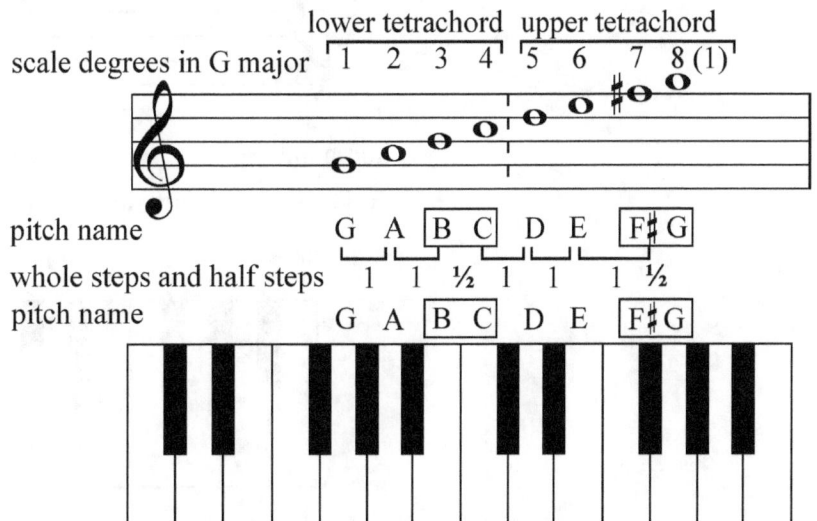

If we now begin on G, scale degree 1 of G major, and go up 3½ steps to D, scale degree 5 of G major, then our next scale will be found within the D octave (example 3–6).

Example 3–6

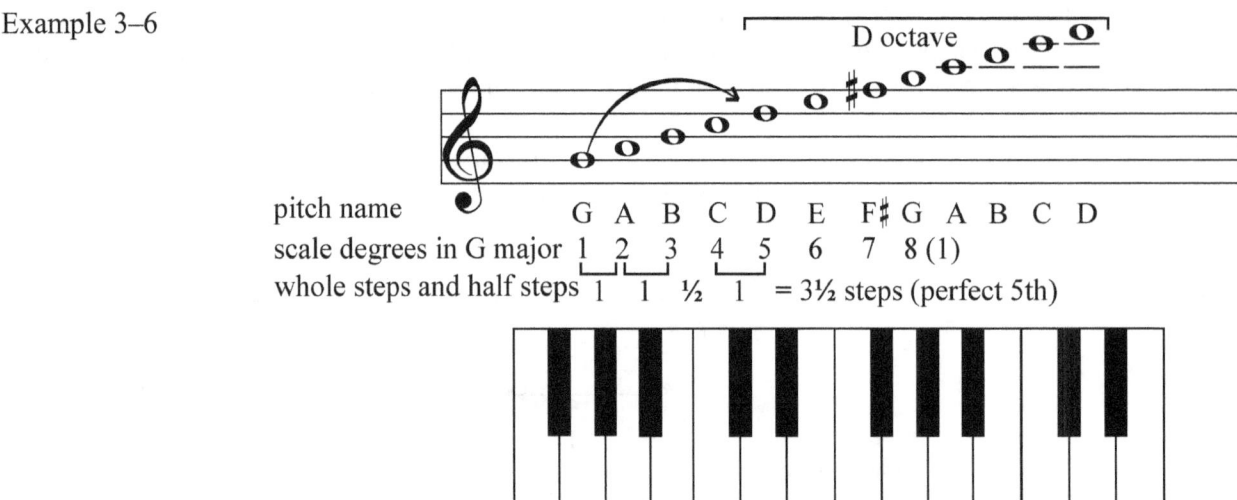

With the D octave so identified, it would be well to bring it down into the prime and double prime registers in order to keep the octave within the limits of the staff (example 3–7). We are now ready to construct the D major scale. First of all, retain the F♯ from the G major scale. *As long as the starting note of each scale is 3½ steps above the one that preceded it, all of the sharps added previously for each scale will be used in subsequent formations.*

Accordingly, retaining the F♯ from the previous G major scale preserves the profile of half steps and whole steps for the lower tetrachord of D major, as well as the half steps between scale degrees 3 and 4. The upper tetrachord of D major (scale degrees 5 to 8), however, requires one additional sharp, C♯. The inclusion of C♯ produces the requisite half step between scale degrees 7 and 8 and thereby maintains the structure of D major's upper tetrachord (whole step, whole step, half step).

Example 3–7

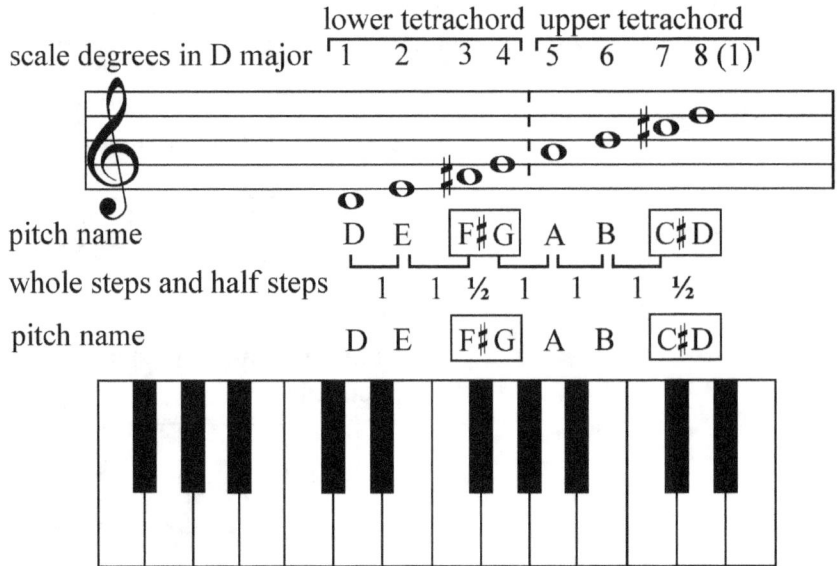

Our construction of the major scale began with C major, which has no sharps (or flats). We proceeded upwards 3½ steps to G major, which has one sharp, and then continued upwards 3½ steps to D major, which has two sharps. Since a pattern of adding sharps is evident, let us amend our earlier statement to read as follows: as long as the starting note of each scale is 3½ steps above the one that preceded it, all of the sharps added previously for each scale will be used in subsequent formations; *and, each new scale will add one sharp to those that have been retained from previous formations*. That additional sharp will create the leading tone (scale degree 7) of the new scale *within the upper tetrachord*.

And so, moving upwards 3½ steps from D identifies A as the octave in which to construct the next major scale (example 3–8); A is scale degree 5 of D major. The formation of the A major scale retains the F♯ and C♯ from the previous D major and adds a third sharp to bring the total number of sharps up to three; the question is, where does the third sharp appear?

Scale degrees 1 to 4 present no problem, as the C♯ from the previous D major maintains the structure of the lower tetrachord (example 3–9). The upper tetrachord, however, requires the addition of G♯ to preserve the structure of whole steps and half steps. Thus, the inclusion of G♯ (the leading tone) produces the half step between scale degrees 7 and 8.

Example 3–8

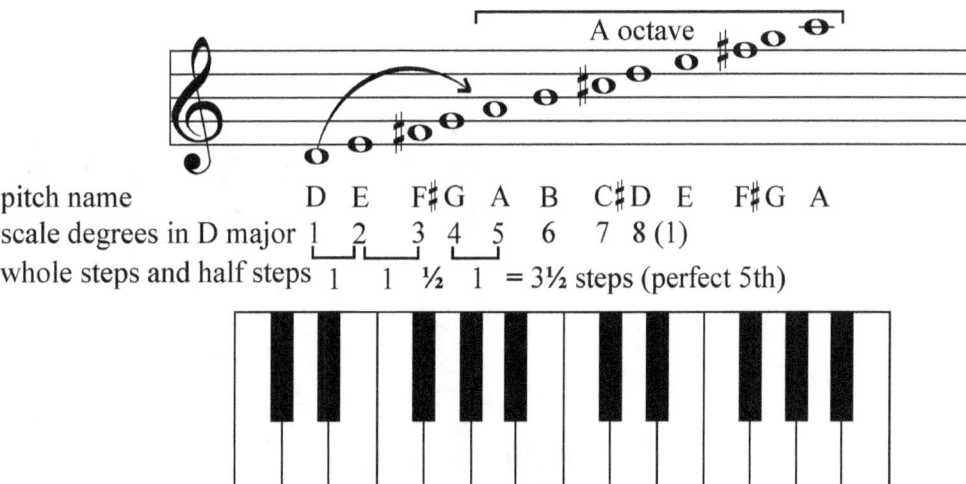

Example 3–9

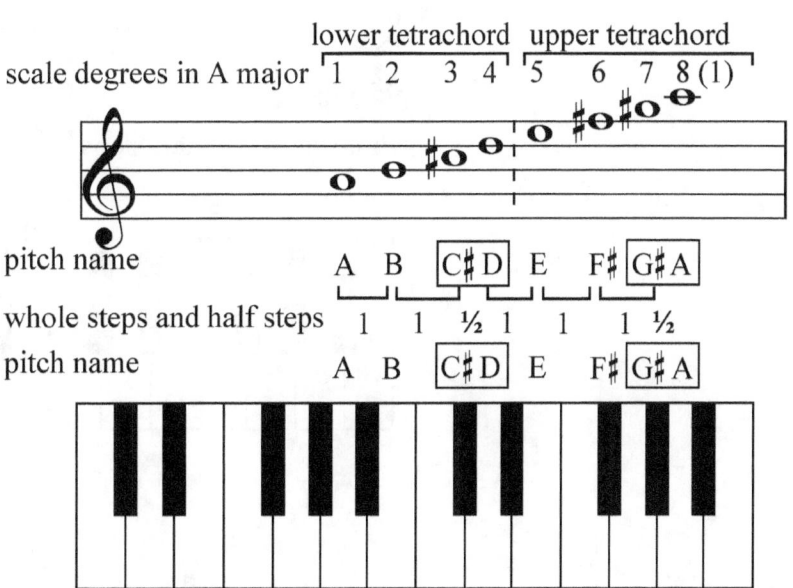

36   Chapter 3 The Major Scale

In order to identify the next octave in which to build the major scale, continue upwards 3½ steps from A to E (example 3–10). Bringing the E octave down into the prime and double prime registers keeps the octave within the limits of the staff (example 3–11). The E major scale retains the F♯, C♯, and G♯ of A major and adds a fourth sharp; but once again, the question is: where does the fourth sharp appear?

The lower tetrachord of E major already exhibits the correct arrangement of whole steps and half steps (whole step, whole step, half step), as well as the requisite half steps between scale degrees 3 and 4. For the upper tetrachord, the addition of D♯ produces the half step between scale degrees 7 and 8.

Example 3–10

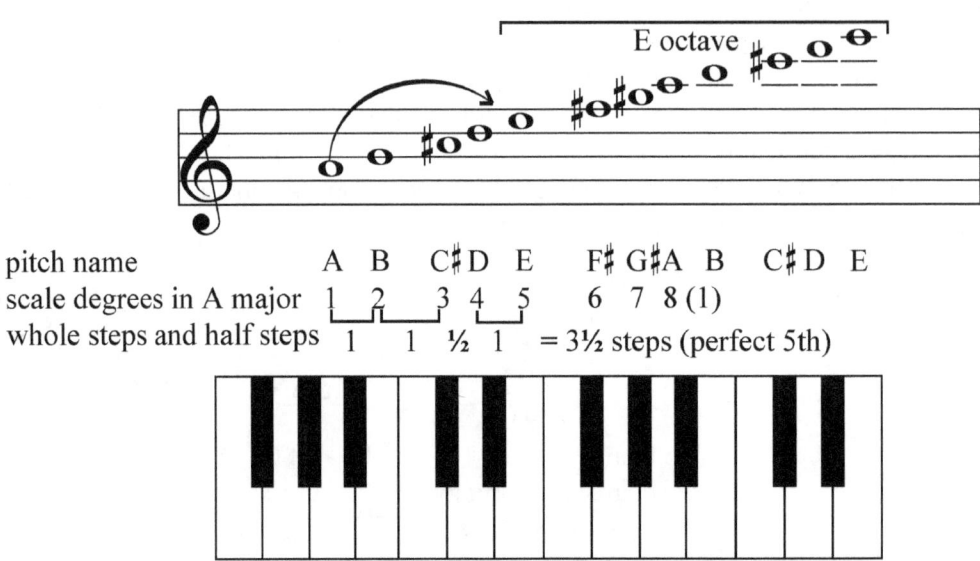

Example 3–11

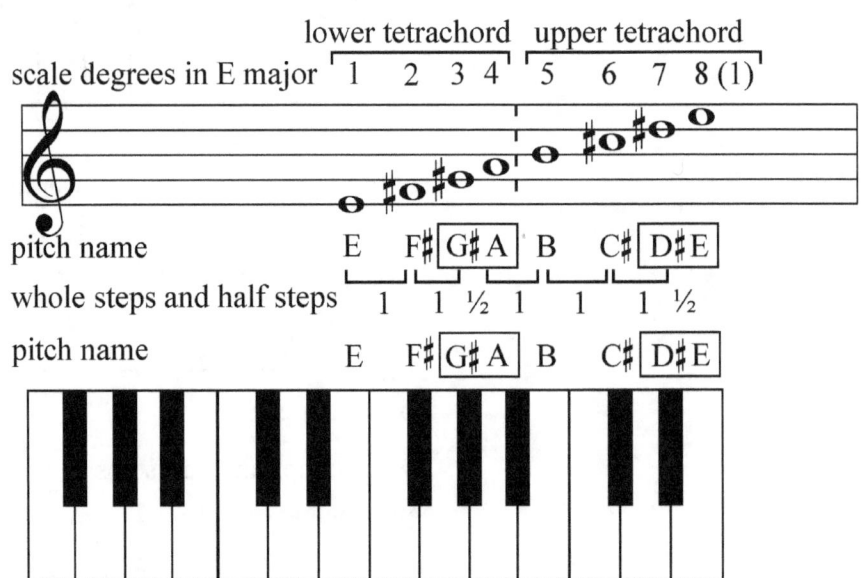

Chapter 3 The Major Scale 37

The octave in which to build the major scale with five sharps stands on B, 3½ steps above E (example 3–12). As in previous scale constructions, we retain the four sharps of E major and add a fifth sharp to complete the structure of both tetrachords (example 3–13). The addition of A♯ to the upper tetrachord maintains the half step between scale degrees 7 and 8.

Example 3–12

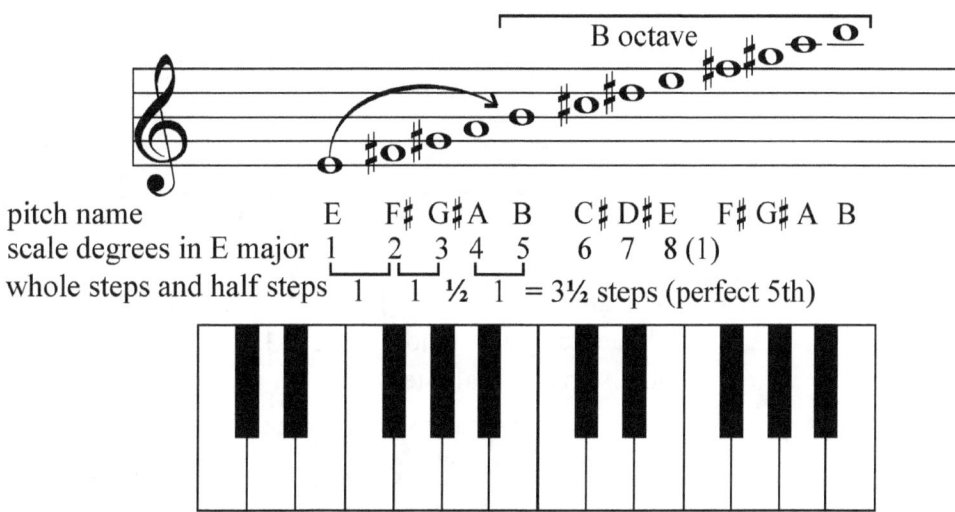

Example 3–13

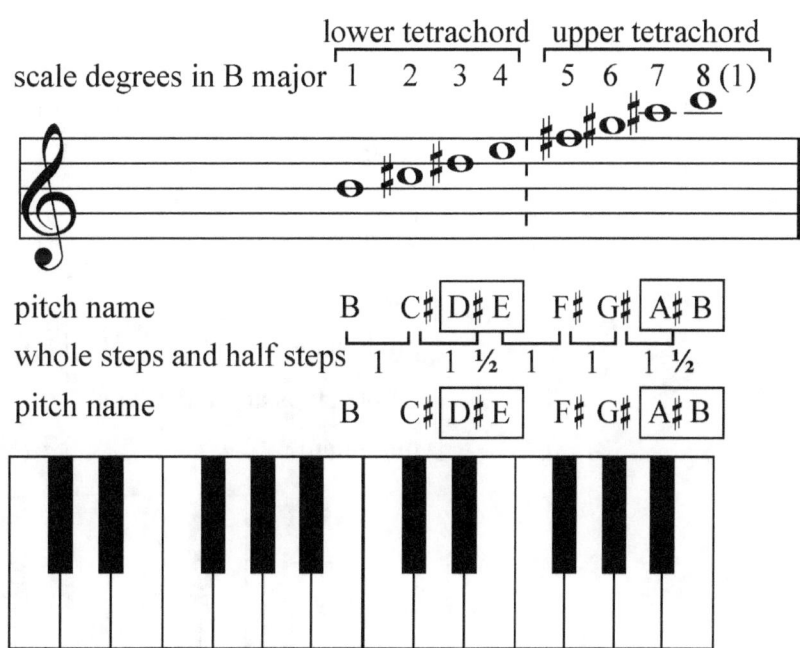

38   Chapter 3 The Major Scale

Proceeding upwards 3½ steps from B brings us to the F♯ octave (example 3–14). Here, we shall add a sixth sharp, E♯, to create an F♯ major scale (example 3–15). The lower tetrachord remains unchanged, retaining all of the sharps from the previous B major and preserving the half step between scale degrees 3 and 4. The addition of E♯ to the upper tetrachord completes its structure and establishes the half step between scale degrees 7 and 8.

Example 3–14

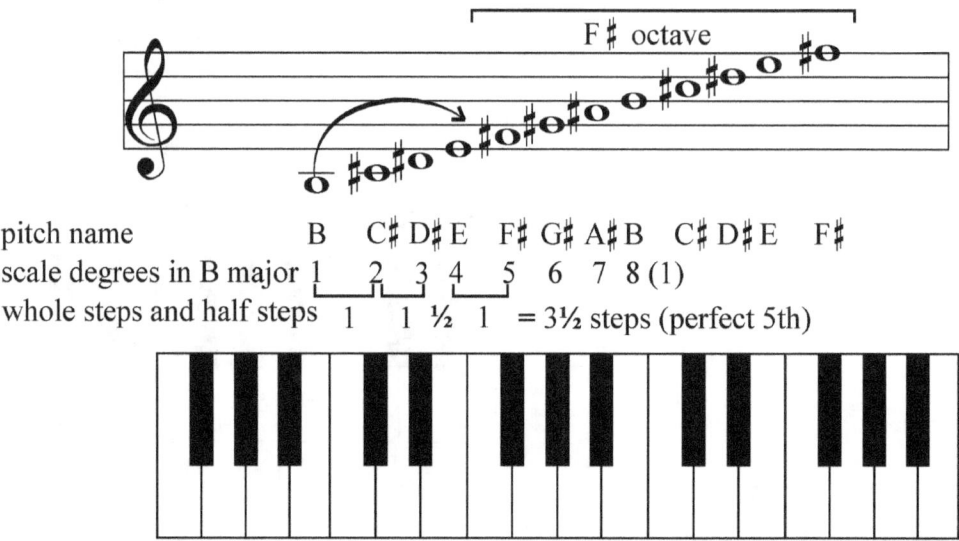

Example 3–15

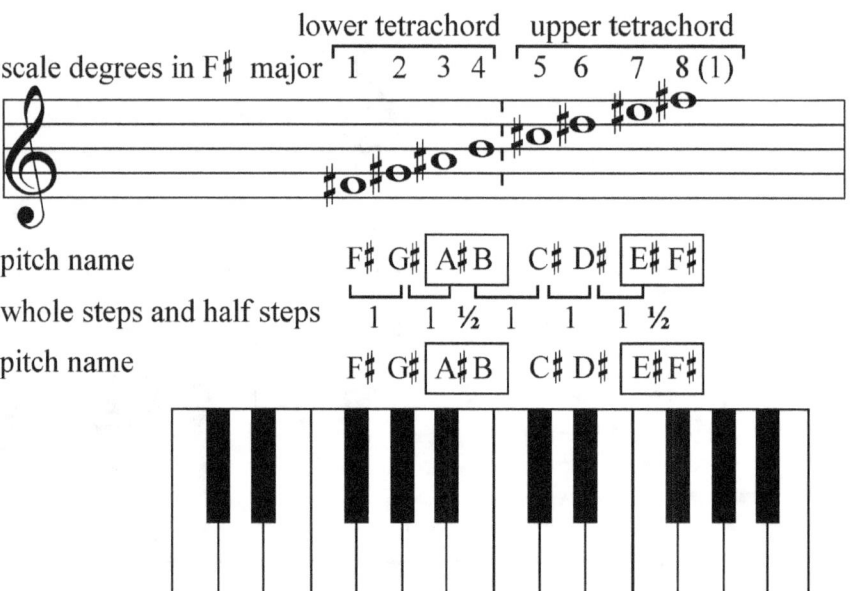

The C♯ octave is located 3½ steps above F♯ (example 3–16). The sharps from the previous scale, F♯ major, maintain the structure of C♯ major's lower tetrachord with half steps between scale degrees 3 and 4 (example 3–17). Let us also bring the C♯ octave down into the prime and double prime registers in order to keep most of the pitches within the limits of the staff. The addition of B♯ to the upper tetrachord, produces the half step between scale degrees 7 and 8. All seven tones of the major scale now carry a sharp.

Example 3–16

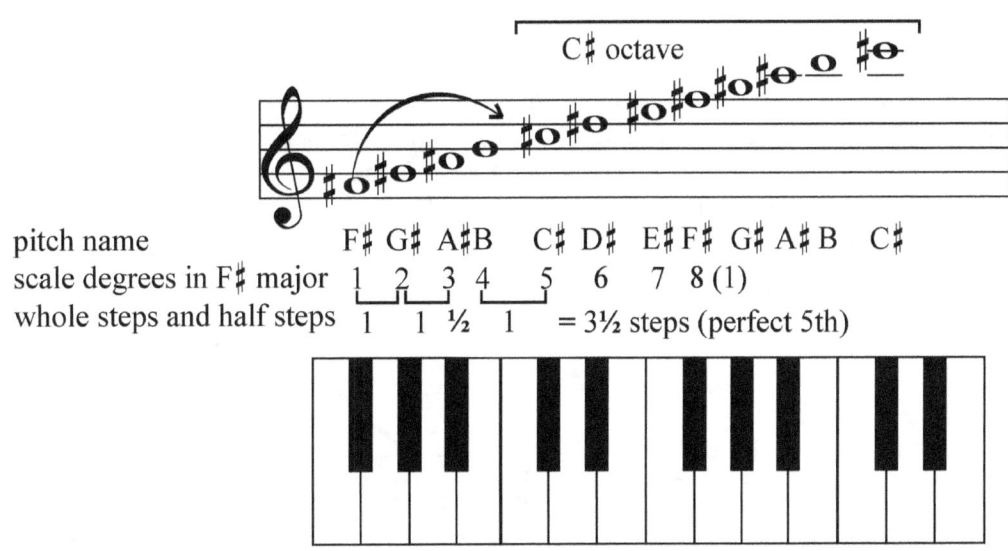

Example 3–17

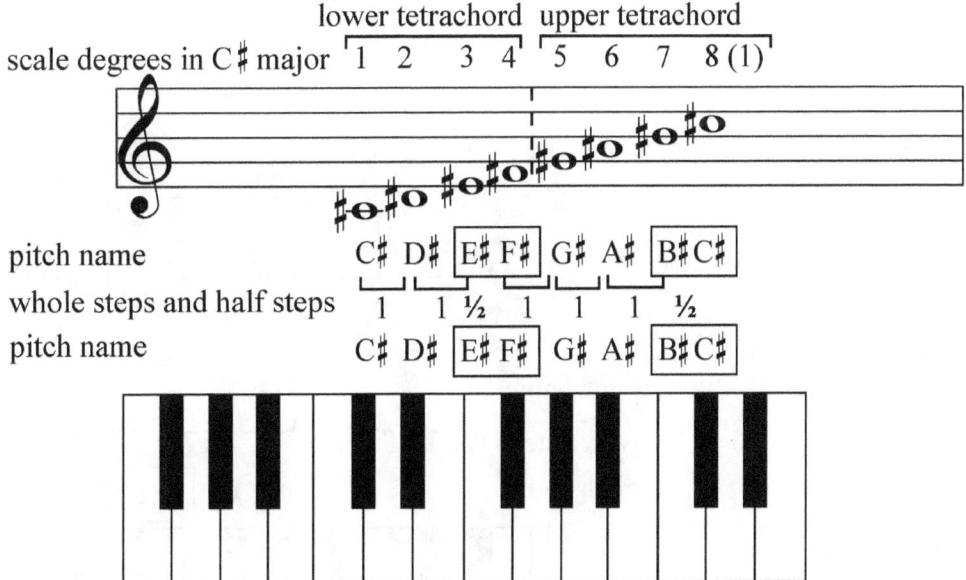

40 Chapter 3 The Major Scale

In the foregoing scale constructions, we developed the following principle with respect to those scales that employ sharps: as long as the starting note is 3½ steps above the one that preceded it, all of the sharps added previously for each scale are used in subsequent formations, and each new scale adds one sharp to those that have been retained from previous formulations (the sharps occur in the following order: F♯, C♯, G♯, D♯, A♯, E♯, and B♯). The sharp added to the previous ones creates the leading tone (scale degree 7) of the new scale. Moving upwards in 3½-step increments from C, then, takes us through the following major scales: G, D, A, E, B, F♯, and C♯.

It is theoretically possible, though not practical, to locate the next octave in which to build a major scale by continuing upwards 3½ steps from C♯ to G♯ (example 3–18). The structure of G♯ major's lower tetrachord remains complete, as it incorporates the sharps from C♯ major (example 3–19). The upper tetrachord, however, requires the addition of an eighth sharp. Since all the pitches already have one sharp, a double sharp replaces the F♯ on scale degree 7. Hence, the half step between scale degrees 7 and 8 is established by raising F♯ one half step to F𝄪, the leading tone of G♯ major. Again, building a major scale on G♯ is a useful theoretical exercise but not a practical one. We shall see that it is far more desirable to re-evaluate the G♯ enharmonically as A♭, and there construct a major scale that will require four flats rather than eight sharps.

Example 3–18

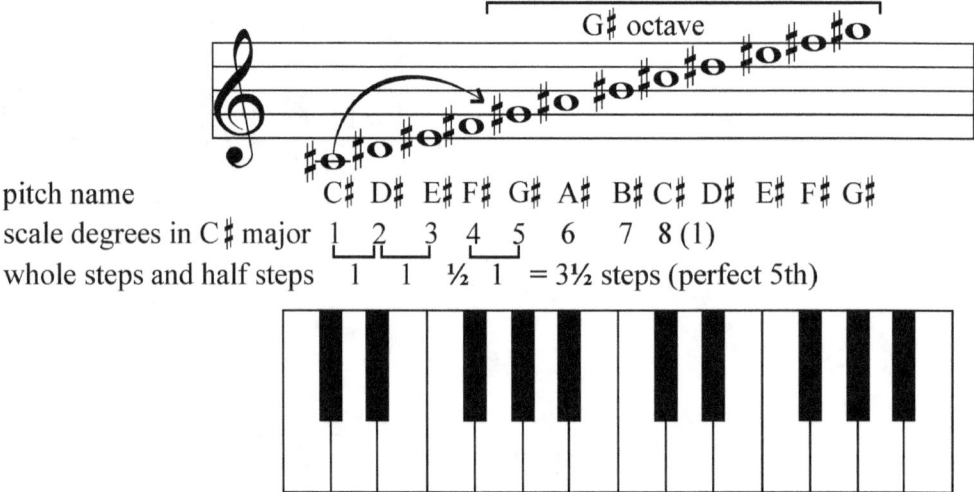

Example 3–19

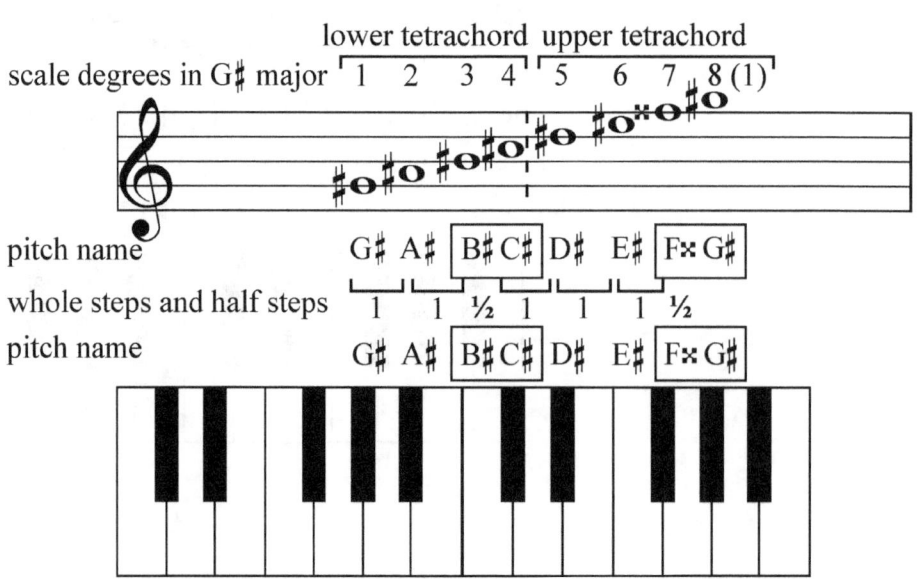

Moving the Major Scale to Octaves Other Than C with the Addition of Flats

To locate the first octave in which to construct a major scale with flats, count downwards 3½ steps from C to F (example 3–20). As we shall see, moving downwards in 3½-step increments from C takes us through the following octaves: F, B♭, E♭, A♭, D♭, G♭, and C♭. In order to best illustrate each of these octaves and their respective scale constructions, it will be easier to move upwards in 2½-step increments. Later, in Chapter 5, we shall refer to this distance as a **perfect 4th**.

Looking at example 3–20, notice that if we start on c prime (c^1) and continue upwards 2½ steps, our destination will be f prime (f^1). Proceeding downwards 3½ steps from c prime leads to small f. Therefore, the same pitch letter can be reached by moving either up 2½ steps (a perfect 4th) or down 3½ steps (a perfect 5th) from any given pitch (in this instance, c prime); however, each pitch of the same letter will be in a different octave register.

In any case, having located the F octave, let us build the F major scale. In order to preserve the half step between scale degrees 3 and 4, a B♭ must be added to the *lower tetrachord* (example 3–21). The upper tetrachord requires no changes, as a half step already exists between E and F, scale degrees 7 and 8.

Example 3–20

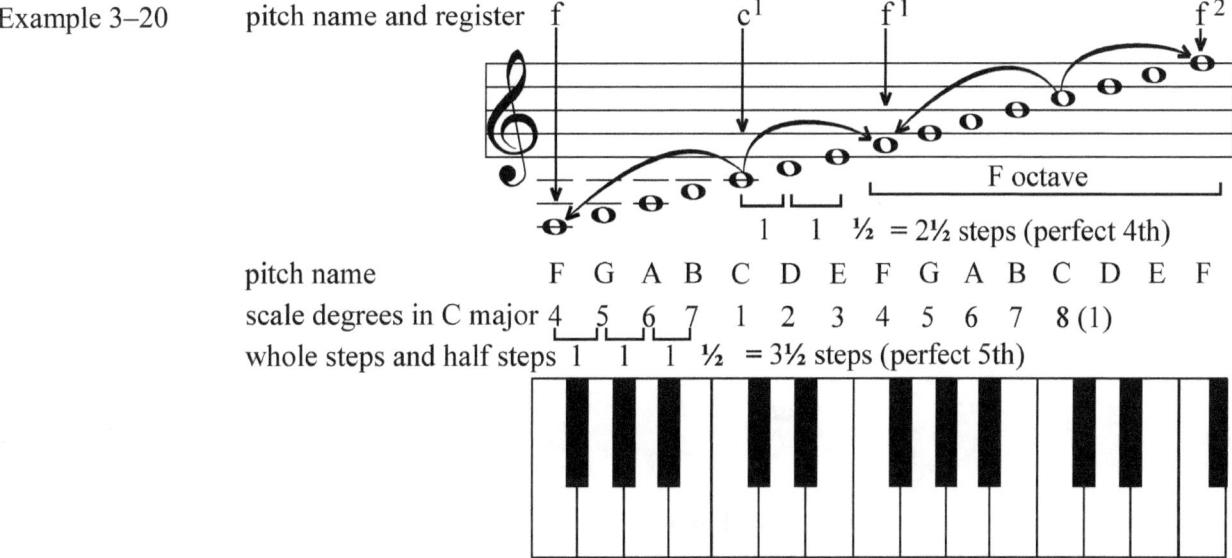

Example 3–21

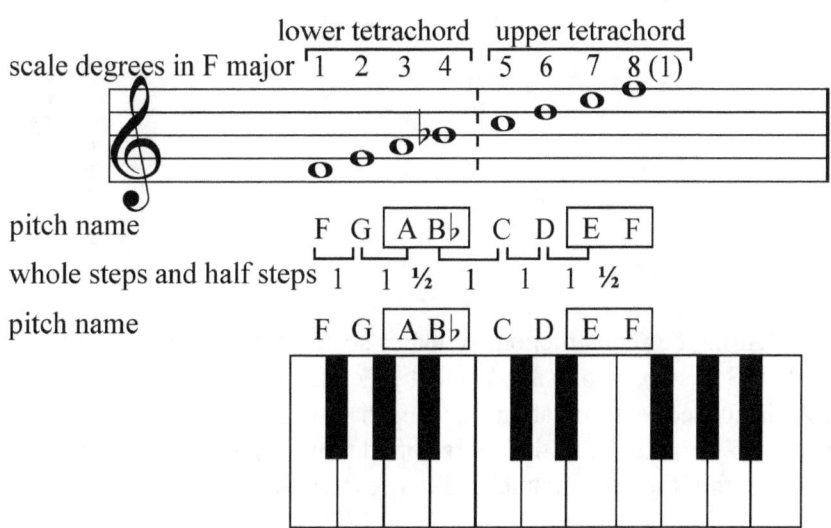

The B♭ octave is located 2½ steps above F (example 3–22); B♭ is scale degree 4 of F major. As we shall see, the scale for B♭ major requires the addition of one flat, E♭ (example 3–23). Since the structure of B♭ major's upper tetrachord already contains a half step between scale degrees 7 and 8, no additional changes are needed. The lower tetrachord, however, must take an E♭ to produce the requisite half step between scale degrees 3 and 4.

Example 3–22

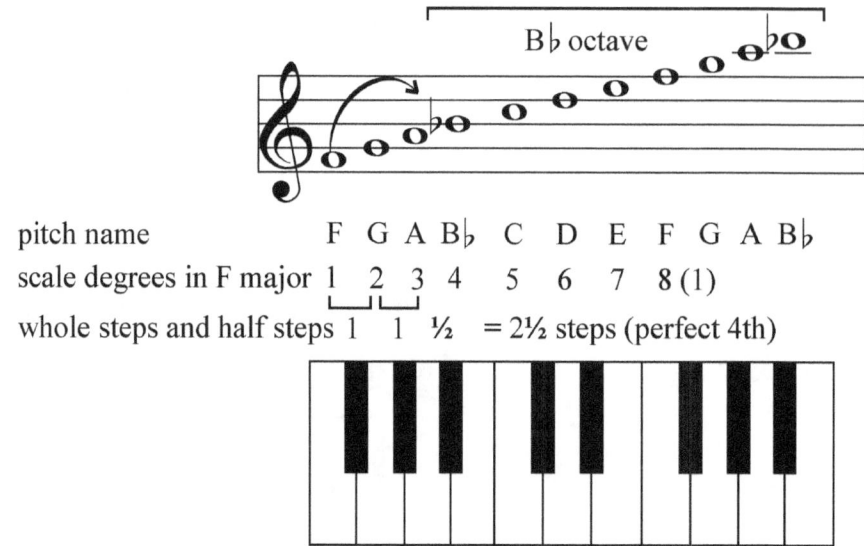

Example 3–23

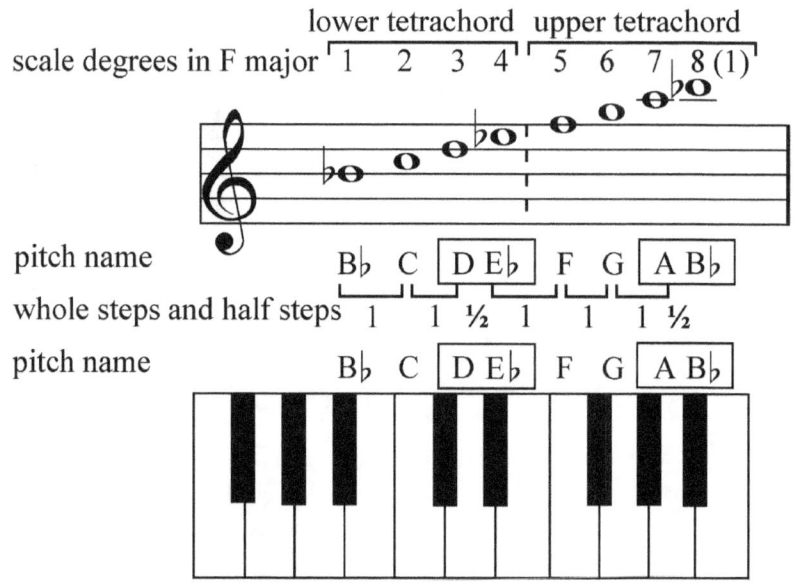

During our constructions of major scales with sharps, we said that as long as the starting note of each scale is 3½ steps above the one that preceded it, all of the sharps added previously for each scale will be used in subsequent formations; and, each new scale will add one sharp to those that have been retained from previous formations. In the course of adding a sharp to each new scale, we saw that these additions were made within the upper tetrachord to preserve the half step between scale degree 7 and 8.

With respect to the construction of major scales with flats, the addition of each new flat will occur within the *lower tetrachord*, as long as the starting note of each scale is 2½ steps above the one that preceded it (or 3½ steps below the one that preceded it). Therefore, moving upwards 2½ steps from B♭ brings us to the E♭ octave (example 3–24); E♭ is scale degree 4 of B♭ major. The lower tetrachord of E♭ major takes an A♭ to maintain the half step between scale degree 3 and 4 (example 3–25). The upper tetrachord of E♭ retains the B♭ from the previous scale and requires no further additions.

Example 3–24

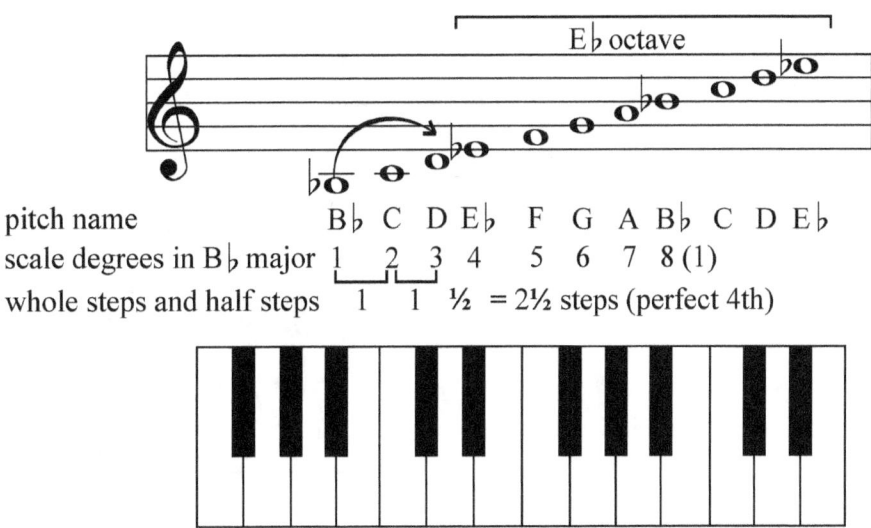

Example 3–25

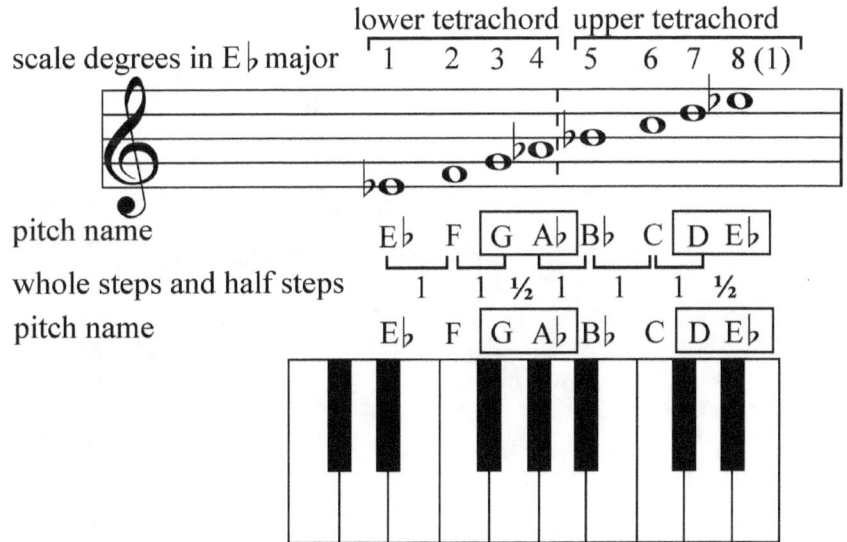

A♭ major, the next scale to add a flat, begins 2½ steps above E♭ (example 3–26). The upper tetrachord requires no additional flats; however, the lower tetrachord must have a D♭ in order to maintain its structure and to effect the half step between scale degree 3 and 4 (example 3–27).

Example 3–26

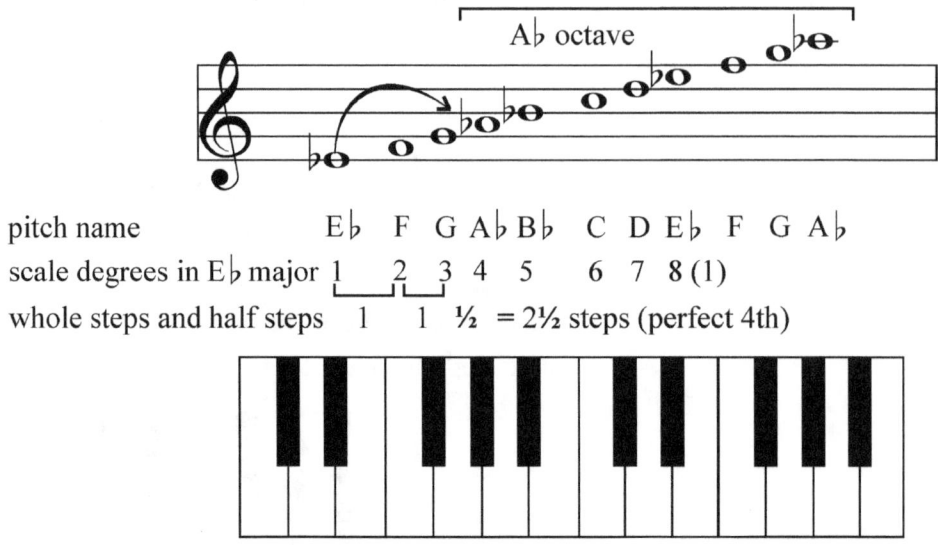

Example 3–27

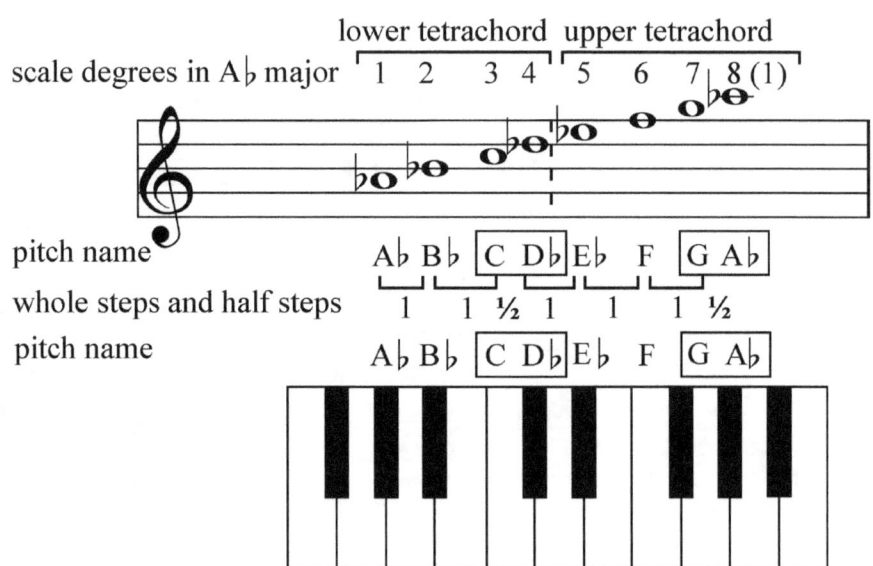

The process of maintaining the flats from previous scale constructions continues if we proceed upwards 2½ steps from A♭ to D♭ (example 3–28). Once again, the lower tetrachord requires the addition of a flat, G♭ (example 3–29). The upper tetrachord remains unchanged. Notice that for the flat side of major, the addition of a flat in the lower tetrachord occurs on scale degree 4 and that once the alteration has been made, the distance between scale degrees 1 and 4 is now 2½ steps, that is, a perfect 4th.

Example 3–28

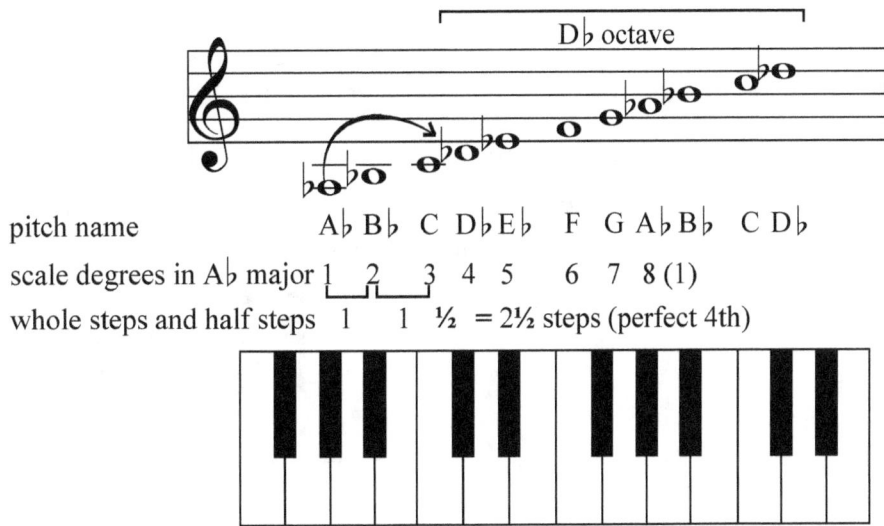

Example 3–29

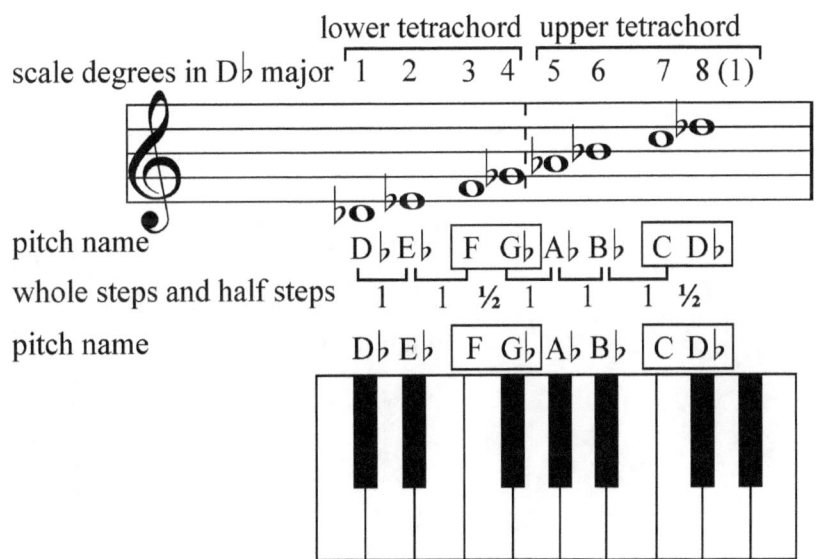

Ascending 2½ steps from D♭ brings us to the G♭ octave (example 3–30). The upper tetrachord retains all of the flats from the previous D♭ major scale (example 3–31). The lower tetrachord, however, takes a C♭ to preserve the half step between scale degrees 3 and 4. Again, the addition of C♭ also creates a 2½-step (perfect 4th) span between scale degrees 1 and 4.

Example 3–30

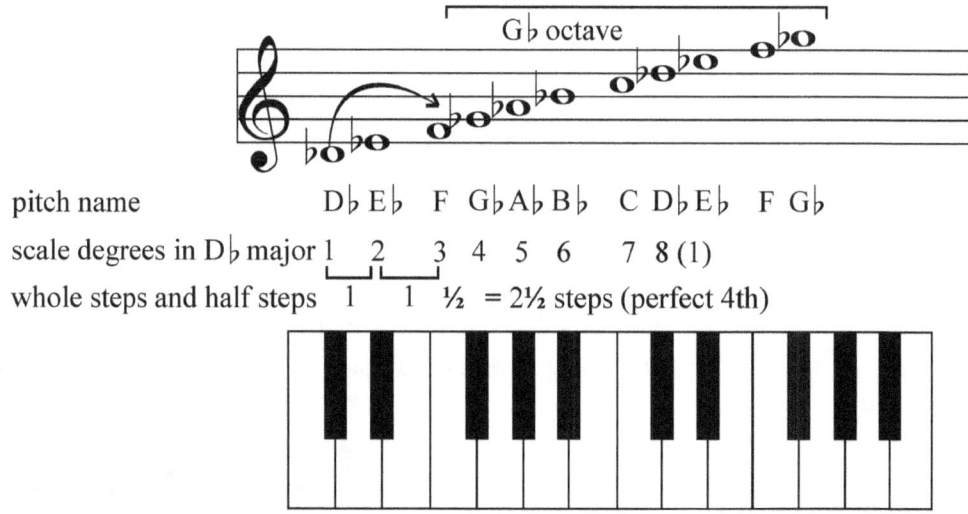

Example 3–31

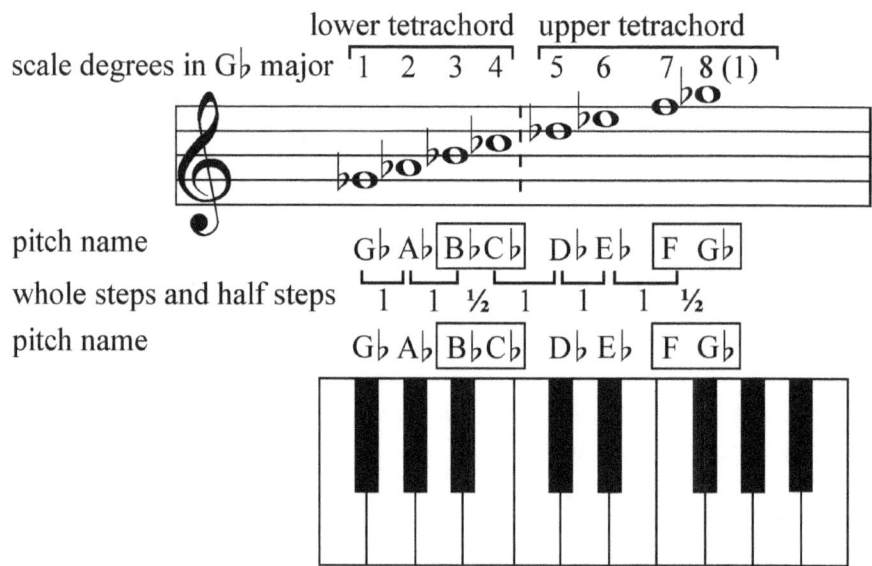

Standing 2½ steps above G♭ is C♭, the starting note for the next octave in which to build a major scale and add a flat (example 3–32). The lower tetrachord requires the inclusion of an F♭ to produce the needed half step between 3 and 4 (example 3–33). All seven tones of the major scale now carry a flat.

Example 3–32

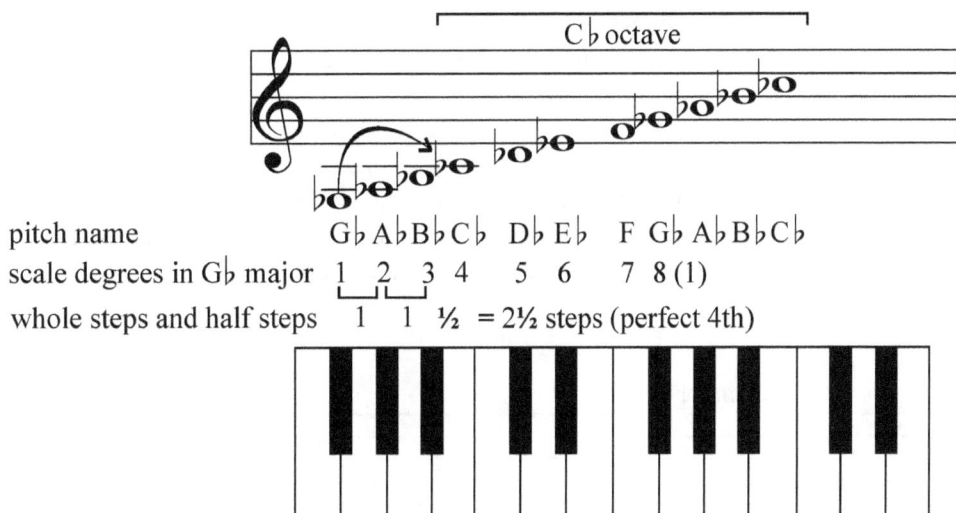

Example 3–33

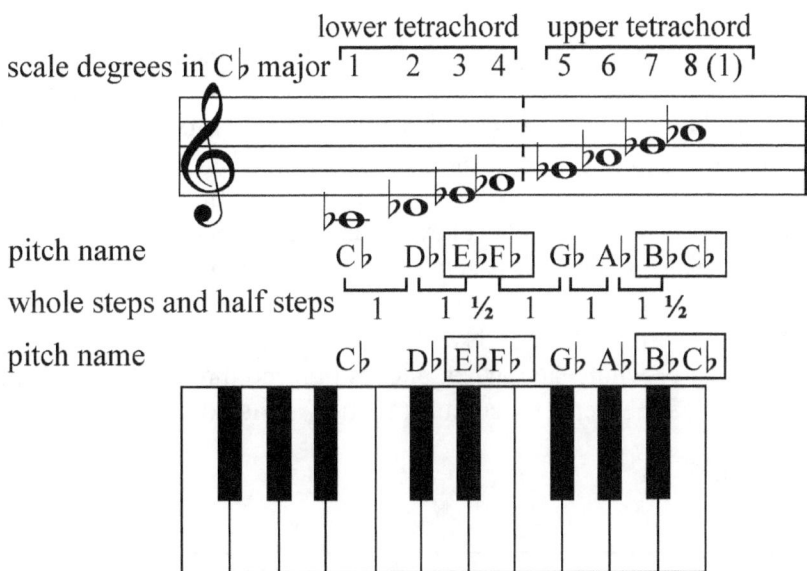

And so, as we have said, in scale constructions with flats, the addition of each new flat will occur within the lower tetrachord, as long as the starting note of each scale is 2½ steps above the one that preceded it (or 3½ steps below the one that preceded it). Moreover, the adjustment to the lower tetrachord will always involve the subdominant scale degree, that is, scale degree 4.

Singing the Major Scale

Earlier in this chapter, we said that a scale was an alphabetical inventory of pitches abstracted from the music. The scale has two practical purposes: first of all, the scale shows the pitch content for the key and mode in which the music is written; and secondly, a scale is a succession of pitches that musicians practice on their respective instruments, usually as a "warm up" exercise before playing or singing actual music. One of the ways to sing a major scale is to assign syllables to each scale degree. This approach is generally referred to as "solmization."

The most common method for singing the major scale assigns the syllables *do, re, mi, fa, sol, la, ti,* and *do* (pronounced doe, ray, mee, fah, soh or soul, lah, tee, and doe) to scale degrees 1, 2, 3, 4, 5, 6, 7, and 8 respectively. As shown in example 3–34, when the scale is moved from the C octave to any other octave, such as F, the syllables remain attached to the scale degrees rather than to the pitches. Thus, scale degrees 1, 2, 3, 4, 5, 6, 7, and 8 in both C major and F major carry the syllables *do, re, mi, fa, sol, la, ti,* and *do*.

Example 3–34

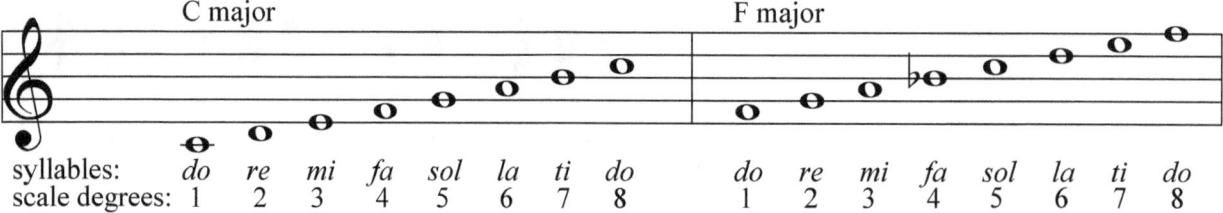

To learn how to sing these syllables and pitches, you should first play the pitches on the piano (if one is available) and then try to match the pitches with your voice. Since the C octave already projects a major scale without incorporating any black keys, first try to play the pitches of C major on the piano, starting in either the small or prime register; secondly, try matching the pitches with your voice using the syllables.

If the range of the C octave is not suitable, you may have to play the scale in a different octave and thereby use some of the black keys. In any case, once you have found a suitable register and octave range, sing the major scale in its ascending and descending form, using the syllables *do, re, mi, fa, sol, la, ti, do* when singing upwards and then *do, ti, la, sol, fa, mi, re, do* when singing downwards (see examples 3–35a and 35b). Both examples 3–34 and 35 involve movement between adjacent scale degrees separated by either a half step or whole step; when pitches proceed through musical space in this way, it is called **conjunct motion**. Another term for conjunct motion is **melodic motion**.

Example 3–35

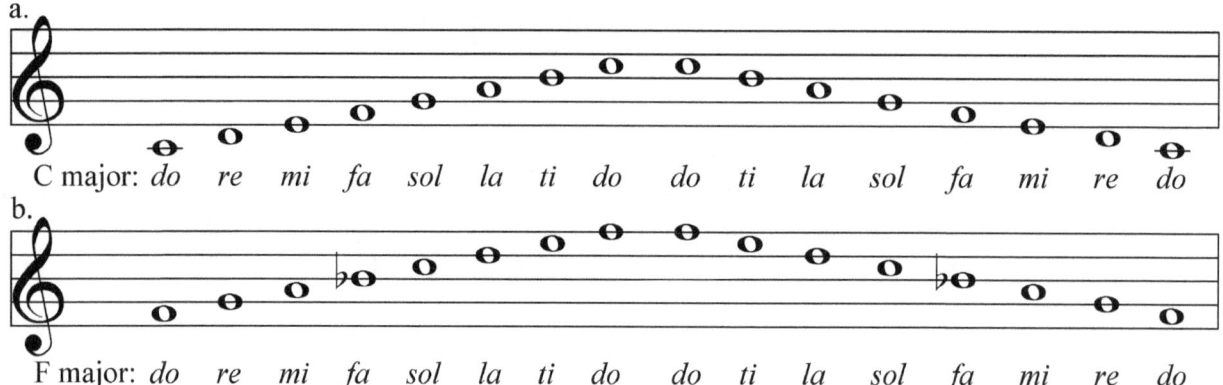

Examples 3–36 and 37 show **disjunct motion**, a type of movement between adjacent scale degrees and pitches separated by an interval greater than a whole step. Example 3–36 begins with conjunct motion but then moves disjunctly with increasingly larger distances between the pitches. In 3–37, the motion between the pitches consists partially of disjunct intervals called 3rds (see Chapter 5).

Example 3–36

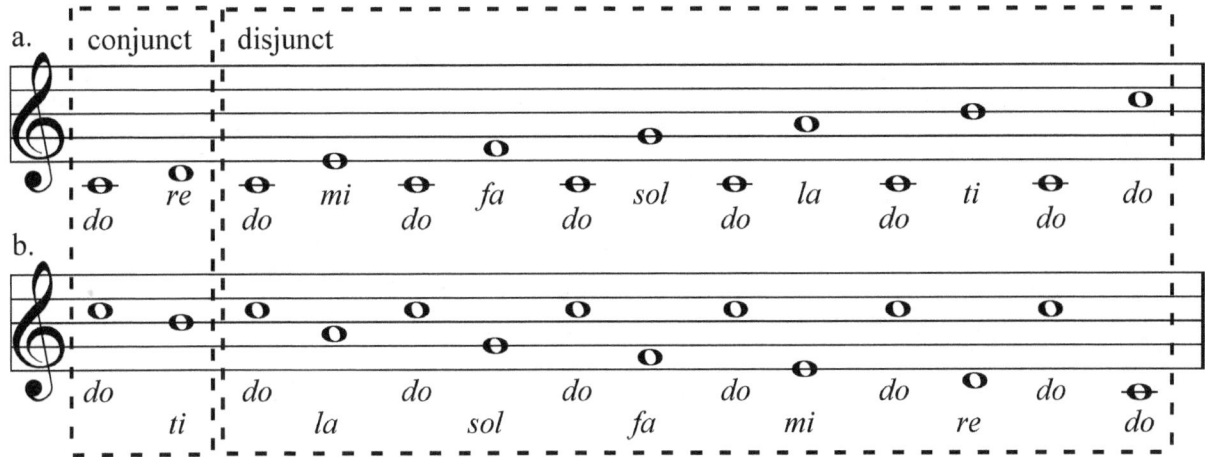

Example 3–37

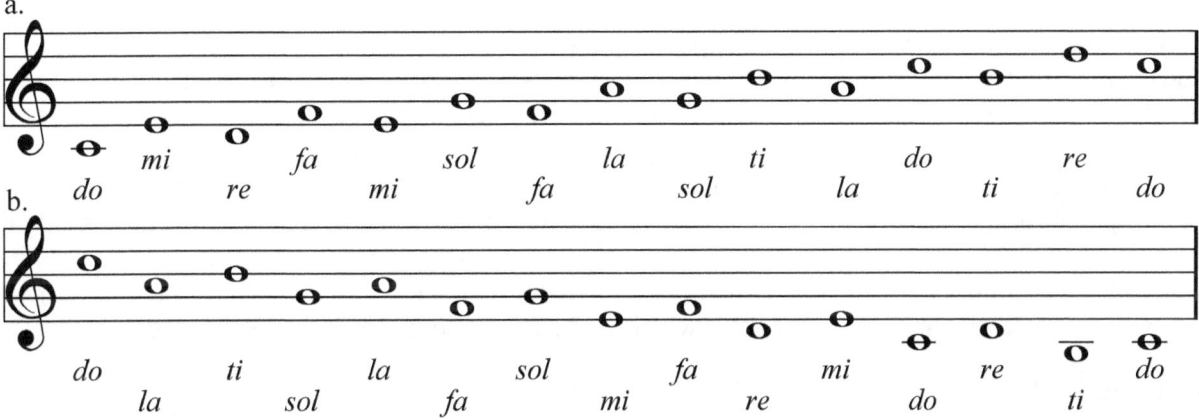

Articulation Marks

In Chapter 1, we encountered performance marks for tempo and dynamics (see above, pp. 16–17). Another performance direction for shaping the expression of a composition involves how musical sounds are connected. Connections between musical sounds may be either smooth or detached; that is, the score may contain instructions to play a composition by either connecting pitches and rhythms smoothly to one another or delivering them in a separated manner; the Italian words *legato* and *staccato* refer to each of these methods respectively. These instructions fall under the general category of articulation marks.

The smooth style of playing, *legato*, is indicated in the musical score with a curved line placed either above or below the notes. This curved line is called a **slur** and is similar to a tie, except that a tie connects two notes of the same pitch whereas a slur connects two or more different pitches together and directs the performer to move from pitch to pitch as seamlessly as possible. The intention is for the one note to flow smoothly into the next without any apparent break between them.

The detached style of playing, *staccato*, is indicated most commonly in the musical score with dots appearing either above or below the notes. Here, the performer is directed to make a clear separation between the pitches; in essence, separating the pitches results in each note receiving a little less than its full value. Example 3–38 illustrates how slurs and dots are used to indicate either a *legato* or *staccato* performance.

Example 3–38

Singing the Chromatic Scale

It is also possible to attach syllables to the pitches of the twelve-tone chromatic scale in both its ascending and descending forms (example 3–39). Since the chromatic scale consists primarily of pairs of pitches that involve two different versions of the same letter name, the syllables must change as each pitch moves from one version of itself to the other. We call this type of change **syllable inflection**.

Just as the pitch names change depending upon the upward or downward direction of the scale, some of the syllable inflections in the ascending chromatic scale are not the same as those of the descending form (*re-ra, mi-me, si-se, li-le*). (Notice that *di* occurs only in the ascending form while *te* appears only in the descending form.) In Chapter 6 and Appendix C, we shall find it helpful to use some of the syllables of the ascending and descending chromatic scale when singing modes other than the major mode.

Example 3–39

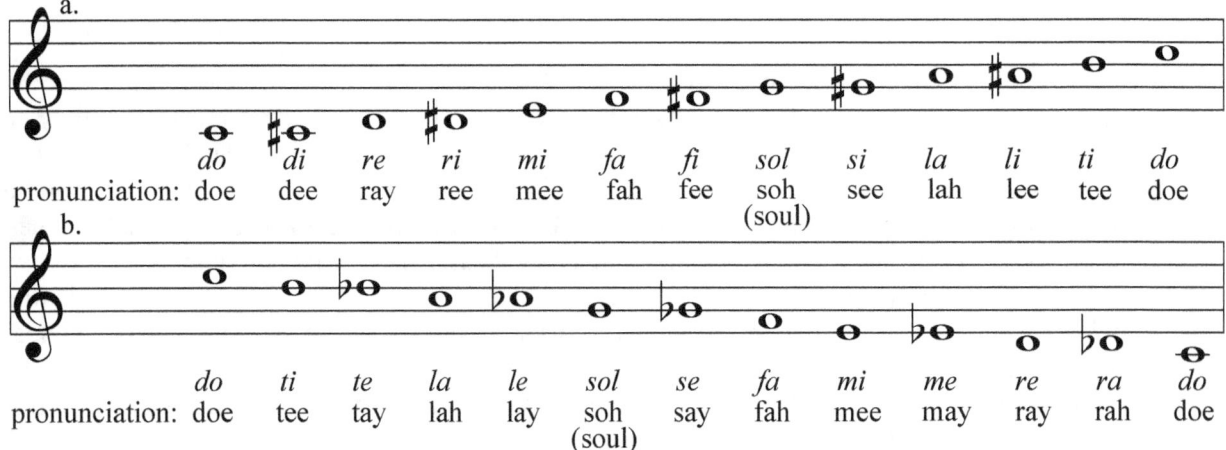

Chapter 4 Major Key Signatures

In Chapter 3, we learned that when moving the major scale to octaves other than C, the half steps between scale degrees 3 and 4 and scale degrees 7 and 8 can be maintained only with the inclusion of one or more black notes of the piano. It is, however, unwieldy to place all of the sharps or flats of the mode throughout the notated score of a music composition. Accordingly, the accidentals (sharps or flats) of any mode appear in a type of shorthand notation known as a **key signature**.

The key signature identifies the specific notes that are appropriate to the mode of a musical work. Before we investigate the construction and configuration of key signatures for the major mode, it would be well to reconsider how each major scale adds one sharp or flat to those that have been retained from previous scale formations.

As we have seen, there are two sides to the major mode: a flat side and a sharp side. We shall discuss these two sides presently and then find the connection between them in the next section, The Circle of 5ths. Starting on C and proceeding downwards in 3½-step increments (a perfect 5th) or upwards in 2½-step increments (a perfect 4th) brings us to the flat side of major. Each new scale formation adds one flat to those that preceded it. Example 4–1 shows the ascending or descending order of scales on the flat side of major: F, B♭, E♭, A♭, D♭, G♭, and C♭.

Example 4–1

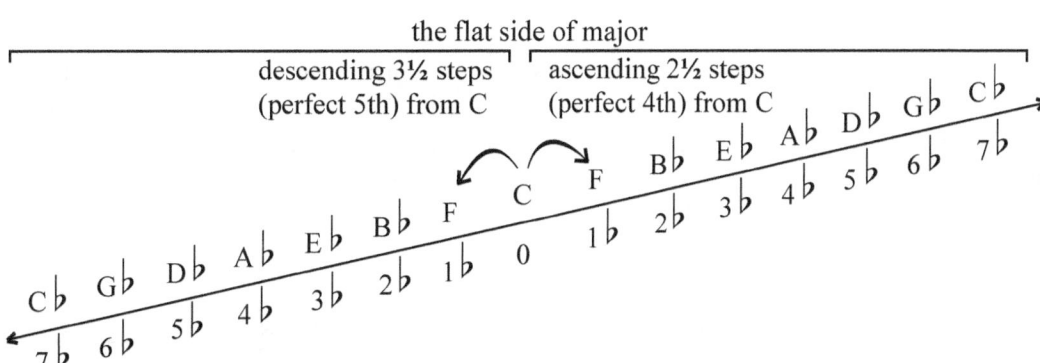

It is possible to apply the process of moving in either direction from C to the sharp side of major by continuing upwards in 3½-step increments or downwards in 2½-step increments. Each new scale construction adds one sharp to those that preceded it. Example 4–2 illustrates the ascending or descending order of scales on the sharp side of major: G, D, A, E, B, F♯, and C♯.

Example 4–2

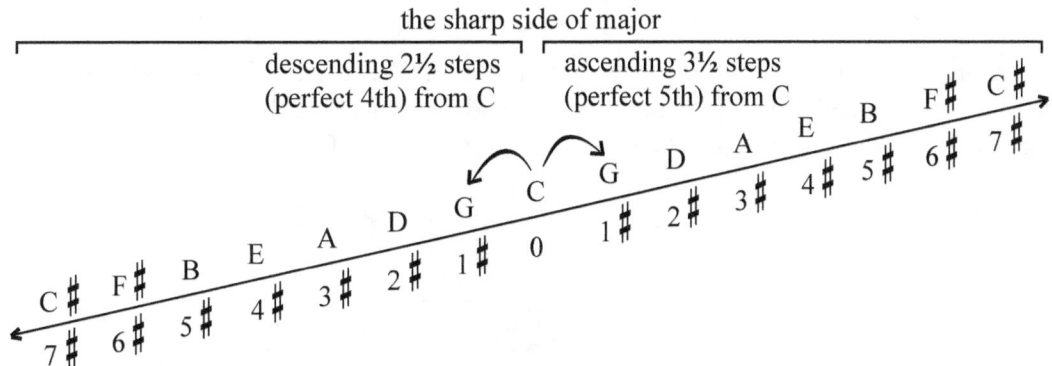

Example 4–3 combines the descending portion of example 4–1 and the ascending portion of example 4–2, with the sharp side of major rising 3½ steps above C and the flat side falling 3½ steps below C.

Example 4–3

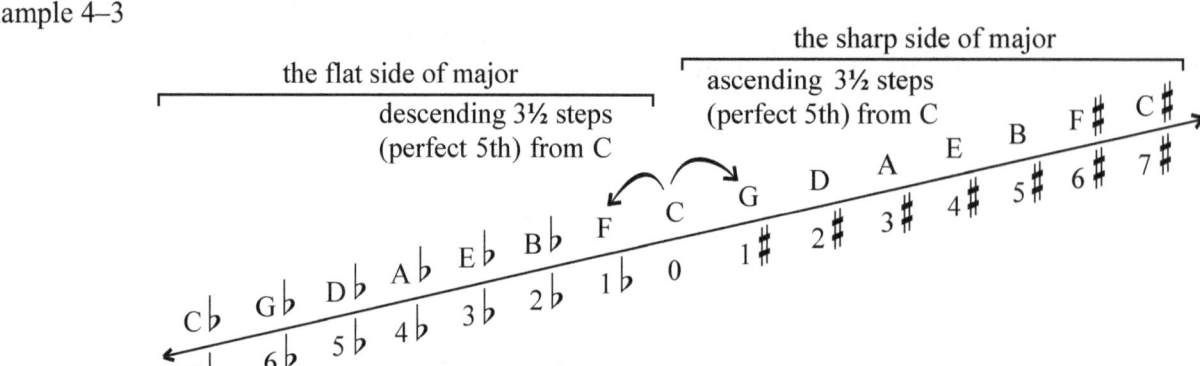

Look at the configurations of the key signatures for C♯ major and C♭ major as they appear on both the G clef (treble clef) and the F clef (bass clef). Examples 4–4a and 4b present the key signature as a collection of accidentals that appears between the clef sign and the time signature. The key signature forms a pattern that is logically designed to keep all of the accidentals within the limits of the staff and to facilitate reading.

The pattern for both sharp and flat keys is consistently maintained except in one place. Starting with F♯, the pattern for sharp keys is down a 4th and up a 5th, except for the A♯, which continues down another 4th before the pattern resumes. Determine the intervals of a 4th and 5th by counting each line and space on the staff. The key signature pattern for flat keys contains no irregularities: up a 4th and down a 5th.

Example 4–4

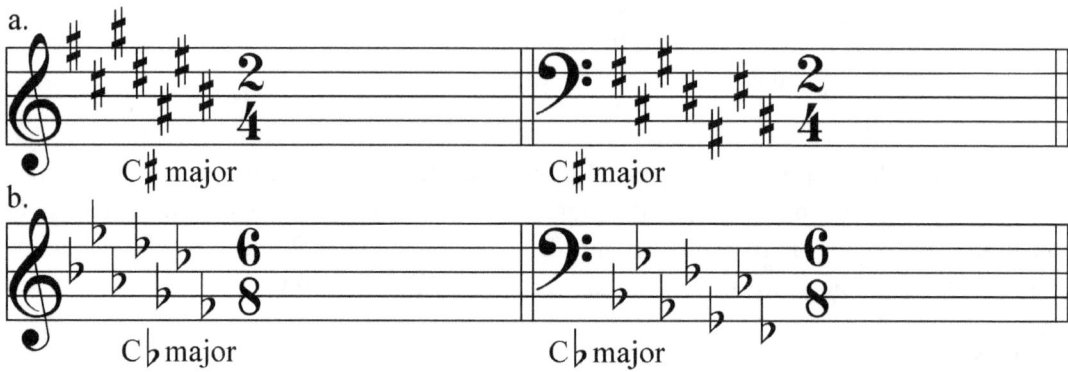

Consider what would have happened to the A♯ if the pattern of descending 4ths and ascending 5ths had been consistently observed. Both the A♯ and the B♯ would have required ledger lines and thereby exceeded the limits of the staff (example 4–5).

Example 4–5

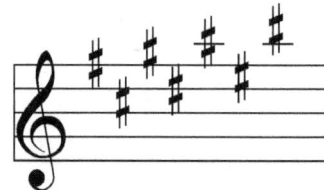

The Circle of 5ths

In example 4–3, we used C major as a starting point and ascended in perfect-5th intervals through G, D, A, E, B, F♯, and C♯, increasing by one the number of sharps for each successive key. Similarly, we descended from C in perfect-5th intervals through F, B♭, E♭, A♭, D♭, G♭, and C♭, increasing by one the number of flats for each successive key. Out of these formations, fifteen major keys emerge, seven with sharps, seven with flats, and C major, which has neither sharps nor flats.

As shown in example 4–6, the procession of ascending perfect 5ths on the sharp side of major and descending perfect 5ths on the flat side of major forms a circle, a **circle of 5ths**. Remember each key's position in the circle and you will be able to determine how many accidentals any given major key has.

For example, the third key from C on the sharp side, A major, has three sharps. The fourth key from C on the flat side, A♭ major, has four flats. Notice the three pairs of keys located on the lower portion of the circle, namely, D♭ and C♯, G♭ and F♯, and C♭ and B. Play the scales for these three pairs of keys on the piano and you will find that each pair sounds the same; they are **enharmonic keys**. The enharmonic keys close the circle of 5ths by bringing the sharp and flat sides of major together.

Example 4–6: the sharp and flat sides of major in the circle of 5ths

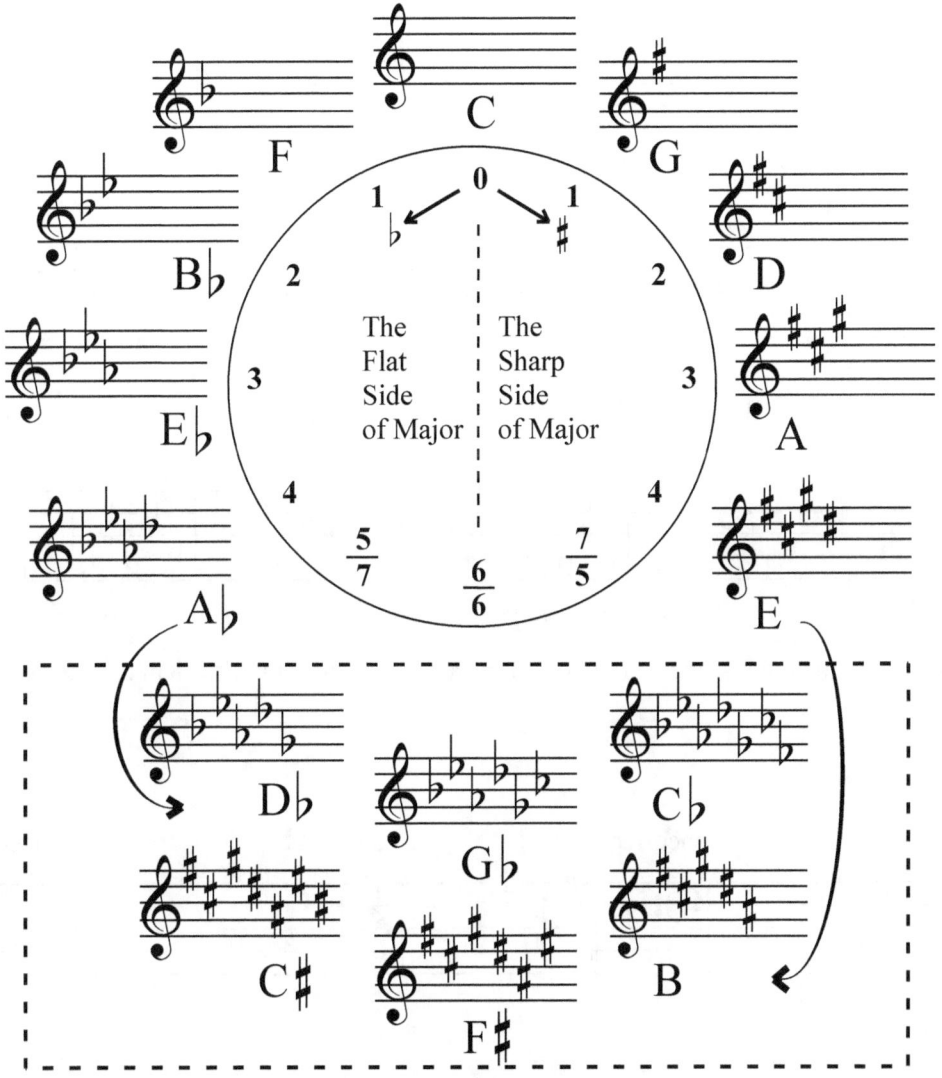

54   Chapter 4 Major Key Signatures

Examples 4–7a, 7b, 7c, and 7d show both the sharp and flat key signatures in their respective treble and bass clefs. As stated above, the arrangement for sharps is down a 4th and up a 5th, except for the A♯, which continues down another 4th before the initial pattern is resumed. For the flat keys, the pattern reverses the configuration of the sharp keys: up a 4th and down a 5th, with no irregularities.

A useful way to remember the order of sharps as they appear on the staff is to associate them respectively with the first letter of each word of the sentence "friends can go dancing at Ernie's bar." For flats, remember that the first four flats spell the word BEAD, followed by the letters GCF, which we could read as an abbreviation for "good cars fast."

Example 4–7

Example 4–8 illustrates some of the common mistakes that music students make when writing key signatures.

Example 4–8

Identifying Major Key Signatures

There is a paradox in the relationship between key signatures and the scales and modes they signify. The paradox involves the difference in the order of accidentals that appear in the construction of a scale versus the order of accidentals as they appear in that scale's key signature. Consider the scale construction for C♯ major (example 4–9a); here, the order of sharps is C♯, D♯, E♯, F♯, G♯, A♯, and B♯. Compare the sequence of sharps in the construction of the C♯-major scale to the order of sharps in the key signature (4–9b): F♯, C♯, G♯, D♯, A♯, E♯, and B♯.

The only common factor of significance between the order of accidentals in the construction of a scale with sharps and the order of accidentals in that scale's key signature is as follows: the last sharp added to the scale (not including scale degree 8 which is a duplication of scale degree 1) is scale degree 7 and the last sharp of the key signature is also scale degree 7. In the case of C♯ major, scale degree 7 is B♯.

The fact that the last pitch of the key signature is scale degree 7 helps us to identify the keynote of any sharp key, as the note following scale degree 7 is scale degree 8, the keynote (see the upward arrow pointing to C♯ in 4–9b). And so, for all of the sharp key signatures, look at the last sharp and realize that the keynote is one half step above that last sharp.

Example 4–9: C♯ major

For flat keys, we find the same paradox in the relationship between key signatures and the scales and modes they signify (examples 4–10a and 10b); however, the last flat of the signature cannot help us identify the keynote. Rather, a different principle must be applied to acquire this information. If the flat key has two or more flats in its key signature, the next-to-the-last flat will be the keynote. The key with one flat is F major and you will simply have to memorize this fact.

Example 4–10: C♭ major

Diatonicism, Chromaticism, Tonality, and Atonality

The terms diatonic and chromatic can be used in a variety of ways. In Chapter 2, we noted that a half step occurring between two pitches that involve two different consecutive letter names is referred to as a diatonic half step. A half step between two different versions of the same letter name is called a chromatic half step. In Chapter 3, we distinguished between diatonic scales and the chromatic scale, the former having one version only of the seven available pitch names and the latter dividing the octave into twelve half steps and consisting primarily of pairs of pitches that involve two different versions of the same letter name.

We also learned that the pattern of half steps and whole steps in the major scale reflects two things, namely, key and mode. The mode of a composition expresses certain characteristic designs that confirm and establish the key. The key is that pitch to which all other pitches are related and toward which they ultimately move. The key represents the **tonality** of the mode.

Tonality in music is analogous to the gravitational force exerted by the Sun upon any object that comes within its field of attraction. Tonality is a system of pitch organization that establishes its own field of attraction around one central tone. All of the other tones of the mode seek to revolve around and gravitate toward this central tone in a hierarchical order.

The tonic, as the principal tone of this hierarchy, exerts its gravitational force upon all of the other tones of the mode, each of which assumes a position of relative strength and stability within the tonic's field of attraction. In other words, within the framework of the key and mode, some tones have a stronger relationship to the tonic than others. We shall explore further the hierarchical relationships of tonal music in Chapter 8.

In broad terms, the concepts of key, mode, and tonality bring us to a consideration of the principles of **diatonicism** and **chromaticism**. The study of music fundamentals deals largely with diatonic usages in music. Perhaps the best way to understand diatonicism is to recognize that every mode (including those that we have yet to examine) has certain tones that represent its unique profile of half steps and whole steps. The tones that are specific and appropriate to the mode are diatonic elements; these tones are part of the key's orbital system.

In most cases, the diatonic elements will be reflected in the key signature. However, the key signature may not represent all of the pitch content of a music composition. The tones that are neither native to the mode nor reflected in the key signature are referred to as chromatic pitches. Chromaticism, if used extensively in a musical work, can not only undermine both the key and mode, it can eliminate them altogether. In the early twentieth century, certain composers began creating music that expressed no key at all, generally referred to as **atonality**.

Atonal music is based upon a system of pitches, either strictly or loosely organized, in which all tones are of equal importance—there is no key center toward which other tones seek to move, no tonal hierarchy. Moreover, in atonal music, there is no distinction between something known as **consonance** and **dissonance**. We shall encounter consonance and dissonance again in the next chapter.

Chapter 5 Intervals

In Chapter 2, the term interval was introduced to describe the distance from one pitch to any other pitch. It is possible to measure the numerical distance between two pitches by counting the letter names from the lower pitch to the higher pitch or from the higher pitch to the lower pitch. For example, C to D, is called a 2nd, C to E a 3rd, C to F a 4th, C to G a 5th, C to A a 6th, and C to B a 7th (example 5–1a). When speaking of the numerical distance from C to C (the second C is a duplication of the first in a higher register), we use the term octave rather than the number 8. The abbreviation for octave is 8ve.

When two or more musicians perform the same pitch in the same register, the terms unison or prime are used to designate the interval. If two pitches occur simultaneously, then the interval is called a **harmonic interval**. Example 5–1a illustrates some of the harmonic intervals that may exist within the range of a single C octave; intervals no larger than an octave are called **simple intervals**.

Example 5–1b demonstrates what happens if the upper pitch of each pair of simple intervals is moved into the next higher octave; this action produces what are referred to as **compound intervals**, intervals exceeding the span of an octave. To determine the numerical designation for a compound interval, add the number 7 to its simple intervallic counterpart: 2+7 becomes a 9th, 3+7 a 10th, 4+7 an 11th, 5+7 a 12th, 6+7 a 13th, 7+7 a 14th, and 8+7 a 15th. Since the top pitch of the octave duplicates the bottom pitch, we add 7 rather than 8 to the simple interval in order to avoid counting the same pitch twice.

Example 5–1: harmonic intervals

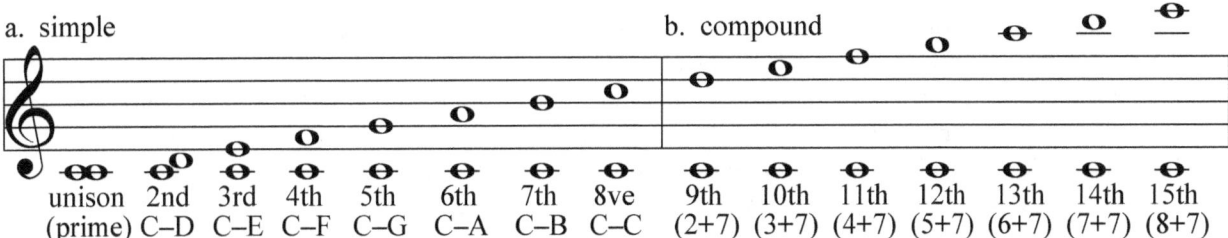

Example 5–2 shows the appearance on the staff of various harmonic intervals irrespective of clef but with the bottom note placed on either a space or a line (except for the unison, which has no bottom note). Notice that with the unison, 3rd, 5th, and 7th, both notes of the interval are placed on either spaces or lines. With the 2nd, 4th, 6th, and octave, however, one note of the interval will always be on a line and the other note will be on a space.

Example 5–2: harmonic intervals on the staff

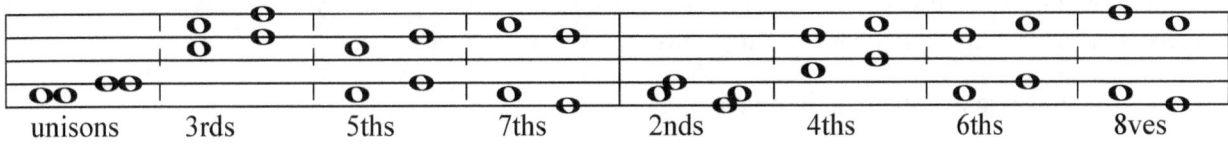

If two pitches occur in succession, then the interval is called a **melodic interval**. Example 5–3 reproduces some of the pitch content of example 3–36, one of the singing exercises from Chapter 3 that demonstrates conjunct motion and disjunct motion between adjacent pitches. Conjunct motion involves movement between pitches that are either a half step or whole step apart, whereas disjunct motion occurs when movement between pitches is greater than a whole step. In Example 5–3, the distance between the bottom C and the upper pitches of each melodic interval becomes increasingly larger until the octave is reached.

Example 5–3: melodic intervals

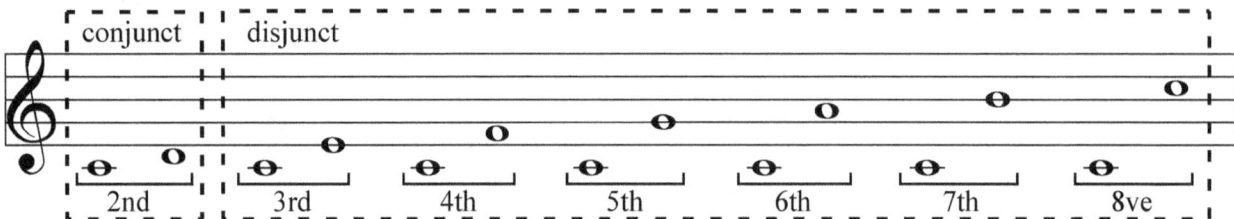

The Essential Diatonic Intervals of Major

In order to recognize and calculate the exact distance between two pitches, you must understand the intervallic relationships between scale degree 1 and all of the other scale degrees of the major mode. As stated above, the numerical size of an interval in major can be determined by counting the pitch names between the bottom note and each note above it.

Intervals can be measured not only in terms of their numerical value but also according to their quality. "Perfect," "major," "minor," "diminished," "doubly diminished," "augmented," and "doubly augmented" are all qualitative descriptions applied to the distance between two pitches. Doubly diminished and doubly augmented intervals are far less common than the other five varieties; however, you will encounter them if your study of music theory continues beyond the purview of music fundamentals and basic harmony.

In C major, the intervals formed between scale degree 1 and the diatonic scale degrees that occur above scale degree 1 are described as either major or perfect Major and perfect intervals are the two categories of "essential diatonic intervals" from which all invervallic relationships are determined; and when we move these intervals to keys other than C major, such as G major, the same numerical and qualitative relationships are preserved.

If, as shown in example 5–4, the interval's numerical distance from scale degree 1 is a 2nd, 3rd, 6th, or 7th, *and* if the top note of the interval is part of the scale (and therefore part of its key signature), then the quality of the interval is always major in a major mode. Moreover, the term major can be applied only to 2nds, 3rds, 6ths, and 7ths.

If the interval's numerical distance from scale degree 1 is a 4th, 5th, octave, or even a unison, *and* if the top note of the interval is part of the scale, then the quality of the interval is always perfect in a major mode (a perfect unison, however, does not have a top note since both pitches of the interval are identical). The term perfect can be applied only to 4ths, 5ths, octaves, and unisons.

Example 5–4: the essential diatonic intervals in C major

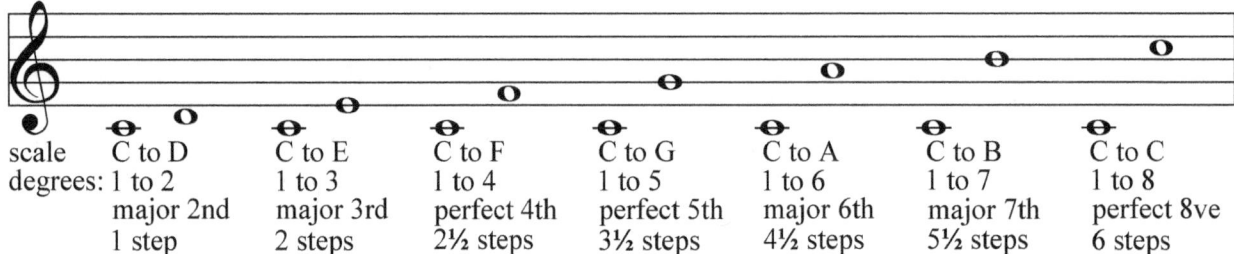

Study the essential diatonic intervals as they appear in example 5–5; for here we have the major scale and mode transposed to G, which requires the addition of F♯ to maintain the correct profile of half steps between scale degrees 3 and 4 and scale degrees 7 and 8. As long as the mode's half-step profile is preserved, the same intervallic relationships found in C major above scale degree 1 will be found also in G major above its scale degree 1.

Example 5–5: the essential diatonic intervals in G major

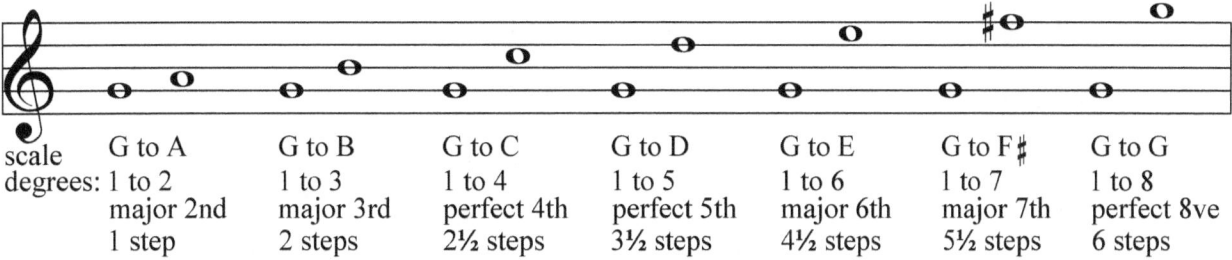

| scale degrees: | G to A
1 to 2
major 2nd
1 step | G to B
1 to 3
major 3rd
2 steps | G to C
1 to 4
perfect 4th
2½ steps | G to D
1 to 5
perfect 5th
3½ steps | G to E
1 to 6
major 6th
4½ steps | G to F♯
1 to 7
major 7th
5½ steps | G to G
1 to 8
perfect 8ve
6 steps |

Example 5–6 summarizes the two categories of essential intervals found above scale degree 1 in the major mode.

Example 5–6

Perfect Intervals	Major Intervals
unison	2nd
4th	3rd
5th	6th
8ve	7th

Two Principles for Recognizing and Constructing the Qualities of Intervals

In the foregoing section, we stated that if the bottom note of an interval is scale degree 1 of a major scale and if the top note of the interval coincides with a diatonic scale degree of the scale, then the quality of the interval is either major or perfect. The coincidence of the top note of the interval with a diatonic scale degree is the *first principle* for recognizing and constructing the qualities of intervals.

The *second principle*, referred to here as the re-sizing principle, is applied when the top note does not appear as a diatonic scale degree above scale degree 1. As demonstrated in 5–7 below, the re-sizing principle uses the following qualitative terms: minor, diminished, doubly diminished, augmented, and doubly augmented. Accordingly,

(1) decreasing the size of a perfect interval by one half step produces a diminished interval (5–7a);
(2) a diminished interval reduced in size by one half step gives us a doubly diminished interval;
(3) increasing the size of a perfect interval by one half step becomes an augmented interval;
(4) an augmented interval expanded by one half step results in a doubly augmented interval;
(5) decreasing the size of a major interval by one half step yields a minor interval (5–7b);
(6) reducing the size of a minor interval by one half step creates a diminished interval; and,
(7) a major interval increased in size by one half step becomes an augmented interval.

Example 5–7: the re-sizing principle

a. re-sizing perfect intervals (principle two)

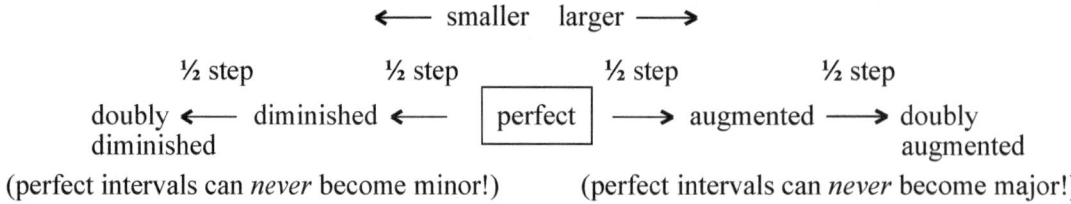

(perfect intervals can *never* become minor!)   (perfect intervals can *never* become major!)

b. re-sizing major intervals (principle two)

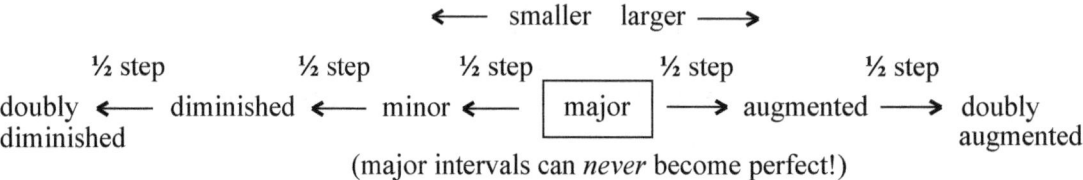

(major intervals can *never* become perfect!)

And so, to calculate the quality of an interval, evaluate the lower note as scale degree 1 of a major mode, if the top note coincides with a diatonic scale degree of that mode (based upon the mode's half-step profile and key signature), then according to principle one, the quality is either major or perfect. If, however; the top note does not constitute a diatonic scale degree of a major mode, then determine the quality according to the re-sizing principle as put forward in 5–7 above.

The diagrams in examples 5–8a and 8b show how to use the re-sizing principle to visualize the decrease or increase in the size of an interval without the benefit of a piano keyboard, clef, or pitch names as references.

Example 5–8

a. decreasing the size of perfect and major intervals by one half step

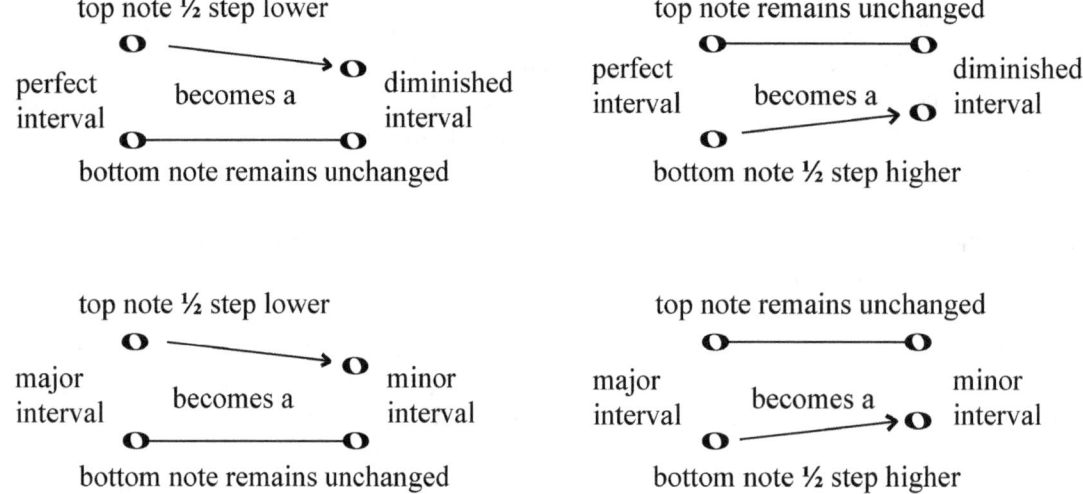

b. increasing the size of perfect and major intervals by one half step

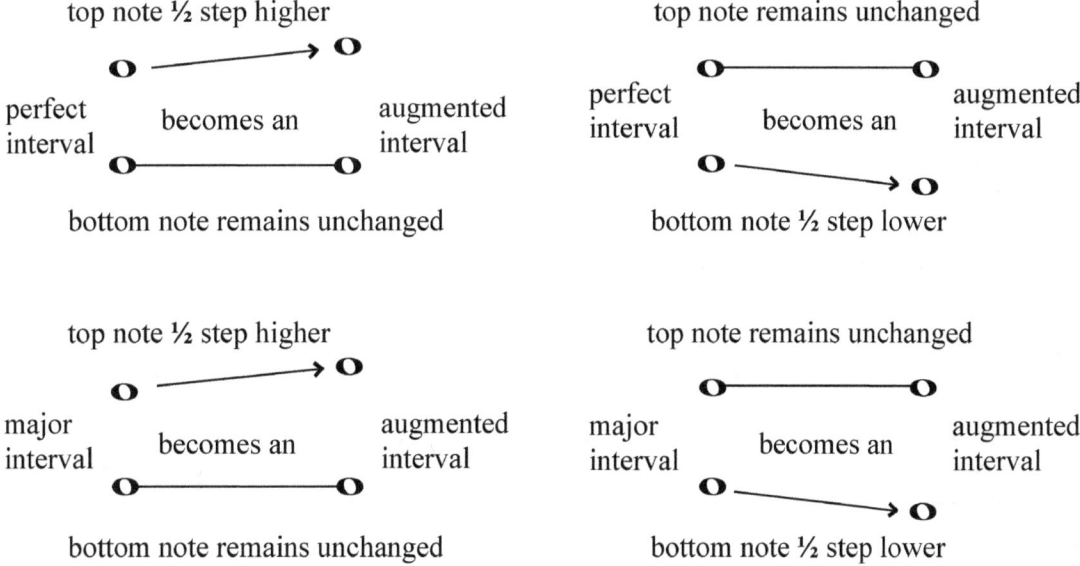

In examples 5–8a and 8b above, the diagrams demonstrate how perfect and major intervals may be decreased or increased in size by moving one of the two notes of the interval up or down one half step while the other note remains stationary. It is possible, however, to keep one note stationary while moving the other note two half steps, a move equivalent to that of one whole step. Indeed, as we saw in examples 5–7a and 7b, decreasing the size of a perfect interval by two half steps produces a doubly diminished interval, while increasing its size by two half steps results in a doubly augmented interval. Decreasing the size of a major interval by two half steps produces a diminished interval, while increasing its size by two half steps results in a doubly augmented interval.

Example 5–9 demonstrates another option for changing the size of an interval by two half steps; here, both notes move from their original position:

Example 5–9: decreasing or increasing the size of perfect and major intervals by two half steps

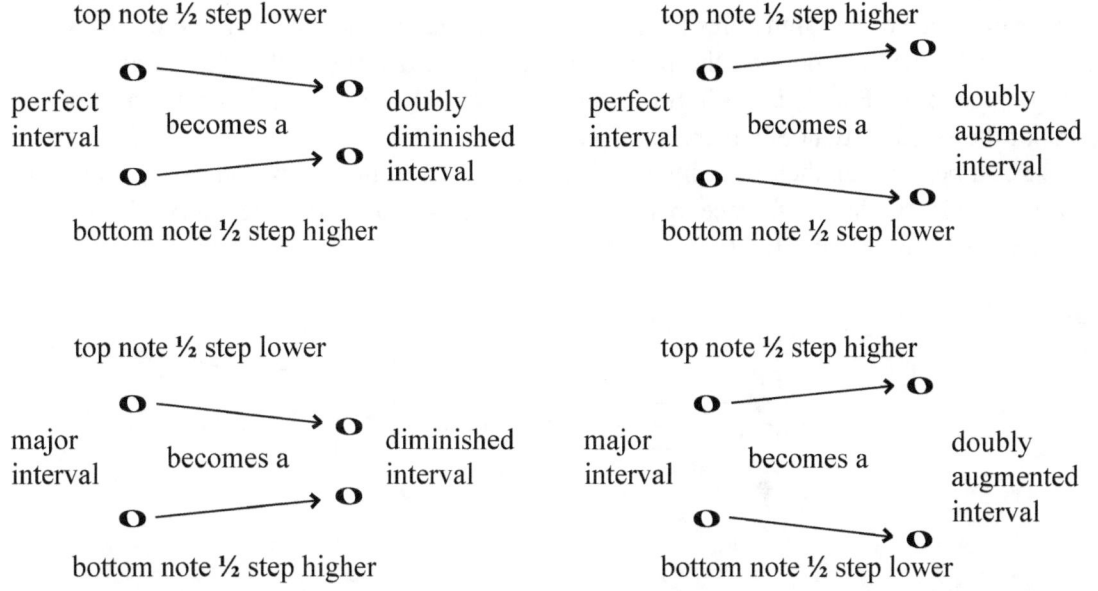

Let us return to our reference key and mode of C major and consider some of the intervals that may occur when the diatonic pitches above scale degree 1 are either raised or lowered by one half step with the addition of either a sharp or flat. You will notice that these alterations produce minor, diminished, and augmented qualities (example 5–10).

All qualitative descriptions of intervals take the following abbreviations: major as M, minor as m, diminished as d, and augmented as A. Uppercase and lowercase letters are used to distinguish between intervallic qualities. The filled-in note heads without stems in the example do not represent specific durational values.

Example 5–10: producing minor, diminished, and augmented intervals above C

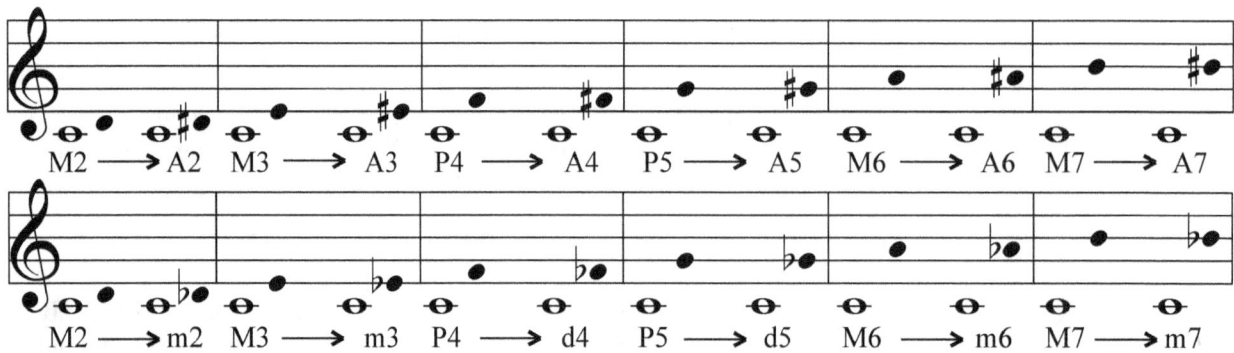

When the Bottom Pitch of the Interval Is Not Scale Degree 1 of C Major

Recognizing or calculating the numerical distance and quality of an interval is a relatively simple task when the bottom pitch is scale degree 1 of C major. But when the bottom pitch is not scale degree 1 of C major, we are confronted with a new set of challenges and one central fact: the key signatures that arise from the fourteen transpositions of the C major scale and mode must be committed to memory; for our study of music fundamentals cannot progress without meeting this requirement.

The following examples will focus on the difficulties that underlie these challenges. We begin with the problem of building intervals above pitches other than C. Example 5–11a starts with the pitches F and B♮ (natural). Our knowledge of key signatures tells us that F major takes one flat, B♭. Therefore, B♮ is not a diatonic member of F major. Counting the pitch names, we can determine that the numerical distance between F to B♮ (counting F as 1) is a 4th. Since B♭ is native to F major, F to B♭ must be a perfect 4th (i.e., P4), one of the essential diatonic intervals of F major.

If F to B♭ is a perfect 4th, then what interval is produced when the B♭ becomes B♮? Visualize the perfect 4th from F to B♭ without reference to a clef or staff and ask yourself if the interval becomes larger or smaller when the B♭ becomes a B♮ (5–11b).

Example 5–11

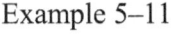

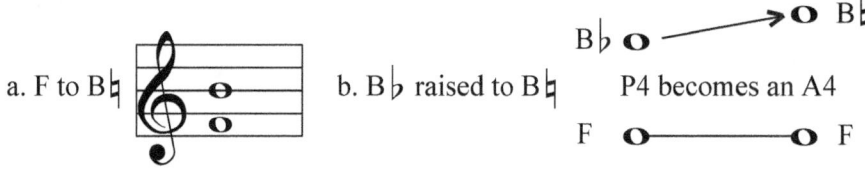

The question posed in the preceding paragraph may well be the most difficult one to address because finding the correct answer requires you to understand that the move from B♭ to B♮ constitutes a raising of the pitch by one half step. Remember that when we proceed from left to right on the piano keyboard, each piano key produces a pitch that is incrementally higher and its equivalent frequency faster (see above, p. 19).

Once you are able to recognize that B♮ is one half step higher than B♭, it should be clear that F to B♮ is one half step larger than F to B♭. *If the size of a perfect interval is increased by one half step, then the quality changes from perfect to augmented;* hence, F to B♮ is an augmented 4th (A4). An inspection of the piano keyboard reveals that F to B♮ is the *only* place within the octave where the interval of an augmented 4th occurs between white keys. Committing this fact to memory now will help significantly to calculate the qualities of certain intervals and chords later.

Before we consider some of the more complex issues associated with interval recognition and construction, it would be well to look at a few examples in which the bottom pitch of the interval carries an **inflection**, in other words, a note that has been altered with the addition of an accidental. In example 5–12a, both the bottom and top pitches of the interval are inflected, that is, C♯ and A♯.

In order to identify the exact quality of the interval, our first question should be: "what is the numerical distance between these two notes?" Counting the pitch names between C♯ and A♯ (counting C♯ as 1), we find that A♯ is 6 steps away from the bottom pitch; hence, the numerical distance is a 6th. (The interval of the 6th can *never* be associated with the term perfect because only 4ths, 5ths, octaves, and unisons belong to the category of perfect intervals.)

Secondly: "in C♯ major, is there an A♯?" If you have memorized the key signatures for the fourteen transpositions of C major, then you will determine quite easily that A♯ is a diatonic member of C♯ major because C♯ major has seven sharps, one of which is A♯. Since the interval here is a 6th, the qualitative description is major because A♯ is part of the C♯-major scale. And so, the interval would be called a major 6th (M6).

Example 5–12

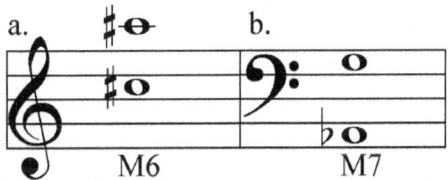

The interval in 5–12b above presents a slightly different challenge in that only one of its two pitches has an accidental, namely, A♭. Once you have asked and answered the question of the numerical distance between A♭ and G and determined that the interval is a 7th, you must call upon your memory to tell you that A♭ major has four flats, none of which involve G. However, it is important to recognize that G, C, and F are all native to A♭ major, despite the fact that none of these pitches carry a flat. Indeed, except for C♯ major and C♭ major, there will be pitches in the key signature that are not inflected with an accidental. Since G is scale degree 7, the leading tone of A♭ major, the interval between A♭ and G is a major 7th (M7).

In example 5–13a, the interval from B♭ to D♯ consists of two different types of accidentals, a flat and a sharp. As before, the first question we address is the numerical distance between the two pitches. Since the distance between B♭ and D♯ is a 3rd, the interval can never be described as perfect. The next step is to determine if D♯ is a diatonic scale degree of B♭ major. Drawing upon our knowledge of key signatures, we know that B♭ major has two flats and no D♯. Therefore, the quality of the 3rd cannot be major. If the pitches had been B♭ to D, then the interval would have been a major 3rd because D is scale degree 3 of B♭ major. (If the pitches had been B♭ to D♭, then the interval would have been a minor 3rd.)

And so, what is B♭ to D♯? Once again, the challenge is recognizing that D♯ is one half step higher in pitch than D and that the distance from B♭ to D♯ is one half step larger than the distance from B♭ to D. If the size of a major interval is increased by one half step, then the quality changes from major to augmented; hence, B♭ to D♯ is an augmented 3rd (A3). The diagram to the right of 5–13a will help you to visualize the change in the size of the interval.

Example 5–13

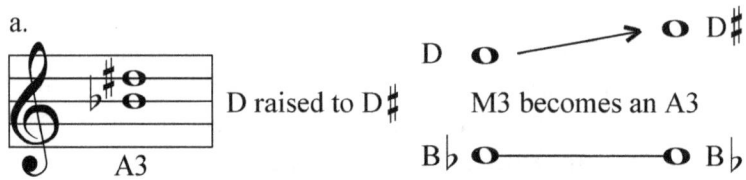

The next interval is built on C♭ and contains an E♭♭ as its upper component (example 5–13b). The numerical distance between the pitches C♭ and E♭♭ is a 3rd; but is there an E♭♭ in C♭ major? We know that C♭ major has seven flats, one of which is E♭ rather than E♭♭. Therefore, C♭ to E♭ constitutes a diatonic major 3rd. If E♭ is lowered to E♭♭, is the interval larger or smaller? The diagram to the right of 5–13b illustrates the change in size that occurs when E♭ is lowered to E♭♭, a change in size that produces a minor 3rd (m3); for *when the size of a major interval is decreased by one half step, the quality changes from major to minor.*

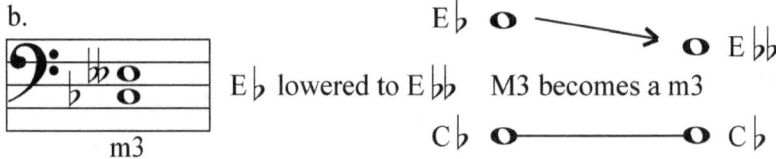

Counting the letter names from the F♯ to the E♭ in 5–13c confirms the numerical distance to be a 7th. But now we want to know if there is an E♭ in F♯ major. Since F♯ major has six sharps, the answer is no. The sixth sharp of F♯ major's key signature is E♯. E♯ is scale degree 7; therefore, the quality from F♯ to E♯ is a major 7th, one of the essential diatonic intervals of major. If we lower E♯ to E, does the interval get larger or smaller?

Study the diagram to the right of 5–13c and notice that the move from E♯ to E decreases the size of the interval by one half step. When a major interval (F♯ to E♯) is reduced in size by one half step, the quality changes from major to minor (F♯ to E♮). Let us move the E to E♭, recognizing that the interval has now decreased in size another half step. If the size of a minor interval is reduced by one half step, then the quality becomes diminished; thus, F♯ to E♭ is a diminished 7th (d7).

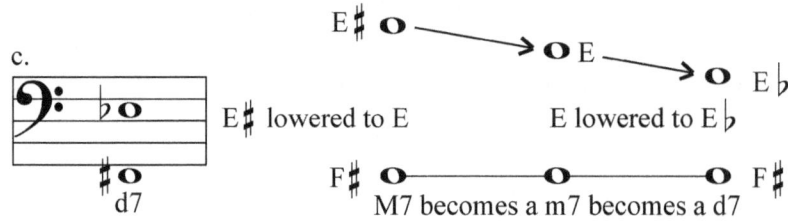

When the Bottom Pitch Does Not Correspond to One of the Fourteen Transpositions of C Major

In the examples 5–12 and 13, we assumed the bottom pitch of the interval to be scale degree 1 of the major mode and then used the two principles for recognizing and calculating the qualities of intervals to determine the exact distance between the two pitches. Thus, if the bottom note represents C major or corresponds to one of its fourteen transpositions (G, D, A, E, B, F♯, C♯, F, B♭, E♭, A♭, D♭, G♭, or C♭), then identifying the top note as a diatonic scale degree is a relatively simple task. On the other hand, if the top pitch is not a diatonic scale degree, then we can derive the quality of the interval according to the re-sizing principle.

But as we shall see presently, not all intervals have bottom pitches that correspond to one of the fourteen transpositions of C major. Consider example 5–14a, an interval consisting of F𝄪 and B♯. We can see from counting the letter names that the interval is some kind of 4th; however, there is no F𝄪 major key signature to use as a reference. Consequently, we must employ some alternative strategies to find the exact distance between the two pitches, to find the quality of the interval. Since the problem is with the F𝄪, simply remove the double sharp as well as the sharp attached to the B, evaluate the interval with no inflections (as F♮ to B♮), re-introduce the sharps, and then, apply principles one and two as needed.

(1) Starting with F♮ as the bottom note and assuming it to be scale degree 1 of F major, does its key signature have a B♮? The answer is no. F major has a B♭; therefore, B♮ is not a diatonic scale degree. The distance from F♮ to B♭ constitutes a perfect 4th.
(2) If we raise B♭ to B♮, the interval is one half step larger and as such becomes an augmented 4th.
(3) Raising the F♮ to F♯ makes the interval one half step smaller and brings us again to a perfect 4th.
(4) At this point, add back the sharp attached to the B; the move from B♮ to B♯ expands the perfect 4th by one half step and creates an augmented 4th (F♯ to B♯).
(5) Finally, re-introducing the double sharp to the bottom note contracts the augmented 4th by one half step and produces a perfect 4th. F𝄪 to B♯ is a perfect 4th.

Example 5–14

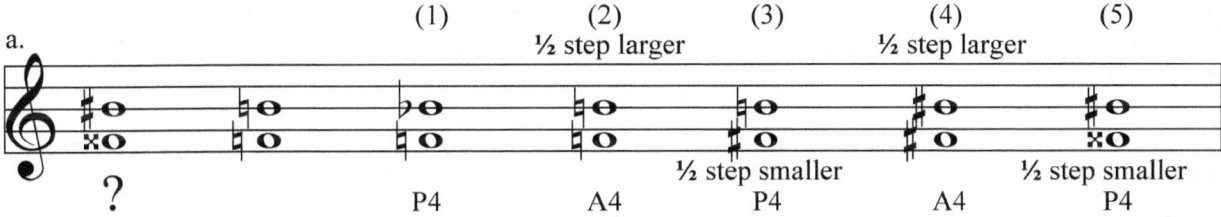

The diagram in 5–14b presents an alternative view of the five-step process outlined above.

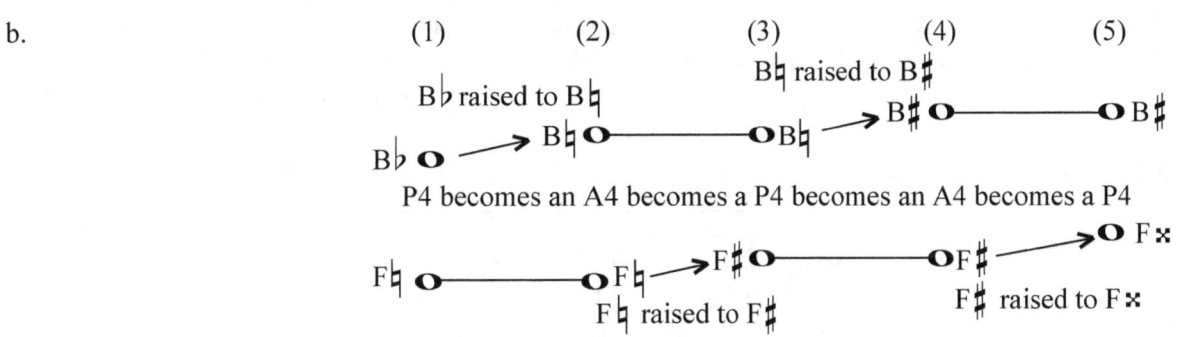

The Principle of Like Inflection

Although the foregoing exercise provides reliable results for recognizing the quality of an interval, it involves too many steps. This section will demonstrate how to streamline the process. Skipping the move to the perfect 4th between F♯ and B♮ eliminates the third re-sizing step displayed in example 5–14.

But what principle would allow us to bypass one of the steps outlined above? As example 5–15a shows, once we determine that F♮ to B♮ is an augmented 4th, inflecting both F♮ and B♮ with a sharp does not change the augmented quality of the 4th. Example 5–15a skips the perfect 4th from F♯ to B♮ and proceeds directly to the augmented 4th between F♯ and B♯. Raising the F♯ to F𝄪 produces a perfect 4th from F𝄪 to B♯.

We can conclude from this observation that *if both pitches of an interval are inflected equally in the same direction, upwards or downwards, then the quality of the interval does not change.* This phenomenon may be referred to as "the principle of like inflection." The only aspect of the interval that does change is that it occurs at a higher or lower pitch level depending on whether sharps or flats are used. Example 5–15b illustrates this fact.

Example 5–15: using the principle of like inflection to identify intervals

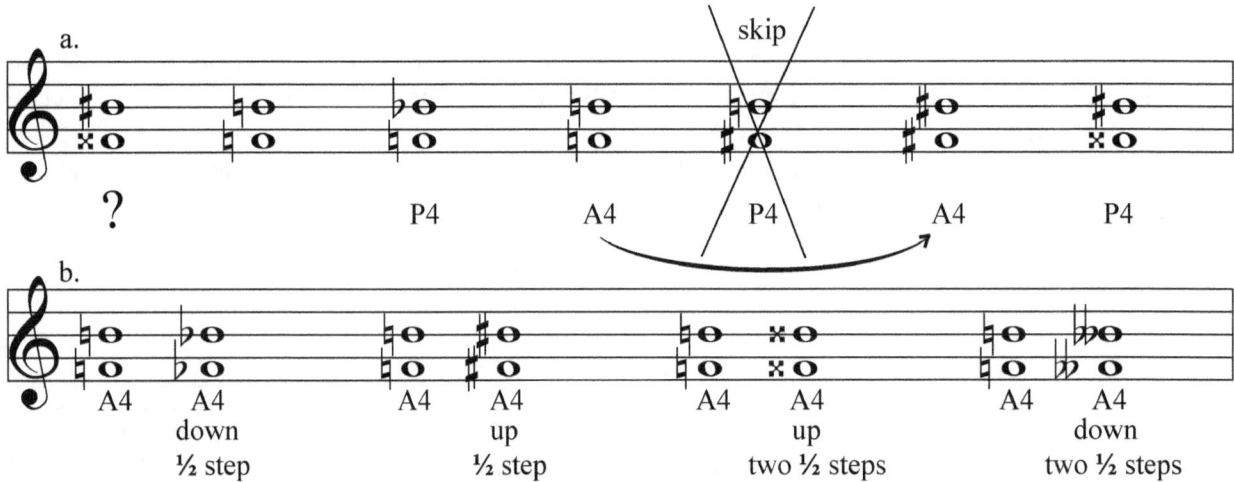

There is a simpler way to identify an interval with a complicated spelling, such as the one in 5–14, if you use your knowledge of enharmonic equivalency to re-interpret the pitch inflections. As directed in example 5–16, respell the F𝄪 and B♯ as G and C respectively. The numerical distance remains unchanged, as the interval is still a 4th; therefore, assume that G is scale degree 1 of the major mode and draw upon your knowledge of key signatures to determine if C is a diatonic component of G major. C is, in fact, native to G major which means that the 4th between the two pitches is perfect. Once you have identified the quality of the re-interpreted interval, simply reinstate the original spelling (in this case, G as F𝄪 and C as B♯).

Example 5–16

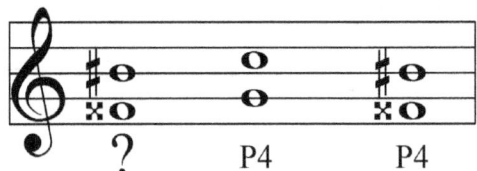

Compound Intervals

At the outset of this chapter, we noted that intervals may exceed the span of an octave. As shown in example 5–17b, the numerical designation for a compound interval is determined by adding the number 7 to its simple intervallic counterpart: 2+7 becomes a 9th, 3+7 a 10th, 4+7 an 11th, 5+7 a 12th, 6+7 a 13th, 7+7 a 14th, and 8+7 a 15th. Since the top pitch of the octave duplicates the bottom pitch, we add 7 rather than 8 to the simple interval in order to avoid counting the same pitch twice.

Although the numerical designation of a compound interval changes, its qualitative description does not. All minor intervals remain minor in their compound forms, major intervals remain major, perfect intervals remain perfect, diminished intervals remain diminished, and augmented intervals remain augmented. Thus, a major 2nd becomes a major 9th, a major 3rd becomes a major 10th, a perfect 4th becomes a perfect 11th, a perfect 5th becomes a perfect 12th, a major 6th becomes a major 13th, a major 7th becomes a major 14th, and a perfect octave becomes a perfect 15th.

Example 5–17

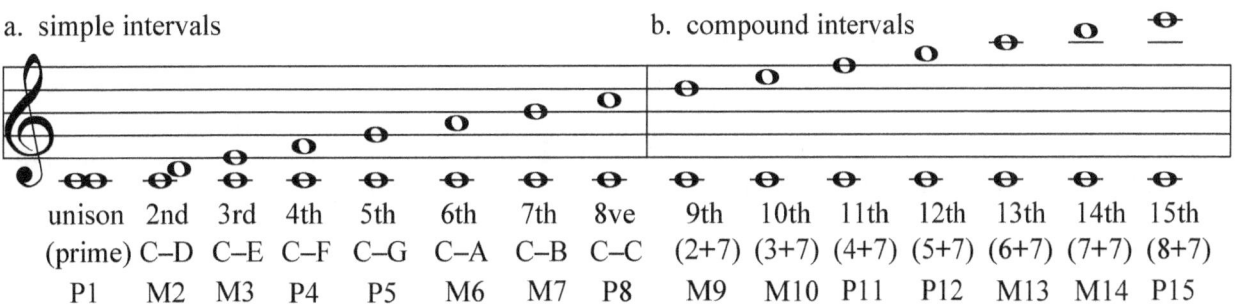

Consider the compound interval in example 5–18. To identify the numerical distance of the compound interval in its simple form, move either the top note of the compound interval down one octave or the bottom note of the interval up one octave: move c^1 down to small c or great A up to small a. Either adjustment will confirm the numerical distance to be a 3rd; therefore, adding 7 to that 3rd reveals the interval from great A to c^1 to be a 10th.

With the numerical distance identified as a 10th (or as a 3rd), determine the quality of the interval according to principles one and two (see above, pp. 59-62). Since there is a C♯ in A major rather than a C♮, the quality of the interval is minor; hence, the interval in its compound form is a minor 10th (m10). Had the C carried a sharp, the interval would have been a major 10th.

Example 5–18

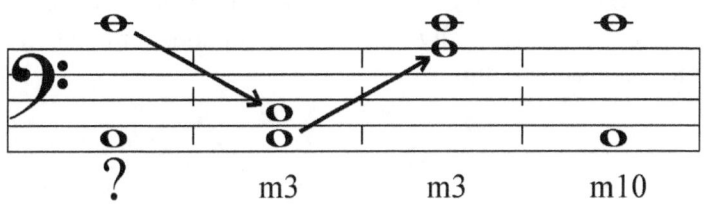

Interval Inversion

In 5–18 above, we identified the numerical distance of a compound interval in its simple form by shifting either the top note of the interval down one octave or the bottom note of the interval up one octave. It is important to recognize that despite these adjustments, the bottom note of the interval remains an A and the top note of the interval remains a C; in other words, the basic identity of the interval is unchanged.

Moreover, the interval's qualitative description remains intact; for here, the quality of the interval is minor in both its simple and compound forms. To be sure, interpreting a compound interval as a simple interval changes the numerical distance by at least one octave (in this case, a 10th becomes a 3rd); but again, the A retains its status as the bottom note and the C retains its status as the top note. In fact, the minor 10th in 5–18 can also referred to as a compound minor 3rd.

But what happens to the numerical distance and quality of a simple interval when its two pitches are turned upside down or flipped, that is, when either the bottom note of the simple interval is placed one octave higher to become the top note or the top note is moved one octave lower to become the bottom note? Intervals that undergo this type of alteration are said to be inverted. As we shall see, interval inversion changes the numerical distance of the two pitches and *frequently* the quality of the interval.

Using C major as our reference key and mode, let us consider the inversions of intervals in example 5–19a. Notice that when c^1 is moved one octave higher into the c^2 register, the unison (or prime) becomes an octave, the 2nd a 7th, the 3rd a 6th, the 4th a 5th, the 5th a 4th, the 6th a 3rd, the 7th a 2nd, and the octave a unison. If you add the pair of numbers that the interval and its inversion represent, the sum is always nine: 1+8=9, 2+7=9, 3+6=9, 4+5=9, 5+4=9, 6+3=9, 7+2=9, and 8+1=9. As indicated in 5–19b, perfect intervals (P) remain perfect upon inversion, whereas major intervals (M) become minor (m).

Example 5–19

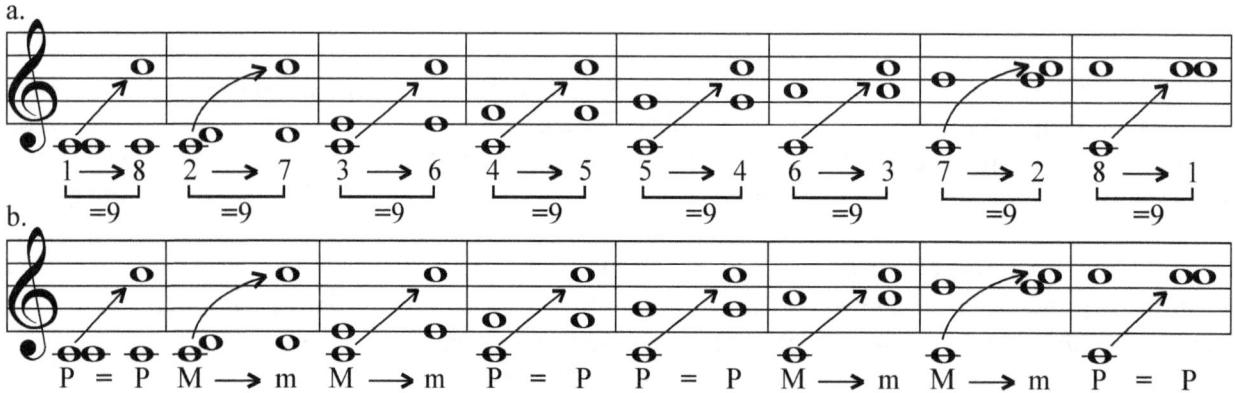

Example 5–20 summarizes the numerical and qualitative changes that occur when an interval is inverted. Note carefully that upon inversion, diminished intervals become augmented and augmented intervals become diminished.

Example 5–20

Upon inversion:

the unison (prime) becomes an octave	1 ⟶ 8 (= 9)	
the 2nd becomes a 7th	2 ⟶ 7 (= 9)	Therefore,
the 3rd becomes a 6th	3 ⟶ 6 (= 9)	upon inversion:
the 4th becomes a 5th	4 ⟶ 5 (= 9)	
the 5th becomes a 4th	5 ⟶ 4 (= 9)	P1 ⟶ P8 ⟶ P1
the 6th becomes a 3rd	6 ⟶ 3 (= 9)	M2 ⟶ m7 ⟶ M2
the 7th becomes a 2nd	7 ⟶ 2 (= 9)	M3 ⟶ m6 ⟶ M3
the octave becomes a unison	8 ⟶ 1 (= 9)	P4 ⟶ P5 ⟶ P4
		P5 ⟶ P4 ⟶ P5
		M6 ⟶ m3 ⟶ M6
		M7 ⟶ m2 ⟶ M7
Upon inversion:		P8 ⟶ P1 ⟶ P8
perfect intervals remain perfect	P = P	
major intervals become minor	M ⟶ m	A4 ⟶ d5 ⟶ A4
minor intervals become major	m ⟶ M	d5 ⟶ A4 ⟶ d5
diminished intervals become augmented	d ⟶ A	
augmented intervals become diminished	A ⟶ d	

Constructing Intervals Below a Given Tone: the Practical Application of Interval Inversion

Earlier in this chapter, we learned how to recognize and construct intervals based upon the premise that the bottom note of the interval is the implied scale degree 1 of a major scale. Principle one tells us that if the top note of the interval coincides with a diatonic scale degree of the scale, then the quality of the interval is either major or perfect. If the top note does not coincide with a diatonic scale degree, then we apply the second principle, the re-sizing principle, to determine whether the interval is either minor, diminished, or augmented. But what if we want to construct an interval *below* a given tone? In this instance, there is no bottom note on which to base our calculations.

There are three ways to construct an interval below a given tone. First, it is possible to count down whole steps and half steps to find the right pitch; but this approach is slow and somewhat unwieldy. Another alternative would be to count down the required number of letter names until the correct letter name for the bottom tone is reached and then, if needed, raise or lower the bottom tone with a sharp or flat until the desired interval has been created; this method can be effective but it can also lead to mistakes.

The most consistent method for constructing an interval below a given tone involves the use of interval inversion. Let us consider some examples to see how principles one and two are used in conjunction with the inversion of intervals. Depending on the interval involved, finding the right pitch will require either a couple of steps or several, but all steps are contingent upon having the major key signatures committed solidly to memory.

Example 5–21a presents the following problem: construct a minor 6th (m6) below the tone B. In order to employ interval inversion to solve the problem, we ask the following question: "what is the inversion of a minor 6th?" We know that upon inversion, 6ths become 3rds and minor intervals become major; therefore, the inversion of a minor 6th is a major 3rd. This is important information because in order to locate the minor 6th *below* the tone B, the first thing we are going to do is construct a major 3rd *above* B (remember that the span between scale degrees 1 and 3 of major constitutes one of the essential diatonic intervals of the major mode.). Once we have found the right pitch above B, we will then move that pitch down one octave. That adjustment will give us the minor 6th below the given tone B.

(1) Interpret the given tone B as scale degree 1 of the major mode. Counting three letter names up from B (counting B as 1), we find that a 3rd above the tone B involves some version of D, either D♯, D♭, or D♮.

(2) Since B major has five sharps, one of which is D♯, the correct version of D for the major 3rd above B is D♯.

(3) Once the D♯ has been identified as the correct pitch, the final step is to move the D♯ down one octave from the double prime register to the prime register to create the minor 6th below B.

Example 5–21

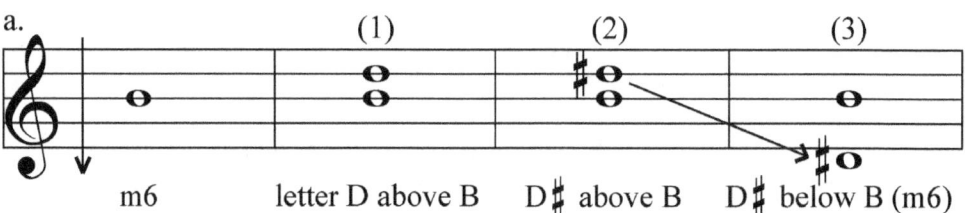

Example 5–21b shows the construction of a diminished 7th (d7) below the given tone G♭. After you have determined that the inversion of a diminished 7th is an augmented 2nd (A2), interpret G♭ as scale degree 1 of the major mode and count up two letter names from G♭ (counting G♭ as 1).

(1) Two letter names above the tone G♭ involves some version of A. Since we are looking for an augmented 2nd, it would be well to first find the diatonic major 2nd that normally occurs between scale degrees 1 and 2 of G♭ major. Subsequently, use principle two, the re-sizing principle, to find the augmented 2nd above G♭.

(2) The key of G♭ major has six flats, one of which is A♭. Thus, a major 2nd above G♭ is A♭. Our task, however, is to find an augmented 2nd above G♭.

(3) Drawing upon principle two, we know that increasing the size of a major interval by one half step creates an augmented interval. In order to increase the size of the interval between G♭ and A♭ by one half step, raise the A♭ to A♮. G♭ to A♮ is an augmented 2nd.

(4) Now that the A♮ has been selected correctly, move the A♮ down one octave from the small register to the great register. This final adjustment creates the diminished 7th below G♭. (The natural sign in parentheses in measure 4 of example 5–21b serves as a reminder to not repeat the A♭ from the previous measure and to read the pitch accurately as an A♮. When the A♮ is moved down from the small register to the great register, the natural in parentheses is unnecessary because of the change in register.)

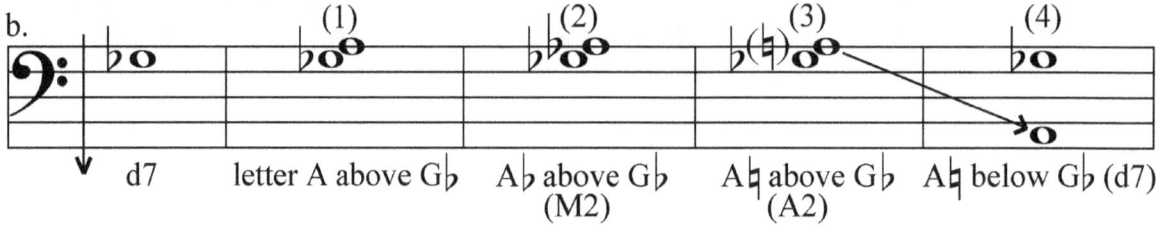

Example 5–21c provides a five-step guide for constructing a diminished 5th (d5) below the given tone D♯. Here we have an additional challenge in that there is no key signature to which D♯ can be associated. Unraveling this problem begins with the recognition that diminished 5ths invert to become augmented 4ths. In the course of this five-step process, we will place the augmented 4th above D♯. After a few intermediary steps, we will move the top note of that augmented 4th down one octave to establish the diminished 5th below D♯.

(1) The diminished 5th below D♯ can be constructed more easily by temporarily removing the sharp from the D, interpreting D as scale degree 1 of the major mode, and counting up four letter names from D (counting D as 1). We count up four letter names from D because eventually we will have to find an augmented 4th above the given tone before moving that tone into the lower octave. Presently, however, we need to locate the perfect 4th that normally occurs between scale degrees 1 and 4 of D major.

(2) Our knowledge of key signatures enables us to determine that a perfect 4th up from D is G.

(3) Having established the perfect 4th between D and G, let us employ the principle of like inflection to add a sharp to both D and G. Remember that the principle of like inflection states that if both pitches of an interval are inflected with the same accidental, then the quality of the interval does not change. Thus, adding a sharp to both the D and G does not change the size of the interval; the addition merely shifts the interval up one half step from D and G to D♯ and G♯.

(4) With the perfect 4th between D♯ and G♯ in place, all that remains is to enlarge the interval one half step to create the augmented 4th and then take the top note down one octave to establish the diminished 5th below the D♯. Since at this stage of the construction we cannot change the D♯, the perfect 4th that stands above it can be expanded to an augmented 4th only by raising the G♯ to G𝄪.

(5) Finally, moving the G𝄪 down from the double prime register into the prime register brings this task to a successful conclusion.

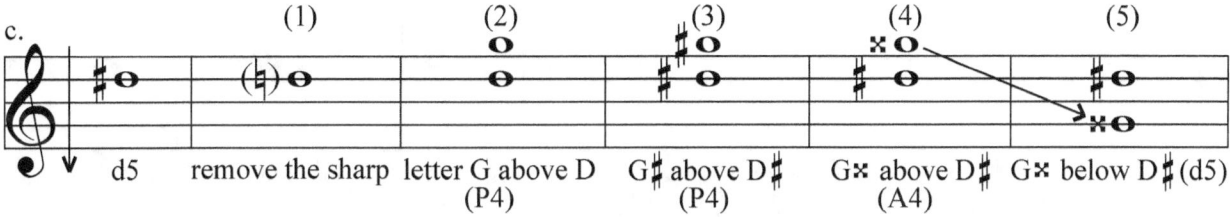

Before continuing with another challenge involving interval inversion, it should be pointed out that both the diminished 5th and the augmented 4th are notable for their sound and construction. Both intervals are often referred to as the **tritone** because each of its forms consists of three whole tones (i.e., three whole steps). The tritone stands exactly in the middle of the octave, dividing it in half. The sound of the tritone remains the same when it inverts because it always consists of three whole tones. The only change that occurs with the inversion of the tritone is within the context its numerical size: 4ths always invert to become 5ths and *vice versa*.

Historically, musicians and music theorists have perceived the tritone as an unstable interval, classified it as dissonance, and accordingly handled it with care. The stability and instability of intervals as well as the treatment of the tritone and other unstable intervals will be discussed in the final section of this chapter, Consonance and Dissonance. But first, one final problem associated with the process of interval inversion remains.

Examples 5–21a, 21b, and 21c have shown how to construct simple intervals below the given tone. In 5–21d, the right pitch ultimately stands more than an octave below the given tone, a compound interval. Placing an augmented 9th (A9) below the given tone A♯ requires six steps. As in 5–21c above, there is no key signature to which A♯ can be associated.

Before undertaking the six steps that will enable us to locate the augmented 9th below A♯, it is necessary to identify the numerical distance of the augmented 9th in its simple form and then find the inversion of that simple interval. Subtracting 7 from 9 gives us 2; hence, the simple form of an augmented 9th is an augmented 2nd (A2). The inversion of an augmented 2nd is a diminished 7th (d7). Steps 1–4 of 5–21d outlines the formation of a diminished 7th above A♯.

(1) Remove the sharp from the A and interpret A as scale degree 1 of the major mode. Count seven letter names up from A (counting A as 1) to reach the letter G.
(2) Since we have already removed the sharp from the A, find a major 7th (M7) above A. The key of A major has three sharps, one of which is G♯; therefore, a major 7th above A is G♯.
(3) Adding back the A♯ raises the lower tone of the major 7th by one half step and decreases the size of the interval by one half step. When a major 7th is contracted by one half step, the interval becomes minor; A♯ to G♯ is a minor 7th. Decreasing the size of a minor interval by one half step produces a diminished interval.
(4) At this stage of the construction, the given tone A♯ cannot be changed, which means that the only way to decrease the size of the minor 7th by one half step involves changing the G♯. Lowering the G♯ to G♮ produces the diminished 7th above A♯.
(5) The next step is to transfer the G♮ down one octave from the prime register to the small register to place an augmented 2nd below the A♯.
(6) Moving the G♮ down one more octave from the small register to the great register transforms the augmented 2nd below A♯ into an augmented 9th and completes the task of 5–21d.

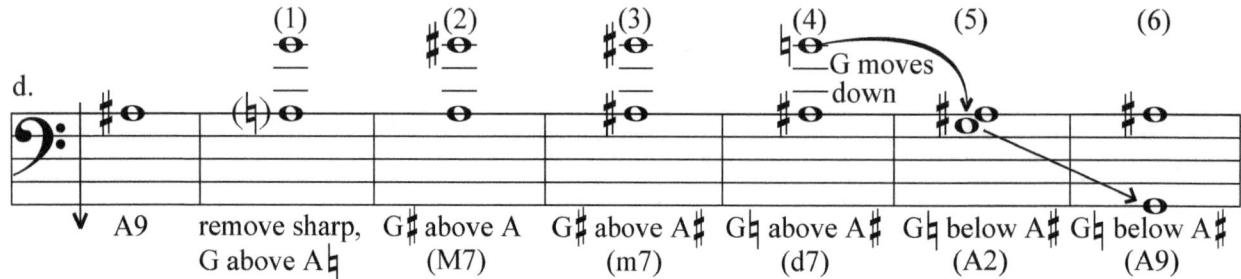

Consonance and Dissonance

The distinction between consonance and dissonance in music is a means by which intervals are classified according to whether they are perceived by listeners as either stable or unstable. Consonant intervals exhibit a feeling of rest, while dissonant intervals exude a sense of tension. Dissonant intervals usually seek to form connections to consonant intervals in a process known as resolution. Traditionally, dissonances resolve to consonances. When a dissonant interval is resolved to a consonance, a feeling of relaxation is produced. Resolutions of dissonance endow most of the tonal music of the Western tradition with a sense of forward motion, as the alternation between tension and relaxation propels the music ever forward.

There are two classes of consonant intervals, perfect consonances and imperfect consonances. The perfect consonances are the unison, the perfect octave, the perfect 5th, and *sometimes the perfect 4th*. The imperfect consonances consist of both major and minor 3rds and 6ths. The dissonant intervals include 2nds, 7ths, the tritone (augmented 4th and diminished 5th), and *sometimes the perfect 4th*.

In music, the lowest pitch of the musical texture is called the **bass** (pronounced bās), even if the source of the sound is an instrument rather than a human voice. If the perfect 4th occurs between the bass and an upper note, then the interval is treated as a dissonance (example 5–22a). If, however, the perfect 4th does not occur between the bass and an upper note, then the interval is consonant (5–22b).

Therefore, the consonant perfect 4th is a 4th that occurs between two pitches above the bass; neither of the two upper pitches form the interval of a 4th with the bass. Example 5–22 illustrates the difference between the consonant and dissonant 4th. The brackets show the two pitches that form the interval of the perfect 4th. Notice that both the consonant and the dissonant 4th can appear as either a simple or compound interval (a perfect 11th).

Example 5–22

Example 5–23 demonstrates how dissonant 7ths, 4ths, 2nds, and tritones are usually treated. The conventional way for dissonant intervals to resolve is by either a whole step or by a half step, in other words, by conjunct motion. All of the resolutions in 5–23 are conjunct. The numerical distances of the intervals shown here are given below the staff, except for the augmented 4th (A4) and the diminished 5th (d5), which are also identified according to quality (5–23c). The example below shows how the tritone interval is typically used: as an augmented 4th, it expands to a 6th; as a diminished 5th, it contracts to a 3rd. (The principle of stem direction mentioned on p. 1 does not apply when two individual melodic lines appear simultaneously on one staff.)

Example 5–23

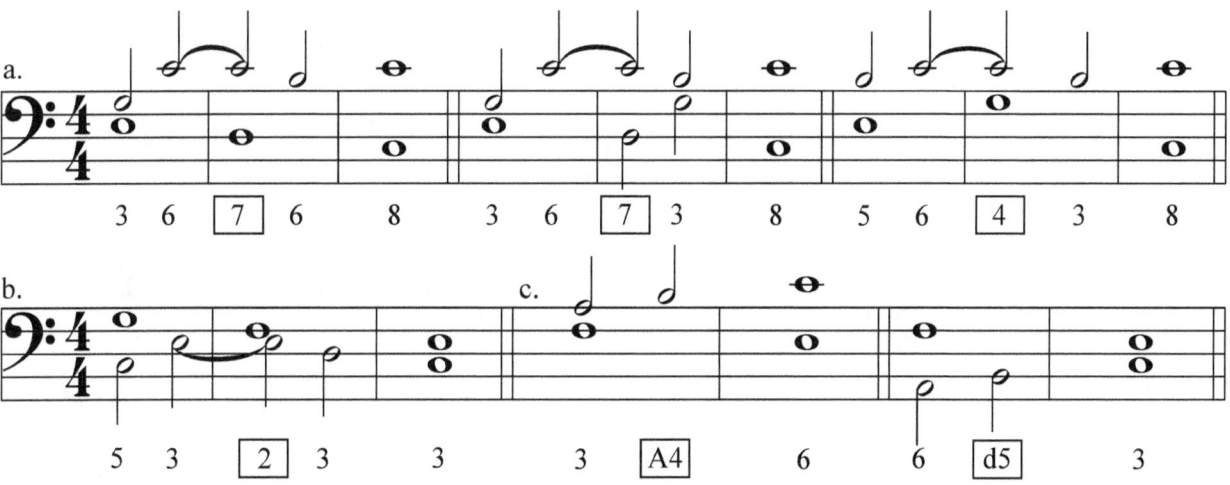

Chapter 6 The Minor Mode

The major mode is not the only mode in music that has a tonal center; however, as mentioned in Chapter 3, its profile of half steps and whole steps distinguishes major from the profiles of other diatonic modes. In this chapter, we shall learn about the properties of the minor mode and discover the ways in which it resembles and differs from the major mode.

In major, certain scale degrees are relatively stable, while other scale degrees are relatively unstable. That is to say, some scale degrees seek to move to other scale degrees, while some scale degrees have less of a tendency to move. Scale degrees 1, 3, 5, and 8 are comparatively stable and can be referred to as **rest tones**. The scale degrees between the rest tones, scale degrees 2, 4, 6, and 7, are unstable; the unstable scale degrees seek to move to one of the more stable rest tones. The unstable scale degrees shall be called **active tones**.

Scale degree 2 usually moves to either scale degrees 1 or 3, scale degree 4 to either 3 or 5, and scale degree 6 to either 5 or 7. If scale degree 6 proceeds to 7, the leading tone, then the motion frequently continues upwards to the tonic note (8). It is important to understand the relatively unstable nature of active tones because their tendency to attach themselves to the more stable rest tones accounts for some of the melodic patterns that occur in both the major and minor modes. In this text, we refer to the major and minor modes collectively as the **major-minor tonal system**.

The Natural Minor Mode

The minor mode has three forms, the harmonic minor, the melodic minor, and the natural minor, which is also known as the pure minor and the Aeolian mode (for a discussion of the Aeolian mode and the other modes that have Greek names, see Appendix C). The natural minor can be located on the piano keyboard by finding the A octave in any register. As shown in example 6–1, the natural minor in the A octave consists of white keys only; no black keys are involved and no pitches inflected. Since the pitches E to F and B to C constitute the only two places within the octave where there are half steps between two adjacent white keys, the combined distribution of whole steps and half steps across the A octave produces a profile of half steps between scale degrees 2 and 3 and scale degrees 5 and 6.

Example 6–1

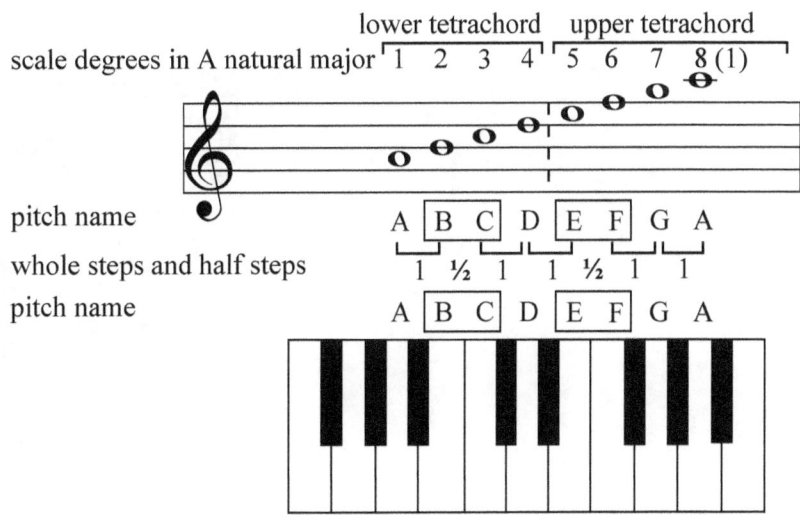

The natural minor takes from the major mode the names of the tonic, supertonic, mediant, subdominant, dominant, and submediant to designate scale degrees 1, 2, 3, 4, 5, and 6 respectively. Scale degree 7, however, is a special case. Unlike the major mode, the natural minor contains a whole step rather than a half step between scale degrees 7 and 8. Scale degree 7 of the natural minor is called the subtonic in order to distinguish it from the leading tone of the major mode. The natural minor does not share the major mode's compelling drive to move upwards by half step from scale degree 7 to scale degree 8. It is therefore more difficult to define and hear the tonic of the natural minor. The presence of the subtonic note may well be the natural minor's most distinctive feature. (Appendix C discusses other modes that also have the subtonic scale degree.)

The natural minor contains two tetrachords, each of which is separated by a whole step (see example 6–1 above). Unlike the major mode, the tetrachords for the natural minor are non-matching; in other words, the profile of half steps and whole steps for the lower tetrachord from scale degrees 1 to 4 (whole step, half step, and whole step) does not match the profile of half steps and whole steps for the upper tetrachord from scales 5 to 8 (half step, whole step, whole step).

Following the method introduced in Chapter 5 for describing major and minor intervals, we shall use lowercase letters when referring to the tonic of any minor mode. Therefore, the minor mode in the A octave will be written as "a minor" rather than as "A minor" (and pronounced as ā minor, not ă minor). On the other hand, major keys such as C major, F♯ major, and D♭ major use uppercase letters.

The Relative Minor

Since no black keys are involved in the construction of a minor, its key signature is identical to that of C major. Having neither sharps nor flats, both modes possess exactly the same pitch content and therefore *share the same key signature* (example 6–2). The principal differences between C major and a minor are their tonics and ranges. C major's scale degree 1 is C; its range extends across the C octave. Scale degree 1 of a minor is A; its range falls within the A octave.

Despite these differences, the common pitch content between C major and a minor constitutes an important *relationship* between the two modes. Indeed, within the context of C major, a minor is described as the **relative minor** key area of C major. The relative minor key area always occurs on scale degree 6 of the corresponding major mode.

Example 6–2

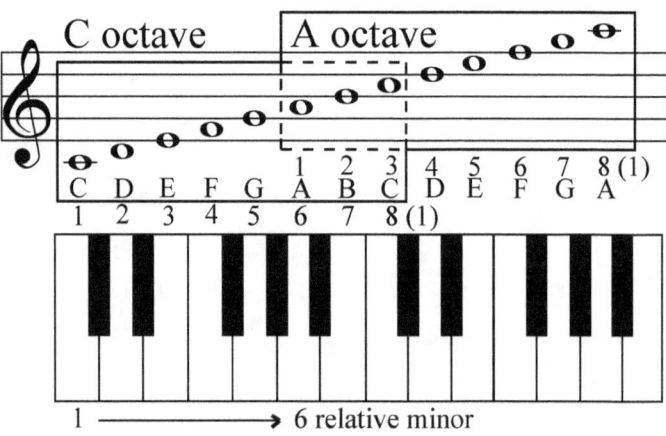

Each of the fourteen transpositions of C major has a relative minor. To find the relative minor of any transposed major mode, transpose the relationship between C major and a minor. In other words, locate scale degree 6 of any transposed major mode and that pitch will be the relative minor key area. For example, what is the relative minor key of G major? Scale degree 6 of G major is E. Therefore, e minor is the relative minor of G major; and both modes have one sharp (F♯) in their key signatures.

Another way to find the relative minor of any transposed major mode is to recognize that scale degree 6 is always a major 6th above the tonic note. Also, remember that the inversion of a major 6th is a minor 3rd; accordingly, we can find the relative minor of any major mode by proceeding either up a major 6th *or* down a minor 3rd from the tonic note.

Either direction from scale degree 1 leads to scale degree 6 (example 6–3). Let us answer two more questions: what is the relative minor of F major? A major 6th above (or a minor 3rd below) F is D; thus, d minor is the relative minor of F major. Both F major and d minor have one flat (B♭). What is the relative minor of E major? A minor 3rd below (or a major 6th above) E is C♯; and so, c♯ minor has four sharps (F♯, C♯, G♯, and D♯)—the same sharps that occur in E major.

Example 6–3

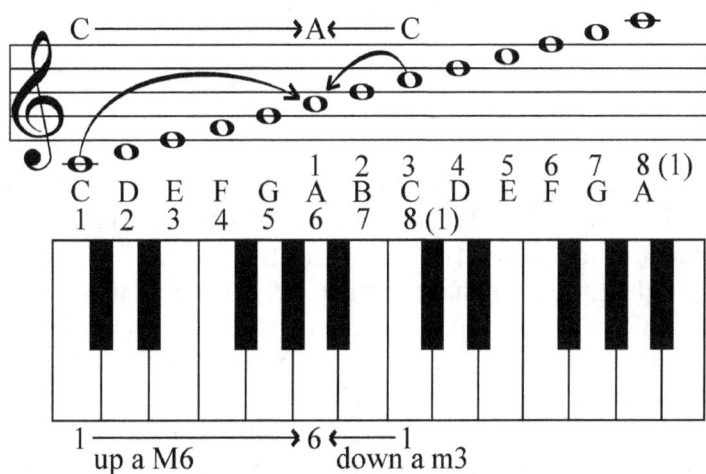

The Parallel Minor and the Parallel Major

In the foregoing paragraphs, we saw how major and minor modes standing in a relative relationship to one another share the same key signature (and therefore the same pitch content) but always have different tonics and different ranges. Another type of modal relationship involves two modes that have different key signatures but share the same tonic and the same range. Because both modes have the same tonic note, they are considered to be *parallel* to one another. Every major mode has a **parallel minor** mode, every minor mode a **parallel major**. Using C as scale degree 1, examples 6–4a and 4b illustrate the differences and the similarities between two parallel modes.

Example 6–4

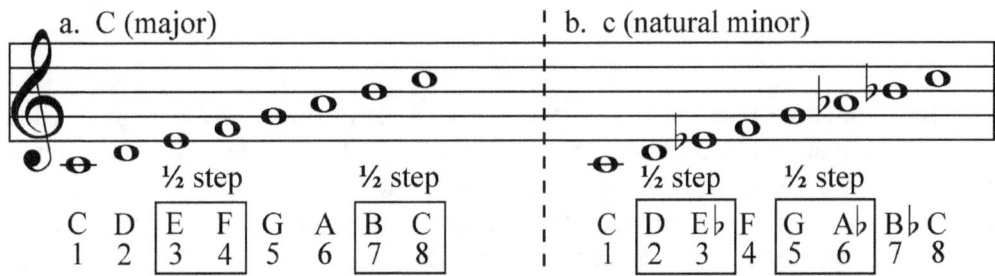

As we have observed, the major mode contains half steps between scale degrees 3 and 4 and scale degrees 7 and 8, whereas the natural minor has half steps between scale degrees 2 and 3 and scale degrees 5 and 6. When the major mode and the natural minor are parallel, having the same tonic and range, the pitch content between them will be different; specifically, their scale degrees 3, 6, and 7 cannot be the same.

Example 6–4b above presents the scale formation for the natural minor within the C octave. Since C is the tonic, the mode must include an E♭, A♭, and B♭ (scale degrees 3, 6, and 7) in order to preserve the profile of half steps between scale degrees 2 and 3 and scale degrees 5 and 6. On the other hand, C major maintains its profile of half steps with E♮, A♮, and B♮.

The Relative Major

Although it is possible to construct the scale for the natural minor on any pitch and add the appropriate accidentals to preserve its half-step profile, there is a faster and easier way to find the accidentals that comprise the key signature for the minor mode. In the preceding section, we noted that every major mode has a parallel minor and every minor a parallel major. And just as every major mode has a relative minor, every minor mode has a **relative major**.

To find the relative major, proceed to scale degree 3 of the minor mode by counting up a minor 3rd from the minor mode's tonic pitch. Once you have located the relative major, its key signature will provide the pitch content and the key signature for the natural minor.

Let us clarify this point with a few practice questions. What is the relative major of b♭ minor? Counting up a minor 3rd from B♭ brings us to D♭; since D♭ major has five flats (B♭, E♭, A♭, D♭, and G♭), the same five flats are found in the key signature of b♭ minor. What is the relative major of e minor (count up a minor 3rd)? G is the relative major of e minor. The key signature of G major has one sharp; accordingly, e minor has one sharp. What is the relative major of d minor? The answer is F major. Thus, the key of d minor has the same key signature as F major: one flat.

Examples 6–5a and 5b show the various options for finding relative major and minor key areas. We know that the relative minor of a major mode can be found by counting either up a major 6th or down a minor 3rd from the major mode's tonic pitch (6–5a). Similarly, it is possible to locate the relative major key area of any minor mode by counting either down a major 6th *or* up a minor 3rd from the minor mode's tonic pitch (6–5b).

Example 6–5

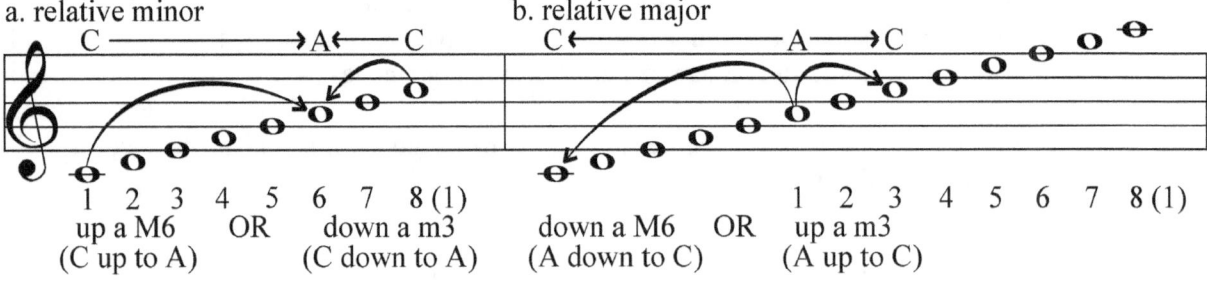

To summarize parallel and relative modal relationships: any two modes that stand in a parallel relationship to one another will share the same tonic pitch and range but have different key signatures. Any two modes that stand in a relative relationship to one another will share the same key signature but have different tonics and different ranges. Scale degree 6 of the major mode is the relative minor key area. Scale degree 3 of the natural minor is the relative major key area.

The Circle of 5ths for Minor

In Chapter 4, we assembled a group of ascending and descending perfect 5ths to form a circle of 5ths for the major mode (example 4–6 above), a circle that has a sharp side of ascending perfect 5ths and a flat side of descending perfect 5ths. Three of the keys located in the lower portion of the circle (D♭ and C♯, G♭ and F♯, and C♭ and B) constitute enharmonic keys that close the circle of 5ths and bring the sharp and flat sides of major together.

The minor mode also has a circle of 5ths (example 6–6) and it is organized in exactly the same way as the circle of 5ths for the major mode. As with the major mode, the minor mode has fifteen key and scale formations, seven with sharps, seven with flats, and the key of a minor, which has neither sharps nor flats.

On the sharp side of minor, the circle begins with a minor and ascends in perfect 5ths through the keys of e, b, f♯, c♯, g♯, d♯, and a♯, increasing by one the number of sharps for each successive key. Similarly, on the flat side of minor, the circle begins on a minor and descends in perfect 5ths through d, g, c, f, b♭, e♭, and a♭. Three pairs of enharmonic keys located in the lower position of the circle, namely, b♭ and a♯, e♭ and d♯, and a♭ and g♯, close the circle of 5ths and bring the sharp and the flat sides of minor together.

Example 6–6: the sharp and flat sides of minor in the circle of 5ths

80 Chapter 6 The Minor Mode

Example 6–7 places all of the major keys next to the minor keys in order to show the relationship between each pair of relative major and minor modes (uppercase letters represent major keys, while lowercase letters signify minor keys). Notice that moving clockwise two perfect 5ths from a minor and C major brings us to b minor and D major—both of which have two sharps in their key signatures. The relative major of b minor is D major; D major's relative minor is b minor. If we proceed counterclockwise four perfect 5ths from a minor and C major, we arrive at f minor and A♭ major—both of which have four flats in their key signatures. The relative major of f minor is A♭ major; A♭ major's relative minor is f minor.

Example 6–7: the sharp and flats sides of major and minor in the circle of 5ths

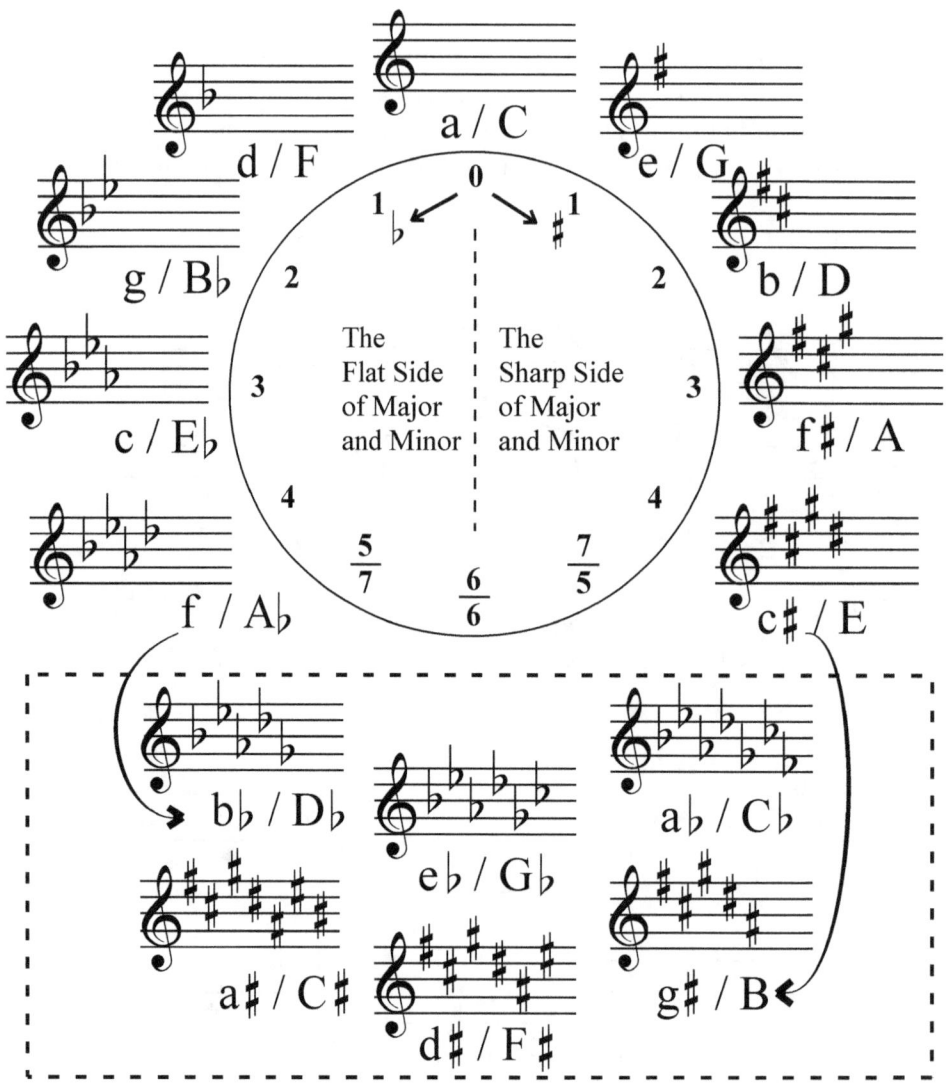

The Harmonic Minor Mode

The harmonic minor and the natural minor are almost identical—except for one *very* important difference. The natural minor employs the subtonic, which is one whole step below the tonic. The harmonic minor, on the other hand, borrows the leading tone from the parallel major; which in effect raises the subtonic by one half step and produces a half step between scale degrees 7 and 8 (examples 6–8a and 8b).

The harmonic minor's use of the leading tone (instead of the natural minor's subtonic scale degree) intensifies the melodic motion upwards to the tonic note. Moreover, the drive upwards by half step from scale degree 7 to scale degree 8 helps to firmly establish the key center. Conversely, the subtonic scale degree lacks the leading tone's compelling drive to move upwards by half step to the tonic; thus, as we have said, the key center is more clearly defined in those modes that employ the leading tone and more difficult to hear in modes that have subtonics, such as the natural minor.

Example 6–8: the harmonic minor and its parallel major

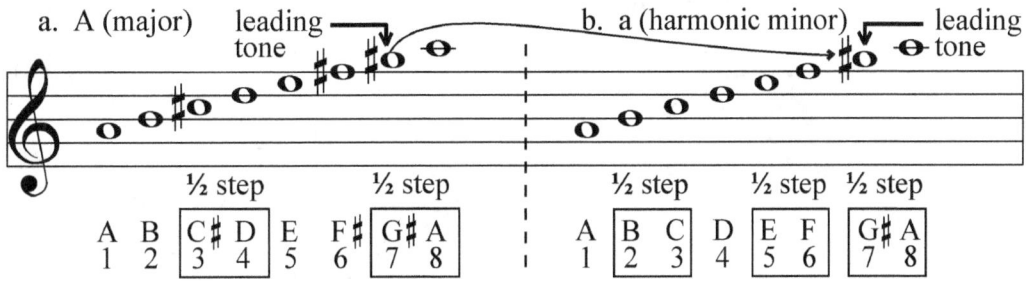

As shown in examples 6–9a and 9b, the harmonic minor retains all of the pitch content of the natural minor *except* for the incorporation of the major mode's leading tone. This one difference, however, produces a very unusual mode and scale. First, the harmonic minor has half steps between scale degrees 2 and 3, scale degrees 5 and 6, and scale degrees 7 and 8—a mode and scale with three pairs of half steps. Secondly, by raising the subtonic one half step to produce a half step approach to scale degree 8, an augmented 2nd (1½ steps) is created between scale degrees 6 and 7. The augmented 2nd is far more difficult to sing than either the major or minor 2nd.

Finally, the leading tone of the harmonic minor is never indicated in the key signature for the minor mode. Notably, both the harmonic minor and the melodic minor (to be discussed below) base their key signatures on the pitch content of the natural minor, despite the fact that both modes have tones that do not occur in the natural minor.

Example 6–9

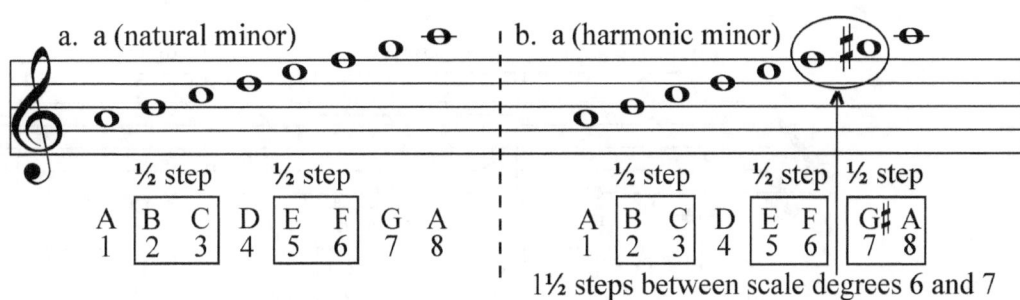

The Melodic Minor Mode

The melodic minor contains elements of the major mode and the natural minor. The melodic minor arises from two important factors:
(1) the inherent tendency of active tones to move to more stable rest tones; and,
(2) the preference of composers to create conjunct (i.e., stepwise) melodic structures that avoid awkward intervals such as the augmented 2nd.

The Ascending Form of the Melodic Minor

When a melody in the harmonic minor moves upwards towards scale degree 8, composers usually raise scale degree 6 by one half step in order to eliminate the augmented 2nd that would otherwise occur between scale degrees 6 and 7 (example 6–10).

Example 6–10

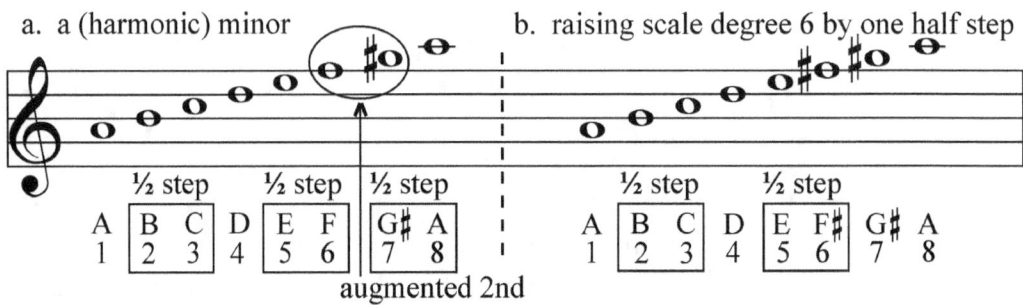

Raising scale degree 6 by one half step to avoid the augmented 2nd of the harmonic minor results in an upper tetrachord with a profile of half steps and whole steps that is identical to the upper tetrachord of the major mode, that is: whole step, whole step, half step (example 6–11). Borrowing the upper tetrachord of the major mode produces what is referred to as the "ascending" form of the melodic minor. Whenever the melodic activity of a composition written in the minor mode moves upwards in the direction of scale degree 8, the ascending form of the melodic minor is usually preferred.

Notice that the key signature for c minor in the second measure of example 6–11 has three flats but that an A♮ (rather than an A♭) is used to avoid the augmented 2nd that would occur in the harmonic minor between scale degrees 6 and 7. Henceforth, we shall refer to scale degrees 6 and 7 as "raised 6" and "raised 7" when the ascending melodic minor is used. The symbols for raised 6 and raised 7 are ♯6 and ♯7 respectively.

Example 6–11: borrowing the upper tetrachord of major to produce the ascending melodic minor

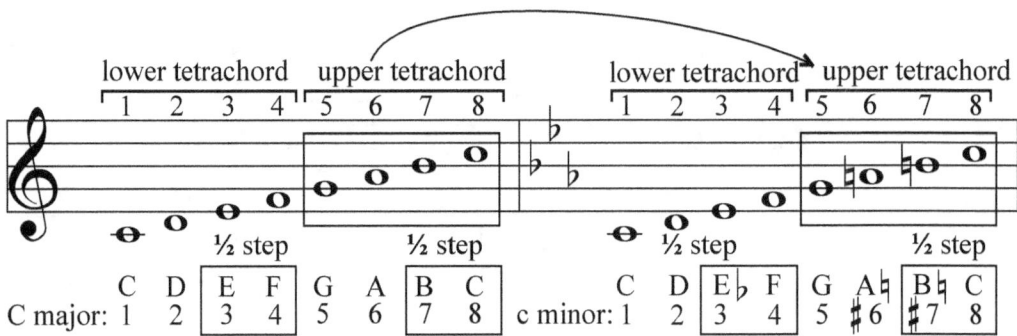

The use of the sharp (♯) in front of the number does not necessarily mean that the pitch itself carries a sharp. Indeed, in 6–11 above, the pitches for ♯6 and ♯7 are A♮ and B♮. (The reason for not referring to the leading tone of the harmonic minor as raised 7 will be explained below.)

It is central to our understanding of the minor mode to recognize that scale degrees ♯6 and ♯7 are not reflected in the minor key signature. If, therefore, a composition is written in a key such as c minor, which has three flats in its key signature (B♭, E♭, and A♭), the music will probably also include an A♮ and/or a B♮, particularly when the melody moves upwards towards scale degree 8. And so, when reading music in the minor mode, it would be well to expect that tones representing scale degrees ♯6 and ♯7 are likely to appear and that their presence will contradict the implied pitch content of the key signature.

The Descending Form of the Melodic Minor

If the minor mode descends towards scale degree 5, scale degrees 6 and 7 are each lowered by one half step from their raised counterparts, scale degrees ♯6 and ♯7. Lowering scale degrees 6 and 7 produces what is called the "descending" melodic minor (example 6–12). We call the lowered forms of scale degrees 6 and 7 "lowered 6" and "lowered 7" to distinguish them from their raised counterparts, scale degrees ♯6 and ♯7. The symbols for lowered 6 and lowered 7 are ♭6 and ♭7. Notably, the pitch content of the descending form of the melodic minor is identical to that of the natural minor.

Let us consider the key of c minor in example 6–12 to see how the process of lowering scale degrees 6 and 7 works. The ascending form of the melodic minor in the key of c minor shows A♮ and B♮ as scale degrees ♯6 and ♯7. But when the c-minor scale moves down in the direction of scale degree 5 (G) in the descending form of the melodic minor, both the A♮ and B♮ are lowered by one half step to A♭ and B♭.

Example 6–12: the ascending and descending forms of the melodic minor

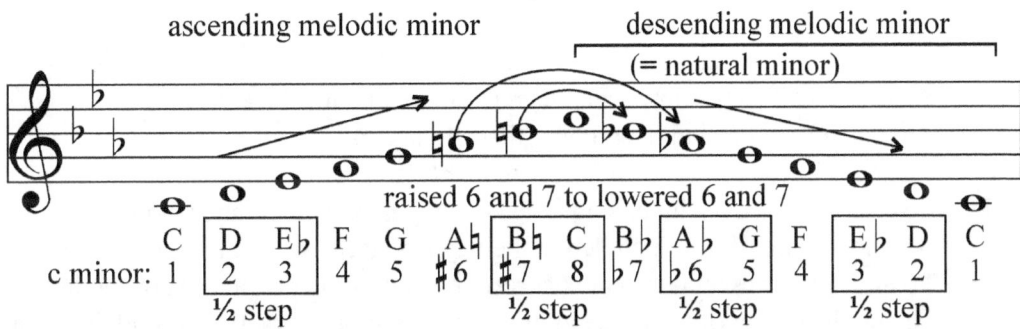

The use of scale degrees ♭6 and ♭7 intensifies the melodic motion downwards to scale degree 5 by creating a half-step approach from scale degree ♭6 to scale degree 5. We term scale degrees 6 and 7 raised or lowered and apply symbols to them (either ♯ or ♭) because on each of these scale degrees, the melodic minor has two different versions of the same letter name. For example, in c minor, scale degrees 6 and 7 may be either A♮ or A♭ and B♮ or B♭, according to whether the tones are either raised or lowered. The sharp or flat in front of the number merely indicates that there are two pitches with the same letter name and that one pitch is either raised or lowered *in relation to the other pitch*.

Having two versions of the same letter name, scale degrees 6 and 7 are *variable* tones in the melodic minor; we therefore refer to scale degrees 6 and 7 as "variable scale degree 6" and "variable scale degree 7." A more complete and specific verbal description of the variable scale degrees in the melodic minor would be as follows: "variable scale degree raised 6," "variable scale degree raised 7," "variable scale degree lowered 6," and "variable scale degree lowered 7."

It is important to understand that the flat (♭) in front of the number 6 and 7 does not necessarily mean that the pitch itself carries a flat. For example, compare the keys of c minor and a minor. In c minor (6–12 above), the lowered variables happen to take flats (A♭ and B♭), whereas in the key of a minor (example 6–13), the lowered variables do not carry flats (F♮ and G♮).

Example 6–13

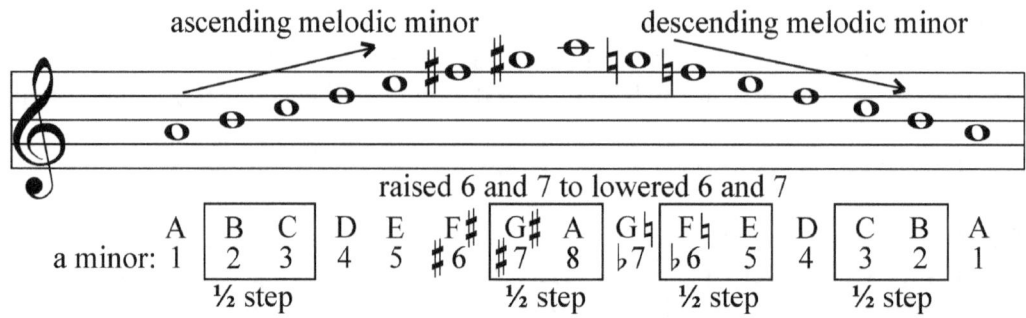

The foregoing examples 6–11, 12, and 13 demonstrate that the sharp or flat in front of the number only means that the variable scale degree is either raised or lowered by one half step; the act of raising or lowering the pitch by one half step could be indicated just as easily with an arrow pointing upwards or downwards in front of the scale degree.

Finding the Variable Scale Degrees of the Melodic Minor

Variables ♯6, ♯7, ♭6, and ♭7 may be located in any key according to the following guidelines:
  (1) ♭6 is one half step above scale degree 5 (and a minor 6th above scale degree 1).
  (2) ♭7 is one whole step below scale degree 1 (and a minor 7th above scale degree 1).
  (3) ♯6 is one whole step above scale degree 5 (and a major 6th above scale degree 1).
  (4) ♯7 is one half step below scale degree 1 (and a major 7th above scale degree 1).
  (5) ♭6 and ♭7 are one half step lower than ♯6 and ♯7.
  (6) ♯6 and ♯7 are one half step higher than ♭6 and ♭7.
  (7) ♯6 and ♯7 are *never* included in the key signature of the minor mode.
  (8) ♭6 and ♭7 are *always* included in the key signature of the minor mode.
  (9) ♯6 and ♯7 correspond to scale degrees 6 and 7 of the parallel major mode.
  (10) The pitch content of the descending melodic minor is exactly the same as the natural minor.
  (11) Since ♯6 and ♯7 of the melodic minor correspond to scale degrees 6 and 7 of the parallel major mode, ♯6 and ♯7 can be found easily if you know the key signature of that minor key's parallel major mode. For example: what are variables ♯6 and ♯7 in the key and mode of a minor?
    (a) The parallel major of a minor is A major, which has three sharps (F♯, C♯, and G♯).
    (b) Scale degrees 6 and 7 in A major are F♯ and G♯.
    (c) Therefore, variables ♯6 and ♯7 in the key and mode of a minor are also F♯ and G♯.

Comparing the Three Forms of Minor

The key signature of all three forms of the minor mode is derived from the pitch content of the natural minor (again, despite the fact that both the harmonic minor and the melodic minor have tones that do not occur in the natural minor).

In the natural minor, the harmonic minor, and the melodic minor, scale degrees 1, 2, 3, 4, and 5 are all invariable tones with one pitch name only for each mode's five respective scale degrees. For all three forms of minor, the profile of half steps and whole steps from scale degrees 1 to 5 is the same; therefore, all three forms of minor have the same pitch content for their invariable tones.

With respect to the melodic minor, if all of its pitch content is taken into account, then strictly speaking, the mode is not a seven-tone diatonic scale. On the other hand, the harmonic minor is diatonic to the extent that it has one pitch name only for each of its seven scale degrees; as a consequence, the term leading tone is sufficient to describe its scale degree 7. Since the harmonic minor does not have a lowered 7 scale degree, there is no need to refer to the leading tone as raised 7.

Example 6–14 shows all three forms of minor together in order to facilitate comparison; additionally, each mode appears untransposed in the key of a minor and then transposed to the key of c minor. Attaching the accidentals directly to the notes rather than using key signatures underscores both the differences and the similarities between the three forms.

Example 6–14

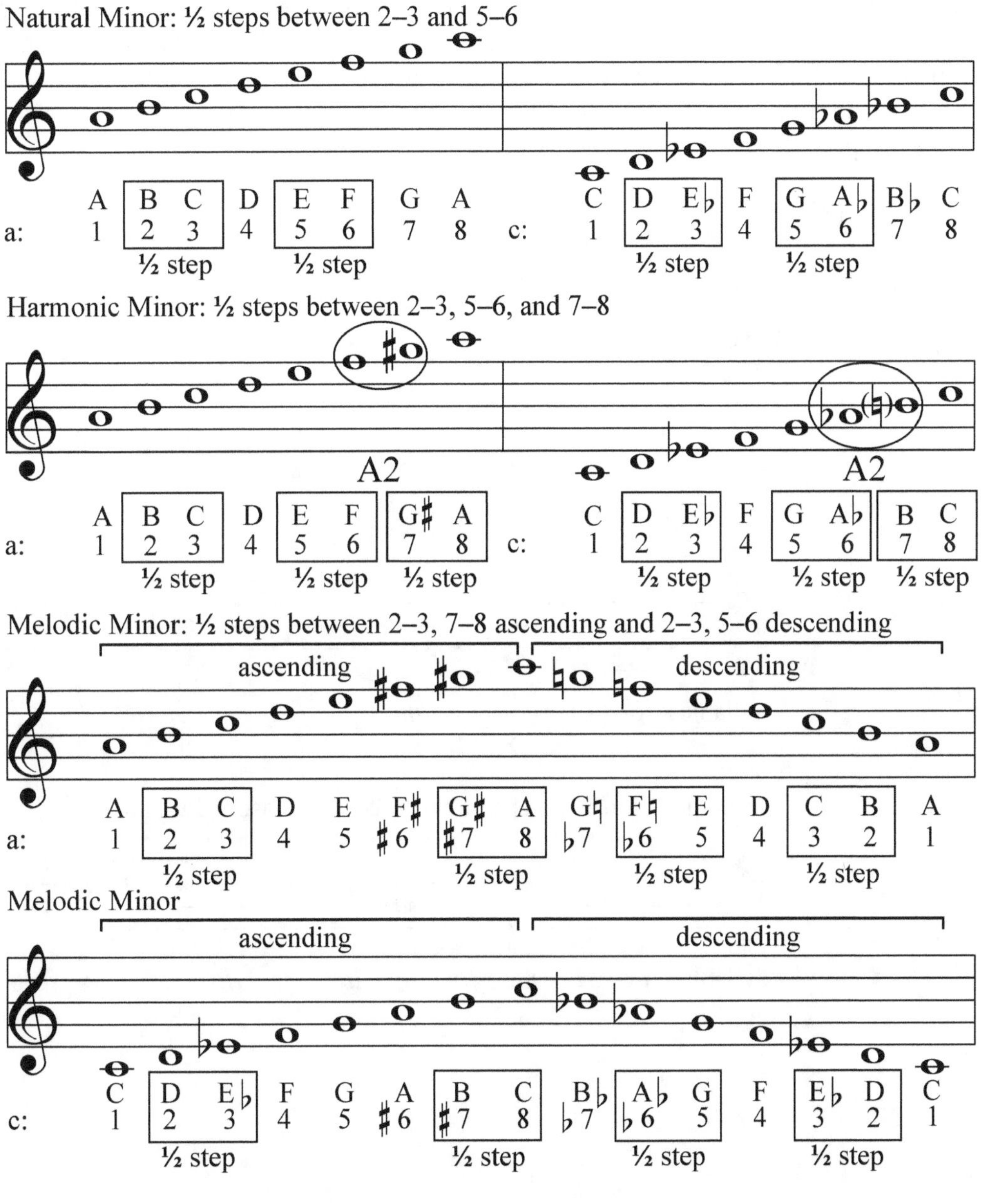

A comparison of the three forms of minor shown above in 6–14 reveals that the natural minor and the harmonic minor do not share all of the same pitches and that the melodic minor contains all of the pitches found in both the natural minor and the harmonic minor. Since the pitch content of the melodic minor exceeds that of the natural and harmonic forms of minor and therefore presents the most complete inventory of pitches, we shall prefer the melodic minor for the purpose of demonstrating the formation of triads in Chapter 8.

Singing the Three Forms of Minor

At the conclusion of Chapter 3, we assigned syllables to each of the seven scale degrees of the major mode in order to sing simple conjunct and disjunct melodic patterns. Using syllable inflection, other syllables were attached to the pitches that span the ascending and descending chromatic scale.

Example 6–15 presents the three forms of minor with the appropriate syllables for singing each scale pattern. When singing the natural minor, scale degrees 3, 6, and 7 carry the syllables *me*, *le*, and *te* respectively, instead of *mi*, *la*, and *ti*. The harmonic minor uses *me* and *le* (scale degrees 3 and 6) instead of *mi* and *la*; however, *ti* is used instead of *te* because it constitutes the leading tone. The melodic minor employs *la* and *ti* (scale degrees ♯6 and ♯7) in its ascending form and *le* and *te* (scale degrees ♭6 and ♭7) in its descending form; *me* is retained in both forms. (To review the correct pronunciation of the syllables, see above, p. 50.)

Example 6–15

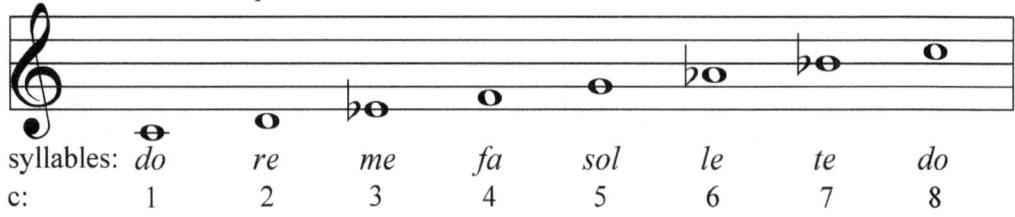

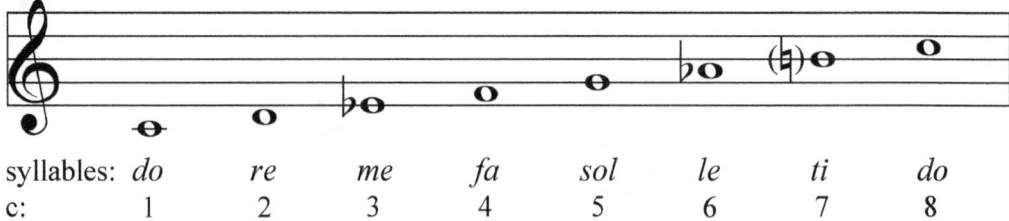

Chapter 7 Advanced Concepts in Meter

This chapter explores some of the more complex expressions of rhythm and meter, arranged here in four sections. Sections 1 and 4 are recommended for study, sections 2 and 3 as reference:
(1) simple and compound meter exchange in which irregular groupings of notes occur either within the span of a single beat or extend across two or more beats of the measure (pp. 87–97);
(2) irregular groupings of notes that occur within the span of a single beat other than those involving simple and compound meter exchange (pp. 98–101);
(3) irregular groupings of notes other than those involving simple and compound meter exchange that extend across two or more beats of the measure (pp. 101–104); and,
(4) asymmetrical distributions of beats within the measure (pp. 105–106).

Section 1: Simple and Compound Meter Exchange

In music, it is possible and often desirable to place either a simple division of the beat into a compound meter or a compound division of the beat into a simple meter. A simple (two-part) division of the beat occurring in a compound meter is referred to as the **duplet**. A compound (three-part) division of the beat used in a simple meter is called the **triplet**.

Triplets

To understand the triplet, let us compare two duple meters: $\frac{2}{4}$ and $\frac{6}{8}$. In $\frac{2}{4}$ time (example 7–1a), the value of the beat occurs at the level of the quarter note; in $\frac{6}{8}$ time (7–1b), however, the value of the beat is the dotted quarter note. The first division of the beat for both meters is the eighth note. Because both $\frac{2}{4}$ and $\frac{6}{8}$ are duple meters and have beat values of the same note denomination (i.e., the quarter note and the dotted quarter note), we shall refer to these meters as "parallel duple meters."

Example 7–1: parallel duple meters

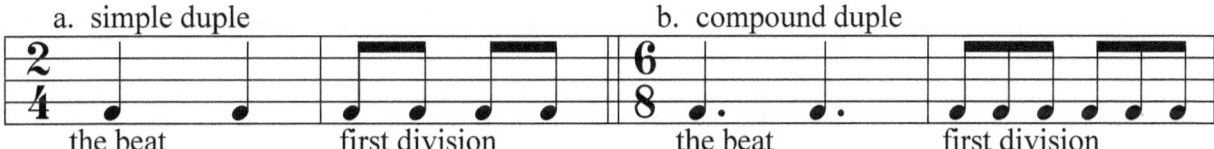

When a simple meter borrows the first division of the beat from a compound meter, the first division carries the number 3 above the note group and is referred to generally as the triplet; in this text, the triplet of the first division is termed "the small triplet." Examples 7–2a and 2b show how the triplet appears in $\frac{2}{4}$, first with all three notes beamed together (7–2a) and then expressed as a quarter note and eighth (7–2b). The method for counting the triplet is taken from compound meter (1 + a 2 + a).

If the triplet is not beamed (7–2b), then the figure adds a bracket to the number 3 in order to show the correct grouping of the notes. In example 7–2b, the first two eighth notes of the triplet are replaced by a quarter note, thereby modifying the triplet's basic three-note framework.

Example 7–2: the small triplet

87

88   Chapter 7 Advanced Concepts In Meter

The triplet on beat 2 of 7–2a above occurs within the same span of time as the two eighth notes that normally constitute the first division of the beat. In simple meter, the triplet forms an irregular grouping of notes that conflicts with the two-part division of the beat. Example 7–3 shows the placement of the triplet in relation to the two eighth notes of the first division. Here, the triplet is notated with stems down and combined with another rhythmic line with stems up; the latter shows the first simple division of the beat. The second half of beat 2 (measure 1) falls between the second and third notes of the triplet.

Example 7–3: placement of the small triplet

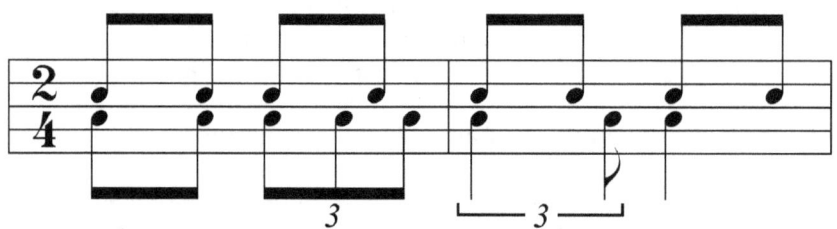

As we have said, any triplet with note values that are equivalent to the note values of the meter's first division will be referred to as the small triplet. Other varieties of triplets discussed in this chapter include "the micro triplet," "the large triplet," and the "macro triplet." These other triplets use note values that either correspond to the second division of the beat or span two or four beats within the measure.

In example 7–4, we can see how it is possible to replace any of the first-division values of the triplet with smaller note denominations, such as those of the second division. In each instance, the basic three-note framework of the triplet figure has been changed: either two sixteenths replace one eighth (examples 7–4a and 4b) or four sixteenths replace two eighths (7–4c). Notice that the second sixteenth note of each pair of sixteenths does not receive a count (or syllable).

Example 7–4: using second-division notes values with the small triplet

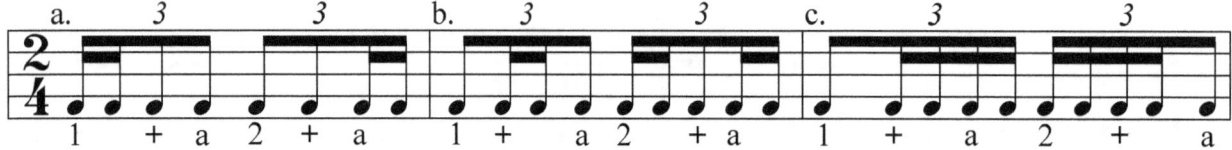

Example 7–5 illustrates another type of triplet, one that occurs at the level of the second division, the sixteenth note in $\frac{2}{4}$ time. We shall refer to this triplet as the micro triplet. The micro triplet is notated with stems down in the example and is combined with another rhythmic line with stems up; the line with stems up shows both the first division of the beat in eighths (7–5a) and the second division of the beat in sixteenths (7–5b, the second half of beat 2). Each micro triplet carries the number 3.

Example 7–5: the micro triplet

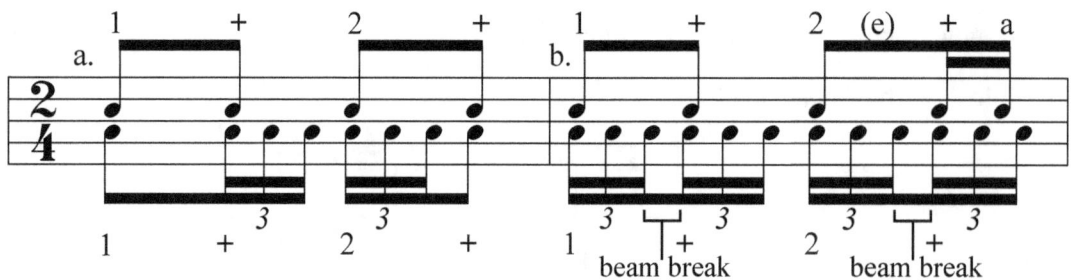

The micro triplet may appear on the first part of the beat, the second part, or both. In 7–5a, the micro triplet falls alternately on each half of the beat, whereas in 7–5b, it is placed on both halves. When the micro triplet appears on both parts of the beat, there is usually a *break in the beam* to make the second half of the beat easier to read.

Example 7–6a shows where the small triplet falls in relation to both the first and second simple divisions of the beat. Example 7–6b presents a decidedly different operation at the level of the second division; for here, we have two micro triplets beamed into a single group of six notes on each beat. The six notes carry the number 6 instead of the number 3.

The notation for the group of six notes changes because the accompanying rhythmic line (i.e., the line with stems up) does not emphasize the second half of the beat. On beat 1 of 7–6b, the second half of the beat has been subsumed within the eighth note that falls on the syllable "e" (see the circled "e"). On beat 2, the second half of the beat occurs within the larger context of four equally-spaced sixteenth notes. Thus, in the line that has the six notes, there is no need to clarify the second half of the beat with a beam break. In effect, each pair of micro triplets has become a single group of six notes called the **sextuplet**.

Example 7–6: the small triplet, sextuplet, and second division of the beat

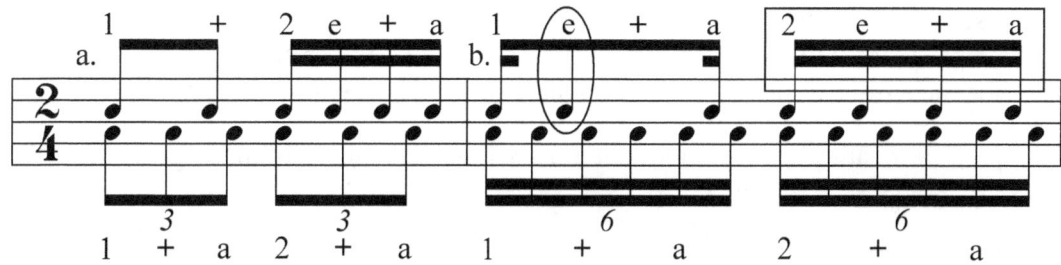

We have seen how the small triplet substitutes three notes for two notes of the first simple division. The micro triplet can replace either one half of the beat or it can occur on both halves of the beat, resulting in a single group of six notes. Although the small triplet and the micro triplet are each confined to the duration of one beat, they can be repeated in a series of successive beats in a variety of combinations and configurations. The large triplet, however, extends its note values across two beats.

Example 7–7 demonstrates how the large triplet is created and placed over two beats: the six eighth notes of two small triplets in $\frac{4}{4}$ time are tied together in pairs, which ultimately produces the equivalent of three quarter-note durations that in turn fill the space of two quarter-note beats. (Remember that only the first note of any tied pair of notes is articulated.)

Since both the value of the beat and the note value for the large triplet in $\frac{4}{4}$ time are exactly the same (i.e., the quarter note), it follows that *the note value of any large triplet corresponds to the value of the beat for the meter in which the large triplet occurs.*

Example 7–7: converting two small triplets in $\frac{4}{4}$ time into one large triplet

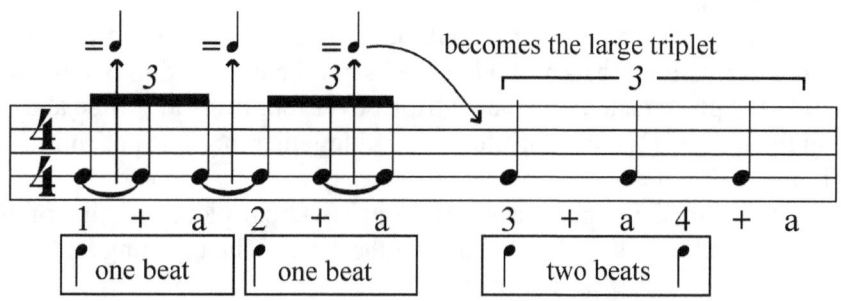

In example 7–8, the large triplet exists in $\frac{4}{2}$ time at the level of the half note and extends across two half-note beats. Since the first division of the beat occurs at the level of the quarter note, the small triplet also uses the quarter note.

Example 7–8: converting two small triplets in $\frac{4}{2}$ time into one large triplet

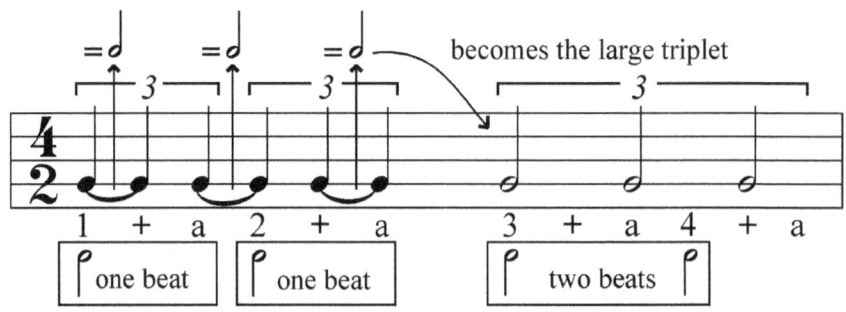

Example 7–9 shows the relationship between the note values of the small triplet (tied together in pairs) and those of the large triplet in $\frac{4}{4}$ time and in $\frac{4}{2}$ time. The counting and articulation for the large triplets in the example are as follows: 1 + a 2 ± a 3 + a 4 ± a (the underlined characters indicate the articulated notes for each group of tied durations and therefore each note of the large triplet).

Example 7–9: relating the note values of the small triplet to those of the large triplet

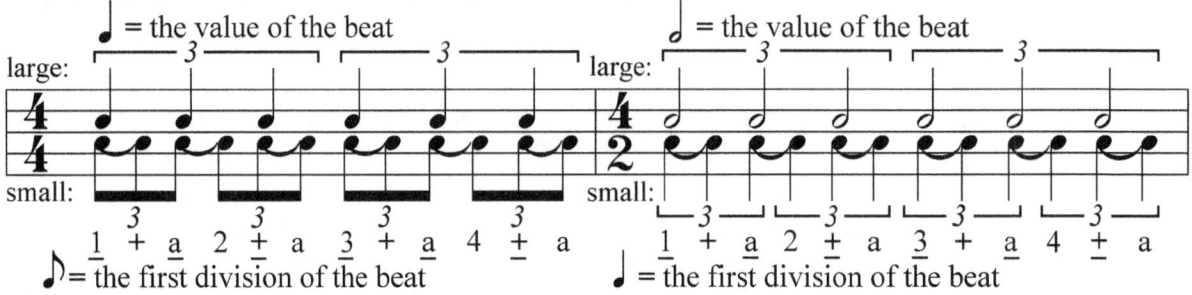

To summarize how the large triplet, the small triplet, and the micro triplet each relate the value of the beat and its potential divisions:
(1) the note value of any large triplet corresponds to the value of the beat for the meter in which the large triplet appears, substituting three notes for two notes at the level of the beat;
(2) the note value of any small triplet corresponds to the first division of the beat for the meter in which the small triplet appears, substituting three notes for two notes at the level of the first division;
(3) the note value of any micro triplet corresponds to the second division of the beat for the meter in which the micro triplet appears, substituting three notes for two notes at the level of the second division.

Finally, we come to what shall be termed here the macro triplet. The macro triplet extends its note values across four beats and therefore cannot be used within one measure of triple meter. Example 7–10 shows the placement of the macro triplet over four beats in $\frac{4}{4}$ time and in $\frac{4}{2}$ time. In 7–10a, notice how the eighth notes of four small triplets are tied together in groups of four to produce a macro triplet consisting of three half notes.

In 7–10b, the same process results in a macro triplet consisting of three whole notes. In both cases, the macro triplet overlays all four beats of the meter. The counting and articulation for the macro triplet is as follows: 1 + a 2 ± a 3 + a 4 + a.

Example 7–10: relating the note values of the small triplet to those of the macro triplet

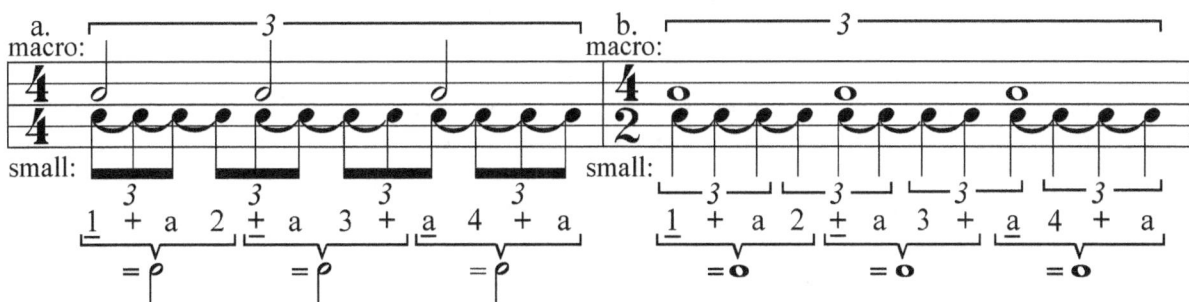

Earlier, in examples 7–2b and 4, we saw how the basic three-note framework of the small triplet could be modified with the inclusion of note values that are either larger or smaller than the first division of the beat. Example 7–11 displays a few of the many ways in which the principle of modification may be applied to the large triplet to alter its structure.

Example 7–11: modifying the three-note framework of the large triplet

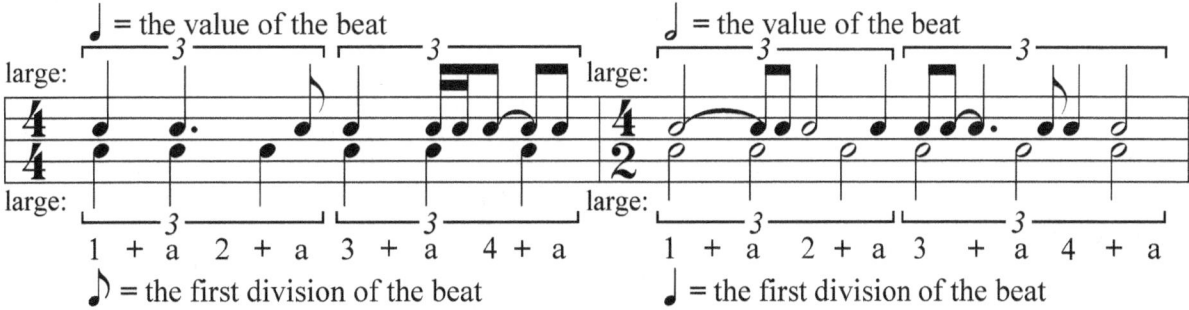

The alterations shown above underscore the rhythmic flexibility that comes from placing compound divisions of beats into simple meter. The possibilities are increased even further when the process of meter exchange is reversed: when simple divisions of beats are used in compound meter.

Duplets

A simple (two-part) division of the beat occurring in a compound meter is referred to as a duplet. When a compound meter borrows the first division of the beat from a simple meter, the first division carries the number 2 above the note group and is identified as a duplet. Example 7–12 shows how the duplet appears in the compound duple meter of $\frac{6}{8}$; the origin of the eighth-note duplet in $\frac{6}{8}$ can be traced to the first division of the beat in $\frac{2}{4}$ (the parallel duple meter of $\frac{6}{8}$). The example below displays two methods for counting the duplet in compound duple meter, in 2 and in 6. We shall explore further the formation of the duplet and its counting in examples 7–13 and 14.

Example 7–12: the duplet

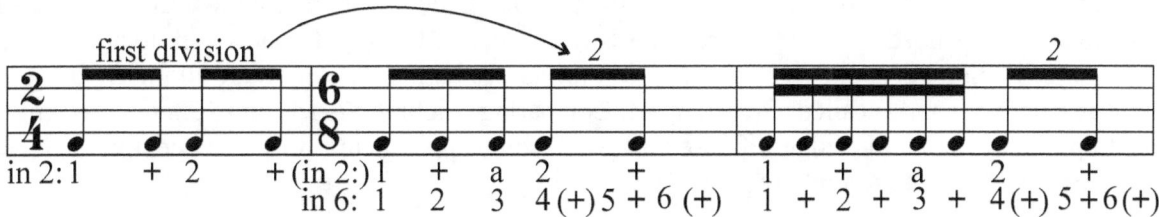

Although the duplet arises when a compound meter borrows the first division of the beat from a simple meter, the duplet can also be generated from within the compound meter itself. Example 7–13a illustrates the process by which six sixteenth notes of the second division in $^6_8$ are tied together to produce two groups of three sixteenth notes (interpreting the meter in 2, see beat 1, stems up).

Each group of sixteenths is rewritten in example 7–13a as a dotted eighth note (beat 2, stems up), as a dotted eighth spans the same duration of time as three sixteenths. In effect, a duplet figure consisting of two dotted eighth notes arises from the tied sixteenths. Once the 2 is placed over that figure, as shown in 7–13b (and below the figure if the stems are down), the dot is no longer needed and the rhythm is counted just as it would be in the parallel duple meter, $^2_4$: 1 + 2 + . In compound meter, the duplet constitutes an irregular grouping of notes that conflicts with the normal three-part division of the beat.

Example 7–13: producing the duplet from within compound meter

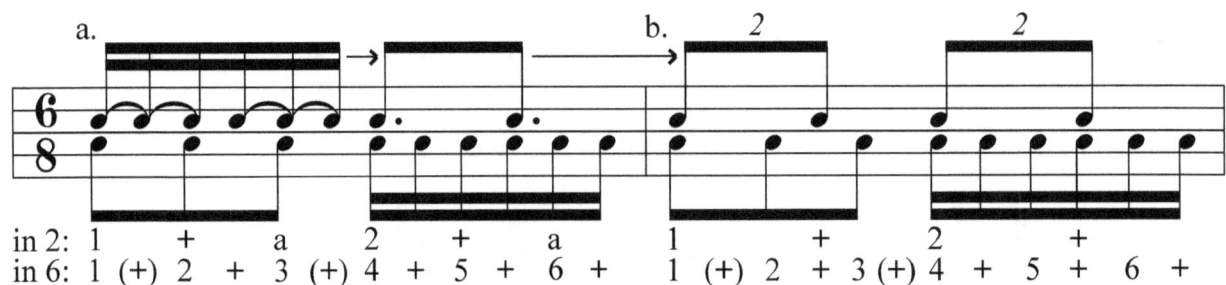

Notably, the duplet may also occur in simple meter. Example 7–14 presents the most common usage of the duplet within simple meter. The duplet in the second and third measures of the example transforms a simple triple meter ($^3_4$) into a simple duple meter ($^2_4$). In Chapter 1, we referred this type of transformation as the hemiola. Here, the duplet constitutes an irregular grouping of notes that conflicts with the normal three-part distribution of beats across the measure.

Example 7–14: using the duplet to transform simple triple meter into simple duple meter

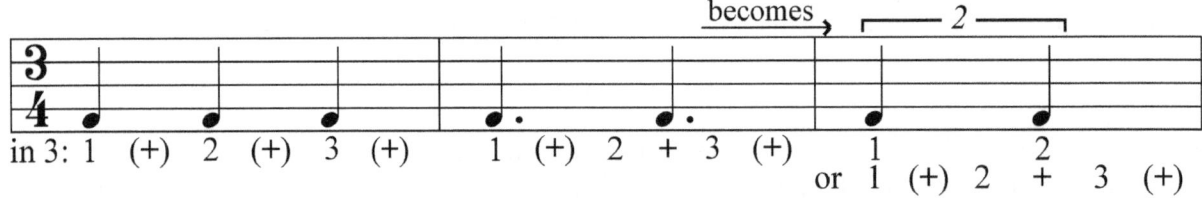

The previous discussions in this chapter have explored some of the ways in which simple and compound divisions of beats are exchanged within simple and compound meters. Triplets exceed the standard number of note values for each beat (or half beat) in simple meter and may even extend across two or four beats in the measure. It is also possible to modify the basic three-note framework of the triplet with either larger or smaller note values.

By contrast, the duplet has fewer note values than are found normally within the triple divisions of compound meter. Still, as demonstrated with the parallel duple meters of $^6_8$ and $^2_4$ in example 7–15, the duplet can be expanded to include more notes by replacing its two eighth notes with four sixteenth notes (four sixteenth notes span the same duration of time as two eighth notes). The resulting figure carries the number 4 above it and is called a **quadruplet**. Comparing examples 7–15a and 15b, it is evident that the quadruplet may be interpreted as a figure borrowed from simple meter; for the sixteenth-note quadruplet in $^6_8$ corresponds to the second division of the beat in $^2_4$.

Example 7–15: expanding the duplet

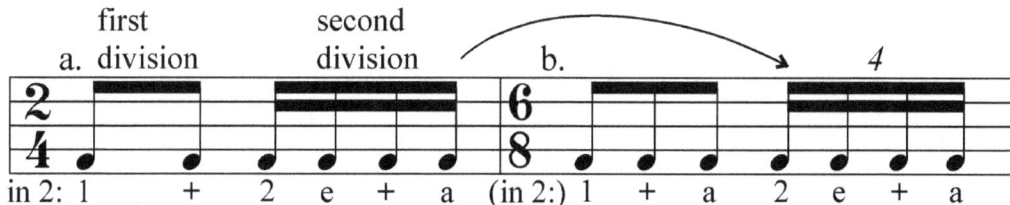

Despite the apparent derivation of the quadruplet from the second division of the beat in simple meter, it is also possible to generate the quadruplet from within the compound meter itself. Example 7–16a shows how twelve thirty-second notes of the third division in $^6_8$ may be tied together to produce four groups of three thirty-second notes (interpreting the meter in 2, see the dotted brackets on beat 1, stems up).

Each group of tied thirty-seconds in 7–16a is rewritten as a dotted sixteenth note (beat 2, stems up), as a dotted sixteenth is equivalent to three thirty-seconds. In effect, a quadruplet figure consisting of four dotted sixteenth notes results from the tied thirty-seconds (the placement of the four dotted sixteenths in relation to the three eighth notes of the first division in $^6_8$ is indicated in parentheses above the four-note figure). Once we place the number 4 over the quadruplet figure (7–16b), the dot becomes unnecessary and counting the figure proceeds as it would in the parallel duple meter of $^2_4$: 1 e + a 2 e + a.

Example 7–16: producing the quadruplet from within compound meter

94   Chapter 7 Advanced Concepts In Meter

As we have seen in examples 1–18b, 18c, 21, 22, and 23 of Chapter 1, four sixteenth notes can be arranged and configured in numerous ways within the context of simple meter. The most common expressions of sixteenth notes and sixteenth rests in simple meter are presented here in example 7–17 (remember that a dotted eighth is equivalent to three sixteenth notes).

Example 7–17

Example 7–18 demonstrates some of the ways in which the rhythms based upon a group of four sixteenth notes may be transferred to compound meter as a quadruplet. Notice how complex the articulations of the quadruplet become in relation to the three notes of the first division in compound meter when one of the notes of the quadruplet is lengthened (7–18a), or when the quadruplet is syncopated (interpreting the meter in 2, see beat 1 of 7–18b), or when the quadruplet contains one or more rest values (interpreting the meter in 2, see beat 2 of 7–18b).

Example 7–18: modifying the quadruplet

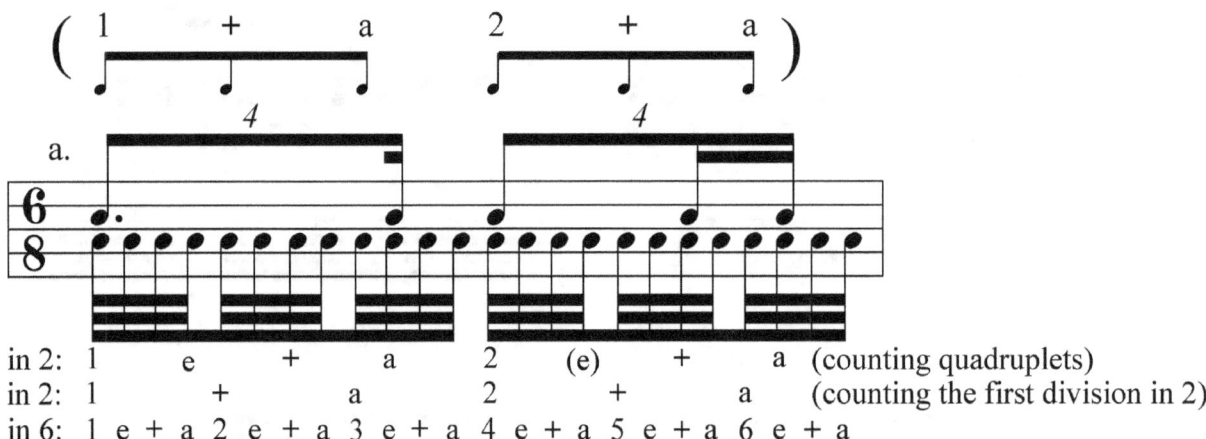

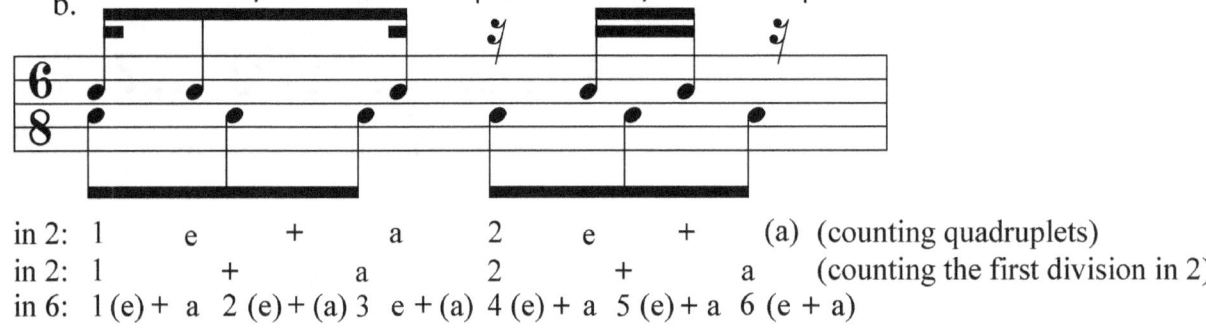

Alternative Notation

Before we continue exploring some of the challenges associated with irregular groupings of notes, it should be understood that composers and publishers often put forward inconsistent methods of notation that prevent the emergence of a common practice. For instance, an alternative way to notate the quadruplet is to use the note value of the first division rather than that of the second division. Example 7–19 illustrates the quadruplet in $\frac{6}{8}$ time, expressed initially with the second division in sixteenths (the preferred notation of this text) and then with the first division in eighths (the alternative notation).

Example 7–19: alternative notations for the quadruplet

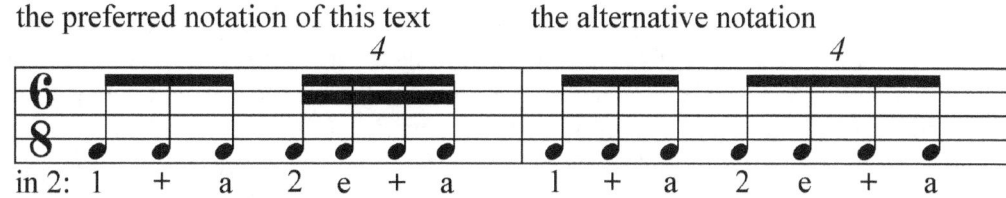

Fitting an Irregular Group into the Meter at the Level of the Beat or the Division of the Beat

The introduction of the triplet and the duplet into the meter produces a condition of conflict. Typically, the triplet places three beats or divisions of beats into the space of two beats or divisions of beats; the expression "three against two" is often used to describe the relationship between the beats (or divisions of beats). The macro triplet extends its note values across four beats, producing a "three-against-four" conflict. The duplet, on the other hand, places two beats or divisions of beats into the space of three beats or divisions of beats. The conflict of the duplet would be referred to as "two against three."

One means for showing the relationship between the beats is to place a colon (:) between the numbers; thus, three against two (or three in the space of two) becomes 3:2. Three against four (or three in the space of four) would be 3:4. Two against three (or two in the space of three) would be 2:3. In $\frac{2}{4}$ time, the large triplet produces a three-against-two conflict between beats (example 7–20a). In $\frac{4}{4}$ time, the macro triplet creates a three-against-four conflict between beats (7–20b). Placing the duplet into $\frac{3}{4}$ time brings about a two-against-three conflict between beats (7–20c).

Example 7–20: the conflict of meter exchange at the level of the beat

96   Chapter 7 Advanced Concepts In Meter

Consider the conflict between the first and second divisions of the beat in example 7–21. The issue involves the integration of a second-division quadruplet (in sixteenth notes) into the metric structure of $\frac{6}{8}$ time. Since $\frac{6}{8}$ is a compound meter, the beat is divided into three equal parts (or multiples of three). Beat 1 of the example illustrates the four-against-three relationship (4:3) between the two rhythmic parts.

The method for determining the correct placement of the quadruplet in relation to the three-part division of the beat involves finding the *fewest number of notes into which each group of notes may be divided*. In practice, multiplying the respective number of notes that each conflicting group contains provides the number common to both groups.

Multiplying the numbers 4 and 3, the two numbers that represent the conflict between the quadruplet and the three-part division of the beat in $\frac{6}{8}$ time, produces the number 12. The number 12 is common to both 4 and 3 and is also divisible by either number. To find out how the twelve notes should be grouped, or arranged, divide the number 4 (representing the sixteenth-note quadruplet) into the number 12. The quotient, 3, indicates that the twelve notes are to be arranged into *three* groups of four notes each. Since the quadruplet is expressed in sixteenth notes at the level of the second division, the twelve notes will be written with thirty-second notes at the level of the third division.

Beat 2 of 7–21 shows exactly where each note of the quadruplet falls in relation to the twelve thirty-second notes of the third division. Using the twelve notes of the third division enables us to see precisely how each sixteenth note of the quadruplet relates to both the eighth notes of the first division and the thirty-second notes of third division. The third division thus indicates the correct placement of each note of the quadruplet within the compound duple framework. Each note of the quadruplet coincides with the underlined characters of the following rhythmic syllables: 4 e + a 5 e + a 6 e + a.

Example 7–21: four-against-three (4:3) between the first and second divisions of the beat

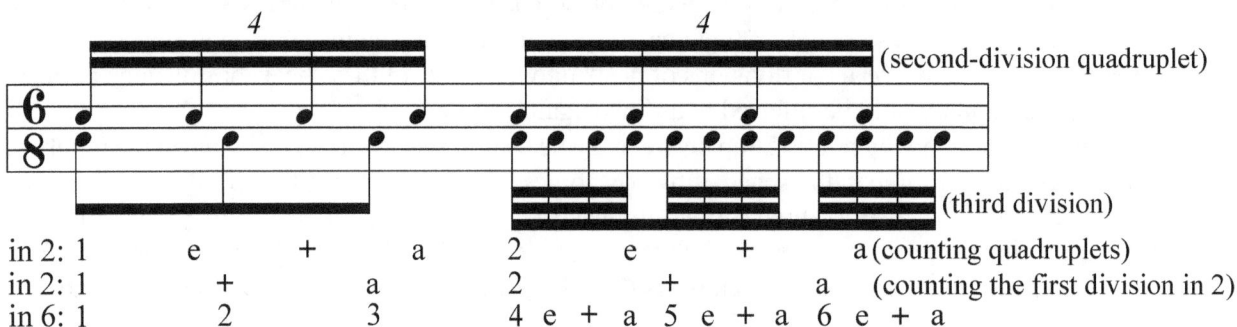

In example 7–22, the large quarter-note triplet in $\frac{2}{4}$ time constitutes a three-against-two relationship (3:2) at the level of the beat. Understanding the relationship between the large triplet and the quarter-note beat in $\frac{2}{4}$ time requires finding the fewest number of notes into which 3 and 2 can be divided. Multiplying the numbers 3 (the large triplet) and 2 (the beat) produces the number 6. The number 6 is common to both 3 and 2 and is divisible by either number. We therefore start with six notes, six eighth notes.

Example 7–22: three-against-two (3:2) at the level of the beat

In order to see exactly where each note of the large triplet falls within the context of $\frac{2}{4}$ in example 7–22, we must place six eighth notes into the three quarter-note span of the irregular group (the triplet). If we divide the number 3 (representing the large triplet) into the number 6, a quotient of 2 confirms that the six eighth notes must be arranged into *two* groups of three notes each. The only way that six eighth notes will fit into a measure of $\frac{2}{4}$ is to arrange them into two small triplets. The large triplet uses the count of the small triplet: $\underline{1}$ + a 2 $\underline{+}$ a. The underlined characters indicate where each note of the large triplet falls.

Example 7–23 shows a quarter-note duplet in $\frac{3}{4}$ time, a two-against-three relationship (2:3) at the level of the beat. Multiplying the numbers 2 and 3 produces the number 6. Once again, we start with six eighth notes. However, in order to see precisely where each note of the duplet falls within the context of $\frac{3}{4}$ requires the placement of six eighth notes into the span of the *measure* rather than into the span of the irregular group (the duplet). Unlike the previous example in $\frac{2}{4}$ time, six eighth notes in $\frac{3}{4}$ time constitute three regular groups of notes at the level of the first division (see the notes with downward stems in measure 1 of 7–23).

Since six eighth notes already fit into one measure of $\frac{3}{4}$ time, we must divide the number 3 (representing the beat) into the number 6 to find out how they should be grouped within the measure. The six eighth notes are divided into two groups of three notes each; the tie creates two three-note pairs. Converting three eighth notes into a dotted quarter produces the note value for the duplet. As we have said, the dot can be replaced with the number 2 above the group. Each note of the duplet coincides with the underlined characters of the following rhythmic syllables: $\underline{1}$ + 2 $\underline{+}$ 3 +.

Example 7–23: two-against-three (2:3) at the level of the beat

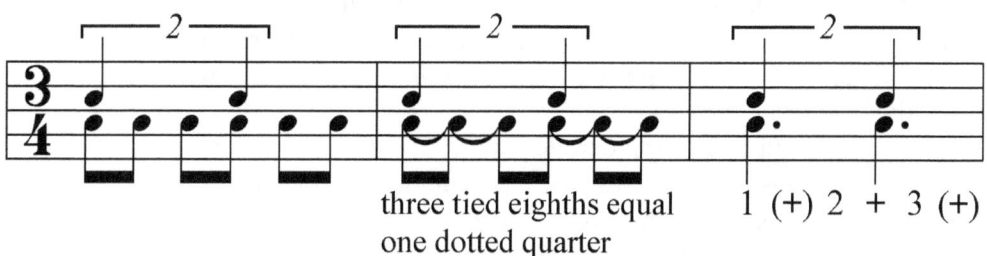

In example 7–21 above, the sixteenth-note quadruplet creates a four-against-three conflict between the first and second divisions of the beat in $\frac{6}{8}$ time. In example 7–24, the quadruplet in quarters occurs within the context of $\frac{3}{4}$ time, creating a four-against-three conflict at the level of the beat. Multiplying the numbers 4 and 3 produces the number 12, the fewest number of notes divisible by 4 and 3 (dividing the number 4 into the number 12 gives us *three* groups of four notes each). Twelve notes of the second division fill the three quarter-note beats of the meter. Each note of the quadruplet coincides with the underlined characters of the following rhythmic syllables: $\underline{1}$ e + $\underline{a}$ 2 e $\underline{+}$ a 3 $\underline{e}$ + a.

As we shall see in Section 3, the assigned note value for an irregular group in simple meter depends on whether that note value exceeds twice the number of beats for the meter. For instance, a group of seven notes in $\frac{3}{4}$ time is written with eighths rather than quarters (see example 7–39 below).

Example 7–24: four-against-three (4:3) at the level of the beat

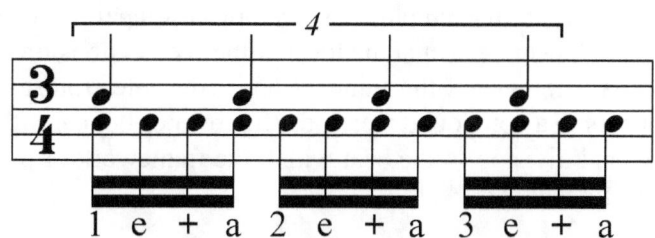

Section 2: Other Irregular Groupings of Notes Occurring within the Span of a Single Beat

As we have seen, in simple and compound meters, beats are normally divided into either two equal parts (or multiples of two) or three equal parts (or multiples of three) respectively. It is also possible to replace regular divisions of the beat with irregular divisions of the beat. In addition to the duplet, triplet, and quadruplet figures discussed in the foregoing pages of this chapter, other irregular groups of notes may fill the span of a single beat.

A **quintuplet** is an irregular group of five notes that replaces either the two notes of the first division in simple meter or the three notes of the first division in compound meter. In both cases, the five notes carry a 5 above the note group and are notated at the level of the second division. Thus, if the value of the beat were a quarter note (or a dotted quarter note), then the group of five notes would occur at the level of the second division and therefore consist of sixteenth notes. Example 7–25 shows how the quintuplet appears in both $\frac{2}{4}$ and $\frac{6}{8}$ time.

Example 7–25

In theory, any number of notes could occur within the span of a single beat and be marked as equivalent to the durational value of that beat by simply placing the appropriate number over the note group. Because a large number of notes might be used, counting such groups with rhythmic syllables could become unwieldy.

Still, one could find an appropriate polysyllabic word to accompany an irregular grouping of notes, for example: *u-ni-ver-si-ty* works well for the quintuplet. Another solution would be to count the number of notes in each group. In a simple quadruple meter such as $\frac{4}{4}$, a series of four quintuplets would be counted as follows: 1 2 3 4 5 1 2 3 4 5 1 2 3 4 5 1 2 3 4 5 (example 7–26).

Example 7–26

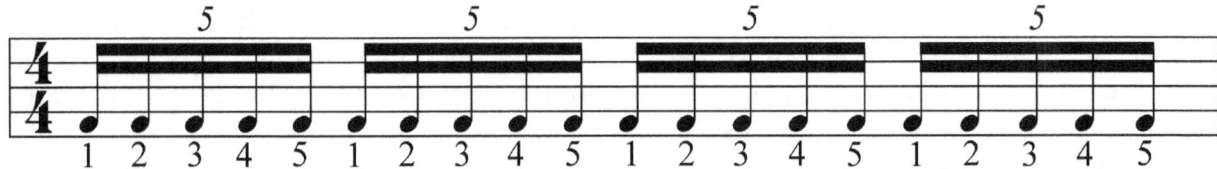

Regardless of the method used for counting irregular groups, if the tempo of the music and the number of notes within the beat increase beyond a certain threshold, all methods for counting become impractical. In this instance, the musician must rely upon his or her own abilities and understanding of the musical context in order to fit a given number of notes into the duration of a single beat.

Earlier, in example 7–6b, we saw how a pair of micro triplets in simple meter could unfold within the span of a single beat at the level of the second division and be reinterpreted as a single group of six notes. The six notes carry the number 6 above the note group and are referred to as a sextuplet. When the sextuplet occurs in a compound meter, the figure does not carry the 6 above the note group because it *is* the normal second division of the beat within the framework of the meter rather than an irregular grouping of notes (example 7–27).

Example 7–27

Adding one note to the sextuplet produces a note group called the **septuplet**, a seven-note figure. In both simple and compound meters, the septuplet carries the number 7 above the note group and is expressed at the level of the second division (example 7–28).

Example 7–28

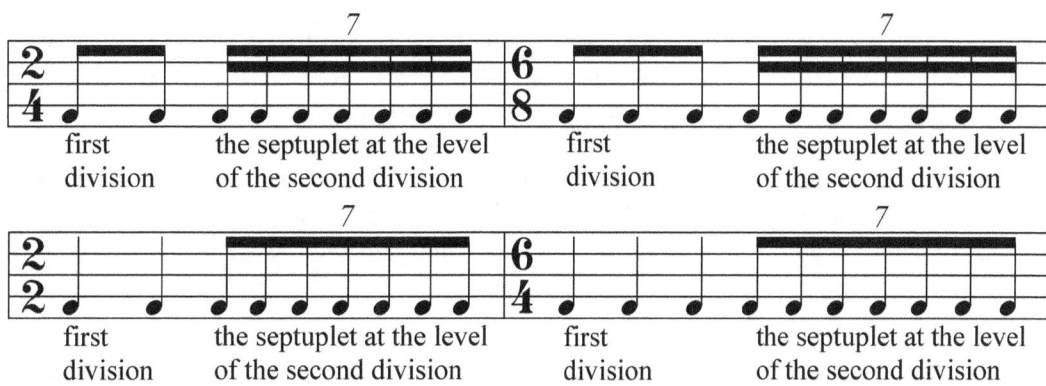

Once the number of notes in the group doubles that of the second division in simple meter, the group uses the next smaller note denomination and constitutes a normal third division of the beat rather than an irregular grouping of notes. Thus, the eight-note figure otherwise known as the **octuplet** does *not* carry an 8 above the note group because it has exactly twice the number of notes as the second division and therefore assumes the level of the third division (example 7–29). If the value of the beat were the quarter note, then the third division of the beat would be thirty-second notes. If the value of the beat were the half note, then the third division of the beat would be sixteenth notes.

Example 7–29

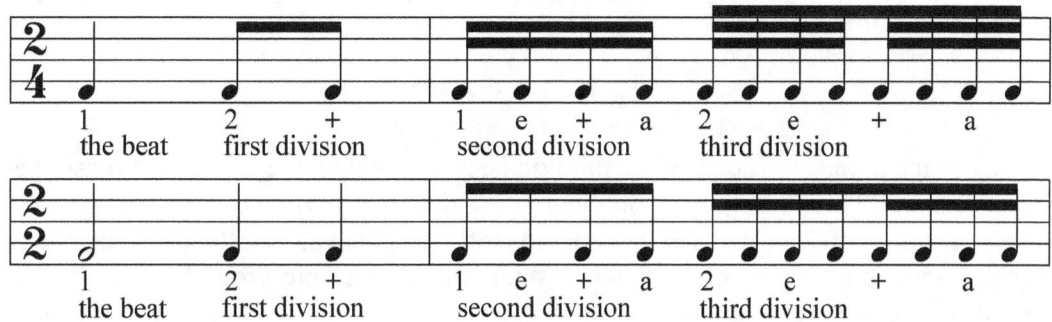

In compound meters such as $\frac{6}{8}$ or $\frac{6}{4}$, however, the octuplet neither doubles nor exceeds the number of notes of the second division. Accordingly, it remains an irregular division of the beat, carries an 8 above the note group, and uses the second division of the beat rather than the third division (example 7–30).

Example 7–30

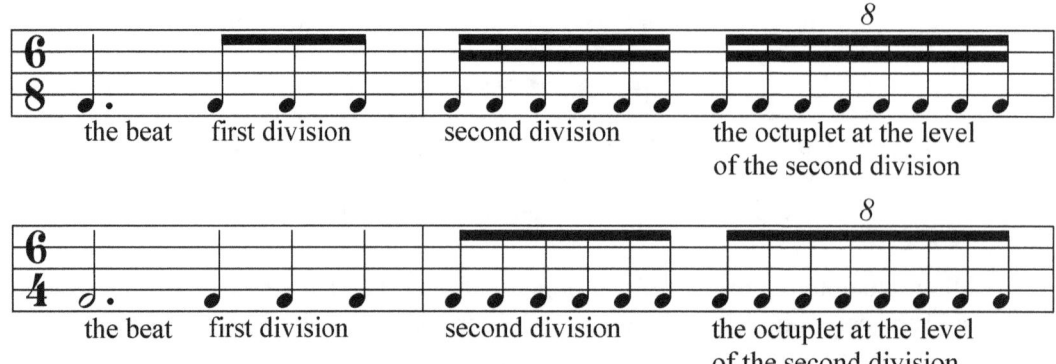

As we have said, once the number of notes in the group doubles that of the second division, the group uses notes that are one denomination smaller. Therefore, if the group consists of twelve notes in compound meter, as shown in the second measure of example 7–31, then the figure would have exactly twice the number of notes as the second division and be expressed at the level of the third division.

Because it doubles the number of notes of the second division, the twelve-note group constitutes a normal division of the beat and does not require a number to identify itself as a note group. The group of eleven, however, which precedes the group of twelve in the example, is expressed at the level of the second division and takes a number above the note group to indicate that it is an irregular division of the beat (7–31, beat 1 of the second measure).

Example 7–31

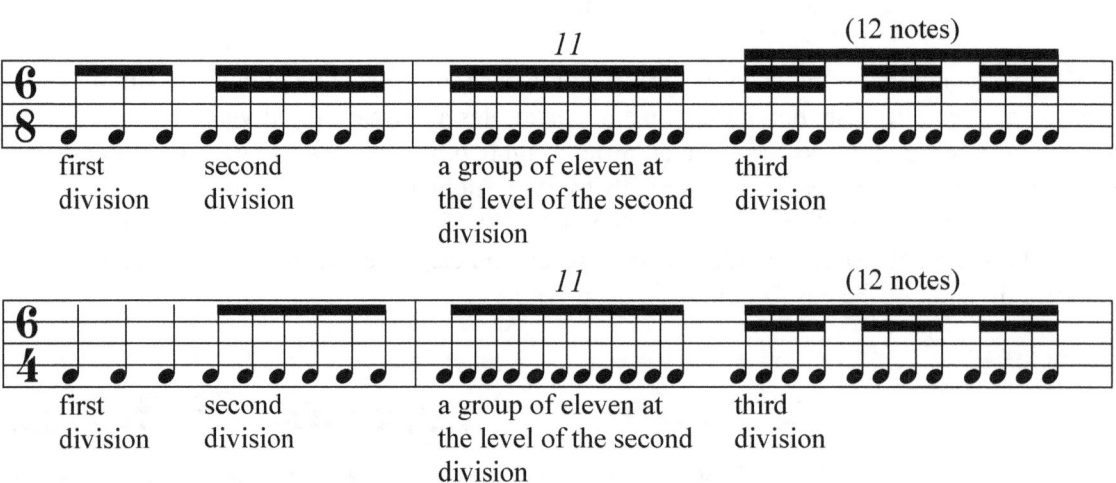

Once the number of notes of the third division is doubled, the figure is expressed at the level of the fourth division. Thus, the sixteen-note figure in $\frac{2}{4}$ time shown in example 7–32 has twice the number of notes as the third division and assumes consequently the note value of the fourth division. A number is not required above the sixteen notes to identify the figure as a note group because it constitutes a normal division of the beat.

Examples 7–32 and 33 summarize what we know about the notation of irregular groups of notes occurring within the span of a single beat other than those involving simple and compound meter exchange: In simple meter (7–32),
(1) irregular groups of five to seven notes employ the durational value of the second division;
(2) groups ranging from eight to fifteen notes use the third division and thus take the next smaller note denomination; and,
(3) groups with more than fifteen notes use the next smaller note denomination and are notated at the level of the fourth division.

Example 7–32: notation of note groups in simple meter

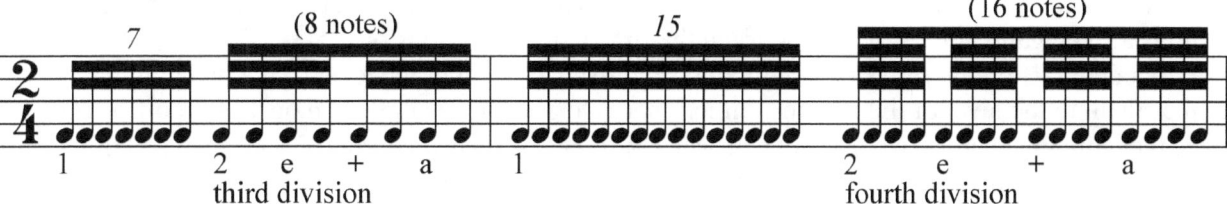

In compound meter (7–33),
(1) the level of the second division is employed for groups ranging from four to eleven notes;
(2) a range of twelve to twenty-three notes uses the durational value of the third division; and,
(3) groups with more than twenty-three notes are expressed with the next smaller note denomination and are notated at the level of the fourth division.

Example 7–33: notation of note groups in compound meter

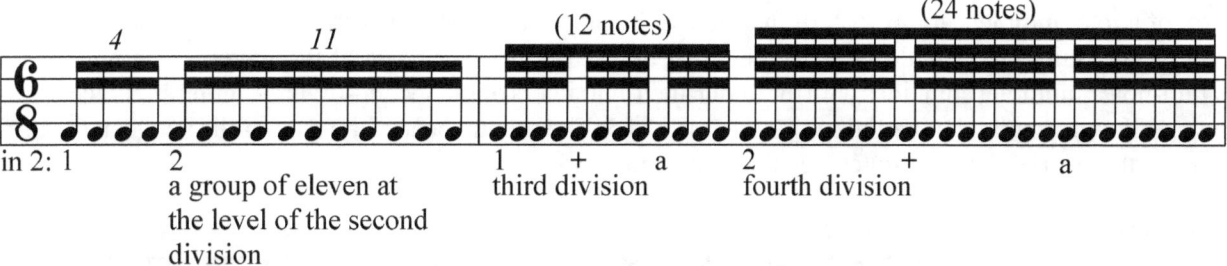

Section 3: Other Irregular Groupings of Notes Extending Across Two or More Beats

The triplet, duplet, and quadruplet are all irregular groupings of notes within the context of the meters in which that are placed. As stated earlier, any number of notes could occur within the span of a single beat and be marked as equivalent to the durational value of that beat by simply placing the appropriate number over the note group.

Using the triplet, duplet, and quadruplet, we formulated a methodology for determining how a group of notes conflicting with either the beat or the division of the beat fits into the prevailing meter. The method involves finding the fewest number of notes into which each conflicting group may be divided. Multiplying the respective number of notes that each group contains provides the number common to both groups.

With this approach, we are able to see how the quintuplet and other irregular groups occur at the level of the beat and extend across two or more beats of the measure. In order to demonstrate how these other irregular groups extend beyond the confines of a single beat, let us revisit the quintuplet shown in example 7–25 above, reproduced here as example 7–34.

Example 7–34

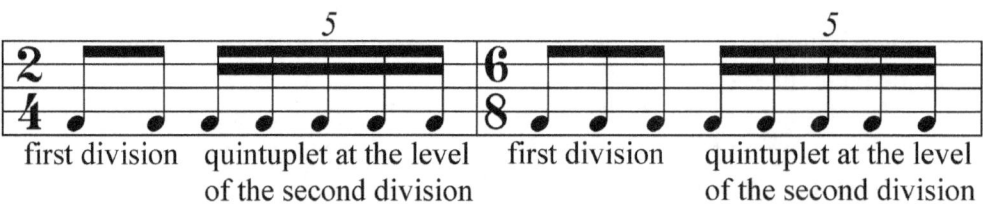

first division | quintuplet at the level of the second division | first division | quintuplet at the level of the second division

The sixteenth-note quintuplet in 7–34 takes place at the level of the second division within the span of a single beat and replaces either two eighth notes of the first division in simple meter or three eighth notes of the first division in compound meter. In simple meter, the quintuplet constitutes a five-against-two conflict between the levels of the first and second divisions (5:2). In compound meter, the quintuplet exhibits a five-against-three conflict between the first and second divisions (5:3).

Example 7–35 reinterprets the conflicting rhythms that occur at the level of the division in 7–34 and applies them to the level of the beat in $\frac{2}{4}$ time. That is to say, the example demonstrates how to correctly place the quintuplet across two beats of a measure, a five-against-two conflict (5:2) at the level of the beat. If we were to use a quarter-note quintuplet to fill out the measure, then it would exceed twice the number of beats for the meter; therefore, the quintuplet will assume the value of the next smaller note denomination, namely, the eighth. In simple meter, if the note denomination of the irregular group takes a reduction, then it occurs at the level of the first division. In $\frac{2}{4}$ time, the first division yields four eighth notes (see Chapter 1, example 1–13); accordingly, an irregular group of five notes would also be written with eighths.

Once again, for the problem put forward in 7–35, find the fewest number of notes into which each group of notes may be divided, in this instance, the group of five and the group of two. Multiplying 5 and 2 produces the number 10. The number 10 is common to both 5 and 2 and is divisible by either number.

The best way to fit ten notes into $\frac{2}{4}$ time is to proceed to the level of the second division and arrange the ten notes into *two* quintuplets (divide the number 5 into the number 10). Introducing ten notes in the form of two quintuplets at the level of the second division (stems down) enables us to see exactly how the eighth-note quintuplet should be placed against the two prevailing beats of the meter. Each note of the eighth-note quintuplet coincides with the underlined characters of the second-division quintuplets according to the following method of counting: 1̲ 2 3̲ 4 5̲ 1̲ 2 3̲ 4 5̲. The second beat of the meter falls between the third and fourth notes of the quintuplet (see the arrows in 7–35).

Example 7–35

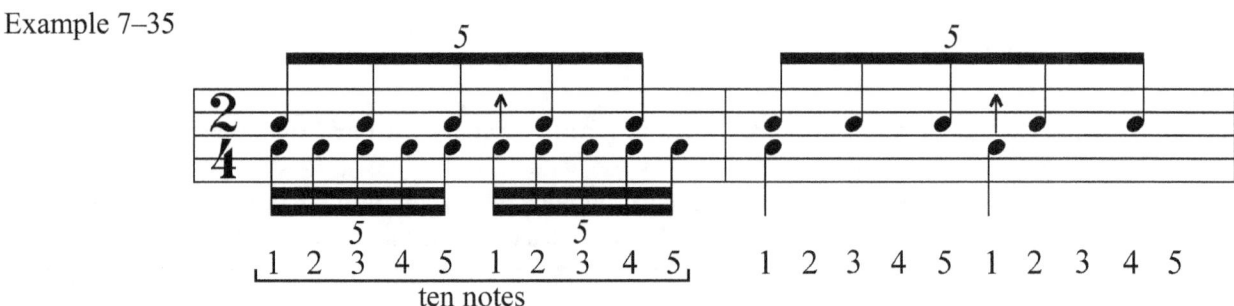

1 2 3 4 5 1 2 3 4 5 | 1 2 3 4 5 1 2 3 4 5
ten notes

Example 7–36 illustrates the placement of the quintuplet into a measure of triple meter, a conflict of five-against-three (5:3) at the level of the beat. Fifteen notes are needed to determine where each beat of the meter falls (5 multiplied by 3 produces 15). The number 15 is common to both 5 and 3 and is divisible by either number. Integrating the fifteen notes into $\frac{3}{4}$ time requires that they be arranged into *three* quintuplets at the level of the second division (divide the number 5 into the number 15). The second beat of the meter falls between the second and third notes of the quintuplet; the third beat is situated between the fourth and fifth notes of the quintuplet (see the arrows in 7–36).

Chapter 7 Advanced Concepts In Meter   103

Since five quarter notes do not exceed twice the number of beats per measure for the meter, the quintuplet retains the quarter-note value of the beat rather than assuming the next smaller note denomination. If the irregular group had consisted of seven notes, then we would use the next smaller note denomination because seven quarter notes would exceed six quarter notes—twice the number of quarter notes in $\frac{3}{4}$ time (see example 7–39 below).

Example 7–36

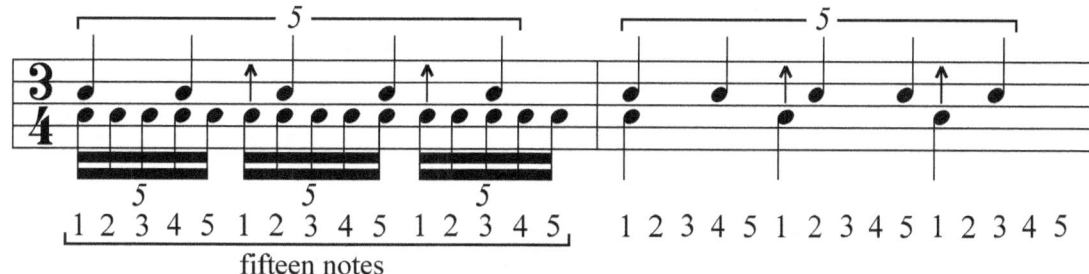

Let us consider another irregular group, namely, the sextuplet (example 7–37). Within the context of $\frac{4}{4}$ time, the sextuplet presents a six-against-four conflict (6:4) at the level of the beat. Multiplying the numbers 6 and 4 produces the number 24. The number 24 is common to both 6 and 4 and is divisible by either number.

In order to place twenty-four notes into $\frac{4}{4}$ time, we must employ *four* groups of six sixteenth notes at the level of the second division (divide the number 6 into the number 24). Each group constitutes a second-division sextuplet. The second beat of the meter occurs between the second and third notes of the quarter-note sextuplet. Beat 3 of the meter coincides with the fourth note of the quarter-note sextuplet, the fourth beat of the meter falls between the fifth and sixth notes of the quarter-note sextuplet (see the arrows in 7–37).

Example 7–37

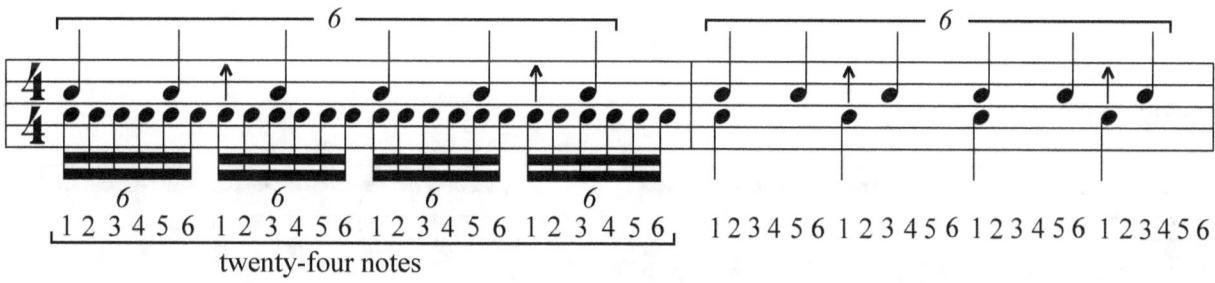

Before looking at the next conflict between an irregular grouping of notes and the meter into which it is placed, it should be noted that the six-against-four relationship constitutes an exceptional case that merits further consideration here; for the number 24 does not represent the *fewest* number of notes into which the numbers 6 and 4 can be divided. The smallest number common to both 6 and 4 is 12.

To be sure, the number 24 can be used successfully to integrate the two conflicting groups of numbers together (as 7–37 above confirms); but in this case, preference should be given to the smaller number (12). Accordingly, twelve notes can be fit into $\frac{4}{4}$ time at the level of the first division by arranging them into four groups of three notes each, resulting in the formation of four small eighth-note triplets. Example 7–38a demonstrates how the four small triplets fit with the quarter-note sextuplet in $\frac{4}{4}$ time.

104   Chapter 7 Advanced Concepts In Meter

Notice that the quarter-note values of the sextuplet in 7–38a are virtually identical to the quarter-note values of the two large triplets shown in 7–38b. We first saw this pair of large triplets in measure 1 of example 7–9. As with the sextuplet of 7–38a, the large triplets of 38b are accompanied by four small triplets. Each respective note of the sextuplet and the large triplet coincides with the underlined characters of the following rhythmic syllables: 1 + a 2 + a 3 + a 4 + a.

In any case, the sextuplet is expressed with quarter notes rather than the next smaller note denomination because six quarter notes do not exceed twice the number of quarter notes for the meter. If the irregular group had consisted of nine notes, then we would use the next smaller note denomination because nine quarter notes would exceed eight quarter notes—twice the number of quarter notes in $\frac{4}{4}$ time.

Example 7–38

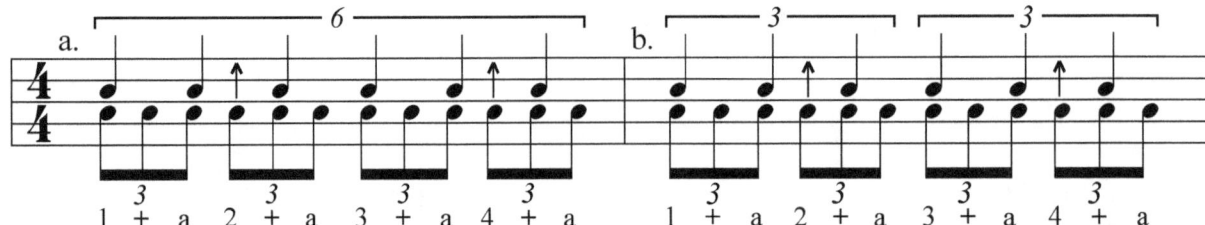

Look at the septuplet, shown in example 7–39 as an irregular group of seven notes extending across three beats in $\frac{3}{4}$ time. The example illustrates a seven-against-three conflict at level of the beat. Since seven quarter notes would more than double the three quarter-note beats of the meter, the septuplet should be notated with the next smaller note denomination, namely, the eighth note.

Multiplying 7 and 3 tells us that twenty-one notes are required to find the precise location of the meter's three beats in relation to the septuplet. The number 21 is common to both 7 and 3 and is divisible by either number. Dividing the number 7 into the number 21 indicates that *three* groups of septuplets written at the level of the second division provides the appropriate distribution and arrangement of the twenty-one notes across the framework of $\frac{3}{4}$. Both the eighth-note septuplet and the second-division septuplets should be counted according to the following method: 1 2 3 4 5 6 7 1 2 3 4 5 6 7 1 2 3 4 5 6 7 (the underlined characters indicate each articulation of the eighth-note septuplet). The second beat of the meter falls between the third and fourth notes of the septuplet, the third beat between the fifth and sixth (see the arrows in 7–39).

Example 7–39

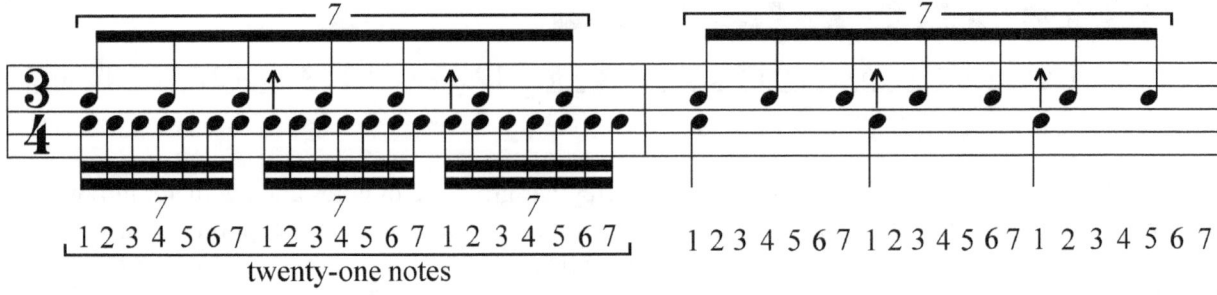

Throughout this section, our discussion of irregular groupings of notes extending across two or more beats has been confined to examples in simple meter. It would be well to examine briefly the notation for irregular groups in compound meter. As illustrated in example 7–40, if the figure spanning the measure exceeds the number of notes for the second division of the meter, then retain the note value of the second division.

Although the limits of space preclude a thorough investigation of how beats are positioned in compound meter, suffice it to say that the placement of beats should be the same as in the parallel simple meter. Let us consider the placement and notation of an irregular group in $\frac{6}{8}$ time. The second division of $\frac{6}{8}$ time consists of twelve sixteenth notes (7–40a). Therefore, an irregular group of thirteen notes should retain the note value of the second division and also use sixteenths (7–40b). In fact, referring to examples 7–16b and 7–21 above, we find that even a group of eight notes extending across one measure of $\frac{6}{8}$ takes the note value of the second division. Finally, in 7–40b, the second beat of the meter falls between the seventh and eighth sixteenth note.

Example 7–40

Section 4: Asymmetrical Meter

We know that duple, triple, and quadruple meters are all considered to be symmetrical meters because they are divisible by either 2 or 3. Most of the time, a single, symmetrical meter will be used *consistently* throughout a piece of music. In other words, compositions that begin in, say, duple meter, usually remain in duple meter until the end. Sometimes, however, a piece of music might begin in one meter but subsequently change to another meter or a series of meters before the conclusion. Further, it is possible to have a meter with an odd number of beats per measure, a meter that is not divisible by either 2 or 3. Such meters are usually referred to as either **asymmetrical meters** or **odd meters**.

Let us consider a meter with five beats per measure. A meter "in 5" results when duple and triple meters are combined. There are a few ways in which to indicate a meter in 5. One method involves using two different time signatures in succession, such as the combination of $\frac{2}{4}$ and $\frac{3}{4}$ shown in example 7–41a. An alternative approach would be to place the two time signatures at the beginning of the composition and separate them with a plus sign, that is: $\frac{2}{4} + \frac{3}{4}$. If the bottom number for both time signatures represents the same note value, then the following option is available: $\frac{2+3}{4}$. In either instance, the person reading the music would understand that each pair of measures alternates between the two time signatures until the end or until a change in the metric structure occurs. This method avoids having to notate each measure of $\frac{2}{4}$ and $\frac{3}{4}$ throughout the entire composition.

Example 7–41

The most common way to express a meter in 5, however, would be to simply consolidate $\frac{2}{4}$ and $\frac{3}{4}$ into $\frac{5}{4}$ time, as displayed in 7–41b above. We classify $\frac{5}{4}$ time as a *simple* asymmetrical meter because dividing the number 3 into the top number of the time signature does not produce a whole number quotient greater than 4 (such as 5 or 7). Accordingly, the meter is simple rather than compound. The dotted line in 7–41b indicates what would otherwise be a measure of $\frac{2}{4}$ and a measure of $\frac{3}{4}$.

Again, combining duple and triple meters produces a meter in 5: either a measure of duple meter is followed by measure of triple meter ("two plus three") or a measure of triple meter is followed by a measure of duple meter ("three plus two"). Thus, a meter with five beats per measure can be subdivided and counted as either 1-2 1-2-3 (two plus three) or 1-2-3 1-2 (three plus two).

Example 7–42 displays three measures of $\frac{7}{8}$ time, an asymmetrical meter with seven beats per measure. The value of the beat is the eighth note. This asymmetrical meter can be classified as simple because dividing the number 3 into the top number of the time signature does not produce a quotient greater than 4. Each of the seven beats would be divided into two equal parts (or multiples of two). The first division of the beat occurs at the level of the sixteenth note. The subdivision of the meter is three plus two plus two; an alternative notation for 7–42 would be $\frac{3}{8} + \frac{2}{8} + \frac{2}{8}$ or $\frac{3+2+2}{8}$.

Example 7–42

We conclude this chapter with one final asymmetrical meter, $\frac{15}{16}$ time, as shown in example 7–43. Dividing the number 3 into the top number yields a quotient of 5. This information tells us that the meter is compound asymmetrical with five beats per measure. To determine the value of the beat, we take the note value that the bottom number represents (the sixteenth note) and proceed to the note value that is one denomination higher (the eighth note), adding a dot to that note value. The value of the beat in $\frac{15}{16}$ time is a dotted eighth. The first division of the beat is the sixteenth.

Example 7–43

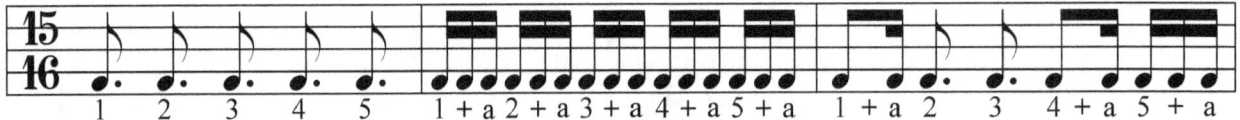

As for the subdivision of the meter, a grouping of three plus two begins to emerge only in the third measure of the example. We would need a few more measures of differentiated rhythms to confirm a clear subdivision of three plus two; for the pattern of notes could change to reveal a grouping of two plus three, a mixture of both possibilities, or an asymmetrical structure with no subdivisions at all beyond the basic five beats of the meter.

The fifteen notes of the first division in $\frac{15}{16}$ time could even be configured in such a way as to deny the five-beat implication of the time signature. For example, it is quite possible to arrange fifteen sixteenth notes into three groups of five notes each (five plus five plus five). Alternatively, we might encounter one group of seven notes and one group of eight notes (seven plus eight). Of course, within the context of $\frac{15}{16}$ time, these subdivisions could be viewed as irregular rhythmic patterns occurring at the level of the first division, a division that normally has three sixteenth notes for each dotted eighth.

Chapter 8 Triads

Since the ninth century of the Common Era in Western Europe, music makers have combined two or more musical tones together, creating sounds that are either pleasing or displeasing to the ear. The perception of what constitutes a good or bad combination of musical tones at any point in history changes over time. Moreover, the many diverse cultures of the world do not necessarily share the same musical values and therefore may have different opinions and beliefs regarding the qualities of musical sounds.

For example, someone accustomed to listening to the music of the Western European tradition might have difficulty appreciating the performance of *ganga* songs found in the mountainous regions of Bosnia and Herzegovina, which exhibit close combinations of tones, particularly the interval of the 2nd. The performers of *ganga* songs consider the sounds of 2nds to be pleasing to the ear; conversely, we in the West are more accustomed to the perceived richness of 3rds.

In Chapter 5, we learned that when two pitches occur simultaneously, the resulting sound is a harmonic interval. Any time two or more pitches occur simultaneously, it produces an effect known as **harmony**. When three or more *different* pitches sound simultaneously, the resulting harmony is called a **chord**.

Examples 8–1a, 1b, and 1c demonstrate three forms of harmony that assume chord status; in each instance, the chord has five different pitches and at least four intervals. The first type of chord, shown in 8–1a, is **secundal**; a secundal chord results from a combination of major and/or minor 2nds. (Although secundal harmonies must contain major and/or minor 2nds, they may also have 3rds.) Example 8–1b illustrates **quartal** harmony, a chord formation consisting of 4th intervals.

The most common harmonic construction to appear in the music of the Western European tradition and the one with which we are concerned here is **tertian** harmony. As illustrated in 8–1c, tertian chords have two or more superimposed 3rds. When notated on the staff, secundal and quartal harmonies involve a combination of spaces and lines. On the other hand, tertian harmonies (when positioned in a close structure on a single staff) are placed on either spaces or lines, rather than a combination of both.

The tertian harmony in 8–1c displays intervals of the 3rd, 5th, 7th, and 9th above the lowest pitch of the chord; so constructed, we have a chord of the ninth, or ninth chord (C E G B D). Removing the ninth produces a chord of the seventh, or seventh chord (C E G B).

Example 8–1

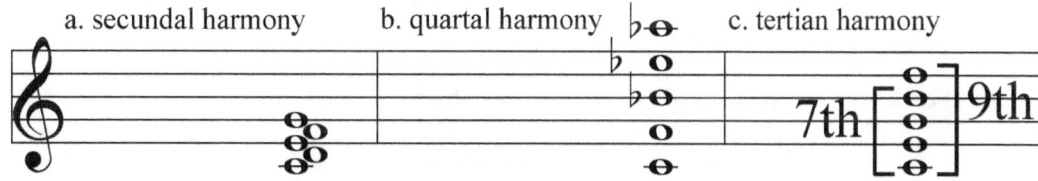

The pitches of a chord may be performed either simultaneously or in succession. A chord given a simultaneous performance of its pitches is called a **block chord** (example 8–2a). Successive presentation of some or all of a chord's pitches is described variously as **arpeggio, arpeggiated chord,** or **broken chord** (8–2b).

Example 8–2

108   Chapter 8   Triads

Tertian harmony has been an important component of Western music for more than five hundred years. As early as the fifteenth century, people in Western Europe began to have a decided preference for the interval of the 3rd and its inversion, the 6th. Today, chords built from the interval of the 3rd are still favored in nearly every style of music in the Western world.

When a tertian harmony contains three different pitches and two intervals of the 3rd, the chord is referred to as a triad. The triad in example 8–3 contains the pitches C, E, and G and has two 3rds formed above C, the lowest pitch of the musical texture and the foundation of the chord.

Example 8–3: the triad

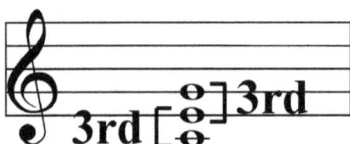

The lowest pitch upon which the other two pitches of the triad are built is called the root. In example 8–4, C is identified as the root of the triad (R). The remaining tones of the triad, E and G, are known as the third (3) and the fifth (5) because they are located at the intervals of a 3rd and a 5th above the root. The triad in 8–4 is said to be in **root position** because the root is positioned as the lowest pitch of the musical texture.

Example 8–4: the components of the triad

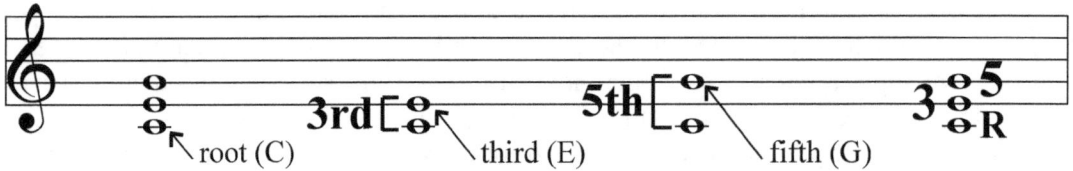

The triad derives its name from the root. For example, if the triad is built on the subdominant scale degree of the major mode (scale degree 4), then the chord would be termed the subdominant triad. Since there are seven tones in a major key and scale, it is possible to build a triad on each of these seven tones. Example 8–5 shows how each of the root-position triads occurring in C major receives the name of the scale degree with which it is associated.

Example 8–5: root-position triads in the key of C major

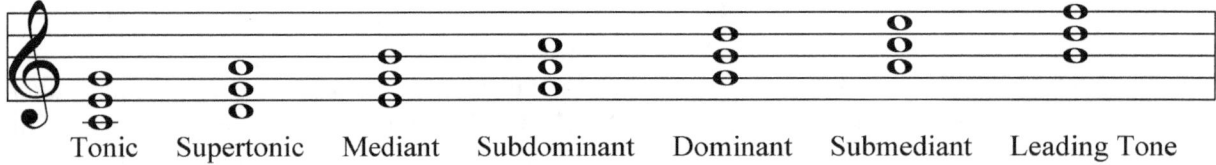

The root-position triads exhibited in 8–5 fall into two groups based upon their respective locations on either the lines or spaces of the staff: triads of the tonic, mediant, dominant, and leading tone on the one hand and those of the supertonic, subdominant, and submediant on the other. When triads from either group are formed above each tone of the major scale, their placement on the staff is determined by the position of the tonic note on the staff.

If the tonic note begins on a line, then the first group of triads (tonic, mediant, dominant, and leading tone) uses lines, the second group (supertonic, subdominant, and submediant) spaces. Thus, with c^1 as the starting note of the major mode (see example 8–5 above), the tonic, mediant, dominant, and leading-tone triads occupy lines on the staff, whereas the supertonic, subdominant, and submediant triads are placed on spaces. Starting the tonic one octave lower on small c (a space) would put the first group on spaces and the second group on lines.

In example 8–6, the C-major scale is transposed to D major. All of the pitches that make up the triads are diatonic elements of the key and mode and therefore include the addition of F♯ and C♯. With d^1 as the starting note of the scale, the tonic, mediant, dominant, and leading-tone triads occur on spaces instead of lines, whereas the supertonic, subdominant, and submediant triads utilize the lines of the staff instead of spaces. Starting the tonic one octave lower on small d (a line) would put the first group on lines and the second group on spaces.

Example 8–6: root-position triads in the key of D major

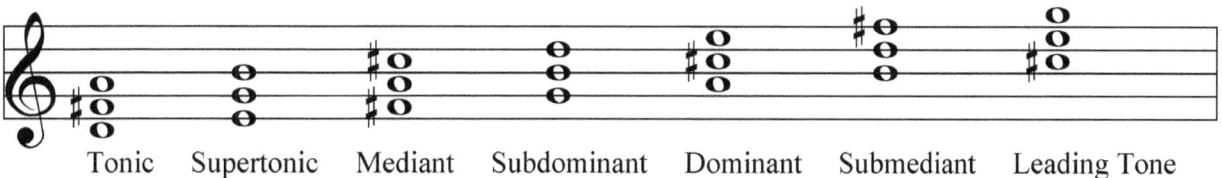

Triad Quality

Triads, like intervals, may be classified according to their quality. There are four types of triad qualities: the **major triad** (MT), the **minor triad** (mt), the **diminished triad** (d°t), and the **augmented triad** (A+T). The quality of a triad is based upon the intervallic distance between the root and the third, the third and the fifth, and the root and the fifth.

Example 8–7 illustrates the configuration of intervals for the four triad qualities, all of which share the common tone C as the root. R – 3 represents the distance from the root to the third, 3 – 5 the distance from the third to the fifth, and R – 5 the distance from the root to the fifth. The superscript circle in the chord symbol d°t is a conventional sign for indicating diminished quality; it can be used with diminished chords and with diminished intervals (e.g., 5° or °5 = diminished 5th). The plus sign in the A+T chord symbol is the traditional designation for showing augmented quality; it appears in connection with augmented chords and with augmented intervals (e.g., 5+ or +5 = augmented 5th).

Example 8–7: the configuration of intervals for the four triad qualities rooted on C

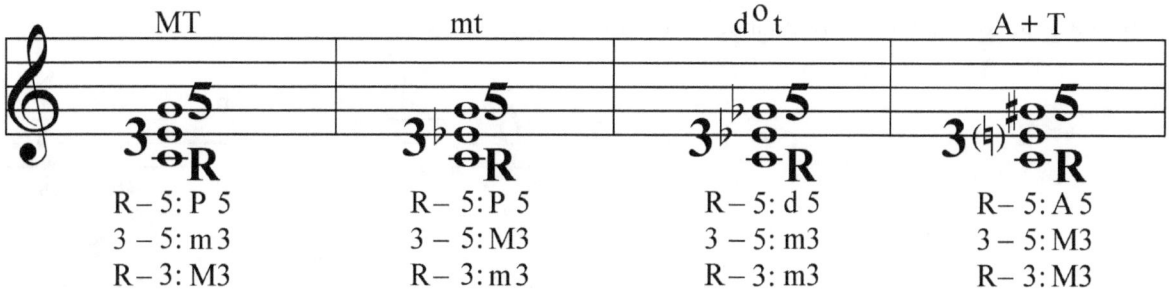

The major triad in example 8–8a contains a major 3rd from the root to the third (C to E) and a minor 3rd from the third to the fifth (E to G). Additionally, the chord has a perfect 5th from the root to the fifth (C to G). The minor triad, shown in 8–8b, has a minor 3rd from the root to the third (C to E♭), a major 3rd from the third to the fifth (E♭ to G), and a perfect 5th from the root to the fifth (C to G).

Although both major and minor triads are made up of a combination of major 3rds and minor 3rds, the internal configuration of 3rds in the minor triad is the reverse of that of the major triad. The ordering of thirds up from the root of the major triad is: M3/m3. The ordering of thirds up from the root of the minor triad is: m3/M3.

The pitch that represents the third of the minor triad is one half step lower than the corresponding third of the major triad with the same root. Accordingly, changing the major triad C E G into a minor triad requires lowering the third of the major triad one half step, from E to E♭: C E♭ G. Conversely, changing the minor triad C E♭ G into a major triad involves raising the third of the minor triad one half step from E♭ to E (♮): C E G.

Example 8–8: root-position major and minor triads

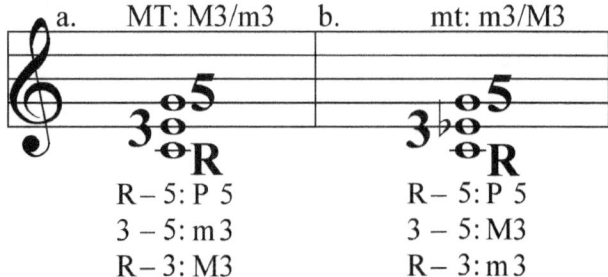

The diminished triad in example 8–9a bears a similarity to the minor triad in 8–9b in that it has a minor 3rd from the root to the third (C to E♭). Instead of having a perfect 5th from the root to the fifth, however, the diminished triad has a diminished 5th from the root to the fifth (C to G♭). From the third to the fifth, the diminished triad has a minor 3rd (E♭ to G♭). Thus, the ordering of thirds up from the root of the diminished triad is: m3/m3.

One way to build a diminished triad up from any given tone is to first construct a minor triad and then lower the fifth of the chord one half step. Remember, lowering the top note of a perfect 5th one half step produces a diminished 5th. For example, changing the minor triad C E♭ G into a diminished triad involves lowering the fifth of the minor triad one half step, from G to G♭: C E♭ G♭. Changing the diminished triad C E♭ G♭ into a minor triad necessitates raising the fifth of the diminished triad one half step from G♭ to G (♮): C E♭ G. (Musicians with either a commercial or jazz background often interpret the diminished triad as a minor triad with a lowered fifth.)

Example 8–9: root-position diminished and minor triads

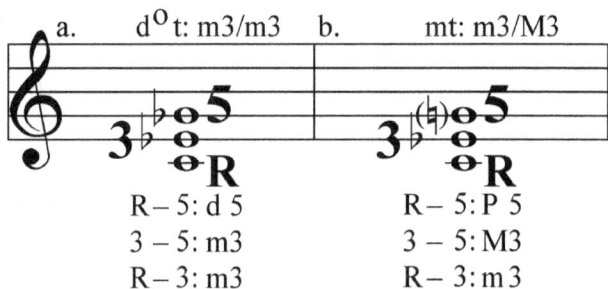

The augmented triad in example 8–10a, like the major triad shown in 8–10b, has a major 3rd from the root to the third (C to E). The distance from the root to the fifth of the augmented triad, however, is an augmented 5th (C to G♯), exceeding by one half step the perfect 5ths of the major and minor triads. From the third to the fifth, the augmented triad has a major third (E to G♯). The ordering of the thirds up from the root of the augmented triad is: M3/M3.

One way to construct an augmented triad up from any given tone is to form a major triad and then raise the fifth of the chord one half step to change the perfect 5th into an augmented 5th. Thus, changing the major triad C E G into an augmented triad requires raising the fifth of the major triad one half step, from G to G♯: C E G♯. Reversing the procedure by lowering the fifth of the augmented triad one half step from G♯ to G (♮) turns the chord into a major triad: C E G.

Example 8–10: root-position augmented and major triads

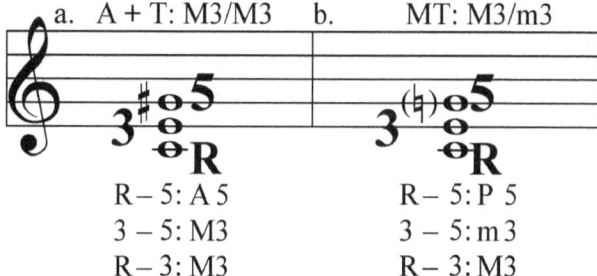

Triad Qualities in Major

In example 8–11, we return to the root-position triads constructed above each of the seven scale degrees of C major and identify the combinations of intervals in each chord. In C major, the major triad appears on the tonic (C E G), the subdominant (F A C), and the dominant (G B D), whereas the minor triad resides in the supertonic (D F A), the mediant (E G B), and the submediant (A C E). The diminished triad occurs in the scale degree area of the leading tone (B D F).

Notice that the diatonic pitch content of C major cannot support the formation of the augmented triad; therefore, the augmented triad cannot exist in any transposition of C major. Later in this chapter, however, we shall see that the augmented triad can be formed in the minor mode.

Example 8–11: triad qualities in C major

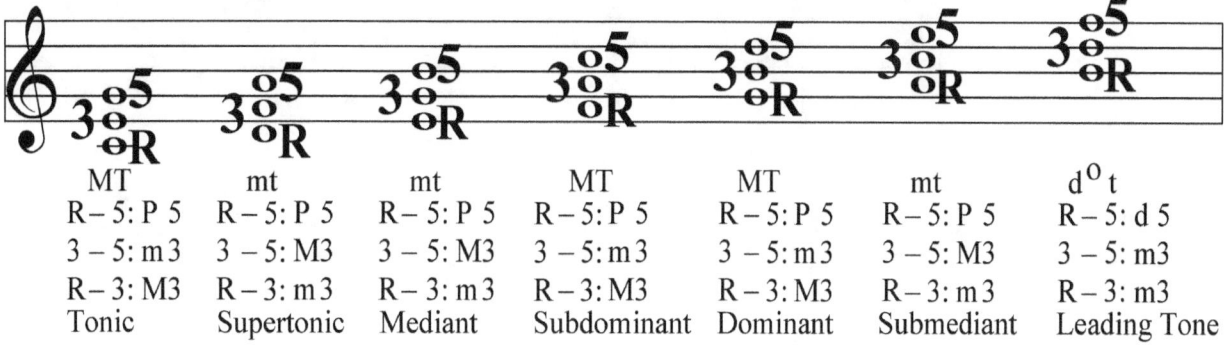

In Example 8–12, the C-major scale is transposed to B♭ major (note the addition of the B♭ and the E♭). As shown below, the same triad qualities that occurred in C major may be formed in B♭ major: the major triad appears in the tonic (B♭ D F), the subdominant (E♭ G B♭), and the dominant (F A C), whereas the minor triad resides in the supertonic (C E♭ G), the mediant (D F A), and the submediant (G B♭ D). The scale degree area of the leading tone supports the diminished triad (A C E♭). Again, the augmented triad is not possible in a diatonic major mode.

Example 8–12: triad qualities in B♭ major

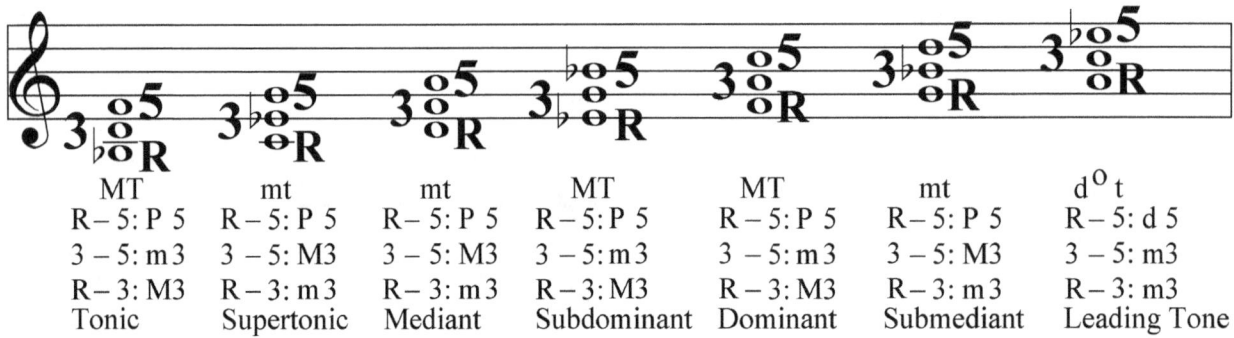

MT	mt	mt	MT	MT	mt	d°t
R–5: P 5	R–5: P 5	R–5: P 5	R–5: P 5	R–5: P 5	R–5: P 5	R–5: d 5
3–5: m 3	3–5: M 3	3–5: M 3	3–5: m 3	3–5: m 3	3–5: M 3	3–5: m 3
R–3: M 3	R–3: m 3	R–3: m 3	R–3: M 3	R–3: M 3	R–3: m 3	R–3: m 3
Tonic	Supertonic	Mediant	Subdominant	Dominant	Submediant	Leading Tone

In the following exercises, we shall attempt to solve a few problems involving major, minor, and diminished triads in keys other than C major. Since the augmented triad cannot exist in major, it is excluded here.

In the key of E♭ major, spell the submediant triad in root position (example 8–13).
  (1) Find the *letter name* for the submediant (scale degree 6) of the E♭-major scale. The answer is C.
  (2) E♭ major has three flats, B♭, E♭, and A♭; therefore, the submediant scale degree is C (natural).
  (3) What is the interval of a 3rd and a 5th above C? The answer is E and G.
  (4) Since E carries a flat in E♭ major and the G is natural, the submediant triad is spelled C E♭ G.
  (5) The submediant triad in E♭ major is a minor triad: C E♭ G.

Example 8–13

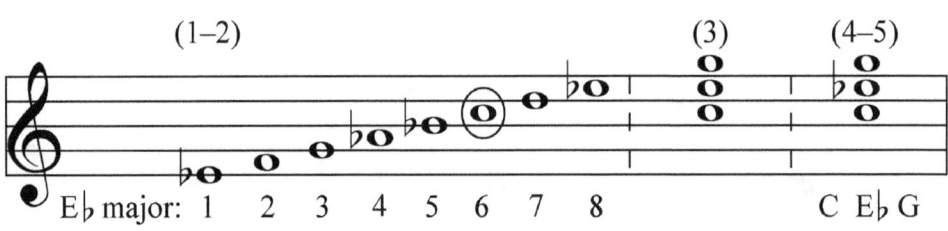

In the key of A major, spell the leading-tone triad in root position (example 8–14).
  (1) Find the *letter name* for the leading tone (scale degree 7) of the A-major scale. The answer is G.
  (2) A major has three sharps, one of which is G♯; therefore, the leading-tone scale degree is G♯.
  (3) What is the interval of a 3rd and a 5th above G♯? The answer is B and D.
  (4) Since B and D do not carry sharps in A major, the leading-tone triad is spelled G♯ B D.
  (5) The leading-tone triad in A major is a diminished triad: G♯ B D.

Example 8–14

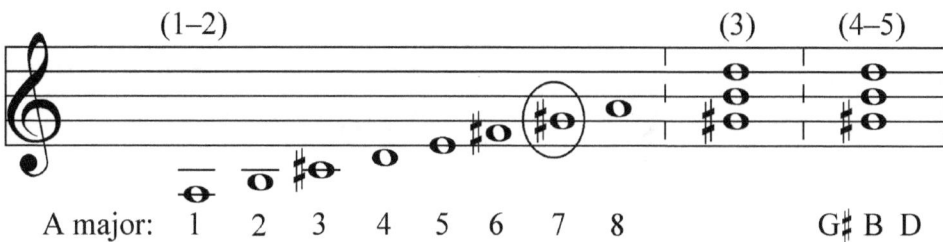

In the key of G major, spell the mediant triad in root position (example 8–15).
  (1) Find the *letter name* for the mediant (scale degree 3) of the G-major scale. The answer is B.
  (2) G major has one sharp, F♯; therefore, the mediant scale degree is B (natural).
  (3) What is the interval of a 3rd and a 5th above B? The answer is D and F.
  (4) Since F carries a sharp in G major and D is natural, the mediant triad is spelled B D F♯.
  (5) The mediant triad in G major is a minor triad: B D F♯.

Example 8–15

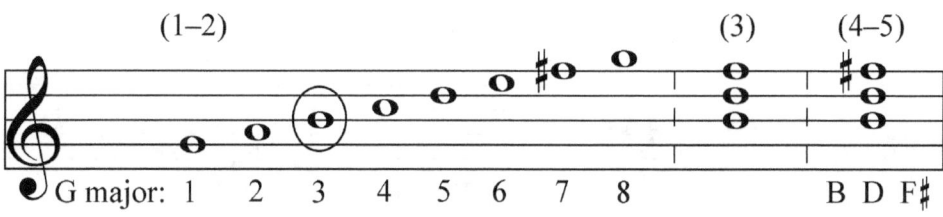

In the key of F major, spell the subdominant triad in root position (example 8–16).
  (1) Find the *letter name* for the subdominant (scale degree 4) of the F-major scale. The answer is B.
  (2) F major has one flat, B♭; therefore, the subdominant scale degree is B♭.
  (3) What is the interval of a 3rd and a 5th above B♭? The answer is D and F.
  (4) Since D and F are both natural, the subdominant triad is spelled B♭ D F.
  (5) The subdominant triad in F major is a major triad: B♭ D F.

Example 8–16

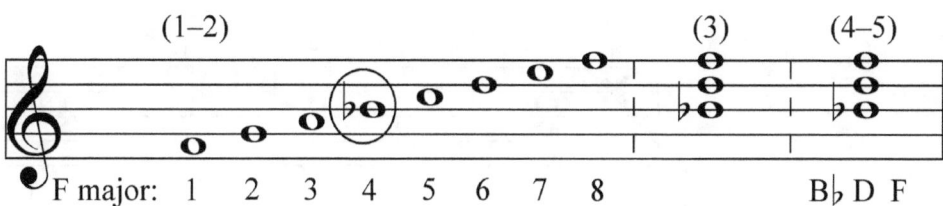

114   Chapter 8   Triads

In the key of D major, spell the supertonic triad in root position (example 8–17).
  (1) Find the *letter name* for the supertonic (scale degree 2) of the D-major scale. The answer is E.
  (2) D major has two sharps, F♯ and C♯; therefore, the supertonic scale degree is E (natural).
  (3) What is the interval of a 3rd and a 5th above E? The answer is G and B.
  (4) Since G and B are both natural, the supertonic triad is spelled E G B.
  (5) The supertonic triad in D major is a minor triad: E G B.

Example 8–17

In the key of A♭ major, spell the dominant triad in root position (example 8–18).
  (1) Find the *letter name* for the dominant (scale degree 5) of the A♭-major scale. The answer is E.
  (2) A♭ major has four flats, one of which is E♭; therefore, the dominant scale degree is E♭.
  (3) What is the interval of a 3rd and a 5th above E♭? The answer is G and B.
  (4) Since G is natural in A♭ major and B carries a flat, the dominant triad is spelled E♭ G B♭.
  (5) The dominant triad in A♭ major is a major triad: E♭ G B♭.

Example 8–18

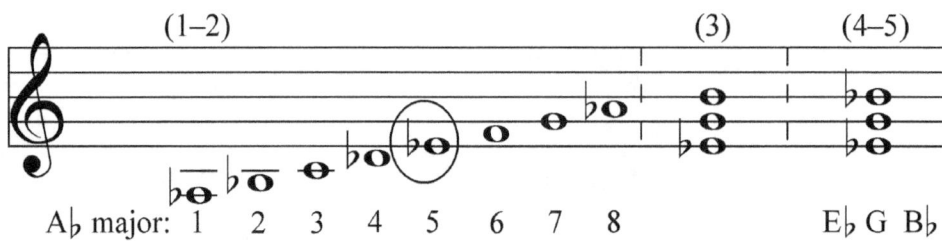

Inverting the Major Triad

Triads are created from combinations of intervals, intervals of the 3rd in particular. The 3rd can be transformed into the interval of the 6th by placing the bottom note of the 3rd one octave higher (example 8–19a) or by moving the top note of the 3rd one octave lower to become the bottom note (8–19b).

Example 8–19: inverting the interval of the 3rd

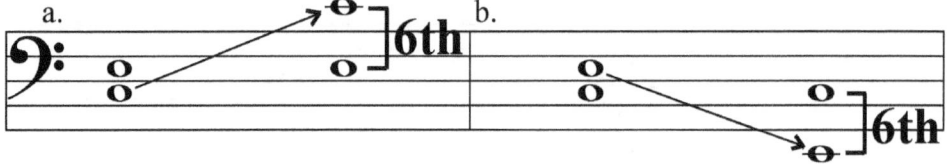

Example 8–20 shows how interval inversion changes the structure of the major triad in root position. Again, the two elements of the triad standing above the root are referred to respectively as the third and the fifth because they are located at the intervals of a 3rd and a 5th above the root. The three elements of the major triad in root position appear in the following order from the lowest to the highest pitch: root, third, and fifth.

Example 8–20a presents an alternative description for the intervallic structure of the root-position triad, designating the chord in "$^5_3$ position." The Arabic numbers indicate the placement of certain intervals and pitches (in this case, E and G) above the lowest note of the musical texture (C); the numbers are referred to as **figured bass** ("figuring" means counting the intervals and pitches up from the bass note).

In 8–20b, the **first inversion** of the major triad is displayed. Shifting the root of the major triad into the next higher octave leaves the third of the chord (E) as the bass pitch. The figured bass for the first inversion of the triad is $^6_3$, which means that the intervals of a 3rd (E to G) and a 6th (E to C) occur above the lowest note (E). The three elements of the major triad in first inversion appear in the following order from the lowest to the highest pitch: third, fifth, and root.

Example 8–20c illustrates the **second inversion** of the major triad. Moving the third component of the first-inversion triad up one octave leaves the fifth of the chord (G) in the bass. The figured bass for the second inversion of the triad is $^6_4$, which means that the intervals of a 4th (G to C) and a 6th (G to E) occur above the lowest note (G). The three elements of the major triad in second inversion appear in the following order from the lowest to the highest pitch: fifth, root, and third.

Example 8–20: the major triad in root position, first inversion, and second inversion

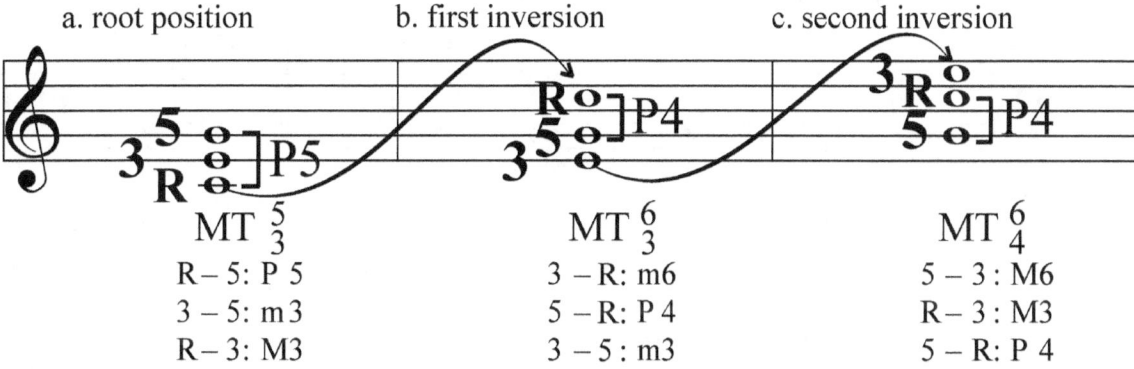

Before considering the inversions of minor, diminished, and augmented triads, let us compare the intervals that comprise the major triad in its root position, first inversion, and second inversion. We know that in root position (8–20a), the major triad has a major 3rd from the root to the third, a minor 3rd from the third to the fifth, and a perfect 5th from the root to the fifth.

In first inversion (8–20b), the perfect 5th from the root up to the fifth (C to G) is transformed into a perfect 4th from the fifth up to the root (G to C). The minor 3rd between the third and the fifth (E to G) remains unchanged from the root position because the two elements of the chord have not been inverted. However, the relationship between the root and the third does change, as the first inversion places the root above the third. The major 3rd between the root and the third (C to E) becomes a minor 6th between the third and the root (E to C).

In second inversion (8–20c), the fifth up to the root is, once again, a perfect 4th (G to C). A major 3rd remains between the root and the third (C to E). The fifth up to the third is a major 6th (G to E). Finally, remember that in the major mode, the major triad occurs in three scale degree areas: the tonic, the subdominant, and the dominant.

Inverting the Minor Triad

Earlier in this chapter, we said that the only difference between a major triad and a minor triad with the same root is the middle component of each respective chord, the third. In the minor triad, the third is one half step lower than the corresponding third of the major triad. Raising the third of the minor triad by one half step produces a major triad.

As shown in example 8–21a, the minor triad in root position has a perfect 5th between the root and the fifth (C to G). In first inversion (8–21b), a perfect 4th spans the distance from the fifth up to the root (G to C). The major 3rd between the third and the fifth (E♭ to G) remains unchanged from the root position because the interval has not been inverted. On the other hand, first inversion changes the relationship between the root and the third by placing the root above the third, leaving the latter element of the chord as the lowest note of the texture (E♭). The minor 3rd between the root and the third (C to E♭) becomes a major 6th between the third and the root (E♭ to C).

In second inversion, we find the root situated above the fifth of the chord (8–21c). As with the first inversion, the distance from the fifth up to the root constitutes a perfect 4th (G to C). The interval between the root and the third (C to E♭) remains a minor 3rd because the two elements of the chord have not been inverted. The fifth up to the third is a minor 6th (G to E♭). Remember that in the major mode, the minor triad occurs in three scale degree areas: the supertonic, the mediant, and the submediant.

Example 8–21: the minor triad in root position, first inversion, and second inversion

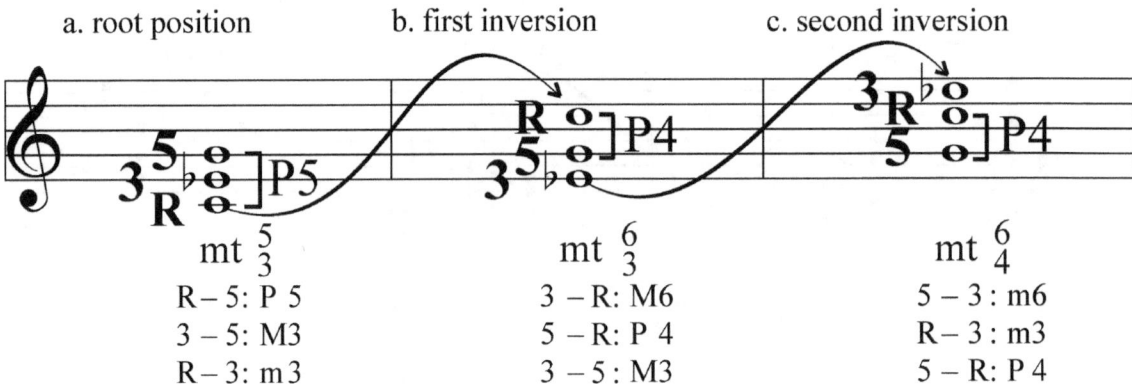

Inverting the Diminished Triad

The diminished triad (example 8–22a) has a diminished 5th between the root and the fifth (C to G♭). When the diminished triad inverts (examples 8–22b and 22c), the diminished 5th becomes an augmented 4th, as the root is placed above the fifth (G♭ to C). Two minor 3rds comprise the structure of the chord in root position. A minor 3rd occurs between the root and the third (C to E♭) and between the third and the fifth (E♭ to G♭).

In first inversion (8–22b), the third and the fifth retain their original relationship (a minor 3rd). The relationship between the root and the third, however, changes. Here, the root appears as an inverted tone above the third, producing a major 6th between the two elements of the chord (E♭ to C).

In second inversion (8–22c), the distance between the root and the third remains the same as it was in root position, a minor 3rd. The fifth up to the third is a major 6th (G♭ to E♭). Remember that in the major mode, the diminished triad occurs in one scale degree area only: the leading tone.

Example 8–22: the diminished triad in root position, first inversion, and second inversion

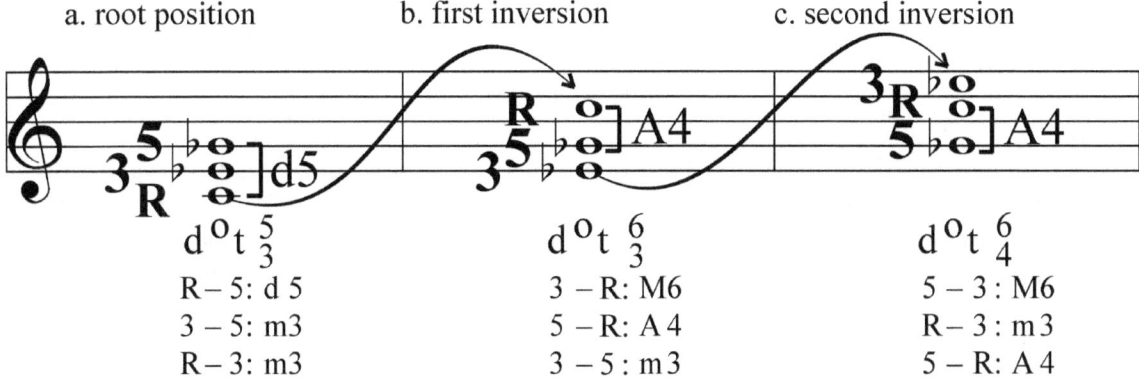

Inverting the Augmented Triad

We know that the intervallic structures of the diminished triad and the minor triad are the same except for the distances between their respective roots and fifths. The minor triad has a perfect 5th from the root to the fifth, whereas the diminished triad has a diminished 5th from the root to the fifth.

There are also certain similarities between the intervallic structures of the augmented triad and the major triad. Both the augmented triad and the major triad are the same except for the distances between their respective roots and fifths. As we have seen, the distance from the root to the fifth of the major triad is a perfect 5th, whereas the distance from the root to the fifth of the augmented triad is an augmented 5th.

Example 8–23 shows the augmented triad in root position, first inversion, and second inversion. In 8–23a, which illustrates the root position of the chord, we have two major 3rds, one between the root and the third (C to E) and the other between the third and the fifth (E to G♯). When the augmented triad inverts, as demonstrated in examples 8–23b and 23c, the root is placed above the fifth, changing the augmented 5th between the root and the fifth (C to G♯) into a diminished 4th (G♯ to C).

Example 8–23: the augmented triad in root position, first inversion, and second inversion

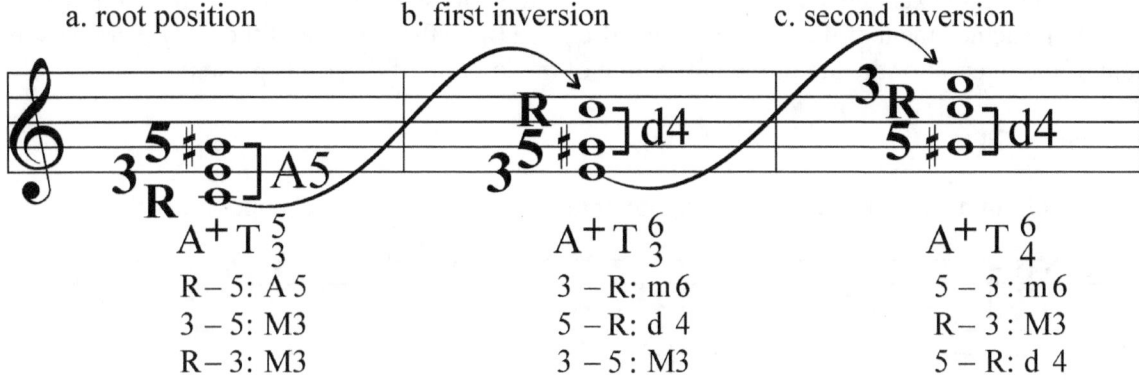

It should be understood that the diminished 4th between the fifth and the root of the augmented triad exists only within the *written context* of the chord because the *sound* of the diminished 4th is identical to that of another interval, the major 3rd. Therefore, the diminished 4th should be referred to properly as a **contextual interval**.

Although the diminished 4th and the major 3rd are both identifiable within the written context, the major 3rd may also be classified as an **acoustic interval** because it has only one aural interpretation—the major 3rd cannot be heard as a diminished 4th. The acoustical major 3rd from the fifth up to the root gives the augmented triad a neutral-sounding profile that precludes hearing the chord as an inverted structure. Regardless of its written position, the augmented triad sounds like two superimposed major 3rds (see example 8–37 below).

The augmented 5th (the inversion of the diminished 4th) is also a contextual interval because the *sound* of the augmented 5th is identical to that of another interval, the minor 6th. Later in this study, we shall see that the status of the augmented triad as a genuine chord is somewhat questionable because of its intervallic structure and because it usually occurs in conjunction with another chord and depends on that chord for its own existence, so to speak.

The augmented triad in 8–23a above contains two major 3rds, one between the root and the third (C to E) and the other between the third and the root (E to G♯). In first inversion (8–23b), the third and the fifth retain their original configuration (a major 3rd). The relationship between the root and third changes, however. Since the inversion of the chord places the root above the third, the distance from the third up to the root is now a minor 6th (E to C).

In second inversion (8–23c), the distance between the root and the third remains a major third, as the third still appears above the root. Since the inversion of the chord finds the third above the fifth, the distance from the fifth up to the third becomes a minor 6th (G♯ to E).

Identifying Triad Position

In order to identify the position of the triad, we must find the location of the root within the structure of the chord. Finding the root of the triad provides us with the requisite information to determine which of the three elements of the chord is in the bass: the root, the third, or the fifth. In $^5_3$ position (i.e., root position), the bottom note of the interval of the 5th indicates the location of the root. In both $^6_3$ position (i.e., first inversion) and $^6_4$ position (i.e., second inversion), the process of interval inversion changes the structure of the triad, as the root of the chord now occurs above the fifth, converting the interval of the 5th into the interval of the 4th. Therefore, the upper note of the 4th indicates the location of the root when the triad is inverted.

As shown in example 8–24, if the triad is notated on the staff, then the root can be found even without assigning each element of the chord to a specific pitch (note the absence of the clef) as long as the bottom note of the interval of the 5th or the upper note of the interval of the 4th is present.

Example 8–24

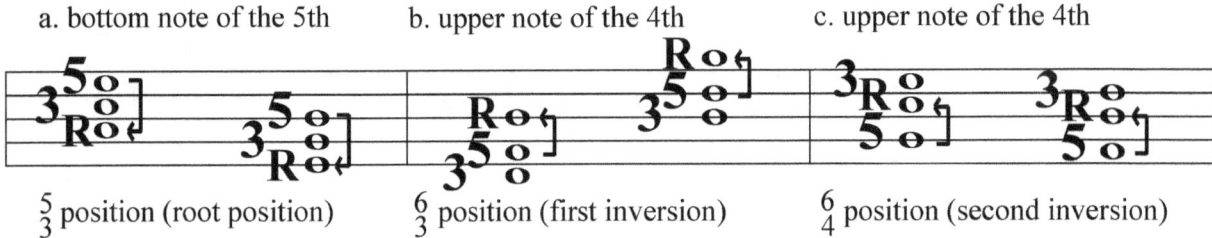

a. bottom note of the 5th   b. upper note of the 4th   c. upper note of the 4th

$^5_3$ position (root position) $^6_3$ position (first inversion) $^6_4$ position (second inversion)

Example 8–25 shows another view of the elements of the triad up from the bass for all three positions of the chord. The example assumes that the three elements of the triad are placed as closely together on the staff as possible for all three chord positions. Later, we shall see how the structure of the triad in root position, $^6_3$ position, or $^6_4$ position may extend across more than one octave, producing a spacing of the chord that is more "open" than those configurations that hold the three elements of the chord within a single octave.

Example 8–25

$$\text{Bass:} \begin{matrix} 5 \\ 3 \\ R \end{matrix} \quad \begin{matrix} R \\ 5 \\ 3 \end{matrix} \quad \begin{matrix} 3 \\ R \\ 5 \end{matrix}$$

$^5_3$ position $^6_3$ position $^6_4$ position

Identifying Triad Quality in Root Position

When the triad in root position occupies three adjacent spaces or three adjacent lines on the staff with the root standing as the lowest note of the musical texture, we can identify easily the intervallic structure and the quality of the triad.

Examples 8–26 and 27 present four different triad qualities, each of which is in root position. As we have said, the bottom note of the interval of the 5th indicates the location of the root in the root-position triad. Once the root of the triad has been located, the next step would be to measure the distance between the root and fifth of each respective chord. Any triad with a perfect 5th between its root and fifth must be either major or minor. Any triad with a diminished 5th between its root and fifth must be diminished, while any triad with an augmented 5th between its root and fifth must be augmented.

The triads for both examples 8–26a and 26b have perfect 5ths between their respective roots and fifths; hence, the only possible qualities for the triads are major and minor. Measuring the distance from the root to the third reveals the quality of each chord. In 8–26a, the interval from A♭ to C is a major 3rd; therefore, the triad is major. In 8–26b, the interval from F♯ to A is a minor 3rd; therefore, the triad is minor.

Example 8–26: root-position triads

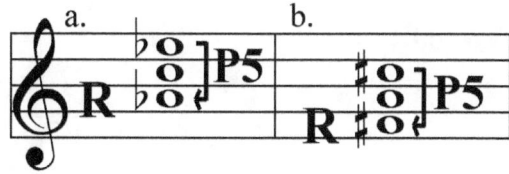

The triads for both examples 8–27a and 27b do not have perfect 5ths between their respective roots and fifths; hence, the only possible qualities for the triads are diminished and augmented. Measuring the distance from the root to the fifth reveals the quality of each chord. In 8–27a, the interval from G to D♭ is a diminished 5th; therefore, the triad is diminished. In 8–27b, the interval from E♭ to B is an augmented fifth; therefore, the triad is augmented.

Example 8–27: root-position triads

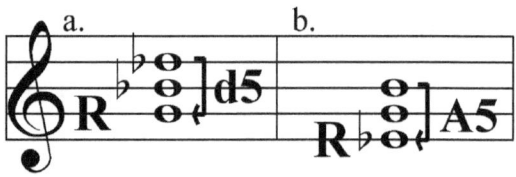

Applying the Principle of Like Inflection to Triads

In Chapter 5, the principle of like inflection was introduced to indicate that if both pitches of an interval are inflected equally in the same direction, upwards or downwards, then the quality of the interval does not change (see above, p. 66). The principle of like inflection may be applied to any combination of intervals that produces triads and other chords. Thus, if C E G is a major triad, assigning a sharp or a flat to each pitch does not change the quality of the chord. In example 8–28, each pitch of the major triad on C is inflected equally, upwards (sharps) or downwards (flats).

Example 8–28

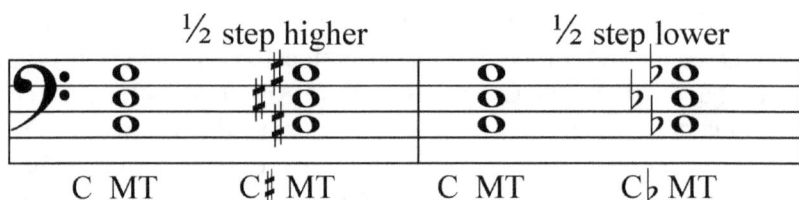

In example 8–29, each pitch of the major triad on D (D F♯ A) is inflected equally, upwards or downwards; however, the only way to maintain the quality of the chord is to use a combination of different accidentals.

Example 8–29

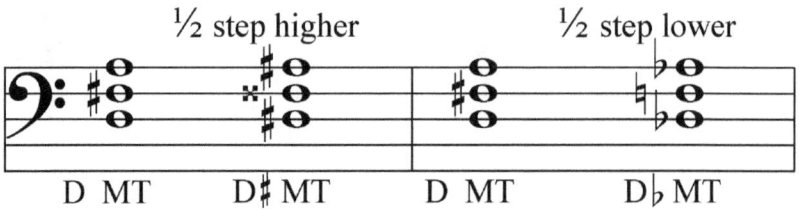

When the Root of the Triad Does Not Represent One of the Fourteen Transpositions of C Major

In the foregoing examples in this chapter, the root of the triad was given as either C or as one of the fourteen transpositions of C. Identification of triad quality and/or triad location within the context of the major scale and mode requires a thorough knowledge of major key signatures and the ability to measure intervals.

We shall call upon these skills presently when working with the roots of three triads that do not represent one of the transpositions of C. The triads put forward here have roots with which no practical key signature can be associated. Temporarily removing accidentals from these roots makes it easier to analyze the intervallic structures of each triad.

(1) The root in example 8–30 is F𝑥, a pitch that does not correspond to one of the transpositions of C.

(2) Since there is no key signature for F𝑥, removing one of the sharps from the double sharp converts the root into a pitch that does correspond to one of the transpositions of C, namely, F♯ major. The key of F♯ major has six sharps, including A♯ and C♯. Therefore, F♯ A♯ C♯ constitutes the tonic triad for the key of F♯ major. As we have said, the quality of the tonic triad in the major mode is major (see above, p. 111), with a major 3rd from the root to the third (F♯ to A♯) and a minor 3rd from the third to the fifth (A♯ to C♯).

(3) If we re-add the double sharp to the F♯, then the size of the major 3rd from the root to the third (F♯ to A♯) is decreased by one half step, producing a minor 3rd (F𝑥 to A♯). Any triad with a minor 3rd from root to third (F𝑥 to A♯) and a minor 3rd from third to fifth (A♯ to C♯) is diminished. The distance from the root to the fifth of the chord is a diminished 5th (F𝑥 to C♯). F𝑥 A♯ C♯ is a diminished triad.

Example 8–30

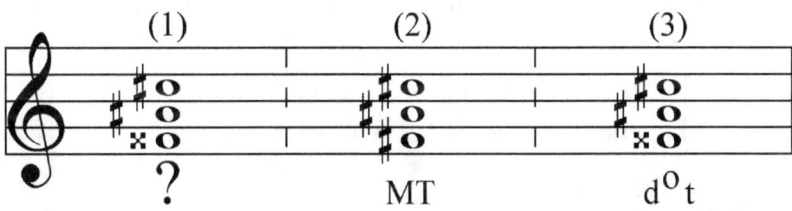

(1) The root in example 8–31 is F♭, a pitch that does not correspond to one of the transpositions of C.
(2) Since there is no key signature for F♭, removing the flat converts the root into a pitch that does correspond to one of the transpositions of C, namely, F major. The key of F major has one flat, B♭. Removing the flats from the other two elements of the triad creates the tonic chord for the key of F major. The quality of the tonic triad in the major mode is major, with a major 3rd from the root to the third (F to A) and a minor 3rd from the third to the fifth (A to C).
(3) If we apply the principle of like inflection to the major triad F A C by adding a flat to each element of the chord, then a major triad is created: F♭ A♭ C♭.

Example 8–31

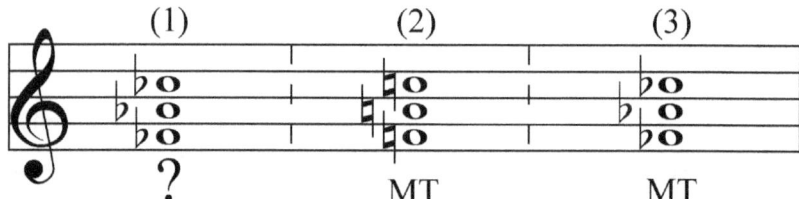

(1) The root in example 8–32 is D♯, a pitch that does not correspond to one of the transpositions of C.
(2) Since there is no key signature for D♯, removing the sharp converts the root into a pitch that does correspond to one of the transpositions of C, namely, D major. The key of D major has two sharps, one of which is F♯.
(3) Since the F𝄪 and the A♯ do not belong to the key signature of D major, remove the accidentals from both pitches and proceed with the triad D F A.
(4) What is the quality of D F A? A perfect 5th spans the root to the fifth (D to A). The distance from the root to the third is a minor 3rd (D to F). D F A is a minor triad.
(5) If we apply the principle of like inflection to the minor triad D F A by adding a sharp to each element of the chord, then a minor triad is created: D♯ F♯ A♯.
(6) Finally, re-adding the double sharp converts the F♯ into F𝄪 and *increases* the size of the minor 3rd between the root and the third of the triad by one half step, producing a major 3rd between the root and the third (D♯ to F𝄪). Thus, D♯ F𝄪 A♯ is a major triad.

Example 8–32

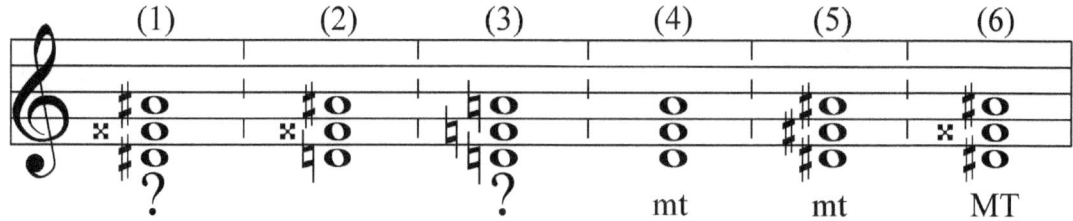

Solving the problem of 8–32 appears to require an excessive number of steps; however, once you have mastered the major key signatures and the measurement of intervals, the procedure outlined above takes place very quickly. Later in this chapter, we shall find better alternatives for identifying chords that are difficult to read (see below, p. 137).

Identifying Triad Quality in $^6_3$ and $^6_4$ Positions

Identifying the quality of the triad in $^6_3$ or $^6_4$ position has the additional challenge of first finding the root and then analyzing the intervallic structure of the chord to determine its quality. As we have said, the upper note of the interval of the 4th indicates the location of the root within the inverted triad. Once the root has been found, it becomes possible to determine whether the chord is in $^6_3$ or $^6_4$ position and therefore what element of the chord is in the bass. Since the process of inversion converts the interval of the 5th into the interval of the 4th, identifying the quality of the 4th between the fifth and the root will help to ascertain the quality of the inverted triad.

If the 4th is perfect from the fifth up to the root, then the triad is either major or minor. If the 4th is augmented from the fifth up to the root, then the triad is diminished. If the 4th is diminished from the fifth up to the root, then the triad is augmented. If the 4th is perfect from the fifth up to the root, then an additional step is required to determine the distance from the root to the third of the chord. A major 3rd between the root and the third indicates a major triad, a minor 3rd between the root and the third indicates a minor triad.

(1) What is the position and the quality of the given triad in example 8–33?
(2) Locate the root of the triad by finding the upper note of the 4th. The root is E♭.
(3) Recalling example 8–25, we can see that the fifth of the triad (B♭) is located immediately below the root (E♭) and that the third (G) is below the fifth as the lowest note of the musical texture. The three elements of the triad appear in the following order from the lowest to the highest pitch: third, fifth, and root.
(4) It would be well to memorize that if the third of the triad is in the bass, then the chord is in $^6_3$ position (i.e., first inversion); however, you could also measure the numerical distance of the intervals that occur above the bass pitch (G) to determine the position of the triad. Thus, G up to B♭ is a 3rd and G up to E♭ a 6th; therefore, the triad is in $^6_3$ position. Alternatively, this step (step 4) can be used initially or in conjunction with step 2 to locate the three elements of the triad.
(5) Having found the root and identified which element of the triad is in the bass, we can now determine the quality of the triad. The interval of the 4th from the fifth (B♭) up to the root (E♭) is perfect; therefore, the quality of the triad is either major or minor.
(6a) Since the interval from the fifth up to the root is a perfect 4th, here is a shortcut: measuring the interval between the third and the fifth will tell us if the triad is major or minor. The interval between the third and the fifth is a minor 3rd; therefore, the triad is major because the distance from third to the fifth is always a minor 3rd in a major triad.
(6b) As an alternative to the shortcut in step 6a, reassemble the triad in root position and identify the quality of the intervals between the root and the third and the third and the fifth. The ordering of thirds up from the root is M3/m3.
(7) The chord is a major triad in $^6_3$ position.

Example 8–33

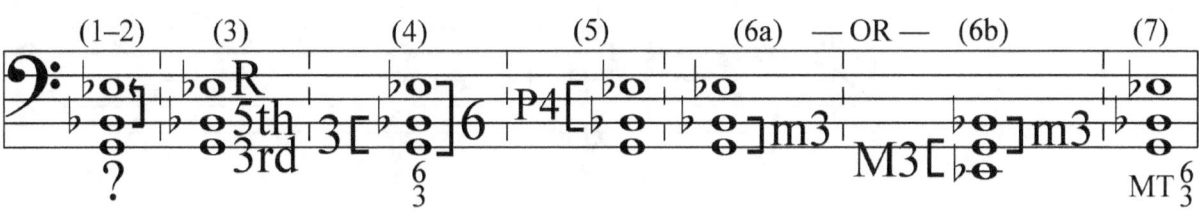

124   Chapter 8 Triads

(1) What is the position and the quality of the given triad in example 8–34?
(2) Locate the root of the triad by finding the upper note of the 4th. The root is C♯.
(3) Recalling example 8–25, we can see that the fifth of the triad (G♯) is located immediately below the root (C♯) and that the third (E) is situated above the root. The fifth (G♯) is in the bass, the lowest note of the musical texture. The three elements of the triad appear in the following order from the lowest to the highest pitch: fifth, root, and third.
(4) Measuring the numerical distance of the intervals that occur above the bass pitch (G♯) shows the triad to be in $^6_4$ position. Indeed, G♯ up to C♯ is a 4th and G♯ up to E a 6th; thus, the intervals of the 4th and the 6th occur over the G♯ bass.
(5) Having found the root and identified which element of the triad is in the bass, we can now determine the quality of the triad. The interval of the 4th from the fifth (G♯) up to the root (C♯) is perfect; therefore, the quality of the triad is either major or minor.
(6a) Since the interval from the fifth up to the root is a perfect 4th, measuring the interval between the root and the third will tell us if the triad is major or minor. The interval between the root and the third is a minor 3rd; therefore, the triad is minor.
(6b) As an alternative to step 6a, reassemble the triad in root position and determine the quality of the intervals between the root and the third and the third and the fifth. The ordering of thirds up from the root is m3/M3.
(7) The chord is a minor triad in $^6_4$ position.

Example 8–34

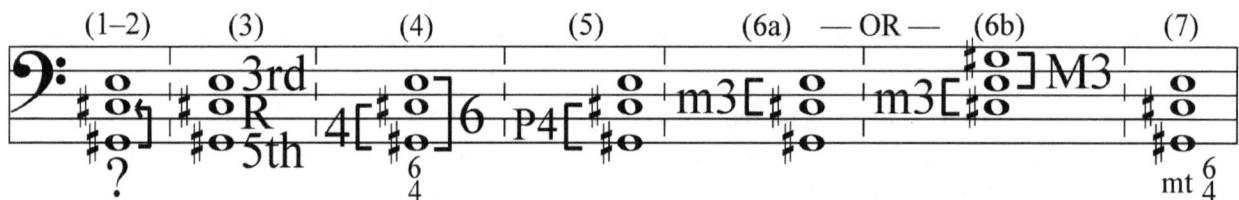

(1) What is the position and the quality of the given triad in example 8–35?
(2) Locate the root of the triad by finding the upper note of the 4th. The root is F.
(3) Recalling example 8–25, we can see that the fifth of the triad (C♭) is located immediately below the root (F) and that the third (A♭) is below the fifth as the lowest note of the musical texture. The three elements of the triad appear in the following order from the lowest to the highest pitch: third, fifth, and root.
(4) Measuring the numerical distance of the intervals that occur above the bass pitch (A♭) shows the triad to be in $^6_3$ position.
(5) The interval from the fifth (C♭) up to the root (F) is an augmented 4th (the inversion of a diminished 5th).
(6) Therefore, the chord is a diminished triad in $^6_3$ position.

Example 8–35

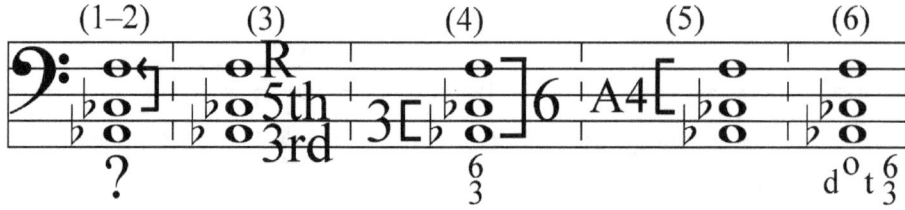

(1) What is the position and the quality of the given triad in example 8–36?
(2) Locate the root of the triad by finding the upper note of the 4th. The root is D.
(3) Recalling example 8–25, we can see that the fifth of the triad (A♯) is located immediately below the root (D) and that the third (F♯) is situated above the root. The fifth (A♯) is in the bass, the lowest note of the musical texture. The three elements of the triad appear in the following order from the lowest to the highest pitch: fifth, root, and third.
(4) Measuring the numerical distance of the intervals that occur above the bass pitch (A♯) shows the triad to be in $^6_4$ position.
(5) The interval from the fifth (A♯) up to the root (D) is a diminished 4th (the inversion of an augmented 5th).
(6) Therefore, the chord is an augmented triad in $^6_4$ position.

Example 8–36

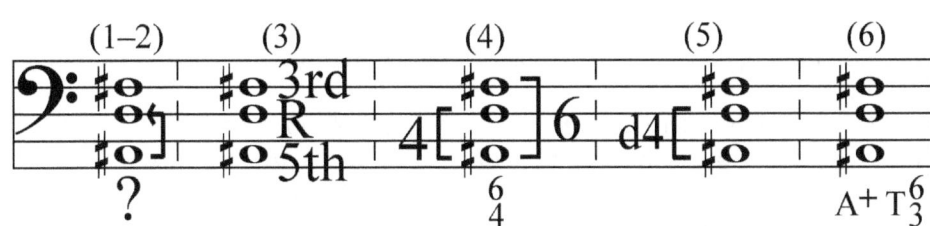

It should be remembered that the diminished 4th between the fifth and the root of the augmented triad shown above in 8–36 exists only within the *written context* of the chord because the *sound* of the diminished 4th is identical to that of the major 3rd. Therefore, the diminished 4th from A♯ up to D is a contextual interval that sounds identical to the acoustical major 3rd, B♭ to D, for the A♯ and B♭ are enharmonically equivalent.

Example 8–37 demonstrates how regardless of the written position of the augmented triad, the chord will always sound like two superimposed major 3rds, an intervallic structure that precludes *hearing* the augmented triad as an inverted chord. Let us reconsider the D F♯ A♯ augmented triad in root position, $^6_3$ position, and $^6_4$ position.

In 8–37a, the augmented triad in spelled in root position as D F♯ A♯ and contains two major thirds, D/F♯ and F♯/A♯. Example 8–37b illustrates the D F♯ A♯ augmented triad in the written $^6_3$ position; but notice that the D is the enharmonic equivalent of C𝄪. Therefore, if the F♯ is the bass pitch, the chord will be heard as F♯ A♯ C𝄪. In 8–37c, the D F♯ A♯ augmented triad is written in $^6_4$ position, with the A♯ as the lowest pitch of the musical texture. The problem is that the A♯ and the B♭ are enharmonically equivalent. Therefore, if A♯ is the bass pitch, then the chord will be heard as B♭ D F♯.

Example 8–37

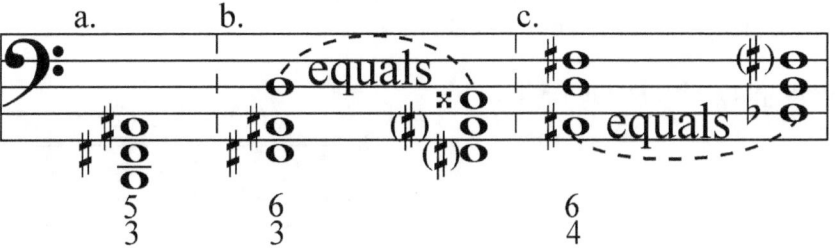

Constructing the Four Triad Qualities in Root Position

In the foregoing sections of this chapter, we examined and *identified* the intervallic structures for major, minor, diminished, and augmented triads. Presently, we shall *construct* triads above roots involving pitches other than C. A couple of options for working with root-position triads are available and both depend upon a thorough knowledge of major key signatures and intervals. In the fullness of time, with sufficient practice, finding the right pitches for all four triad qualities above any given root will become a relatively simple task.

Option 1: Using the Major Triad as a Prototype for Root-Position Constructions

For option 1, we assume that the given tone is the root of the triad, assigning the major triad the status of a prototype from which modifications can be made to create minor, diminished, and augmented triads. According to the prototype option, the given root represents the tonic pitch for any of the fourteen transpositions of C major. Thus, the first step in this process entails forming the tonic major triad on any of the following pitches: G, D, A, E, B, F♯, C♯, F, B♭, E♭, A♭, D♭, G♭, and C♭.

Spell the tonic major triad for the key of D major (example 8–38).
 (1) The challenge is to build a major triad on D, the root of the chord.
 (2) Using letter names rather than specific pitches initially, place a 3rd and a 5th above the D on the staff. The answer is F and A.
 (3) What versions of F and A occur in the key of D major? D major has two sharps, one of which is F♯. The A in D major does not carry an accidental; therefore, the correct pitches above D are F♯ and A (natural).
 (4) The major triad on D is D F♯ A.

Example 8–38: D MT $^5_3$

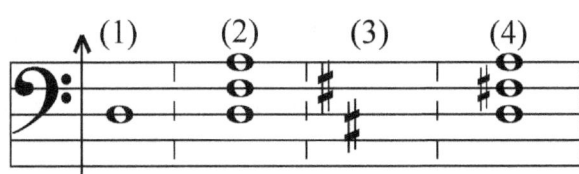

Spell the minor triad above the given tone D (example 8–39).
 (1) D is the root of the chord.
 (2) Using letter names rather than specific pitches initially, place a 3rd and a 5th above the D on the staff. The answer is F and A.
 (3) As in example 8–38 above, build the tonic major triad on D. The answer is D F♯ A.
 (4) Since the third of the minor triad is one half step lower than that of the major triad, lower the third, F♯, one half step. The answer is F (natural).
 (5) The minor triad on D is D F A.

Example 8–39: D mt $^5_3$

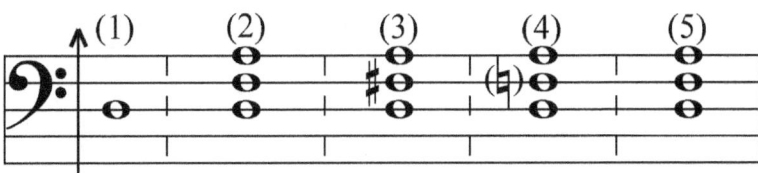

Spell a diminished triad above the given tone D (example 8–40).
  (1) D is the root of the chord.
  (2) Using letter names rather than specific pitches initially, place a 3rd and a 5th above the D on the staff. The answer is F and A.
  (3) Build the tonic major triad on D. The answer is D F♯ A.
  (4) As in example 8–39 above, convert the major triad on D to the minor triad on D. The answer is D F A.
  (5) Since the fifth of the diminished triad is one half step lower than that of the minor triad, lower the fifth, A, one half step. The answer is A♭.
  (6) The diminished triad on D is D F A♭.

Example 8–40: D d° t $\begin{smallmatrix}5\\3\end{smallmatrix}$

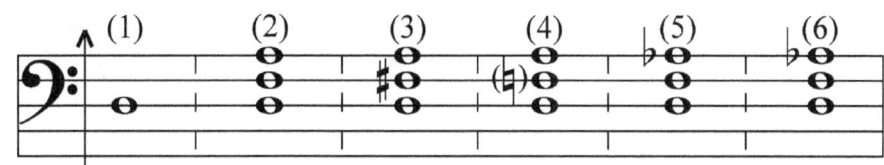

Spell an augmented triad above the given tone D (example 8–41).
  (1) D is the root of the chord.
  (2) Using letter names rather than specific pitches initially, place a 3rd and a 5th above the D on the staff. The answer is F and A.
  (3) Build the tonic major triad on D. The answer is D F♯ A.
  (4) Since the fifth of the augmented triad is one half step higher than that of the major triad, raise the fifth, A, one half step. The answer is A♯.
  (5) The augmented triad on D is D F♯ A♯.

Example 8–41: D A+T $\begin{smallmatrix}5\\3\end{smallmatrix}$

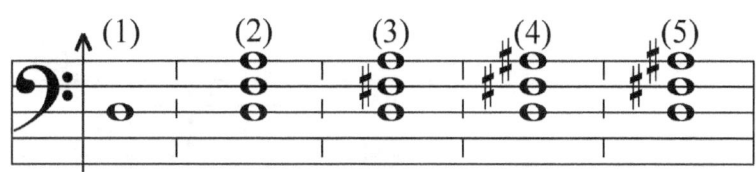

Spell the tonic major triad for the key of C♯ major (example 8–42).
  (1) The challenge is to build a major triad on C♯, the root of the chord.
  (2) Using letter names rather than specific pitches initially, place a 3rd and a 5th above the C♯ on the staff. The answer is E and G.
  (3) What versions of E and G occur in the key of C♯ major? Since C♯ major has seven sharps, the correct pitches above C♯ are E♯ and G♯.
  (4) The major triad on C♯ is C♯ E♯ G♯.

Example 8–42: C♯ MT $\begin{smallmatrix}5\\3\end{smallmatrix}$

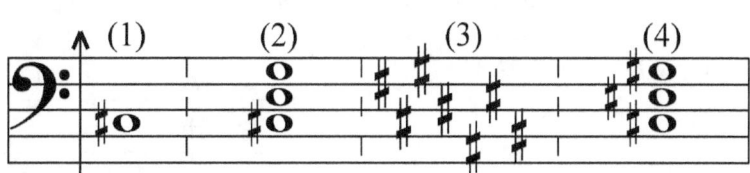

128   Chapter 8 Triads

Spell a minor triad above the given tone C♯ (example 8–43).
  (1) C♯ is the root of the chord.
  (2) Using letter names rather than specific pitches initially, place a 3rd and a 5th above the C♯ on the staff. The answer is E and G.
  (3) Build the tonic major triad on C♯. The answer is C♯ E♯ G♯.
  (4) Since the third of the minor triad is one half step lower than that of the major triad, lower the third, E♯, one half step. The answer is E (natural).
  (5) The minor triad on C♯ is C♯ E G♯.

Example 8–43: C♯ mt $\frac{5}{3}$

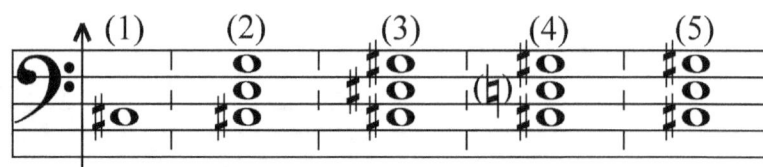

Spell a diminished triad above the given tone C♯ (example 8–44).
  (1) C♯ is the root of the chord.
  (2) Using letter names rather than specific pitches initially, place a 3rd and a 5th above the C♯ on the staff. The answer is E and G.
  (3) Build the tonic major triad on C♯. The answer is C♯ E♯ G♯.
  (4) Convert the major triad on C♯ to the minor triad on C♯. The answer is C♯ E G♯.
  (5) Since the fifth of the diminished triad is one half step lower than that of the minor triad, lower the fifth, G♯, one half step. The answer is G (natural).
  (6) The diminished triad on C♯ is C♯ E G.

Example 8–44: C♯ d°t $\frac{5}{3}$

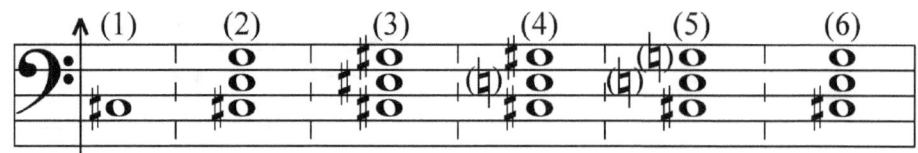

Spell an augmented triad above the given tone C♯ (example 8–45).
  (1) C♯ is the root of the chord.
  (2) Using letter names rather than specific pitches initially, place a 3rd and a 5th above the C♯ on the staff. The answer is E and G.
  (3) Build the tonic major triad on C♯. The answer is C♯ E♯ G♯.
  (4) Since the fifth of the augmented triad is one half step higher than that of the major triad, raise the fifth, G♯, one half step. The answer is G𝄪.
  (5) The augmented triad on C♯ is C♯ E♯ G𝄪.

Example 8–45: C♯ A+T $\frac{5}{3}$

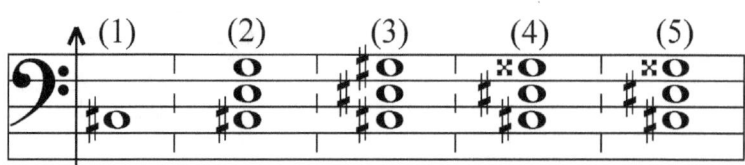

Spell the tonic major triad for the key of G♭ major (example 8–46).
  (1) The challenge is to build a major triad on G♭, the root of the chord.
  (2) Using letter names rather than specific pitches initially, place a 3rd and a 5th above the G♭ on the staff. The answer is B and D.
  (3) What versions of B and D occur in the key of G♭ major? Since G♭ major has six flats, two of which are B♭ and D♭, the correct pitches above G♭ are B♭ and D♭.
  (4) The major triad on G♭ is G♭ B♭ D♭.

Example 8–46: G♭ MT $^5_3$

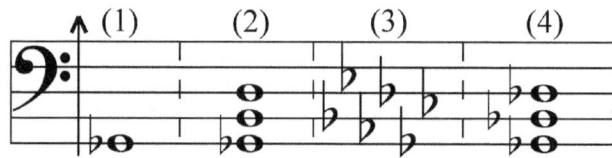

Spell a minor triad above G♭ (example 8–47)
  (1) G♭ is the root of the chord.
  (2) Using letter names rather than specific pitches initially, place a 3rd and a 5th above the G♭ on the staff. The answer is B and D.
  (3) Build the tonic major triad on G♭. The answer is G♭ B♭ D♭.
  (4) Since the third of the minor triad is one half step lower than that of the major triad, lower the third, B♭, one half step. The answer is B♭♭.
  (5) The minor triad on G♭ is G♭ B♭♭ D♭.

Example 8–47: G♭ mt $^5_3$

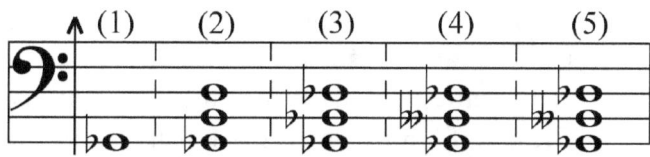

Spell a diminished triad above G♭ (example 8–48)
  (1) G♭ is the root of the chord.
  (2) Using letter names rather than specific pitches initially, place a 3rd and a 5th above the G♭ on the staff. The answer is B and D.
  (3) Build the tonic major triad on G♭. The answer is G♭ B♭ D♭.
  (4) Convert the major triad on G♭ to the minor triad on G♭. The answer is G♭ B♭♭ D♭.
  (5) Since the fifth of the diminished triad is one half step lower than that of the minor triad, lower the fifth, D♭, one half step. The answer is D♭♭.
  (6) The diminished triad on G♭ is spelled G♭ B♭♭ D♭♭ (later, we shall see that as a practical matter, this chord would be respelled enharmonically as F♯ A C).

Example 8–48: G♭ d°t $^5_3$

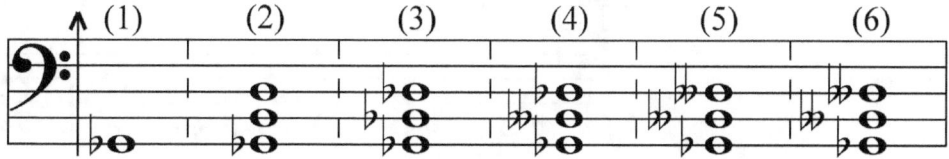

Spell an augmented triad above the given tone G♭ (example 8–49).
  (1) G♭ is the root of the chord.
  (2) Using letter names rather than specific pitches initially, place a 3rd and a 5th above the G♭ on the staff. The answer is B and D.
  (3) Build the tonic major triad on G♭. The answer is G♭ B♭ D♭.
  (4) Since the fifth of the augmented triad is one half step higher than that of the major triad, raise the fifth, D♭, one half step. The answer is D (natural).
  (5) The augmented triad on G♭ is G♭ B♭ D.

Example 8–49: G♭ A+T $^5_3$

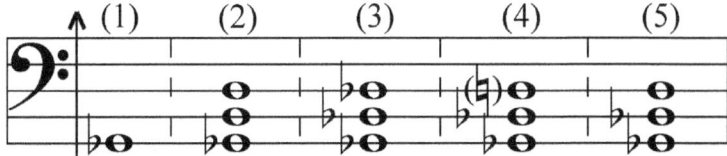

Option 2: Measuring the Intervallic Content of the Triad for Root-Position Constructions

As with option 1, option 2 starts from the premise that the given tone is the root of the triad. The first step measures the intervallic quality of the 3rd from the root to the third of the triad. After the quality of the bottom 3rd has been determined, measure either the top 3rd from the third to the fifth or the outer 5th from the root to the fifth.
  (1) Build a major triad above the given tone C♭ (example 8–50).
  (2) Using letter names rather than specific pitches initially, place a 3rd and a 5th above the C♭ on the staff. The answer is E and G.
  (3) The ordering of thirds up from the root of the major triad is M3/m3. What is a major 3rd above C♭? The key of C♭ major has seven flats, one of which is E♭. A major 3rd above C♭ is E♭.
  (4) The fourth step has two options: either build a perfect 5th above C♭ or a minor 3rd above E♭.
    (a) What is a perfect 5th above the root, C♭? A perfect 5th above C♭ is G♭, as the key of C♭ major has a G♭.
    (b) What is a minor 3rd above the third, E♭? Here, we must draw upon the key signature of E♭ major to calculate the interval. First, build a major 3rd above E♭ and then lower it one half step to find the minor 3rd. Since G does not carry a flat in E♭ major, the major third above E♭ is G. Lowering G one half step brings us to G♭. A minor 3rd above E♭ is G♭.
  (5) The major triad on C♭ is spelled C♭ E♭ G♭. As we have seen, the principle of like inflection frequently offers the simplest solution to the problem of chord construction. If C E G constitutes a major triad, then lowering each of its components by one half step brings us to a major triad on C♭ E♭ G♭.

Example 8–50

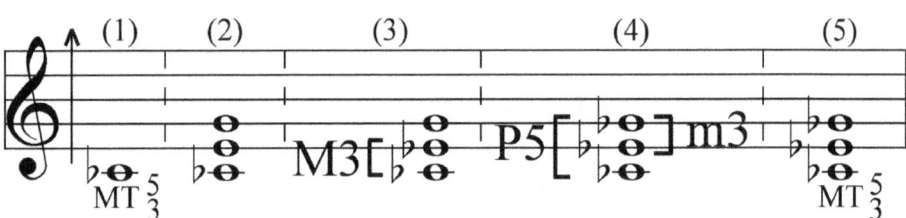

(1) Build a major triad above the given tone A♯ (example 8–51).

(2) Using letter names rather than specific pitches initially, place a 3rd and a 5th above the A♯ on the staff. The answer is C and E.

(3) The ordering of thirds up from the root of the major triad is M3/m3. What is a major 3rd above A♯? Since there is no key signature for A♯ major, it would be well to remove the sharp from the A♯ and build a major 3rd above A. The key of A major has three sharps, one of which is C♯. A major 3rd above A is C♯.

(4) The fourth step has two options: either build a perfect 5th above A or a minor 3rd above C♯.
   (a) What is a perfect 5th above the root, A? A perfect 5th above A is E, as the key of A major has an E.
   (b) What is a minor 3rd above the third, C♯? Here, we must use the key signature of C♯ major to calculate the interval; C♯ major has seven sharps. First, build a major 3rd above C♯ and then lower it one half step to find the minor 3rd. Since E carries a sharp in the key of C♯ major, the major third above C♯ is E♯. Lowering E♯ one half step brings us to E (natural). C♯ to E is a minor 3rd. We now have a major triad on A; however, the initial problem of building a major triad above the given tone A♯ remains.

(5) And so, let us re-add the sharp to the A to produce the given tone A♯. Since A was raised one half step to A♯, we shall use the principle of like inflection to raise the C♯ of step 4 one half step to C𝄪. If the distance from A to C♯ is a major 3rd, then A♯ to C𝄪 is also a major 3rd.

(6) Having constructed the major 3rd from the root (A♯) to the third of the chord (C𝄪), there are a few options available for completing the A♯-major triad. Here are two:
   (a) What is a perfect 5th above the root, A♯? A perfect 5th above A♯ is E♯. How do we know that the correct tone is E♯? Since the perfect 5th above A is E (see step 4a), the principle of like inflection moves both A and E up one half step to A♯ and E♯ without changing the quality of the interval, the perfect 5th.
   (b) Alternatively: after having found the major triad on A in step 4 (A C♯ E), use the principle of like inflection to move all three elements of the chord up one half step to spell the major triad on A♯.

(7) The major triad on A♯ is A♯ C𝄪 E♯.

Example 8–51

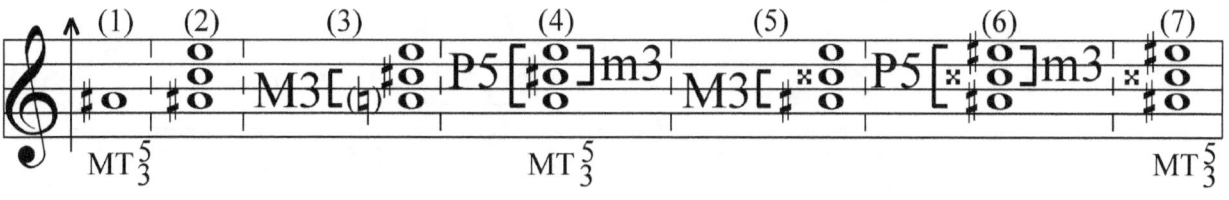

(1) Build a minor triad above the given tone D♭ (example 8–52).
(2) Using letter names rather than specific pitches initially, place a 3rd and a 5th above the D♭ on the staff. The answer is F and A.
(3) The ordering of thirds up from the root of the minor triad is m3/M3. What is a minor 3rd above D♭? The key of D♭ major has five flats, none of which involve F. The tone F is a diatonic member of D♭ major; therefore, a major 3rd above D♭ would be F. Our task, however, is to find a minor 3rd above D♭. We can decrease the size of the major 3rd between D♭ and F by lowering the F one half step to F♭. D♭ to F♭ is a minor 3rd.
(4) The fourth step has two options: either build a major 3rd above F♭ or a perfect 5th above D♭.
   (a) Find a major 3rd above the third of the chord, F♭. Since we do not have a key signature for F♭, the following three steps would be necessary: first, remove the flat to establish the major 3rd above F (natural) as A; secondly, reintroduce the flat to the F; and finally, use the principle of like inflection to establish the major 3rd above F♭ as A♭.
   (b) Alternatively, find the perfect 5th above the root (D♭). The perfect 5th above D♭ is A♭, as there is an A♭ in the key D♭ major.
(5) The minor triad on D♭ is D♭ F♭ A♭. (If you already know that D F A is a minor triad, then using the principle of like inflection tells you that D♭ F♭ A♭ is also a minor triad).

Example 8–52

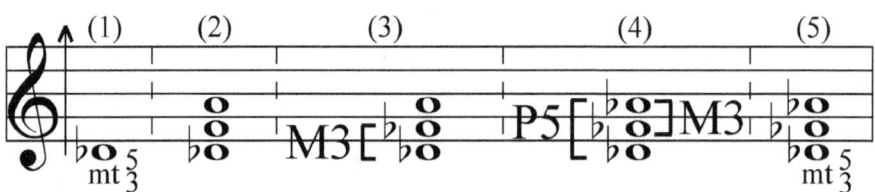

(1) Build a diminished triad above the given tone F (example 8–53).
(2) Using letter names rather than specific pitches initially, place a 3rd and a 5th above the F on the staff. The answer is A and C.
(3) The ordering of thirds up from the root of the diminished triad is m3/m3. What is a minor 3rd above F? The key of F major has only one flat, B♭. Therefore, F to A is a major 3rd. Our task, however, is to find a minor 3rd above F. We can decrease the size of the major 3rd between F and A by lowering the A one half step to A♭. F to A♭ is a minor 3rd.
(4) The fourth step has two options: either build a diminished 5th above F or a minor 3rd above A♭.
   (a) What is a diminished 5th above the root, F? We know that a perfect 5th above F is C, as the key of F major has a C. Our task, however, is to find a diminished 5th above F. We can decrease the size of the perfect 5th by lowering the C one half step to C♭. F to C♭ is a diminished 5th.
   (b) What is a minor 3rd above the third, A♭? Drawing upon the key signature of A♭ major to calculate the interval, we first build a major 3rd above A♭ and then lower it one half step to find the minor 3rd. Since C does not carry a flat in A♭ major, the major third above A♭ is C. Lowering C one half step brings us to C♭. A♭ to C♭ is a minor 3rd.
(5) The diminished triad on F is F A♭ C♭.

Example 8–53

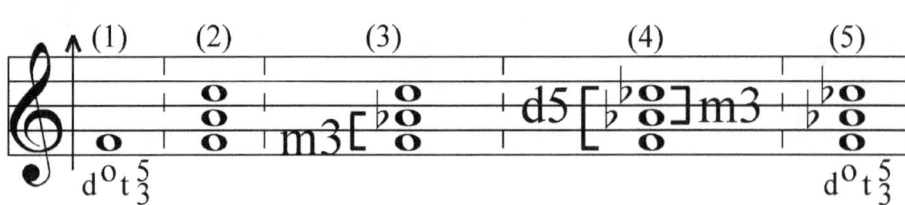

(1) Build an augmented triad above the given tone B (example 8–54).
(2) Using letter names rather than specific pitches initially, place a 3rd and a 5th above the B on the staff. The answer is D and F.
(3) The ordering of thirds up from the root of the augmented triad is M3/M3. What is a major 3rd above B? The key of B major has five sharps, one of which is D♯. B to D♯ is a major 3rd.
(4) The fourth step has two options: either build a major 3rd above D♯ or an augmented 5th above B.
   (a) Find a major 3rd above the third of the chord, D♯. Since we do not have a key signature for D♯, the following steps would be necessary: Remove the sharp and build a major 3rd above D (natural). The answer is F♯. Reintroduce the sharp to the D to create a minor 3rd between D♯ and F♯. Raise F♯ one half step to produce a major 3rd between D♯ and F𝄪.
   (b) Find the perfect 5th above B. The answer is F♯, as there is an F♯ in the key of B major. Secondly, convert the perfect 5th into an augmented 5th by raising F♯ one half step to F𝄪.
(5) The augmented triad on B is B D♯ F𝄪.

Example 8–54

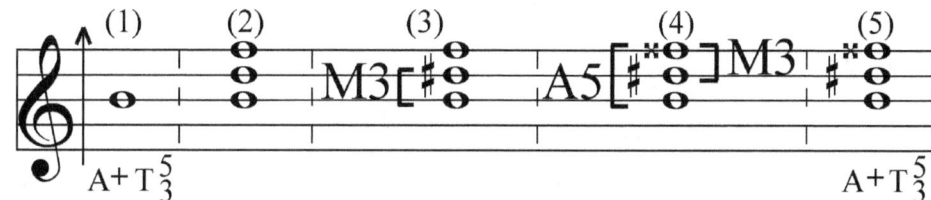

Constructing the Four Triad Qualities in $^6_3$ and $^6_4$ Positions

(1) Build a major triad above the given tone D (example 8–55), understanding that the D is not the root of the chord. The figured bass $^6_3$ indicates that D is the third of the triad and the lowest note of the musical texture.
(2) The figured bass $^6_3$ means that the intervals of a 3rd and a 6th occur above the lowest note (D). Using letter names rather than specific pitches initially, place a 3rd and a 6th above the D on the staff. The answer is F and B.
(3) The distance from the third up to the fifth of the major triad is a minor 3rd. What is a minor 3rd above D? The key of D major has two sharps, one of which is F♯. If a major 3rd above D is F♯, then the interval must be decreased in size by one half step to produce the minor 3rd. The D cannot be altered, as it is the given tone. Therefore, lowering the F♯ by one half step to F natural converts the major 3rd into a minor 3rd. D to F is a minor 3rd.
(4) The next step is to find a perfect 4th above the fifth, F. A perfect 4th above F is B♭, as the key of F major has a B♭.
(5) Rearrange all of the elements of the chord so that it stands in root position and then check both the bottom and top thirds to make sure that the ordering of thirds up from the root is M3/m3.
(6) The major triad in $^6_3$ position above the given tone D is D F B♭.

Example 8–55

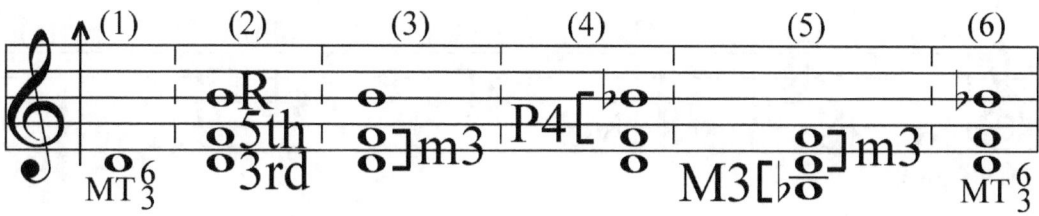

(1) Build a major triad above the given tone D♭ (example 8–56), understanding that the figured bass $^6_4$ indicates that D♭ is the fifth of the triad and the lowest note of the musical texture.

(2) The figured bass $^6_4$ means that the intervals of a 4th and a 6th occur above the lowest note (D♭). Using letter names rather than specific pitches initially, place a 4th and a 6th above the D♭ on the staff. The answer is G and B.

(3) The distance from the fifth up to the root of the major triad is a perfect 4th. What is a perfect 4th above D♭? The key of D♭ major has five flats, one of which is G♭. D♭ to G♭ is a perfect 4th.

(4) The next step is to find a major 3rd above the root, G♭. A major 3rd above G♭ is B♭, as the key of G♭ major has a B♭.

(5) Rearrange all of the elements of the chord so that it stands in root position and then check both the bottom and top thirds to make sure that the ordering of thirds up from the root is M3/m3.

(6) The major triad in $^6_4$ position above the given tone D♭ is D♭ G♭ B♭.

Example 8–56

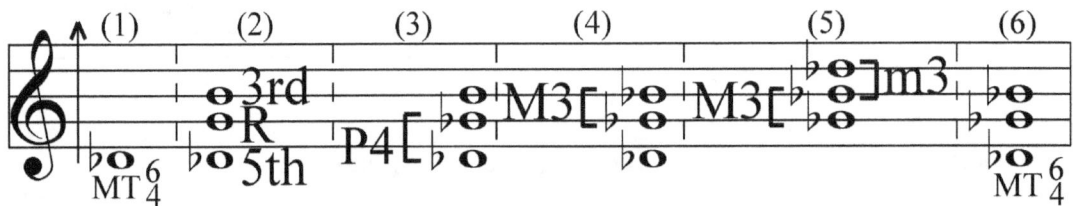

(1) Build a minor triad above the given tone F♯ (example 8–57), understanding that the figured bass $^6_3$ indicates that F♯ is the third of the triad and the lowest note of the musical texture.

(2) Following the figured bass and using letter names rather than specific pitches initially, place a 3rd and a 6th above the F♯ on the staff. The answer is A and D.

(3) The distance up from the third to the fifth of the minor triad is a major 3rd. What is a major 3rd above F♯? The key of F♯ major has six sharps, one of which is A♯. F♯ to A♯ is a major 3rd.

(4) The next step is to find a perfect 4th above the fifth, A♯.
   (a) Since the fifth is A♯, it would be well to remove the sharp and find a perfect 4th above A natural. The perfect 4th above A is D.
   (b) If we reintroduce the sharp to the A, then we can use the principle of like inflection to raise D one half step to D♯. A perfect 4th above A♯ is D♯.

(5) Rearrange all of the elements of the chord so that it stands in root position and then check both the bottom and top thirds to make sure that the ordering of thirds up from the root is m3/M3.

(6) The minor triad in $^6_3$ position above the given tone F♯ is F♯ A♯ D♯.

Example 8–57

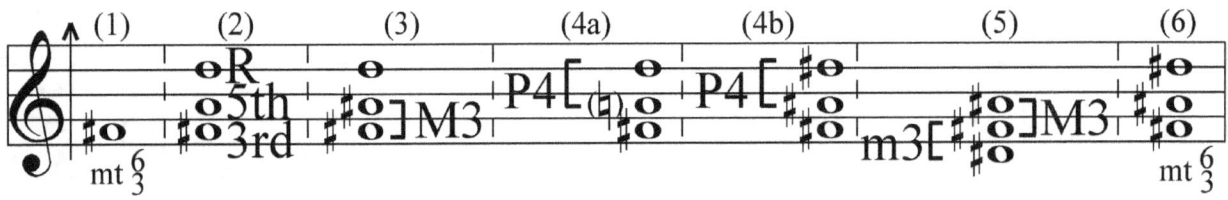

(1) Build a minor triad above the given tone G♯ (example 8–58), understanding that the figured bass $^6_4$ indicates that G♯ is the fifth of the triad and the lowest note of the musical texture.

(2) Following the figured bass and using letter names rather than specific pitches initially, place a 4th and a 6th above the G♯ on the staff. The answer is C and E.

(3) The distance from the fifth up to the root of the major triad is a perfect 4th. What is a perfect 4th above G♯? Since there is no key signature for G♯, the following steps are necessary:
   (a) Remove the sharp to establish the perfect 4th above G (natural) as C.
   (b) Reintroduce the sharp to the G and use the principle of like inflection to establish the perfect 4th above G♯ as C♯.

(4) The next step is to find a minor 3rd above the root, C♯. A major 3rd above C♯ is E♯, as the key of C♯ major has an E♯. Lowering the E♯ by one half step to E natural converts the major 3rd into a minor 3rd. C♯ to E is a minor 3rd.

(5) Rearrange all of the elements of the chord so that it stands in root position and then check both the bottom and top thirds to make sure that the ordering of thirds up from the root is m3/M3.

(6) The minor triad in $^6_4$ position above the given tone G♯ is G♯ C♯ E.

Example 8–58

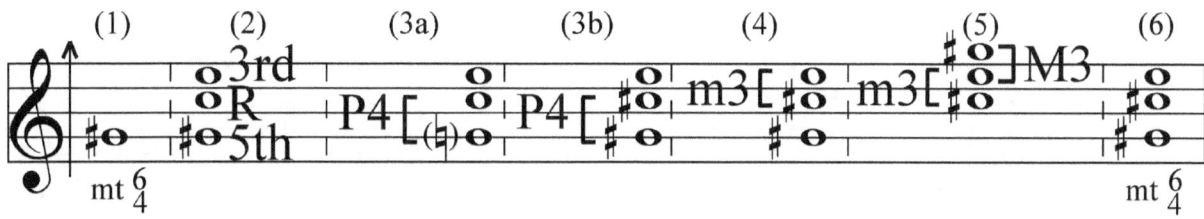

(1) Build a diminished triad above the given tone B (example 8–59), understanding that the figured bass $^6_3$ indicates that B is the third of the triad and the lowest note of the musical texture.

(2) Following the figured bass and using letter names rather than specific pitches initially, place a 3rd and a 6th above the B on the staff. The answer is D and G.

(3) The distance from the third up to the fifth of the diminished triad is a minor 3rd. What is a minor 3rd above B? The key of B major has five sharps, one of which is D♯. If a major 3rd above B is D♯, then the interval must be decreased in size by one half step to produce the minor 3rd. The B cannot be altered, as it is the given tone. Therefore, lowering the D♯ by one half step to D natural converts the major 3rd into a minor 3rd. B to D is a minor 3rd.

(4) The next step is to find an augmented 4th above the fifth, D. We know that a perfect 4th above D is G, as the key of D major has a G. Our task, however, is to find an augmented 4th above D. Raising the G one half step to G♯ transforms the perfect 4th (D/G) to an augmented 4th (D/G♯).

(5) Rearrange all of the elements of the chord so that it stands in root position and then check both the bottom and top thirds to make sure that the ordering of thirds up from the root is m3/m3.

(6) The diminished triad in $^6_3$ position above the given tone B is B D G♯.

Example 8–59

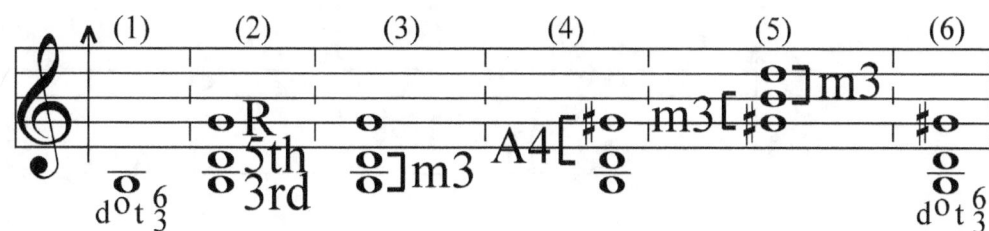

(1) Build a diminished triad above the given tone G♭ (example 8–60), understanding that the figured bass $^6_4$ indicates that G♭ is the fifth of the triad and the lowest note of the musical texture.
(2) Following the figured bass and using letter names rather than specific pitches initially, place a 4th and a 6th above the G♭ on the staff. The answer is C and E.
(3) The distance from the fifth up to the root of the diminished triad is an augmented 4th. We know that a perfect 4th above G♭ is C♭, as the key of G♭ major has a C♭. Our task, however, is to find an augmented 4th above G♭. We can increase the size of the perfect 4th by raising the C♭ one half step to C (natural). G♭ to C is an augmented 4th. The root of the chord is C.
(4) The distance from the root up to the third of the diminished triad is a minor 3rd. First of all, what is a major 3rd above C? The key of C major has neither flats nor sharps. And so, if a major 3rd above C is E (natural), then the interval must be decreased in size by one half step to produce the minor 3rd. The C cannot be altered, as it is the root of the triad. Therefore, lowering the E by one half step to E♭ converts the major 3rd into a minor 3rd. C to E♭ is a minor 3rd.
(5) Rearrange all of the elements of the chord so that it stands in root position and then check both the bottom and top thirds to make sure that the ordering of thirds up from the root is m3/m3.
(6) The diminished triad in $^6_4$ position above the given tone G♭ is G♭ C E♭.

Example 8–60

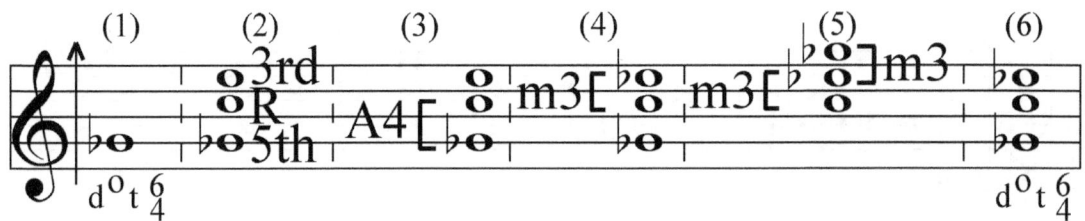

(1) Build an augmented triad above the given tone G (example 8–61), understanding that the figured bass $^6_3$ indicates that G is the third of the triad and the lowest note of the musical texture.
(2) Following the figured bass and using letter names rather than specific pitches initially, place a 3rd and a 6th above the G on the staff. The answer is B and E.
(3) The distance from the third up to the fifth of the augmented triad is a major 3rd. What is a major 3rd above G? The key of G major has one sharp, F♯. Therefore, G to B is a major 3rd.
(4) The next step is to find a diminished 4th above the fifth, B. We know that a perfect 4th above B is E, as the key of B major has an E. Our task, however, is to find a diminished 4th above B. We can decrease the size of the perfect 4th by lowering the E one half step to E♭. B to E♭ is a diminished 4th.
(5) Rearrange all of the elements of the chord so that it stands in root position and then check both the bottom and top thirds to make sure that the ordering of thirds up from the root is M3/M3.
(6) The augmented triad in $^6_3$ position above the given tone G is G B E♭.

Example 8–61

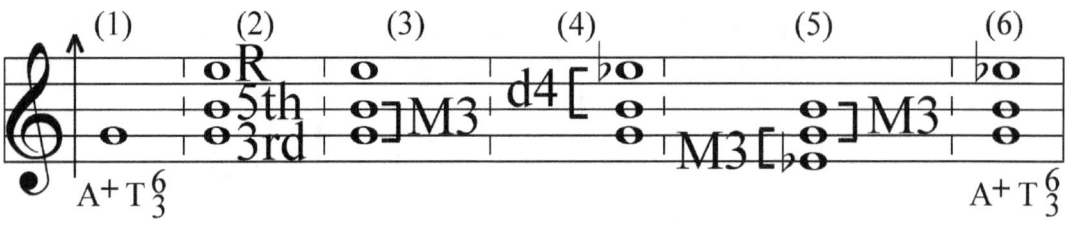

(1) Build an augmented triad above the given tone C𝄪 (example 8–62), understanding that the figured bass $^6_4$ indicates that C𝄪 is the fifth of the triad and the lowest note of the musical texture.

(2) Following the figured bass and using letter names rather than specific pitches initially, place a 4th and a 6th above the C𝄪 on the staff. The answer is F and A.

(3) The distance from the fifth up to the root of the augmented triad is a diminished 4th. What is a diminished 4th above C𝄪?

    (a) Since there is no key signature for C𝄪, remove one of the its two sharps.

    (b) Establish a perfect 4th above C♯ as F♯. (The key signature of C♯ major contains an F♯.)

    (c) Use the principle of like inflection to recognize that if C♯ to F♯ is a perfect 4th, then C𝄪 to F𝄪 is also a perfect 4th.

    (d) Decrease the size of the perfect 4th between C𝄪 and F𝄪 by lowering F𝄪 one half step to F♯. C𝄪 and F♯ is a diminished 4th.

(4) The next step is to find a major 3rd above the root, F♯. A major 3rd above F♯ is A♯, as the key of F♯ major has an A♯.

(5) Rearrange all of the elements of the chord so that it stands in root position and then check both the bottom and top thirds to make sure that the ordering of thirds up from the root is M3/M3.

(6) The augmented triad in $^6_4$ position above the given tone C𝄪 is C𝄪 F♯ A♯.

Example 8–62

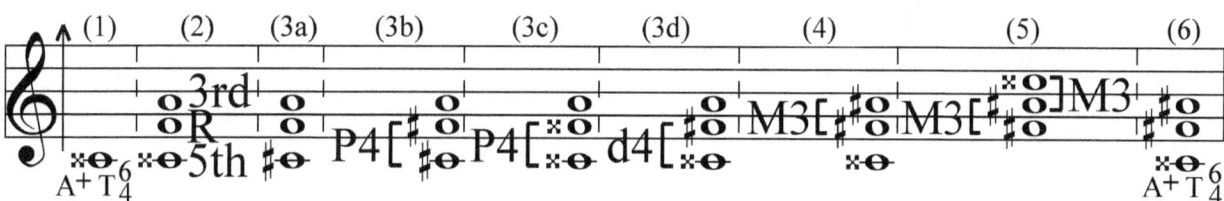

Enharmonic Respelling of Triads

Just as every pitch has at least one enharmonic equivalent, every triad can be respelled enharmonically. In some instances, the triad is easier to read if it is respelled with different letter names; in other situations, however, respelling the triad fails to improve the legibility of the chord.

    As demonstrated in example 8–63, there are times when it is better to respell the root, third, and fifth of the triad, especially if the chord contains double sharps or double flats. A chord with the pitches B♭ D F is easier to recognize as a major triad than one written as A♯ C𝄪 E♯ (8–63a). A diminished triad with the tones G♭ B♭♭ D♭♭ is harder to identify than the alternative F♯ A C (8–63b).

Example 8–63: enharmonic triads

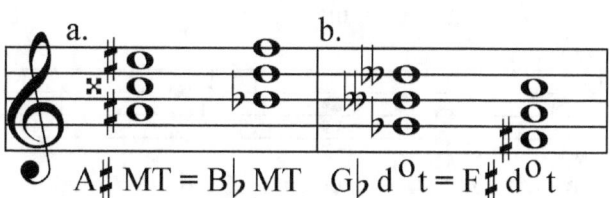

Note the respelled triads in examples 8–64a and 64b. There is virtually no difference between the C♯-major triad and the D♭-major triad (8–64a), nor between the G♭-major triad and the F♯-major triad (8–64b).

Example 8–64: enharmonic triads

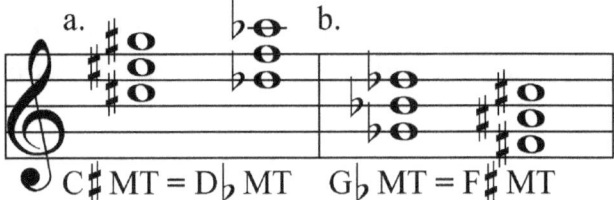

C♯ MT = D♭ MT   G♭ MT = F♯ MT

Triad Qualities in Minor

As we have said, the augmented triad cannot be formed in the major mode, nor can it appear in the natural minor. All four qualities of the triad do occur, however, in the other two forms of minor: the harmonic minor and the melodic minor. Since the melodic minor contains the most complete inventory of pitches of all three forms of minor, we shall use the melodic minor to demonstrate the formation of triads in the minor mode.

Before constructing triads in the minor mode, let us review the pitch content and half-step profile of the melodic minor in the key of C, as presented in example 8–65. Remember that the symbols ♯6 and ♯7 indicate the raised variable scale degrees of the ascending melodic minor and that ♭6 and ♭7 represent the lowered variable scale degrees of the descending melodic minor.

Example 8–65

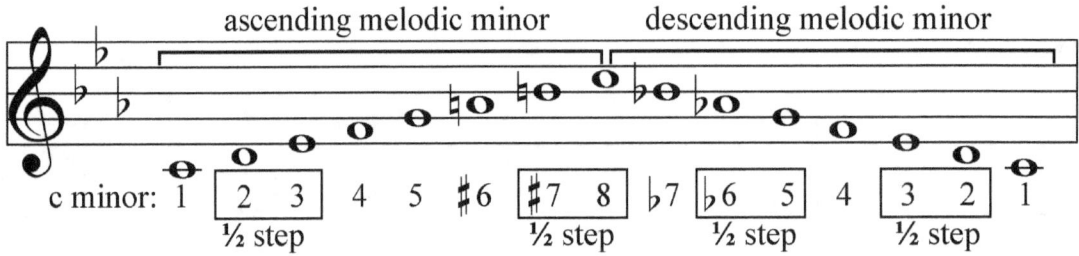

Example 8–66 shows the triads that occur in the ascending melodic minor. With the exception of the tonic triad (C E♭ G), all of the triads in the ascending melodic minor contain either variable ♯6 or variable ♯7 within their respective chord structures. The filled-in note heads in examples 8–66, 67, and 68 designate the variable scale degrees as the root, third, or fifth of the triad.

Using ♯6 (A) as the fifth of the chord, a minor triad (D F A) is formed in the supertonic area. An augmented triad (E♭ G B) occurs in the mediant, with ♯7 (B) as the fifth of the chord. Variables ♯6 and ♯7 appear as third components of two major triads: the subdominant (F A C) and the dominant (G B D). Variables ♯6 and ♯7 constitute the roots of two diminished triads: the submediant (A C E♭) and the leading tone (B D F).

Example 8–66: ascending melodic minor

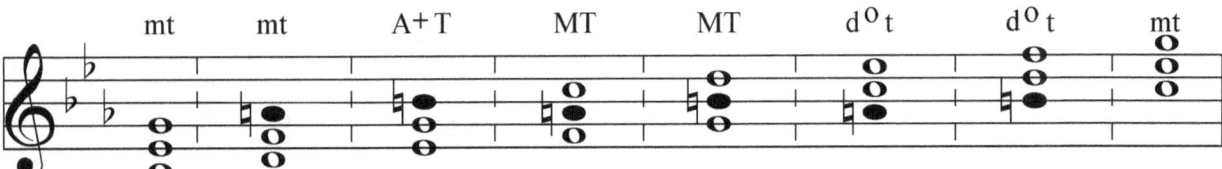

On the descending side of the melodic minor, as displayed in example 8–67, variable ♭7 (B♭) serves as the root of the major triad in the subtonic (B♭ D F) and as the fifth of the major triad in the mediant (E♭ G B♭); variable ♭6 (A♭) forms the root of the major triad in the submediant (A♭ C E♭). Excluding the tonic triad (C E♭ G), the descending melodic minor has two other minor triads, both of which contain a variable scale degree as an element of their chord structures. Variable ♭7 appears as the third of the minor dominant triad (G B♭ D); variable ♭6 constitutes the third of the minor subdominant triad (F A♭ C). Finally, variable ♭6 occurs as the fifth of the diminished supertonic triad (D F A♭).

Example 8–67: descending melodic minor

Example 8–68 incorporates elements of both the ascending and descending forms of the melodic minor into a single ascending scale that projects various chord qualities in each of its seven scale degree areas for a total of thirteen triads. Comparing the number and qualities of triads available in the melodic minor with the triad content of both the natural minor and the harmonic minor, as presented in examples 8–69 and 70, we can see that the melodic minor yields a much richer vocabulary of chords than either the natural minor or harmonic minor.

Example 8–68: the thirteen triads of the melodic minor

Example 8–69: the seven triads of the natural minor

Example 8–70: the seven triads of the harmonic minor

Roman Numeral Chord Symbols

In Chapter 3, we learned that each note of the scale and mode can be referred to as a scale degree and assigned a number according to its position within the scale in relation to the tonic pitch, with the tonic identified as scale degree 1. Additionally, each scale degree has one of the following names: tonic, supertonic, mediant, subdominant, dominant, submediant, and leading tone. When scale degree 7 is located one whole step below the tonic note, as in the natural minor, we use the term subtonic to distinguish it from the leading tone of the major mode, the harmonic minor, and the ascending form of the melodic minor. The subtonic lacks the compelling drive to move upwards by half step to scale degree 8, the tonic.

Ultimately, the numbers and names that represent the scale degrees of the mode constitute an important means for providing information about music; as such, the numbers and names are referential, serving as symbols for communication between those who create music and those who listen to and/or study it. Another method for providing information about music designates Roman numerals for the chords that can be formed on each scale degree of the mode; in other words, it is possible to represent each chord, or triad, with a Roman numeral according to the scale degree on which its root occurs. A longstanding convention of Roman numeral chord symbols maintains the following two practices:

(1) if the chord, or triad, has a major 3rd between the root and its third, then the Roman numeral is expressed in uppercase (e.g., major and augmented triads);
(2) if the chord, or triad, has a minor 3rd between the root and its third, then the Roman numeral is expressed in lowercase (e.g., minor and diminished triads).

Both practices cited here are related to the use of the uppercase for major and augmented intervals and the lowercase for minor and diminished intervals. The two practices also correspond to the designation of major modes with uppercase letters and minor modes with lowercase letters.

In addition to using uppercase and lowercase Roman numerals to distinguish major and augmented triads from minor and diminished triads, augmented triads are further identified with a plus sign (+), diminished triads with a superscript circle (°). As stated earlier, the plus sign is the traditional designation for showing augmented quality, while the superscript circle is a conventional sign for indicating diminished quality.

Example 8–71 presents the Roman numeral chord symbols for the triads that occur in the major mode. The three major triads are indicated as I, IV, and V, the minor triads as ii, iii, and vi, and the diminished triad as vii°.

Example 8–71

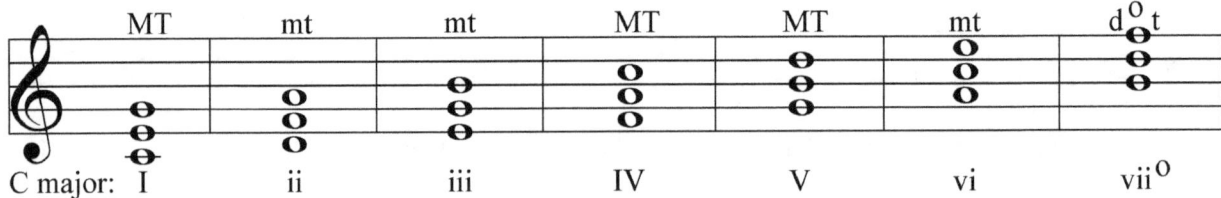

Notice that scale degree 3 in C major stands one *major* 3rd above the tonic pitch and that the quality of the mediant triad formed above scale degree 3 is minor (E G B). Conversely, the intervallic relationship between scale degree 3 and the tonic pitch in c minor, as shown in example 8–72 below, is that of a *minor* 3rd. Moreover, the quality of the mediant triad in the minor mode presents two possibilities: major and augmented. Finding the right pitch upon which the mediant triad is formed in the major mode and in the minor mode and distinguishing between the respective qualities of the chord in both modes counts among the most difficult challenges confronting the student of music fundamentals.

Mastering the triadic content of the melodic minor constitutes a formidable challenge indeed, as it has a much richer vocabulary of chords than either the major mode, the natural minor, or the harmonic minor (compare examples 8–68, 69, 70, and 71 above). Example 8–72 revisits the thirteen triads that are formable above each scale degree of the melodic minor. The increased number of triads in the melodic minor is attributed to the presence of variable scale degrees 6 and 7 as either the root, third, or fifth elements of each chord (again, the filled-in note heads designate the variable scale degrees).

Except for the tonic triad, the basic quality for triads in the melodic minor is determined by the presence of a variable scale degree and identified with uppercase and lowercase Roman numerals and the addition of either the plus sign for the augmented triad or the superscript circle for the diminished triad. If the root of the triad is a variable scale degree, then the Roman numeral is preceded by either a flat or a sharp (8–72), just as the individual pitches for the variable scale degrees of the melodic minor are indicated as either ♯6 and ♯7 or ♭6 and ♭7.

As we have said, the use of a sharp or a flat in front of the variable scale degree does not necessarily mean that the pitch carries either a sharp or a flat; rather, the sharp or flat indicates that the pitch is either raised or lowered (see above, pp. 82–84). We apply the same principle to the flat or sharp in front of the Roman numeral. Thus, the major triads of the melodic minor are represented as III, IV, V, ♭VI, and ♭VII, the minor triads as i, ii, iv, and v, the diminished triads as ii°, ♯vi°, and ♯vii°, and the augmented triad as III+.

Example 8–72

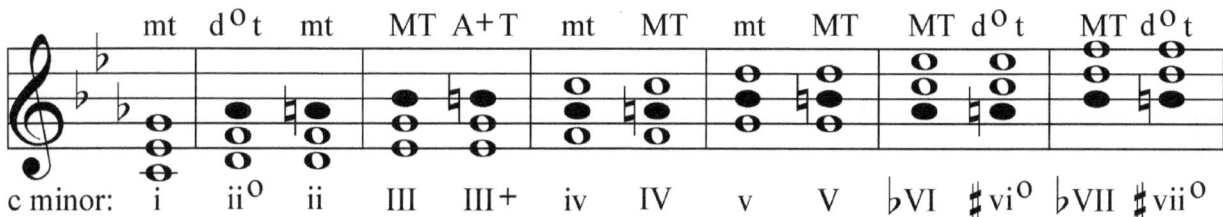

The following list is a guide for verbalizing the Roman numeral chord symbols for the minor mode. As demonstrated in example 8–72, there is more than one chord quality available in every scale degree area of the melodic minor except for the tonic. The quality of the triad is included in the description for the supertonic, mediant, subdominant, and dominant areas. The triads of the ♭VI, the ♯vi°, the ♭VII, and the ♯vii°, however, are all distinguished from one another without including the chord quality in the description. Since there is only one quality for the triad formed on scale degree 1 of the minor mode, we omit the reference to the quality of the chord and describe it simply as "the tonic triad."

Triads with Lowered Variables

ii°	the diminished supertonic triad
III	the major mediant triad
iv	the minor subdominant triad
v	the minor dominant triad
♭VI	the lowered submediant triad
♭VII	the subtonic triad

Triads with Raised Variables

ii	the minor supertonic triad
III+	the augmented mediant triad
IV	the major subdominant triad
V	the major dominant triad
♯vi°	the raised submediant triad
♯vii°	the leading-tone triad

The various chord symbols shown above enable us to determine easily whether the quality of the triad is major (uppercase letters), minor (lowercase letters), diminished (lowercase letters with a superscript circle) or augmented (uppercase letters with a plus sign).

As with the tonic triad of the minor mode, the triads for the major mode can be described more simply because there is only one chord quality for each scale degree area:

I   the tonic triad
ii   the supertonic triad
iii   the mediant triad
IV   the subdominant triad
V   the dominant triad
vi   the submediant triad
vii°   the leading-tone triad

Contextualization of Triads

Now that we have explored the possibilities for triads appearing in C major and c minor, let us place some of these chords within the context of key centers other than C: first, in root position, and subsequently, in $^6_3$ and $^6_4$ positions. As the examples in this section demonstrate, whenever a Roman numeral represents a triad in root position, it is not necessary to use figured bass to indicate the chord position; for the absence of $^5_3$ implies that the chord is in root position. Whenever a Roman numeral represents a triad in $^6_3$ position, it is not necessary to include 3 under 6. With the $^6_4$ position, however, 4 below 6 cannot be removed because the omission of the 4 would render the figured bass for the first and second inversions indistinguishable.

Triads in $^5_3$ Position

(1) Given the key, mode, clef, and chord symbol, construct the appropriate triad (example 8–73).
(2) The key and mode is F♯ major.
 (a) The uppercase letter F designates the major mode.
 (b) The Roman numeral iii denotes the triad of the mediant.
 (c) The lowercase iii means that the quality of the triad is minor.
(3) Find the root of the mediant triad by locating scale degree 3 of F♯ major. F♯ major has six sharps, one of which is A♯. A♯ is scale degree 3 and the root of the mediant triad. In the major mode, scale degree 3 is a major 3rd above scale degree 1 (F♯).
(4) Construct an A♯-minor triad using any of the methods presented earlier in this chapter. F♯ major also has a C♯ and E♯. Therefore, the iii chord in F♯ major is A♯ C♯ E♯.

Example 8–73

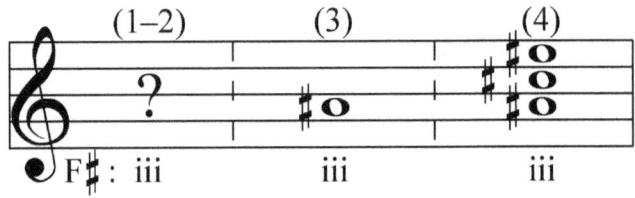

Let us consider the pitch content for the mediant triad within the context of f♯ minor, the parallel minor of F♯ major. The following problem brings into focus the challenge of the mediant triad mentioned earlier (see above, p. 140); as we have said, the intervallic distance between the tonic and scale degree 3 is a minor 3rd. Unlike the pitch content of the major mode, which allows only one possible triad quality in the mediant area, the pitch content of the melodic minor supports the formation of both the major and augmented triad.

(1) Given the key, mode, clef, and chord symbol, construct the appropriate triad (example 8–74). Again, the absence of $^5_3$ implies that the chord is in root position.
(2) The key and mode is f♯ minor.
   (a) The lowercase letter f designates the minor mode.
   (b) The Roman numeral III denotes the triad of the mediant.
   (c) The uppercase III and absence of the plus sign means that the quality of the triad is major (rather than augmented).
(3) Find the root of the mediant triad by locating scale degree 3 of f♯ minor. The key and mode of f♯ minor has three sharps: F♯, C♯, and G♯. A is scale degree 3 of f♯ minor.
(4) Construct an A-major triad. The major triad in the mediant area of the melodic minor uses scale degrees 3, 5, and ♭7 as the its root, third, and fifth respectively (to review the structure and pitch content of the III chord in c minor, see example 8–72 above). Since the lowered variables are *always* indicated in the key signature of the minor mode, use the key signature of f♯ minor to find ♭7. Therefore, ♭7 (E natural) is in the key signature of f♯ minor. The III chord in f♯ minor is A C♯ E.

Example 8–74

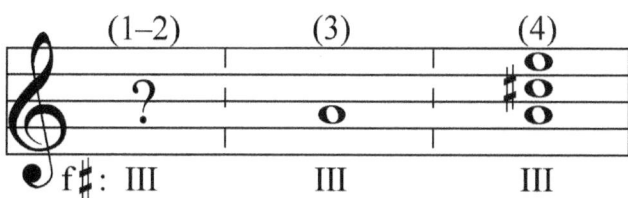

(1) Given the key, mode, clef, and chord symbol, construct the appropriate triad (example 8–75).
(2) The key and mode is f♯ minor. Both the uppercase III and the presence of the plus sign indicate that the quality of the triad is augmented.
(3) Find the root of the mediant triad by locating scale degree 3 of f♯ minor. The answer is A.
(4) Construct an A-augmented triad. The fifth of the augmented triad in the mediant area of the melodic minor uses scale degree ♯7, the leading tone. Since the raised variables are *never* indicated in the key signature of the minor mode, use any of the methods presented in Chapter 6 for locating ♯7. For example, find variable ♭7 (E) using the minor key signature; variable ♯7 (E♯) is one half step higher. The III+ chord in f♯ minor is A C♯ E♯.
(5) Finally, as stated above, the fifth of the augmented mediant is the leading tone (♯7), a scale degree that usually seeks to move upwards by half step to scale degree 8. Accordingly, the E♯ in 8–75 proceeds upwards by half step to F♯. Notice that if we repeat both the root and third of the mediant triad as the fifth moves to scale degree 8, the operation produces the pitches A C♯ F♯, the tonic triad in first inversion. As shown below, then, the augmented triad is usually not autonomous; typically, the augmented triad is associated with another chord. (Whenever a Roman numeral is used to represent a triad in $^6_3$ position, *it is not necessary to include 3 under 6*. And so, the first-inversion tonic is expressed here as i^6 rather than as i$^6_3$.)

Example 8–75

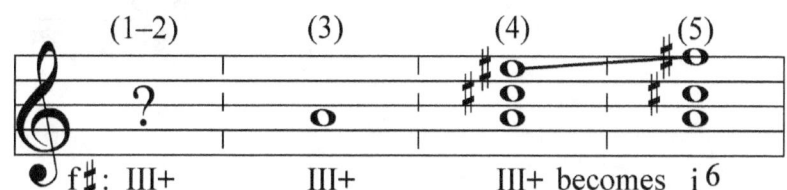

We shall now turn our attention to some of the other triads that occur in the major and minor modes, starting with the submediant.

(1) Given the key, mode, clef, and chord symbol, construct the appropriate triad (example 8–76).
(2) The key and mode is B♭ major.
  (a) The uppercase letter B designates the major mode.
  (b) The Roman numeral vi denotes the triad of the submediant.
  (c) The lowercase vi means that the quality of the triad is minor.
  (d) Note carefully that *the third element of any submediant triad is scale degree 1, the tonic pitch.*
(3) Find the root of the submediant triad by locating scale degree 6 of B♭ major. B♭ major has two flats: B♭ and E♭. In the major mode, scale degree 6 is a major 6th above scale degree 1 (B♭). G is scale degree 6 and the root of the submediant triad.
(4) Construct a G-minor triad. In addition to having two flats, B♭ major has a D (natural). Since the third element of any submediant triad is scale degree 1, the vi chord in B♭ major is G B♭ D.

Example 8–76

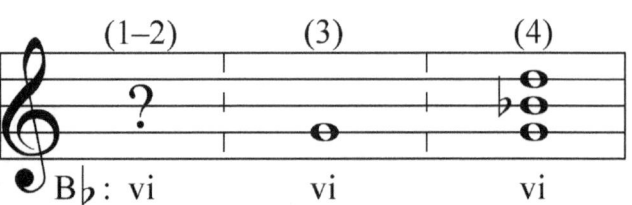

(1) Given the key, mode, clef, and chord symbol, construct the appropriate triad (example 8–77).
(2) The key and mode is b♭ minor.
  (a) The lowercase letter b designates the minor mode.
  (b) The Roman numeral VI denotes a triad on one of the variable 6 scale degrees in minor.
  (c) Both the uppercase VI and the absence of the superscript circle indicate that the quality of the triad is major.
  (d) The flat in front of the numeral VI identifies variable ♭6 as the root of the lowered submediant triad.
(3) Find the root of the lowered submediant triad by locating variable ♭6 of b♭ minor. Since the lowered variables are *always* indicated in the key signature of the minor mode; use the key signature of b♭ minor to find ♭6. The key and mode of b♭ minor has five flats: B♭, E♭, A♭, D♭, and G♭. The root of the lowered submediant triad is G♭.
(4) Construct a G♭-major triad. The fifth of the ♭VI chord is D♭, scale degree 3 of the key and mode. Since the third of any submediant triad is scale degree 1, the ♭VI chord in b♭ minor is G♭ B♭ D♭.

Example 8–77

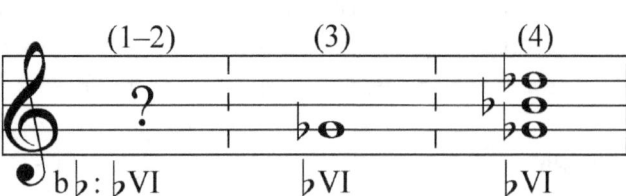

(1) Given the key, mode, clef, and chord symbol, construct the appropriate triad (example 8–78).
(2) The key and mode is b♭ minor.
    (a) The lowercase letter b designates the minor mode.
    (b) The Roman numeral vi denotes a triad on one of the variable 6 scale degrees in minor.
    (c) Both the lowercase vi and the presence of the superscript circle indicate that the quality of the triad is diminished.
    (d) The sharp in front of the numeral vi identifies variable ♯6 as the root of the raised submediant triad.
(3) Find the root of the raised submediant triad by locating variable ♯6 of b♭ minor. Variable ♯6 is *never* indicated in the key signature of the minor mode; however, variable ♯6 corresponds to scale degree 6 of the parallel major mode, B♭ major, and is therefore a major 6th above scale degree 1. The root of the raised submediant triad is G.
(4) Construct a G-diminished triad. The key and mode of b♭ minor has five flats: B♭, E♭, A♭, D♭, and G♭. The fifth of the ♯vi° chord is D♭, scale degree 3 of the key and mode. Since the third of any submediant triad is scale degree 1, the ♯vi° chord in b♭ minor is G B♭ D♭.

Example 8–78

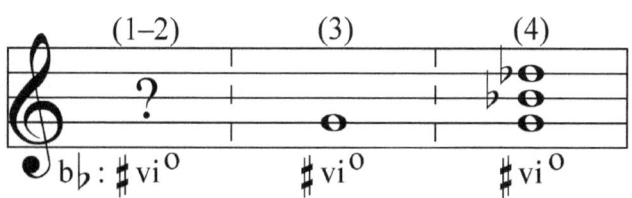

(1) Given the key, mode, clef, and chord symbol, construct the appropriate triad (example 8–79).
(2) The key and mode is E major.
    (a) The uppercase letter E designates the major mode.
    (b) The Roman numeral ii denotes the triad of the supertonic.
    (c) The lowercase ii means that the quality of the triad is minor.
(3) Find the root of the supertonic triad by locating scale degree 2 of E major. E major has four sharps: F♯, C♯, G♯, and D♯. F♯ is scale degree 2 and the root of the supertonic triad. In both the major mode and the minor mode, scale degree 2 is a major 2nd above scale degree 1.
(4) Construct an F♯-minor triad using any of the methods presented earlier in this chapter. E major also has an A (natural). Therefore, the ii chord in E major is F♯ A C♯.

Example 8–79

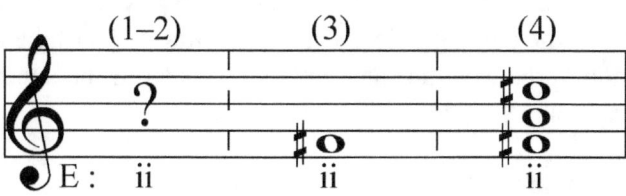

(1) Given the key, mode, clef, and chord symbol, construct the appropriate triad (example 8–80).
(2) The key and mode is e minor.
   (a) The lowercase letter e designates the minor mode.
   (b) The Roman numeral ii denotes the triad of the supertonic.
   (c) The lowercase ii and presence of the superscript circle indicate that the quality of the triad is diminished.
(3) Find the root of the diminished supertonic triad by locating scale degree 2 of e minor. The key and mode of e minor has one sharp: F♯. F♯ is scale degree 2 and the root of the supertonic triad.
(4) Construct an F♯-diminished triad. The diminished triad in the supertonic area of the melodic minor uses scale degrees 2, 4, and ♭6 as the its root, third, and fifth respectively (to review the structure and pitch content of the ii° chord in c minor, see example 8–72 above). Since the lowered variables are *always* indicated in the key signature of the minor mode, use the key signature of e minor to find ♭6. Variable ♭6 in the key and mode of e minor is C (natural). Therefore, the ii° chord in e minor is F♯ A C.

Example 8–80

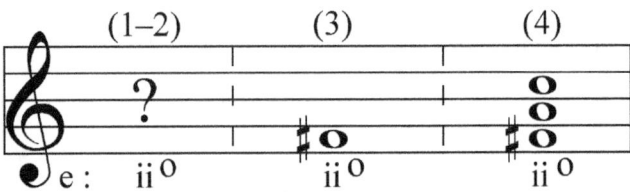

(1) Given the key, mode, clef, and chord symbol, construct the appropriate triad (example 8–81).
(2) The key and mode is e minor.
   (a) The lowercase letter e designates the minor mode.
   (b) The Roman numeral ii denotes the triad of the supertonic.
   (c) The lowercase ii and absence of the superscript circle indicate that the quality of the triad is minor.
(3) Find the root of the minor supertonic triad by locating scale degree 2 of e minor. The key and mode of e minor has one sharp: F♯. F♯ is scale degree 2 and the root of the supertonic triad.
(4) Construct an F♯-minor triad. The minor triad in the supertonic area of the melodic minor uses variable ♯6 as its fifth. Variable ♯6 is *never* indicated in the key signature of the minor mode; however, variable ♯6 corresponds to scale degree 6 of the parallel major mode, E major. Scale degree 6 of E major is C♯, a major 6th above the tonic note. Therefore, the fifth of the minor supertonic is C♯. The ii chord in e minor is F♯ A C♯.

Note: the correspondence between variable ♯6 of the minor mode and scale degree 6 of the parallel major mode produces the same F♯-minor triad in the supertonic area of both E major and e minor (compare examples 8–79 and 81).

Example 8–81

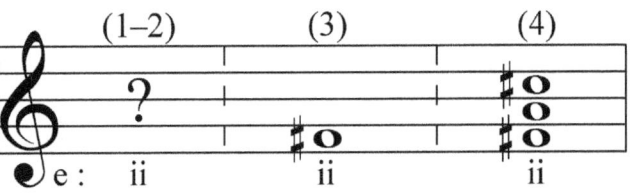

(1) Given the key, mode, clef, and chord symbol, construct the appropriate triad (example 8–82).
(2) The key and mode is E♭ major.
   (a) The uppercase letter E designates the major mode.
   (b) The Roman numeral vii denotes the triad of the leading tone.
   (c) Both the lowercase vii and the presence of the superscript circle indicate that the quality of the triad is diminished.
(3) Find the root of the leading-tone triad by locating scale degree 7 of E♭ major. E♭ major has three flats: B♭, E♭, and A♭. D is scale degree 7 and the root of the leading-tone triad.
(4) Construct a D-diminished triad. The leading-tone triad in the major mode uses scale degrees 7, 2, and 4 as the root, third, and fifth respectively. In addition to having an A♭ as scale degree 4, E♭ major has an F as scale degree 2. Therefore, the vii° chord in E♭ major is D F A♭.

Example 8–82

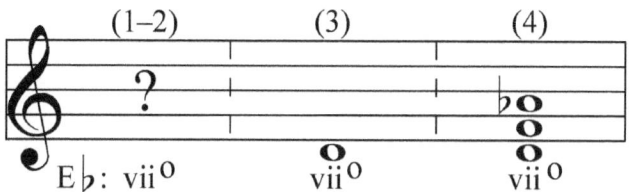

(1) Given the key, mode, clef, and chord symbol, construct the appropriate triad (example 8–83).
(2) The key and mode is e♭ minor.
   (a) The lowercase letter e designates the minor mode.
   (b) The Roman numeral vii denotes a triad on one of the variable 7 scale degrees in minor.
   (c) Both the lowercase vii and the presence of the superscript circle indicate that the quality of the triad is diminished.
   (d) The sharp in front of the numeral vii identifies variable ♯7 as the root of the leading-tone triad.
(3) Find the root of the leading-tone triad by locating variable ♯7 of e♭ minor. Variable ♯7 is *never* indicated in the key signature of the minor mode; however, variable ♯7 corresponds to scale degree 7 of the parallel major mode, E♭ major, and is therefore a major 7th above scale degree 1. The root of the leading-tone triad is D.
(4) Construct a D-diminished triad. The key and mode of e♭ minor has six flats: B♭, E♭, A♭, D♭, G♭, and C♭. The third of the ♯vii° chord is F (natural), scale degree 2. The fifth of the ♯vii° chord is A♭, scale degree 4. Therefore, the ♯vii° chord in e♭ minor is D F A♭.

Note: the correspondence between variable ♯7 of the minor mode and scale degree 7 of the parallel major mode produces the same D-diminished triad in the leading-tone area of both E♭ major and e♭ minor (compare examples 8–82 and 83).

Example 8–83

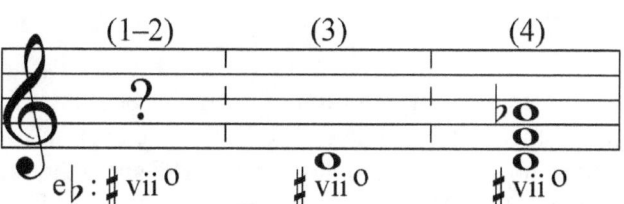

148   Chapter 8 Triads

(1) Given the key, mode, clef, and chord symbol, construct the appropriate triad (example 8–84).
(2) The key and mode is e♭ minor.
   (a) The lowercase letter e designates the minor mode.
   (b) The Roman numeral VII denotes a triad on one of the variable 7 scale degrees in minor.
   (c) Both the uppercase VII and the absence of the superscript circle indicate that the quality of the triad is major.
   (d) The flat in front of the VII identifies the subtonic scale degree (♭7) as the root of the triad.
(3) Find the root of the subtonic triad by locating variable ♭7 of e♭ minor. Since the lowered variables are *always* indicated in the key signature of the minor mode; use the key signature of e♭ minor to find ♭7. The key and mode of e♭ minor has six flats: B♭, E♭, A♭, D♭, G♭, and C♭. The root of the subtonic triad is D♭.
(4) Construct a D♭-major triad. The third of the ♭VII chord is F, scale degree 2 of the key and mode. The fifth of the ♭VII chord is A♭, scale degree 4 of the key and mode. Therefore, the ♭VII chord in e♭ minor is D♭ F A♭.

Example 8–84

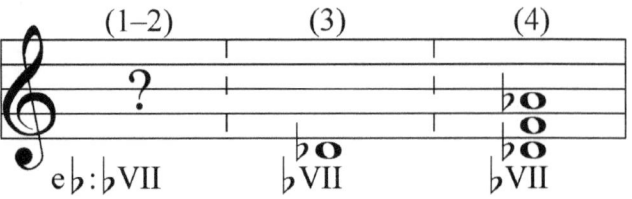

(1) Given the key, mode, clef, and chord symbol, construct the appropriate triad (example 8–85).
(2) The key and mode is A♭ major.
   (a) The uppercase letter A designates the major mode.
   (b) The Roman numeral IV denotes the triad of the subdominant.
   (c) The uppercase IV indicates that the quality of the triad is major.
   (d) Note carefully that *the fifth element of any subdominant triad in both the major and minor modes is scale degree 1, the tonic pitch.*
(3) Find the root of the subdominant triad by locating scale degree 4 of A♭ major. A♭ major has four flats: B♭, E♭, A♭, and D♭. In the major mode (and in the minor mode), scale degree 4 is a perfect 4th above scale degree 1. D♭ is scale degree 4 and the root of the subdominant triad.
(4) Construct a D♭-major triad. Standing a major 3rd above the root, the third of the D♭-major triad is F, scale degree 6 of A♭ major. Since the fifth element of any subdominant triad in the major or minor mode is scale degree 1, the IV chord in A♭ major is D♭ F A♭.

Example 8–85

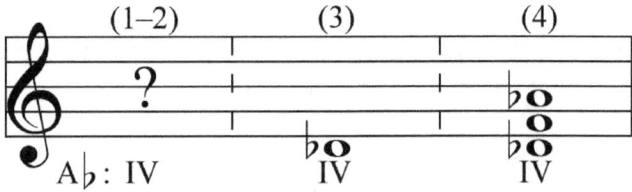

    From our consideration of examples 8–79, 81, 82, and 83, we conclude that it is possible for parallel modes to share the same chord. Before we examine another chord within the context of two more parallel modes, notice that examples 8–84 and 85 show the same chord occurring within two different keys; in this instance, the D♭-major triad can be either a chord of the subtonic in e♭ minor or a chord of the subdominant in A♭ major.

(1) Given the key, mode, clef, and chord symbol, construct the appropriate triad (example 8–86).
(2) The key and mode is a♭ minor.
   (a) The lowercase letter a designates the minor mode.
   (b) The Roman numeral IV denotes the triad of the subdominant.
   (c) The uppercase IV indicates that the quality of the triad is major.
   (d) Again, the fifth element of any subdominant triad in the major or minor mode is scale degree 1, the tonic pitch.
(3) Find the root of the major subdominant triad by locating scale degree 4 of a♭ minor. The key and mode of a♭ minor has seven flats: B♭, E♭, A♭, D♭, G♭, C♭, and F♭. As in the major mode, scale degree 4 of the minor mode is a perfect 4th above scale degree 1 (A♭). D♭ is scale degree 4 and the root of the major subdominant triad.
(4) Construct a D♭-major triad. Standing a major 3rd above the root, the third of the D♭-major triad is F, variable ♯6 of a♭ minor. Variable ♯6 is *never* indicated in the key signature of the minor mode; however, variable ♯6 corresponds to scale degree 6 of the parallel major mode, A♭ major. Scale degree 6 of A♭ major is F, a major 6th above the tonic note. The fifth element of the major subdominant triad is scale degree 1; therefore, the IV chord in a♭ minor is D♭ F A♭.

Note: the correspondence between variable ♯6 of the minor mode and scale degree 6 of the parallel major mode produces the same D♭-major triad in the subdominant area of both A♭ major and a♭ minor (compare examples 8–85 and 86)

Example 8–86

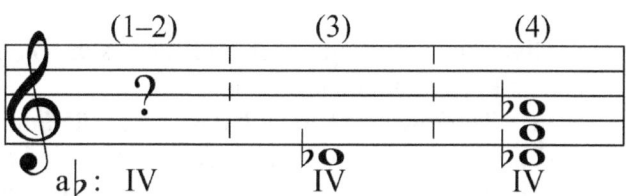

(1) Given the key, mode, clef, and chord symbol, construct the appropriate triad (example 8–87).
(2) The key and mode is a♭ minor.
   (a) The lowercase letter a designates the minor mode.
   (b) The Roman numeral iv denotes the triad of the subdominant.
   (c) The lowercase iv indicates that the quality of the triad is minor.
(3) Find the root of the minor subdominant triad by locating scale degree 4 of a♭ minor. As in example 8–86 above, D♭ is scale degree 4 and the root of the chord.
(4) Construct a D♭-minor triad. Standing a minor 3rd above the root, the third of the D♭-minor triad is F♭, variable ♭6 of a♭ minor. As we have said, the lowered variables are *always* reflected in the key signature of the minor mode. Therefore, the iv chord in a♭ minor is D♭ F♭ A♭.

Example 8–87

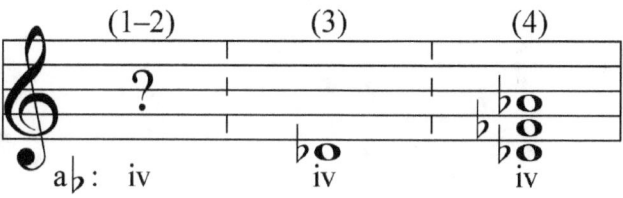

150   Chapter 8 Triads

(1) Given the key, mode, clef, and chord symbol, construct the appropriate triad (example 8–88).
(2) The key and mode is B major.
   (a) The uppercase letter B designates the major mode.
   (b) The Roman numeral V denotes the triad of the dominant.
   (c) The uppercase V means that the quality of the triad is major.
   (d) *Note carefully that the third element of any major triad of the dominant in both the major and minor modes is scale degree 7 or variable ♯7 respectively, the leading tone.*
(3) Find the root of the dominant triad by locating scale degree 5 of B major. B major has five sharps: F♯, C♯, G♯, D♯, and A♯. F♯ is scale degree 5 and the root of the dominant triad. In both the major mode and the minor mode, scale degree 5 is a perfect 5th above scale degree 1 (B).
(4) Construct an F♯-major triad. A♯ is the leading tone of B major and therefore the third of the dominant. The V chord in B major is F♯ A♯ C♯.

Example 8–88

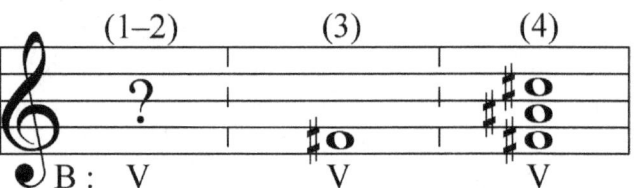

(1) Given the key, mode, clef, and chord symbol, construct the appropriate triad (example 8–89).
(2) The key and mode is b minor.
   (a) The lowercase letter b designates the minor mode.
   (b) The Roman numeral V denotes the triad of the dominant.
   (c) The uppercase V means that the quality of the triad is major.
   (d) Again, the third element of any major triad of the dominant in both the major and minor modes is scale degree 7 or variable ♯7 respectively, the leading tone.
(3) Find the root of the major dominant triad by locating scale degree 5 of b minor. The key and mode of b minor has two sharps: F♯ and C♯. As in 8–88 above, F♯ is scale degree 5 and the root of the dominant triad.
(4) Construct an F♯-major triad. A♯ is variable ♯7, the leading tone of b minor, and therefore the third of the dominant. The V chord in b minor is F♯ A♯ C♯.

Note: the correspondence between variable ♯7 of the minor mode and scale degree 7 of the parallel major mode produces the same F♯-major triad in the dominant area of both B major and b minor (compare examples 8–88 and 89).

Example 8–89

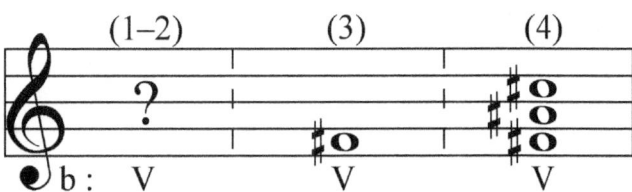

(1) Given the key, mode, clef, and chord symbol, construct the appropriate triad (example 8–90).
(2) The key and mode is b minor.
   (a) The lowercase letter b designates the minor mode.
   (b) The Roman numeral v denotes the triad of the dominant.
   (c) The lowercase v means that the quality of the triad is minor.
   (d) Note carefully that *the third element of any minor triad of the dominant in the minor mode is variable ♭7, the subtonic pitch.*
(3) Find the root of the minor dominant triad by locating scale degree 5 of b minor. As in examples 8–88 and 89 above, F♯ is scale degree 5 and the root of the dominant triad.
(4) Construct an F♯-minor triad. A is variable ♭7, the subtonic of b minor, and therefore the third of the minor dominant. The v chord in b minor is F♯ A C♯.

Example 8–90

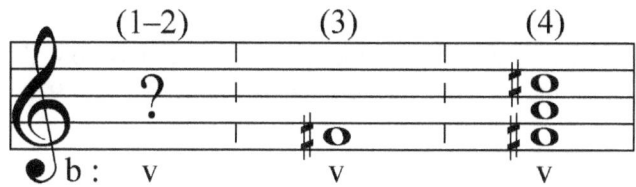

Triads in $\frac{6}{3}$ and $\frac{6}{4}$ Positions

(1) Given the key, mode, clef, chord symbol, *and* figured bass, construct the appropriate triad (example 8–91).
(2) The key and mode is A major.
(3) Find the root of the leading-tone triad by locating scale degree 7 of A major. The key of A major has three sharps: F♯, C♯, and G♯. G♯ is scale degree 7 and the root of the leading-tone triad.
(4) Construct a G♯-diminished triad in $\frac{5}{3}$ position. The leading-tone triad in the major mode uses scale degrees 7, 2, and 4 as the root, third, and fifth respectively. Therefore, the vii° chord in $\frac{5}{3}$ position in A major is G♯ B D.
(5) Once the G♯-diminished triad has been constructed in $\frac{5}{3}$ position, move the root of the chord up one octave so that the third of the chord is exposed as the lowest note of the musical texture. With the third in the bass (B), the chord is in $\frac{6}{3}$ position, first inversion. (Again, whenever a Roman numeral is used to represent a triad in $\frac{6}{3}$ position, *it is not necessary to include 3 under 6.* Therefore, the leading-tone triad shown below is expressed as vii°⁶ rather than as vii°$\frac{6}{3}$.)

Example 8–91

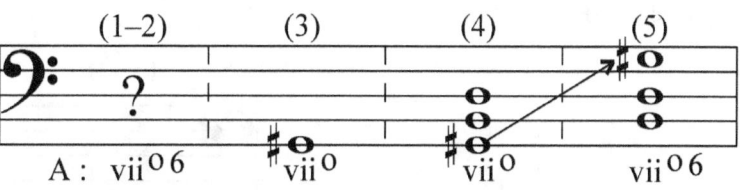

(1) Given the key, mode, clef, chord symbol, *and* figured bass, construct the appropriate triad (example 8–92).
(2) The key and mode is a minor.
(3) Find the root of the leading-tone triad by locating variable ♯7 of a minor. Variable ♯7 corresponds to scale degree 7 of the parallel major mode, A major; therefore, the root of the leading-tone triad is G♯.
(4) Construct a G♯-diminished triad in $\frac{5}{3}$ position. The leading-tone triad in the minor mode uses scale degrees ♯7, 2, and 4 as the root, third, and fifth respectively. In the key and mode of a minor, the ♯vii° chord in $\frac{5}{3}$ position is G♯ B D.
(5) Once the G♯-diminished triad has been constructed in $\frac{5}{3}$ position, move the root of the chord up one octave so that the third of the chord is exposed as the lowest note of the musical texture. With the third in the bass (B), the chord is in $\frac{6}{3}$ position, first inversion.

Note: as stated in step 3 above, the correspondence between variable ♯7 of the minor mode and scale degree 7 of the parallel major mode produces the same G♯-diminished triad in the leading-tone area of both A major and a minor (compare examples 8–91 and 92).

Example 8–92

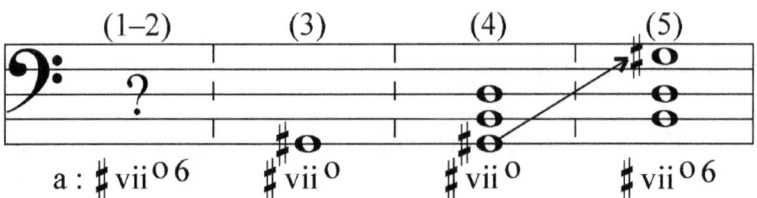

(1) Given the key, mode, clef, chord symbol, *and* figured bass, construct the appropriate triad (example 8–93).
(2) The key and mode is a minor.
(3) Find the root of the subtonic triad by locating variable ♭7 of a minor. Since the lowered variables are *always* indicated in the key signature of the minor mode; use the key signature of a minor to find ♭7. The key and mode of a minor has neither flats nor sharps. The root of the subtonic triad is G.
(4) Construct a G-major triad in $\frac{5}{3}$ position. The ♭VII chord in a minor is G B D.
(5) Once the G-major triad has been constructed in $\frac{5}{3}$ position, move both the root and third of the chord (G and B) up one octave so that the fifth of the chord is exposed as the lowest note of the musical texture. With the fifth in the bass (D), the chord is in $\frac{6}{4}$ position, second inversion.

Example 8–93

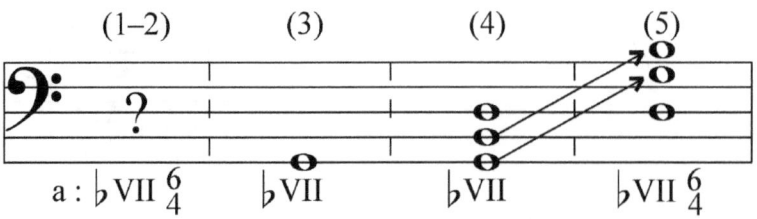

(1) Given the key, mode, clef, chord symbol, *and* figured bass, construct the appropriate triad (example 8–94).
(2) The key and mode is D major.
(3) Find the root of the dominant triad by locating scale degree 5 of D major. D major has two sharps: F♯ and C♯. A is scale degree 5 and the root of the dominant triad.
(4) Construct an A-major triad in $^5_3$ position. C♯ is the leading tone of D major and therefore the third of the dominant. The V chord in D major is A C♯ E.
(5) Once the A-major triad has been constructed in $^5_3$ position, move the fifth of the chord (E) down one octave so that it becomes the lowest note of the musical texture. With the fifth in the bass, the chord is in $^6_4$ position, second inversion.

Example 8–94

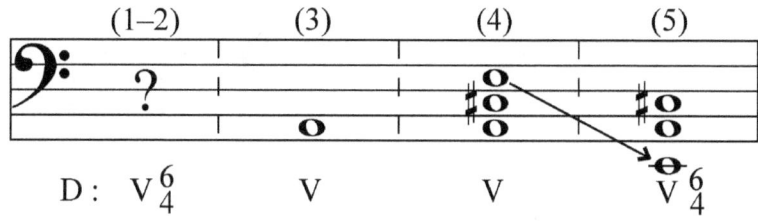

(1) Given the key, mode, clef, chord symbol, *and* figured bass, construct the appropriate triad (example 8–95).
(2) The key and mode is d minor.
(3) Find the root of the major dominant triad by locating scale degree 5 of d minor. The key and mode of d minor has one flat: B♭. A is scale degree 5 and the root of the dominant triad.
(4) Construct an A-major triad in $^5_3$ position. C♯ is variable ♯7, the leading tone of d minor, and therefore the third of the dominant. The V chord in d minor is A C♯ E.
(5) Once the A-major triad has been constructed in $^5_3$ position, move fifth of the chord (E) down one octave so that it becomes the lowest note of the musical texture. With the fifth in the bass, the chord is in $^6_4$ position, second inversion.

Note: the correspondence between variable ♯7 of the minor mode and scale degree 7 of the parallel major mode produces the same A-major triad in the dominant area of both D major and d minor (compare examples 8–94 and 95).

Example 8–95

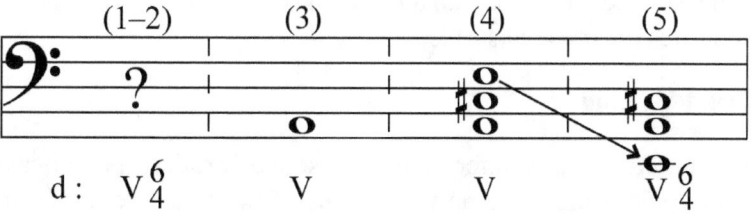

(1) Given the key, mode, clef, chord symbol, *and* figured bass, construct the appropriate triad (example 8–96).
(2) The key and mode is d minor.
(3) Find the root of the minor dominant triad by locating scale degree 5 of d minor. The key and mode of d minor has one flat: B♭. A is scale degree 5 and the root of the dominant triad.
(4) Construct an A-minor triad in $^5_3$ position. C (natural) is variable ♭7, the subtonic of d minor, and therefore the third of the minor dominant. The v chord in d minor is A C E.
(5) Once the A-minor triad has been constructed in $^5_3$ position, move the root of the chord up one octave so that the third of the chord is exposed as the lowest note of the musical texture. With the third in the bass (C), the chord is in $^6_3$ position, first inversion.

Example 8–96

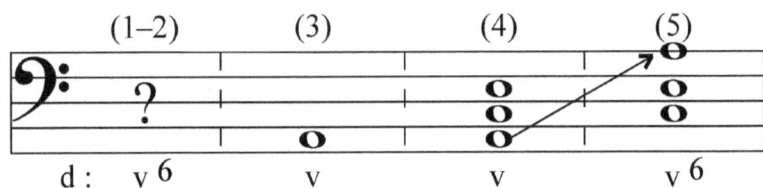

Four-Part Texture

Most of the vocal and instrumental music written during the eighteenth and nineteenth centuries either implies four parts or is reducible to four parts. Frequently, we may add a fourth part to music with three parts without disturbing the harmonic framework of the original setting. Conversely, a composition whose texture seems to exhibit a high level of density is often the result of part doubling; once we remove the doublings, a chord structure in four parts emerges.

When expressing a triad in four parts, at least one of the three elements of the chord must be doubled to produce the fourth part; however, as suggested here, additional duplications of chord tones may result in textures that are more apparent than real. (The doubling of chord tones is a separate and complex issue that will be addressed later in this chapter.)

Regardless of how we configure the triad, any combination of instruments and/or human voices may perform each of the various elements of the chord. Notably, we refer to chord tones as voices even if instruments constitute the only medium of performance. Moreover, if an instrument performs any of the chord's voices, then that instrument will probably exhibit the same simplicity of design and lyrical quality that would inform a vocal setting.

The complexity of expression found in instrumental writing is generally absent in four-part textures. To be sure, performance media such as the string quartet often contain technical challenges that are impossible to duplicate with the human voice; but even in these instances, a simpler four-part texture usually underlies the musical surface.

Triad Voicing

Not only does **voice** refer to musical sounds produced by vocal cords and/or instruments, we also use the term voice to describe how the tones of the triad are configured on the staff, in other words, how the elements of the chord are spaced or distributed. In the previous examples of this chapter, we spaced the root, third, and fifth of the triad as closely together as possible within the confines of the octave.

This type of triad structure is known as **close voicing**, **close structure**, or **close position**. When limiting the expression of the triad to one octave, a single staff is sufficient for representing a close arrangement of tones. It is possible, however, to voice the triad with a close structure on more than one staff, especially if we double one of the chord tones to produce four parts. When the triad in close structure has four parts and is written on two staves, the upper three parts will fit into a single octave (see example 8–97c below).

When the three elements of the triad extend across more than one octave and are *not* voiced as closely together as possible, the configuration of tones is referred to as **open voicing**, **open structure**, or **open position**. Although we may express an open disposition of the triad on one staff, the great staff is usually preferred when the voicing of the chord exceeds the span of a single octave.

Example 8–97 illustrates the following possible configurations for the triad: close structure on one staff (8–97a), open structure on one staff (8–97b), close structure on two staves (8–97c), and open structure on two staves (8–97d). The differences between close and open triad structures are discussed later in this chapter; for now, notice how the open structure appears in relation to the close structure (and how the two structures sound if you have access to a music keyboard).

Example 8–97

Vocal Range

A basic four-part texture consists of the following designated voices: soprano, alto, tenor, and bass, often abbreviated as SATB. Remember that it is possible to perform each of these parts with any combination of instruments and/or human voices. The guiding principle for SATB texture is that the voices maintain a simplicity of design and lyrical quality comparable to that found in a vocal composition.

The ranges for the soprano, alto, tenor, and bass voices are given in example 8–98. The high and low extremes of each voice might be extended or contracted by one pitch depending on the actual performance situation; for example, some alto singers might struggle to produce the high D in the double prime register, while some bass singers could possibly manage a low E in the great register (the filled-in note head in the example). Hence, the ranges provided in this book assume that the vocalists possess neither exceptional nor professional capabilities.

Example 8–98

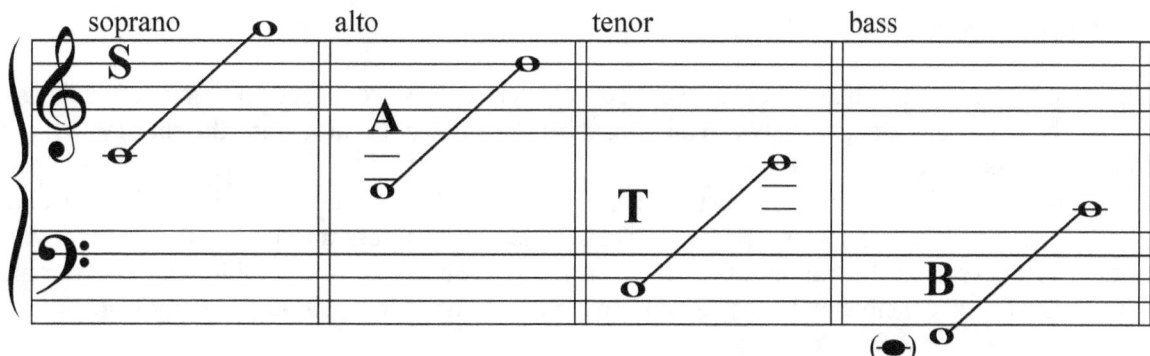

156   Chapter 8   Triads

Close and Open Structure

Throughout this chapter, we have seen that spacing the elements of the triad as closely together as possible results in what is referred to as close voicing, close structure, or close position. Further, when a triad in close structure appears on two staves, the upper three parts fit into the span of a single octave. *Voicing a triad in open structure requires at least one octave between the soprano and tenor voices.*

Using the C-major triad in root position, example 8–99 exhibits various dispositions of close and open structure. When two staves are used, the soprano and alto voices are written in the treble clef, whereas the tenor and bass voices are in the bass clef.

Example 8–99

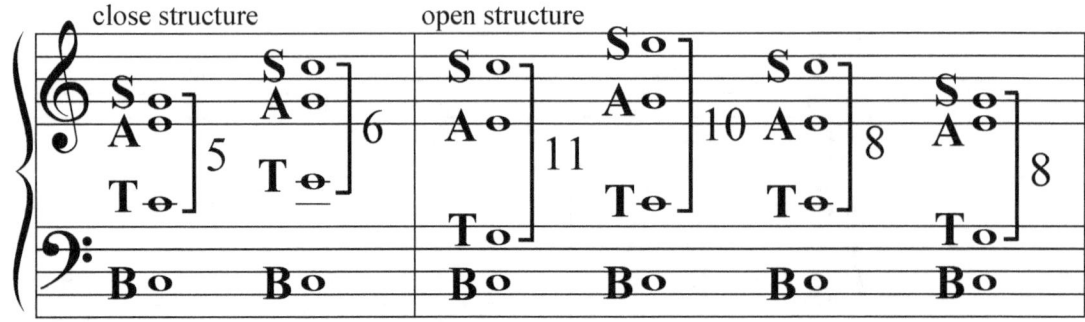

As demonstrated in example 8–100, *open chord structures allow for at least one potential chord tone to be placed between the soprano and alto voices, alto and tenor voices, or between both pairs of voices* (the filled-in note heads represent potential chord tones).

Example 8–100

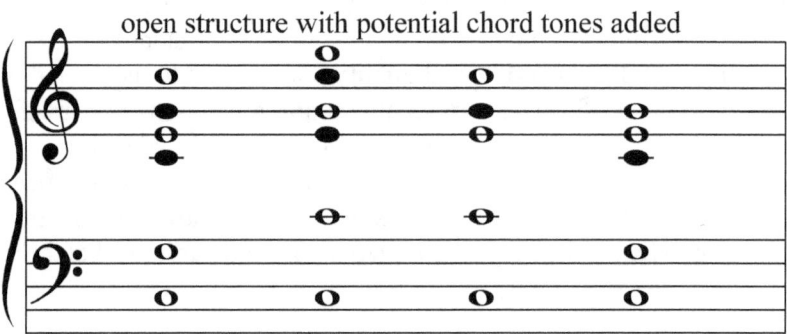

Spacing Between Adjacent Voices

There should be no more than one octave between adjacent voices except between the tenor and bass voices. If more than one octave occurs between the soprano, alto, and tenor voices, then the chord will likely sound thin and imbalanced.

Although a close positioning between the tenor and bass voices of the chord is acceptable, an arrangement between the lower voices that is too close sounds dark and perhaps even muddy. A wider spacing of intervals at the bottom of the chord usually produces more desirable results. Example 8–101 illustrates a few acceptable and unacceptable spacings for the C-major triad in root position.

Example 8–101

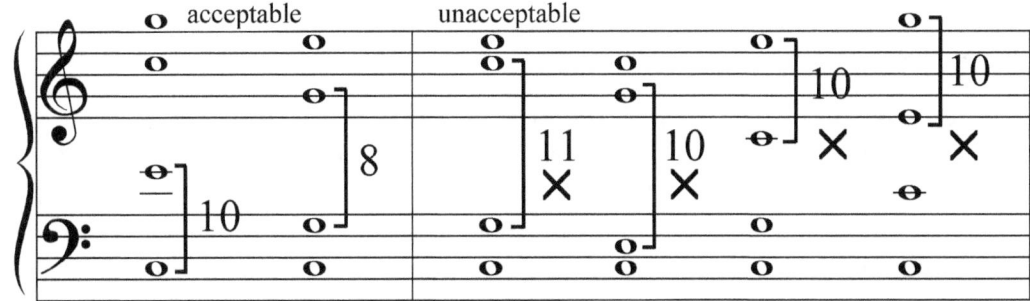

Stem Direction

Heretofore, all of the triads shown in both close and open structure have used whole-note values. Obviously, actual music is expressed with a variety of note values, most of which include stems. As demonstrated in example 8–102, when two voices are written on one staff, the soprano and tenor voices have upward stems, whereas the alto and bass voices have downward stems.

Example 8–102: stem direction in four-voice texture

The Doubling of Chord Tones in Four-Voice Texture

The doubling of chord tones in four-voice texture is a complex issue that involves two important considerations:
  (1) The goal of good four-voice writing is to assure the individuality of each melodic line while at the same time blending the parts together to produce a harmonious vertical sound.
  (2) The conventional expression of tonality in music conveys a sense of forward motion, best effected in chordal textures by successions between unlike chords, that is, chords whose roots are different. A sense of motion in tonal music is less evident when melodic activity does not produce a chord change. In order to create a feeling of movement in chordal music, careful attention must be given as to how the voices of one chord connect to those of the next chord.

Improper doubling of chord tones usually produces a poor connection between chords, a loss of melodic integrity, and vertical structures that sound imbalanced. Example 8–103 illustrates some general guidelines for doubling the chord tones of triads. The triads in the example are related to each other as a unit of musical expression called a "chord progression." The progression is in the key and mode of f minor.

158   Chapter 8 Triads

The principles cited below are keyed to the progression in 8–103. These principles are general recommendations; the actual context of any given music composition may demand doublings that contradict some of the guidelines presented here.

(1) When triads are used in a four-voice texture, the preference—subject to exceptions—is to double scale degrees 1, 4, and 5 of the tonic key (examples 8–103a, 103e, 103f, 103g, 103h, 103i, and 103j).

(2) Avoid doubling the variable scale degrees of the minor mode. (Examples 103b, 103c, 103d, 103e, and 103f show the correct usage for variables ♭6, ♭7, and ♯7. Example 8–103i demonstrates an exceptional treatment of the leading tone in the alto voice, which moves to scale degree 5 in 103j instead of the tonic; we shall see this special license again in Appendix F, pp. 244–245).

(3) For major and minor triads in $\frac{5}{3}$ position, double the root (examples 103f, 103i, and 103j), the fifth, or third—usually in that order. However, doubling the third of the tonic chord is always a good secondary choice.

(4) For major and minor triads in $\frac{6}{3}$ position, double whatever chord tone appears in the soprano voice; alternatively, double the root (8–103a), fifth, and third—in that order.

(5) For triads in $\frac{6}{4}$ position, double the fifth, that is, the bass voice (examples 103b and 103h).

(6) Avoid doubling the leading tone; therefore,
   (a) do not double the root of the vii° chord,
   (b) do not double the third of the V chord.

(7) The diminished triad is best limited to $\frac{6}{3}$ position; in this context, double the third (8–103e) or the fifth.

Example 8–103

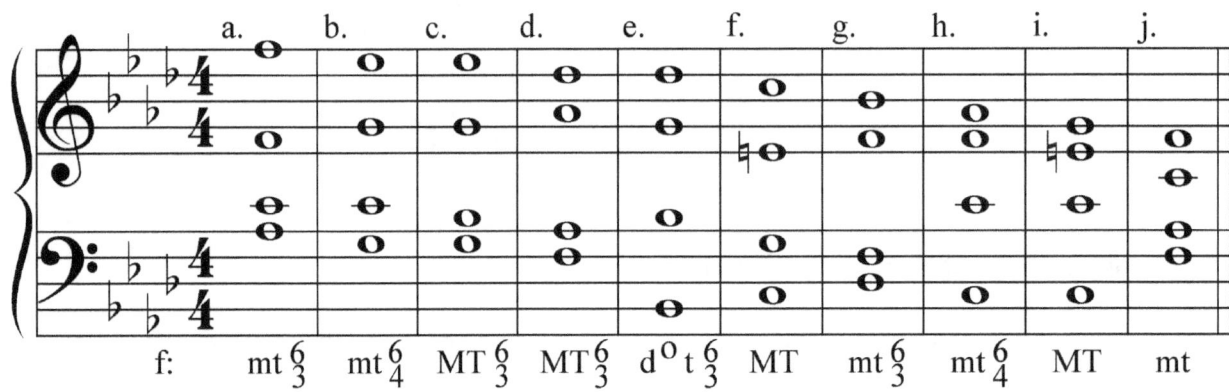

As shown in example 8–104, the $\frac{5}{3}$ and $\frac{6}{4}$ positions of the diminished triad are usually avoided because of the tritone (augmented 4th or diminished 5th) interval between the lowest voice of the texture and one of the upper voices. In $\frac{6}{3}$ position, the tritone in the diminished triad is somewhat hidden because it occurs between two upper voices—in other words, the lowest voice is not one of the components of the tritone interval. For this reason, the diminished triad is usually expressed in $\frac{6}{3}$ position.

Example 8–104

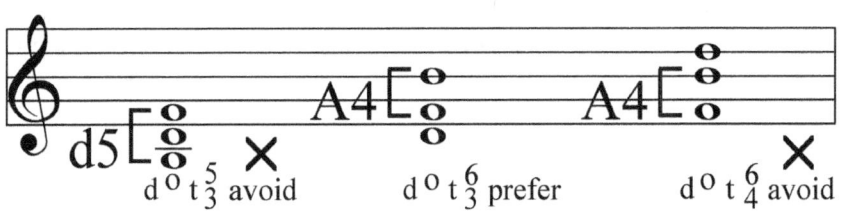

Tonality and the Names of the Scale Degrees

We have discovered that the major mode is not the only mode in music that has a tonal center, that the numbers 1 through 7 can be used to represent each of the scale degrees of the mode, and that each of the scale degrees of the mode has one of the following names: tonic, supertonic, mediant, subdominant, dominant, submediant, and leading tone. When scale degree 7 is located one whole step below the tonic note, the term subtonic is used to distinguish it from the leading tone, as the subtonic lacks the compelling drive of the leading tone to *lead* upwards by half step to the tonic. In this section, we shall see that the names of the scale degrees are derived from their position and function in relation to the tonic, which represents the tonality of the mode.

As stated in Chapter 4, tonality in music is analogous to the gravitational force exerted by the Sun upon any object that comes within its field of attraction. Tonality is a system of pitch organization that establishes its own field of attraction around one central tone. All the other tones of the key and mode seek to revolve around and gravitate toward this central tone in a hierarchical order.

The tonic, as the principal tone of this hierarchy, exerts its gravitational force upon all of the other tones, each of which holds a position of relative strength and stability within the tonic's field of attraction. Since the pitch content of the key and mode provides the material from which chords may be formed on each of the seven scale degrees, the chords also assume a hierarchical position within the tonal framework. Thus, some tones and chords have a stronger relationship to the tonic than others.

Standing at the interval of the perfect 5th above the tonic and serving as the primary definer of a composition's tonality, the dominant scale degree forms the strongest relationship with the tonic. The perfect 5th, which has its origin in a natural phenomenon known as the **harmonic series** (see below, pp. 161–162), constitutes the closest intervallic relationship between two unlike pitches. The field of attraction between the dominant and the tonic is based upon the prominence of the perfect 5th within the harmonic series.

In example 8–105, we have the triad of the dominant addressing the tonic in a falling perfect 5th and rising perfect 4th root and bass relationship. Movement in the bass of either the perfect or tritone 5th and 4th is called **harmonic motion**. The falling perfect 5th (and its inversion, the rising perfect 4th) presents the strongest expression of harmonic motion in tonal music.

When the dominant triad is major, it contains as its chord third the second most important scale degree within the tonal hierarchy, namely, the leading tone. Therefore, as shown in 8–105, the movement between the dominant and tonic chords produces two optimal conditions for affirming the tonality of a musical work: the compelling melodic drive upwards from the leading tone to the tonic and the strong harmonic motion of a falling perfect 5th or a rising perfect 4th in the bass.

Example 8–105: the harmonic root and bass relationship between the dominant and tonic triads

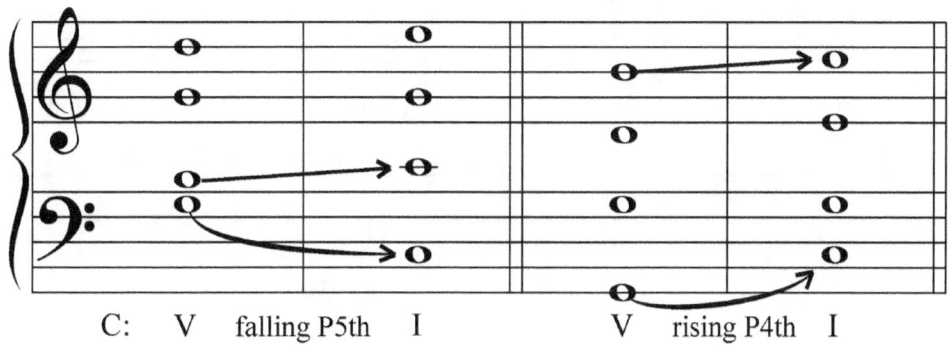

The next chord within the tonal hierarchy is the triad of the leading tone, which shares two pitches in common with the triad of the dominant. The root and the third of the leading-tone triad are the same pitches as the third and the fifth of the corresponding dominant triad. Example 8–106 demonstrates the common pitch content of the two chords in the key and mode of C major.

For the purpose of comparison in the example, the leading-tone triad is expressed in $^5_3$ position; however, it should be remembered that limiting the diminished triad to its $^6_3$ position (first inversion) avoids the dissonant tritone between the bass and one of the upper voices. The remaining areas of the supertonic, mediant, subdominant, and submediant assume subordinate status within the key and mode and are so-named largely because of their respective positions in relation to the tonic and dominant.

Example 8–106: common pitch content between the leading-tone and dominant triads

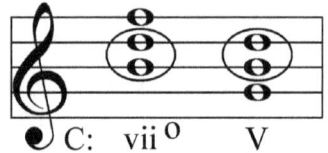

C: vii°   V

Examples 8–107a and 107b display all of the scale degree areas of the key and mode of C major. The areas of the supertonic, the mediant, and the dominant are the focus of 8–107a. Scale degree 2 receives the name supertonic because it stands one step above the tonic. Scale degree 5, the dominant, occurs one fifth above the tonic (see the upward arrow).

Scale degree 3 is called the mediant because it falls midway between the tonic and the dominant (see the dotted slurs). The mediant helps to distinguish the major and minor modes because of its third relationship to the tonic. In the major mode, there is a major 3rd between scale degrees 1 and 3, whereas in the minor mode, the distance between scale degrees 1 and 3 is a minor 3rd.

The areas of the subdominant, the submediant, and leading tone are shown in 8–107b. Scale degree 4, the subdominant, occurs one 5th below the tonic (see the downward arrow) and a 2nd below the dominant. Scale degree 6 is called the submediant because it is located below the tonic and falls midway between the tonic and subdominant (see the dotted slurs). The leading tone is one half step below the tonic. (Remember that the term subtonic is used in the minor mode to distinguish it from the leading tone, as the subtonic lacks the compelling drive of the leading tone to *lead* upwards by half step to the tonic.)

Example 8–107

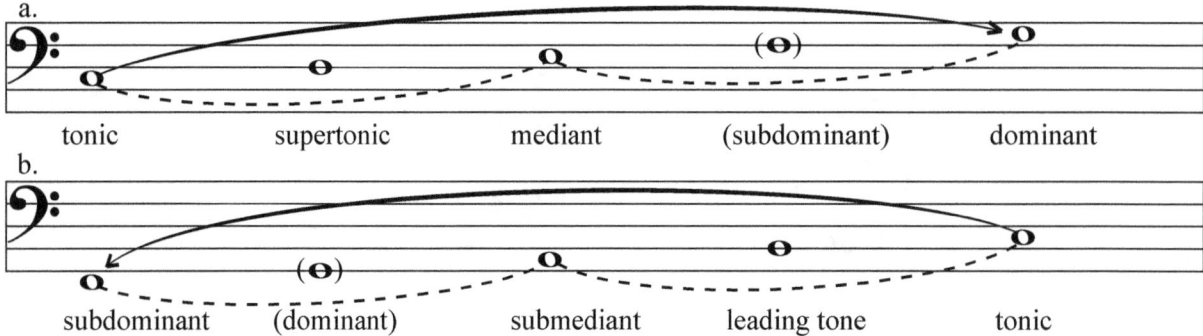

The Harmonic Series

In the foregoing section, we stated that the interval of the perfect 5th is of central importance to the definition of a music composition's tonality. Additionally, it spans the distance from the root to the fifth of the major and minor triad. Both major and minor triads are relatively stable chords, while diminished and augmented triads are relatively unstable. The diminished triad has a diminished 5th from its root to fifth. The augmented triad has a contextual 5th from its root to fifth but not an acoustical 5th (see above, p. 118). As we shall see, the major triad is the most stable of all four chord qualities.

The stability of the major triad and the role of the dominant as the chief definer of the tonality is associated with the harmonic series. A portion of the harmonic series with a starting pitch of C is shown below in example 8–108 (the series can begin on any pitch). Before we consider how this series works and how it relates to the strength of the dominant and the stability of the major triad, it would be well to review briefly the nature of musical tones and how they are created.

In Chapter 2, we learned that an object moved by force produces vibrations that are carried through a medium of transmission to the human ear. A sound that generates a regular number of frequencies at a steady rate is perceived as a musical tone. The relative lowness or highness of any pitch corresponds to the rate of the vibrating frequency of the sound-producing object. Slower vibrating frequencies result in lower pitches, while faster vibrating frequencies produce higher pitches. The rate of vibration generating the pitch is called the **fundamental frequency**, also known as the **first partial** or **first harmonic**.

A musical tone is a combination of two components: the fundamental pitch and a spectrum of higher frequencies called **overtones**. Projecting varying degrees of intensity (volume) from within the harmonic series, overtones are usually not loud enough to be heard as pitches in their own right. Rather, the fundamental frequency and its overtones are blended together into a single composite sound. This composite sound is referred to variously as tone quality, tone color, or **timbre** (pronounced *tam*ber).

Although the individual overtones cannot be heard as distinct pitches, they do *color* the fundamental frequency and collectively generate the timbre of a musical instrument—overtones enable us to identify the source of the musical sound. On any given instrument, some overtones are relatively stronger than others. The reason two different instruments sound differently is due to the fact that each makes its own unique selection of overtones from a much larger inventory of weaker overtones. For example, we can distinguish the sound of the clarinet and the violin even when both instruments are playing the exact same pitch because each instrument projects its own unique profile of overtones, its own sonic fingerprint.

The fundamental frequency and its overtones together produce the harmonic series, which is why the harmonic series is also called the **overtone series**. The number of overtones that are generated above the fundamental pitch is potentially infinite; however, in order to maintain a reasonable degree of simplicity, discussions of the harmonic series in publications are usually limited to the first sixteen pitches.

Example 8–108 restricts our view of the harmonic series to the first five pitches, starting with the fundamental on great C. These five pitches reveal two important bits of information:
(1) the first tone that is *not* a duplication of the fundamental is a compound perfect 5th (circled G) and
(2) the first five tones of the harmonic series produce the major triad (measure 2).

Example 8–108: the first five pitches of the harmonic series

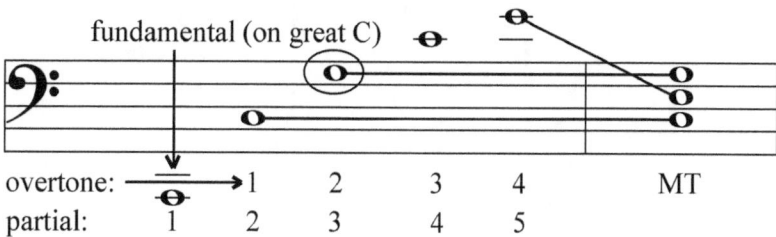

As noted earlier, the fundamental is also called the first partial or first harmonic. When discussing the harmonic series, a distinction should be made between the fundamental and the overtones that occur above it. Although the fundamental is the first partial (or first harmonic), it is *not* the first overtone. Examples 8–108 above and 109 below indicate that the first overtone is actually the second partial (or second harmonic), the second overtone is the third partial (or third harmonic), and so on. Therefore, we never refer to the fundamental frequency as the first overtone.

Example 8–109: the first five pitches of the harmonic series on great C

	Overtone Series		Harmonic Series
great C :	fundamental		fundamental (first partial or first harmonic)
small c :	first overtone	=	second partial (second harmonic)
small g :	second overtone	=	third partial (third harmonic)
c^1 :	third overtone	=	fourth partial (fourth harmonic)
e^1 :	fourth overtone	=	fifth partial (fifth harmonic)

Omitting the Fifth in Four-Voice Texture

The strength of the perfect 5th within the harmonic series makes it possible in four-voice textures to omit the fifth of major and minor triads in root position, using an additional root or third as the fourth part. In this instance, the missing fifth is understood to be generated by the harmonic series.

It is also possible to omit the 5th with root-position seventh chords in a four-voice texture if the underlying triad is either a major or minor triad. The omission produces a seventh chord with a doubled root, a third, and a seventh (see Appendix G, example G–8a, beat 1).

Singing the Four Triad Qualities in All Chord Positions

There are a few different ways in which to sing triads. One approach, shown in example 8–110, involves finding a starting note near the bottom of an individual's vocal range and singing each successive tone of the major triad in root position above the selected pitch. Subsequently, the singer moves up by a whole step (or by half step) from the initial root and produces another major triad in root position. This pattern is continued until the singer reaches the top note of his or her vocal range. Example 8–110 designates 1, 3, and 5 as the root, third, and fifth respectively (1-3-5-1-5-3-1).

Example 8–110

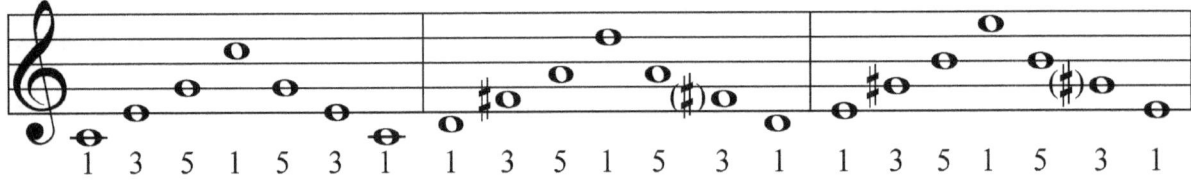

A more rewarding (though challenging) alternative involves singing all four triad qualities in all three chord positions above a common-tone bass. Using the major triad with C as the common tone, example 8–111 demonstrates the application of this highly useful approach. When moving through the three positions, the notes above the common tone must be adjusted to preserve the major quality of the triad while still retaining the C-octave between the outside pitches ($c^1 - c^2$).

The challenge of the exercise is in preserving the outside octave while adjusting the internal intervals to maintain the correct chord quality and position. The numbers 1, 3, and 5 designate the root, third, and fifth of the chord respectively (1-3-5-1-5-3-1). As you proceed with the inversions of the triad, both the intervals (indicated between each element of the chord) and the numbers change as the common-tone C becomes the third of the major triad in $^6_3$ position (3-5-1-3-1-5-3) and then the fifth of the chord in $^6_4$ position (5-1-3-5-3-1-5).

In $^5_3$ position (8–111a), the third of the C-major triad is E; however, in $^6_3$ position (8–111b), the chord formed above C is an A♭-major triad, with an E♭ producing the minor 3rd between the third and the fifth. In $^6_4$ position (8–111c), the C in the bass becomes the fifth of an F-major triad. In all positions of the major triad, the distance from the fifth up to the root is a perfect 4th.

Additionally, we shall apply the technique of common-tone singing to minor, diminished, and augmented triads in examples 8–112 through 114. For all of the common tone exercises shown below, the upper note of the fourth identifies both the written and sounding root of the chord, *except for the augmented triad which has no acoustical fourth* (see example 8–114).

Finally, consider these two factors when singing the three chord positions of all four triad qualities:
(1) the root position projects a "root triad" upwards from the bass pitch (*1–3–5*–1); and,
(2) the $^6_4$ position projects a root triad among its three upper pitches (5–*1–3–5*).

Example 8–111: singing the major triad using a common-tone bass

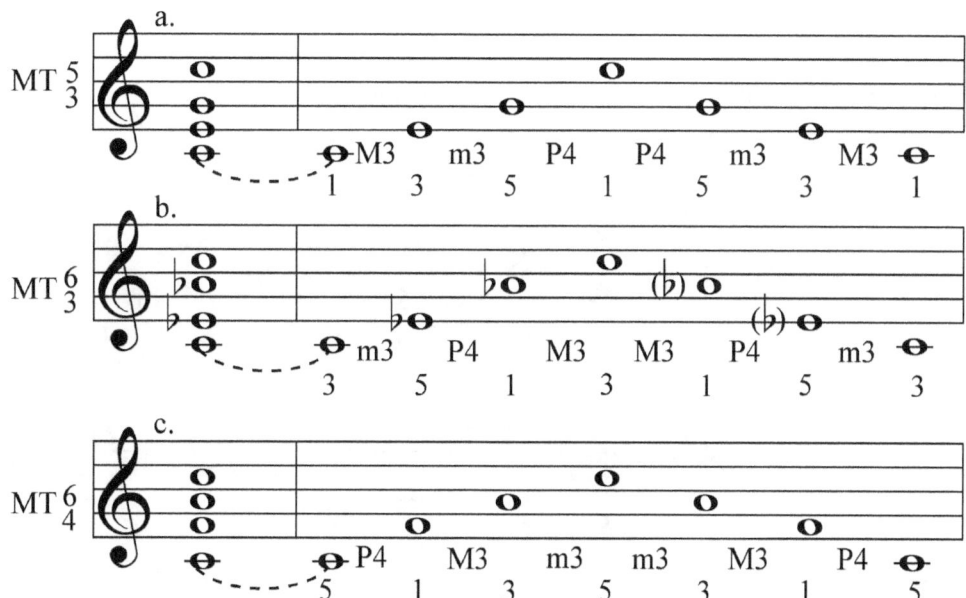

The singing of the minor triad, as shown in example 8–112, requires a change in the pitch content of the chord above the common tone C. In $\frac{5}{3}$ position (8–112a), the third of the C-minor triad is E♭; however, in $\frac{6}{3}$ position (8–112b), the chord formed above C is an A-minor triad, with an E natural producing the major 3rd between the third and the fifth. In $\frac{6}{4}$ position (8–112c), the C in the bass becomes the fifth of an F-minor triad. In all positions of the minor triad, the distance from the fifth up to the root is a perfect 4th.

Example 8–112: singing the minor triad using a common-tone bass

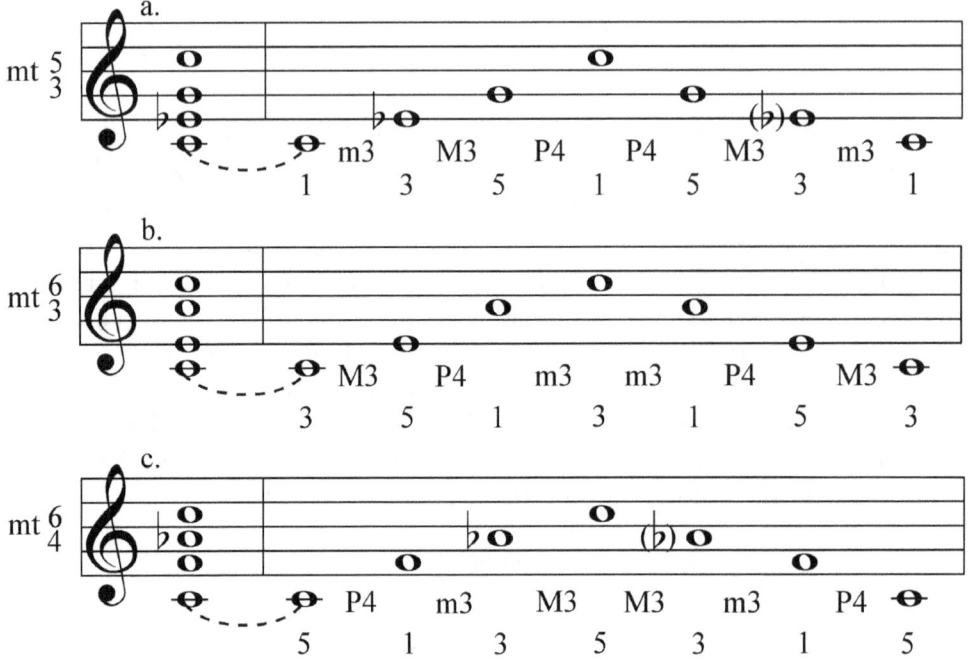

Example 8–113: singing the diminished triad using a common-tone bass

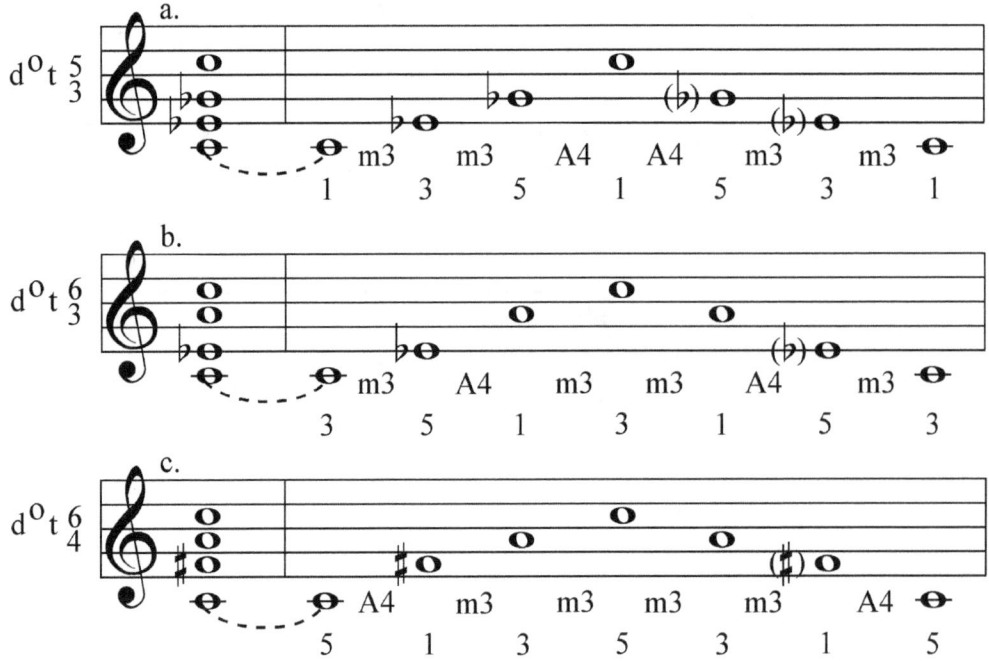

The singing of the diminished triad, illustrated in example 8–113 above, presents one additional problem: namely, the tritone that occurs between the root and the fifth (a diminished 5th) and between the fifth and the root (an augmented 4th). Of all the acoustical intervals, the tritone is the most difficult to sing. When using the common tone for singing the diminished triad in all three chord positions, the best suggestion we can offer is to focus on the outside octave interval, as this interval is the easiest to hear. To be sure, the challenge of adjusting of the pitches within that octave remains.

Finally, singing the augmented triad presents a different set of challenges (example 8–114). As we have said (see above, p. 125 and example 8–37), regardless of its written position, the augmented triad will always sound like two superimposed major 3rds, an intervallic structure that precludes *hearing* the augmented triad as an inverted chord. Hence, the augmented triad projects a neutral-sounding profile. Even the diminished 4th between the fifth and the root of the augmented triad exists only within the *written context* of the chord because the *sound* of the diminished 4th is identical to that of the major 3rd.

Singing the augmented triad using the common-tone method results in performing the same acoustical pitches three times as you proceed through all three chord positions; however, each time, the numbers assigned to those same pitches will change: 1-3-5-1-5-3-1 is used for the $\frac{5}{3}$ position, 3-5-1-3-1-5-3 for the $\frac{6}{3}$ position, and 5-1-3-5-3-1-5 for the $\frac{6}{4}$ position. Once you are accustomed to singing major, minor, and diminished triads using the common tone, you may find that performing the augmented triad with the same pitches while changing the numbers for each chord position is not without its difficulties.

Example 8–114: singing the augmented triad using a common-tone bass

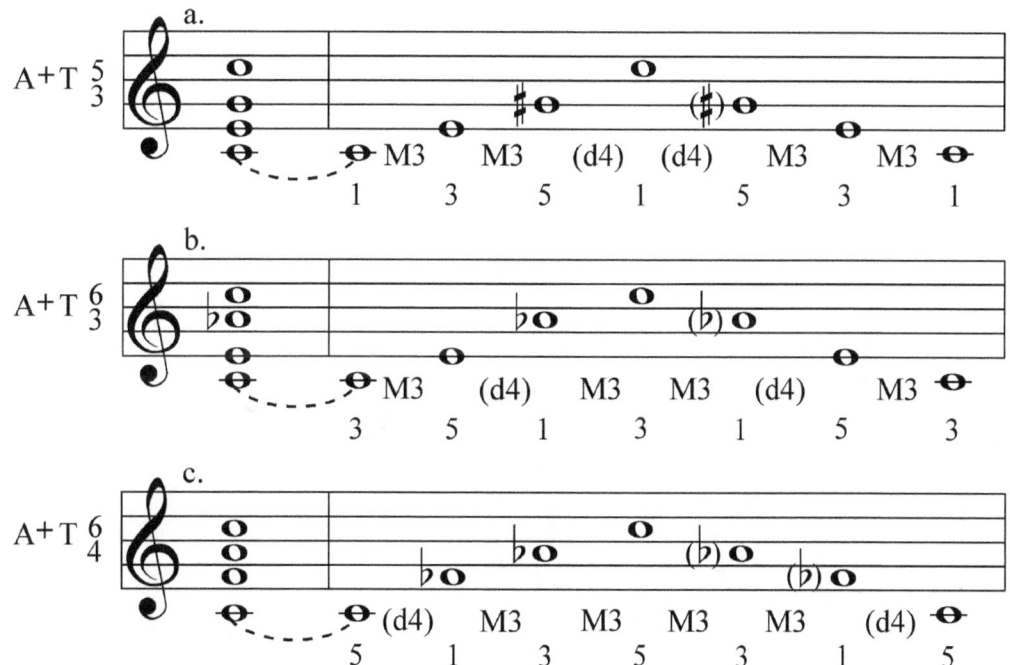

Appendix A   Rhythmic Exercises

The rhythmic exercises contained herein may be played by tapping on a table or clapping with hands while sitting down. As you execute the rhythms, you should tap both feet with the basic pulse of the meter. You should also try counting the rhythmic syllables aloud while playing the exercises.

Rhythmic Exercise A–1

168 Appendix A Rhythmic Exercises

Rhythmic Exercise A–2

Appendix A Rhythmic Exercises

Rhythmic Exercise A–3

a.
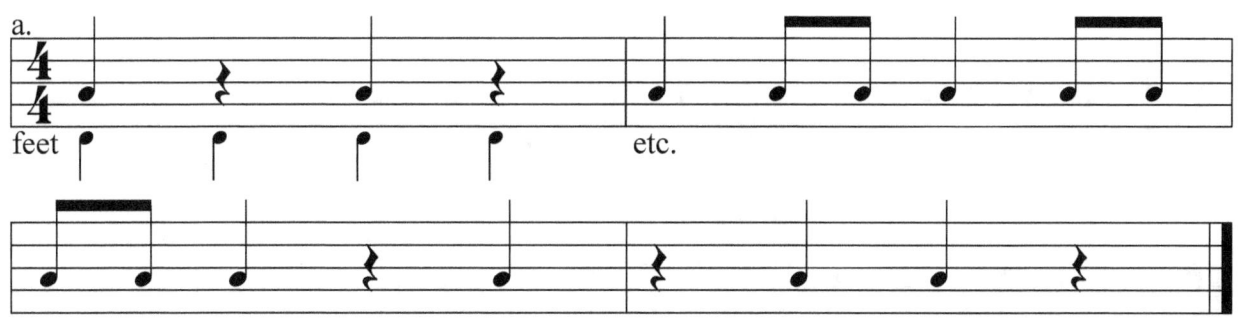

b.
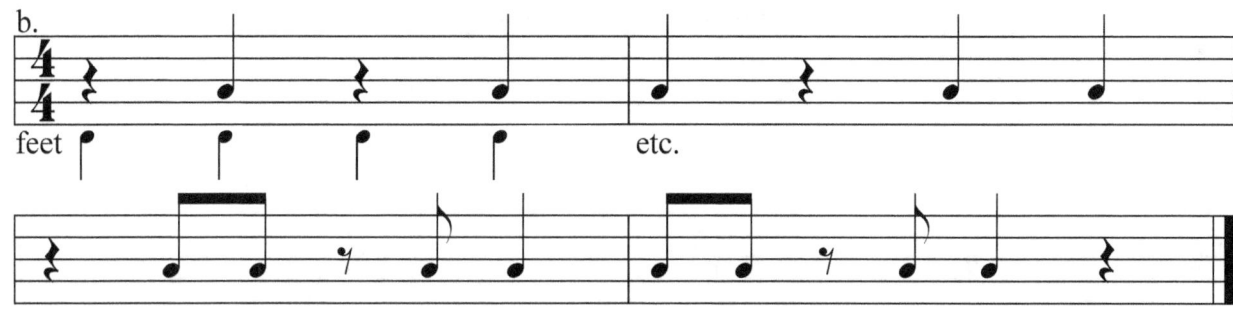

c.
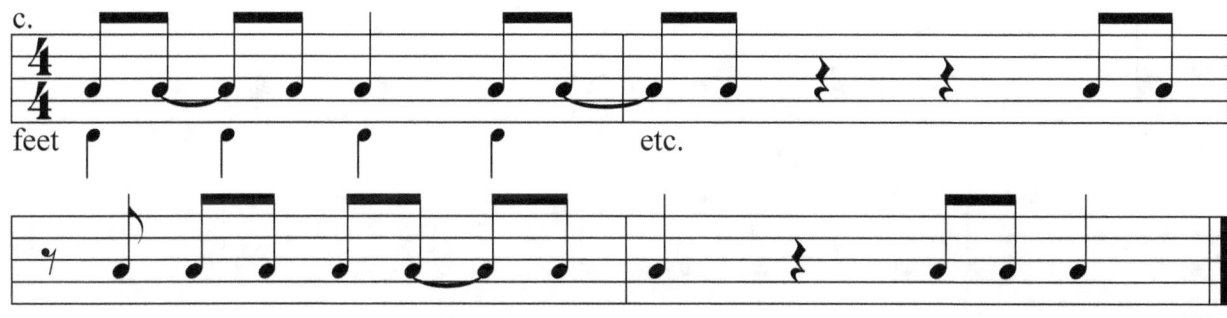

d.

Appendix A Rhythmic Exercises

Rhythmic Exercise A–4

a.
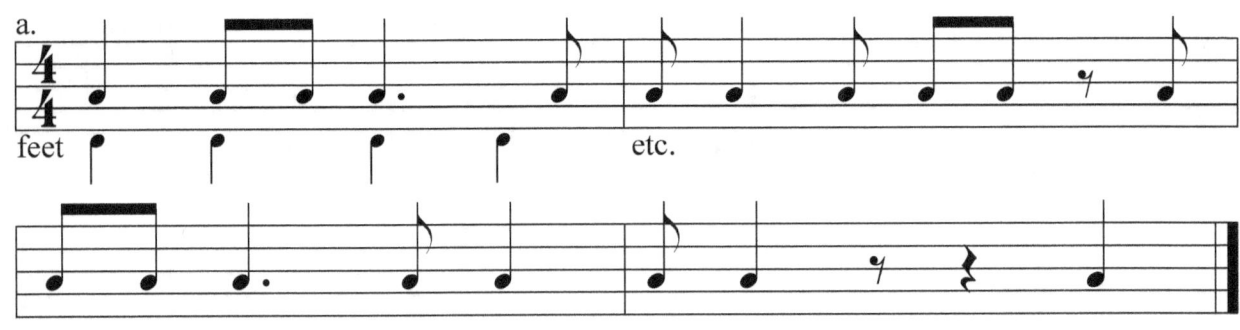

b.
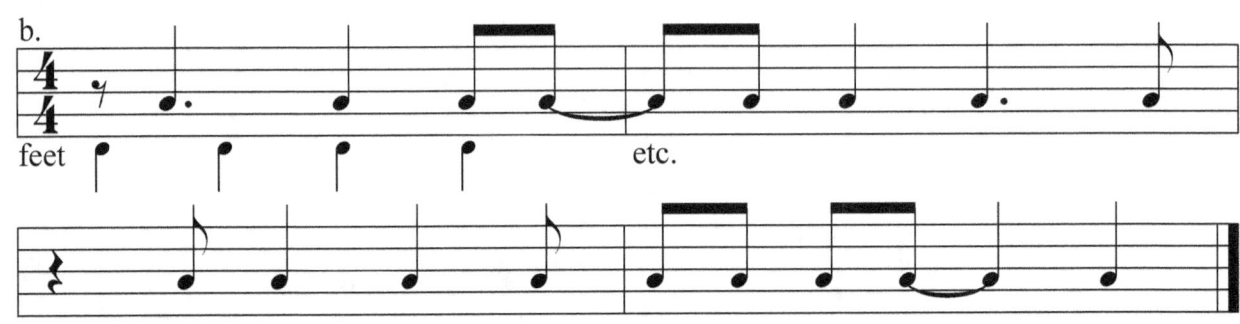

c.
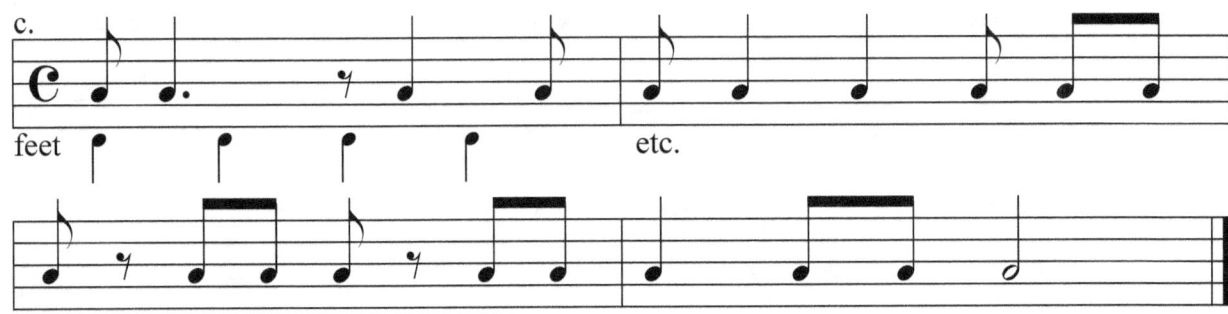

d.
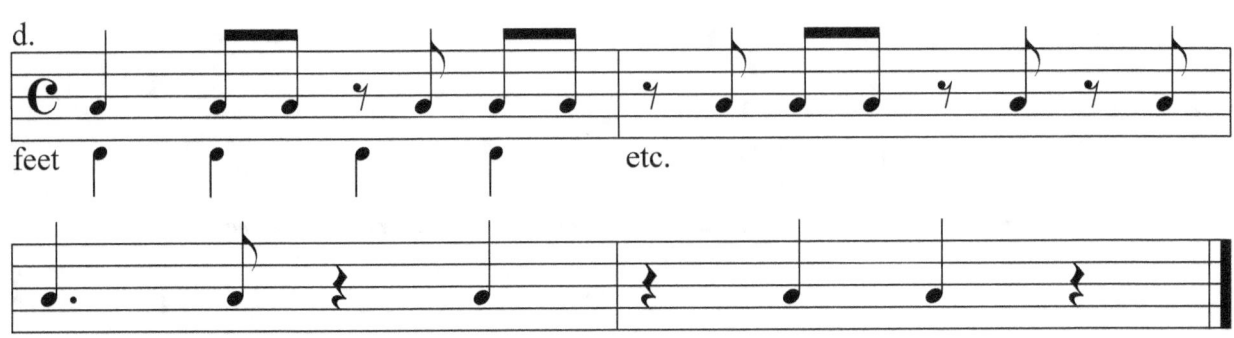

Appendix A Rhythmic Exercises 171

Rhythmic Exercise A–5

172 Appendix A Rhythmic Exercises

Rhythmic Exercise A–6

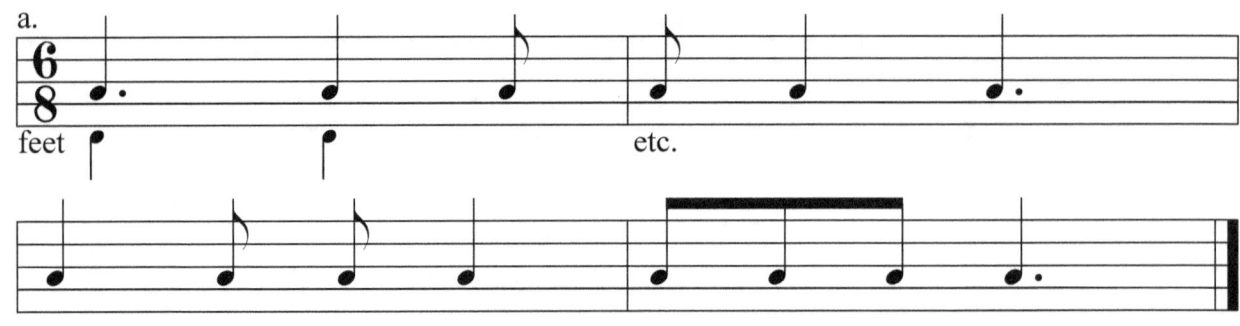

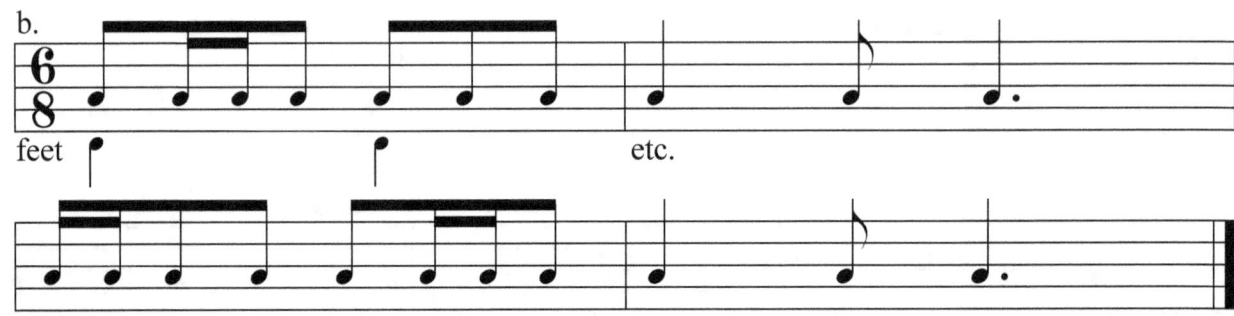

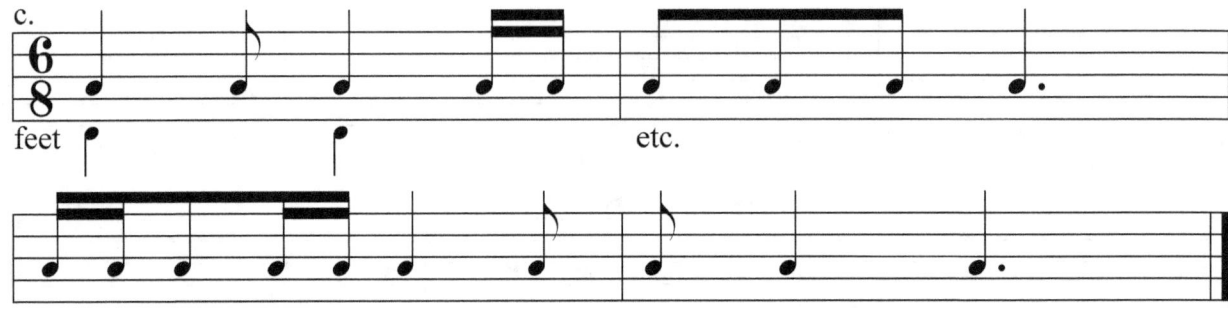

Rhythmic Exercise A–7

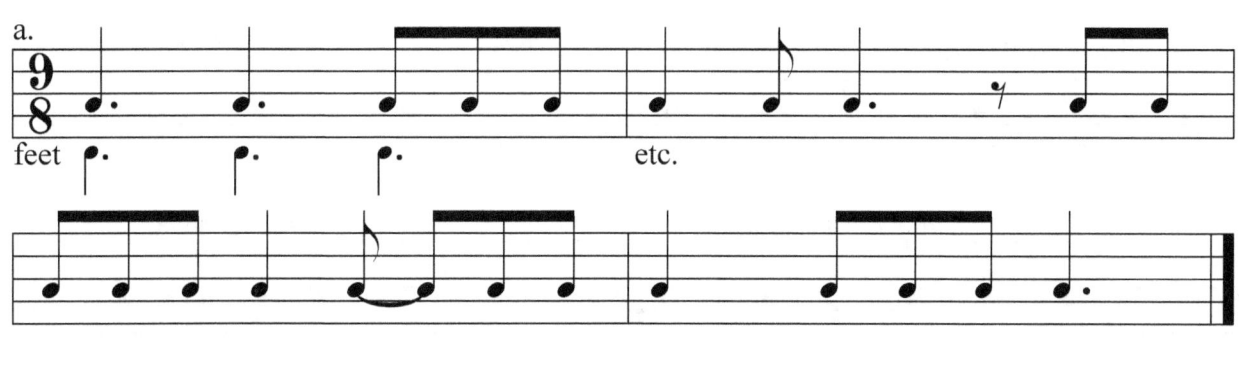

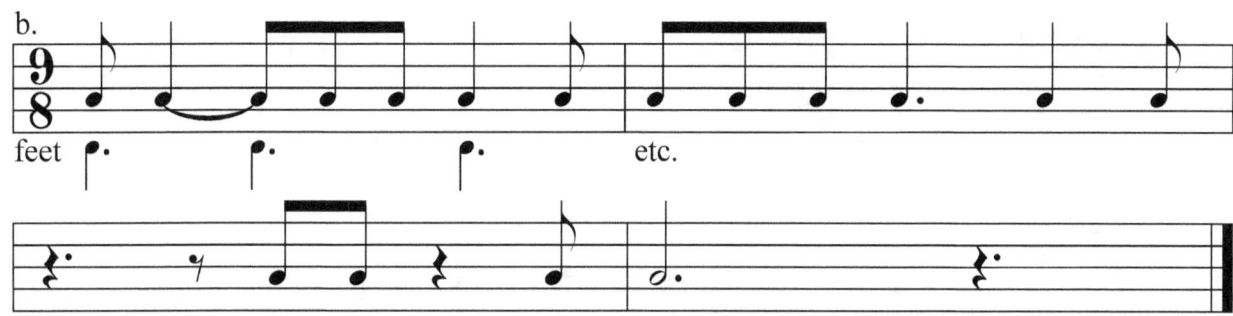

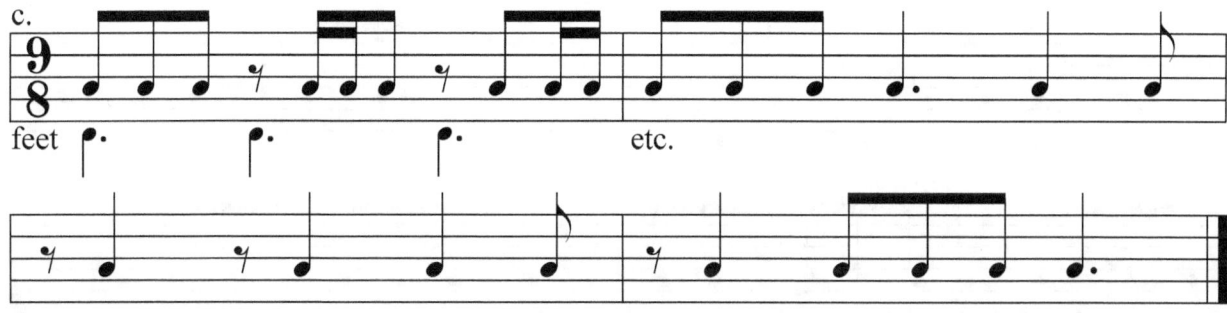

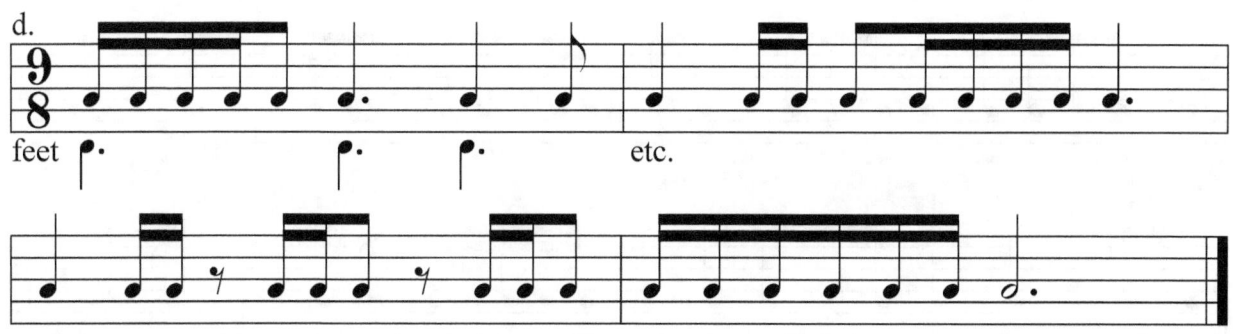

Appendix A Rhythmic Exercises

Rhythmic Exercise A–8

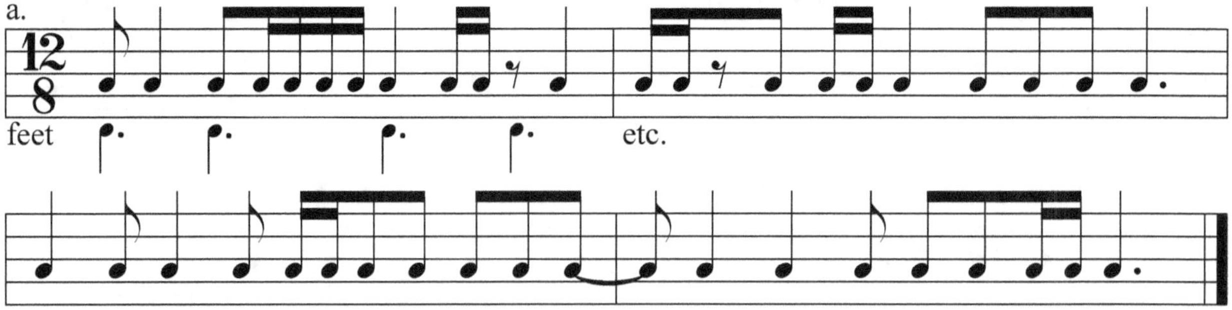

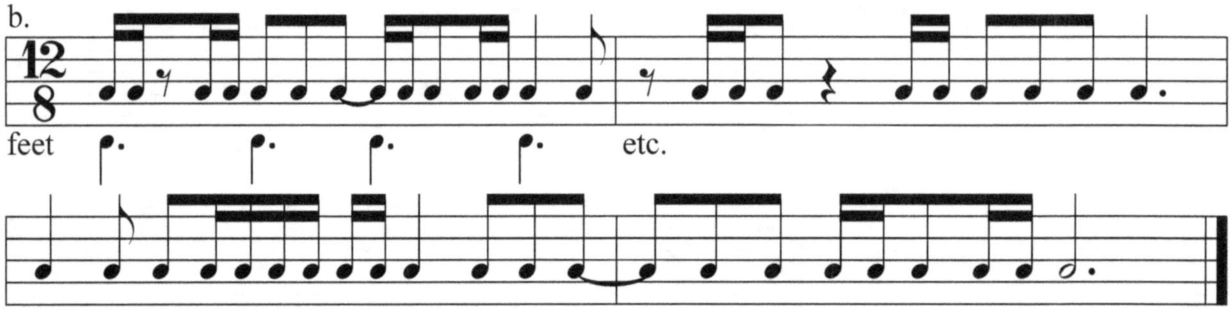

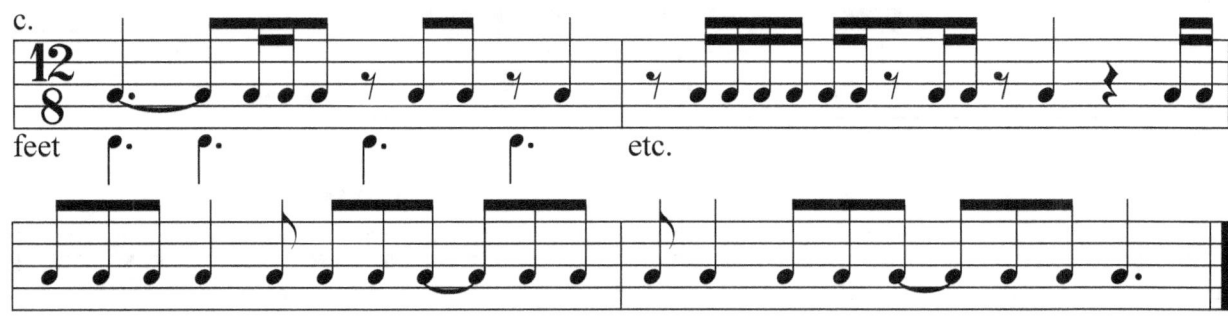

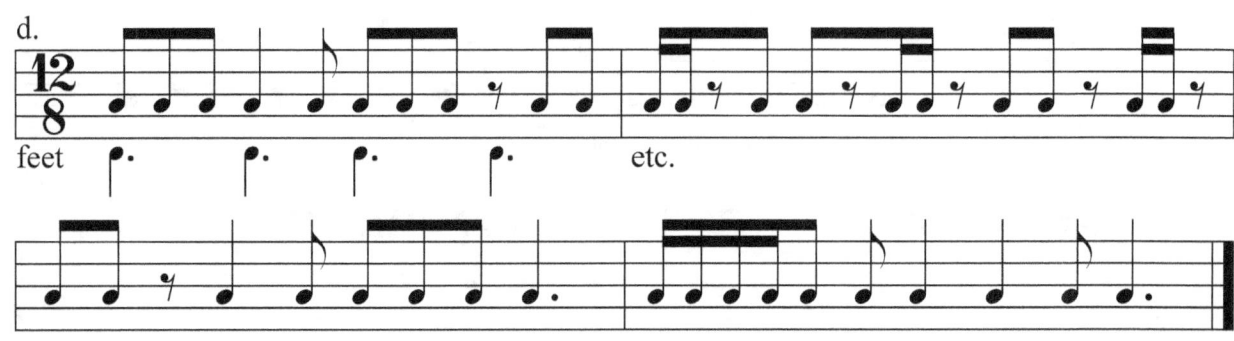

Appendix A Rhythmic Exercises

Rhythmic Exercise A–9

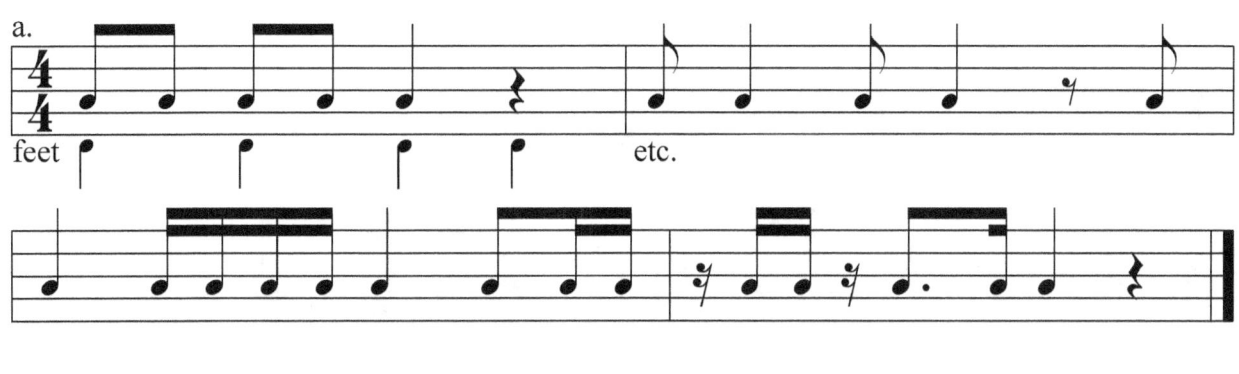

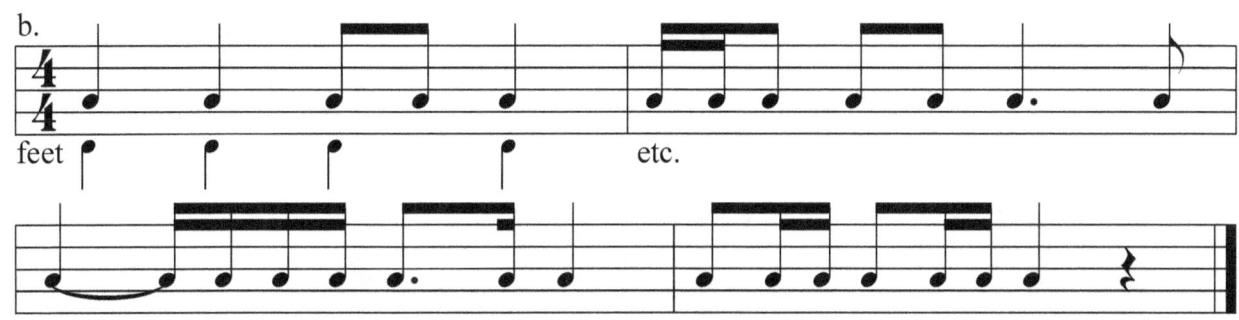

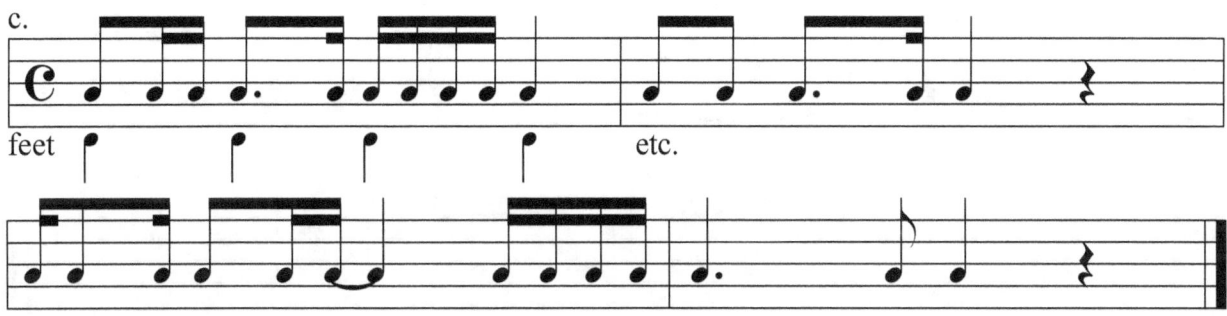

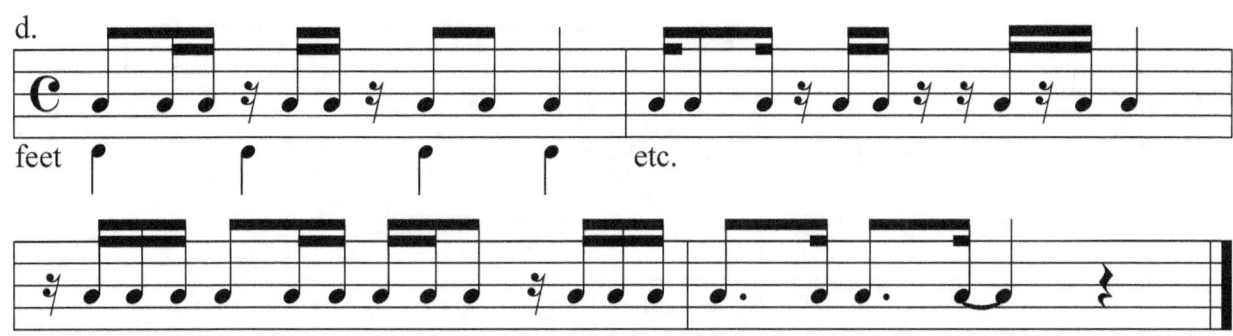

176   Appendix A Rhythmic Exercises

Rhythmic Exercise A–10

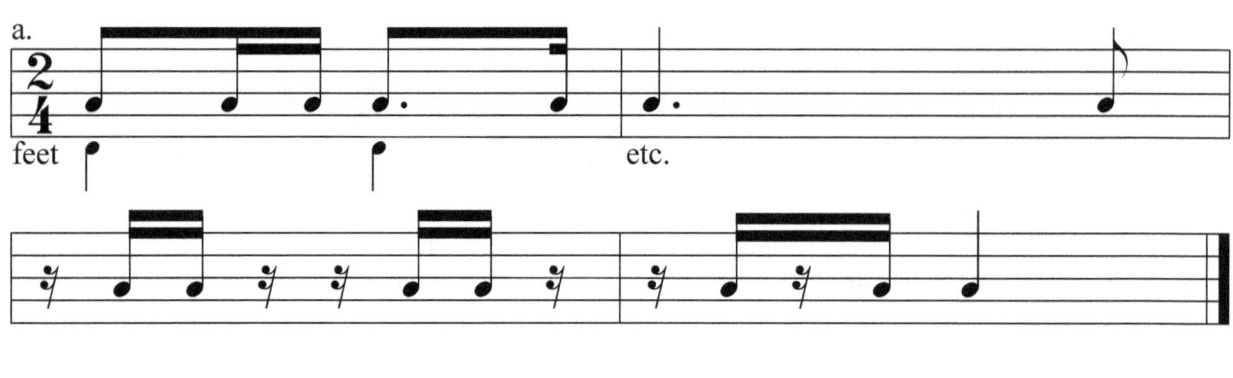

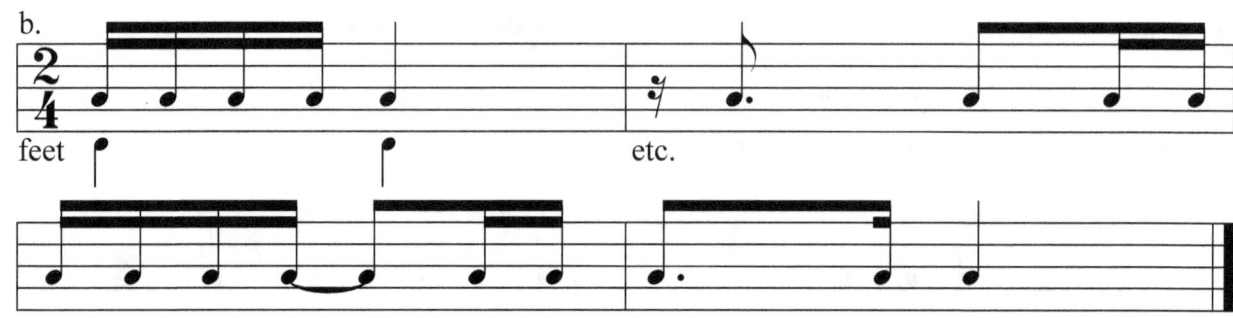

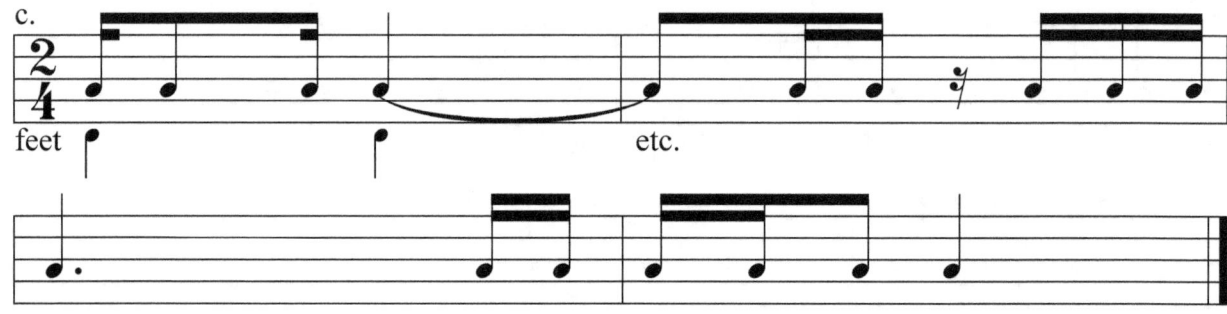

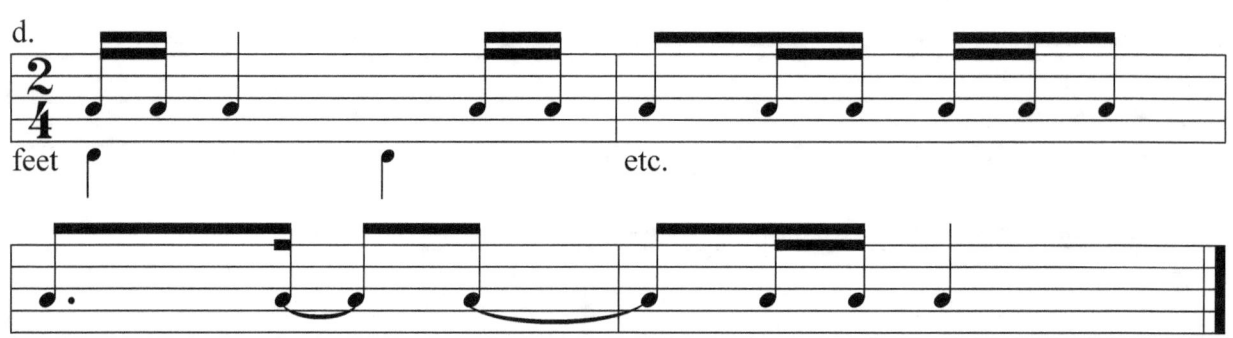

Appendix A Rhythmic Exercises 177

Rhythmic Exercise A–11

a.

b.

c.
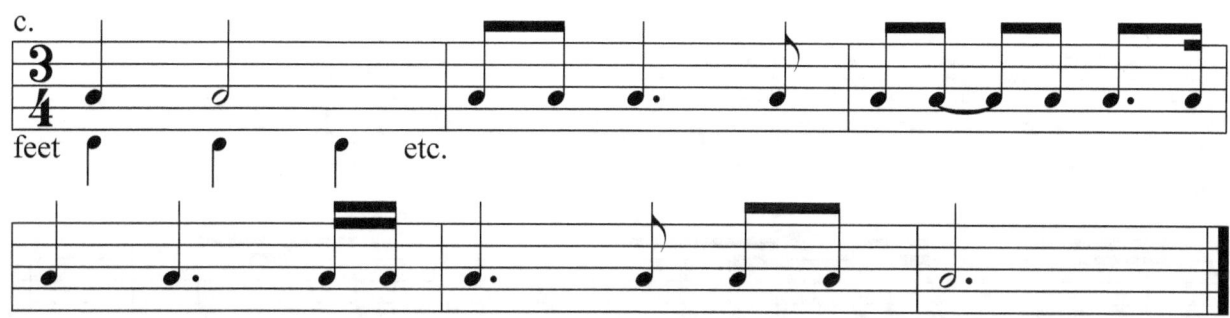

d.
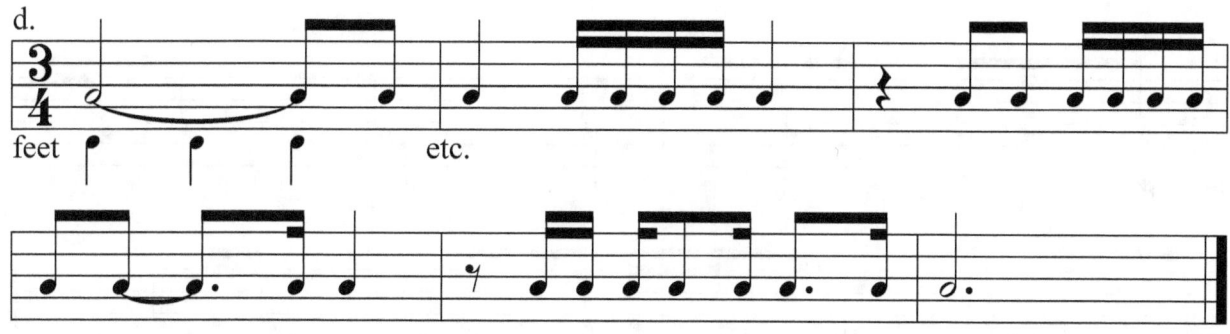

Rhythmic Exercise A–12

Rhythmic Exercise A–13

180 Appendix A Rhythmic Exercises

Rhythmic Exercise A–14

Appendix A Rhythmic Exercises 181

Rhythmic Exercise A–15

Rhythmic Exercise A–16

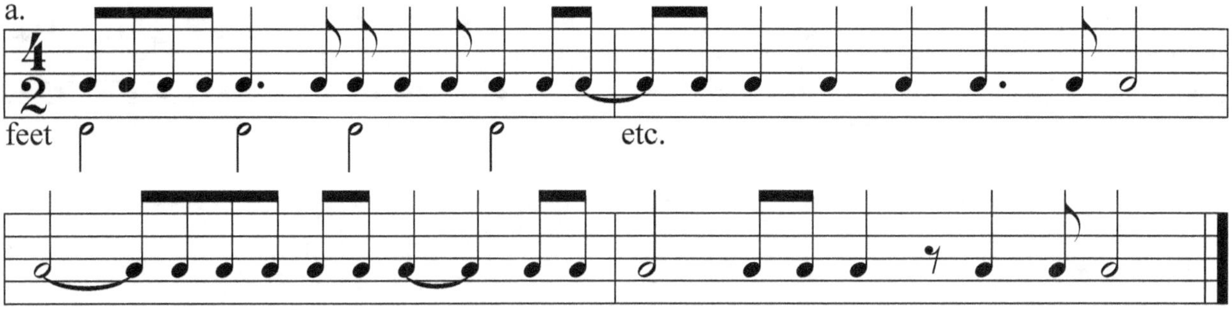

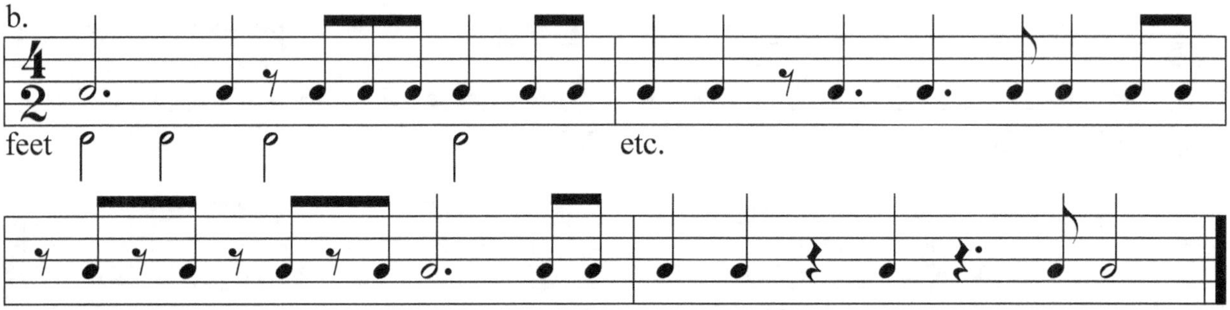

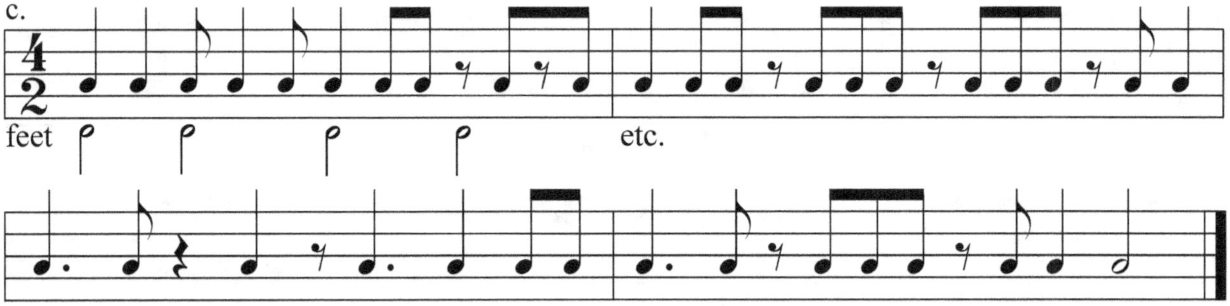

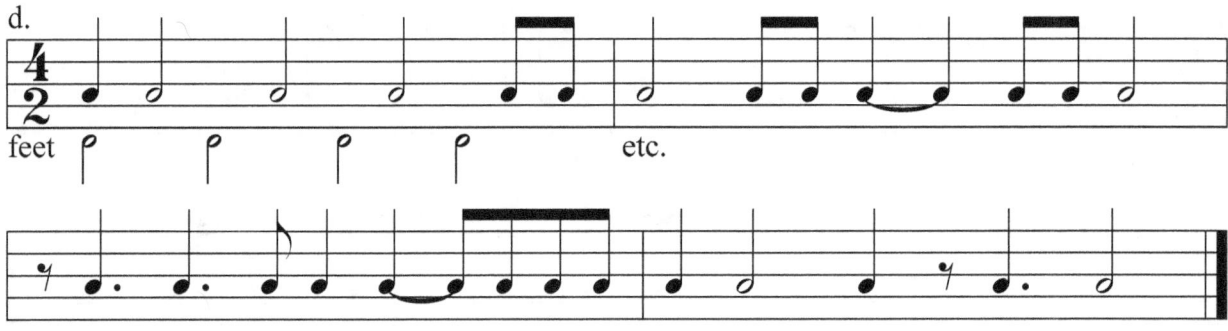

Appendix A Rhythmic Exercises 183

Rhythmic Exercise A–17

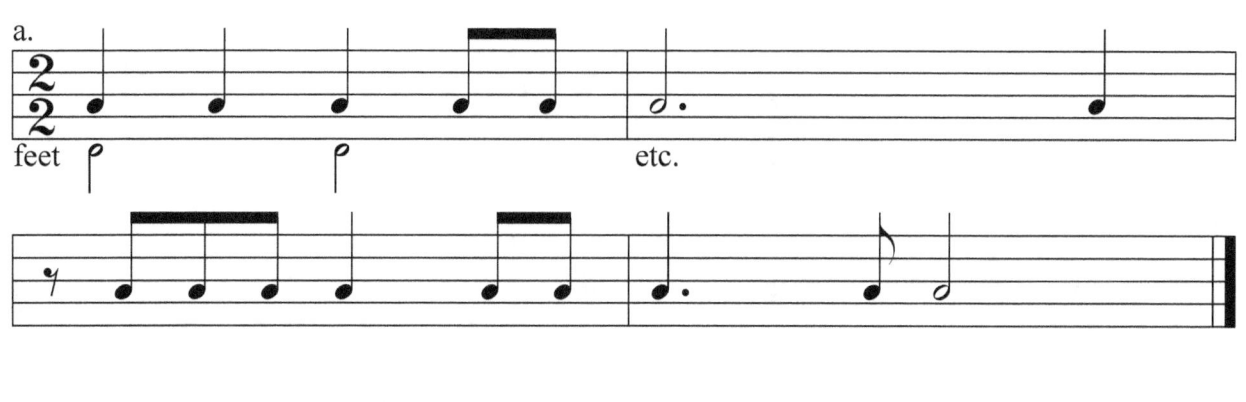

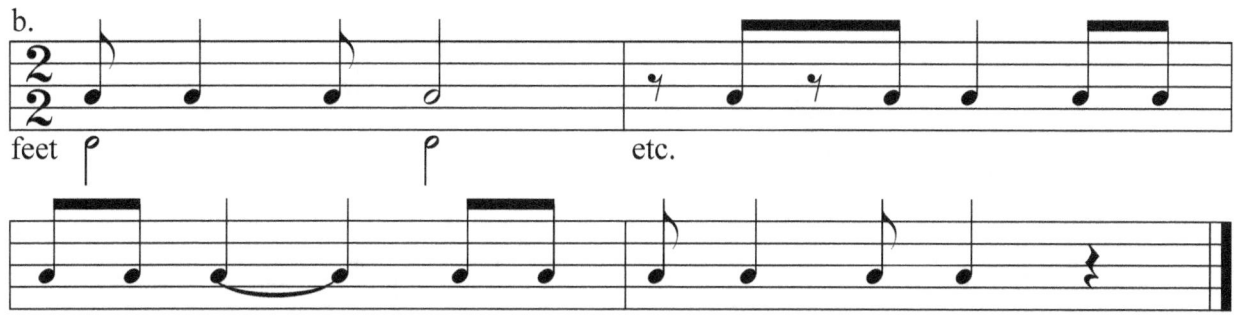

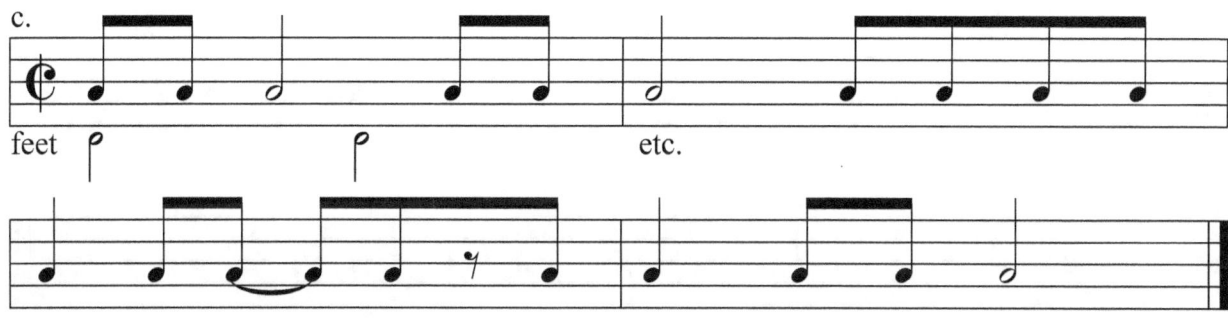

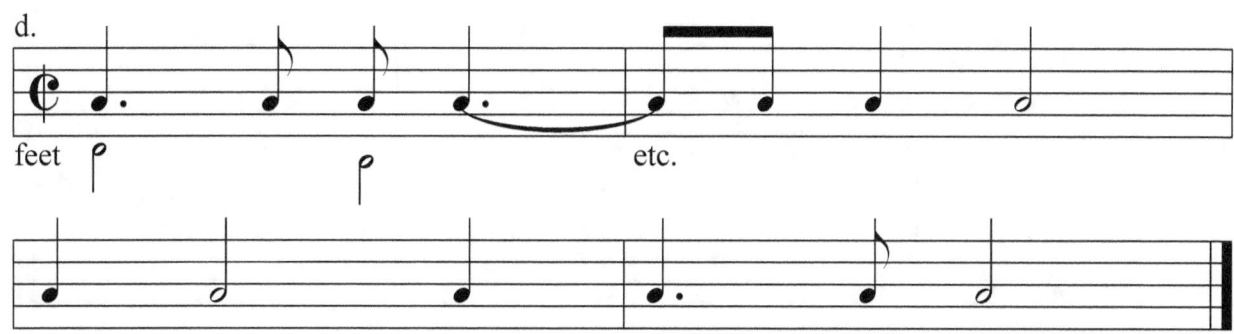

Rhythmic Exercise A–18

a.
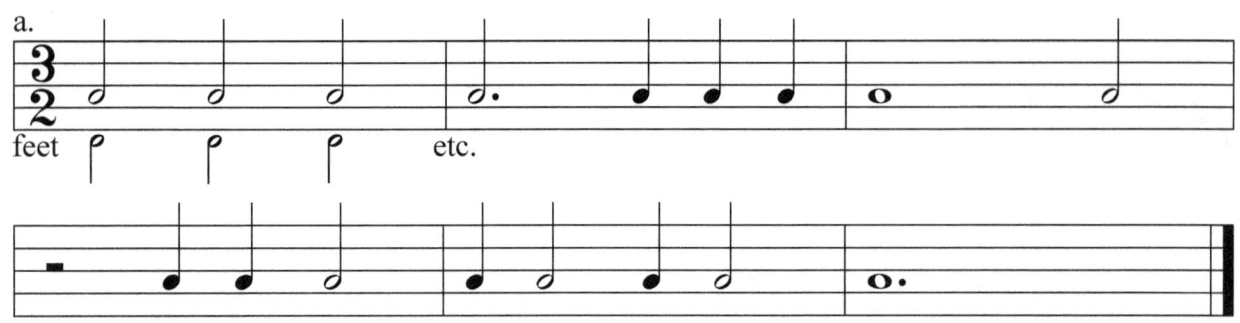

b.
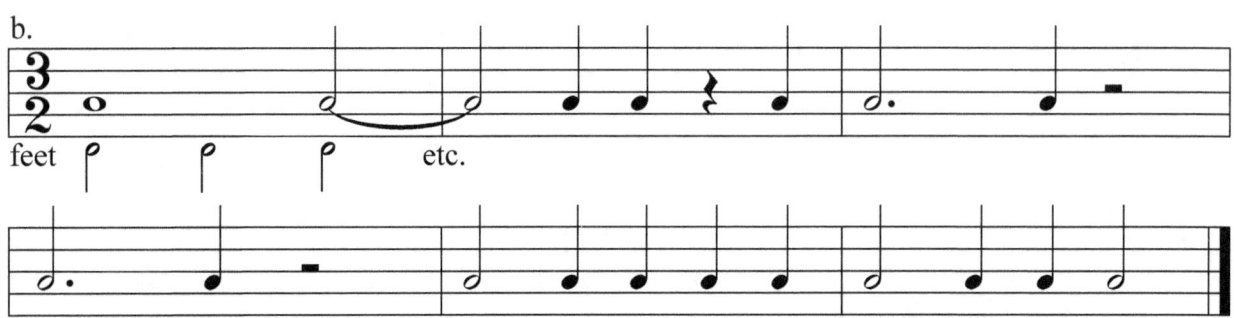

c.
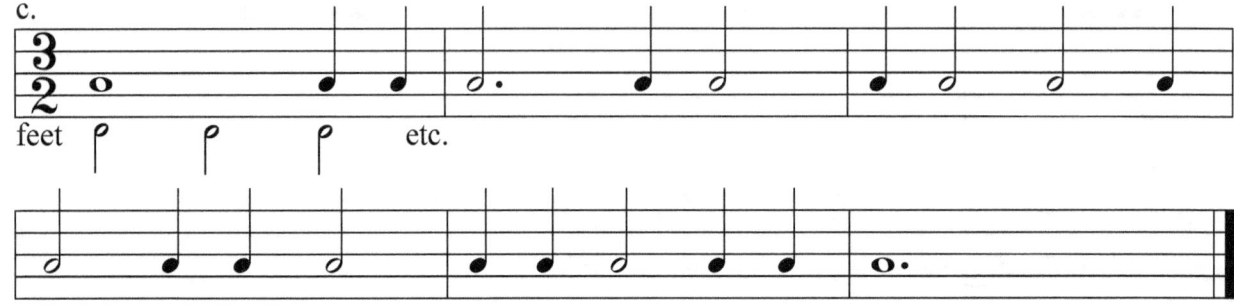

d.

Rhythmic Exercise A–19

The basic pulse for the following 6/4, 9/4, and 12/4 meters is indicated below the staff.

Appendix A Rhythmic Exercises

Rhythmic Exercise A–20

Appendix A Rhythmic Exercises 187

Rhythmic Exercise A–21

Rhythmic Exercise A–22

Rhythmic Exercise A–23

190 Appendix A Rhythmic Exercises

Rhythmic Exercise A–24

Rhythmic Exercise A–25

Appendix A Rhythmic Exercises

Rhythmic Exercise A–26

Rhythmic Exercise A–27

Appendix B   Rhythmic Exercises: Two Hands

Rhythmic Exercise B–1: Two Hands

Using the pitches of the bass clef to designate small c as the right hand and great A as the left, play the following two-hand rhythm. You should tap both feet with the basic pulse of the meter. The > symbol on beats 2 and 4 indicates that the note to which it is attached should be played louder than the notes that do not carry this marking. We call this type of symbol a dynamic accent. The double dots and bars at both the beginning and end of the exercise indicate that you should play all four measures twice before stopping. It would be well, however, to repeat the exercise several times in order to develop a level of comfort with the rhythm.

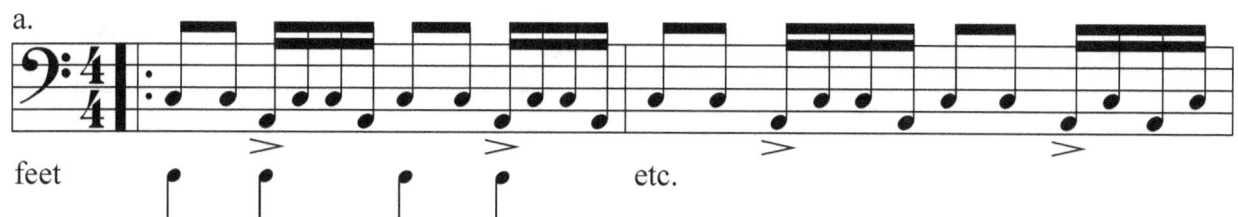

Once you have mastered Exercise B–1a, try this slight variation of the same rhythm:

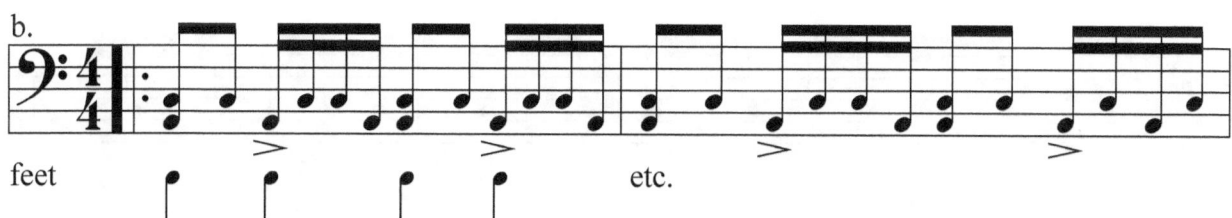

196 Appendix B Rhythmic Exercises: Two Hands

Rhythmic Exercise B–2: Two Hands

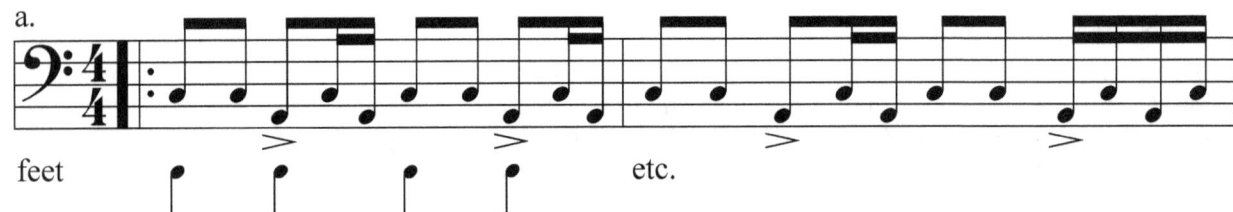

Once you have mastered Exercise B–2a, try this slight variation of the same rhythm:

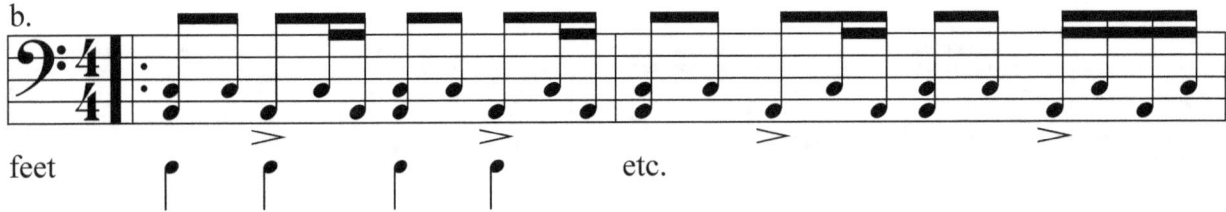

Appendix B Rhythmic Exercises: Two Hands   197

Rhythmic Exercise B–3: Two Hands

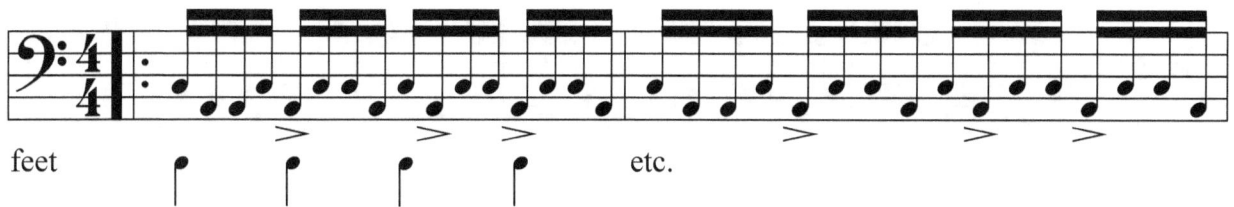

feet

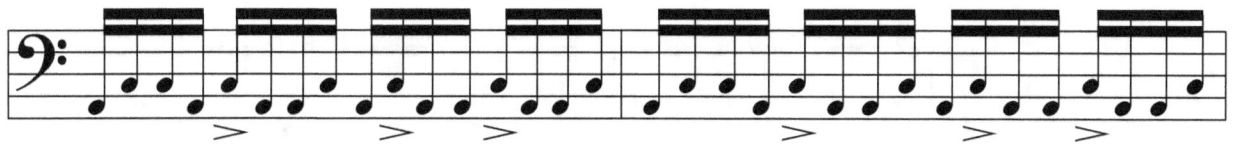

Appendix B Rhythmic Exercises: Two Hands

Rhythmic Exercise B–4: Two Hands

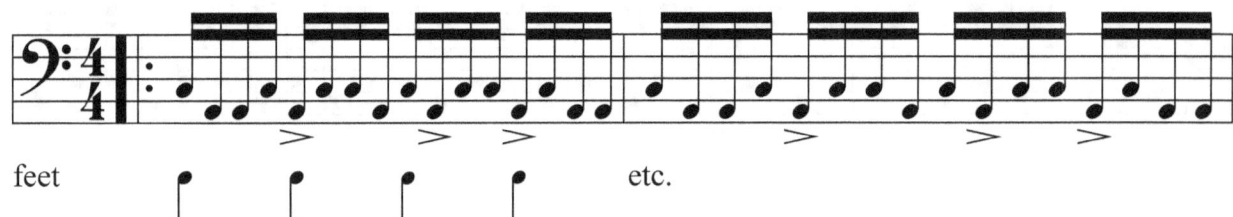

feet   etc.

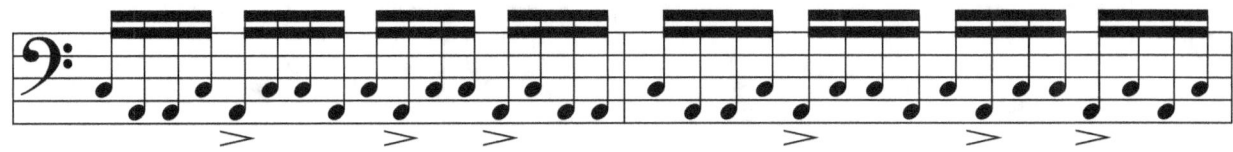

Rhythmic Exercise B–5: Two Hands

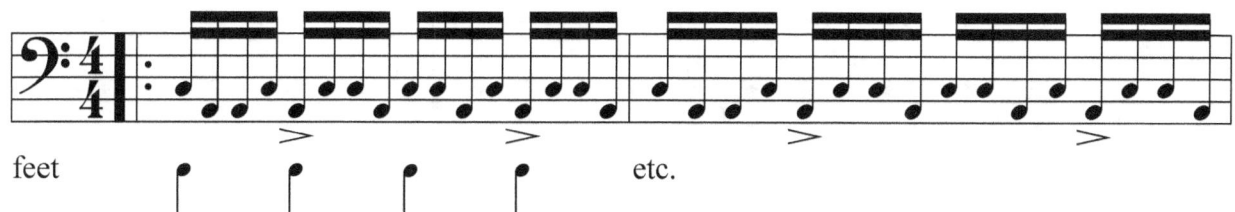

feet

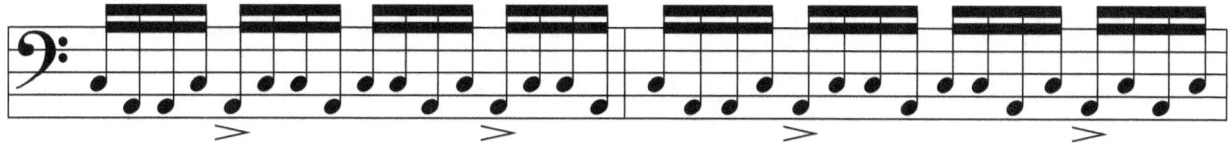

Rhythmic Exercise B–6: Two Hands

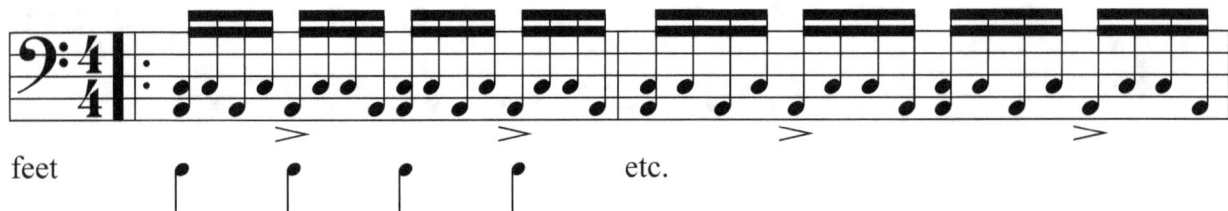

feet

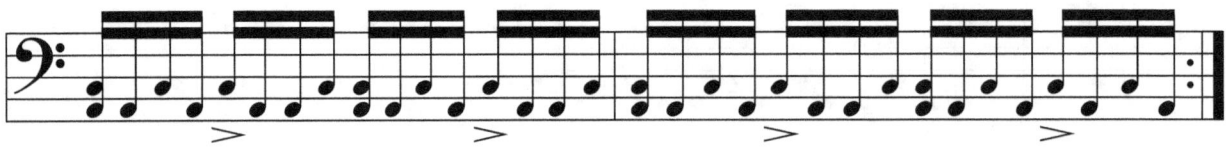

Appendix B Rhythmic Exercises: Two Hands   201

Rhythmic Exercise B–7: Two Hands

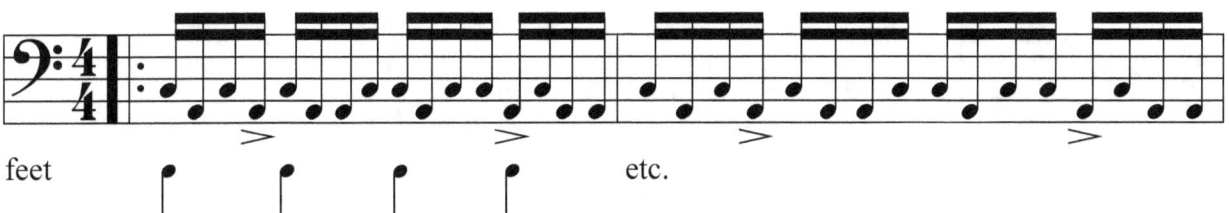

feet   etc.

202 Appendix B Rhythmic Exercises: Two Hands

Rhythmic Exercise B–8: Two Hands

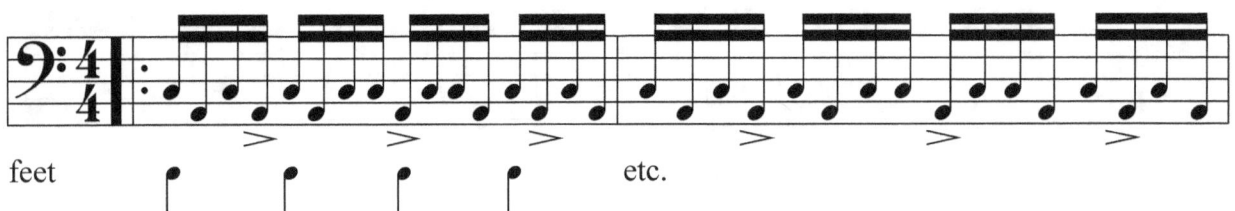
feet   etc.

Rhythmic Exercise B–9: Two Hands

Beats 2 and 4 have dynamic accents in the left hand (great A) for measures 1–4 and in the right hand (small c) for measures 5–8.

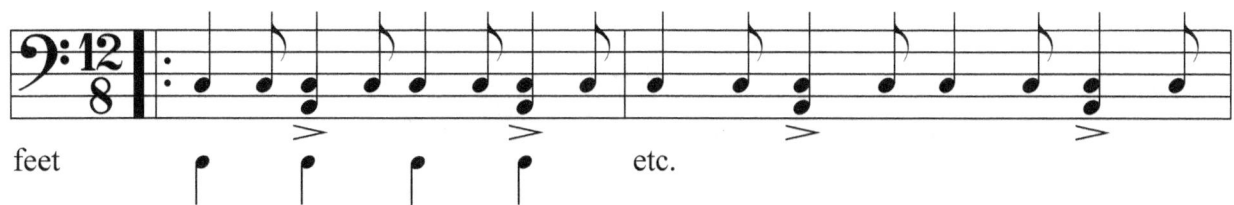

Rhythmic Exercise B–10: Two Hands

Beats 2 and 4 have dynamic accents in the left hand (great A) for measures 1–4 and in the right hand (small c) for measures 5–8.

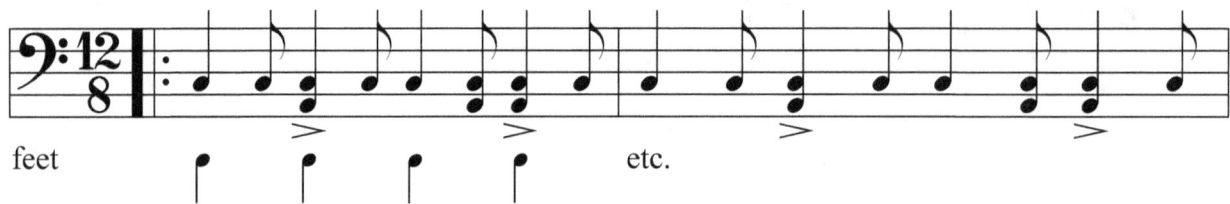

feet   etc.

Rhythmic Exercise B–11: Two Hands

Beats 2 and 4 have dynamic accents in the left hand (great A) for measures 1–4 and in the right hand (small c) for measures 5–8.

206　Appendix B Rhythmic Exercises: Two Hands

Rhythmic Exercise B–12: Two Hands

Beats 2 and 4 have dynamic accents in the left hand (great A) for measures 1–4 and in the right hand (small c) for measures 5–8.

Rhythmic Exercise B–13: Two Hands

Beats 2 and 4 have dynamic accents in the left hand (great A) for measures 1–4 and in the right hand (small c) for measures 5–8.

Appendix B Rhythmic Exercises: Two Hands

Rhythmic Exercise B–14: Two Hands

Beats 2 and 4 have dynamic accents in the left hand (great A) for measures 1–4 and in the right hand (small c) for measures 5–8.

Rhythmic Exercise B–15: Two Hands

Beats 2 and 4 have dynamic accents in the left hand (great A) for measures 1–4 and in the right hand (small c) for measures 5–8.

Rhythmic Exercise B–16: Two Hands

Beats 2 and 4 have dynamic accents in the left hand (great A) for measures 1–4 and in the right hand (small c) for measures 5–8.

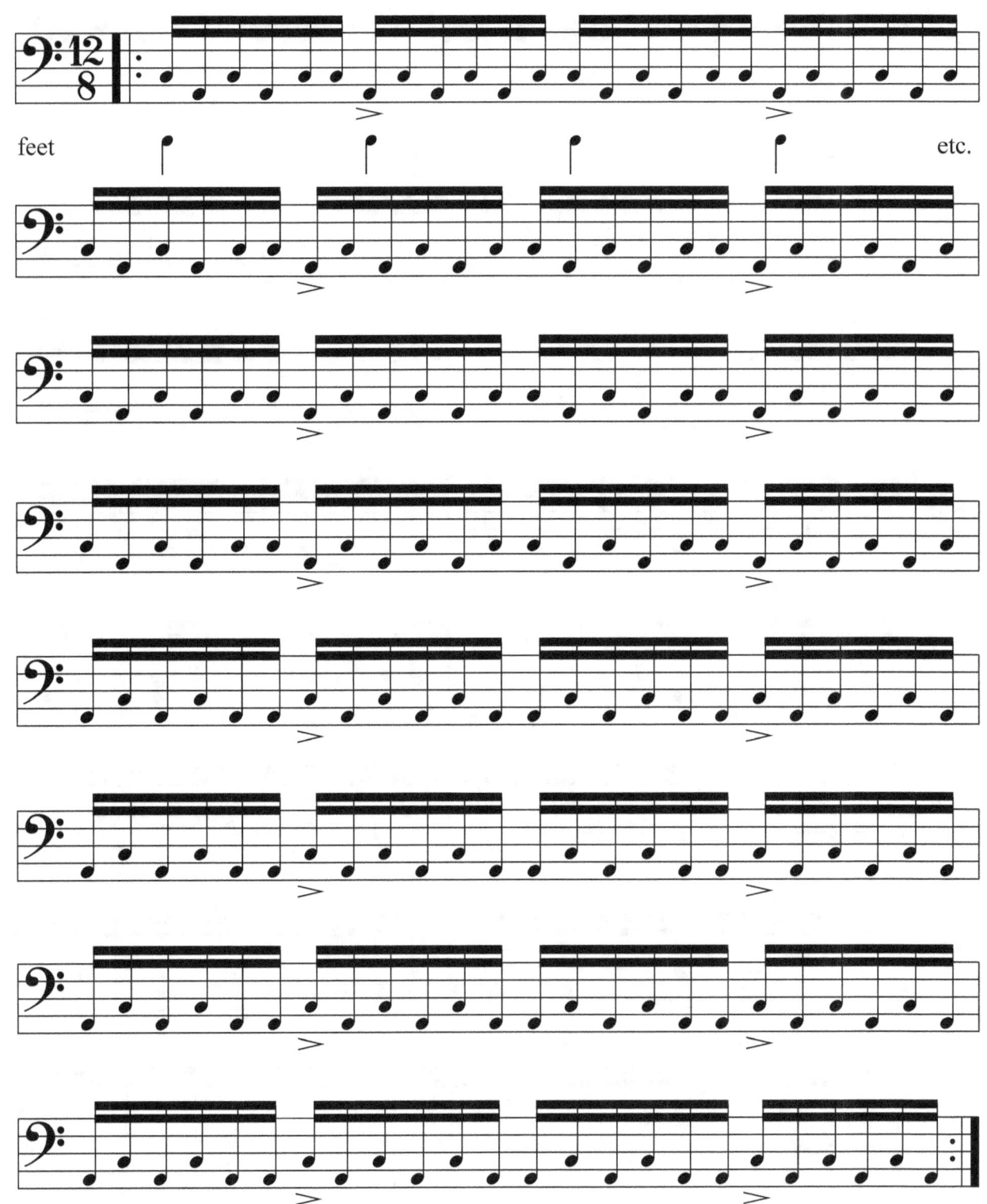

Appendix B Rhythmic Exercises: Two Hands   211

Rhythmic Exercise B–17: Two Hands

Beats 2 and 4 have dynamic accents in the left hand (great A) for measures 1–4 and in the right hand (small c) for measures 5–8.

Rhythmic Exercise B–18: Two Hands

Beats 2 and 4 have dynamic accents in the left hand (great A) for measures 1–4 and in the right hand (small c) for measures 5–8.

Appendix B Rhythmic Exercises: Two Hands   213

Rhythmic Exercise B–19: Two Hands

Beats 2 and 4 have dynamic accents in the left hand (great A) for measures 1–4 and in the right hand (small c) for measures 5–8.

Rhythmic Exercise B–20: Two Hands

As in the previous exercises, the dynamic accents will occur first in the left hand (great A) for measures 1–4 and then in the right hand (small c) for measures 5–8. For this exercise, however, you will be counting in 6 for the two-hand part while tapping both feet on counts 1, 3, and 5, resulting in a subtle feeling of two against three. In the two-hand part, the dynamic accent in parentheses on the second half of the fourth count can be executed instead of or in addition to the first accent of the measure; alternatively, the accent in parentheses can be omitted.

Rhythmic Exercise B–21: Two Hands

As in the previous exercises, the dynamic accents will occur first in the left hand (great A) for measures 1–4 and then in the right hand (small c) for measures 5–8. This exercise also presents a challenge similar to that of exercise B–20 if you choose to execute the optional accents in parentheses. Tapping your feet to the quarter note while observing the accents will produce a feeling of two rhythms at once. Play this exercise very slowly at first.

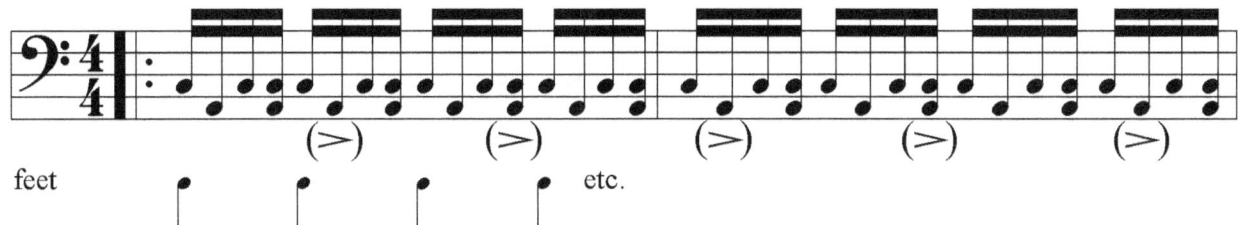

Appendix C   The Church Modes

Mode, or modality, is a collection of pitch relationships exhibiting certain characteristic melodic and chordal configurations that confirm and establish the key of a musical work. Our present-day concept of mode is the result of centuries of evolution and practice. Out of this evolution, the major-minor tonal system emerged as the most widely used system of pitch organization in the Western world. But long before the development of this system in the late-seventeenth century, other modes existed.

Known as the **church modes**, or **ecclesiastical modes**, they were used for hundreds of years, through the Middle Ages and the Renaissance. Thereafter, the church modes receded from view for about two hundred years but then recaptured the imagination of composers during the second half of the nineteenth century. Before we consider the modal system in its current state, let us take a brief excursion into the early history of this system.

The church modes were developed during the eighth and ninth centuries of the Common Era as a means for analyzing and classifying the monophonic music of the Roman Catholic Church. **Monophony** is a type of musical texture that consists of a single melodic line. The music of the Roman Church is referred to generally as **plainchant** (*cantus planus*) and more specifically as **Gregorian chant**. The latter reference is an attribution to the charismatic pope St. Gregory I (540?–604), who traditionally receives credit for composing the chant for the services of the Roman Church during his papacy. St. Gregory is a central figure in the history of the Roman Church, one of the four Doctors (teachers) of the Church, along with St. Ambrose (340?–397), St. Augustine (354–430), and St. Jerome (340?–420?).

Although St. Gregory may have helped to bring the chant repertory of the Roman Church together through his extraordinary service as an administrator, it is unlikely that he composed any of the music himself. Still, given the magnitude of St. Gregory's role in establishing both the papacy as a world power and the independence of the Western Church, it is understandable that the surviving corpus of Western chant would bear his name.

The first discussions of the church modes began to appear in the treatises of the ninth century. Based upon certain references to the scale system of the ancient Greeks found in a sixth-century treatise called *De institutione musica* (The Fundamentals of Music), some writers concluded that the modes were of Greek origin. The treatise was written by the Roman statesman Boethius (ca. 480–ca. 524), the most widely read authority on the music theory of antiquity.

Misinterpreting Boethius's account of the Greek scales, medieval theoreticians improperly assigned the Greek names associated with these scales to the modes of the Roman Church. Although the musical scales of ancient Greece had nothing in common with the modal system of the Middle Ages, the church modes as we understand them today retain their Hellenistic names.

The history of the church modes is one in which the usage differs from one era to another, from the Middle Ages through the second half of the nineteenth century. The treatment of the church modes during the last hundred and fifty years or so, however, constitutes a relatively consistent practice. Focusing on the characteristics of the modes as they occur in the music literature of the recent past will deepen our understanding of the concepts that concern beginning music students, especially pitch, key, scale, mode, key signature, interval, and harmony.

Example C–1 below illustrates the seven church modes with their Greek names, tonic triads, and half-step profiles. All of the modes shown in the example appear as diatonic scales, each with five whole steps and two half steps. The placement of the half steps, however, is different for each of the seven modes. Two modes should be recognized immediately, the Ionian mode and the Aeolian mode. The half-step profile of the Ionian mode is identical to that of the major mode, whereas the half-step profile of the Aeolian mode is identical to that of the natural minor.

Appendix C The Church Modes

Example C–1: the seven church modes with their Greek names, tonic triads, and half-step profiles

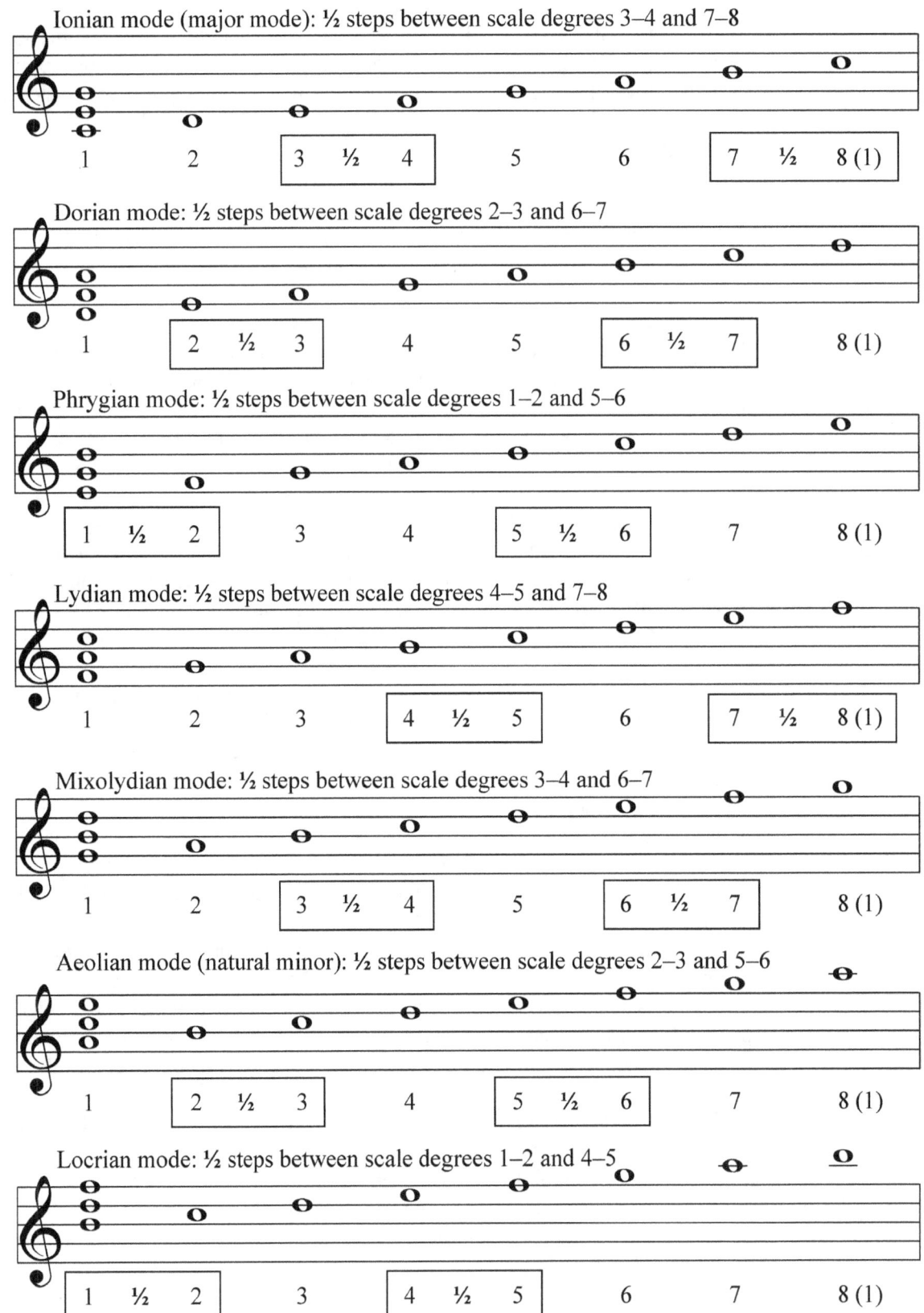

Appendix C The Church Modes 219

The white keys of the piano keyboard contain all of the pitch content for each of the seven modes in their *untransposed* forms. As displayed in example C–1 above, the untransposed Ionian mode (or major mode) spans the white keys of the C octave, the Dorian mode the D octave, the Phrygian mode the E octave, the Lydian mode the F octave, the Mixolydian mode the G octave, the Aeolian mode the A octave, and the Locrian mode the B octave. In the next section, we shall place the seven untransposed modes into two separate categories according to the quality of their respective tonic triads and the intervallic relationship between their tonic and mediant scale degrees.

Major and Minor Prototypes

The Lydian and Mixolydian modes are "major prototypes" because they have both a major triad on the tonic and a major 3rd between their tonic and mediant scale degrees (example C–2).

Compare the untransposed mode of F Lydian to its parallel major, F major. Notice that there are similarities between the two modes, except that F Lydian's scale degree 4 is raised one half step in relation to the F-major scale. F Lydian contains a B natural, F major a B♭ (examples C–2a and 2b). The untransposed Mixolydian mode on G is similar to its parallel major, G major, except that G Mixolydian's scale degree 7 is lowered one half step in relation to the G-major scale. G Mixolydian contains an F natural, G major an F♯ (examples C–2c and 2d).

Example C–2: major prototype modes

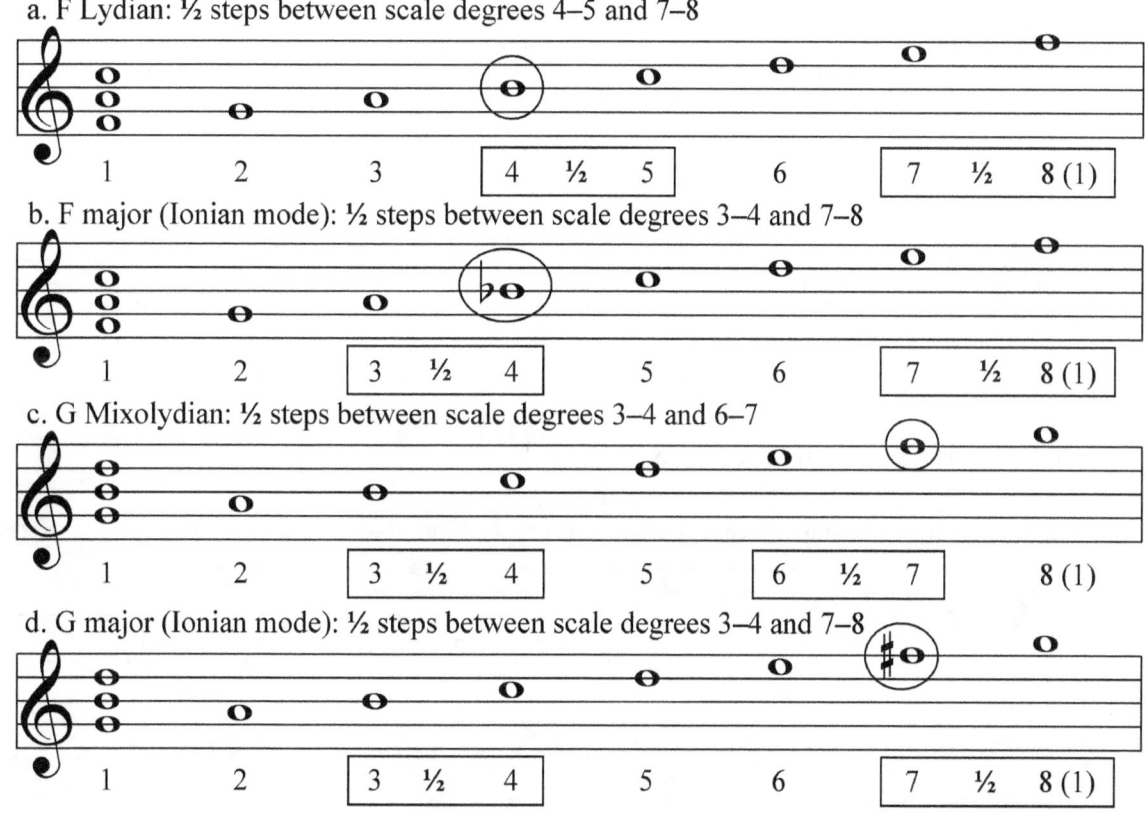

The Dorian and Phrygian modes, on the other hand, are "minor prototypes" because they have both a minor triad on the tonic and a minor 3rd between their tonic and mediant scale degrees (example C–3). The untransposed Dorian mode on D resembles the parallel natural minor on D, except that D Dorian's scale degree 6 is raised one half step in relation to the d-minor scale. D Dorian contains a B natural, d minor a B♭ (examples C–3a and 3b). The untransposed Phrygian mode on E is similar to its parallel natural minor, e minor, except that E Phrygian's scale degree 2 is lowered one half step in relation to the e-minor scale. E Phrygian contains an F natural, e minor an F♯ (examples C–3c and 3d).

Example C–3: minor prototype modes

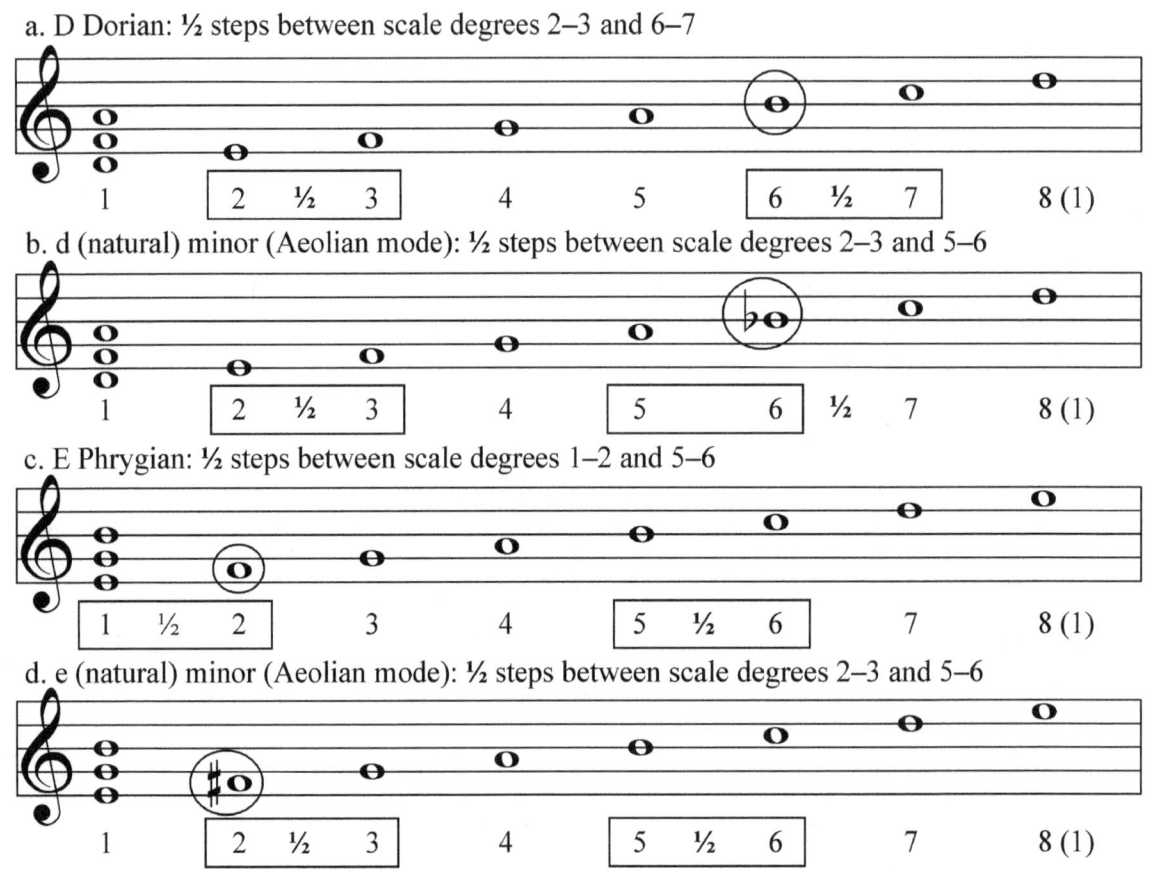

Example C–4: the exceptional Locrian mode

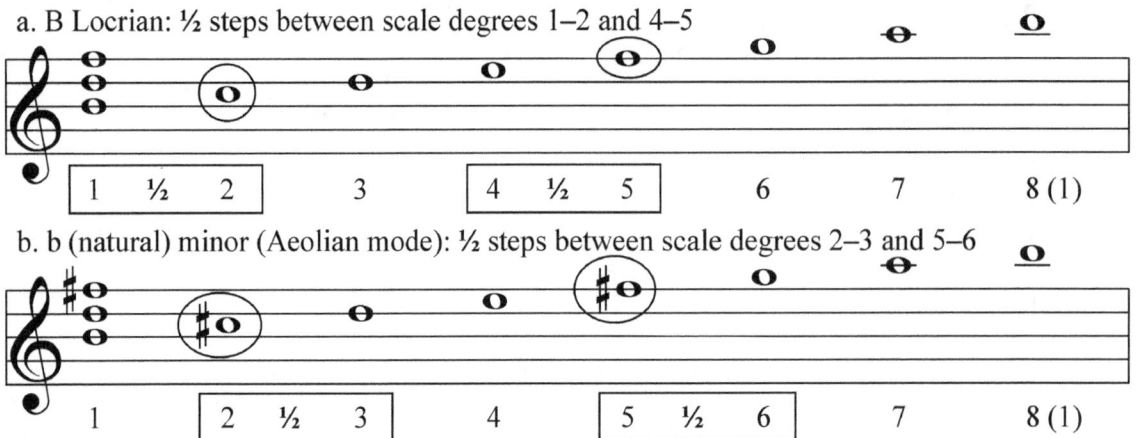

The Locrian mode, as illustrated in C–4 above, is an exceptional case for two reasons: the mode has two scale degrees that differ from the natural minor and its tonic triad is diminished and therefore inherently unstable. B Locrian's scale degrees 2 and 5 are each lowered one half step in relation to its parallel natural minor, b minor. The untransposed Locrian mode on B contains a C natural and an F natural, whereas b minor has both a C♯ and an F♯. Still, because the Locrian mode has a minor 3rd between its tonic and mediant scale degrees (as does the Dorian and Phrygian modes), we classify Locrian as a minor prototype, albeit an unusual one.

Relating the Church Modes to the Major Mode

Earlier in this appendix, we noted that the white keys of the piano keyboard contain all of the pitch content for the seven modes in their untransposed forms. As demonstrated in example C–5, the first note of each mode may be placed within the context of the C-major scale. Accordingly, we assign the names of the seven church modes to each of the seven scale degrees of C major, starting with the untransposed Ionian mode.

Thus, the keynote of the Ionian mode begins on C, the keynote of the Dorian mode on D, the keynote of the Phrygian mode on E, the keynote of the Lydian mode on F, the keynote of the Mixolydian mode on G, the keynote of the Aeolian mode on A, and the keynote of the Locrian mode on B.

Example C–5: the church mode areas within the context of the C-major scale

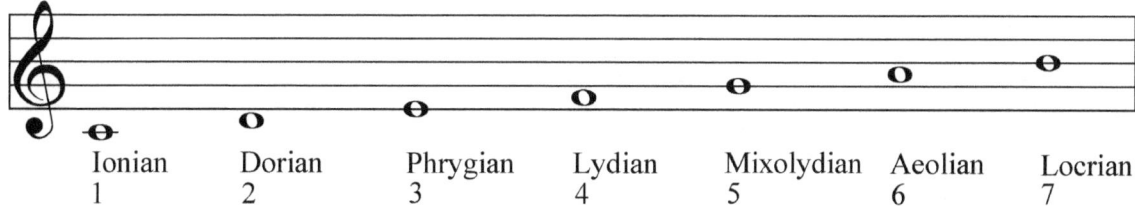

Mode Transposition

Since all seven church modes in their untransposed forms use only the white keys of the piano keyboard and appear within the context of the C-major scale, the respective key signatures and pitch content of D Dorian, E Phrygian, F Lydian, G Mixolydian, A Aeolian, and B Locrian are all *related* to the key signature and pitch content of C major (or C Ionian).

As we observed in Chapter 6, any two modes standing in a relative relationship to one another will share the same key signature and the same pitch content but have different tonics and different octave ranges. For example, any major mode, transposed or untransposed, has a relative minor key area with which it shares the same key signature and pitch content.

Presently, we shall apply the concept of relative relationships between major and minor modes to all of the church modes, designating scale degree 2 of C major as its relative Dorian area, scale degree 3 as its relative Phrygian area, scale degree 4 as its relative Lydian area, scale degree 5 as its relative Mixolydian area, scale degree 6 as its relative Aeolian area, and scale degree 7 as its relative Locrian area (see C–5 above).

As we explore the characteristics of the church modes, our reference point will be the untransposed key and mode of C major. Let us begin with the relationship between the untransposed mode of C major and its relative Dorian, D Dorian, as shown in example C–6 below. Notice that both modes share the same pitch content but have different tonics and different ranges.

Example C–6: D, the relative Dorian of C major (scale degree 2 of C Major)

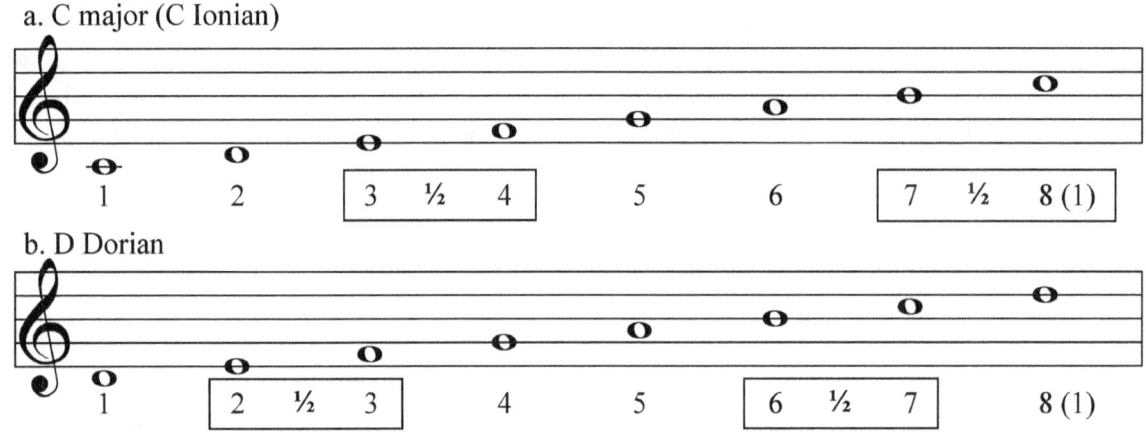

The names of the seven church modes remain unchanged when transposing the C major to another key (example C–7).

Example C–7: the church mode areas of B♭ major

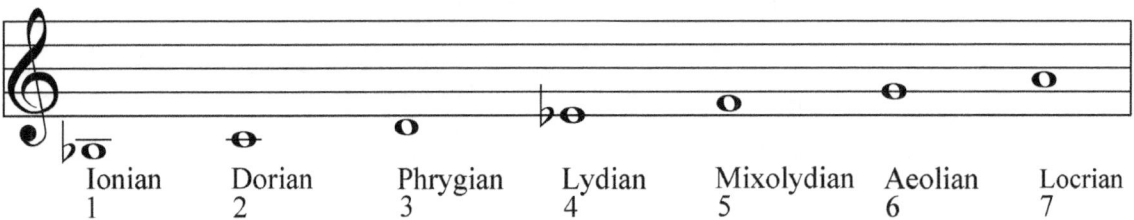

Example C–8 moves the relationship between C major and D Dorian down one whole step, to B♭ major and C Dorian; both modes share the same pitch content, including a B♭ and an E♭, but have different tonics and different ranges.

Example C–8: C, the relative Dorian of B♭ major (scale degree 2 of B♭ major)

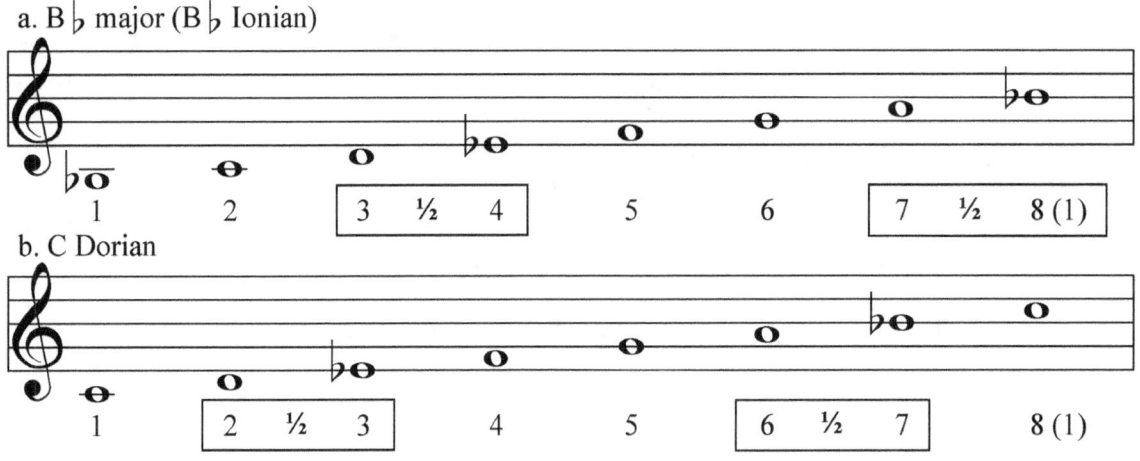

Appendix C The Church Modes   223

Let us stay with B♭ major for a few more examples. If C Dorian has the same pitch content as B♭ major, then any of the other relative modes of B♭ major will also have seven tones in common. In example C–9, we have B♭ major and its relative Phrygian, D Phrygian. Both C Dorian (example C–8b) and D Phrygian (C–9b) have the same key signature as B♭ major: two flats, B♭ and E♭. All three modes (B♭ major, C Dorian, and D Phrygian), however, have different tonics and different ranges.

Example C–9: D, the relative Phrygian of B♭ major (scale degree 3 of B♭ major)

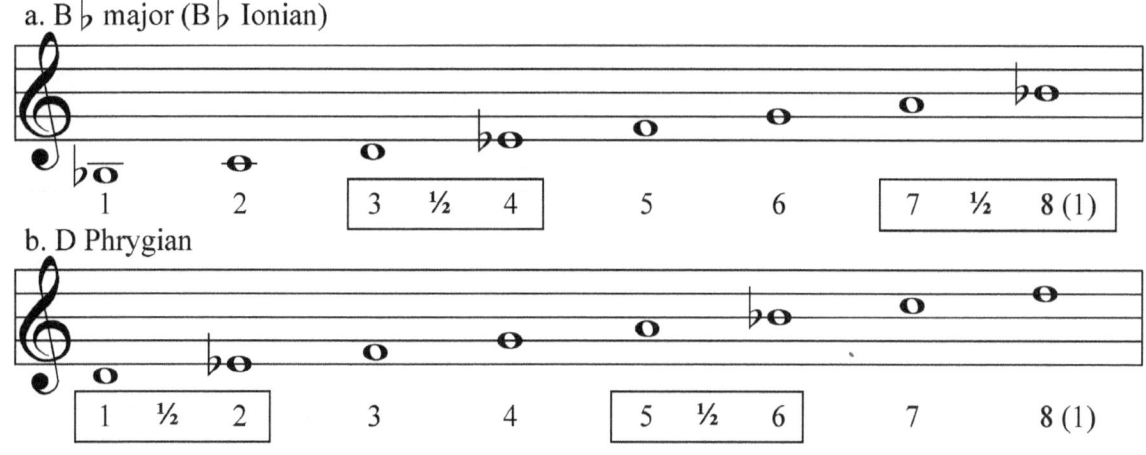

Example C–10 compares B♭ major to its relative Lydian, E♭ Lydian; again, the pitch content is the same for both modes but their respective tonics and ranges are different.

Example C–10: E♭, the relative Lydian of B♭ major (scale degree 4 of B♭ major)

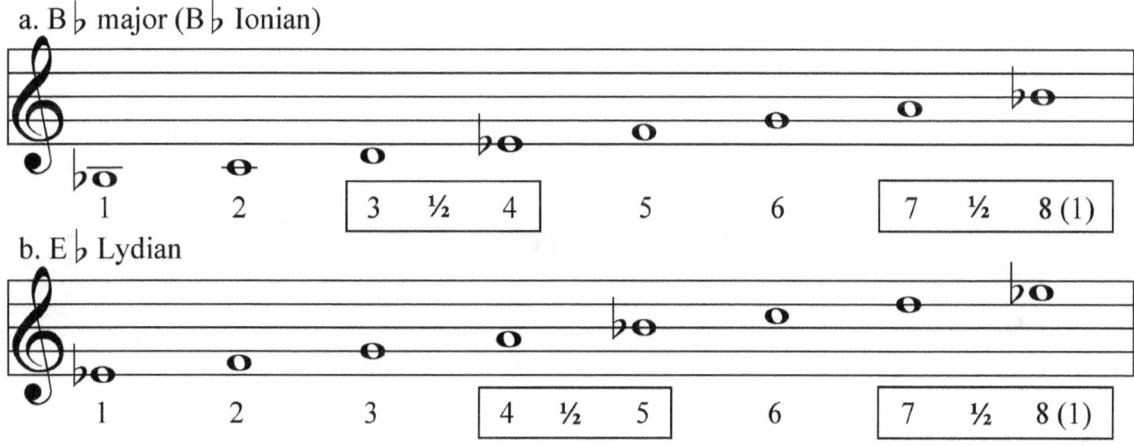

As shown in example C–11, the relative Mixolydian of B♭ major is F Mixolydian. Both modes have the same pitch content but different tonics and different ranges.

Example C–11: F, the relative Mixolydian of B♭ major (scale degree 5 of B♭ major)

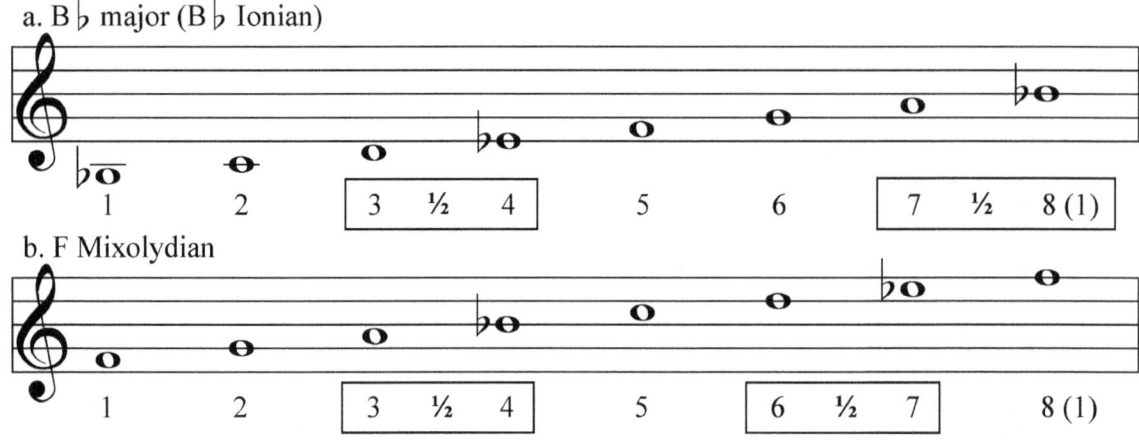

Example C–12 illustrates the relative Aeolian of B♭ major, G Aeolian. As we have observed, the Aeolian mode is identical to that of the natural minor; therefore, the relationship between the two modes shown below is the same as the relationship between B♭ major and its relative minor.

Example C–12: G, the relative Aeolian of B♭ major (scale degree 6 of B♭ major)

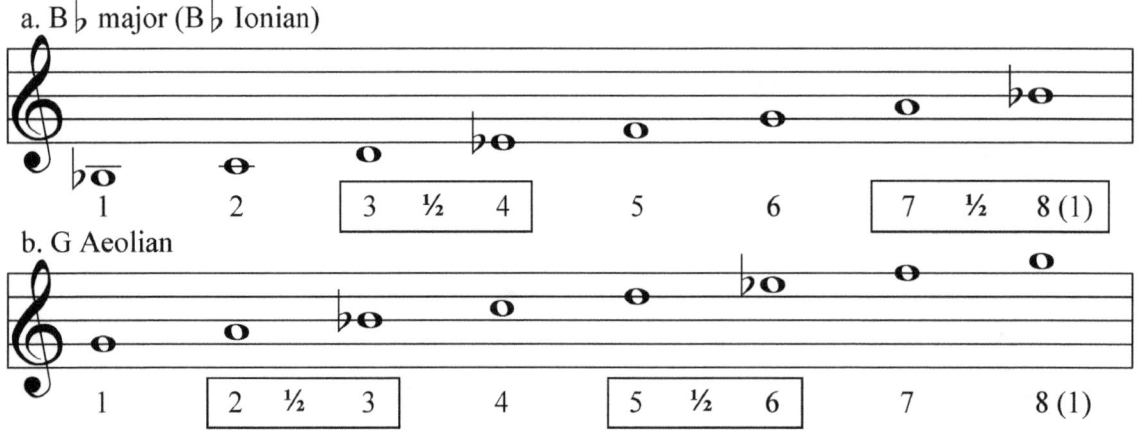

Finally, example C–13 presents the relative Locrian of B♭ major, A Locrian. We know that the Locrian mode's tonic scale degree projects a diminished triad. The Locrian mode is the only church mode that has a diminished 5th between its scale degrees 1 and 5. The unstable properties of the Locrian mode has tended to discourage its use throughout most periods of music history; indeed, the tritone relationship between its tonic and dominant as well as the lack of a stable tonic triad make it difficult to establish a strong tonal center.

Example C–13: A, the relative Locrian of B♭ major (scale degree 7 of B♭ major)

a. B♭ major (B♭ Ionian)

1   2   3 ½ 4   5   6   7 ½ 8 (1)

b. A Locrian

1 ½ 2   3   4 ½ 5   6   7   8 (1)

Given the Key and Mode, Find the Right Key Signature

In the foregoing discussion, we learned that if the relative modal key areas of C major share the same pitch content and key signature as C major, then the relative modal key areas of B♭ major share the same pitch content and key signature as B♭ major. Finding the relative modal key area of any transposed major mode is one way of understanding the principle of mode transposition. There are, however, other ways to approach this inquiry.

Drawing upon the information gleaned from the modal relationships considered in examples C–8 through 13, we shall now arrange two pairs of conditions into the following proposition in order to find the relationship between them: *untransposed major is to untransposed mode as transposed major is to transposed mode*.

As presented in example C–14, the first pair of conditions contains two known values and is therefore complete; the second pair, however, contains one unknown value and is therefore incomplete: C major is to D Dorian as the unknown value (X) is to C Dorian. Finding the correct value will tell us the keynote of the transposed major and provide the answer to the following question:

(1) What is the key signature for the transposed mode of C Dorian (C–14)?
(2) D Dorian is the untransposed mode and scale degree 2 of the untransposed major, C major.
(3) C Dorian occurs on scale degree 2 of what transposed major (X)?
(4) C major is to D Dorian (a major 2nd) as X major is to C Dorian; what is a major 2nd *below* C?
(5) If you cannot find a major 2nd below C, find a minor 7th above C (the inversion of a major 2nd). B♭ is a minor 7th above C and therefore a major 2nd below C.
(6) C major is to D Dorian as B♭ major (X) is to C Dorian.
(7) B♭ major has two flats (B♭ and E♭) and so does C Dorian.

Example C–14: the key signature of C Dorian

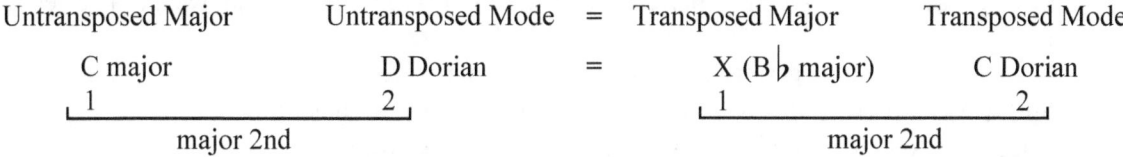

Appendix C The Church Modes

Two skills are absolutely necessary at this point in your study. You must know the major key signatures *and* be able to calculate easily the intervals of the major 2nd, major 3rd, perfect 4th, perfect 5th, major 6th, and major 7th *below* any given tone. In this exercise, the given tone represents the transposed mode; X represents the key signature of that transposed mode.

(1) What is the key signature for the transposed mode of D Phrygian (example C–15)?
(2) E Phrygian is the untransposed mode and scale degree 3 of the untransposed major, C major.
(3) D Phrygian occurs on scale degree 3 of what transposed major (X)?
(4) C major is to E Phrygian (a major 3rd) as X major is to D Phrygian; what is a major 3rd *below* D?
(5) If you cannot find a major 3rd below D, then find a minor 6th above D (the inversion of a major 3rd). B♭ is a minor 6th above D and therefore a major 3rd below D.
(6) C major is to E Phrygian as B♭ major (X) is to D Phrygian.
(7) B♭ major has two flats (B♭ and E♭) and so does D Phrygian.

Example C–15: the key signature of D Phrygian

Untransposed Major	Untransposed Mode	=	Transposed Major	Transposed Mode
C major	E Phrygian	=	X (B♭ major)	D Phrygian
1	3		1	3
major 3rd			major 3rd	

(1) What is the key signature for the transposed mode of E♭ Lydian (example C–16)?
(2) F Lydian is the untransposed mode and scale degree 4 of the untransposed major, C major.
(3) E♭ Lydian occurs on scale degree 4 of what transposed major (X)?
(4) C major is to F Lydian (a perfect 4th) as X major is to E♭ Lydian; what is a perfect 4th *below* E♭?
(5) If you cannot find a perfect 4th below E♭, then find a perfect 5th above E♭ (the inversion of a perfect 4th). B♭ is a perfect 5th above E♭ and therefore a perfect 4th below E♭.
(6) C major is to F Lydian as B♭ major (X) is to E♭ Lydian.
(7) B♭ major has two flats (B♭ and E♭) and so does E♭ Lydian.

Example C–16: the key signature of E♭ Lydian

Untransposed Major	Untransposed Mode	=	Transposed Major	Transposed Mode
C major	F Lydian	=	X (B♭ major)	E♭ Lydian
1	4		1	4
perfect 4th			perfect 4th	

(1) What is the key signature for the transposed mode of F Mixolydian (example C–17)?
(2) G Mixolydian is the untransposed mode and scale degree 5 of the untransposed major, C major.
(3) F Mixolydian occurs on scale degree 5 of what transposed major (X)?
(4) C major is to G Mixolydian (a perfect 5th) as X major is to F Mixolydian; what is a perfect 5th *below* F?
(5) If you cannot find a perfect 5th below F, then find a perfect 4th above F (the inversion of a perfect 5th). B♭ is a perfect 4th above F and therefore a perfect 5th below F.
(6) C major is to G Mixolydian as B♭ major (X) is to F Mixolydian.
(7) B♭ major has two flats (B♭ and E♭) and so does F Mixolydian.

Example C–17: the key signature of F Mixolydian

Untransposed Major	Untransposed Mode	=	Transposed Major	Transposed Mode
C major	G Mixolydian	=	X (B♭ major)	F Mixolydian
1	5		1	5
perfect 5th			perfect 5th	

(1) What is the key signature for the transposed mode of G Aeolian (example C–18)?
(2) A Aeolian is the untransposed mode and scale degree 6 of the untransposed major, C major.
(3) G Aeolian occurs on scale degree 6 of what transposed major (X)?
(4) C major is to A Aeolian (a major 6th) as X major is to G Aeolian; what is a major 6th *below* G?
(5) If you cannot find a major 6th below G, then find a minor 3rd above G (the inversion of a major 6th). B♭ is a minor 3rd above G and therefore a major 6th below G.
(6) C major is to A Aeolian as B♭ major (X) is to G Aeolian.
(7) B♭ major has two flats (B♭ and E♭) and so does G Aeolian.

Example C–18: the key signature of G Aeolian

Untransposed Major	Untransposed Mode	=	Transposed Major	Transposed Mode
C major	A Aeolian	=	X (B♭ major)	G Aeolian
1	6		1	6
major 6th			major 6th	

(1) What is the key signature for the transposed mode of A Locrian (example C–19)?
(2) B Locrian is the untransposed mode and scale degree 7 of the untransposed major, C major.
(3) A Locrian occurs on scale degree 7 of what transposed major (X)?
(4) C major is to B Locrian (a major 7th) as X major is to A Locrian; what is a major 7th *below* A?
(5) If you cannot find a major 7th below A, then find a minor 2nd above A (the inversion of a major 7th). B♭ is a minor 2nd above A and therefore a major 7th below A.
(6) C major is to B Locrian as B♭ major (X) is to A Locrian.
(7) B♭ major has two flats (B♭ and E♭) and so does A Locrian.

Example C–19: the key signature of A Locrian

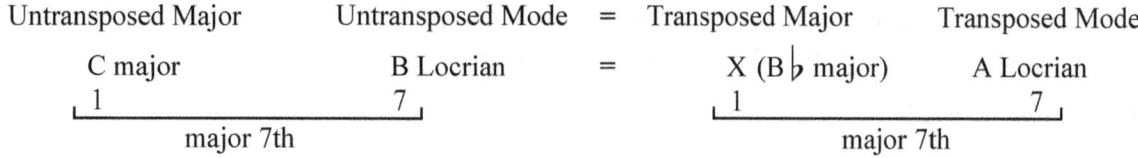

Untransposed Major	Untransposed Mode	=	Transposed Major	Transposed Mode
C major	B Locrian	=	X (B♭ major)	A Locrian
1	7		1	7
major 7th			major 7th	

Up to this point in our study of mode transposition, we have systematically explored the possibilities of modes with two flats from two different but related perspectives. First, we ascended through the modal key areas of B♭ major one scale degree at a time (pp. 222–225). Second, armed with the knowledge of the first perspective, or approach, we held the key signature of B♭ major in the background as an unknown quantity (X) and then endeavored to find the key signatures for the transposed modes of C Dorian, D Phrygian, E♭ Lydian, F Mixolydian, G Aeolian, and A Locrian (pp. 225–227).

Of course, we already knew that all six transposed modes of examples C–14 through 19 would have two flats in their respective key signatures, as that fact was determined from our prior consideration of examples C–8 through 13. For the next several examples, however, let us practice finding the key signatures of transposed modes *without the benefit of knowing from previous exercises* what key would be entered into the unknown quantity of X.

(1) What is the key signature for the transposed mode of F Dorian (example C–20)?
(2) D Dorian is the untransposed mode and scale degree 2 of the untransposed major, C major.
(3) F Dorian occurs on scale degree 2 of what transposed major (X)?
(4) C major is to D Dorian (a major 2nd) as X major is to F Dorian; what is a major 2nd *below* F?
(5) If you cannot find a major 2nd below F, then find a minor 7th above F (the inversion of a major 2nd). E♭ is a minor 7th above F and therefore a major 2nd below F.
(6) C major is to D Dorian as E♭ major (X) is to F Dorian.
(7) E♭ major has three flats (B♭, E♭, and A♭) and so does F Dorian.

Example C–20: the key signature of F Dorian

Untransposed Major	Untransposed Mode	=	Transposed Major	Transposed Mode
C major	D Dorian	=	X (E♭ major)	F Dorian
1	2		1	2
major 2nd			major 2nd	

(1) What is the key signature for the transposed mode of C Lydian (example C–21)?
(2) F Lydian is the untransposed mode and scale degree 4 of the untransposed major, C major.
(3) C Lydian occurs on scale degree 4 of what transposed major (X)?
(4) C major is to F Lydian (a perfect 4th) as X major is to C Lydian; what is a perfect 4th *below* C?
(5) If you cannot find a perfect 4th below C, then find a perfect 5th above C (the inversion of a perfect 4th). G is a perfect 5th above C and therefore a perfect 4th below C.
(6) C major is to F Lydian as G major (X) is to C Lydian.
(7) G major has one sharp (F♯) and so does C Lydian.

Example C–21: the key signature of C Lydian

Untransposed Major	Untransposed Mode	=	Transposed Major	Transposed Mode
C major	F Lydian	=	X (G major)	C Lydian
1	4		1	4
perfect 4th			perfect 4th	

(1) What is the key signature for the transposed mode of F♯ Aeolian (example C–22)?
(2) A Aeolian is the untransposed mode and scale degree 6 of the untransposed major, C major.
(3) F♯ Aeolian occurs on scale degree 6 of what transposed major (X)?
(4) C major is to A Aeolian (a major 6th) as X major is to F♯ Aeolian; what is a major 6th *below* F♯?
(5) If you cannot find a major 6th below F♯, then find a minor 3rd above F♯ (the inversion of a major 6th). A is a minor 3rd above F♯ and therefore a major 6th below F♯.
(6) C major is to A Aeolian as A major (X) is to F♯ Aeolian.
(7) A major has three sharps (F♯, C♯, and G♯) and so does F♯ Aeolian.

Example C–22: the key signature of F♯ Aeolian

Untransposed Major	Untransposed Mode	=	Transposed Major	Transposed Mode
C major	A Aeolian	=	X (A major)	F♯ Aeolian
1	6		1	6
major 6th			major 6th	

Again, a reminder: with respect to the key signature, the relative Aeolian and the relative minor are equivalent terms. The relative minor of A major is F♯ minor; both modes have three sharps.

(1) What is the key signature for the transposed mode of F Phrygian (example C–23)?
(2) E Phrygian is the untransposed mode and scale degree 3 of the untransposed major, C major.
(3) F Phrygian occurs on scale degree 3 of what transposed major (X)?
(4) C major is to E Phrygian (a major 3rd) as X major is to F Phrygian; what is a major 3rd *below* F?
(5) If you cannot find a major 3rd below F, then find a minor 6th above F (the inversion of a major 3rd). D♭ is a minor 6th above F and therefore a major 3rd below F.
(6) C major is to E Phrygian as D♭ major (X) is to F Phrygian.
(7) D♭ major has five flats (B♭, E♭, A♭, D♭, and G♭) and so does F Phrygian.

Example C–23: the key signature of F Phrygian

Untransposed Major	Untransposed Mode	=	Transposed Major	Transposed Mode
C major	E Phrygian	=	X (D♭ major)	F Phrygian
1	3		1	3
major 3rd			major 3rd	

(1) What is the key signature for the transposed mode of D♯ Locrian (example C–24)?
(2) B Locrian is the untransposed mode and scale degree 7 of the untransposed major, C major.
(3) D♯ Locrian occurs on scale degree 7 of what transposed major (X)?
(4) C major is to B Locrian (a major 7th) as X major is to D♯ Locrian; what is a major 7th *below* D♯?
(5) If you cannot find a major 7th below D♯, then find a minor 2nd above D♯ (the inversion of a major 7th). E is a minor 2nd above D♯ and therefore a major 7th below D♯.
(6) C major is to B Locrian as E major (X) is to D♯ Locrian.
(7) E major has four sharps (F♯, C♯, G♯, and D♯) and so does D♯ Locrian.

Example C–24: the key signature of D♯ Locrian

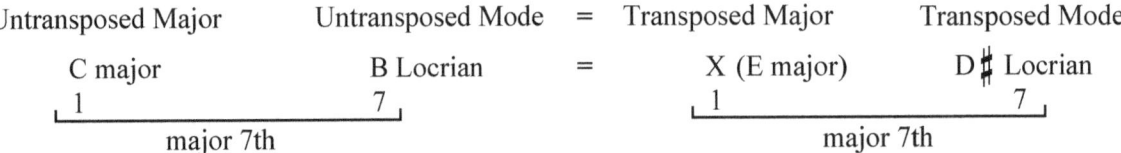

(1) What is the key signature for the transposed mode of D♭ Mixolydian (example C–25)?
(2) G Mixolydian is the untransposed mode and scale degree 5 of the untransposed major, C major.
(3) D♭ Mixolydian occurs on scale degree 5 of what transposed major (X)?
(4) C major is to G Mixolydian (a perfect 5th) as X major is to D♭ Mixolydian; what is a perfect 5th *below* D♭?
(5) If you cannot find a perfect 5th below D♭, then find a perfect 4th above D♭ (the inversion of a perfect 5th). G♭ is a perfect 4th above D♭ and therefore a perfect 5th below D♭.
(6) C major is to G Mixolydian as G♭ major (X) is to D♭ Mixolydian.
(7) G♭ major has six flats (B♭, E♭, A♭, D♭, G♭ and C♭) and so does D♭ Mixolydian.

Example C–25: the key signature of D♭ Mixolydian

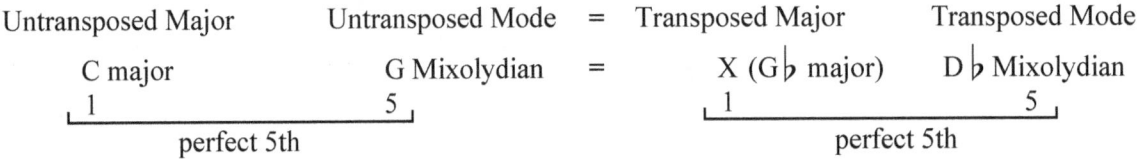

Given the Key and Key Signature, Find the Right Mode

The exercises introduced in the foregoing examples will help you to play (or sing) scales and/or melodies in any key using any of the various diatonic modes discussed in this appendix. Once you have found the key signature of a specified key center and mode, it is a relatively simple task to run through the tones of the mode, assuming that you have some degree of facility with an instrument (or voice).

In examples C–14 through 25, we found the relationship between two pairs of conditions by placing an unknown value (X) into the second pair. In examples C–26 through 31, we find the relationship between two pairs of conditions by moving the unknown value to the first pair, from the transposed major to the untransposed mode. With the first pair of conditions now containing the unknown value, the object of the inquiry becomes the identity of the transposed mode rather than its key signature. Accordingly, given both the key center (transposed mode) and the key signature (transposed major), what is the *mode* of the music?

(1) Given the tonic key of E♭ and a key signature with four flats, what is the name of the transposed mode (example C–26)?
(2) The key signature of four flats represents the transposed major key of A♭ major.
(3) E♭ is scale degree 5 of the transposed major, A♭ major; A♭ is a perfect 5th *below* E♭.
(4) The perfect 5th between A♭ and E♭ must be duplicated between C major and the untransposed mode X. A perfect 5th above C is G. G represents the untransposed Mixolydian mode.
(5) C major is to G Mixolydian as A♭ major is to E♭ Mixolydian
(6) Therefore, the transposed mode is E♭ Mixolydian.
(7) A♭ major has four flats (B♭, E♭, A♭, and D♭) and so does E♭ Mixolydian.

Example C–26: What mode on E♭ has four flats?

Untransposed Major	Untransposed Mode	=	Transposed Major	Transposed Mode
C major	X (G Mixolydian)	=	A♭ major (4 Flats)	E♭
1	5		1	5
perfect 5th			perfect 5th	

(1) Given the tonic key of F♯ and a key signature with four sharps, what is the name of the transposed mode (example C–27)?
(2) The key signature of four sharps represents the transposed major key of E major.
(3) F♯ is scale degree 2 of the transposed major, E major; E is a major 2nd *below* F♯.
(4) The major 2nd between E and F♯ must be duplicated between C major and the untransposed mode X. A major 2nd above C is D. D represents the untransposed Dorian mode.
(5) C major is to D Dorian as E major is to F♯ Dorian.
(6) Therefore, the transposed mode is F♯ Dorian.
(7) E major has four sharps (F♯, C♯, G♯, and D♯) and so does F♯ Dorian.

Example C–27: What mode on F♯ has four sharps?

Untransposed Major	Untransposed Mode	=	Transposed Major	Transposed Mode
C major	X (D Dorian)	=	E major (4 Sharps)	F♯
1	2		1	2
major 2nd			major 2nd	

(1) Given the tonic key of B♭ and a key signature with seven flats, what is the name of the transposed mode (example C–28)?
(2) The key signature of seven flats represents the transposed major key of C♭ major.
(3) B♭ is scale degree 7 of the transposed major, C♭ major; C♭ is a major 7th *below* B♭.
(4) The major 7th between C♭ and B♭ must be duplicated between C major and the untransposed mode X. A major 7th above C is B. B represents the untransposed Locrian mode.
(5) C major is to B Locrian as C♭ major is to B♭ Locrian.
(6) Therefore, the transposed mode is B♭ Locrian.
(7) C♭ major has seven flats (B♭, E♭, A♭, D♭, G♭, C♭, and F♭) and so does B♭ Locrian.

Example C–28: What mode on B♭ has seven flats?

Untransposed Major	Untransposed Mode	=	Transposed Major	Transposed Mode
C major	X (B Locrian)	=	C♭ major (7 Flats)	B♭
1	7		1	7
major 7th			major 7th	

(1) Given the tonic key of B and a key signature with one sharp, what is the name of the transposed mode (example C–29)?
(2) The key signature of one sharp represents the transposed major key of G major.
(3) B is scale degree 3 of the transposed major, G major; G is a major 3rd *below* B.
(4) The major 3rd between G and B must be duplicated between C major and the untransposed mode X. A major 3rd above C is E. E represents the untransposed Phrygian mode.
(5) C major is to E Phrygian as G major is to B Phrygian.
(6) Therefore, the transposed mode is B Phrygian.
(7) G major has one sharp (F♯) and so does B Phrygian.

Example C–29: What mode on B has one sharp?

Untransposed Major	Untransposed Mode	=	Transposed Major	Transposed Mode
C major	X (E Phrygian)	=	G major (1 Sharp)	B
1	3		1	3
major 3rd			major 3rd	

(1) Given the tonic key of E♭ and a key signature with six flats, what is the name of the transposed mode (example C–30)?
(2) The key signature of six flats represents the transposed major key of G♭ major.
(3) E♭ is scale degree 6 of the transposed major, G♭ major; G♭ is a major 6th *below* E♭.
(4) The major 6th between G♭ and E♭ must be duplicated between C major and the untransposed mode X. A major 6th above C is A. A represents the untransposed Aeolian mode.
(5) C major is to A Aeolian as G♭ major is to E♭ Aeolian.
(6) Therefore, the transposed mode is E♭ Aeolian.
(7) G♭ major has six flats (B♭, E♭, A♭, D♭, G♭, and C♭) and so does E♭ Aeolian.

Example C–30: What mode on E♭ has six flats?

Untransposed Major	Untransposed Mode	=	Transposed Major	Transposed Mode
C major	X (A Aeolian)	=	G♭ major (6 Flats)	E♭
1	6		1	6
major 6th			major 6th	

(1) Given the tonic key of G and a key signature with two sharps, what is the name of the transposed mode (example C–31)?
(2) The key signature of two sharps represents the transposed major key of D major.
(3) G is scale degree 4 of the transposed major, D major; D is a perfect 4th *below* G.
(4) The perfect 4th between D and G must be duplicated between C major and the untransposed mode X. A perfect 4th above C is F. F represents the untransposed Lydian mode.
(5) C major is to F Lydian as D major is to G Lydian.
(6) Therefore, the transposed mode is G Lydian.
(7) D major has two sharps (F♯ and C♯) and so does G Lydian.

Example C–31: What mode on G has two sharps?

Untransposed Major	Untransposed Mode	=	Transposed Major	Transposed Mode
C major	X (F Lydian)	=	D major (2 Sharps)	G
1	4		1	4
perfect 4th			perfect 4th	

Examples C–26 through 31 have demonstrated how to identify the mode of a music composition, *if we know both its key center and pitch content* (as represented in the key signature). We must add one caveat to the process of mode identification, however. The melody of the composition may contain tones that are not appropriate to the mode—chromatic notes (see above, p. 56). Upon mastering the fundamentals of music and basic harmony, you will have the requisite knowledge to ferret out these "inappropriate" tones and recognize those components of the music that are native (that is, diatonic) to the mode and those that are not.

Singing the Church Modes

In Chapter 6, we used the techniques of solmization and syllable inflection to sing the three forms of minor, including the natural minor, or Aeolian mode. The choice of syllables is based upon the inflections that were introduced for singing the chromatic scale in Chapter 3 (see above, example 3–39, p. 50).

When singing the natural minor in Chapter 6, we learned that scale degrees 3, 6, and 7 carry the syllables *me*, *le*, and *te* respectively, instead of *mi*, *la*, and *ti*. The harmonic minor uses *me* and *le* (scale degrees 3 and 6) instead of *mi* and *la*; however, *ti* is used instead of *te* because it constitutes the leading tone. Finally, the melodic minor employs *la* and *ti* (scale degrees ♯6 and ♯7) in its ascending form and *le* and *te* (scale degrees ♭6 and ♭7) in its descending form; *me* is retained in both forms.

In example C–32 below, the techniques of solmization and syllable inflection are revisited and demonstrated with all seven church modes, including the Ionian and Aeolian modes.

234 Appendix C The Church Modes

Example C–32

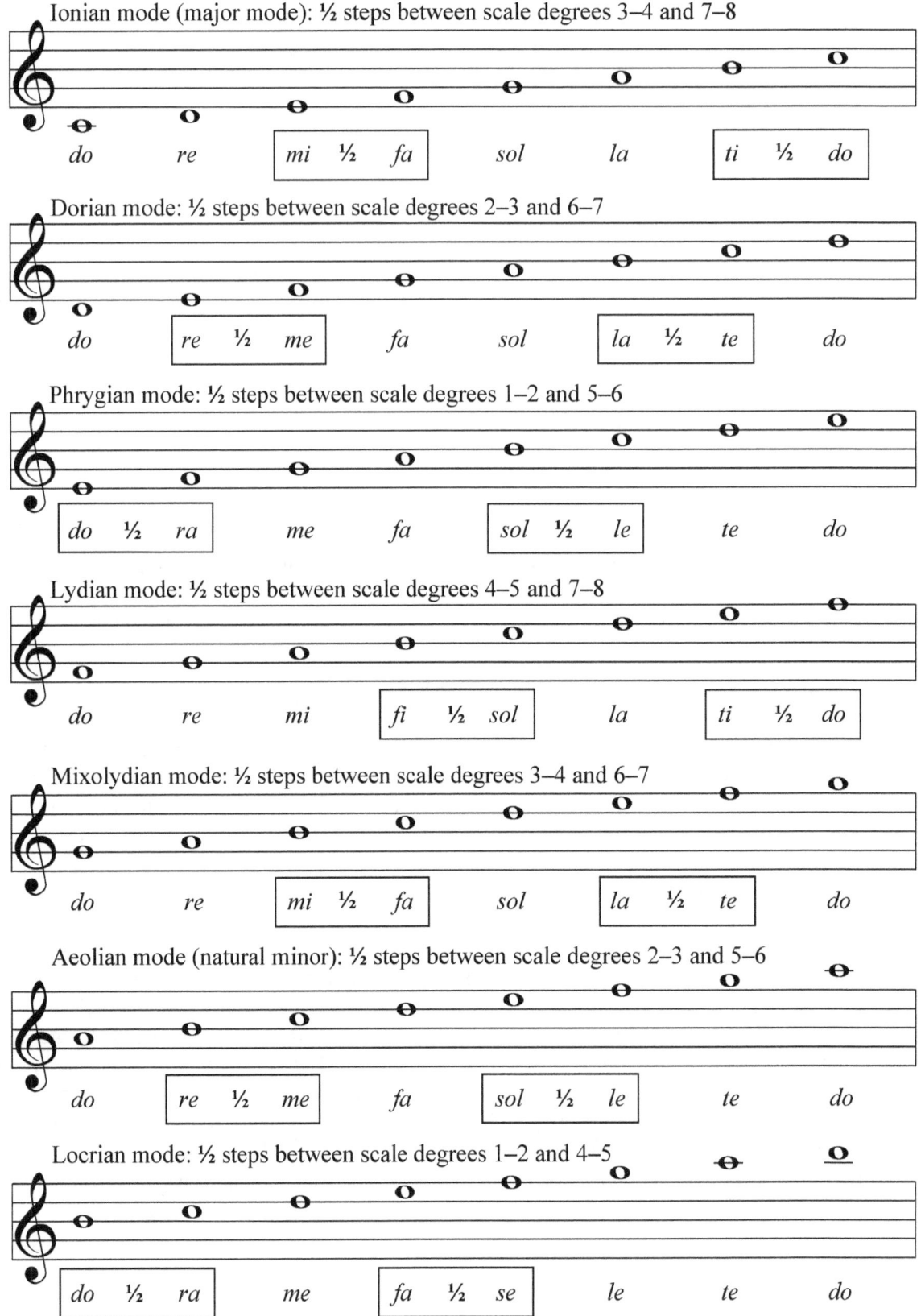

Appendix D The Cadential Six-Four Chord

In Chapter 5, we noted that if the interval of the perfect 4th occurs between the bass and an upper note, then the interval is treated as a dissonance (see above, p. 73). If, however, the perfect 4th does not occur between an upper note and the bass, then the interval is consonant. The first inversion of the triad has the consonant 4th; the second inversion, however, places the 4th in the dissonant position.

This appendix explores one of the most important usages of the $^6_4$ chord, the so-called cadential $^6_4$, a linear and harmonic formation that often appears at the end of a segment of music known as the **phrase**. The phrase is the smallest element of musical form in which a combination of melodic, rhythmic, and chordal components together comprise the beginning, middle, and end of a musical thought.

The Origins of the Cadential $^6_4$

One of the origins of the cadential $^6_4$ is the **passing tone**. Either dissonant or consonant with another voice, the passing tone usually connects two harmonic consonances; it is approached and left by step and may occur on either a strong or weak beat. The passing tone also appears on either a strong or weak portion of a beat.

In example D–1a, the soprano voice moves down a minor 3rd from D to B; the tone C (P) fills in the distance between the two pitches on beat 1 of measure 2. Forming a *dissonant* passing 4th with the bass, C connects two harmonic consonances, a major 6th and a major 3rd (compound intervals in the example are identified in their simple forms). A combination of figured-bass numbers and a dash between them (4—3) indicates the downward movement of the 4th (G/C) to the 3rd (G/B) over a stationary bass. Despite the limitations of the two-voice texture shown in D–1a, the arrival of the major 3rd on beat 3 of measure 2 implies a G-major triad, the dominant of C major (the chord symbols in parentheses indicate the implied chords).

Example D–1b places the passing 4th (P) within the framework of four parts with the addition of the alto and tenor voices. The combination of four voices gives us the tones G G D C on beat 1 of measure 2. The passing 4th *delays* the complete formation of the G dominant. However, with the arrival of B on beat 3 of the second measure, we have the third of the chord and therefore all three components of the G-major triad. These intervals are counted above the bass pitch. Since the 4th occurs on a strong beat, we should refer to it more precisely as an "*accented* passing tone."

Example D–1: the dissonant passing 4th

The cadential $^6_4$ grew out of the desire to rhythmically *delay* the formation of the dominant chord at the end of a musical phrase in a two-chord pattern known as the **cadence** (see Appendix F). The accented passing tone constitutes one means for delaying the appearance of the dominant chord.

Examples D–2a and 2b below demonstrate another technique for delaying certain elements of the dominant chord. As with the dissonant passing tone, the second measure of examples D–2a and 2b contains a dissonant 4th on the first beat of the measure, which once again shifts the third of the G chord to beat 3. However, in this instance, the third of the dominant is delayed by a procedure called **suspension**. As shown in D–2a, the suspension has three parts:

(1) the suspension is *prepared* ("prep"), usually as a consonance (but sometimes as a dissonance); then,

(2) the preparation is held, or *suspended* ("susp"), as the opposing voice (usually the bass) moves to form a dissonance with the suspended voice (though a consonant suspension is also possible); and finally,

(3) the suspended voice moves down by step to *resolve* to a consonance ("res"). In measure 2 of both examples D–2a and 2b, the interval of the 4th (susp) moves down by step to form a consonant 3rd on the second half note (res). We call the suspended 4th the "4–3 suspension."

An essential feature of the suspension is the degree of metric stress each part of the operation receives. First and foremost, the resolution (res) must be metrically weaker than the suspension itself (susp). The initial preparation, however, can be made from either a strong or weak position. In the preparation of D–2a, notice that the second half note of measure 1 is tied into the first half note of measure 2. The result of this tie lengthens the duration of the second half note.

Although the tie is the most common means for executing the suspension, D–2b shows how an actual tie between two note values is not required to employ this technique, as a repeated pitch also lengthens the duration of the second half note (in measure 1). Normally, without either tying or repeating the pitch, the second half note of measure 1 would be weaker than the first half note. However, by increasing its duration, the second half note becomes stronger than the first half note, resulting in syncopation.

Example D–2: the 4–3 suspension

Example D–2b places the suspended 4th within the framework of four parts with the addition of the alto and tenor voices. The complete formation of the dominant triad (G B D) does not occur until the suspended 4th between the bass and soprano voices moves down by step to form a consonant 3rd on beat 3 of the second measure (4—3). The soprano voice in measure 1 prepares the 4th by moving upwards to the subdominant's fifth (C) as the tenor proceeds to its third (A). The alto remains on F, the root of the IV.

Rather than taking the alto down from F to D in measure 2, an alternative disposition holds on to the F and creates a suspended 7th within the dominant chord (G/F). The 7th provides a smoother connection between the two chords (IV and V) and gives us a dominant with a doubled root, a third, a seventh, and an omitted fifth (D). In measure 3, the dissonant 7th resolves to a consonant 3rd within the tonic chord.

The idioms of the passing tone and the suspension both involve pitches that are not inherent components of the chord. Each of these operations counts among the various techniques falling within the category known as the **nonharmonic tone**, or **nonchord tone** (nonharmonic tones are discussed in Appendix G). The nonharmonic tone is an integral feature of the cadential $^6_4$.

The Cadential $^6_4$

The cadential $^6_4$ is also known as the "accented $^6_4$" because it is rhythmically strong, usually falling on the strongest beat of the measure (or, in triple meter, occasionally falling on beat 2 and resolving on beat 3). The cadential $^6_4$ occurs at the conclusion of a musical phrase and is approached either by step (with chords such as the IV or the ii^6), by a supertonic chord in root position, by a tonic chord in root position, or by a tonic chord in first inversion.

In example D–3a, the suspended 4th is first prepared in the soprano as a consonance and then held as the bass moves up to G to create the dissonance. The soprano moves down by step to a consonant 3rd on the second half note of measure 2 while the consonant E in the alto continues down to D. The downward motion of both the soprano and alto voices over the stationary bass is represented by a combination of figured-bass numbers and dashes between them: $^{6\,-\,5}_{4\,-\,3}$.

The figured bass in D–3 indicates what appears to be a succession of two distinct chords: a C-major triad in $^6_4$ position moving to a G-major triad in $^5_3$ position. However, the C and E in the soprano and alto voices are not native to the chord. In other words, what we have here is not a C-major triad in $^6_4$ position, but rather the arrival of the dominant pitch in the bass (G), over which two nonharmonic tones on the strongest beat of the measure occur. The E in both examples D–3a and 3b is a consonant accented passing tone (the 6th above G), while the C in D–3a is part of the dissonant suspension (the 4th above G).

In D–3b, the dissonant 4th is not prepared as a suspension; instead, we have a stepwise approach to both the dissonant 4th and the consonant the 6th of the cadential $^6_4$. The circle around the figured bass $^5_3$ attached to the chord symbol V$^{6\,-\,5}_{4\,-\,3}$ indicates that the real chord, the dominant (G B D), is formed on beat 3 of the second measure when all three elements of the chord are present.

Example D–3: the cadential $^6_4$

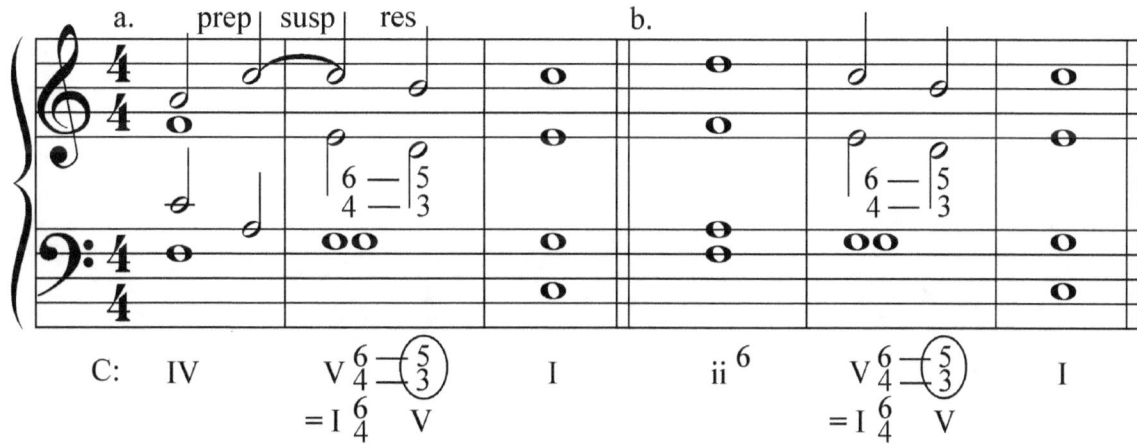

It is instructive to interpret the nonharmonic activity occurring above the stationary root of the dominant chord as an *elaboration* of that chord; as such, we can describe the cadential $^6_4$ as "the elaborated dominant." Indeed, the use of the Roman numeral V in front of the figured bass D–3 is justified because even though a literal tonic $^6_4$ chord is formed on the first half note of the measure, the tonic is *not a real chord*, but rather, an **apparent chord**. Hence, the cadential $^6_4$ has two parts: the apparent $^6_4$ chord and the real chord, the dominant in $^5_3$ position (E and C move to D and B respectively).

Appendix E The Dominant Seventh Chord

The seventh chord is a tertian harmony consisting of four chord tones: a root, third, fifth, and seventh. As shown in example E–1a, the seventh chord is produced by adding the interval of the 3rd above the fifth of the triad. The additional 3rd produces a *dissonant* 7th between the root and the seventh of the chord.

Example E–1

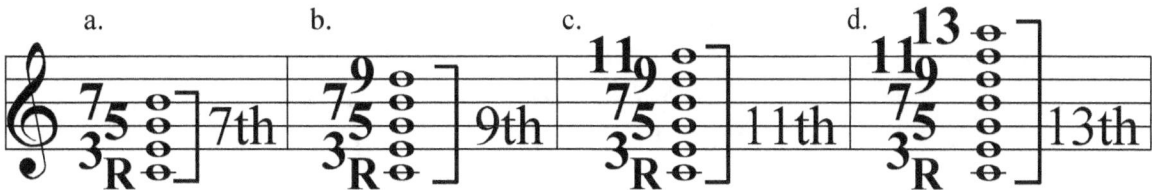

Converting a triad into a seventh chord, regardless of the triad's quality, does not alter the status or function of the chord within the key and mode in which it occurs. The seventh element of the chord is simply an extension of the basic triad, just as ninth, eleventh, and thirteenth elements are all extensions of the underlying seventh chord (examples E–1b, 1c, and 1d).

The creation of *root-position* sevenths chords involves the addition of either a major or minor 3rd above the fifth of the triad; seventh chords are never produced by adding either augmented or diminished 3rds. Therefore, as shown in example E–2 below, if we add a 3rd above the fifth of a root-position C-major triad, the tone is either B♮ (a major 3rd above G) or B♭ (a minor 3rd above G); neither B♯ (an augmented 3rd above G) nor B♭♭ (a diminished 3rd above G) can be used as the seventh of the chord.

Placing a B♯ above the fifth of the C-major triad produces a tone that is enharmonic with the root, resulting in a doubled root (one of which is misspelled as B♯) and no seventh. The addition of a B♭♭ above the fifth creates a chord that contains an enharmonic and acoustical interval of a 6th above the root (C up to A) but no chord seventh. Although it is possible to hear the B♭♭ as the misspelled root (A) of a seventh chord with its third in the bass (C E G A), our concern in this section is with seventh chords in *root position*.

Example E–2

The Dominant Seventh Chord

The dominant seventh is the most important seventh chord for the major-minor tonal system. Both the dominant seventh and the dominant triad are so-named because their root is the dominant scale degree of the major, harmonic, and melodic minor modes. A dominant seventh chord in root position occurring on the dominant scale degree takes the chord symbol V^7. The quality of the dominant seventh is formed from a combination of the major triad and the minor 7th from the root to the seventh (MT / m7).

As demonstrated in example E–3, when the dominant seventh is in root position and addresses the tonic chord, it stands in a falling perfect 5th and rising perfect 4th root *and* bass relationship to the tonic chord. The falling perfect 5th (and its inversion, the rising perfect 4th) presents the strongest expression of harmonic motion in tonal music (see above, p. 159). In both major and minor modes, the dominant seventh contains the leading tone as its chord third. Therefore, the movement between the dominant and tonic chords produces the most effective melodic motion and the most effective harmonic motion for affirming the tonality of a musical work.

Example E–3 illustrates an important principle in the treatment of the dissonant interval of the 7th (G/F): *if a seventh chord stands in a falling 5th or rising 4th root relationship to another chord, then the seventh of the first chord will move down by step in the same voice to become the third of the second chord.* Thus, the seventh of the dominant chord (F) moves down by step in the alto voice to become the third of the tonic triad (E).

Example E–3: the dominant seventh chord

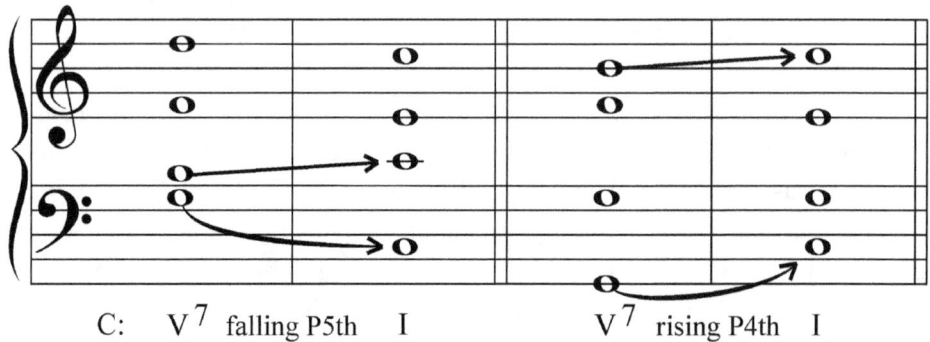

C: V^7 falling P5th   I   V^7 rising P4th   I

Inversions of the Dominant Seventh Chord

Since the dominant seventh chord consists of four tones, it has four chord positions: root position, first inversion, second inversion, and third inversion. In first inversion, the third is the bass pitch, in second inversion the fifth, and in third inversion the seventh. Example E–4 shows all four positions of the dominant seventh in C major. If the seventh chord is in root position, then *the bottom note of the interval of the 7th indicates the location of the root* (see the bracketed arrow).

The *complete* figured-bass description for the intervals above the lowest tone of the dominant seventh in root position is signified with the Arabic numbers $\begin{smallmatrix}7\\5\\3\end{smallmatrix}$. The numbers designate the intervals of the 3rd, 5th, and 7th above the root of the chord. When either an alphabet letter or a Roman numeral precedes the figured bass of the seventh chord in root position, we omit the Arabic numbers 5 and 3 and retain the 7. The term dominant seventh is abbreviated as D^7 (example E–4a).

The first inversion of the seventh chord (E–4b) has the third in the bass. Upon inversion, the interval of the 7th above the root (G/F) becomes the interval of the 2nd (F/G). If the bottom note of the 7th indicates the location of the root, then *the upper note of the 2nd identifies the root of the seventh chord in all three of its inverted positions* (see the bracketed arrows in examples E–4b, 4c, and 4d).

Appendix E The Dominant Seventh Chord

The *complete* figured-bass description for the intervals above the third of the seventh chord in first inversion is signified with the Arabic numbers $\begin{smallmatrix}6\\5\\3\end{smallmatrix}$. The numbers represent the intervals of the 3rd, 5th, and 6th above the third of the chord (B D F G). When either an alphabet letter or a Roman numeral precedes the figured bass of the seventh chord in first inversion, we omit the Arabic number 3 and retain the 6 and the 5 (see E–4b).

Example E–4: inversions of the dominant seventh chord

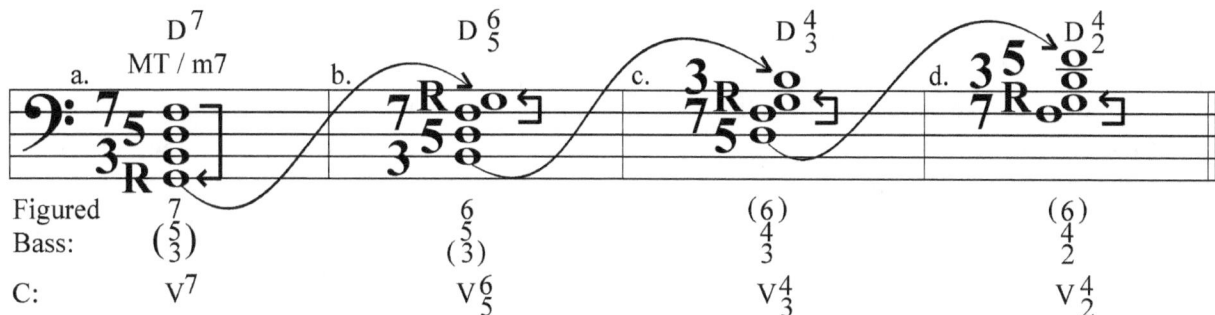

The second inversion of the seventh chord (E–4c) has the fifth in the bass. Again, upon inversion, the upper note of the 2nd identifies the root of the seventh chord. The *complete* figured-bass description for the intervals above the fifth of the seventh chord in second inversion is signified with the Arabic numbers $\begin{smallmatrix}6\\4\\3\end{smallmatrix}$. The numbers denote the intervals of the 3rd, 4th, and 6th above the fifth of the chord (D F G B). When either an alphabet letter or a Roman numeral precedes the figured bass of the seventh chord in second inversion, we omit the Arabic number 6 and retain the 4 and the 3 (E–4c).

The third inversion of the seventh chord (E–4d) has the seventh in the bass. As in examples E–4b and 4c, the upper note of the 2nd identifies the root of the seventh chord. The *complete* figured-bass description for the intervals above the seventh of the seventh chord in third inversion is signified with the Arabic numbers $\begin{smallmatrix}6\\4\\2\end{smallmatrix}$. The numbers indicate the intervals of the 2nd, 4th, and 6th above the seventh of the chord (F G B D). When either an alphabet letter or a Roman numeral precedes the figured bass of the seventh chord in third inversion, we omit the Arabic number 6 and retain the 4 and the 2 (E–4d). In sum, the four positions of the seventh chord are abbreviated as: 7, $\begin{smallmatrix}6\\5\end{smallmatrix}$, $\begin{smallmatrix}4\\3\end{smallmatrix}$, and $\begin{smallmatrix}4\\2\end{smallmatrix}$.

Singing the Dominant Seventh Chord in All Positions

At the end of Chapter 8, we learned how to sing the four qualities of triads in all three chord positions above a common-tone C in the bass. This section applies the same method to the dominant seventh in all four positions. When ascending and descending through each of the four positions, the notes above the common tone must be adjusted to preserve the quality of the chord while retaining the C-octave between the outside pitches (the bass tone is duplicated at the octave).

Appendix E The Dominant Seventh Chord

As with the triads, the challenge is preserving the outside octave while adjusting the internal intervals to maintain the correct chord quality and position. The numbers 1, 3, 5, and 7 designate the root, third, fifth, and seventh of the chord respectively (1-3-5-7-1-7-5-3-1). Notice that both the intervals and the numbers change as the common-tone C becomes the third (3-5-7-1-3-1-7-5-3), fifth (5-7-1-3-5-3-1-7-5), and seventh (7-1-3-5-7-5-3-1-7) of the chord. In the dominant seventh, singing the numbers 7-1 ascending or 1-7 descending produces a major 2nd.

In example E–5, the upper note of the interval of the major 2nd (the inversion of the minor 7th) marks the written and sounding root of the dominant seventh. In root position, the chord has two components: the basic triad (root, third, and fifth) and the interval of the 7th above the root, forming the seventh element. We refer to the basic triad of the dominant seventh chord as the "root triad," which is heard immediately upon arpeggiating the complete chord upwards (see the solid brackets in E–5a).

The root triad also appears in both the second and third inversions above the common-tone bass but not as part of the chord's lowest component (see the solid brackets in examples E–5c and 5d). Put differently, the root triad occurs when 1-3-5 is sung in the upward arpeggiation of the root position, second inversion, and third inversion of the seventh chord. The root triad also appears in the downward arpeggiation when singing 5-3-1.

The first inversion, on the other hand, projects a "false triad" upwards from its bass, consisting of the dominant seventh's third, fifth, and seventh elements. The false triad occurs in the upward arpeggiation when 3-5-7 is sung (see the dotted brackets in E–5b). Additionally, the false triad appears in the downward arpeggiation when 7-5-3 is sung. Immediately following the upward arpeggiation of the false triad (3-5-7) is the actual root of the chord (7-1).

Example E–5: the dominant seventh chord

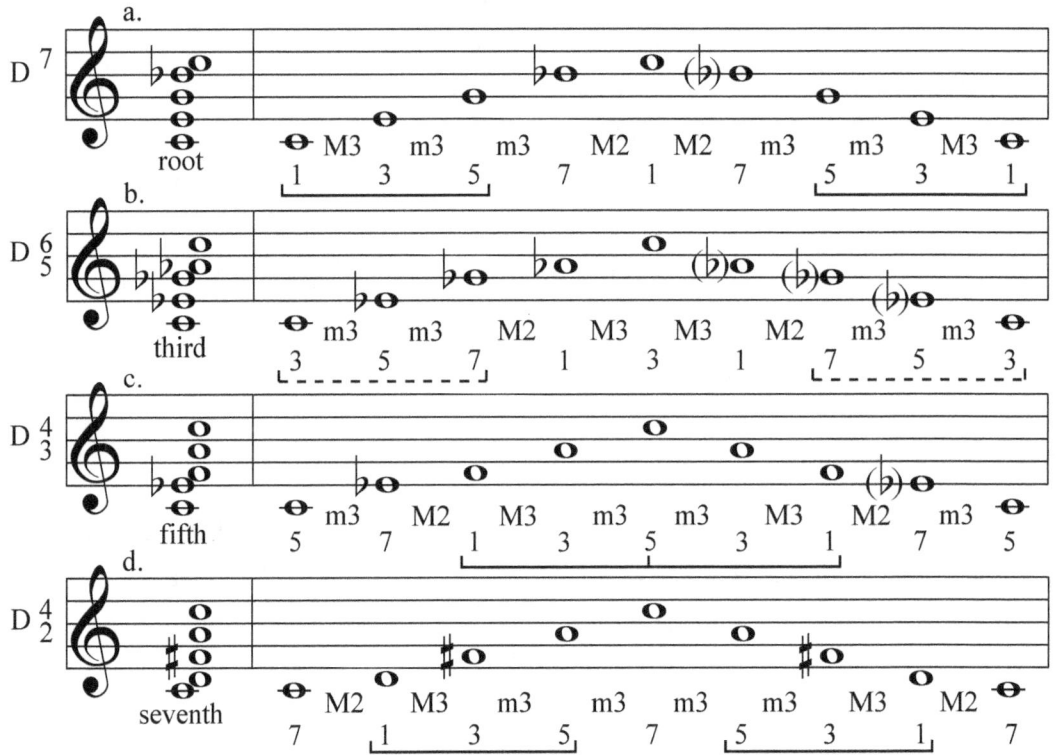

Appendix F The Cadence

The cadence is a two-chord pattern that forms the end of a musical phrase. As stated in Appendix D, the phrase is the smallest element of musical form in which a combination of melodic, rhythmic, and chordal components together comprise the beginning, middle, and end of a musical thought. The ending may be permanent or temporary, whether or not the activity within the phrase is continuous or segmented into smaller units known as sub-phrases. These sub-phrases, if present, may also contain endings marked off by cadences.

The first part of the two-chord pattern is called the *approach chord* because it addresses the second chord, known as the *cadential chord*. The approach chord may include dissonant upper extensions beyond the root, third, and fifth of the basic triad, such as the seventh and the ninth. However, since the cadential chord constitutes either a permanent or temporary ending, avoid dissonant chords here because consonant chords more effectively convey a state of rest.

There are two basic types of cadences, each defined according to how the approach chord addresses the cadential chord:

(1) If the approach to the cadential chord in the bass involves either a falling 5th or rising 4th motion (or a falling 4th or rising 5th motion), then we describe the cadence as a **harmonic cadence**.
(2) If the approach to the cadential chord in the bass involves the melodic interval of a major or minor 2nd, then we describe the cadence as a **contrapuntal cadence**.

The Dominant Family of Chords

In Chapter 8, we noted that when the major triad of the dominant is in root position and addresses the tonic chord, it produces two optimal conditions for affirming the tonality of a music composition: the compelling melodic drive upwards from the leading tone to the tonic and the strong harmonic motion of a falling perfect 5th or a rising perfect 4th in the bass.

Another important triad for defining the tonality of a music composition occurs in the area of the leading tone, which shares two pitches in common with the dominant triad and stands in a rising minor 2nd root relationship to the tonic. The root and the third of the leading-tone triad are the same pitches as the third and the fifth of the corresponding dominant triad (see above, p. 160).

Because of its key-defining function and common pitch content with the dominant, the leading-tone triad functions in most cases as a dominant chord. As such, all of the chords built on the leading tone belong to the "dominant family" of chords. To be sure, there are circumstances in which the chord of the leading tone may not be functioning as a dominant but rather serving some other purpose within a particular musical context. However, in most cases, the leading-tone triad is appropriately recognized as a chord of the dominant family.

Tonic-oriented Cadences: The Authentic Cadence

The authentic cadence is part of a large category of tonic-oriented cadences. The approach chord of the authentic cadence is a dominant-family chord. The cadential chord is the tonic chord. (Note: do not confuse the cadential chord with the elaboration of the dominant known as the cadential $^6_4$.)

There are two general classes of authentic cadences, each defined according to how the approach chord addresses the cadential chord: harmonic authentic cadences and contrapuntal authentic cadences. Additionally, within the general category of the authentic cadence, there are two subclasses, each grouped according to what scale degrees appear in the bass and soprano voices: the **perfect authentic cadence** and the **imperfect authentic cadence**. The most permanent-sounding close to a musical phrase is produced by the authentic cadence, particularly, the perfect authentic cadence.

The following four sections examine each variety of authentic cadence: the harmonic perfect authentic cadence, the harmonic imperfect authentic cadence, the contrapuntal perfect authentic cadence, and the contrapuntal imperfect authentic cadence. Subsequently, we shall consider two other tonic-oriented cadences: the deceptive cadence and the plagal cadence. Finally, our study of cadences concludes with the non-tonic-oriented cadence known as the half cadence.

Tonic-oriented Cadences: the Harmonic Perfect Authentic Cadence

Unlike all of the other types of cadences, the harmonic perfect authentic cadence is described generally as a "closed cadence," or "full cadence" (example F–1). Having either a falling 5th or rising 4th root and bass relationship between its approach chord and cadential chord, the harmonic perfect authentic cadence produces a sense of finality not present in other cadences because it has scale degree 1 in both **outer voices** (that is, the bass and soprano voices) of the tonic chord.

Notice the exceptional treatment of the leading tone (B♮) in the tenor voice of examples F–1c and 1d, which drops back to the fifth of the tonic chord (G); this special license was introduced in Chapter 8 (see above, p. 158). As demonstrated in examples F–1b and 1d, the approach chord for the harmonic perfect authentic cadence may also involve the cadential $\substack{6\\4}$.

Example F–1: the harmonic perfect authentic cadence

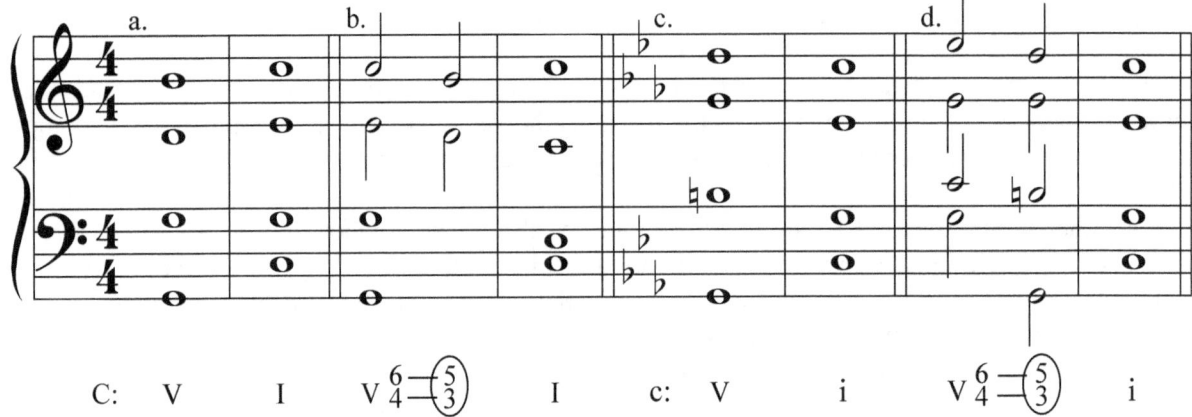

Tonic-oriented Cadences: the Harmonic Imperfect Authentic Cadence

Example F–2 shows various dispositions of the harmonic imperfect authentic cadence, a subclass of the authentic cadence. The chief characteristic of this cadence is the appearance of either scale degree 3 or 5 in the soprano voice of the tonic chord (see the circled pitches). Since the harmonic imperfect authentic cadence must have a falling 5th or rising 4th root and bass relationship between its approach chord and cadential chord, the tonic chord maintains scale degree 1 in the bass.

The cadential $\substack{6\\4}$ may serve as the approach chord for the harmonic imperfect authentic cadence (examples F–2e, 2f, 2g, and 2h). As with every type of cadence other than the harmonic perfect authentic cadence, the imperfect authentic cadence is one of the many types of "open cadences" because scale degree 1 does not appear in both outer voices of the cadential chord. (In the tenor voice of examples F–2b and 2d, the leading tone drops back to the fifth of the tonic chord.)

Example F–2: the harmonic imperfect authentic cadence

Tonic-oriented Cadences: the Contrapuntal Perfect Authentic Cadence

The contrapuntal perfect authentic cadence has scale degree 1 in both outer voices; however, unlike the harmonic perfect authentic cadence, there is a stepwise approach in the bass to the cadential tonic. In example F–3, we have two of the most common approach chords for this cadence: V^6 in major and minor, vii o ^{6} in major, and ♯vii o ^{6} in minor. In their approach to the cadential tonic, these dominant-family chords share important features that ultimately confer upon them a functional description beyond their respective chord symbols. Since both chords contain the leading tone and define the tonic chord while approaching it by step, we shall further call them **contrapuntal leading-tone chords**, a term put forward by Felix Salzer and Carl Schachter in *Counterpoint in Composition* (New York: McGraw-Hill, 1969).

Example F–3: the contrapuntal perfect authentic cadence

Tonic-oriented Cadences: the Contrapuntal Imperfect Authentic Cadence

In the contrapuntal imperfect authentic cadence, the cadential chord has a scale degree other than the tonic in at least one of its outer voices. Example F–4 demonstrates some of the more common possibilities in both major and minor, all of which employ first-inversion chords of the dominant family that approach the cadential tonic by step as contrapuntal leading-tone chords.

Example F–4 the contrapuntal imperfect authentic cadence

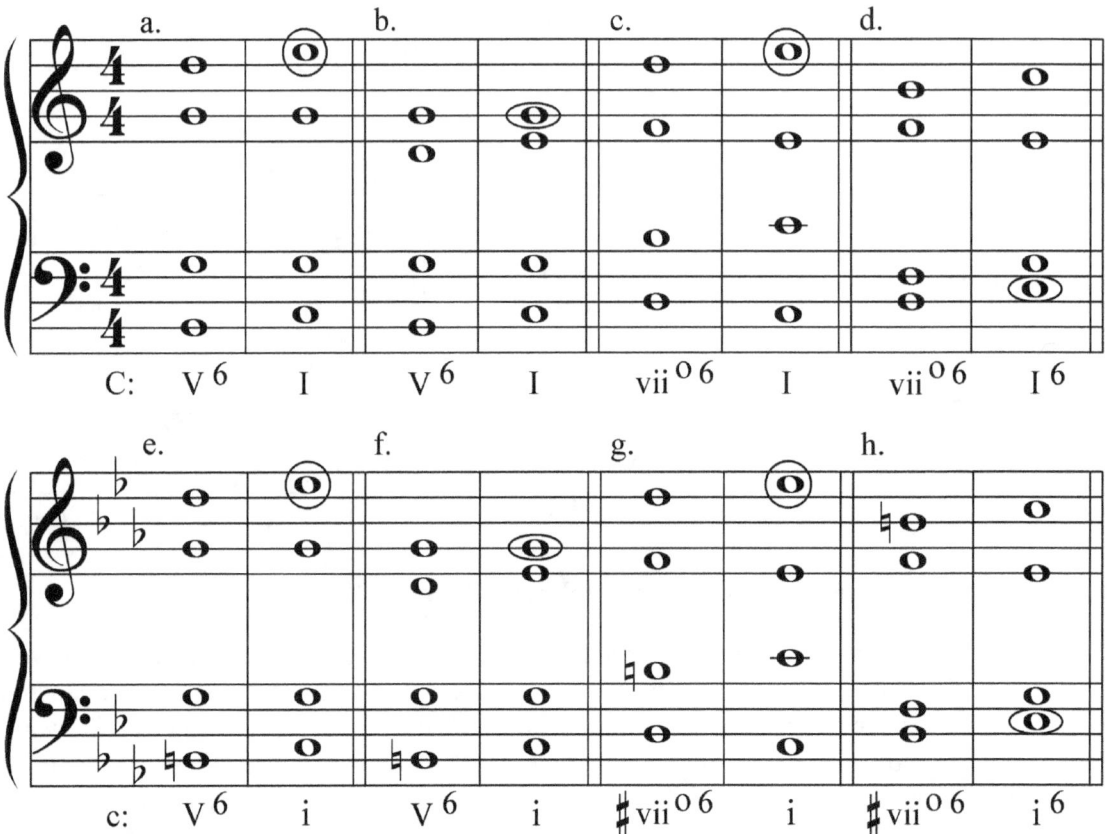

As indicated in F–4 above, the cadential chord can be in either $^5_3$ or in $^6_3$ position but not in $^6_4$ position. Examples F–4a, 4b, 4c, 4e, 4f, and 4g all have scale degree 1 in the bass of the cadential chord. Scale degree 3 occurs in the soprano of examples F–4a, 4c, 4e, and 4g. In examples F–4d and 4h, we have scale degree 3 in the bass. Examples F–4b and 4f both illustrate scale degree 5 in the soprano.

Tonic-oriented Cadences: the Deceptive Cadence

The **deceptive cadence** falls within the category of tonic-oriented cadences because the cadential chord contains scale degree 1 and is approached by the dominant chord. However, even though the leading tone proceeds to scale degree 1 in the cadential chord, the tonic chord itself is usually replaced with either the subdominant or the submediant. Example F–5 exhibits some common dispositions of the deceptive cadence in major and minor, using the submediant as the cadential chord.

With the deceptive cadence, the tone of choice for doubling is the tonic pitch, which is the third of the submediant. Supporting scale degree 1 with the chord of the submediant rather than the tonic produces a state of suspense by delaying the sense of closure, leaving the listener to anticipate the arrival of the tonic chord.

Example F–5: the deceptive cadence with the submediant as the cadential chord

In example F–6, the deceptive cadence consists of two triads: the dominant, G B D, and the subdominant, F A C (or F A♭ C). The F subdominant appears in $^6_3$ position as the cadential chord. The tone of choice for doubling is the fifth of the subdominant, the tonic pitch.

Example F–6: the deceptive cadence with the subdominant as the cadential chord

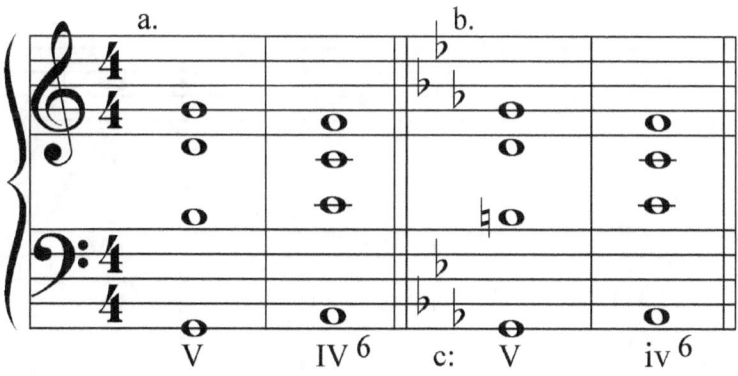

Tonic-oriented Cadences: Perfect and Imperfect Plagal Cadences

The **plagal cadence** often occurs after the actual cadence as a kind of post-cadential extension. The cadential chord (the tonic portion of the plagal cadence) is approached harmonically by a non-dominant chord above scale degree 4 in the bass. Most listeners recognize the plagal cadence as the famous "Amen" closing for many religious forms of music such as the hymn.

Two dispositions of the plagal cadence are possible: the perfect plagal cadence and the imperfect plagal cadence, shown in examples F–7 and 8 respectively. The first disposition, the perfect plagal cadence, has scale degree 1 in both the soprano and bass. Since scale degree 4 is the root of the subdominant triad (examples F–7a and 7c) and the third of the supertonic triad (examples F–7b and 7d), either chord may approach the cadential tonic of the plagal cadence.

Example F–7: the perfect plagal cadence

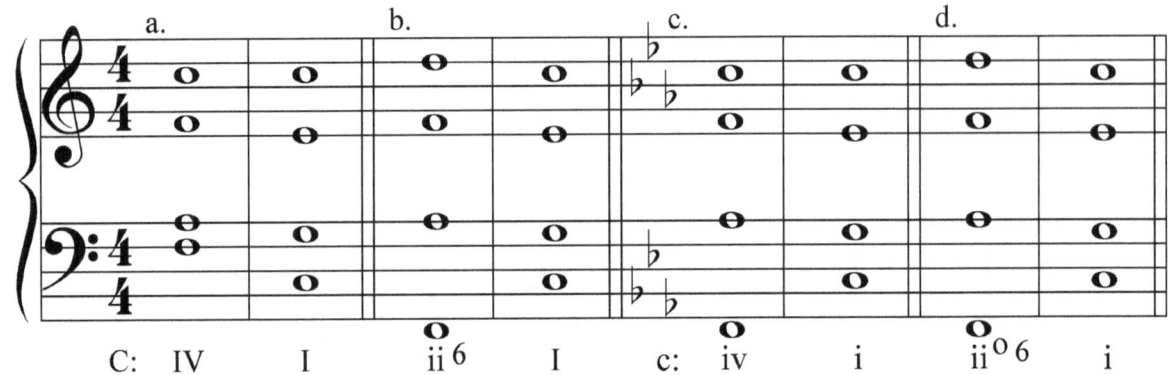

The second disposition of the plagal cadence, the imperfect plagal cadence, takes either scale degree 3 or 5 in the soprano voice (see the circled pitches).

Example F–8: the imperfect plagal cadence

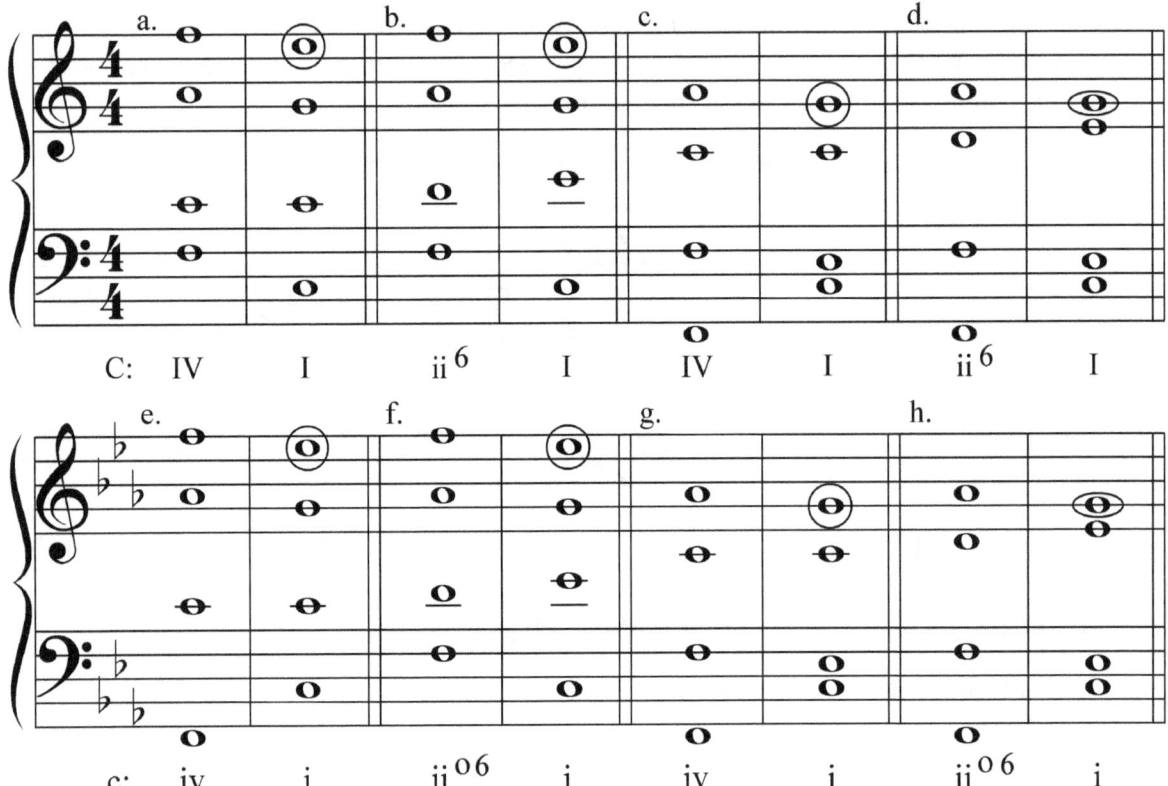

Non-Tonic-oriented Cadences: Harmonic and Contrapuntal Half Cadences

The half cadence, also known as the **semicadence**, consists of a non-dominant approach chord and a cadential chord other than the tonic; it is often analogized to a comma in speech, a stopping point that nonetheless seeks continuation to complete the musical thought. The half cadence exhibits either a harmonic or contrapuntal bass relationship between its two chords.

For the harmonic half cadence in major, illustrated in examples F–9a through 9d, the tonic and the supertonic constitute the most common approaches to the cadential chord. The dominant triad or the cadential $^6_4$ are the most frequently used cadential chords. When either the dominant or the cadential $^6_4$ appears as the cadential chord, a triad rather than a seventh chord is preferred because a consonant chord establishes a feeling of repose more successfully than a dissonant one.

In minor, the tonic often serves as the approach chord of choice (examples F–9e and 9f). The diminished supertonic can be used as an approach chord but not in root position, as the diminished 5th formed above its root is too dissonant (examples F–9g and 9h). The minor supertonic triad is less likely to occur as an approach chord in minor (examples F–9i and 9j) than in major because its fifth is variable ♯6 rather than ♭6; hence, the option to move down to scale degree 5 is not available (♯6 seeks to move up to ♯7 not down to 5).

Finally, remember that in the first part of the cadential $^6_4$, we have the arrival of the dominant pitch in the bass over which two nonharmonic tones on the strongest beat of the measure occur. In examples F–9b and 9f, the nonharmonic tones constitute a double suspension: a dissonant 4th (G/C) and a consonant 6th (G/E♭).

Example F–9: the harmonic half cadence

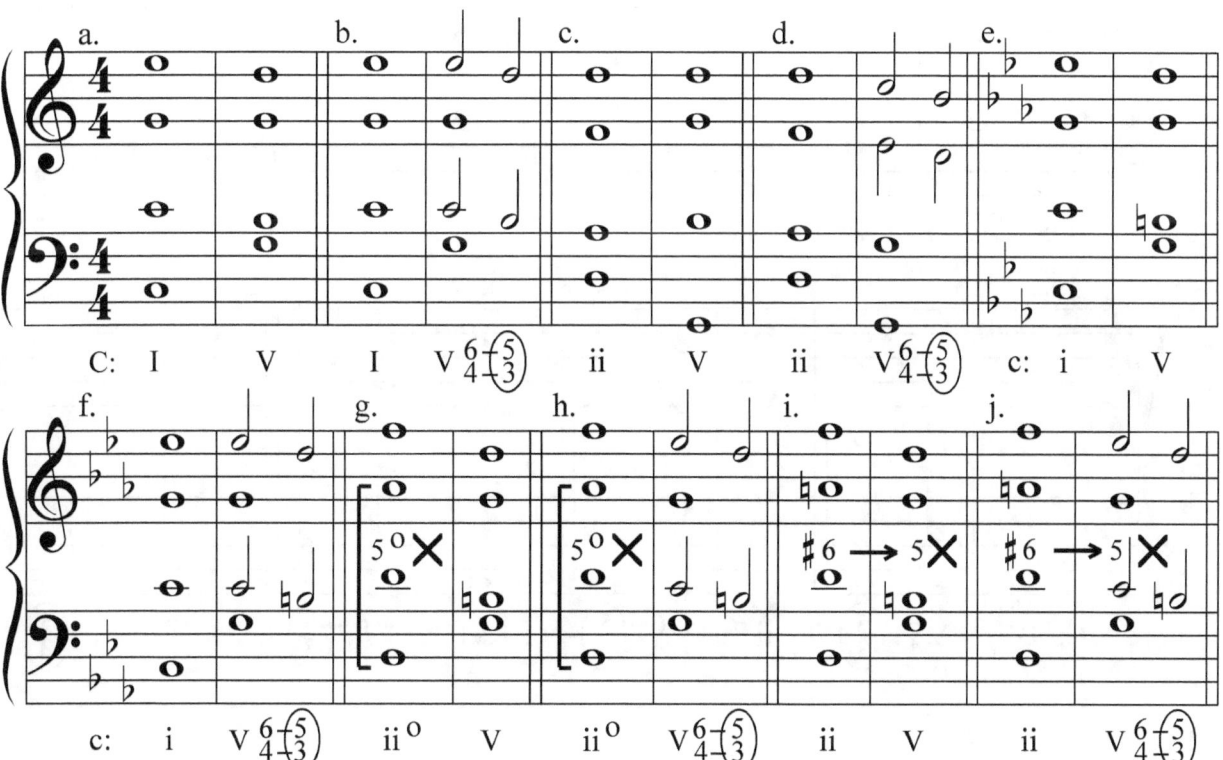

250   Appendix F The Cadence

The contrapuntal half cadence presents more varied possibilities for the approach chord, while the cadential chord is expressed in either root position, first inversion, or as a cadential $^6_4$. The approach to the cadential chord is usually made from above or below by step. Although the limitations of space preclude a complete listing of all the available approach chords for the contrapuntal half cadence, example F–10 demonstrates a few of the simplest ways to address the cadential chord. Examples F–10i, 10j, 10k, and 10l use chords of the subdominant, minor supertonic, submediant, and diminished supertonic to demonstrate the stepwise approach to the cadential $^6_4$.

Example F–10: the contrapuntal half cadence

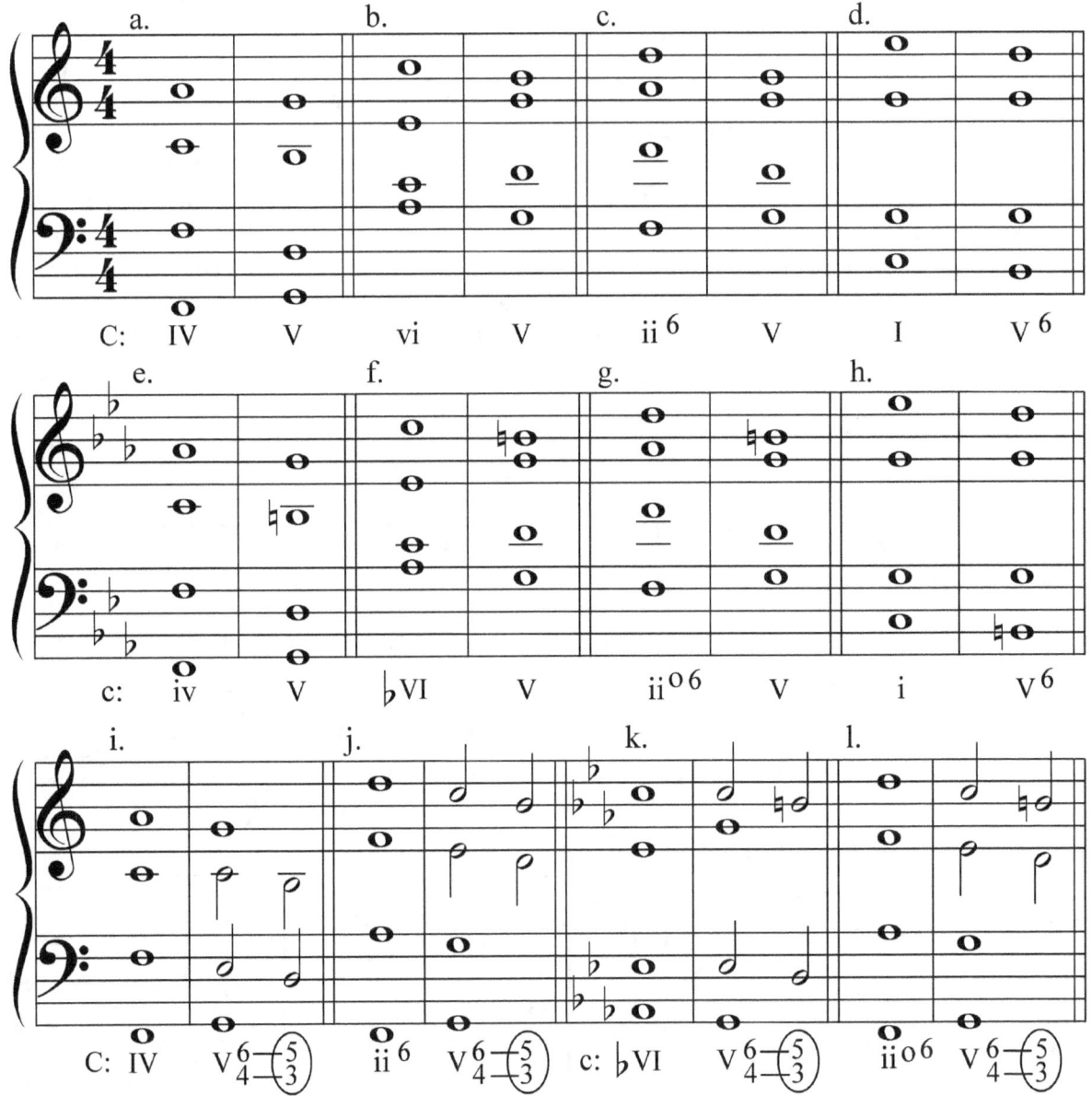

Non-Tonic-oriented Cadences: The Phrygian Half Cadence on V

The final contrapuntal half cadence to consider is the **Phrygian cadence**. A brief review of the properties of the Phrygian mode will shed some light on why we refer to this cadence as Phrygian.

Earlier, we classified the Phrygian mode a minor prototype mode because its tonic triad is minor. The untransposed Phrygian mode on E is similar to its parallel natural minor, e minor, except that E Phrygian's scale degree 2 is lowered one half step in relation to the e-minor scale. E Phrygian contains an F natural, e minor an F♯ (see Appendix C, examples C–3c and 3d).

Frequently, the final tonic of a segment of music written in the Phrygian mode will take a major triad rather than a minor triad. Despite the apparent contradiction in classifying the Phrygian mode as a minor prototype, ending a composition or segment of a composition that is otherwise written in minor with a major tonic triad is based upon a very old tradition.

Around the beginning of the sixteenth century, composers began to show a preference for ending minor compositions with a major triad on the tonic. This practice continued for about two hundred years of music composition. The assignment of the major tonic triad in a composition written in the minor mode was later referred to in French as the *tierce de Picardie*, in English, the **picardy third**. Within the context of the minor mode, the tonic triad is viewed as having a raised 3rd, raised one half step from the characteristic minor 3rd between the root and third of the chord.

The Phrygian cadence occurs in the minor mode and involves a iv^6 approach to a cadential V chord (Example F–11). With the subdominant's third in the bass, the root of the V chord is approached from above by half step. This approach resembles the Phrygian mode's half-step descent from scale degrees 2 down to 1. The half-step relationship between the Phrygian mode's supertonic and tonic scale degrees is sometimes referred to as the "upper leading tone."

Example F–11a demonstrates the contrapuntal Phrygian half cadence in the key and mode of c minor. The best doubling for the subdominant in first inversion is the fifth (scale degree 1). In minor, any chord with variable ♭6 as one of its components (in this instance, the third of the iv chord) followed by a chord with variable ♯7 can potentially produce a melodic augmented 2nd between variables ♭6 and ♯7, an awkward interval to sing that should be avoided whenever possible (see the alto voice of F–11b).

Comparing examples F–11a and 11c, we can see the relationship between the two chords of the Phrygian cadence in both c minor and G Phrygian (G P). In G Phrygian, which has the same key signature as c minor, the relationship becomes that of a first-inversion subtonic proceeding to the tonic G. Note carefully, however, that the tonic triad is major, as it contains the picardy third (the P in parentheses below the chord symbol in uppercase denotes the picardy third).

Example F–11: the Phrygian half cadence on V

Appendix G Nonharmonic Tones

When is the existence of a chord more apparent than real? In our study of the cadential $^6_4$ (Appendix D), we discovered that while certain combinations of tones may be recognized as intervals forming tertian harmonies and placed consequently within the context of a given key and mode, their status as real chords is questionable. The cadential $^6_4$ is ultimately an elaboration of the dominant chord with two pitches that are not inherent components of that chord—they are nonharmonic tones.

There are two classes of nonharmonic tones: **appoggiaturas** and non-appoggiaturas. Appoggiaturas are rhythmically stressed, non-appoggiaturas unstressed. The following outline presents a brief overview of these two categories:

(1) Non-Appoggiaturas: rhythmically *unaccented* nonharmonic tones
    (a) the passing tone
    (b) the complete and incomplete neighbor tone
    (c) the anticipation tone

(2) Appoggiaturas: rhythmically *accented* nonharmonic tones
    (a) the passing tone
    (b) the complete and incomplete neighbor tone (the "appoggiatura itself")
    (c) the suspension

We base our classification of nonharmonic tones on the understanding that rhythmically unstressed tones are those occurring on weak beats in relation to stronger beats or those falling on weak divisions of beats. What we are recognizing here differs somewhat from the distinction made between primary and secondary accents in Chapter 1. That distinction enables us to define the meter by measuring the distance between two primary accents, a distance marked by the number of intervening secondary accents. In order to define nonharmonic tones, however, secondary accents may be considered strong beats, particularly in relation to their divisions.

In example G–1a, which has the half note as the value of the beat in $^2_2$ time, the second and fourth quarter notes are divisions of the beat and therefore weaker in relation to the first and third quarter notes. Using the same note durations in $^4_4$ time, G–1b conveys a feeling of two beats per measure rather than four—despite the fact that now the quarter note rather than the half note represents the value of the beat. Thus, simulating duple meter within the framework of quadruple meter renders the quarters on the second and fourth beats weak in relation to the quarters on the first and third beats, just as they were in G–1a.

If, however, the quadruple meter exhibits a clear expression of four beats, as proposed in the expression of $^4_4$ time in G–1c, and if our intention is to define or use a nonharmonic tone, then we may want to recognize that *all four beats* would be strong in relation to their respective divisions.

To a great extent, then, the strength or weakness of a beat depends on how the meter is expressed and what questions we are asking. Moreover, such factors as syncopation, cross accent, and hemiola further complicate the task of determining whether the nonharmonic tone is rhythmically stressed or unstressed. We will, for the most part, avoid rhythmic procedures that would impede our study of nonharmonic tones within their most natural and demonstrable settings.

Example G–1: simple duple meter ($^2_2$ time) versus simple quadruple meter ($^4_4$ time)

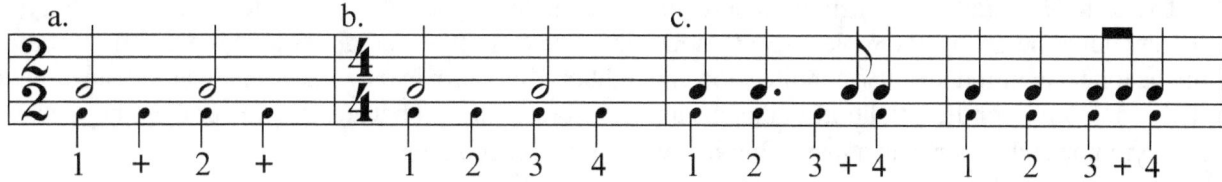

Non-Appoggiaturas

There are three types of non-appoggiaturas: the passing tone, the neighbor tone, and the anticipation tone. In general, all non-appoggiatura types constitute unaccented nonharmonic motions that usually precede and/or follow the inherent components of the chord. Although there are a few exceptions, nonharmonic tones generally resolve either by whole step or by half step. Examples G–4b and 4c, 6, and 7 illustrate nonharmonic tones that lack stepwise resolutions. In this appendix, a plus sign attached to a note indicates a tone with an unaccented nonharmonic function.

The Passing Tone

The passing tone is approached and left by step and occurs on either a strong or weak beat; it also appears on either a strong or weak portion of a beat. Hence, the passing tone belongs to both classes of nonharmonic tones: appoggiaturas and non-appoggiaturas.

Example G–2 shows the unaccented variety of passing tone, ascending (G–2a) and descending (examples G–2b and 2c). Passing tones are either consonant or dissonant with another voice and may occur within one chord (G–2a) or between different chords (G–2b). Typically, a single passing tone fills in the interval of a 3rd, connecting one chord tone to another; however, more than one passing tone may lead in direct succession to another. Further, the passing tone may serve a *harmonic* function as a component of the chord. For example, the second passing tone in G–2c (E, second eighth note, alto voice) is the chord third of the C-major triad.

Example G–2: the passing tone

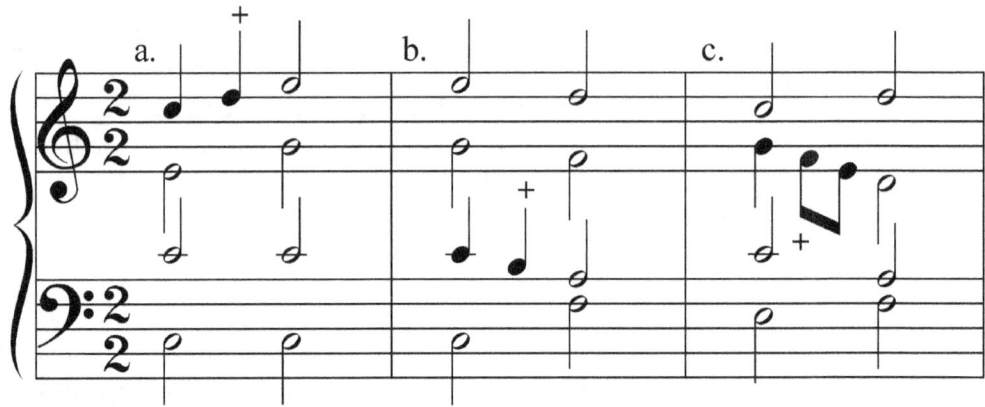

The Complete Neighbor Tone

A neighbor tone usually moves by step, upwards or downwards, from a preceding tone and may be either consonant or dissonant with the bass. Neighbor tones, which are also known as **auxiliary tones**, occur within the same chord or between different chords. As demonstrated in example G–3, a neighbor tone that returns to the tone to which it has left is described as complete. (We shall encounter the incomplete neighbor in subsequent examples.)

Example G–3a (alto voice) shows a neighbor tone moving upwards from the tone that preceded it, a complete upper neighbor. Example G–3b (tenor voice) demonstrates a neighbor tone moving downwards from the tone that introduced it, a complete lower neighbor. The sharp in parentheses indicates that we have an F♯ as an option for the neighbor. In this instance, we prefer the F♯ because the lower neighbor usually stands a minor 2nd rather than a major 2nd below the tone it decorates.

Example G–3: the complete neighbor tone

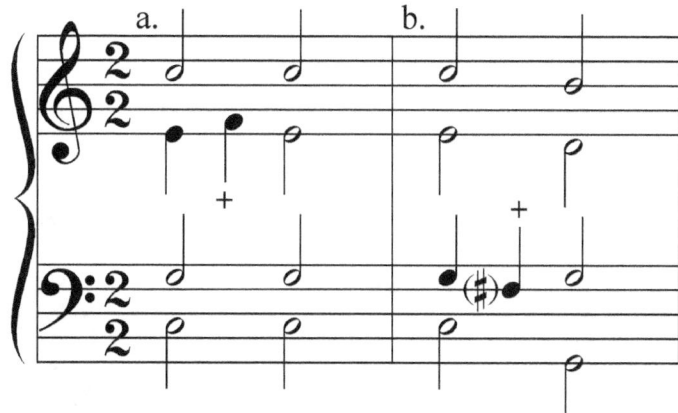

The Complete and Incomplete Changing-Note Group (Double Neighbor)

The **changing-note group**, which is also called the **double neighbor**, has *two* unaccented neighbors occurring in either direct or indirect succession. Example G–4a shows an indirect succession of neighbors in which a chord tone appears between them, whereas examples G–4b and 4c display a direct succession of neighbors without an intervening chord tone. Thus, we apply the term changing-note group to any figure that has two unaccented neighbors (that is, double neighbors) in either direct or indirect succession.

Example G–4 exhibits both complete and incomplete changing-note groups:

(1) if the first of the two neighbors returns to the tone that it has left, that is, the principal tone, then the changing-note group is complete and presents an indirect succession (G–4a: the complete changing-note group);

(2) if the first neighbor proceeds to the second neighbor without returning to the principal tone first, then the group is incomplete and presents a direct succession (examples G–4b and 4c: the incomplete changing-note group).

Ultimately, the second neighbor of the changing-note group (in both its complete and incomplete forms) *resolves by whole step or by half step into the principal tone of the figure* (in this case, E).

If the principal tone does not appear immediately before *and* after the neighbor tone, then the neighbor is referred to as incomplete. The alto F in G–4b is an incomplete upper neighbor to the preceding E; the alto D is an incomplete lower neighbor to the following E. The alto D in G–4c is an incomplete lower neighbor to the preceding E; the alto F is an incomplete upper neighbor to the following E.

Example G–4: complete and incomplete changing-note group

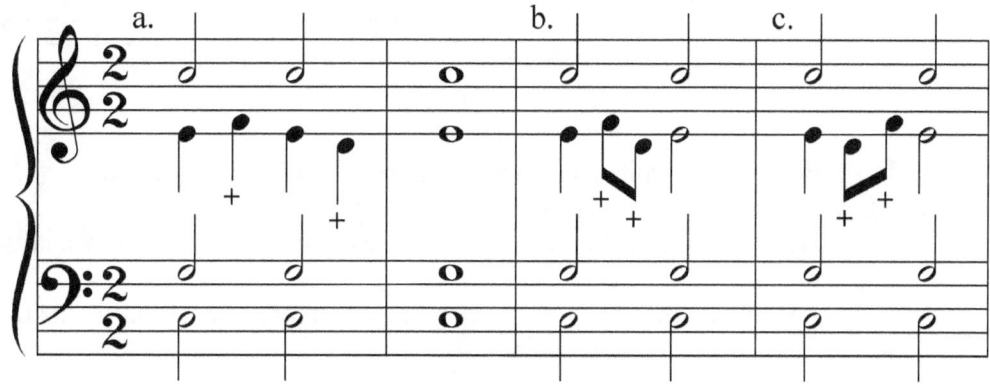

Special Uses of the Incomplete Neighbor Tone: the Cambiata and the Échappée

The cambiata (pronounced cam-bee-yah-tah) *begins with a leap and ends with a stepwise resolution*, becoming an incomplete neighbor to the chord tone it addresses. The arrows in example G–5 demonstrate the operation of the cambiata figure, which leaps one pitch beyond the tone of resolution, overreaching the harmonic component of the next chord before resolving into it. In G–5a, the cambiata figure reaches upwards (in the tenor) from G to B before reversing direction and settling on A; and in G–5b, it moves downwards (in the soprano) from D to B before reversing direction and resolving to C.

Example G–5: the cambiata

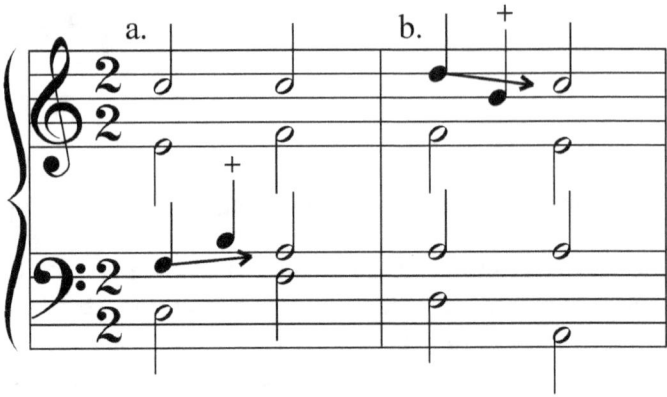

The échappée (pronounced ā-shah-pay), or escape tone, *begins with stepwise motion and ends with a leap into the tone of resolution*, becoming an incomplete neighbor to the chord tone it leaves. If the tone of resolution is part of a descending line, as in example G–6a (E down to D, soprano), then the échappée (F) moves upwards in the opposite direction. If the tone of resolution is part of an ascending line, as in G–6b (E up to F, alto), then the échappée (D) proceeds downwards in the opposite direction.

Example G–6: the échappée

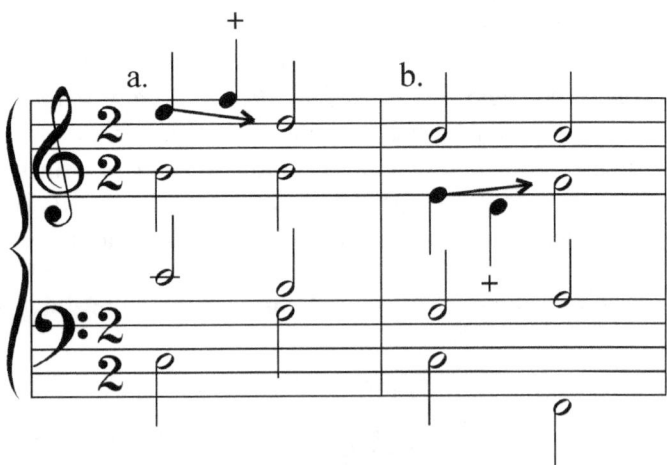

And so, while both the cambiata and the échappée fall within the category of non-appoggiaturas, they present entirely different linear operations:
(1) the cambiata figure leaps to a nonharmonic tone and then moves by whole step or by half step to a chord tone (G–5); whereas,
(2) the échappée figure moves by whole step or by half step to a nonharmonic tone and then leaps to a chord tone (G–6).

Other Incomplete Neighbor Tones

Examples G–7a and 7b present an incomplete neighbor that neither overreaches the harmonic component of the next chord (as in the cambiata) nor moves against the prevailing direction of the line (as in the échappée). However, the respective operations of the incomplete neighbor shown below and the échappée are basically the same: both are approached by stepwise motion and left by leap.

In G–7, the incomplete neighbor reduces the size of the leap into the chord tone on beat 2 from a 5th to a 4th: G up to D becomes A up to D (G–7a) and E down to A becomes D down to A (G–7b). (On beat 2 of G–7a, the inclusion of the F in the alto voice produces a chord consisting of the tones G B D F, a dominant seventh with its third, B, in the bass.)

Example G–7: other incomplete neighbors

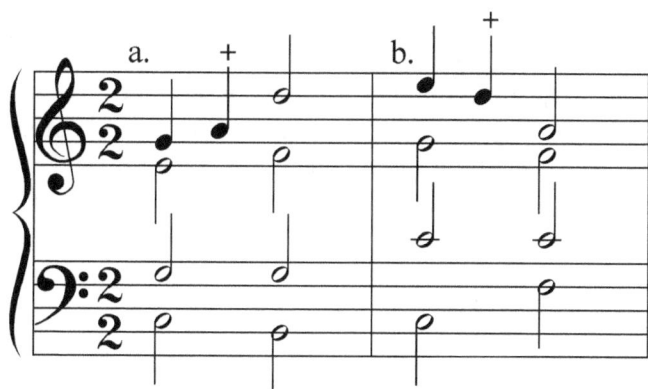

The Anticipation Tone

The anticipation tone previews one of the harmonic components of the following chord, bringing that component forward in time. Since the pitch remains the same when it occurs subsequently within the chord to which it belongs, the previewed tone has no actual resolution and may be either dissonant or consonant with the bass. As example G–8 confirms, the preview (see the plus sign) assumes the status of a chord tone either in the voice of its initial appearance or in another voice.

In examples G–8a and 8b, the preview remains in the same voice as the tone it anticipates. Examples G–8c and 8d exhibit a less typical use of the anticipation in which the preview tone is transferred into another voice when the chord changes (see the dotted line). Ultimately, placing the anticipation tone in another voice produces an incomplete neighbor and transforms the anticipation figure into an échappée (as in examples G–8c and 8d). (Note the dominant seventh with the omitted fifth on beat 1 of G–8a and the complete dominant seventh on beat 1 of 8b.)

Example G–8: the anticipation tone

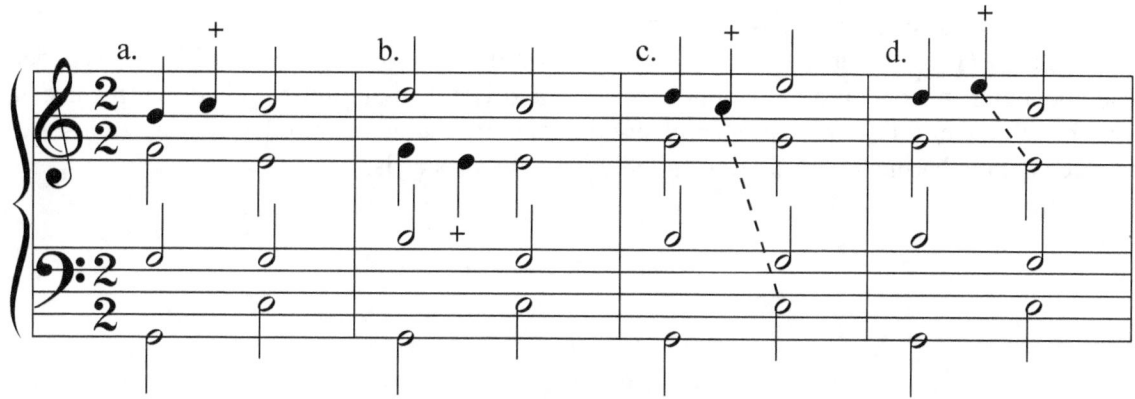

Appoggiaturas

There are four types of appoggiaturas: the passing tone, the complete neighbor tone, the suspension, and finally, the incomplete neighbor, termed here the appoggiatura itself. In general, all appoggiatura types constitute accented nonharmonic motions that usually precede and/or follow inherent components of the chord. As with most of the other nonharmonic tones, appoggiaturas have stepwise resolutions. In this appendix, a circled plus sign identifies the nonharmonic element as an appoggiatura type, as a rhythmically stressed tone.

The Accented Passing Tone

The accented passing tone is virtually the same as the unaccented passing tone except that the former has been shifted to a strong beat or strong portion of a beat. As we have said, the passing tone is approached and left by step. Example G–9 presents the accented passing tone in its ascending (G–9a) and descending (G–9b) forms. (A dominant seventh occurs when the accented passing tone in the soprano of G–9a moves to B.)

Appoggiaturas in general are usually found with a change of harmony. Later in this appendix, however, we shall find a few instances in which the nonharmonic tone appears within the framework of a single chord but nonetheless qualifies as an appoggiatura type.

Example G–9: the accented passing tone

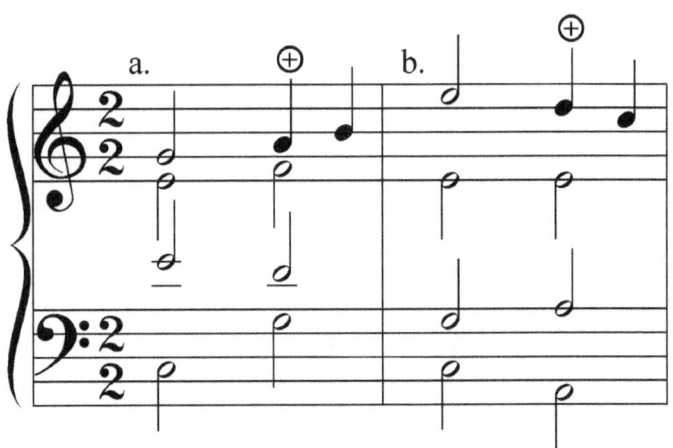

The Accented Complete Neighbor Tone

The accented complete neighbor, like the accented passing tone, is approached and left by stepwise motion (example G–10). In example G–10b, the accented lower neighbor appears as a rhythmically stressed tone resolving upwards by half step to the chord third.

Example G–10b is but one illustration of the upward resolution of a rhythmically stressed tone; we shall also encounter this operation in examples G–11b and G–14. It should be noted that the accented lower neighbor frequently lies one half step below the tone of resolution in order to draw a closer connection between the nonharmonic tone and the pitch to which it proceeds.

Example G–10: the accented neighbor tone

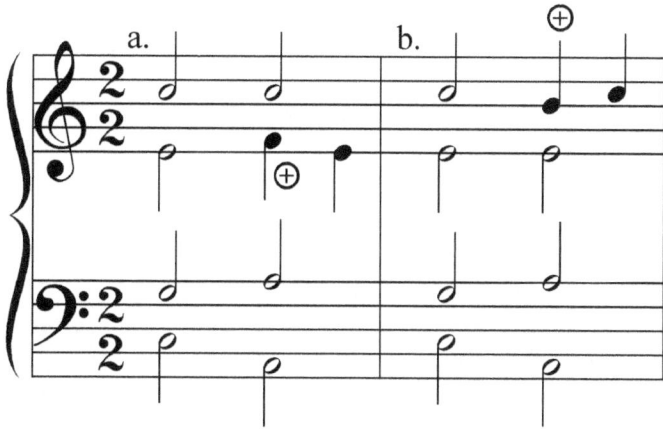

The Appoggiatura Itself (the Incomplete Neighbor Tone)

The Italian term appoggiatura comes from the verb *appoggiare*, one meaning of which is to lean. In musical terms, the appoggiatura refers to an accented dissonance that resolves by step to a consonance (that is, the accented dissonance "leans" into the consonance).

This appendix presents the appoggiatura as a general category within which various subtypes of accented nonharmonic tones are evident. One subtype, which operates as either an accented upper or lower neighbor, is the appoggiatura itself. In order to assume the form of an incomplete neighbor, the appoggiatura itself must be introduced by leap.

The appoggiatura in example G–11a has an upward leap into a major 9th which then resolves downwards to the root of a C-major triad; the nonharmonic tone (D) constitutes an accented incomplete upper neighbor to the tone of resolution (C). In G–11b, an augmented 4th resolves upwards to the chord fifth of an F-major triad; the nonharmonic tone (B) becomes an accented incomplete lower neighbor to the tone of resolution (C).

Example G–11: the appoggiatura itself

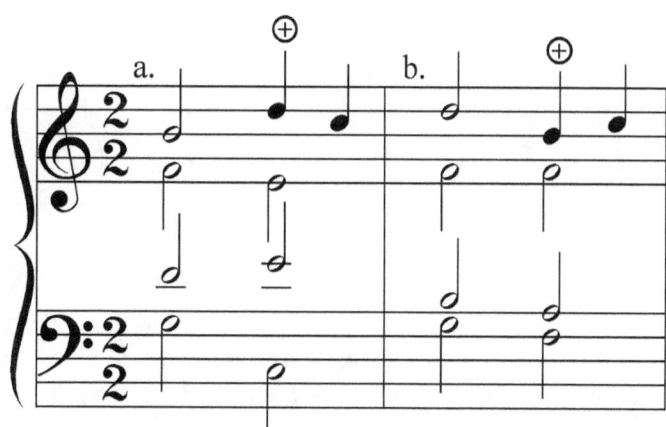

The Suspension

In Appendix D, we found that the operation of the suspension was one of the central factors in the development of the cadential $^6_4$. The suspension has three parts:
  (1) the suspension is *prepared*, usually as a consonance (but not always, see example G–12d below);
  (2) the preparation is held, or *suspended*, as the opposing voice (usually the bass) moves to form a dissonance with the suspended voice (though a consonant suspension is also possible); and finally,
  (3) the suspended voice moves down by step to *resolve* to a consonance. (Example G–14 shows the suspension with an exceptional upward resolution.)

As we have stipulated, the actual suspension (part 2) is metrically stronger than the resolution (part 3). The initial preparation (part 1), however, can be made from either a strong or weak position.

Example G–12a demonstrates a suspended 7th in the soprano voice, producing a 7–6 suspension. Over the stationary bass, the 7th resolves to a consonant 6th on the weak portion of the beat.

In G–12b, the resolution of the dissonant 7th in the soprano from D to C receives a "decoration" in the form of a chromatic passing tone, D♭; this process is referred to properly as a "decorated resolution." It is also possible to use other nonharmonic figures such as the anticipation tone, the cambiata, and the échappée to decorate the resolution. Notice that the tone of resolution falls in the same place within the measure as it would have without the decoration.

Example G–12c is not a suspension. Instead, we have shortened the process introduced in G–12b by leaving out the suspended tone (D) and proceeding directly to the chromatic passing tone (D♭). In so doing, however, we lose the suspension and gain an accented chromatic passing tone.

Example G–12d illustrates a *dissonant* preparation of the suspension in the alto voice. The dissonant 7th of the dominant chord on G is suspended into the tonic chord on C to produce a dissonant 4th, which then resolves to the chord third on the weak portion of the beat (4–3).

Example G–12: the suspension (downward)

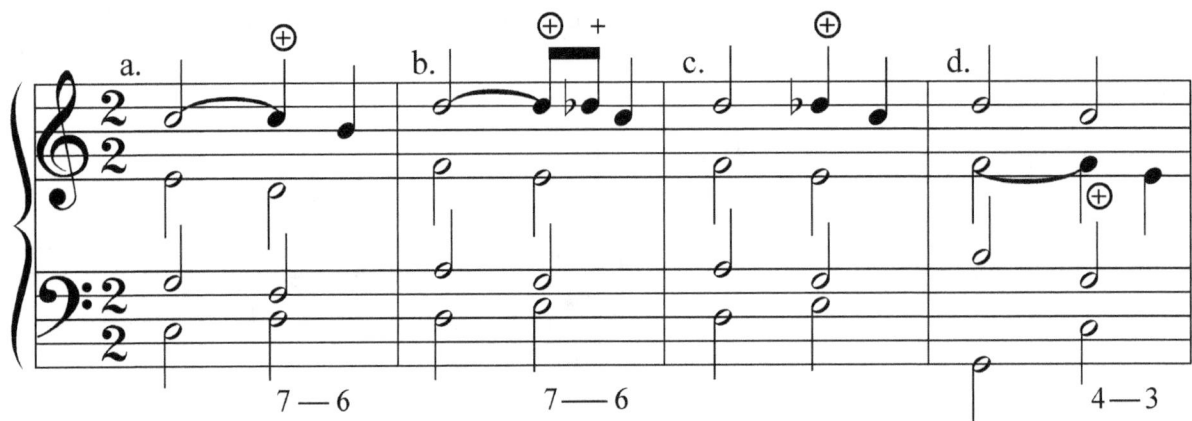

When writing for soprano, alto, tenor, and bass, it is best to withhold the tone of a downward resolution from all of the upper parts except for the suspended voice. In other words, you should not "preview" the tone of resolution in any upper voice other than the suspended voice because it spoils the expected resolution.

Examples G–13a and 13b present two different dispositions of the 7—6 suspension between the bass and the soprano. Play both examples on the piano. You will discover that the suspension in G–13a is more successful than that of 13b because the resolution of the dissonant C is confined to the suspended voice; no other voice above the bass carries B, the tone of resolution. Example G–13b, on the other hand, previews the B in the tenor voice, undermining the strength of the resolution.

Example G–13c illustrates the only exception to our recommendation for avoiding a preview of the resolution. If the suspension involves the interval of the 9th moving to an octave, a 9—8 suspension, then the bottom note of the 9th and the tone of resolution are one and the same. In a four-voice texture, the best position for the bottom note of the 9th is the bass voice. Therefore, the tone of resolution for the 9—8 suspension typically appears in the bass. Previewing the tone of resolution in the bass for the 9—8 suspension is acceptable because the bottom note of the 9th is likely to be the root, which finds its most natural position to be the generating voice for the chord, the bass.

Example G–13: previewing the tone of resolution

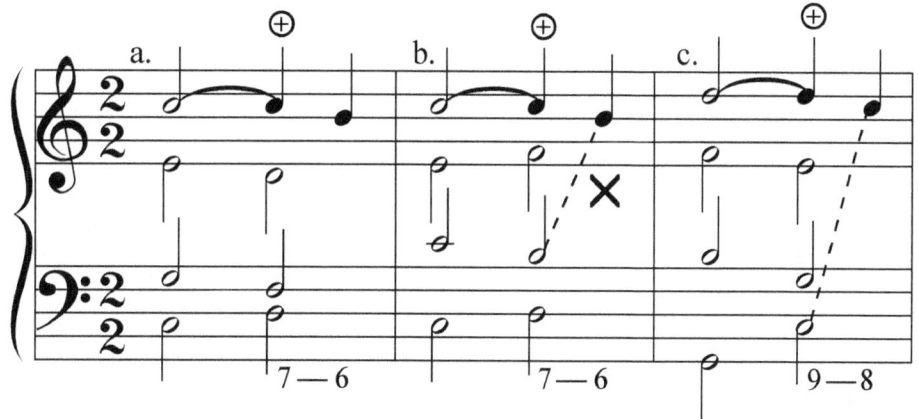

Most suspensions take downward resolutions; however, some suspensions have upward resolutions. Example G–14a demonstrates the most common upward resolution of the suspension. As an upper voice of a dominant-family chord, the leading tone (B) is suspended into the tonic chord. The resolution of the dissonant 7th proceeds upwards to the tonic scale degree, producing a 7—8 motion over the stationary bass (C). The upward resolution of a suspension is sometimes referred to as a **retardation**, a term traditionally reserved for the suspension. However, in a more general sense, retardation may describe any upward resolution of an accented nonharmonic tone.

It is also possible to suspend two or more voices simultaneously, one of which might involve retardation. Example G–14b shows how to suspend the third, fifth, and seventh components of the dominant seventh into the tonic triad, producing multiple 9—8, 7—8, and 4—3 motions over the bass. As with the cadential $^6_4$ chord (see Appendix D), the circle around the figured bass attached to the chord symbol indicates that the real chord is formed on the second half of beat 2.

Example G–14: the suspension (upward)

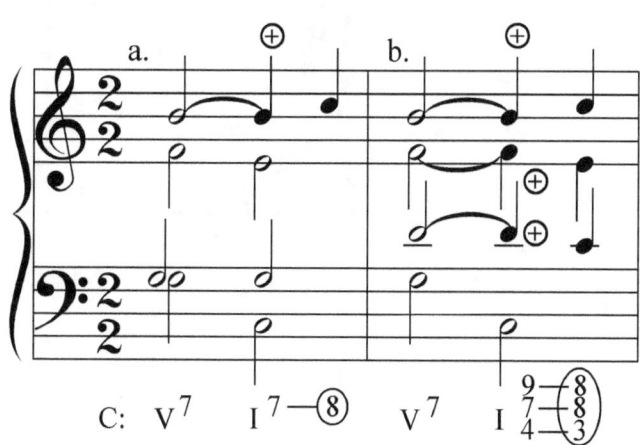

Using Appoggiatura Tones Without a Change of Harmony

As we have said, *accented* nonharmonic tones are usually found with a change of harmony. Indeed, motion between unlike chords strengthens the effect of the nonharmonic tone. However, under certain circumstances, the nonharmonic tone may appear within the framework of a single chord and still constitute an appoggiatura type. As demonstrated in examples G–15 and 16 (see the circled plus signs), a nonharmonic tone that occurs within a single chord is an appoggiatura type if it

(1) falls on beat 1 (G–15a, measure 2);
(2) is syncopated (G–15b, soprano) or otherwise stressed (G–15b, beat 2, tenor);
(3) is an incomplete neighbor on any beat, especially a *chromatic* incomplete lower neighbor (G–15c);

Example G–15: appoggiaturas within the same chord

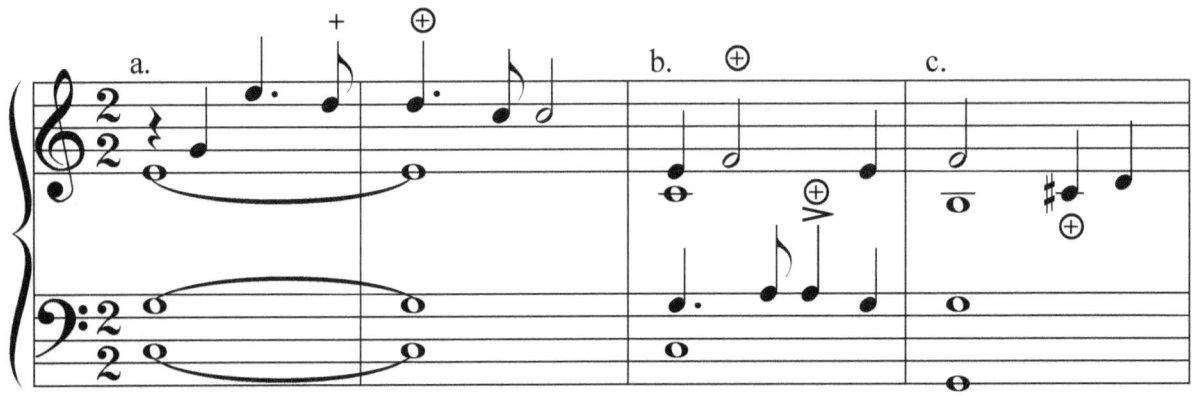

(4) is a complete neighbor or passing tone that resolves to a chord tone within the same beat (G–16a);
(5) is a passing tone that continues to another passing tone within the same beat (G–16b);
(6) is the first component of an incomplete changing-note group (double neighbor) within the same beat (G–16c).

Example G–16: appoggiaturas within the same chord

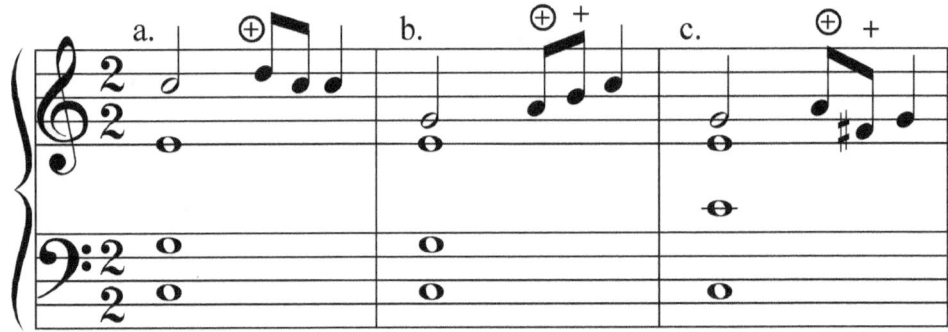

Avoid Conflicts Between the Resolution of the Suspension and Other Nonharmonic Tones

Finally, study example G–17. Notice that a dissonant unaccented upper neighbor in the tenor voice of G–17b occurs simultaneously with the resolution of the suspension in the soprano voice. This is a poor result, as it prevents a complete disposition of the G-major triad from being heard clearly. Therefore, avoid using an unaccented nonharmonic tone in one voice at the same time that another voice resolves any appoggiatura type.

Example G–17c solves the problem by simply lengthening the note value in the tenor, thus delaying the entry of the upper neighbor until *after* the resolution of the suspension has taken place.

Example G–17: avoid interfering with the resolution of an accented nonharmonic tone

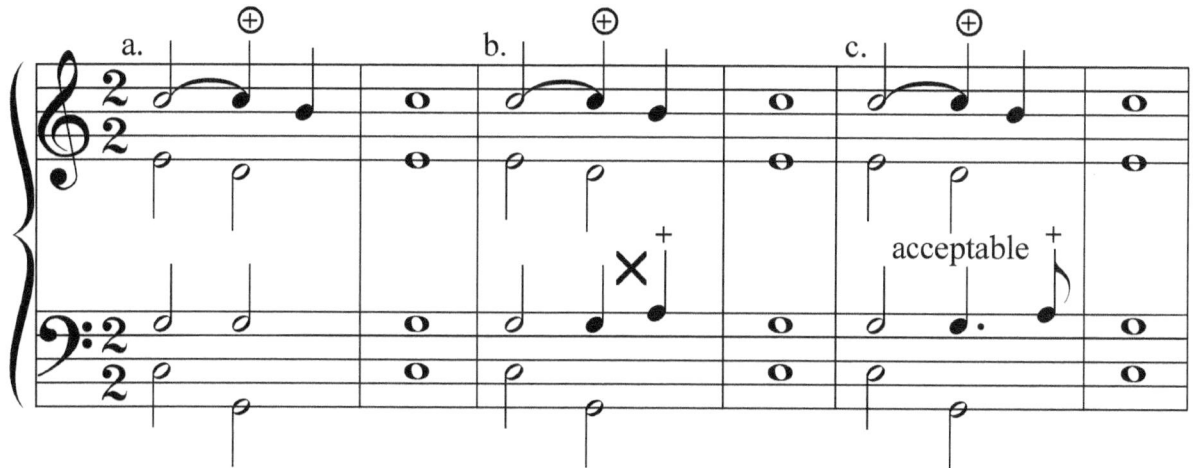

Glossary

accelerando   An expression that directs the performer to gradually increase the speed of a musical passage.

accidental   A sign preceding a note that either raises or lowers both its pitch name and sound.

acoustic interval   An interval whose quality and numerical distance has only one aural interpretation regardless of how it is written. For example, even if a minor 6th is notated as an augmented 5th, the interval always sounds like the former rather than the latter.

active tones   Certain scale degrees of a mode are relatively stable, while other scale degrees are relatively unstable. The relatively unstable scale degrees seek to move to other scale degrees that have less of a tendency to move. The scale degrees that seek to move are called active tones; they include scale degrees 2, 4, 6, and 7.

anticipation tone   A rhythmically unaccented nonharmonic tone, the anticipation previews one of the harmonic components of the following chord, bringing that component forward in time.

apparent chord   A collection of pitches containing one or more nonharmonic tones that together comprise all of the literal components of a chord, a chord whose identity as such is more apparent than real. The real chord usually establishes itself after the nonharmonic tones of the initial chord have moved to actual chord tones. In retrospect, we understand that the first chord was illusory, a coincidence of nonharmonic activity that leads subsequently to the formation of the real chord.

appoggiatura   An Italian term derived from the verb *appoggiare*, one meaning of which is to lean. Within a musical context, the appoggiatura refers to an accented dissonance that resolves by step to a consonance (that is, the accented dissonance "leans" into the consonance).

arpeggiated chord   The successive presentation of a chord's pitches. Also known as **broken chord** and **arpeggio**.

arpeggio   The successive presentation of a chord's pitches. Also known as **broken chord** and **arpeggiated chord**.

asymmetrical meter   A meter with an odd number of beats per measure, a meter that is not divisible by either 2 or 3. Also known as **odd meter**.

atonality   Atonal music is based upon a system of pitches, either strictly or loosely organized, in which no one tone is more important than any other—there is no key center toward which other tones seek to move, no tonal hierarchy.

augmented triad   A triad with a major 3rd from root to third, a major 3rd from third to fifth, and an augmented 5th from root to fifth.

authentic cadence   The authentic cadence is part of a large category of cadences involving the tonic chord. The approach chord of the authentic cadence is a dominant-family chord. The cadential chord is the tonic chord.

auxiliary tone An auxiliary tone usually moves by step, upwards or downwards, to and/or from another tone, referred to as the principal tone. If the principal tone both precedes and follows the auxiliary tone, we call the auxiliary complete. If, however, the principal tone does not both precede and follow the auxiliary tone, we call the auxiliary incomplete. The auxiliary may be either consonant or dissonant with the bass, rhythmically accented or unaccented, and occurs within the same chord or between different chords. Also known as the **neighbor tone**.

bar A unit of musical space created by the distance between two primary accents and enclosed by vertical lines called measure lines or bar lines. Also known as a **measure**.

bar line Vertical line that marks off a unit of measured musical space called a measure or bar.

bass The lowest range for the male voice and/or the lowest part of the musical texture.

bass clef A sign that fixes the pitch F on the fourth line from the bottom of the five-line staff. Also known as the **F clef**.

beam A thick horizontal line that joins two or more notes that would otherwise take flags.

block chord A chord given a simultaneous performance of its pitches.

broken chord The successive presentation of a chord's pitches. Also known as **arpeggio** and **arpeggiated chord**.

cadence A two-chord pattern which forms either a permanent or temporary end of a musical phrase.

cambiata An uncceented nonharmonic tone that begins with a leap and ends with a stepwise resolution.

C clef A sign that encircles the line on which middle C is to be read.

changing-note group A figure that has two unaccented neighbors occurring in either direct or indirect succession. If the first of the two neighbors returns to the tone that it has left, that is, the principal tone, then the changing-note group is complete and presents an indirect succession. If the first neighbor proceeds to the second neighbor without returning to the principal tone first, then the group is incomplete and presents a direct succession. Also known as the **double neighbor**.

chord A combination of three or more different pitches containing at least two intervals sounding either simultaneously or in succession.

chromatic half step Two pitches a half step apart with the same letter name. For example: C and C♯.

chromaticism Pitches that occur in a music composition that are neither native to the mode nor reflected in the key signature.

chromatic scale A scale that divides the octave into twelve half steps.

church modes   Modes that were developed during the eighth and ninth centuries of the Common Era as a means for analyzing and classifying the monophonic music of the Roman Catholic Church. Also known as the **ecclesiastical modes**.

circle of 5ths   Two individual but related patterns of major and minor keys in which each key is one perfect 5th away from the next key and set in a circular clock-like arrangement. The face of each circle shows twelve keys, each of which adds one sharp or flat to its key signature when proceeding clockwise and counter-clockwise from "twelve o'clock" (which represents C major or a minor).

clef   A sign that identifies one pitch on the staff, usually C, F, or G. Once the pitch has been located, it is possible to find the other pitches because they are ordered alphabetically from A to G.

close position   The placement of chord tones as closely together as possible on the staff so that within the span of the chord, none of its elements are omitted from any available line or space. Also known as **close structure** and **close voicing**.

close structure   An equivalent term for **close position** or **close voicing**.

close voicing   An equivalent term for **close position** or **close structure**.

compound intervals   Intervals exceeding the span of the octave.

compound meters   A meter in which each beat is divided into three equal parts or multiples of three.

conjunct motion   Movement between adjacent pitches separated by either a half step or a whole step. Also known as **melodic motion**.

consonance   A consonance is a combination of intervals that conveys a sense of rest and stability. There are two classes of consonant intervals, perfect consonances and imperfect consonances. The perfect consonances are the unison, the perfect octave, the perfect 5th, and sometimes the perfect 4th. The imperfect consonances consist of both major and minor 3rds and 6ths.

contextual interval   An interval that exists only within a written context, such as the diminished 4th, which always sounds like a major 3rd. The augmented 5th (the inversion of the diminished 4th) is also a contextual interval because the *sound* of the augmented 5th is identical to that of another interval, the minor 6th.

contrapuntal cadence   A cadence in which the approach to the cadential chord in the bass involves either a major or minor 2nd.

contrapuntal leading-tone chord   Any dominant-family chord that approaches the tonic chord by half step or by whole step in the bass.

crescendo   A performance direction to gradually play louder.

cross accent   Disrupting the normal rhythmic flow at the level of the beat rather than the division of the beat. Also known as a **displaced accent**.

deceptive cadence   An open type of cadence that falls within the category of tonic-oriented cadences because the cadential chord contains scale degree 1 and is approached by the dominant chord. However, even though the leading tone proceeds to scale degree 1 in the cadential chord, the tonic chord itself is not used.

decrescendo   A performance direction to gradually play softer.

diatonic half step   Two pitches a half step apart with two different letter names. For example: C and D♭.

diatonicism   The principle of diatonicism maintains that every mode has certain tones representing its unique profile of half steps and whole steps, tones reflected in the mode's key signature. The tones specific and appropriate to the pitch content of any given mode are called diatonic tones. Conversely, pitches that are neither native to the mode nor reflected in the key signature are chromatic tones.

diatonic scale   A scale having only one letter name for each of its seven pitches, spanning a single octave, and comprising five whole steps and two half steps.

diminished triad   A triad with a minor 3rd from root to third, a minor 3rd from third to fifth, and a diminished 5th from root to fifth.

disjunct motion   Movement between adjacent pitches separated by an interval greater than a whole step.

displaced accent   Disrupting the normal rhythmic flow at the level of the beat rather than the division of the beat. Also known as a **cross accent**.

dissonance   A dissonance is a combination of intervals that conveys a sense of tension and instability. Dissonant intervals usually seek to form connections to consonant intervals in a process known as resolution. Traditionally, dissonances resolve to consonances. When a dissonant interval is resolved to a consonance, a feeling of relaxation is produced. Resolutions of dissonance endow most of the tonal music of the Western tradition with a sense of forward motion, as the alternation between tension and relaxation propels the music ever forward.

dominant   The name for scale degree 5 of any diatonic mode.

dominant seventh chord   A seventh chord with a major triad and a minor 7th from the root to its seventh.

dots   The addition of a dot extends the duration of a note or rest by one half its original value. Adding a second dot extends the duration of a note or rest by one half the value of the first dot.

double bar lines   Two parallel lines running vertically through the staff or staves. If the double bar has one narrow bar line and one thicker bar line, then it marks the end of a composition. However, if two dots precede the double bar, then it functions as a repeat sign. Another type of double bar, consisting of two narrow bar lines of the same thickness, is used to close off a section of music before the end of the composition.

double neighbor   A figure that has two unaccented neighbors occurring in either direct or indirect succession. If the first of the two neighbors returns to the tone that it has left, that is, the principal tone, then the double neighbor is complete and presents an indirect succession. If the first neighbor proceeds to the second neighbor without returning to the principal tone first, then the double neighbor is incomplete and presents a direct succession. Also known as the **changing-note group**.

duplet   A simple (two-part) division of the beat occurring in a compound meter.

dynamic accent   A sign (>) that instructs the performer to play certain notes louder than others.

dynamics   A term that refers to marks in the musical score that instruct the performer to play within a wide range of volume levels, from barely audible to extremely loud.

ecclesiastical modes   Modes that were developed during the eighth and ninth centuries of the Common Era as a means for analyzing and classifying the monophonic music of the Roman Catholic Church. Also known as the **church modes**.

échappée   An unaccented nonharmonic tone that begins with stepwise motion and ends with a leap into the tone of resolution.

enharmonic equivalents   The application of more than one letter name to the same pitch. Every pitch can have at least three different letter names except for G♯ and A♭. For example, F♭, E, and D𝄪 all represent the same tone.

enharmonic keys   Two keys that sound the same but with different spellings for their respective pitch content. In the circle of 5ths for the major mode, the three pairs of keys located on the lower portion of the circle, namely, D♭ and C♯, G♭ and F♯, and C♭ and B are enharmonic keys, keys that close the circle of 5ths by bringing the sharp and flat sides of major together. In the circle of 5ths for the minor mode, there are three pairs of enharmonic keys, namely, b♭ and a♯, e♭ and d♯, and a♭ and g♯.

F clef   A sign that fixes the pitch F on the fourth line from the bottom of the five-line staff. Also known as the **bass clef**.

fermata   Suspends the counting of the beat and extends the length of the note or rest beyond its original value. There is no precise duration for the extension of the note or rest that carries the fermata, but usually, the suspension of time will be longer in a slow tempo than in a fast tempo.

figured bass   Arabic numbers and other symbols that indicate the placement of certain intervals and pitches above the lowest note of the musical texture, the bass note.

first harmonic   The basic rate of vibration generating the pitch. Also known as the **fundamental frequency** and the **first partial**.

first inversion   Disposition of a tertian chord (usually a triad or a seventh) in which the third of the chord is the lowest tone of the musical texture.

first partial   The basic rate of vibration generating the pitch. Also known as the **fundamental frequency** and the **first harmonic**.

flag A curved notational structure attached to the right side of any stemmed note that has a filled-in note head. In effect, the flag has the opposite function of a dot: the flag shortens the duration of the note value by one half its original value. Thus, one flag transforms a quarter note into an eighth, two flags turns an eighth into a sixteenth, three flags convert a sixteenth into a thirty-second, etcetera.

frequency The number of sound vibrations completed in one second of time when an object is moved by force.

fundamental frequency The basic rate of vibration generating the pitch. Also known as the **first harmonic** and the **first partial**.

G clef A sign that fixes the pitch G on the second line from the bottom of the five-line staff. Also known as the **treble clef**.

grand staff Two staves joined together by a brace in the left margin. The G clef and F clef occupy the top and bottom staves respectively. An additional line called a ledger line between the two staves designates a pitch called "middle C." Also known as the **great staff** and the **piano staff**.

great staff An equivalent term for the **grand staff** and the **piano staff**.

Gregorian chant A type of monophonic music for the Roman Catholic Church originally sung in Latin without instrumental accompaniment. The music is named after St. Gregory I (540?–604), who traditionally receives credit for composing the chant for the services of the Roman Church during his papacy. Although St. Gregory may have helped to bring the chant repertory of the Roman Church together through his extraordinary service as an administrator, it is unlikely that he composed any of the music himself. Also known as **plainchant**.

half cadence A type of cadence consisting of a non-dominant approach chord and a cadential chord other than the tonic. Also known as the **semicadence**.

half step The half step is the smallest possible interval on the piano keyboard and in our Western tradition of music. There are twelve half steps within any single octave. Also known as the **semitone** or the **minor 2nd**.

harmonic cadence A cadence in which the approach to the cadential chord in the bass involves a rising 4th or falling 5th motion or a rising 5th or falling 4th motion.

harmonic interval A type of interval that results from the simultaneous occurrence of two pitches.

harmonic motion Movement in the bass between pitches of either a 4th or a 5th, including the tritone.

harmonic series A spectrum of sounds consisting of both the fundamental frequency and its overtones. Also known as the **overtone series**.

harmony A composite sound resulting from the simultaneous occurrence of two or more pitches.

hemiola   A process by which a composer may displace the accents in such a way that it transforms either a duple meter into what sounds like a triple meter or a triple meter into what sounds like a duple meter. It may occur within the measure or across measures.

imperfect authentic cadence   An open type of cadence that falls within the category of tonic-oriented cadences. It is referred to as an open cadence because scale degree 1 does not appear in both outer voices of the cadential tonic chord.
  (1) In the *harmonic* imperfect authentic cadence, either scale degree 3 or 5 occurs in the soprano voice. The bass presents a rising 4th or falling 5th root and bass relationship between the dominant-family approach chord and cadential chord. The tonic chord maintains scale degree 1 in the bass.
  (2) In the *contrapuntal* imperfect authentic cadence, the cadential chord will have a scale degree other than the tonic in at least one of its outer voices. The approach to the cadential tonic in the bass is either by whole step or half step.

inflection   Refers to either pitch inflection or syllable inflection. Pitch inflection occurs when a note has been altered by the addition of an accidental. Syllable inflection is based upon the solmization syllables associated with singing the chromatic scale, a scale consisting primarily of pairs of pitches that involve two different versions of the same letter name. The syllables change as each pitch moves from one version of itself to the other. Syllable inflection is also applied to the three forms of minor and the church modes.

interval   The distance between two pitches.

key   The principal note of a mode and the pitch to which all other pitches within that mode are related and toward which they ultimately move. Also known as the **keynote**, **tonic**, or **tonal center**.

keynote   The principal note of a mode and the pitch to which all other pitches within that mode are related and toward which they ultimately move. Also known as the **key**, **tonic**, or **tonal center**.

key signature   A type of shorthand notation in which the sharps or flats of any mode appear. The key signature identifies the specific notes that are appropriate to the mode of a musical work.

leading tone   The seventh degree of the scale that is one half step below the tonic.

ledger line   Horizontal line(s) located above and below the staff on which notes that lie beyond the staff are placed. Ledger lines retain within a single clef pitches that exceed the limits of any single staff.

legato   An Italian word that refers to a method of performance in which tones are connected smoothly to one another, a style of playing indicated in the musical score with a curved line placed either above or below the notes. This curved line is called a slur and is similar to a tie, except that a tie connects two notes of the same pitch whereas a slur connects two or more different pitches together and directs the performer to move from pitch to pitch as seamlessly as possible without any apparent break between them.

lower tetrachord   One of two four-note segments comprising scale degrees 1 through 4 of a diatonic scale.

major-minor tonal system   A system of pitch organization that emerged in the late-seventeenth century in Western Europe. The major-minor tonal system developed over time in the course the "common practice period," a span of art music composition that extended from about 1600 to 1900 C. E.

major scale   A seven-tone diatonic scale with half steps between scale degrees 3 and 4 and scale degrees 7 and 8.

major 2nd   Two consecutive half steps. Also known as the **whole step** (sometimes called a "step").

major triad   A triad with a major 3rd from root to third, a minor 3rd from third to fifth, and a perfect 5th from root to fifth.

measure   A unit of musical space created by the distance between two primary accents and enclosed by vertical lines called measure lines or bar lines. Also known as a **bar**.

mediant   The name for the third scale degree of a diatonic mode.

melodic interval   Two pitches occurring in succession rather than simultaneously.

melodic motion   Movement between adjacent pitches separated by either a half step or a whole step. Also known as **conjunct motion**.

meter   A succession of pulses of relative strength and weakness that together produce what is known as meter. The pulses in this text are called primary and secondary accents. The distance between primary accents determines the meter, a distance measured by the number of intervening secondary accents that both precede and follow the primary accents.

meter signature   A sign or symbol that indicates the value of the beat and how many beats are distributed across each measure. The time signature usually consists of two Arabic numbers, one located directly above the other. There are two principal exceptions, each of which involves a symbol that looks somewhat like the letter C. The first symbol ($\mathbf{C}$), known as "common time," is the same as $\frac{4}{4}$ time. The second symbol ($\mathbf{\mathglyph{\cent}}$), referred to as either "cut time" or *alla breve*, is the equivalent of $\frac{2}{2}$ time. Time signature is also known as **time signature**.

metronome   A device that produces a steady and repeated click that helps the musician know exactly how fast or slow to play a composition.

minor 2nd   The smallest numerical distance between two pitches on the piano keyboard and in our Western tradition of music. Also known as the **half step** and the **semitone**.

minor triad   A triad with a minor 3rd from root to third, a major 3rd from third to fifth, and a perfect 5th from root to fifth.

mode   A collection of pitches which demonstrates certain characteristic patterns and configurations, both melodic and chordal, seeking to confirm and establish the key of a musical work.

monophony   A type of musical texture that consists of a single melodic line.

neighbor tone   A neighbor tone usually moves by step, upwards or downwards, to and/or from another tone, referred to as the principal tone. If the principal tone both precedes and follows the neighbor tone, we call the neighbor complete. If, however, the principal tone does not both precede and follow the neighbor tone, we call the neighbor incomplete. The neighbor may be either consonant or dissonant with the bass, rhythmically accented or unaccented, and occurs within the same chord or between different chords. Also known as the **auxiliary tone**.

nonchord tones   Tones that are not inherent components of a chord. Such tones often produce what appear to be chords but which are actually coincidences of melodic activity that subsequently resolve into the real tones of the chord (see **apparent chord**). In other circumstances, the nonchord tone is the result of rhythmic manipulation that either delays the real tone of the chord or brings it forward in time. Also known as **nonharmonic tones** and "tones of figuration."

nonharmonic tones   An equivalent term for **nonchord tones**.

note head   The principal written component representing a musical pitch and/or durational value. The note head appears as either a hollowed-out or filled-in oval structure to which a stem is usually attached. Exceptions are the whole note which has no stem and the double whole note which is sometimes written as a hollowed-out rectangular box with a vertical line on each side of the note box.

octave   Any two pitches of the same letter name that have a frequency ratio of 2:1. An intervallic distance of either 6 whole steps or 12 half steps.

octuplet   A group of eight notes.

odd meter   A meter having an odd number of beats per measure that is not divisible by either 2 or 3. Also known as **asymmetrical meter**.

open position   A disposition of a chord in which its tones are *not* voiced as closely together as possible. In four-part textures, an open-position chord has at least one octave between the soprano and tenor voices and allows for at least one potential chord tone to be placed between the soprano and alto voices, alto and tenor voices, or between both pairs of voices. Also known as **open structure** and **open voicing**.

open structure   An equivalent term for **open position** and **open voicing**.

open voicing   An equivalent term for **open position** and **open structure**.

outer voices   The lowest and highest parts in the texture. In four-voice dispositions, the bass and soprano.

overtones   A spectrum of frequencies of varying degrees of intensity (volume) projected above the fundamental pitch from within the harmonic series. Overtones are usually not loud enough to be heard as pitches in their own right. Rather, the fundamental frequency and its overtones are blended together into a single composite sound. This composite sound is referred to variously as tone quality, tone color, or timbre (pronounced *tam*ber). The first overtone, which sounds one octave above the fundamental, is also called the second partial or second harmonic.

overtone series   A spectrum of sounds consisting of both the fundamental frequency and its overtones. Also known as the **harmonic series**.

parallel major   A major mode that shares both the same tonic and range with another mode; however, the pitch content between the two modes is different.

parallel minor   A minor mode that shares both the same tonic and range with another mode; however, the pitch content between the two modes is different.

passing tone   Usually connects two harmonic consonances, is either dissonant or consonant with another voice, may occur on either a strong or weak beat, and also appears on either a strong or weak portion of a beat. The passing tone is approached and left by step. Although more than one passing tone may be used in direct succession, a single passing tone typically fills in the melodic interval of a 3rd.

perfect authentic cadence   A closed type of cadence, sometimes referred as a full cadence, that falls within the category of tonic-oriented cadences. It is often described as a closed or full cadence because scale degree 1 appears in both outer voices of the cadential tonic chord.
(1) In the *harmonic* perfect authentic cadence, the bass presents a rising 4th or falling 5th root and bass relationship between the dominant-family approach chord and cadential chord.
(2) In the *contrapuntal* perfect authentic cadence, the approach to the cadential tonic in the bass is either by whole step or half step.

perfect 4th   An intervallic distance consisting of either $2\frac{1}{2}$ whole steps or 5 half steps.

perfect 5th   An intervallic distance consisting of either $3\frac{1}{2}$ whole steps or 7 half steps.

phrase   The smallest element of musical form in which a combination of melodic, rhythmic, and chordal components together comprise the beginning, middle, and end of a musical thought. The ending, called the cadence, may be permanent or temporary, whether or not the motion itself within the phrase is continuous or segmented into smaller units known as sub-phrases. These sub-phrases, if present, may also contain endings marked off by cadences.

Phrygian cadence   A type of contrapuntal half cadence that occurs in the minor mode and involves a iv^6 approach to a cadential V chord. With the subdominant's third in the bass, the root of the V chord is approached from above by half step. This approach resembles the Phrygian mode's half-step descent from scale degrees 2 down to 1.

piano staff   Two staves joined together by a brace in the left margin. The G clef and F clef occupy the top and bottom staves respectively. An additional line called a ledger line between the two staves designates a pitch called "middle C." Also known as the **grand staff** and the **great staff**.

picardy third   Around the beginning of the sixteenth century, composers began to show a preference for ending minor compositions with a major triad on the tonic. This practice continued for about two hundred years of music composition. The assignment of the major tonic triad in a composition written in the minor mode was later referred to in French as the *tierce de Picardie*, in English, the picardy third.

pitch   When sound vibrations are produced at a steady rate in one second of time, the human ear perceives them as pitch. These sound vibrations are called frequencies. The relative lowness or highness of any pitch corresponds to the rate of the vibrating frequency. Slower vibrating frequencies result in lower pitches, while faster vibrating frequencies produce higher pitches.

plagal cadence   A tonic-oriented cadence in which the cadential chord (the tonic portion of the plagal cadence) is approached harmonically by a non-dominant family chord above scale degree 4 in the bass. Most listeners recognize the plagal cadence as the famous "Amen" closing for many religious forms of music such as the hymn.

plainchant   A type of monophonic music for the Roman Catholic Church originally sung in Latin without instrumental accompaniment. Also known as **Gregorian chant**.

primary accents   The stronger beats, or stressed beats, in the meter of a music composition. Primary accents are the first accents we perceive when hearing a stream of accents unfold in time as a piece of music is being performed.

quadruplet   A group of four notes.

quartal harmony   A combination of 4th intervals.

quintuplet   A group of five notes.

relative major   Any two modes standing in a relative relationship to one another will share the same key signature and the same pitch content but have different tonics and different octave ranges. Every minor mode has a relative major. To find the relative major, locate scale degree 3 of the minor mode by counting up a minor 3rd from the minor tonic, scale degree 1 (or down a major 6th from the tonic). For example, c minor's relative major is E♭ major; the key signature for both modes is three flats.

relative minor   Any two modes standing in a relative relationship to one another will share the same key signature and the same pitch content but have different tonics and different octave ranges. Every major mode has a relative minor. To find the relative minor, locate scale degree 6 of the major by counting up a major 6th from the major tonic, scale degree 1 (or down a minor 3rd from the tonic). For example, D major's relative minor is b minor; the key signature for both modes is two sharps.

repeat sign   A sign that instructs the performer to play a segment of music again. The most common repeat sign consists of a double bar preceded by two dots on the second and third spaces of the staff, which tells the performer to return to the beginning of the composition or some designated point in the score and repeat that section of music.

rest tones   Certain scale degrees of a mode are relatively stable, while other scale degrees are relatively unstable. The relatively unstable scale degrees, called active tones, seek to move to other scale degrees that have less of a tendency to move. The stable tones are called rest tones; they include scale degrees 1, 3, 5, and 8.

retardation   Any upward resolution of an accented nonharmonic tone.

rhythm   The measurement of both the primary and secondary accents within the meter. Rhythm involves how the accents are organized, or configured. Rhythm is that particular arrangement of notes and rests within each measure that ultimately helps to inform the individuality of a musical composition.

ritardando An expression that directs the performer to gradually slow down the tempo of a musical passage.

root position Disposition of a tertian chord (usually a triad or a seventh) in which the root of the chord is the lowest tone of the musical texture.

scale The term scale derives from the Italian word *scala*, which means ladder. A scale is a ladder of tones: a representation of stepwise pitches, each of which is usually identified by one of seven successive alphabet names that proceed upwards or downwards.

secondary accents The weaker beats, or unstressed beats, in the meter of a music composition. Secondary accents occur after and before the primary accents.

second inversion Disposition of a tertian chord (usually a triad or a seventh) in which the fifth of the chord is the lowest tone of the musical texture.

secundal harmony A combination of major and/or minor 2nds, which may also contain 3rd intervals.

semicadence A type of cadence consisting of a non-dominant approach chord and a cadential chord other than the tonic. Also known as the **half cadence**.

semitone The half step is the smallest possible interval on the piano keyboard and in our Western tradition of music. There are twelve half steps within any single octave. Also known as the **half step** or the **minor 2nd**.

septuplet A group of seven notes.

sextuplet A group of six notes.

simple intervals Intervals that do not exceed the span of the octave.

simple meters Meters in which the beat is divided into two equal parts or multiples of two.

slur A curved line placed either above or below the notes in a musical score that directs the performer to move from pitch to pitch as seamlessly as possible without any apparent break between them. Unlike the tie, which connects two notes of the same pitch, the slur connects two or more different pitches together.

staccato An Italian word that refers to a method of performance in which tones are played in a separated manner. *Staccato* is indicated most commonly in the musical score with dots appearing either above or below the notes. Since the performer is directed to make a clear separation between the pitches, each note receives a little less than its full value.

staff A five-line four-space structure used in music notation.

stem A vertical line attached to all note heads shorter in duration than the whole note. The direction of the stem may be either up or down, depending on the relationship of the note to other notes and its position on the staff.

subdominant The name for the fourth scale degree of a diatonic mode.

submediant The name for the sixth scale degree of a diatonic mode.

subtonic The version of scale degree 7 that is a whole step below the tonic pitch, scale degree 8. The subtonic does not share the compelling drive of the leading tone to move upwards by half step to scale degree 8.

supertonic The name for the second scale degree of a diatonic mode.

suspension A rhythmically accented nonharmonic tone consisting of three basic parts:
  (1) the suspension is prepared usually as a consonance (but sometimes as a dissonance);
  (2) the preparation is held (tied or repeated), or *suspended*, as the opposing voice (the bass) moves to form a dissonance with the suspended voice; and finally
  (3) the suspended voice moves down by step to *resolve* to a consonance.
It is important that the actual suspension (part 2) be metrically stronger than the resolution (part 3). The initial preparation (part 1), however, can be made from either a strong or weak position.

syllable inflection Syllable inflection is based upon the solmization syllables associated with singing the chromatic scale, a scale consisting primarily of pairs of pitches that involve two different versions of the same letter name. The syllables change as each pitch moves from one version of itself to the other. Syllable inflection is also applied to the three forms of minor and the church modes.

symmetrical meters Duple, triple, and quadruple meters in which the top number of the meter signature is divisible by either 2 or 3.

syncopation Disrupting the regular distribution of note values by emphasizing the divisions of beats and/or leaving the strongest part of the primary accent unarticulated or weakened in some way. Syncopation makes strong that which is otherwise weak.

tempo The rate of speed at which the beat in a music composition is performed.

tertian harmony A combination of 3rd intervals.

tetrachords Two four-note segments of a diatonic scale, comprising scale degrees 1 through 4 and 5 through 7 respectively.

third inversion Disposition of a seventh chord in which the seventh of the chord is the lowest tone of the musical texture.

tie A curved line that connects two or more notes together; however, only the first note of any tied pair or group of notes is articulated. The second note of the tied pair (or group of notes) is sustained for the duration of the note values presented. Tied notes are particularly useful for extending the duration of a note across the bar line.

timbre   A composite sound consisting of the fundamental frequency and its overtones, referred to variously as tone quality, tone color, or timbre (pronounced *tam*ber). Although the individual overtones cannot be heard as distinct pitches, they do *color* the fundamental frequency and collectively generate the timbre of a musical instrument, making it possible to identify the source of the musical sound. On any given instrument, some overtones are relatively stronger than others. The reason two different instruments sound differently is due to the fact that each makes its own unique selection of overtones from a much larger inventory of weaker overtones. For example, the sound of the clarinet and the violin are distinguishable even when both instruments are playing the exact same pitch because each instrument projects its own unique profile of overtones, its own sonic fingerprint.

time signature   A sign or symbol that indicates the value of the beat and how many beats are distributed across each measure. The time signature usually consists of two Arabic numbers, one located directly above the other. There are two principal exceptions, each of which involves a symbol that looks somewhat like the letter C. The first symbol (C), known as "common time," is the same as $\frac{4}{4}$ time. The second symbol (₵), referred to as either "cut time" or *alla breve*, is the equivalent of $\frac{2}{2}$ time. Time signature is also known as **meter signature**.

tonal center   The principal note of a mode and the pitch to which all other pitches within that mode are related and toward which they ultimately move. Also known as the **key**, **tonic**, or **keynote**.

tonality   Tonality is a system of pitch organization confirmed and established by certain characteristic designs of the mode. Analogous to the gravitational force exerted by the Sun upon any object that comes within its field of attraction, the tonality of a music composition establishes its own field of attraction around one central tone. All of the other tones of the mode seek to revolve around and gravitate toward this central tone in a hierarchical order. The tonic, as the principal tone of this hierarchy, exerts its gravitational force upon all of the other tones of the mode, each of which assumes a position of relative strength and stability within the tonic's field of attraction. Inherent in the system is the principal of consonant or dissonant relationships between different tones.

tonic   The name for the first scale degree of a diatonic mode.

treble clef   A sign that fixes the pitch G on the second line from the bottom of the five-line staff. Also known as the **G clef**.

triplet   A compound (three-part) division of the beat occurring in a simple meter.

tritone   An intervallic distance consisting of either 3 whole steps or 6 half steps.

upper tetrachord   One of two four-note segments comprising scale degrees 5 through 8 of a diatonic scale.

voice   Used to describe the construction and positioning of triads within a four-voice texture. This texture may involve either a close or wide spacing of pitches, sometimes referred to respectively as "close voicing" or "open voicing." A voice may also constitute a melody performed by either vocal cords or an instrument. Additionally, the term may be used as part of a verbal phrase describing the technique for "voicing" a chord, observing carefully the appropriate guidelines for the spacing and range of the parts.

whole step   Two consecutive half steps. Also known as the **major 2nd** (sometimes called a "step").

INDEX

A

a la quindicesima, 30
accelerando, 16, 265
accented complete neighbor tone, 258–259
    See also nonharmonic tones
accented passing tone, 258
    See also nonharmonic tones
accidentals, 20, 265
  double flats, 20
  double sharps, 20–21
  flat, 20–21
  natural sign, 20
  sharp, 20–21
acoustic interval, 118, 265
active tones, 75, 265
Aeolian mode, 75, 217–219, 221, 224, 227, 228, 229, 233–234
alla breve, 7, 272, 278
all'ottava, 29
alto clef, 25
Ambrose, Saint, 217
anacrusis, 15
anticipation tone, 253, 254, 257, 260, 265
apparent chord, 237, 265, 273
appoggiatura, 253, 258, 262, 265
appoggiatura itself (incomplete neighbor tone), 253, 258–259, 262
arpeggiated chord, 107, 265, 266
arpeggio, 107, 265, 266
articulation marks, 16, 49–50
asymmetrical meter, 87, 105–106, 265, 273
atonality, 55–56, 265
augmented 5th, 109, 111, 117–120, 125, 133, 265, 267
augmented intervals, 58–67, 69, 73, 109, 140
augmented triad, 109, 111, 112, 115, 117–118, 120, 125, 126, 127, 128, 130, 133, 136, 137, 138, 140–141, 142, 143, 161, 163, 265
Augustine, Saint, 217
authentic cadence, 243–246, 265, 271, 274
auxiliary tone, 254, 266, 273

B

bar, 4, 266, 272
baritone clef, 25
bar line, 3–4, 12–13, 266, 268, 272, 277
bass, 73, 115, 118–119, 155, 159–160, 163–165, 235–237, 239–242, 243–249, 251, 254, 257, 260–261, 266–267, 269–271, 273–275, 277
bass clef, 23, 52, 54, 156, 195, 266, 269
beams, 1, 3, 18, 87–89, 266
beat, 4–10, 14, 16, 18, 87–106
bis, 13
    See also repeat signs
block chord, 107, 266
Boethius, Anicius Manlius Severinus, 217
breve, 18
broken chord, 107, 265, 266

C

cadence, 235, 243–251, 266
  authentic cadence, 243–246, 265, 271, 274
  contrapuntal cadence, 243, 244, 245–246, 249–51, 267, 271, 274
  contrapuntal imperfect authentic cadence, 244, 246
  contrapuntal perfect authentic cadence, 244, 245
  deceptive cadence, 244, 247, 268
  half cadence, 244, 249–250, 251, 270, 274, 276
  harmonic cadence, 243–245, 249, 270
  harmonic imperfect authentic cadence, 243–246, 271
  harmonic perfect authentic cadence, 243–245, 274
  plagal cadence, 244, 247–248
  Phrygian cadence, 251, 274
  semicadence, 249, 270, 276
cadential six-four chord, 235–237, 244–245, 249–250
cambiata tone, 256, 257, 260, 266
    See also nonharmonic tones
C clef, 25, 30, 266
changing-note group, 255, 262, 266, 269
    See also nonharmonic tones

chord, 107, 108, 266
   ninth, 107, 243
   quartal harmony, 107, 275
   secundal harmony, 107, 276
   seventh, 107, 239–242, 243
   tertian harmony, 107–108, 239, 253, 269, 276, 277
   triad, 107–111
chromatic half step, 22, 25, 55, 266
chromaticism, 55–56, 266
chromatic scale, 31, 50, 55, 86, 233, 266 271
church modes, 217–234, 267, 269
   Aeolian mode, 75, 217–219, 221, 224, 227, 228, 229, 232–233, 234
   Dorian mode, 218–225, 228, 231, 234
   Ionian mode, 217–219, 221, 222–225, 233–234
   Locrian mode, 218–219, 220–221, 222, 224–225, 227, 228, 230, 232, 234
   Lydian mode, 218–219, 221, 222, 223, 226, 228, 233, 234
   Mixolydian mode, 218–219, 221, 224, 226–227, 228, 230, 231, 234
   Phrygian mode, 218–219, 220–223, 226, 228, 229, 232, 234, 251, 274
circle of 5ths, 51, 53, 79–80, 267, 269
clef, 23–25, 29–30, 57, 60, 62, 118, 267
   alto clef, 25
   baritone clef, 25
   bass clef, 23, 52, 54, 156, 195, 266, 269
   C clef, 25, 30, 266
   F clef, 23, 24, 29, 52, 266, 269, 270, 274
   G clef, 23–25, 29–30, 52, 270, 274, 278
   mezzo-soprano clef, 25
   soprano clef, 25
   tenor clef, 25
   treble clef, 23, 52, 156, 270, 278
close position, 154, 156, 267
close structure, 107, 154–156, 267
close voicing, 154, 156, 267, 278
common time, 7
complete changing-note group, 255, 266
   See also nonharmonic tones
complete neighbor tone, 253–255, 258
   See also nonharmonic tones
compound intervals, 57, 67, 235, 267

compound meters, 5–6, 8, 87, 91, 92–94, 96, 98–102, 267, 269
conjunct motion, 48–49, 57–58, 73, 267, 272
consonance, 56, 71, 72–73, 235–237, 259, 260, 265, 267, 268, 274, 277
consonant 4th, 73, 235
contextual interval, 118, 125, 161, 267
contrapuntal cadence, 243–246, 249–251, 267
contrapuntal imperfect authentic cadence, 246, 271
contrapuntal leading-tone chord, 245–246, 267
contrapuntal perfect authentic cadence, 245
contra register, 26–27, 30
   See also octave registers
crescendo, 17, 267
cross accent, 10–11, 253, 267, 268
cut time, 7

D

Da Capo al Coda, 14–15
Da Capo al Fine, 14
Dal Segno al Coda, 14–15
Dal Segno al Fine, 14
D.C. (*Da Capo*), 14–15
deceptive cadence, 244, 247, 268
decrescendo, 17, 268
diatonic half steps, 22, 23, 25, 31, 55, 268
diatonicism, 55–56, 268
diatonic scale, 31–32, 55, 85, 217, 268
diminished intervals, 58–62, 64, 67–69, 71–73, 109, 140
diminished triad, 109–113, 116–117, 120, 121, 124, 127–129, 132, 135–139, 140–141, 145–147, 151–152, 158, 160–161, 164–165, 224, 268
disjunct motion, 49, 57–58, 268
displaced accent, 10–11, 267, 268
dissonance, 56, 71–73, 235–237, 259–260, 265, 268
dissonant 4th, 72–73, 235–237
dominant, 32, 111, 112, 138–142, 150, 159–160, 161, 162, 235–237, 243–247, 249–251, 268
dominant seventh, 28, 239–242, 257–258, 261, 268
Dorian mode, 218–225, 228, 231, 234
dots, 3, 6, 8, 11, 92, 97, 106, 268
dotted notes, 3, 5, 6, 8, 87, 92–94, 97, 98, 106
dotted rests, 3
double bar lines, 12–14, 195, 268
double dot, 3
double flats, 20–21, 137

double neighbor, 255, 262, 266, 269
    See also nonharmonic tones
double prime register, 26–27
    See also octave registers
double sharps, 20–21, 137
double whole note, 2, 17–18, 273
double whole rest, 17–18
doubly augmented intervals, 58–59, 61
doubly diminished intervals, 58–59, 61
downbeat, 15
D.S. (*Dal Segno*), 14–15
duple meter, 4–5, 7–9, 11, 87, 91–93, 96, 105
duplet, 87, 91–93, 95, 97, 98, 101, 269
dynamic accent, 17, 195–215, 269
dynamic marks, 17
dynamics, 16–17, 269

E

ecclesiastical modes, 217, 267, 269
    See also church modes
échappée, 256–257, 269
    See also nonharmonic tones
eighth note, 1–3, 5–10, 87–97, 102, 104–106
eighth rest, 1, 3, 10
enharmonic equivalents, 20–23, 25, 30, 40, 66, 125, 129, 137, 269
enharmonic keys, 53, 79, 269
essential diatonic intervals, 58–59, 62–65, 70

F

F clef, 23, 24, 29, 52, 266, 269, 270, 274
fermata, 14–15, 269
fifth, 108–111, 115–125
figured bass, 115, 142, 235, 237, 240–242, 261
Fine, 14
    See also repeat signs
first ending, 13
    See also repeat signs
first harmonic, 161–162, 269, 270
first inversion, 115–119, 160, 235, 237, 240–242, 246, 250, 251, 269
    six-five chord ($_5^6$ position), 241–242
    six-three chord ($_3^6$ position), 115–119, 123, 142, 163–165
first partial, 161–162, 269, 270
first principle of intervals, 59–60, 65, 68–69
five-three chord ($_3^5$ position or root position), 108, 115–158, 162–165, 239–242
flags, 1–3, 18, 266, 270
flat, 20–21
four-part texture (four-voice texture), 154–158
    close position, 154, 156, 267
    close structure, 154–156, 267
    close voicing, 154, 156, 267
    open position, 155, 273
    open structure, 155–157, 273
    open voicing, 155, 273
    SATB, 155
four-three chord ($_3^4$ position), 241–242
four-two chord ($_2^4$ position), 241–242
frequency, 19, 63, 161–162, 264, 270, 273, 274
fundamental frequency, 161–162, 269, 270, 273, 278

G

G clef, 23–25, 29–30, 52, 270, 274, 278
grand staff, 23, 270, 274
great register, 26–27, 29, 67, 70, 72, 155, 161–162, 195, 203–215
    See also octave registers
great staff, 23, 25, 26, 155, 270, 274
Gregorian chant, 217, 270, 275
Gregory I, Saint (pope), 217, 270

H

hairpins, 17
half cadence, 244, 249–250, 251, 270, 274, 276
half note, 1–3, 7, 18, 90, 99, 236, 237, 253
half rest, 1
half step, 19, 254–256, 258, 266–268, 270–274, 276
harmonic cadence, 243–245, 249, 270
harmonic imperfect authentic cadence, 243–245, 271
harmonic interval, 57, 107, 270
harmonic minor, 75, 81–86, 138–139, 140, 141, 233
harmonic motion, 159, 240, 243, 270
harmonic perfect authentic cadence, 243–245, 274
harmonic series, 159, 161–162, 270, 273
    fundamental frequency, 161–162, 269, 270, 273, 278
    overtones, 161–162, 270, 273
    overtone series, 161-162, 270, 273

harmony, 107–108, 217, 258, 262, 270
hemiola, 11, 92, 253, 271

I

imperfect authentic cadence, 243–246, 271
imperfect plagal cadence, 244, 247–248
incomplete changing-note group, 255, 262
    See also nonharmonic tones
incomplete neighbor tone, 255–259, 262
    See also nonharmonic tones
inflection, 50, 63, 65, 66, 71, 86, 120, 122, 130–135, 137, 233, 271
interval inversion, 68–69, 71, 115, 118
intervals, 19, 20, 49, 52, 53, 57–73, 271
Ionian mode, 217–219, 221, 222–225, 233–234

J

Jerome, Saint, 217

K

key, 32, 48, 52–56, 271, 272, 278
keynote, 32, 55, 271
key signature, 51–52, 54, 55–56, 271
    parallel major, 77–78, 81, 84, 274
    parallel minor, 77–78, 81, 274
    relative major, 78, 80, 275
    relative minor, 76–78, 80, 275

L

large triplet, 88–92, 95–97, 104
leading tone, 32, 35, 40, 75, 81, 83, 85, 140, 159, 160, 240, 243–245, 247, 261, 271
ledger line, 23, 25, 29, 30, 270, 271, 274
legato, 49–50, 271
like inflection, 66, 71, 120, 122, 130–135, 137
Locrian mode, 218–219, 220–221, 222, 224–225, 227, 228, 230, 232, 234
lower tetrachord, 32–33, 76, 271
Lydian mode, 218–219, 221, 222, 223, 226, 228, 234

M

macro triplet, 88, 90–91, 95
Maelzel, Johann, 16
major intervals, 58–62, 67–69
major-minor tonal system, 75, 217, 239, 272
major scale, 31–32, 48, 51, 56, 272
major 2nd, 20, 272, 278
major triad, 109–112, 114–115, 117, 161–163, 243, 251, 272, 274
measure, 4, 272, 273, 275, 278
mediant, 32, 76, 140–142, 160, 219, 221, 272
melodic intervals, 57–58, 243, 272
melodic minor, 75, 81–86, 138–143, 146, 233, 239
melodic motion, 48, 81, 83, 159, 240, 243, 267, 272
meter, 4–11, 87–106, 167, 195, 237, 253, 272
    asymmetrical meter, 87, 105–106, 265, 273
    compound meters, 5–6, 8, 87, 91, 92–94, 96, 98–102, 267, 269
    duple meter, 4–5, 7–9, 11, 87, 91–93, 96, 105
    quadruple meter, 4–7, 11, 253, 277
    simple meters, 5–8, 87–88, 91–94, 98–99, 101–102, 276
    symmetrical meters, 4, 105, 277
    triple meter, 4–6, 10–11, 90, 92, 95, 97, 102–105
meter exchange, 87, 91, 95, 101
    duplet, 87, 91–93, 95, 97, 98, 101, 269
    large triplet, 88–91, 95–97, 104
    macro triplet, 88, 90–91, 95
    micro triplet, 88–90, 98
    quadruplet, 92–97, 98, 101, 275
    small triplet, 87–91, 96–97, 104
    triplet, 87–92, 95–98, 101, 104, 278
meter signature, 6–7, 272, 277, 278
metronome, 16, 272
mezzo-soprano clef, 25
micro triplet, 88–90, 98
minor intervals, 59–60, 64, 67–69
minor mode, 75–86
    Aeolian mode, 75, 217–219, 221, 224, 227, 228, 229, 232–233, 234
    harmonic minor, 75, 81–86, 138–139, 140, 141, 233
    melodic minor, 75, 81–86, 138–143, 146, 233, 239
    natural minor, 75–76, 78, 81–86, 138–139, 140–141, 217–221, 224, 233–234, 251
minor 2nd, 19, 270, 272

minor triad, 109–112, 116, 117, 119, 151, 161–162, 164, 251, 272
Mixolydian mode, 218–219, 221, 224, 226–227, 228, 230, 231, 234
mode, 32, 48, 50, 51, 56, 159, 217–234, 272
monophony, 217, 272

N

natural minor, 75–76, 78, 81–86, 138–139, 140–141, 217–221, 224, 233–234, 251
natural sign, 20
neighbor tone, 253–259, 262–263, 266, 269
    See also nonharmonic tones
ninth, 107, 243
non-appoggiaturas, 253–257
    See also nonharmonic tones
nonchord tones (nonharmonic tones), 236, 273
nonharmonic tones, 236–237, 249, 253–263, 273
  anticipation tone, 253–254, 257, 260, 265
  appoggiatura, 253, 258, 262, 265
  appoggiatura itself (incomplete neighbor tone), 253, 258–259, 262
  auxiliary tone, 254, 266, 273
  cambiata tone, 256, 257, 260, 266
  changing-note group, 255, 262, 266, 269
  double neighbor, 255, 262, 266, 269
  échappée, 256–257, 269
  neighbor tone, 253–259, 262–263, 266, 269
  non-appoggiaturas, 253–257
  passing tone, 235–237, 253–254, 258, 260, 262, 274
  retardation, 261, 275
  suspension, 236–237, 253, 258, 260–261, 263, 277
note head, 1, 17–18, 273

O

octave, 19–20, 22–23, 25–32, 48, 57, 273
octave registers, 25–30
octave signs, 29–30
  a la quindicesima, 30
  all'ottava, 29
octuplet, 99–100, 273

odd meter, 105, 265, 273
one hundred and twenty-eighth notes, 2, 17–18
one hundred and twenty-eighth rests, 18
open position, 155, 273
open structure, 155–157, 273
open voicing, 155, 273
outer voices, 244–246, 271, 273, 274
overtones, 161–162, 270, 273
overtone series, 161–162, 270, 273

P

parallel major, 77–78, 81, 84, 274
parallel duple meter, 87, 91–93
parallel minor, 77–78, 81, 274
passing tone, 235–237, 253–254, 258, 260, 262, 274
perfect authentic cadence, 243–245, 274
perfect 4th, 41, 51, 72–73, 159, 163–164, 235, 274
perfect 5th, 33, 41, 51, 53, 72, 79–80, 159, 161–162, 274
perfect intervals, 58–62, 67–69
perfect plagal cadence, 244, 247–248
performance marks, 16–17, 49
phrase, 235, 237, 243–244, 266, 274
Phrygian cadence, 251, 274
Phrygian mode, 218–219, 220–223, 226, 228, 229, 232, 234, 251, 274
piano staff, 23, 270, 274
picardy third, 251, 274
pickup, 15
pitch, 1, 16, 19–30, 274
plagal cadence, 247–248, 275
plainchant, 217, 270, 275
primary accents, 4–5, 7, 9–10, 15, 253, 266, 272, 275, 276, 277
prime register, 26–27, 29–30, 34, 36, 39, 41, 48
    See also octave registers

Q

quadruple meter, 4–7, 11, 253, 277
quadruple prime register, 26–27, 29–30
    See also octave registers
quadruplet, 92–97, 98, 101, 275
quartal harmony, 107, 275
quarter note, 1–9, 11, 16, 87, 89–90, 92, 95–97, 98–99, 102–104, 215, 253, 270

quarter rest, 1–3, 5
quintuple prime register, 26–27
    See also octave registers
quintuplet, 98, 101–103, 275

R

relative major, 78, 80, 275
relative minor, 76–78, 80, 275
repeat signs, 12–15, 275
   bis, 13
   Da Capo al Coda, 14–15
   Da Capo al Fine, 14
   Dal Segno al Coda, 14–15
   Dal Segno al Fine, 14
   D.C. (*Da Capo*), 14–15
   D.S. (*Dal Segno*), 14–15
   first ending, 13
   second ending, 13
   two-measure repeat, 13
re-sizing principle, 59–61, 65, 66, 69–70
rest tones, 75, 82, 275
retardation, 261, 275
    See also nonharmonic tones
rhythm, 9–10, 87–89, 91–92, 94, 96–98, 102, 104, 106, 237, 253, 258, 275
rhythmic counting, 7–9
rhythmic syllables, 7–10
ritardando, 16, 276
Roman numeral chord symbols, 140–142
root, 108
root position, 108–120, 126, 130, 143–151, 156, 162–163, 239–240, 242, 249–250, 276

S

SATB, 155
scale, 31–32, 266, 268, 276
scale degrees, 32
secondary accents 4–5, 7, 9–10, 253, 272, 275, 276
second ending, 13
second inversion, 115–119, 142, 235–237, 276
   four-three chord ($^4_3$ position), 241–242
   six-four chord ($^6_4$ position), 115–119, 123, 235–237

second principle of intervals (re-sizing principle), 59–61, 65, 66, 69–70
secundal harmony, 107, 276
semicadence, 249, 270, 276
semitone, 19, 270, 272, 276
septuplet, 99, 104, 276
seventh, 107, 239–242, 243, 257–258, 261, 268, 269, 276, 277
sextuplet, 89, 98–99, 104, 276
sharp, 20–21
simple intervals, 57, 67, 68, 276
simple meters, 5–8, 87–88, 91–94, 98–99, 101–102, 276, 278
six-five chord ($^6_5$ position), 241–242
six-four chord ($^6_4$ position), 115–119, 123–125, 133–137, 152–153, 163–165, 235–237
sixteenth note, 1–3, 5–10, 12–15, 88–89, 92–94, 96–106
sixteenth rest, 1–2
six-three chord ($^6_3$ position), 115–119, 123–125, 133–136, 151–152, 154, 158, 163–165
sixty-fourth note, 1–3, 17–18, 101
sixty-fourth rest, 1–2
slur, 49–50, 271, 276
small register, 26–27, 29–30, 41, 48, 67, 70, 72, 109, 162, 195, 203–215
    See also octave registers
small triplet, 87–91, 96–97, 104
solmization, 48, 233, 271, 277
soprano clef, 25
staccato, 49–50, 276
staff, 1, 12, 16–18, 23–26, 29, 276
stem, 1, 3, 157, 273, 276
sub-contra register, 26–27, 30
    See also octave registers
subdominant, 32, 47, 75–76, 108–109, 111–113, 115, 138–142, 148–149, 159–160, 247–248, 250, 251, 274, 277
submediant, 32, 75–76, 108–109, 111–112, 116, 138–142, 144–145, 159–160, 247, 250, 277
subtonic, 32, 76, 81, 139–141, 148, 151–152, 154, 159–160, 251, 277
supertonic, 32, 75–76, 108–109, 111–112, 114, 116, 138–142, 145–146, 159–160, 235, 237, 277
suspension, 236–237, 249, 253, 260–261, 263, 277
    See also nonharmonic tones

syllable inflection, 50, 86, 233, 271, 277
symmetrical meters, 4, 105, 277
syncopation, 9–10, 236, 253, 277

T

tempo, 14, 16, 49, 98, 269, 276, 277
tenor clef, 25
tertian harmony, 107–108, 239, 253, 269, 276, 277
tetrachords, 32–47, 75–76, 82, 271, 277
third, 108–111, 115–119
third inversion, 241–242, 277
   four-two chord ($\frac{4}{2}$ position), 241–242
thirty-second note, 1–3, 6–9, 14–15, 18, 93–94, 96, 99–101, 270
thirty-second rest, 1–2
ties, 3, 9–11, 49, 89, 90, 92, 93, 236, 277
timbre, 161, 273, 278
time signatures, 5–8, 15, 52, 105–106, 272, 278
tonal center, 32, 72, 159, 224, 271, 278
tonality, 55–56, 157, 159–160, 161, 240, 243, 278
tonic, 32, 56, 75–78, 81, 108, 109, 111, 112, 115, 138–142, 144, 148, 159–160, 237, 240, 243, 271, 278
transposed modes, 221–233
treble clef, 23, 52, 156, 270, 278
triad, 107–111
triple meter, 4–6, 10–11, 90, 92, 95, 97, 102, 103, 104, 105, 237, 271
triple prime register, 26–27, 29–30
   See also octave registers
triplet, 87–91, 95–98, 101, 104, 278
tritone, 71–73, 158, 159, 160, 165, 224, 270, 278
two-measure repeat, 13
   See also repeat signs

U

unaccented passing tone, 253–254, 258
   See also nonharmonic tones
upbeat, 15
upper leading tone, 251
upper tetrachord, 32, 76, 82, 278

V

variable scale degrees, 83–84, 138–139, 141, 151
voice, 25, 48, 73, 154–158, 160, 162, 231, 235–237, 240, 243–246, 248, 251, 254, 257, 260–261, 263, 266, 271, 273, 274, 278

W

whole notes, 1–3, 17, 90–91, 157, 273, 276
whole rests, 1, 3, 18
whole step, 20, 272, 278

Worksheets

Worksheet 1–1

Name _____

Chapter 1: Time and Performance

Given the counts provided in the ten measures below, fill in the missing rhythmic syllables (e, +, a) wherever a blank occurs ("in 2" means that there are two beats to each measure). Counts for the first, second, and third divisions of the beat are as follows:

Worksheet 1–2

Name _____

Chapter 1: Time and Performance

Given the counts provided in the eight measures below, fill in the missing rhythmic syllables wherever a blank occurs. Use both methods for counting compound duple meter as shown here. Accordingly, when counting this meter in 2, the value of the beat is the dotted quarter note. The first division of the beat therefore occurs at the level of the eighth note. Interpreted in a slow 6, however, the value of the beat becomes the eighth note and the first division of the beat is the sixteenth note ("in 2" means that there are two beats to the measure and "in 6" means that there are six beats to the measure).

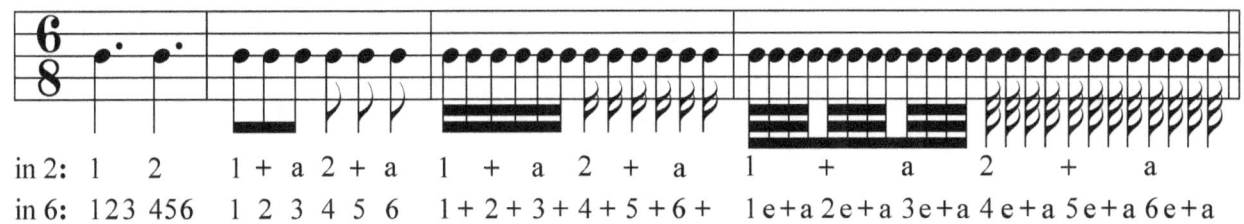

in 2: 1   2   1 + a 2 + a   1 + a 2 + a   1 +   a   2   +   a
in 6: 123 456   1 2 3 4 5 6   1 + 2 + 3 + 4 + 5 + 6 +   1 e + a 2 e + a 3 e + a 4 e + a 5 e + a 6 e + a

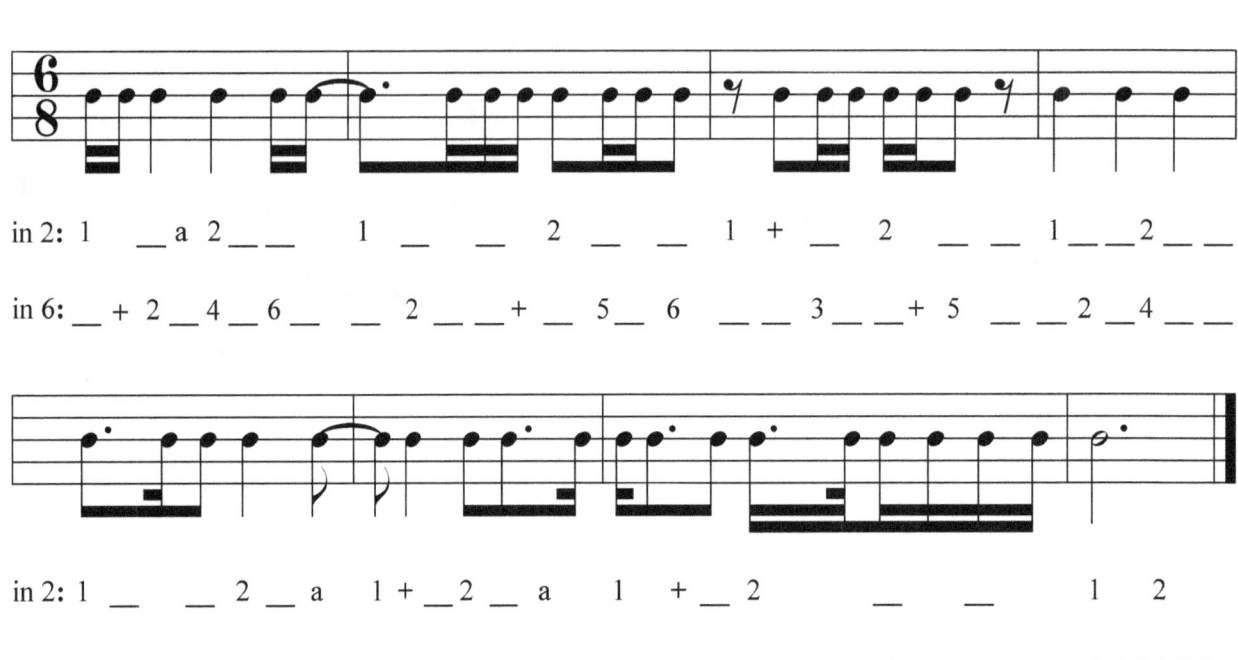

in 2: 1 __ a 2 __ __   1 __ __ 2 __ __   1 + __ 2 __ __   1 __ __ 2 __ __

in 6: __ + 2 __ 4 __ 6 __   __ 2 __ __ + __ 5 __ 6   __ __ 3 __ __ + 5   __ __ 2 __ 4 __ __

in 2: 1 __   __ 2 __ a   1 + __ 2 __ a   1 + __ 2   __   __   1   2

in 6: __ __ + __ __ 5 __   __ __ 3 __ 5 6   __ __ + __ __ __ e + __ 5 __ __ __   1 2 3 4 5 6

Worksheet 1–3

Name _____

Chapter 1: Time and Performance

Given the following counts, notes, and rests, place bar lines in the proper places and fill in the blanks with the remaining counts directly under the appropriate note or rest. The rhythmic syllables in parentheses in the example (and in the exercise) indicate that their inclusion here adds nothing to the basic count and that their absence would not obscure the recognition of any of the beats or divisions of beats.

example

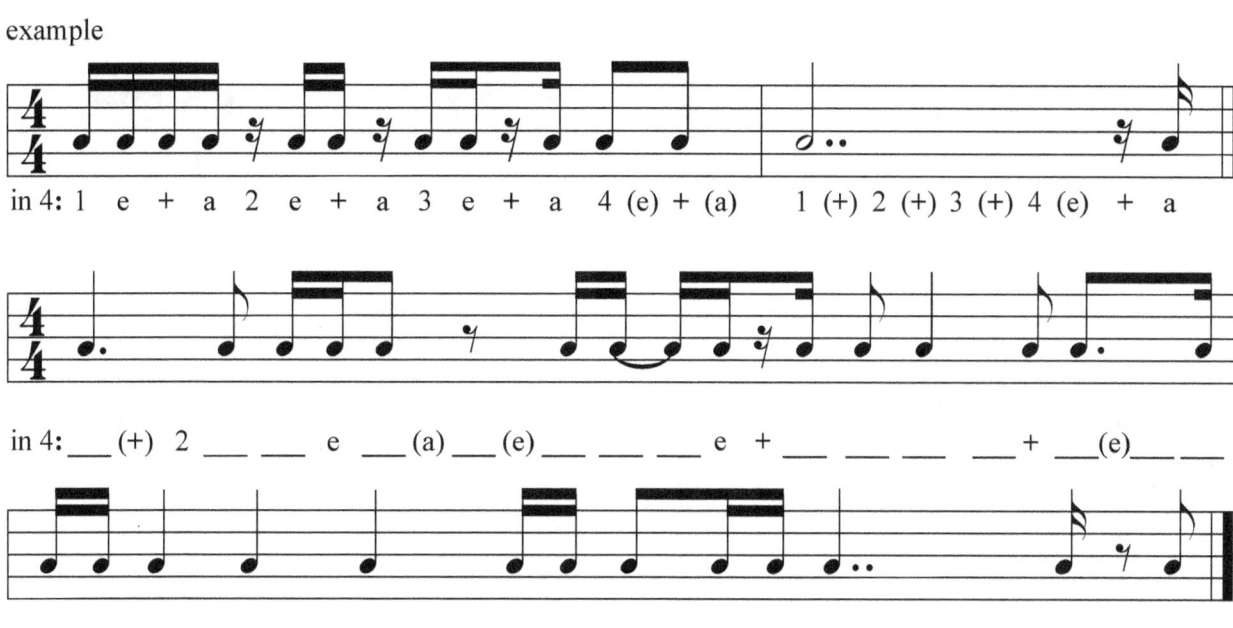

in 4: 1 e + a 2 e + a 3 e + a 4 (e) + (a)   1 (+) 2 (+) 3 (+) 4 (e) + a

in 4: ___ (+) 2 ___ ___ e ___ (a) ___ (e) ___ ___ ___ e + ___ ___ ___ ___ + ___(e)___ ___

___ ___ + 2 ___ ___ ___ (e) ___ ___ (e) ___ ___ ___ + ___ (e) + ___ ___ ___

Worksheet 1–4

Name _____

Chapter 1: Time and Performance

Given the following counts, notes, and rests, place bar lines in the proper places and fill in the blanks with the remaining counts directly under the appropriate note or rest. The rhythmic syllables in parentheses in the exercise indicate that their inclusion here adds nothing to the basic count and that their absence would not obscure the recognition of any of the beats or divisions of beats. As shown in the example, the exercise should be counted with both two and six beats per measure.

example

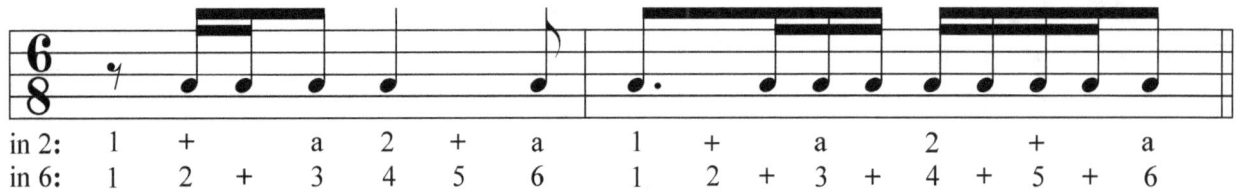

```
in 2:   1   +       a   2   +       a       1   +       a   2   +       a
in 6:   1   2   +   3   4   5   6           1   2   +   3   +   4   +   5   +   6
```

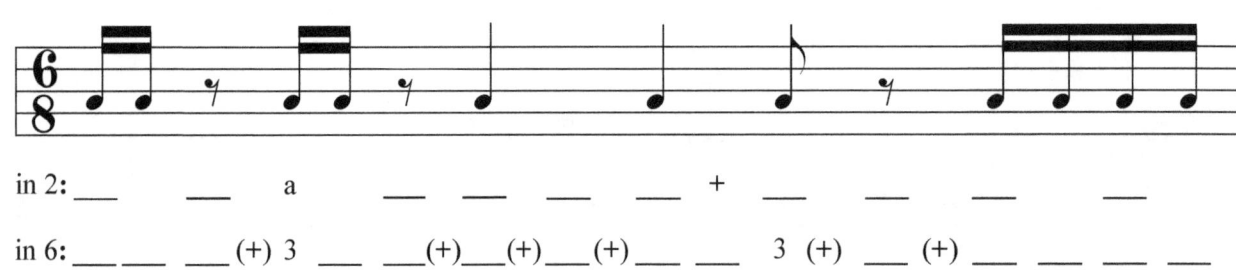

```
in 2: ___  ___  a   ___ ___ ___ ___   +   ___ ___ ___ ___
in 6: ___ ___ ___ (+) 3  ___ ___(+)___(+)___(+)___ ___   3 (+) ___ (+) ___ ___ ___ ___
```

```
in 2: ___ ___  a   ___ ___ ___ ___    +   a   ___ ___ ___
in 6: ___(+)___ + ___   ___(+)___(+)___(+)___(+)___ ___  3 (+) 4  ___ ___ ___ ___ ___
```

Worksheet 2–1

Name _____

Chapter 2: Pitch

Maintaining the same rhythmic values and registers for each of the following pitches, supply one possible enharmonic equivalent in each adjacent space according to the indicated staff and clef. Make sure that the stems for each note are positioned correctly, as discussed in Chapter 1 (see above, p. 1).

Worksheet 2–2

Name _____

Chapter 2: Pitch

Maintaining the same rhythmic values and registers for each of the following pitches, supply one possible enharmonic equivalent in each adjacent space according to the indicated staff and clef. Make sure that the stems for each note are positioned correctly, as discussed in Chapter 1 (see above, p. 1).

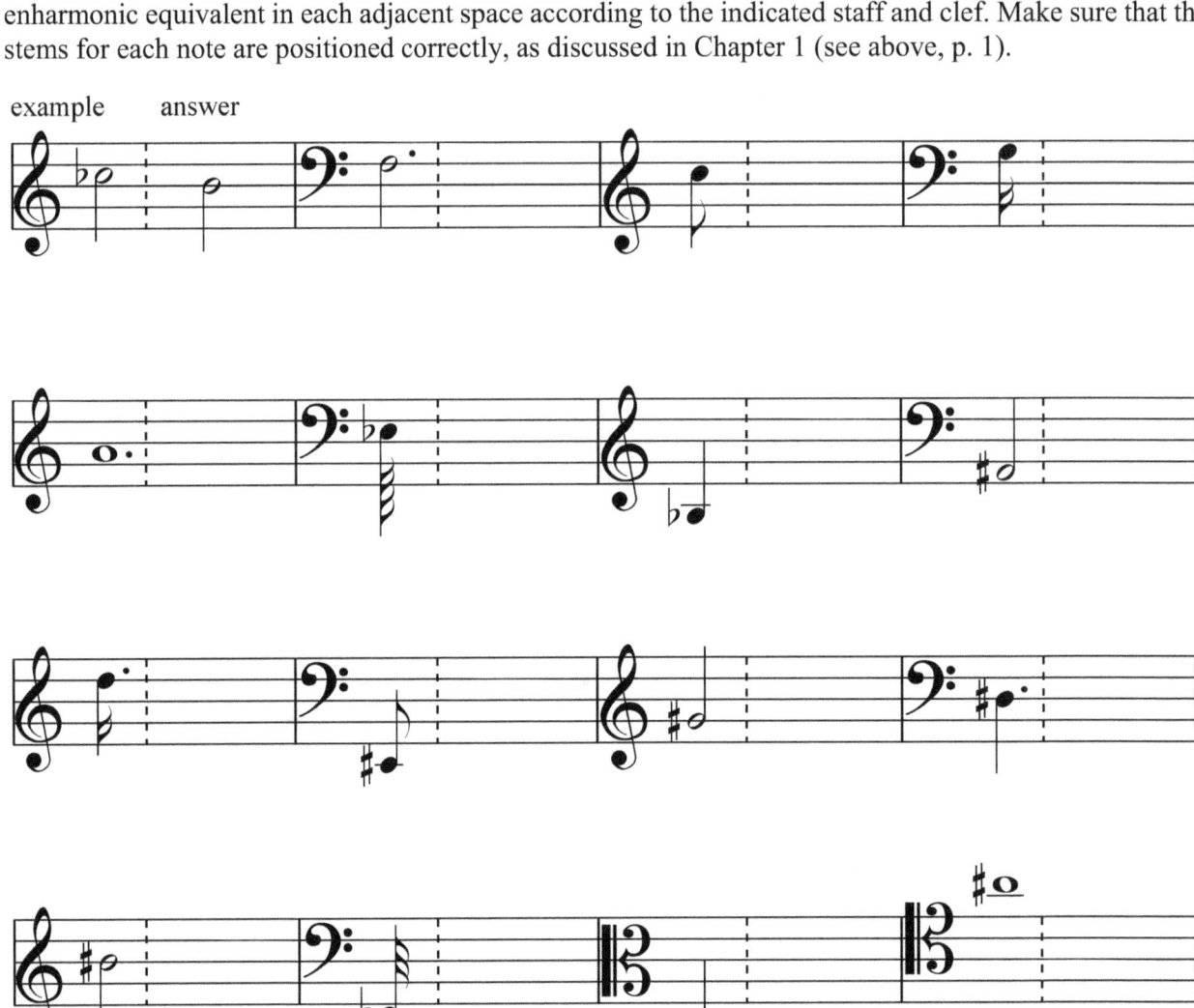

Worksheet 2–3

Name _____

Chapter 2: Pitch

Meter and Rhythm

Given the following counts, notes, and rests, place bar lines in the proper places and fill in the blanks with the remaining counts directly under the appropriate note or rest. The rhythmic syllables in parentheses indicate that their conclusion here adds nothing to the basic count and that their absence would not obscure the recognition of any of the beats or divisions of beats.

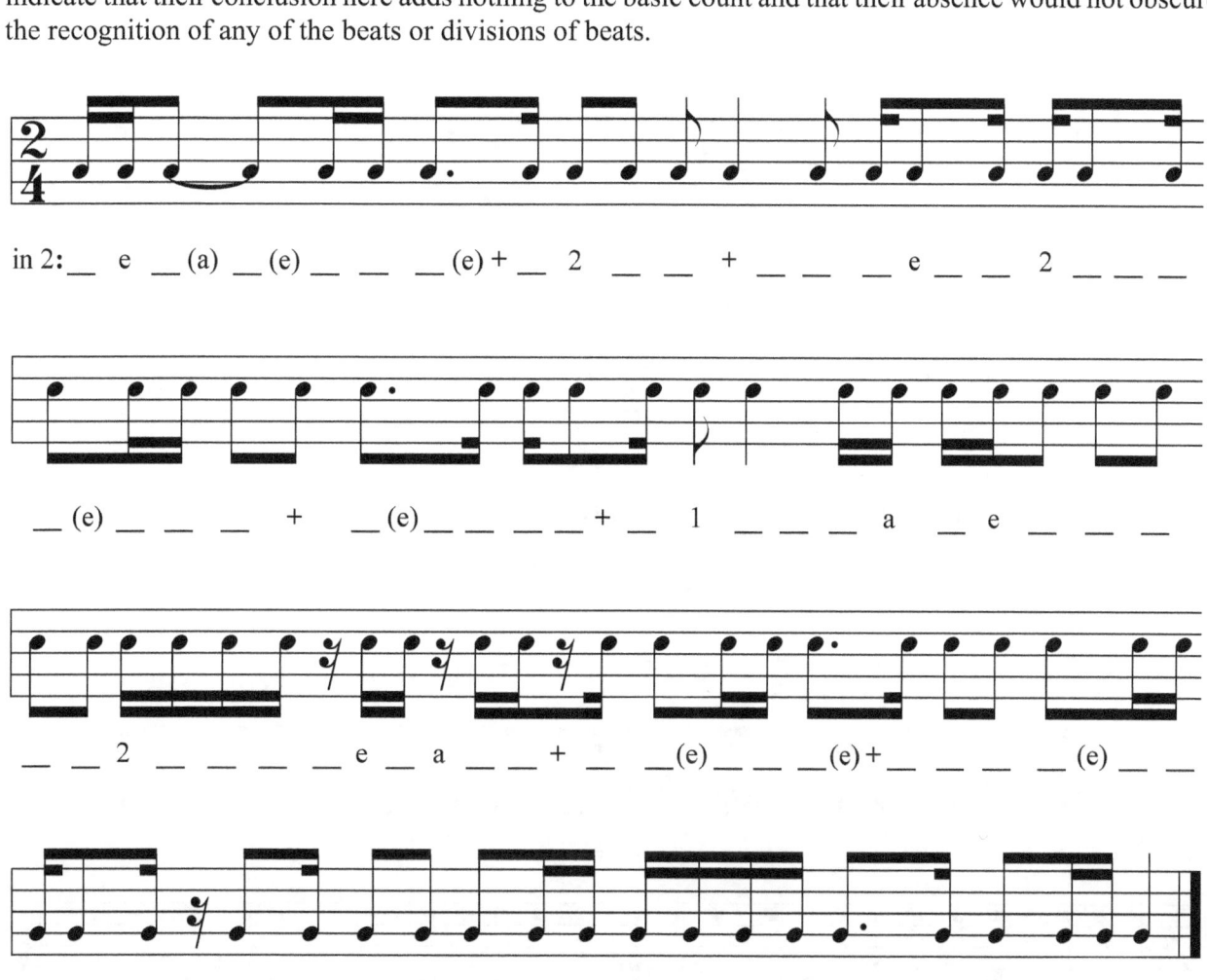

Worksheet 2–4

Name _____

Chapter 2: Pitch

Meter and Rhythm

Given the following counts, notes, and rests, place bar lines in the proper places and fill in the blanks with the remaining counts directly under the appropriate note or rest. The rhythmic syllables in parentheses indicate that their conclusion here adds nothing to the basic count and that their absence would not obscure the recognition of any of the beats or divisions of beats.

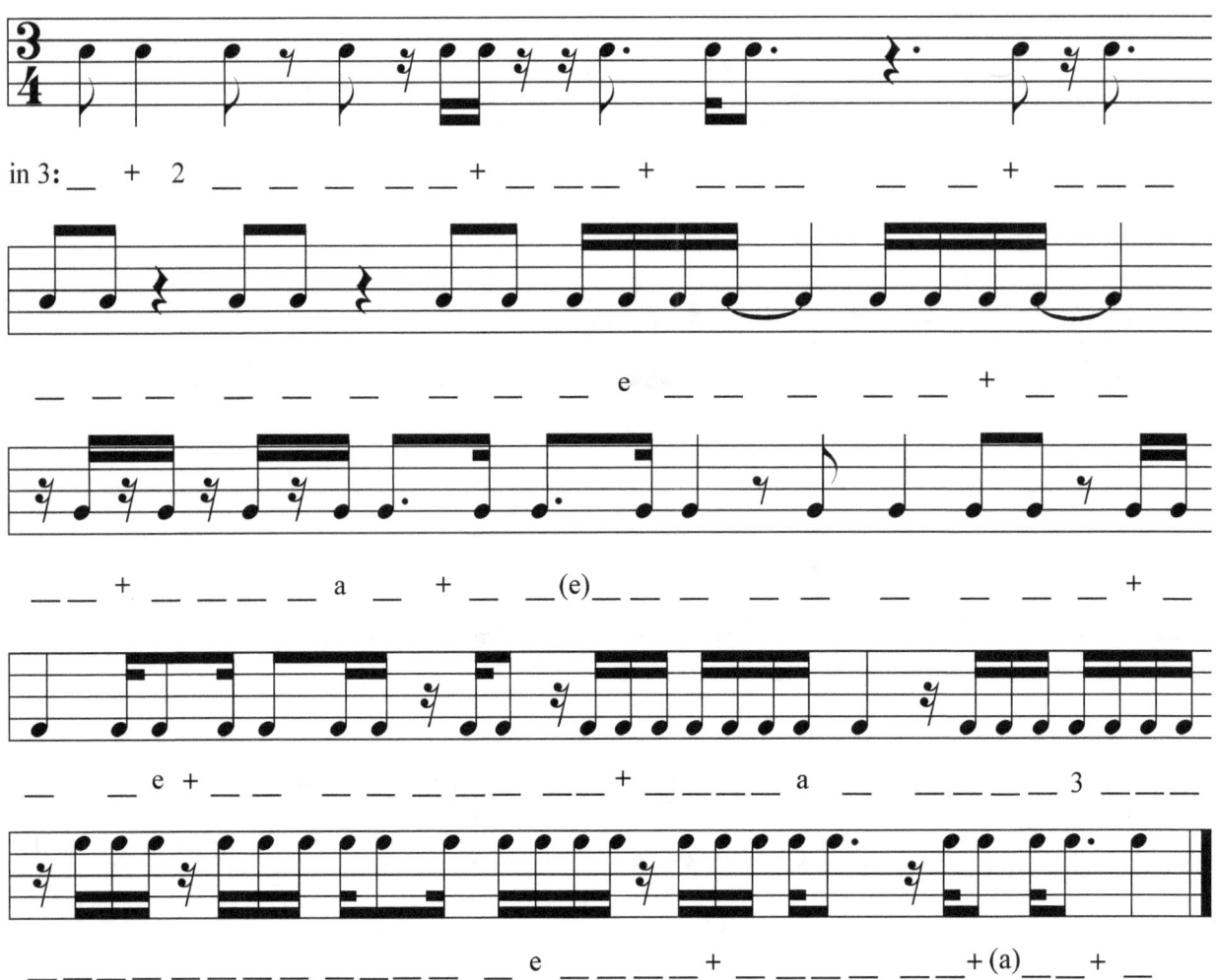

Worksheet 2–5

Name _____

Chapter 2: Pitch

As shown in the two examples below, write the equivalent rest for each given pitch; and then, identify the pitch name, register (either or both methods), and the rhythmic value.

Worksheet 2–6

Name _____

Chapter 2: Pitch

As shown in the example below, write the equivalent rest for each given pitch; and then, identify the pitch name, register (either or both methods), and the rhythmic value.

Worksheet 3–1

Name _____

Chapter 3: The Major Scale

Given the following octave ranges and clefs, create major scales (and modes) by adding the appropriate accidentals; *do not change the first or last note of each octave—that is the keynote.*

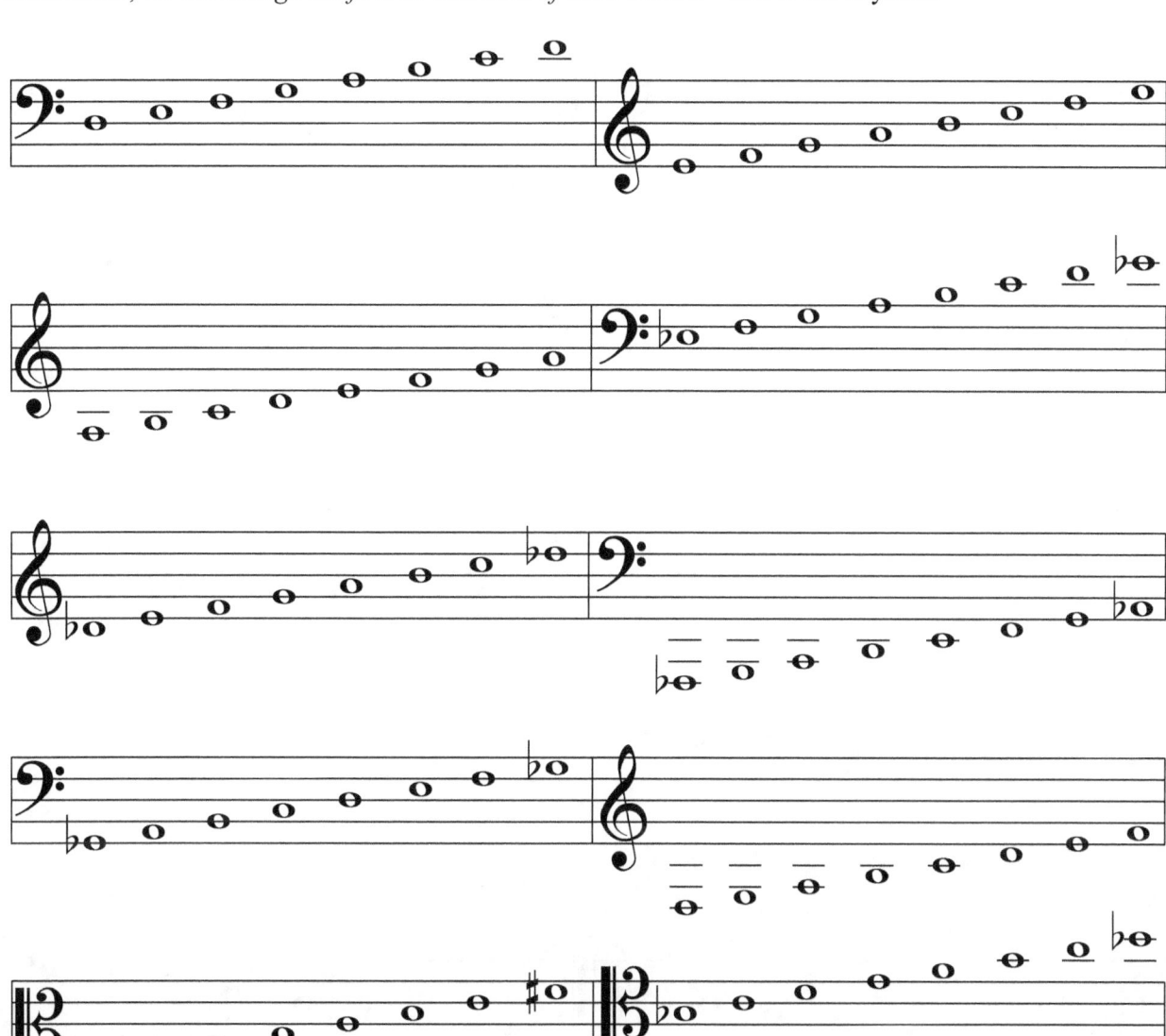

Worksheet 3–2

Name _____

Chapter 3: The Major Scale

Given the following octave ranges and clefs, create major scales (and modes) by adding the appropriate accidentals; *do not change the first or last note of each octave*—that is the keynote.

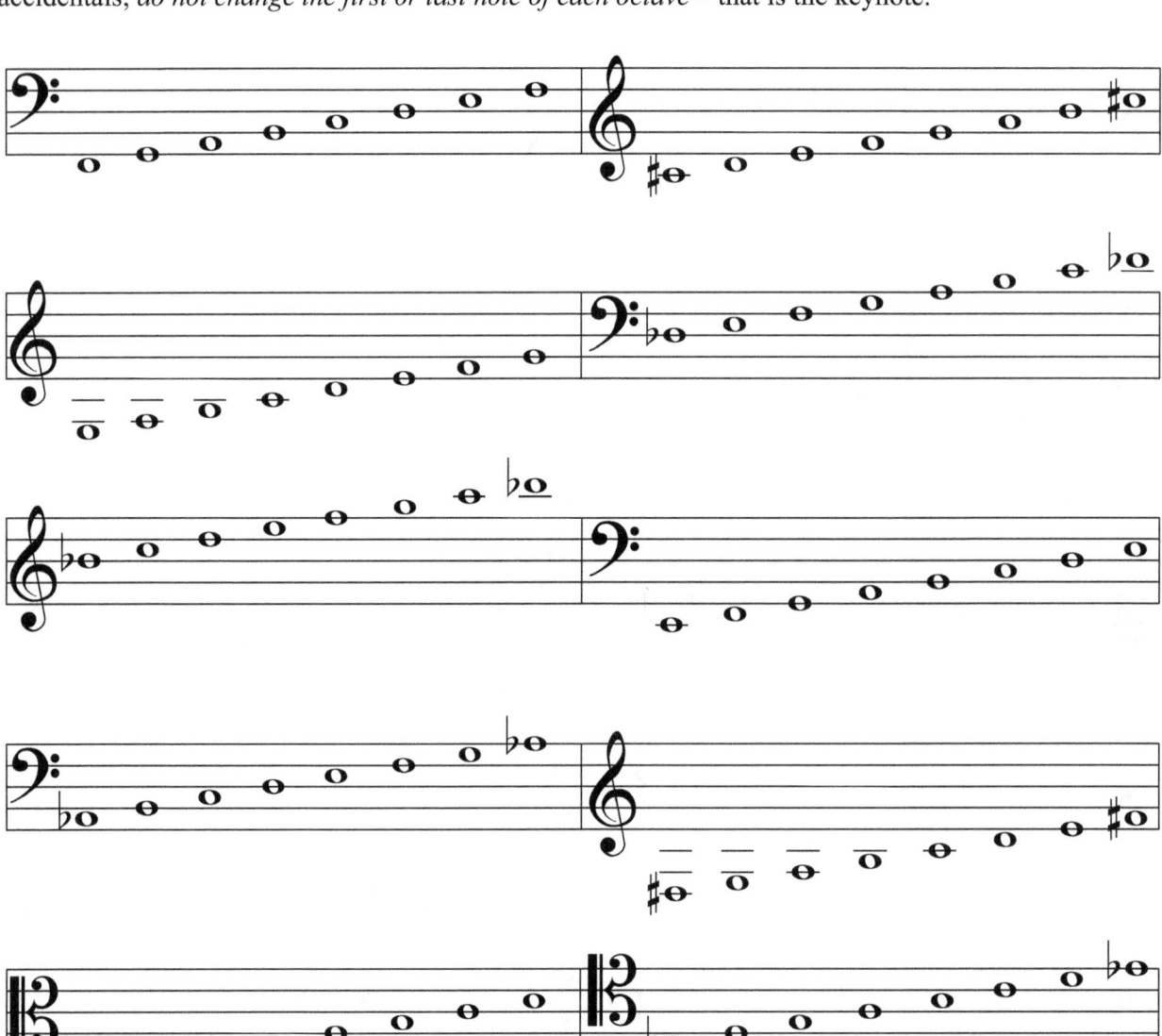

Worksheet 3–3

Name _____

Chapter 3: The Major Scale

Given major keys and scale degrees (indicated with Arabic numbers), supply the missing pitch. Use the scales you built in exercise 3–1 as a reference to find the correct pitches (or construct additional scales as needed). Your answer should appear in only one register; however, as shown in the example, the correct pitch may be written in more than one register.

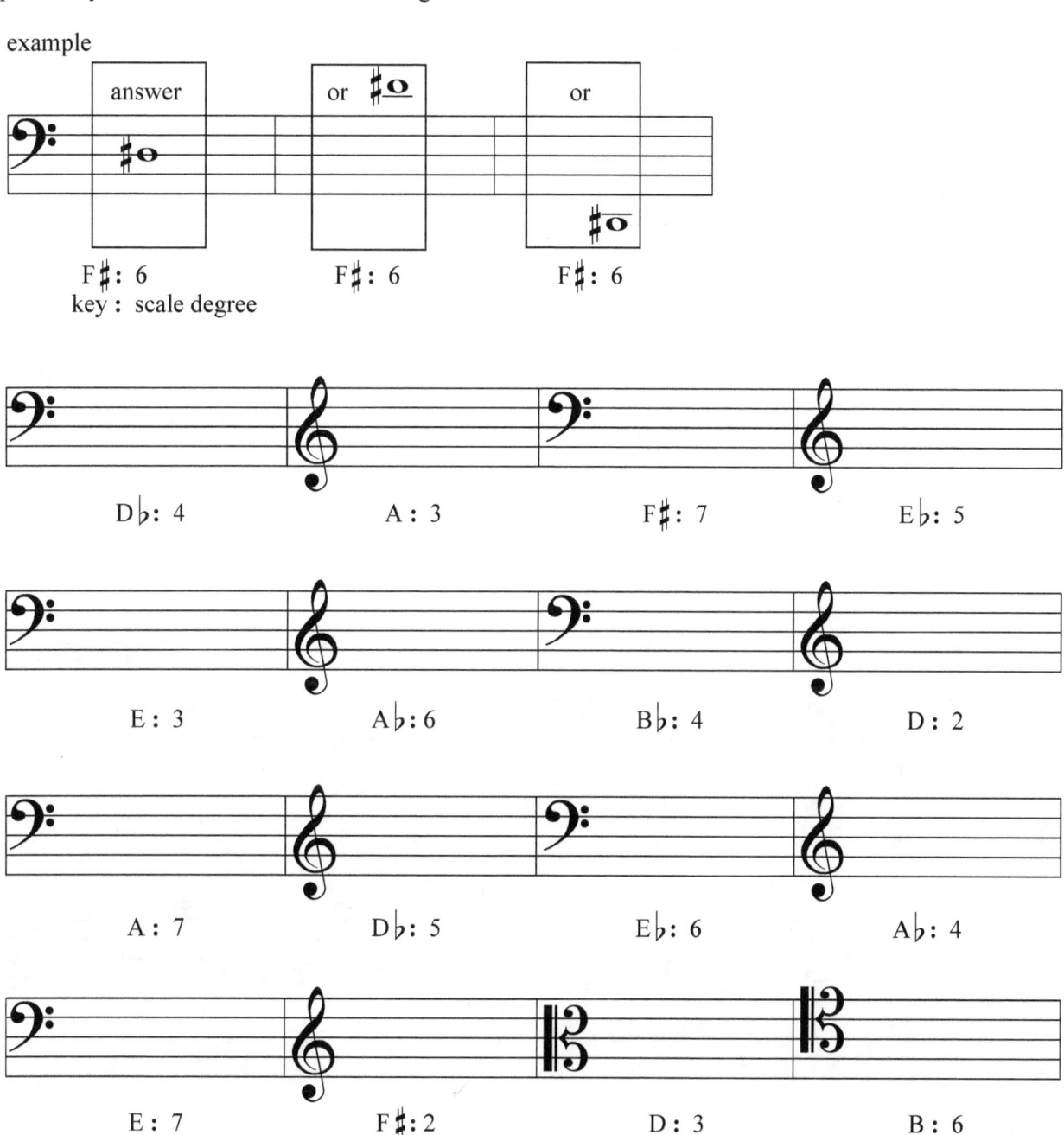

Worksheet 3–4

Name _____

Chapter 3: The Major Scale

Meter and Rhythm

Given the following counts, notes, and rests, place bar lines in the proper places and fill in the blanks with the remaining counts directly under the appropriate note or rest. The rhythmic syllables in parentheses indicate that their inclusion here adds nothing to the basic count and that their absence would not obscure the recognition of any of the beats or divisions of beats (however, any blank in parentheses must be answered). Remember that ¢ is the same as $\frac{2}{2}$ time.

example

in 2: 1   e   +   a   2 (e) +   a   1   e   +   a   2   +

in 2: __   +   2   __ __ __ __ __ __ __   +   __ (__) __   e   __   a

1   __ __ (e) __ __ __ (e) __ __ __ __   __ (__) __ __   2 (__) __   __

1 (__) __ __ __ __   __ __ +   __ __ __ + __   __ (__)

Worksheet 3–5

Name _____

Chapter 3: The Major Scale

Meter and Rhythm

Given the following counts, notes, and rests, place bar lines in the proper places and fill in the blanks with the remaining counts directly under the appropriate note or rest. As shown in the example, use both methods for counting compound duple meter. Accordingly, when counting this meter in 2, the value of the beat is a dotted half note. The first division of the beat therefore occurs at the level of the quarter note. Interpreted in a slow 6, however, the value of the beat becomes the quarter note and the first division of the beat is the eighth note.

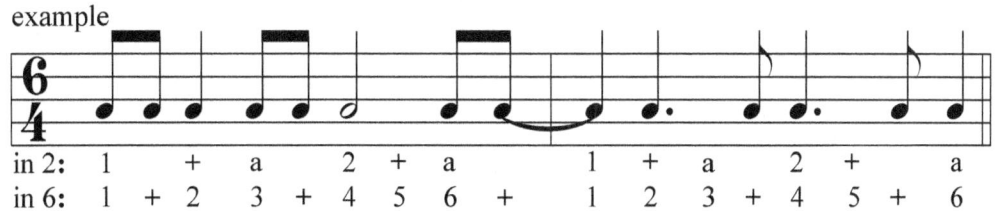

Worksheet 4–1

Name _____

Chapter 4: Major Key Signatures

Provide the correct number of sharps or flats for the following questions:

example

How many sharps are in C♯ major? __7__

1. How many flats in A♭ major? _____
2. How many sharps in G major? _____
3. How many sharps in F♯ major? _____
4. How many flats in B♭ major? _____
5. How many sharps in B major? _____
6. How many flats in C♭ major? _____
7. How many sharps in A major? _____
8. How many flats in G♭ major? _____
9. How many sharps in D major? _____
10. How many flats in D♭ major? _____
11. How many sharps in E major? _____
12. How many flats in E♭ major? _____
13. How many flats in F major? _____

Worksheet 4–2

Name _____

Chapter 4: Major Key Signatures

Identify the following major key signatures:

major: Bb (or B Flat) _____ _____ _____

major: _____ _____ _____ _____

major: _____ _____ _____ _____

Worksheet 4–3

Name _____

Chapter 4: Major Key Signatures

Identify the following major key signatures:

major: _____   _____   _____   _____

major: _____   _____   _____   _____

major: _____   _____   _____   _____

Worksheet 4–4

Name _____

Chapter 4: Major Key Signatures

Supply the key signatures of the following major modes according to the given clef:

F :   C♯:   D♭:   E :

C♭:   G :   A♭:   B :

D :   E♭:   F♯:   B♭:

Worksheet 4–5

Name _____

Chapter 4: Major Key Signatures

Supply the key signatures of the following major mode according to the given clef:

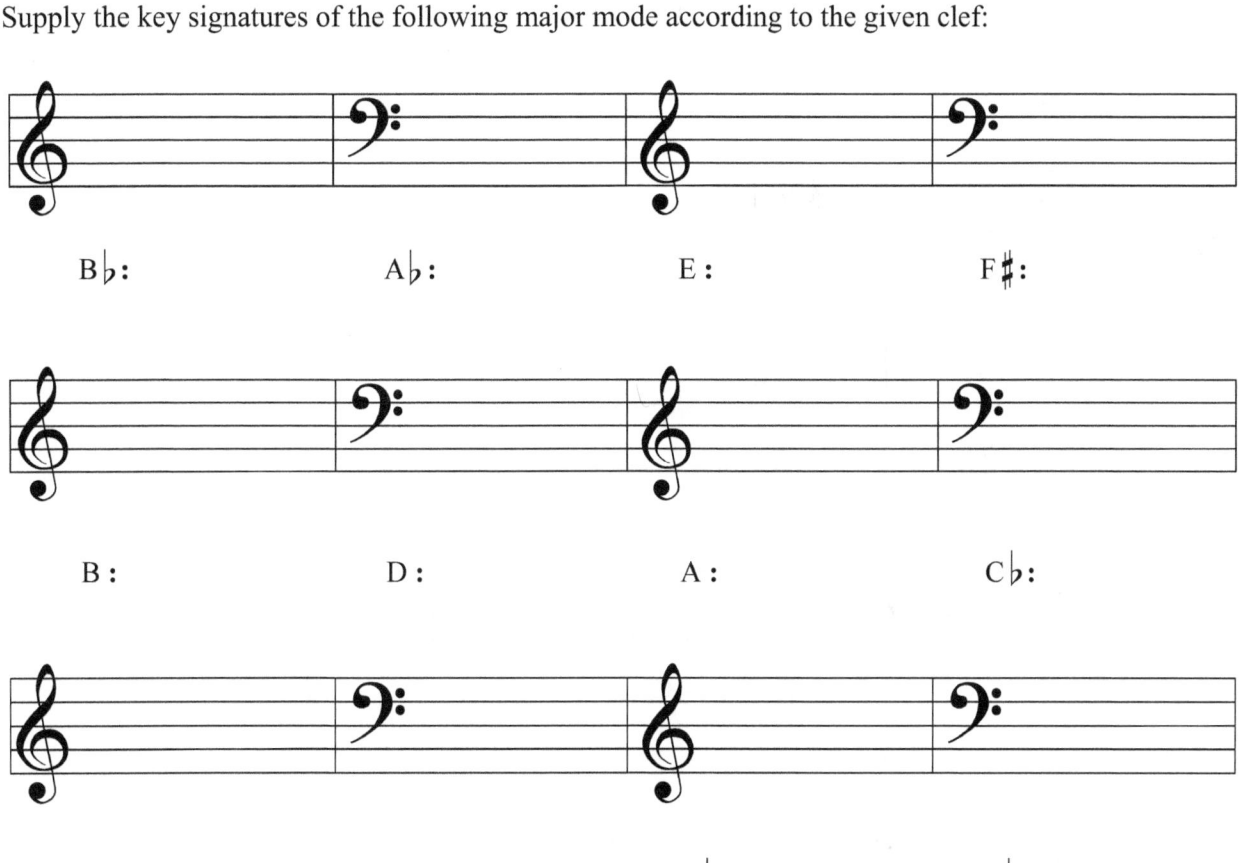

Worksheet 4–6

Name _____

Chapter 4: Major Key Signatures

Given major keys and scale degrees (indicated with Arabic numbers), supply the missing pitch. Your answer should appear in only one register; however, as shown in the example, the correct pitch may be written in more than one register.

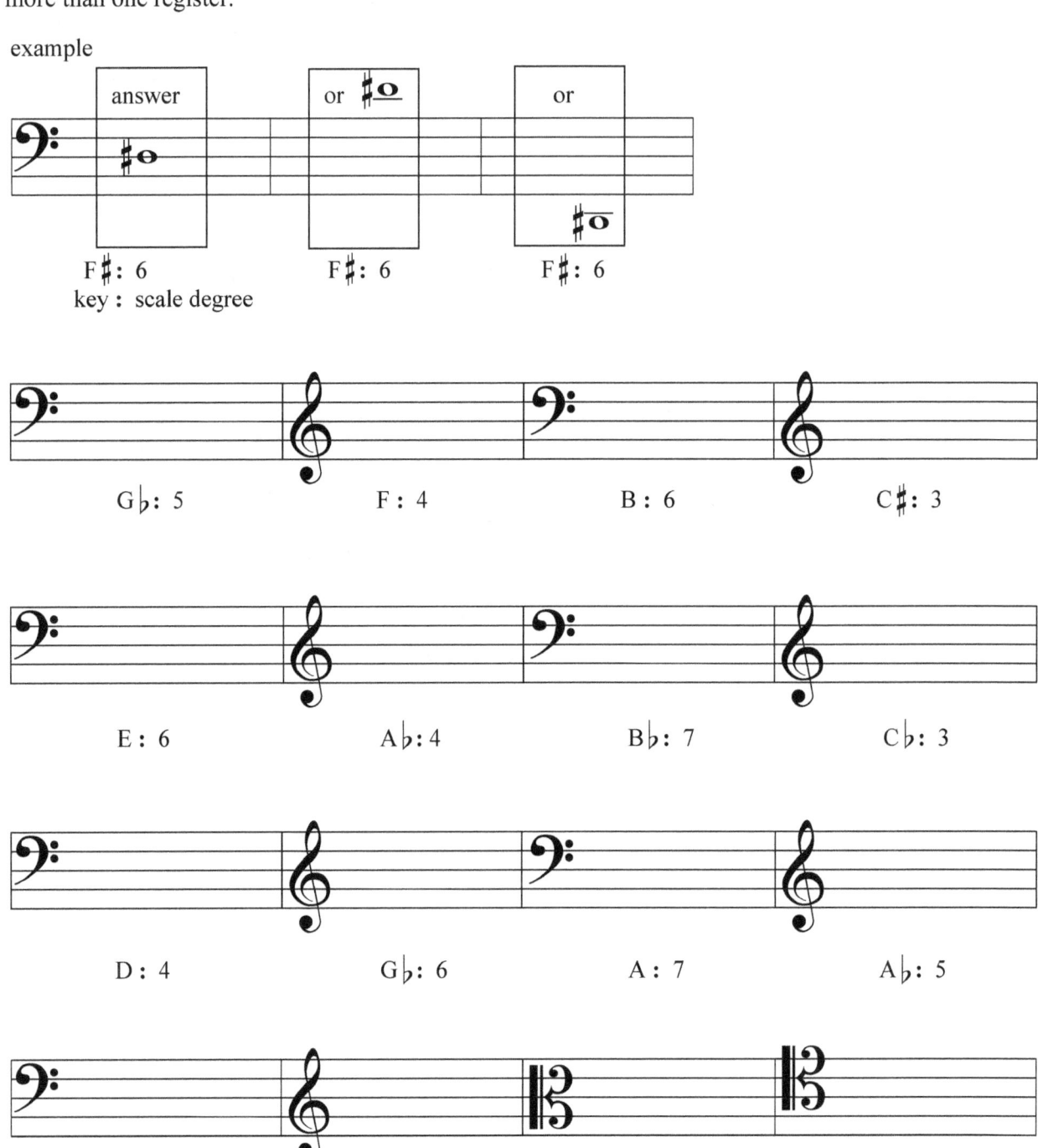

Worksheet 4–7

Name _____

Chapter 4: Major Key Signatures

Given major keys and scale degrees (indicated with Arabic numbers), supply the missing pitch. Your answer should appear in only one register; however, as shown in the example, the correct pitch may be written in more than one register.

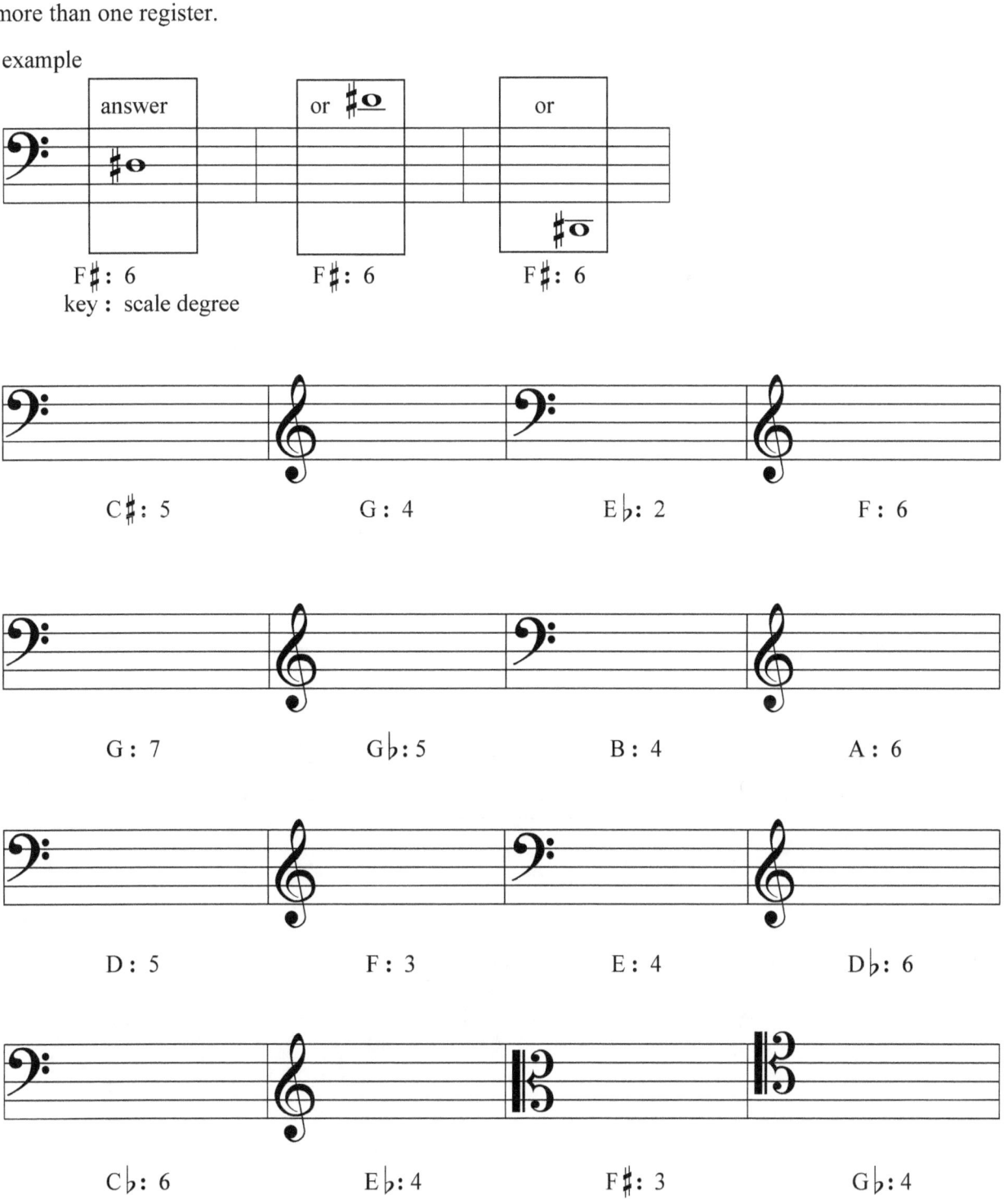

Worksheet 4–8

Name _____

Chapter 4: Major Key Signatures

Given pitches and scale degrees (indicated with Arabic numbers) *or* major keys and pitches, supply the missing factor:

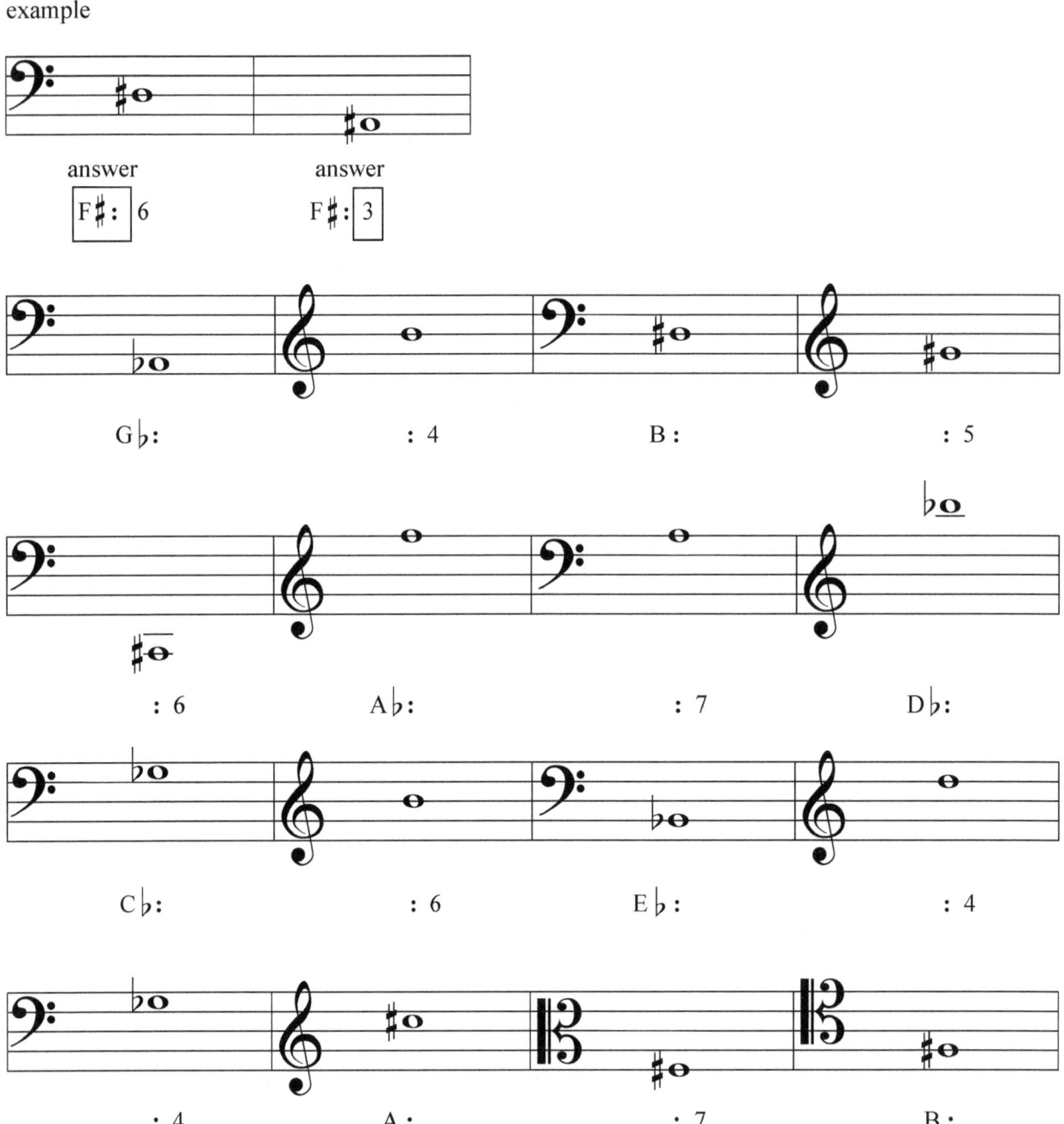

Worksheet 4–9

Name _____

Chapter 4: Major Key Signatures

Meter and Rhythm

Given the following meters, place bar lines in the proper places and write the counts directly under the appropriate note or rest. The final measure requires the addition of a rest (and a count below it); moreover, be sure to observe any incomplete "pickup" measures at the beginning of the exercise when completing the final measure (see above, p. 15 and example 1–23d). Do not forget to write in the bar line at the end of each final measure. Use the supplied counts to help you determine the counts not given.

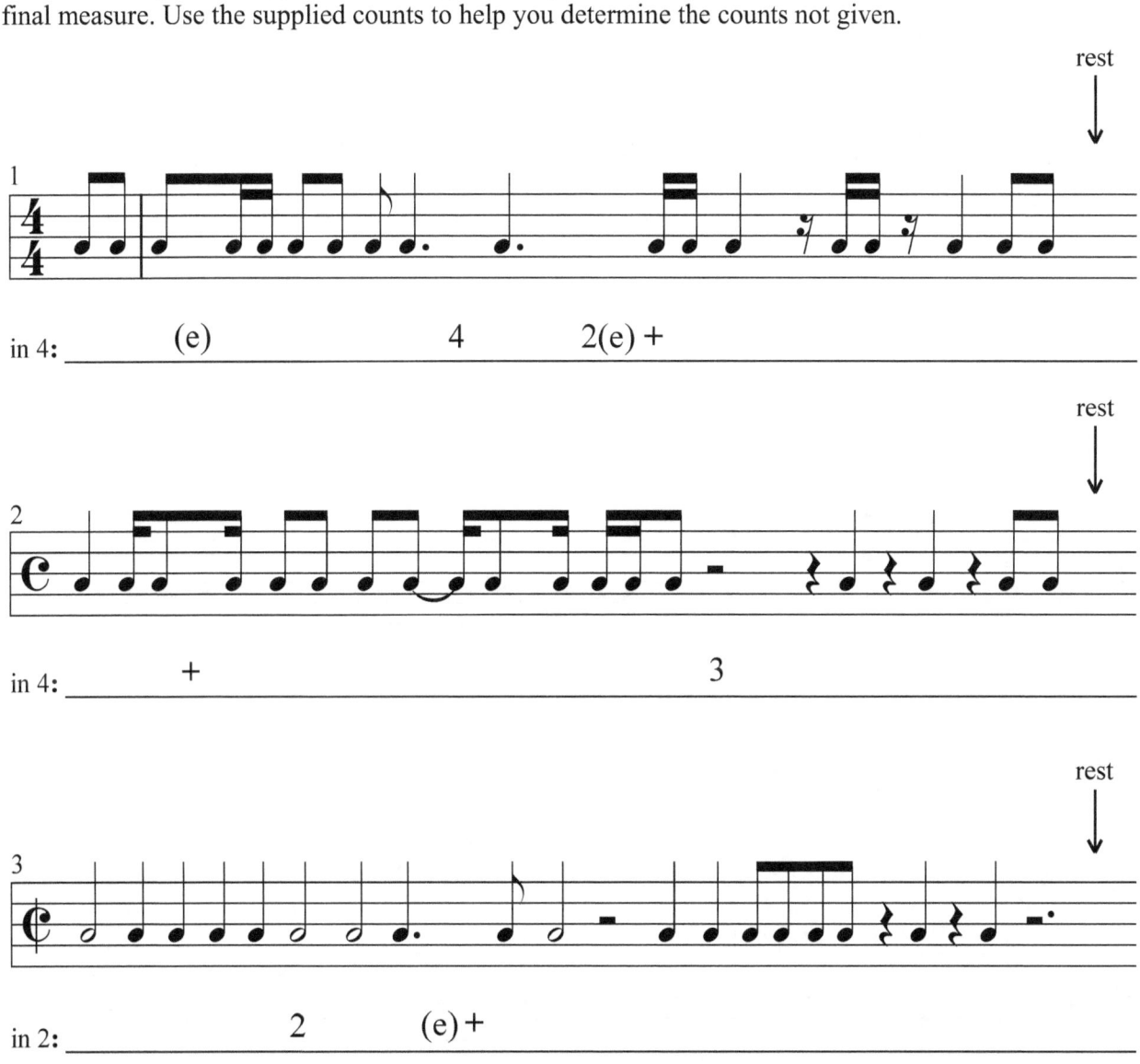

Worksheet 4–10

Name _____

Chapter 4: Major Key Signatures

Meter and Rhythm

Given the following meters, place bar lines in the proper places and write the counts directly under the appropriate note or rest. The final measure requires the addition of a rest (and a count below it); moreover, be sure to observe any incomplete "pickup" measures at the beginning of the exercise when completing the final measure (see above, p. 15 and example 1–23d). Do not forget to write in the bar line at the end of each final measure. Use the supplied counts to help you determine the counts not given.

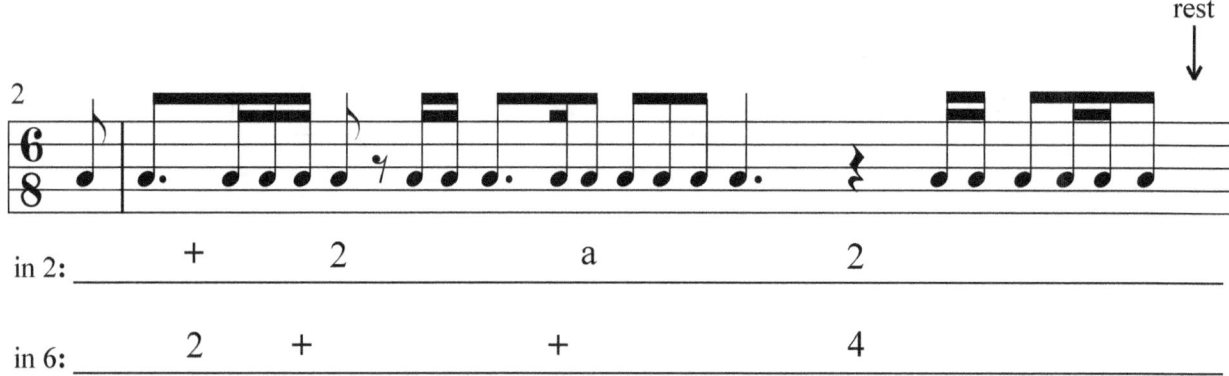

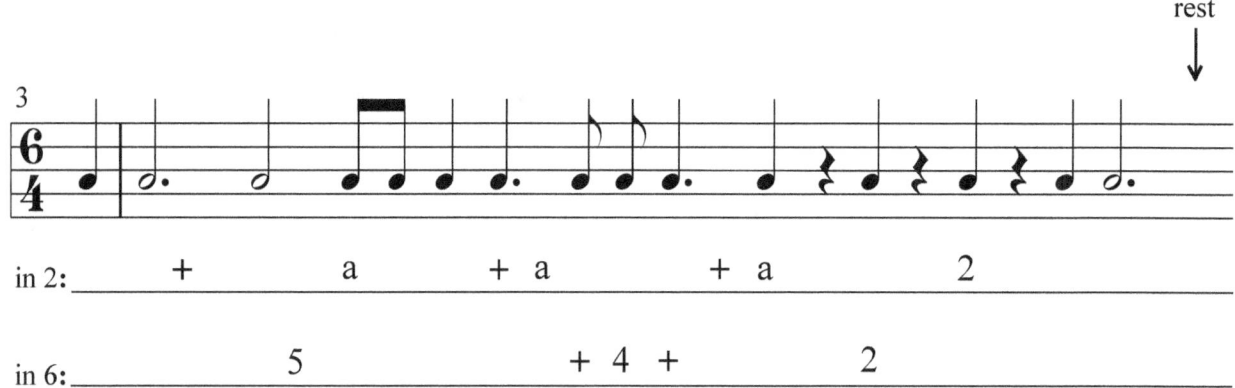

Worksheet 5–1

Name _____

Chapter 5: Intervals

Given pitches and scale degrees (indicated with Arabic numbers) *or* major keys and pitches, supply the missing factor:

example

Worksheet 5–2

Name _____

Chapter 5: Intervals

Given pitches and scale degrees (indicated with Arabic numbers) *or* major keys and pitches, supply the missing factor:

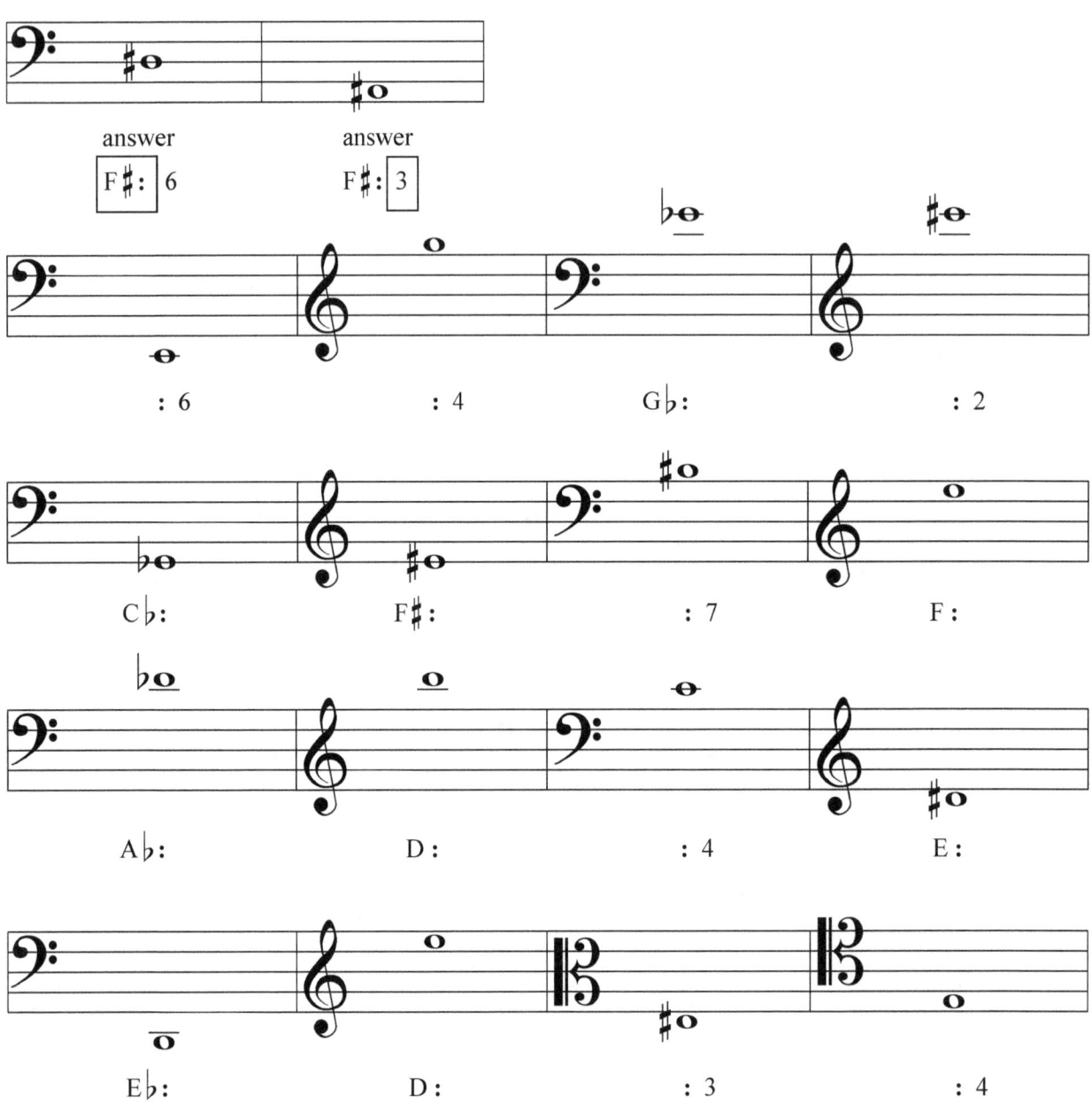

Worksheet 5–3

Name _____

Chapter 5: Intervals

Identify the given intervals according to quality (* M, m, P, d, or A) and numerical distance (2, 3, 4, 5, 6, 7, or 8):

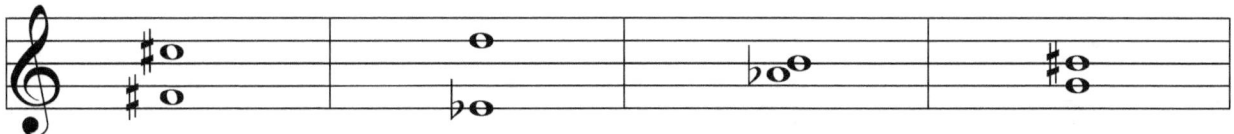

_____   _____   _____   _____

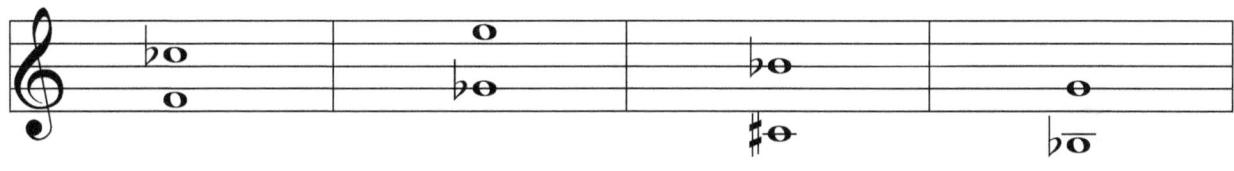

_____   _____   _____   _____

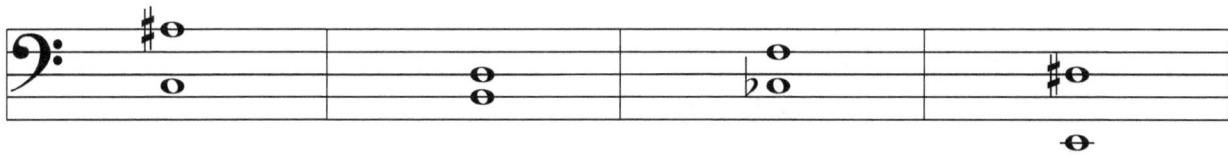

_____   _____   _____   _____

_____   _____   _____   _____

* M = Major, m = minor, P = Perfect, d = diminished, A = Augmented (in order to avoid confusing the upper case M with the lower case m, make the lower case m visibly smaller than the adjoining Arabic number)

Worksheet 5–4

Name _____

Chapter 5: Intervals

Identify the given intervals according to quality (* M, m, P, d, or A) and numerical distance (2, 3, 4, 5, 6, 7, or 8):

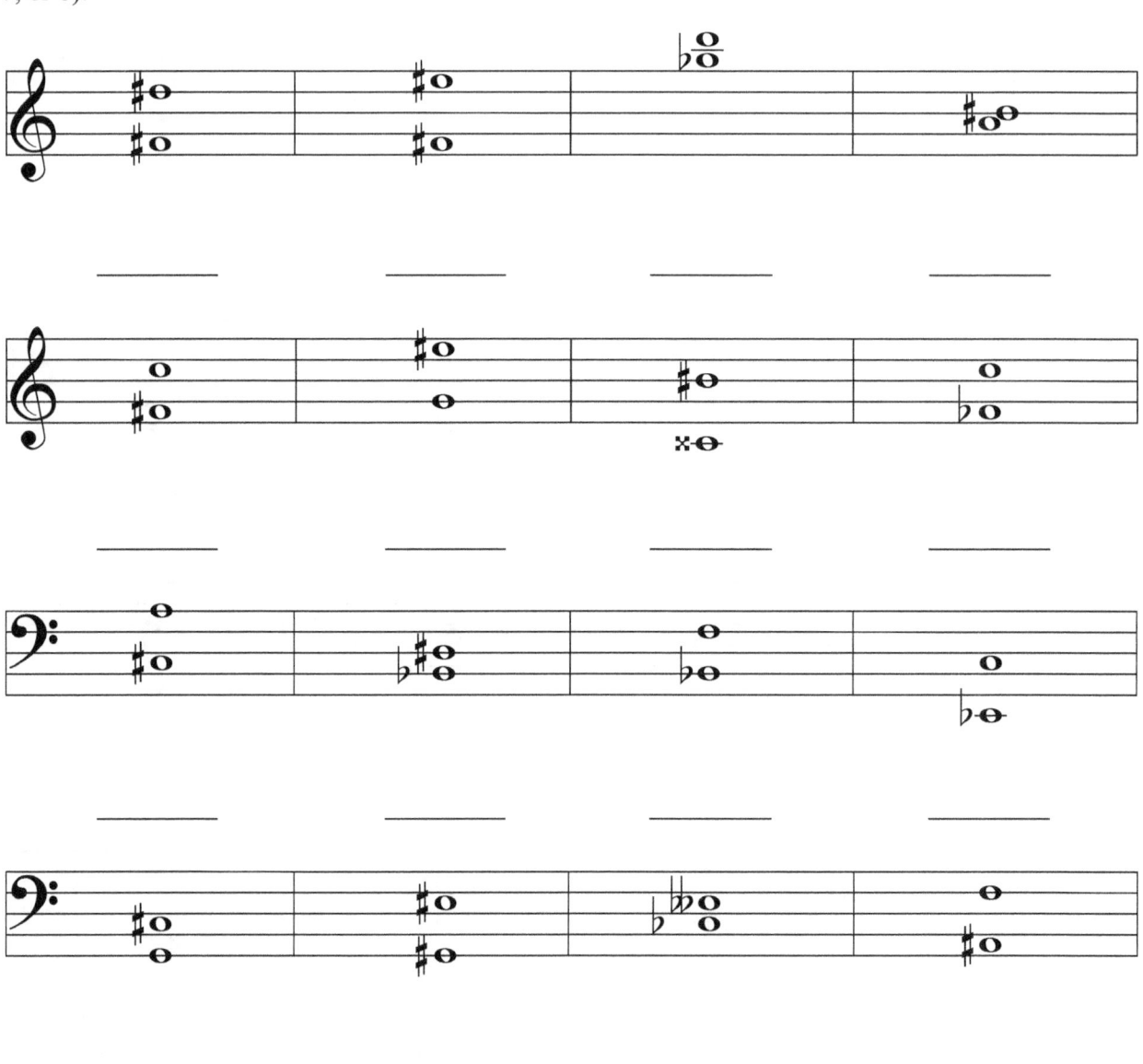

* M = Major, m = minor, P = Perfect, d = diminished, A = Augmented (in order to avoid confusing the upper case M with the lower case m, make the lower case m visibly smaller than the adjoining Arabic number)

Worksheet 5–5

Name _____

Chapter 5: Intervals

Identify the given intervals according to quality (* M, m, P, d, or A) and numerical distance (2, 3, 4, 5, 6, 7, or 8):

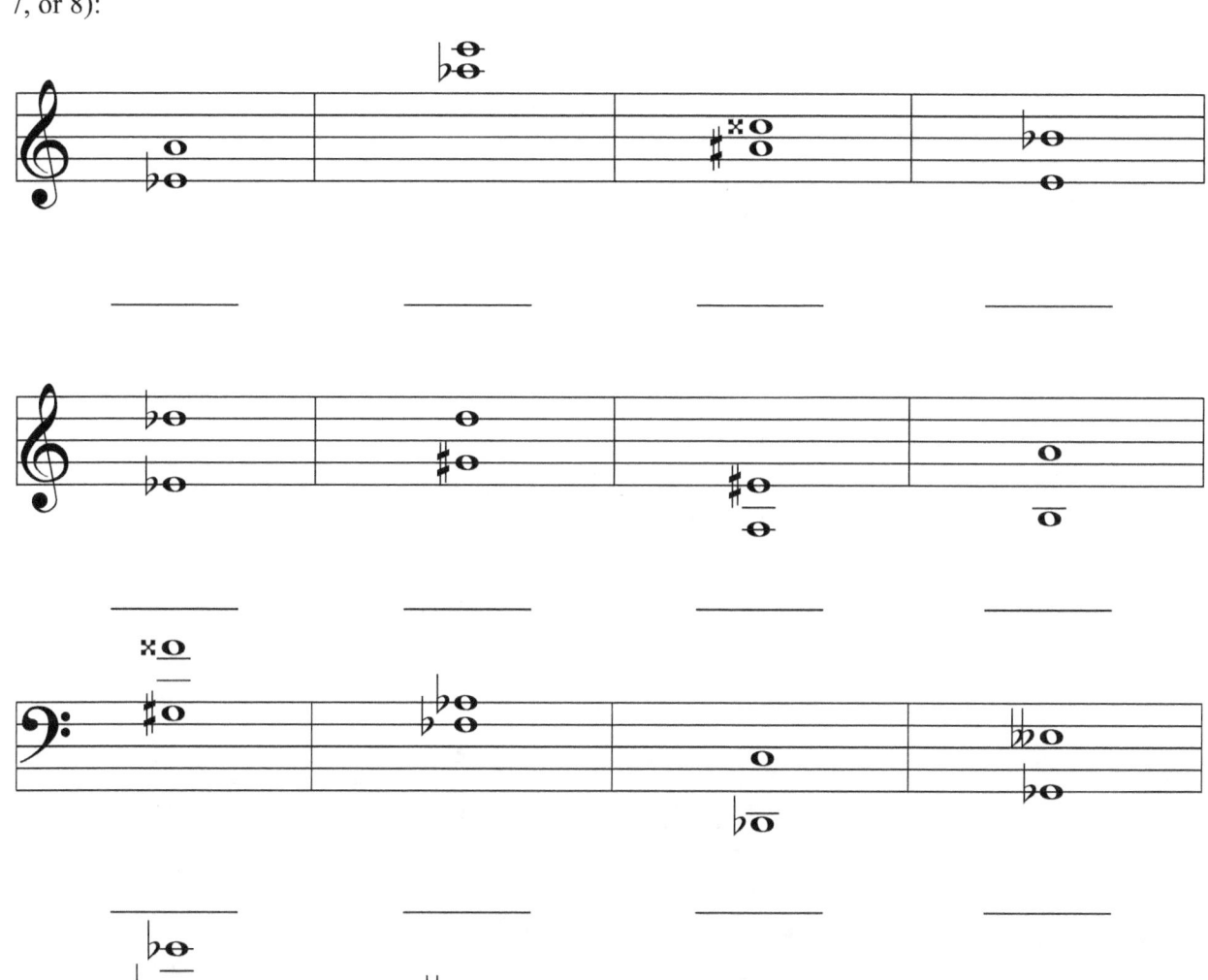

* M = Major, m = minor, P = Perfect, d = diminished, A = Augmented (in order to avoid confusing the upper case M with the lower case m, make the lower case m visibly smaller than the adjoining Arabic number)

Worksheet 5–6

Name _____

Chapter 5: Intervals

Identify the given simple and compound intervals according to quality (* M, m, P, d, or A) and numerical distance (2, 3, 4, 5, 6, 7, 8, 9, 10, 11, 12, 13, etc.):

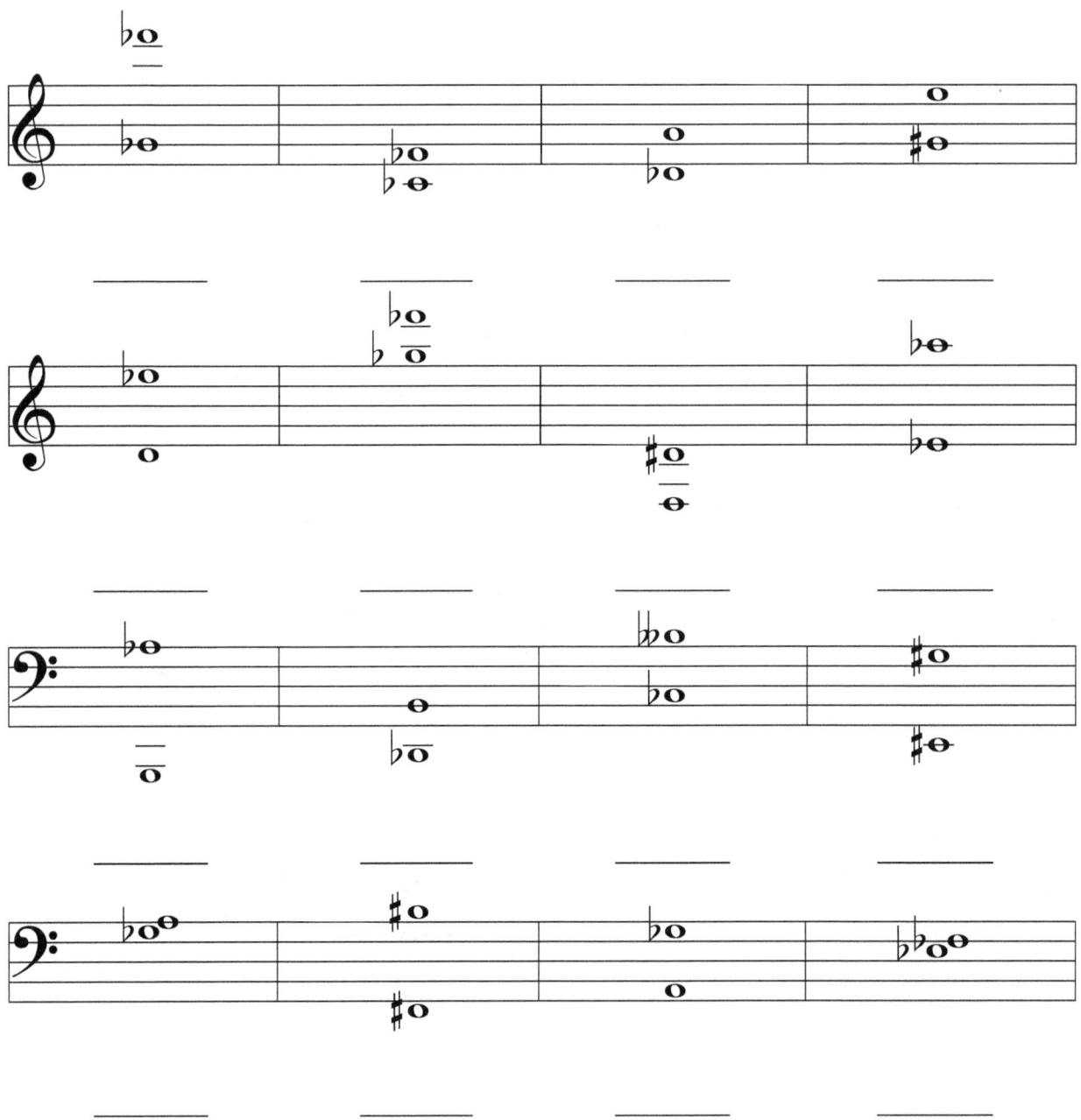

* M = Major, m = minor, P = Perfect, d = diminished, A = Augmented (in order to avoid confusing the upper case M with the lower case m, make the lower case m visibly smaller than the adjoining Arabic number)

Worksheet 5–7

Name _____

Chapter 5: Intervals

Identify the given simple and compound intervals according to quality (* M, m, P, d, or A) and numerical distance (2, 3, 4, 5, 6, 7, 8, 9, 10, 11, 12, 13, etc.):

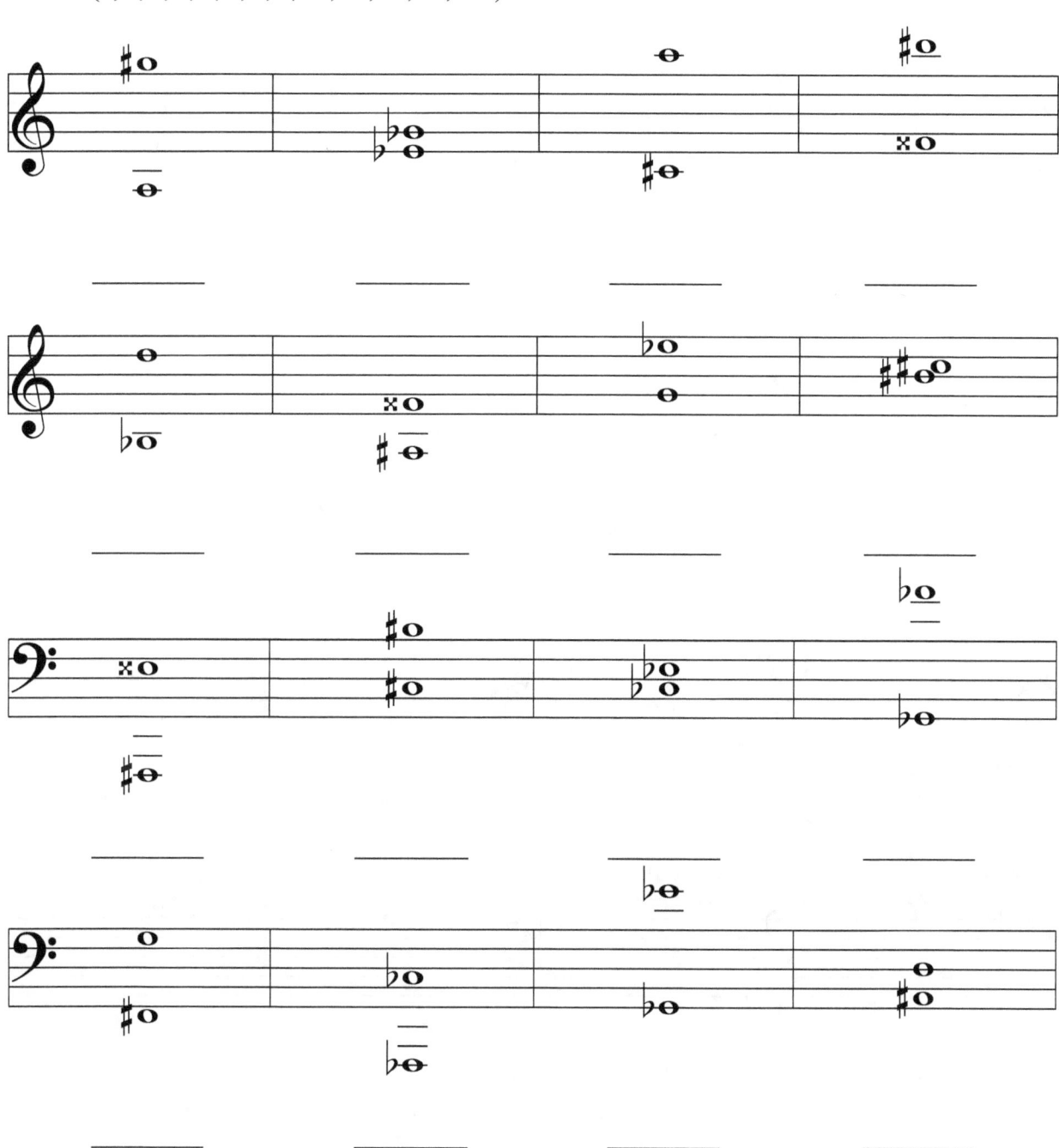

* M = Major, m = minor, P = Perfect, d = diminished, A = Augmented (in order to avoid confusing the upper case M with the lower case m, make the lower case m visibly smaller than the adjoining Arabic number)

Worksheet 5–8

Name _____

Chapter 5: Intervals

Construct the indicated interval above or below the given tone (M = Major, m = minor, P = Perfect, d = diminished, A = Augmented):

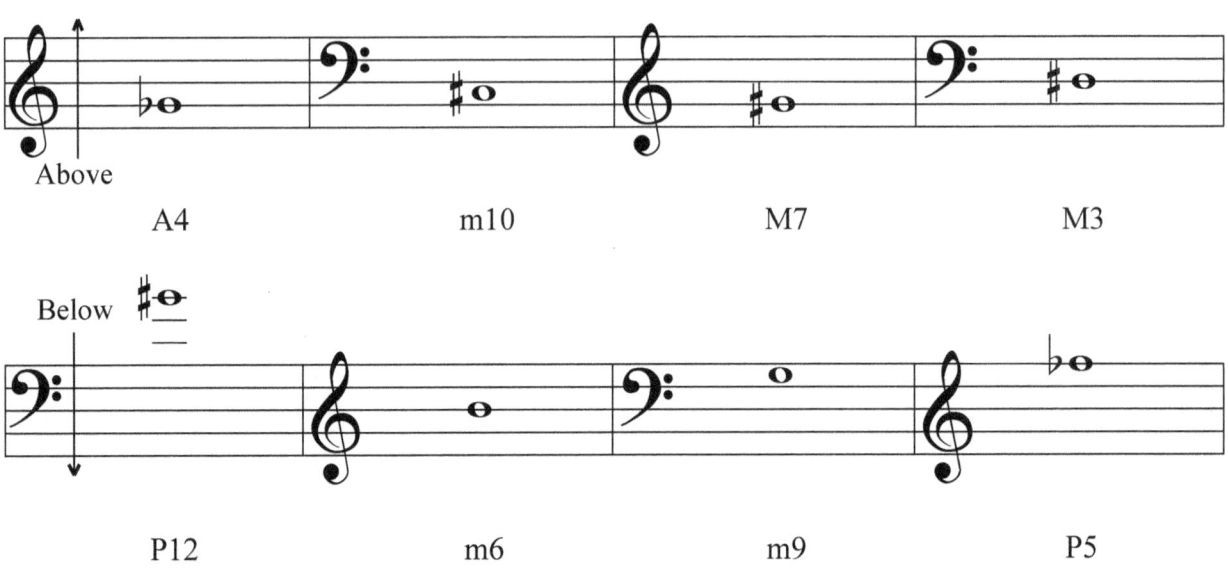

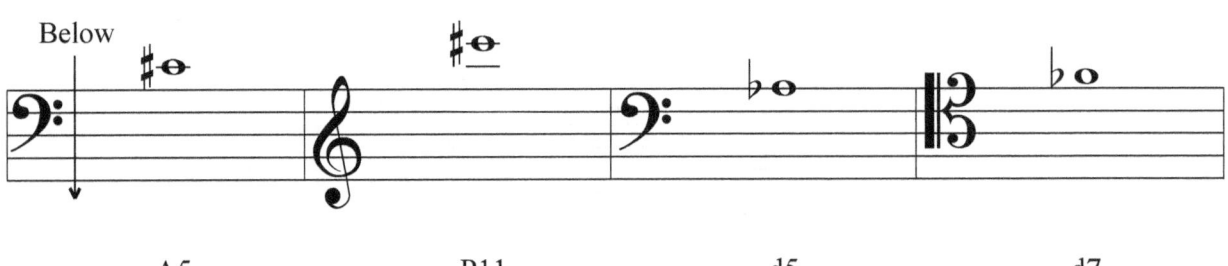

Worksheet 5–9

Name _____

Chapter 5: Intervals

Construct the indicated interval above or below the given tone (M = Major, m = minor, P = Perfect, d = diminished, A = Augmented):

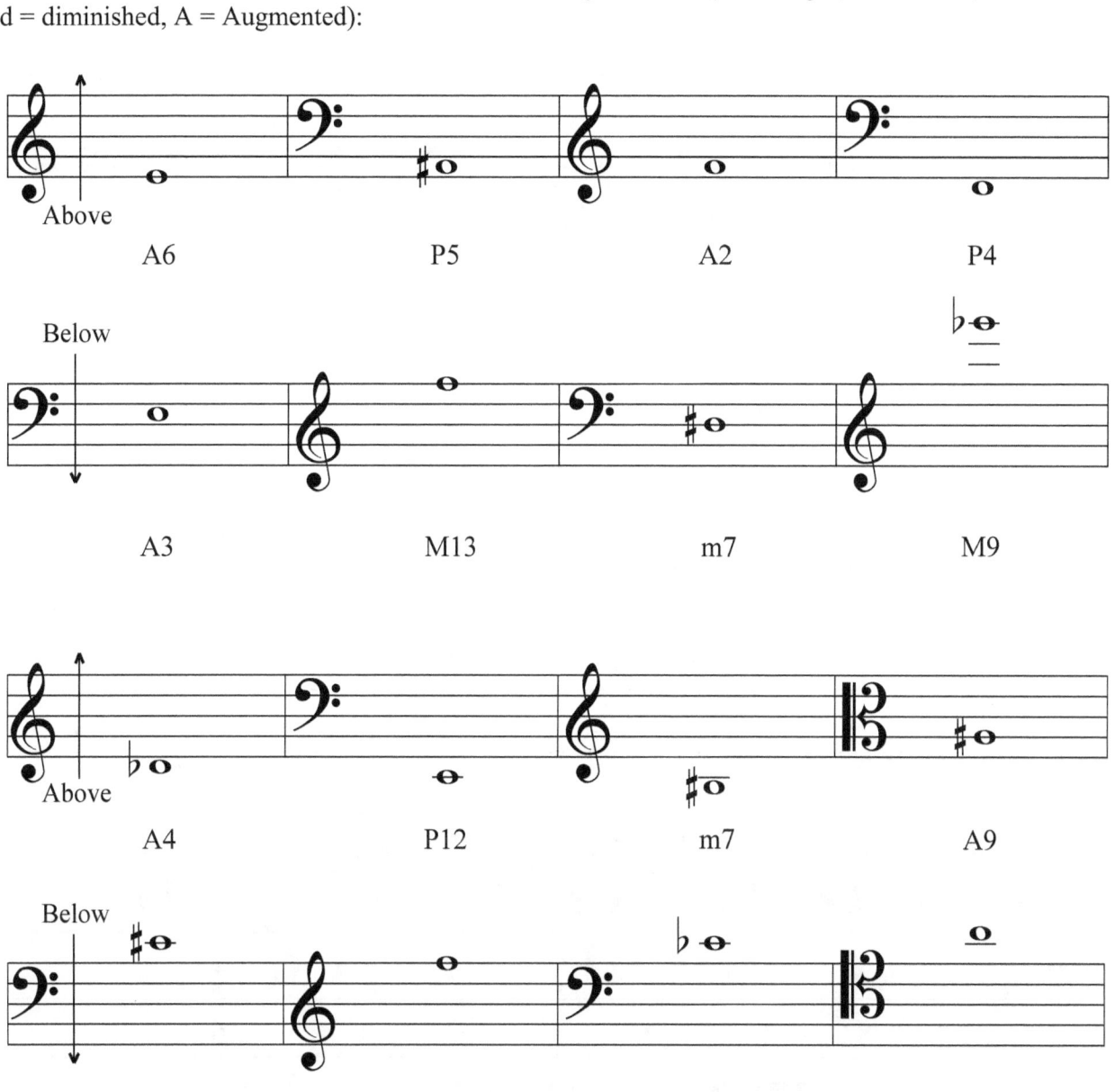

Worksheet 5–10

Name _____

Chapter 5: Intervals

Meter and Rhythm

Given the following meter, place bar lines in the proper places and write the counts directly under the appropriate note or rest. As shown in the example, use both methods for counting compound triple meter.

Worksheet 6–1

Name _____

Chapter 6: The Minor Mode

Given the following octave ranges and clefs, create the indicated minor scale by adding the appropriate accidentals; do not change the first or last note of each octave—that is the keynote. Remember that the ascending and descending forms of the melodic minor require different accidentals for variable scale degrees 6 and 7.

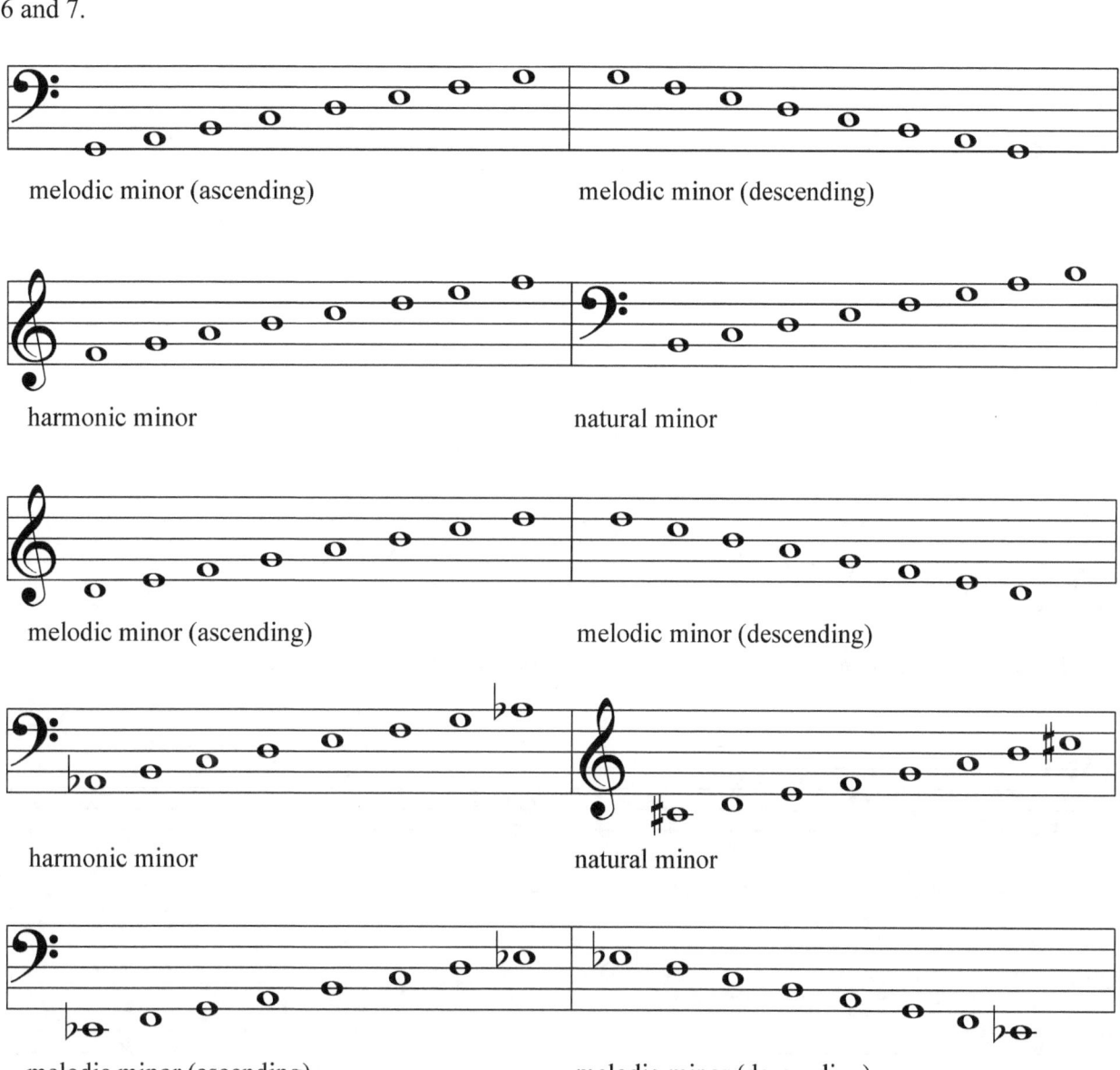

melodic minor (ascending)   melodic minor (descending)

harmonic minor   natural minor

melodic minor (ascending)   melodic minor (descending)

harmonic minor   natural minor

melodic minor (ascending)   melodic minor (descending)

Worksheet 6–2

Name _____

Chapter 6: The Minor Mode

Given the following octave ranges and clefs, create the indicated minor scale by adding the appropriate accidentals; do not change the first or last note of each octave—that is the keynote. Remember that the ascending and descending forms of the melodic minor require different accidentals for variable scale degrees 6 and 7.

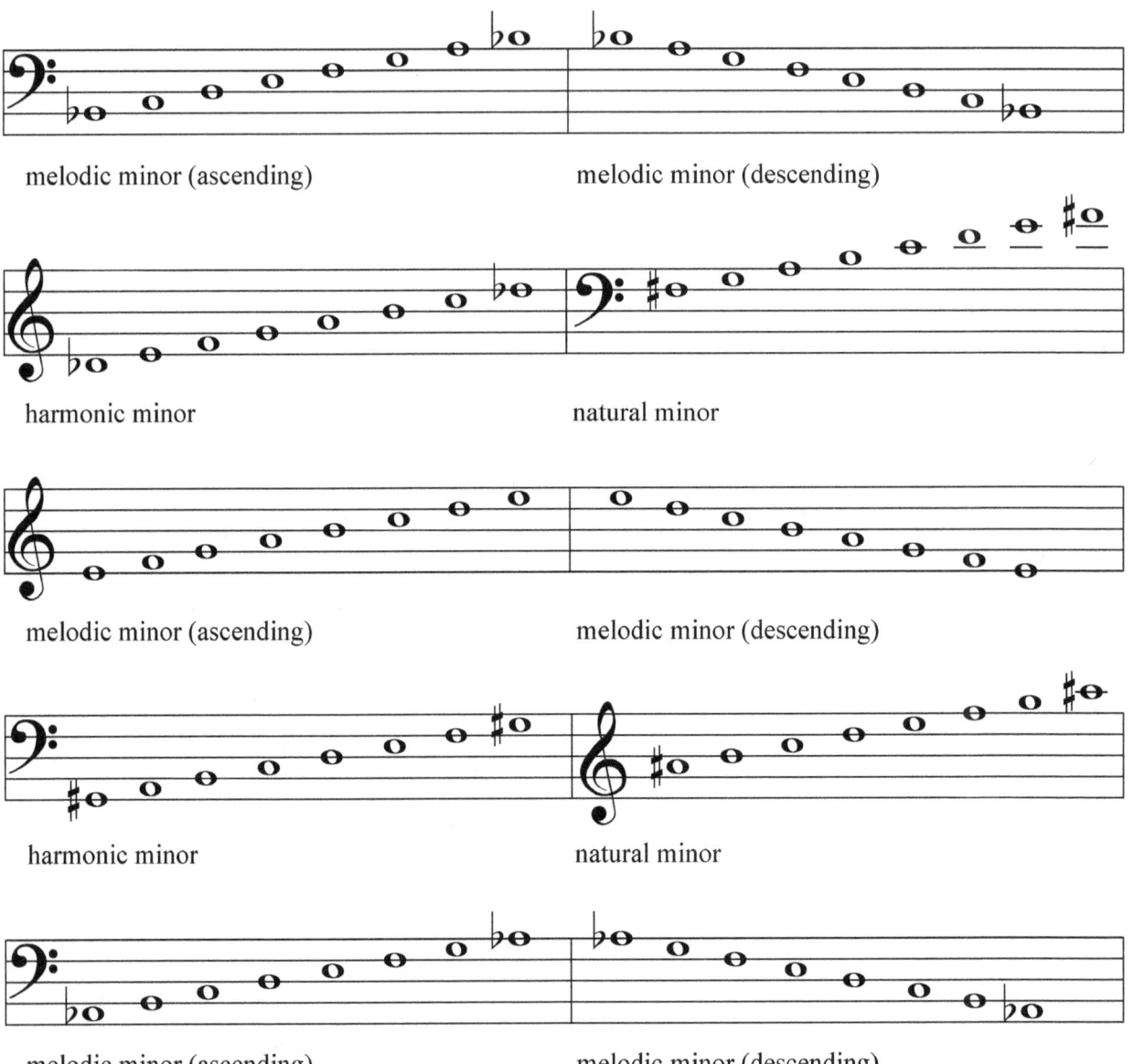

Worksheet 6–3

Name _____

Chapter 6: The Minor Mode

Identify the following key signatures according to both major and minor modes (use upper case letters for major modes and lower case letters for minor modes).

major: B♭ ____ ____ ____

minor: g ____ ____ ____

major: ____ ____ ____ ____

minor: ____ ____ ____ ____

major: ____ ____ ____ ____

minor: ____ ____ ____ ____

Worksheet 6–4

Name _____

Chapter 6: The Minor Mode

Identify the following key signatures according to both major and minor modes (use upper case letters for major modes and lower case letters for minor modes).

major: _____   _____   _____   _____

minor: _____   _____   _____   _____

major: _____   _____   _____   _____

minor: _____   _____   _____   _____

major: _____   _____   _____   _____

minor: _____   _____   _____   _____

Worksheet 6–5

Name _____

Chapter 6: The Minor Mode

Supply the key signatures of the following minor modes according to the given clef:

a♭:   f♯:   b♭:   d♯:

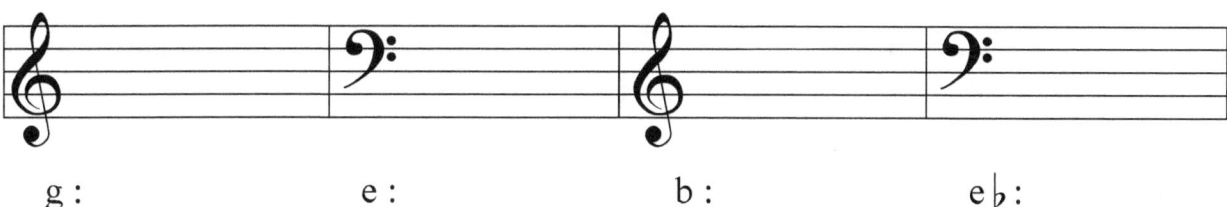

g: e: b: e♭:

c: d: g♯:   a♯:

Worksheet 6–6

Name _____

Chapter 6: The Minor Mode

Supply the key signatures of the following minor modes according to the given clef:

eb :   g# :   d :   c# :

f :   g :   e :   bb :

f# :   b :   a# :   c :

Worksheet 6–7

Name _____

Chapter 6: The Minor Mode

Identify the given intervals according to quality (* M, m, P, d, or A) and numerical distance (6 or 7):

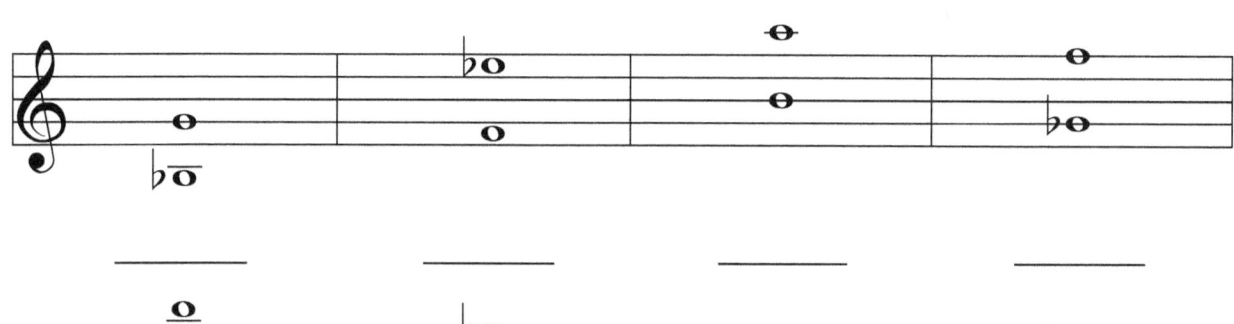

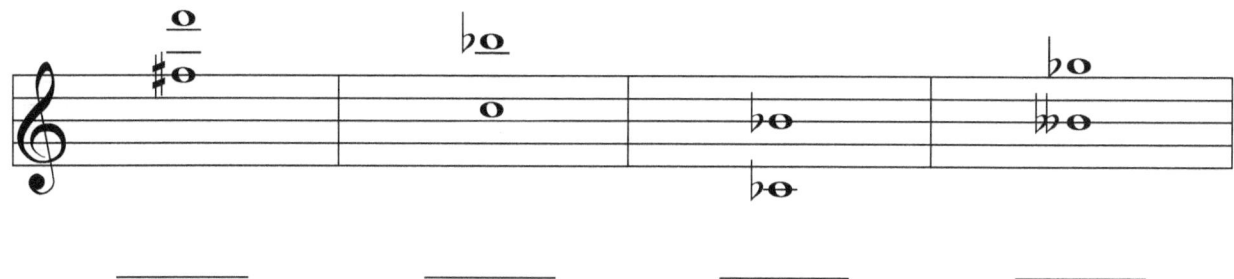

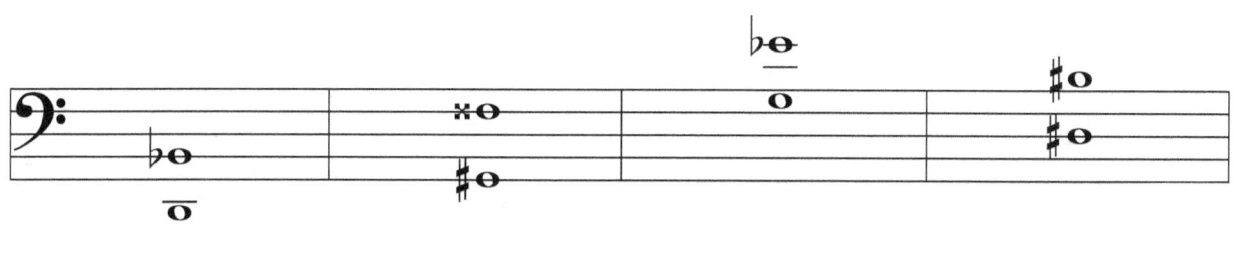

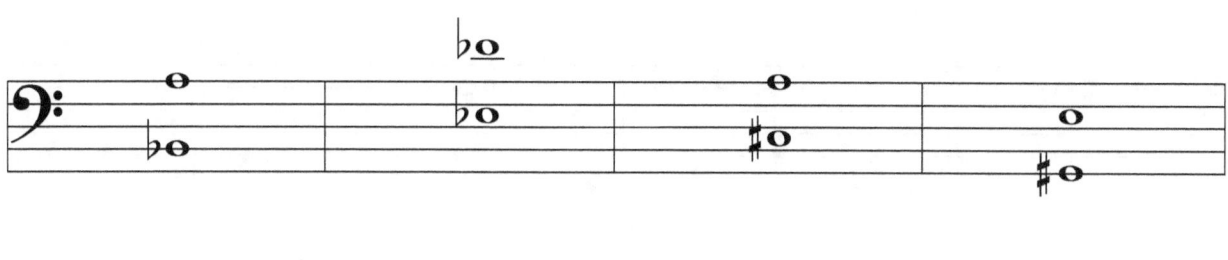

* M = Major, m = minor, P = Perfect, d = diminished, A = Augmented (in order to avoid confusing the upper case M with the lower case m, make the lower case m visibly smaller than the adjoining Arabic number)

Worksheet 6–8

Name _____

Chapter 6: The Minor Mode

Identify the given intervals according to quality (* M, m, P, d, or A) and numerical distance (6 or 7):

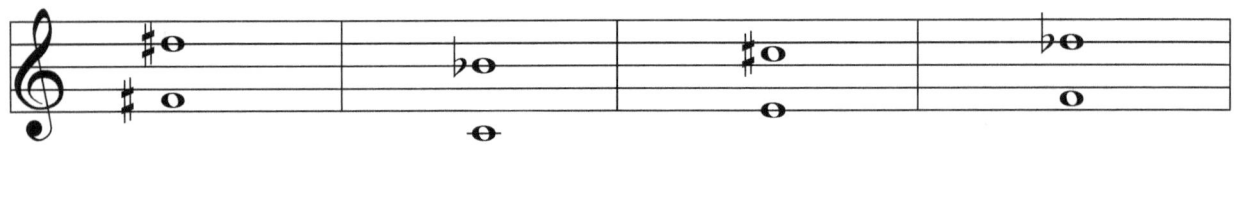

_____   _____   _____   _____

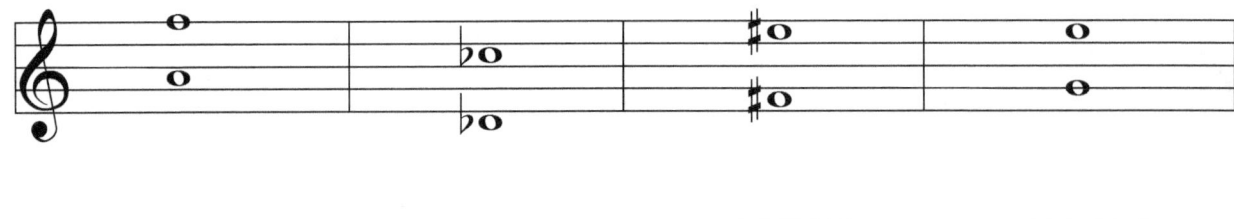

_____   _____   _____   _____

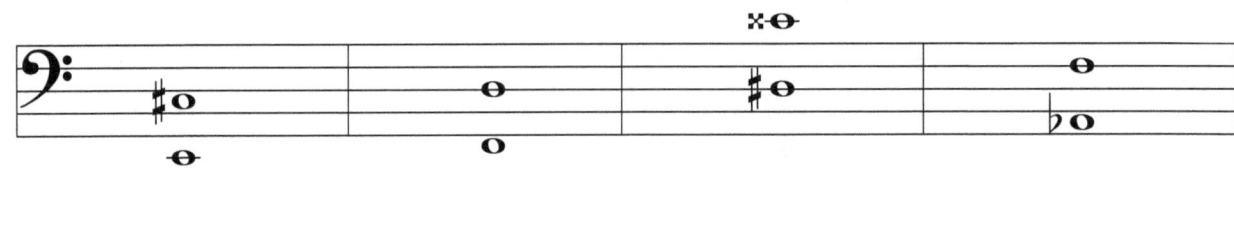

_____   _____   _____   _____

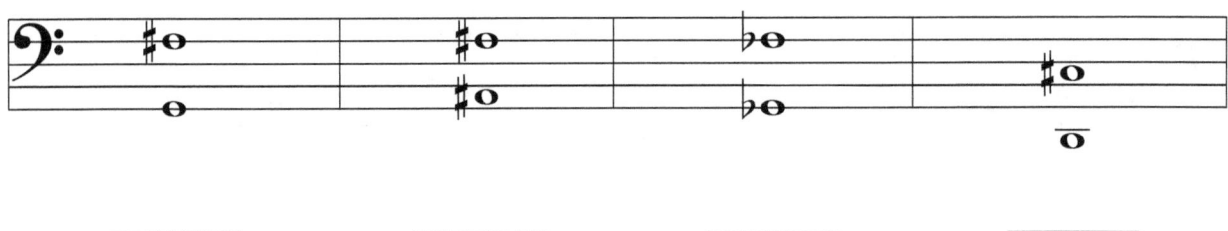

_____   _____   _____   _____

* M = Major, m = minor, P = Perfect, d = diminished, A = Augmented (in order to avoid confusing the upper case M with the lower case m, make the lower case m visibly smaller than the adjoining Arabic number)

Worksheet 6–9

Name _____

Chapter 6: The Minor Mode

Construct the indicated interval above or below the given tone (M = major, m = minor):

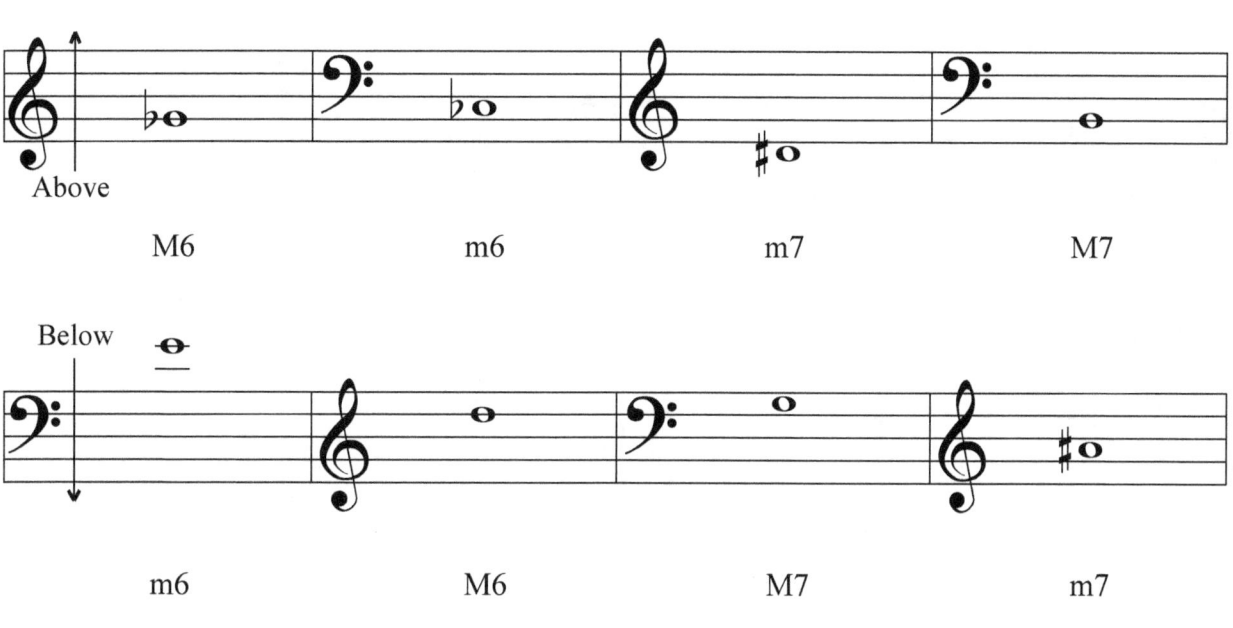

Worksheet 6–10

Name _____

Chapter 6: The Minor Mode

Construct the indicated interval above or below the given tone (M = major, m = minor):

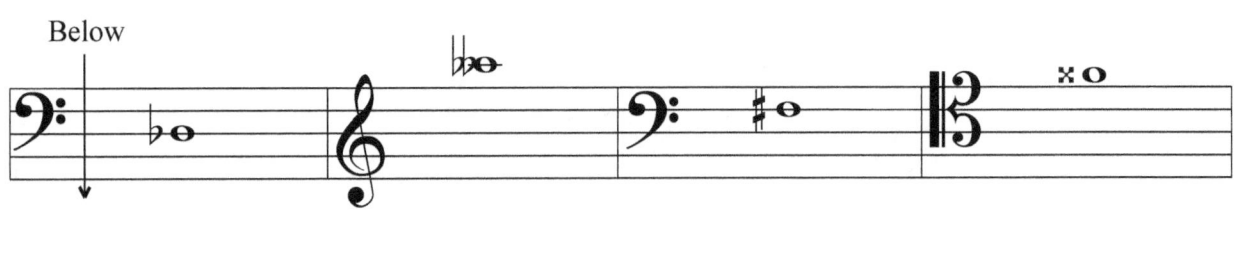

Worksheet 6–11

Name _____

Chapter 6: The Minor Mode

Given the following melodic minor keys and variable scale degrees, supply the missing pitch. Your answer should appear in only one register; however, as shown in the example, the correct pitch may be written in more than one register. Remember that variables ♯6 and ♯7 of the melodic minor correspond to scale degrees 6 and 7 of the parallel major mode and that ♭6 and ♭7 are always one half step lower than ♯6 and ♯7. See p. 84 above for a complete set of guidelines for finding the variable tones of the melodic minor.

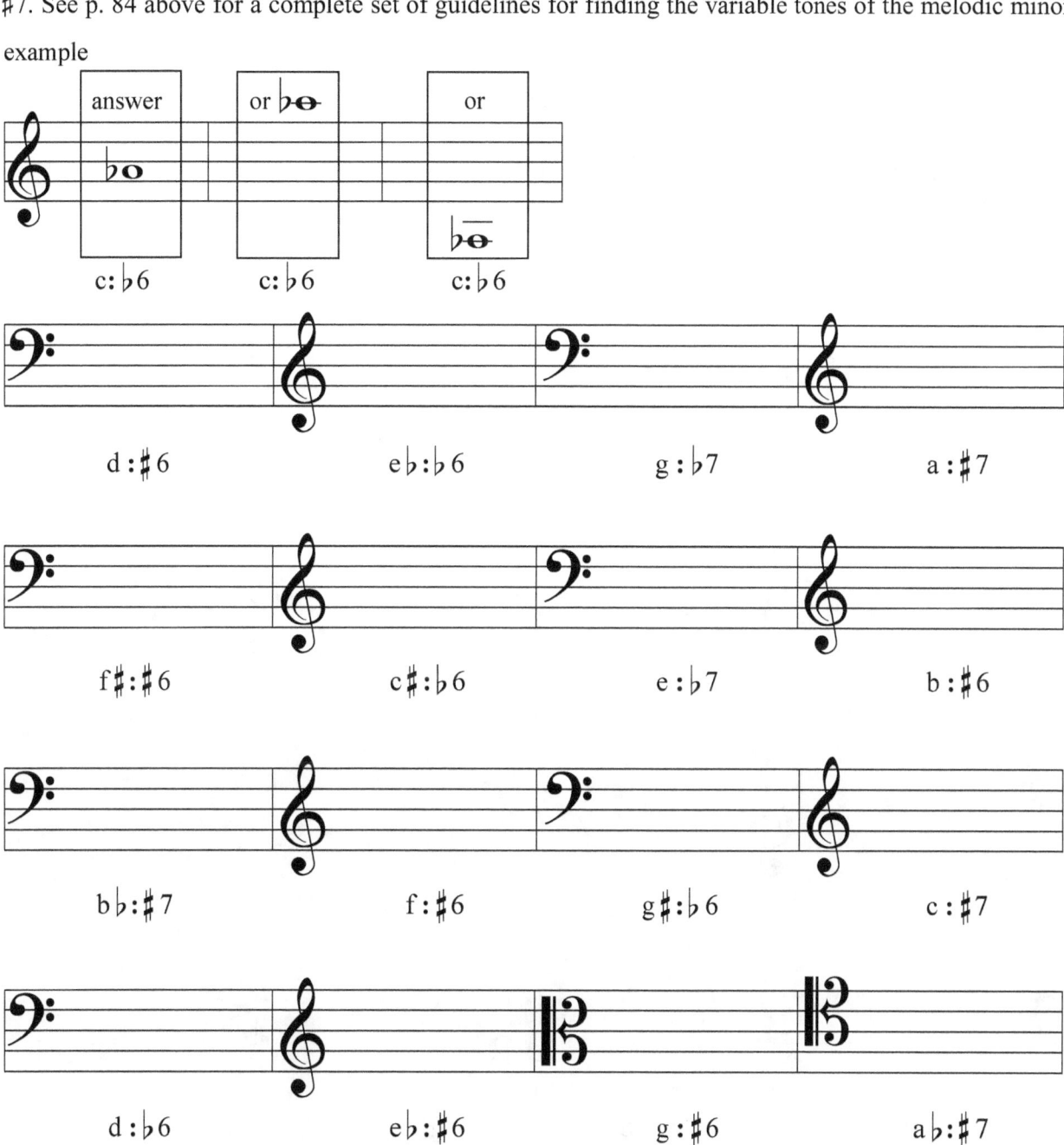

Worksheet 6–12

Name _____

Chapter 6: The Minor Mode

Given the following melodic minor keys and variable scale degrees, supply the missing pitch. Your answer should appear in only one register; however, as shown in the example, the correct pitch may be written in more than one register. Remember that variables ♯6 and ♯7 of the melodic minor correspond to scale degrees 6 and 7 of the parallel major mode and that ♭6 and ♭7 are always one half step lower than ♯6 and ♯7. See p. 84 above for a complete set of guidelines for finding the variable tones of the melodic minor.

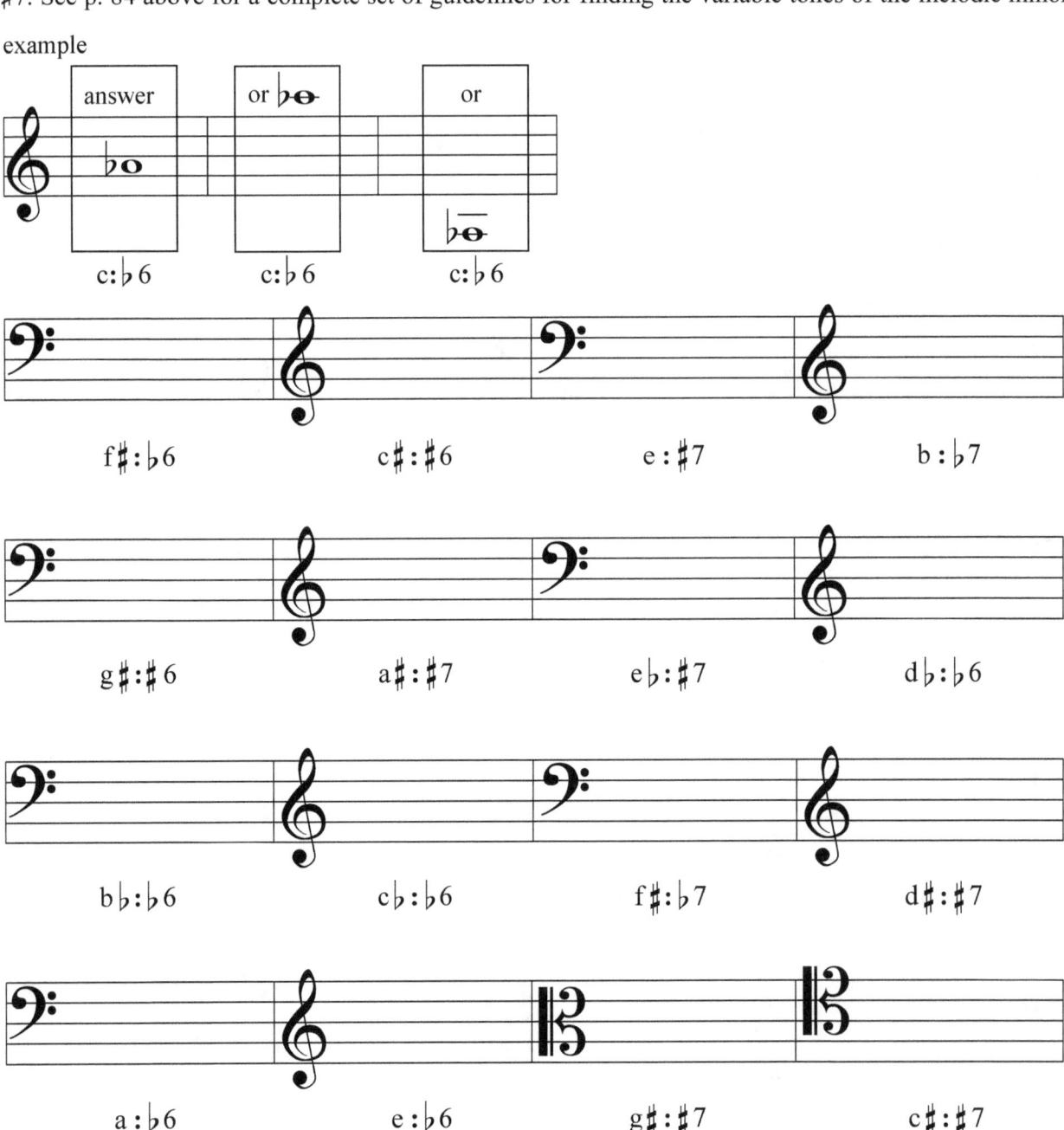

Worksheet 6–13

Name _____

Chapter 6: The Minor Mode

Given the following melodic minor keys and variable scale degrees, supply the missing pitch. Your answer should appear in only one register; however, as shown in the example, the correct pitch may be written in more than one register. Remember that variables ♯6 and ♯7 of the melodic minor correspond to scale degrees 6 and 7 of the parallel major mode and that ♭6 and ♭7 are always one half step lower than ♯6 and ♯7. See p. 84 above for a complete set of guidelines for finding the variable tones of the melodic minor.

example

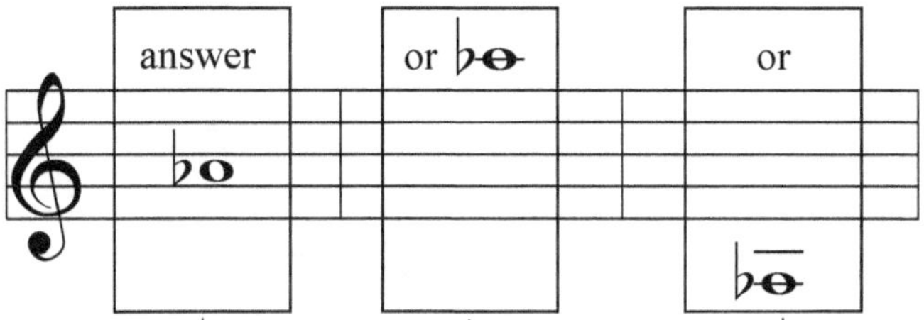

answer	or ♭𝅝	or
♭𝅝		♭𝅝
c: ♭6	c: ♭6	c: ♭6

e : ♯6   g : ♭6   b : ♭6   c : ♭7

d♯ : ♭6   a♯ : ♭6   d♭ : ♯7   f : ♭6

e♭ : ♭7   a♭ : ♭6   f♯ : ♯7   d♯ : ♯6

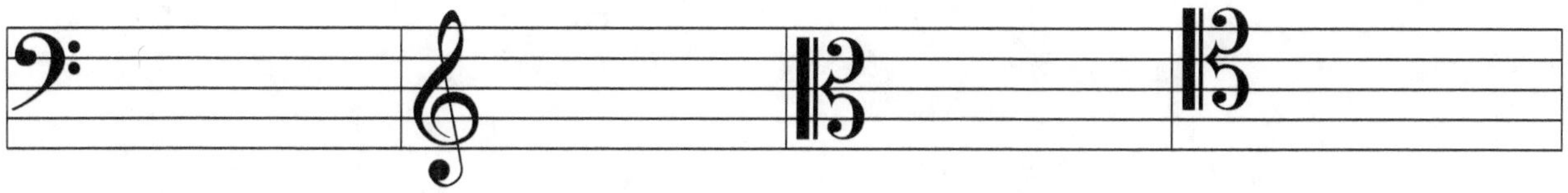

a : ♯6   b♭ : ♯6   a♭ : ♭7   d : ♯7

Worksheet 6–14

Name _____

Chapter 6: The Minor Mode

Given the following melodic minor keys and pitches or scale degrees and pitches, supply the missing factor (remember to use lowercase letters to indicate minor keys):

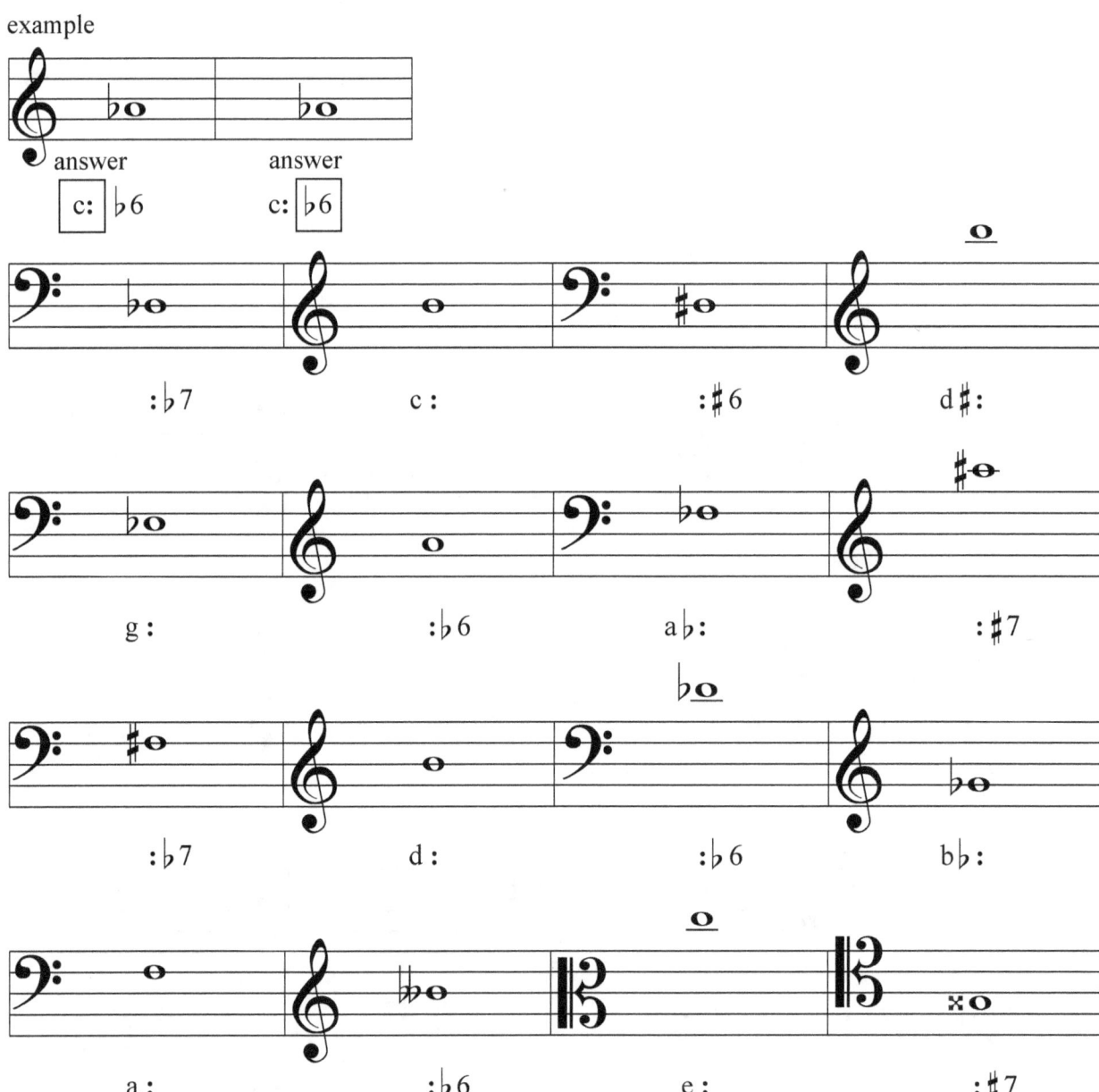

Worksheet 6–15

Name _____

Chapter 6: The Minor Mode

Given the following melodic minor keys and pitches or scale degrees and pitches, supply the missing factor (remember to use lowercase letters to indicate minor keys):

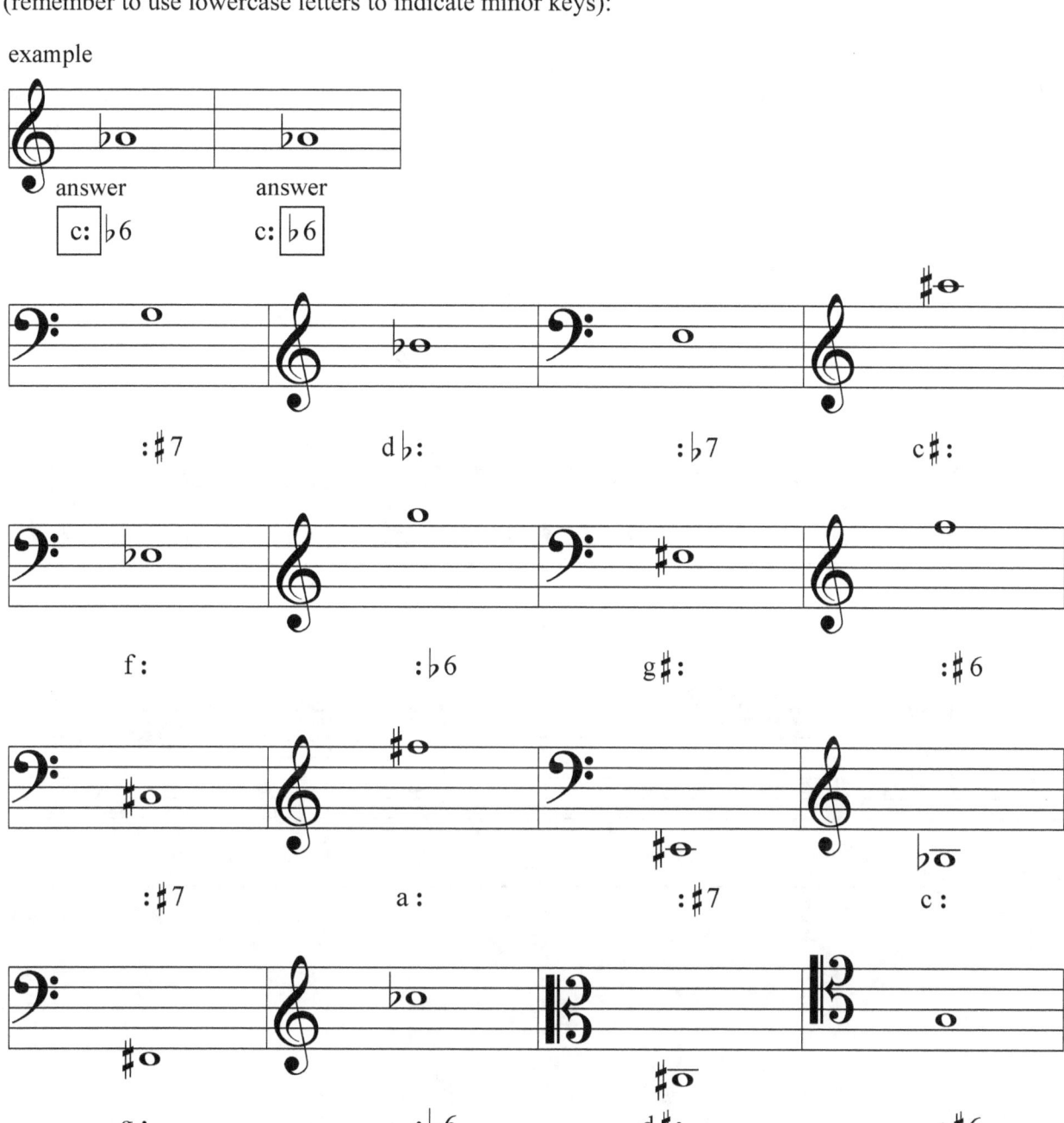

Worksheet 6–16

Name _____

Chapter 6: The Minor Mode

Meter and Rhythm

Given the following meter, place bar lines in the proper places and write the counts directly under the appropriate note or rest. The final measure requires the addition of a rest (and a count below it); moreover, be sure to observe any incomplete "pickup" measures at the beginning of the exercise when completing the final measure (see above, p. 15 and example 1–23d). Do not forget to write in the bar line at the end of the final measure. Use the supplied counts to help you determine the counts not given.

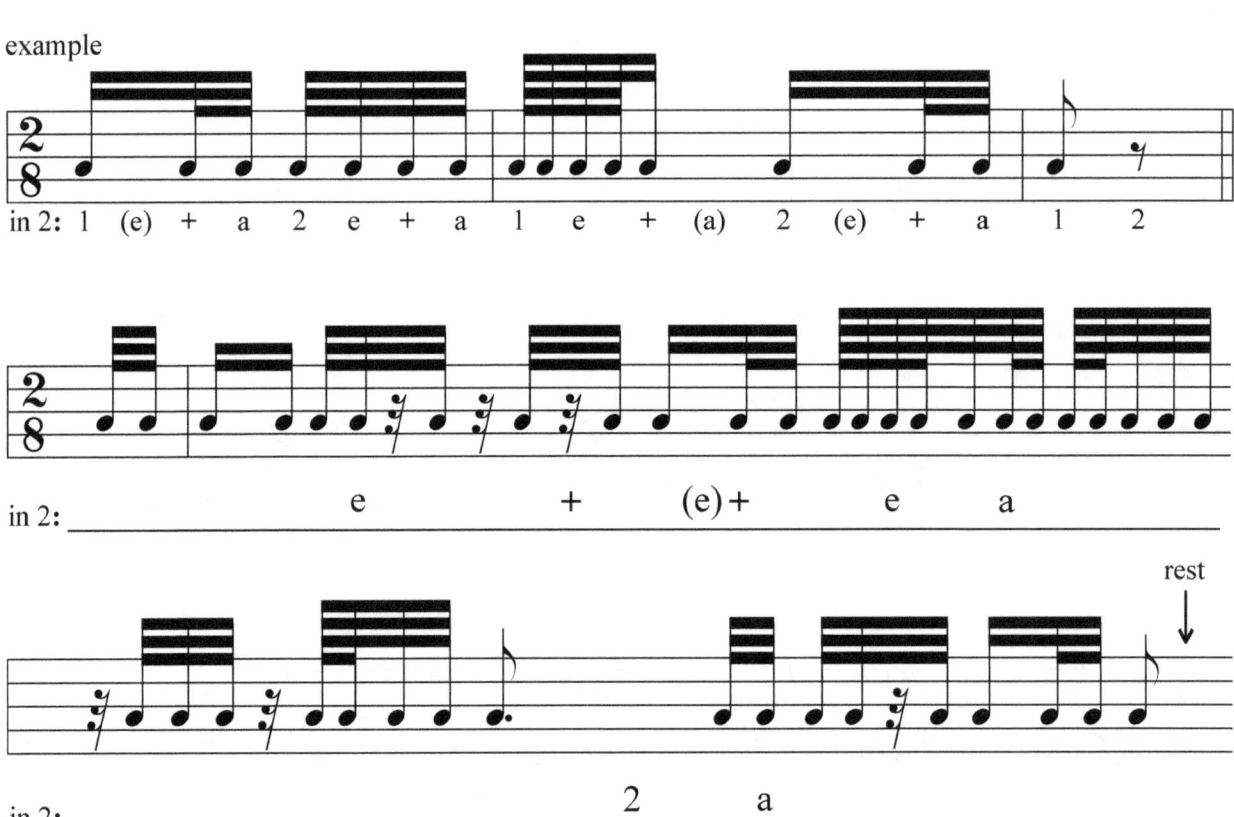

Worksheet 7–1

Name _____

Chapter 7: Advanced Concepts in Meter

Given the following meter, place bar lines in the proper places and write the counts directly under the appropriate note or rest. Do not forget to write in the bar line at the end of the final measure. Use the supplied counts to help you determine the counts not given.

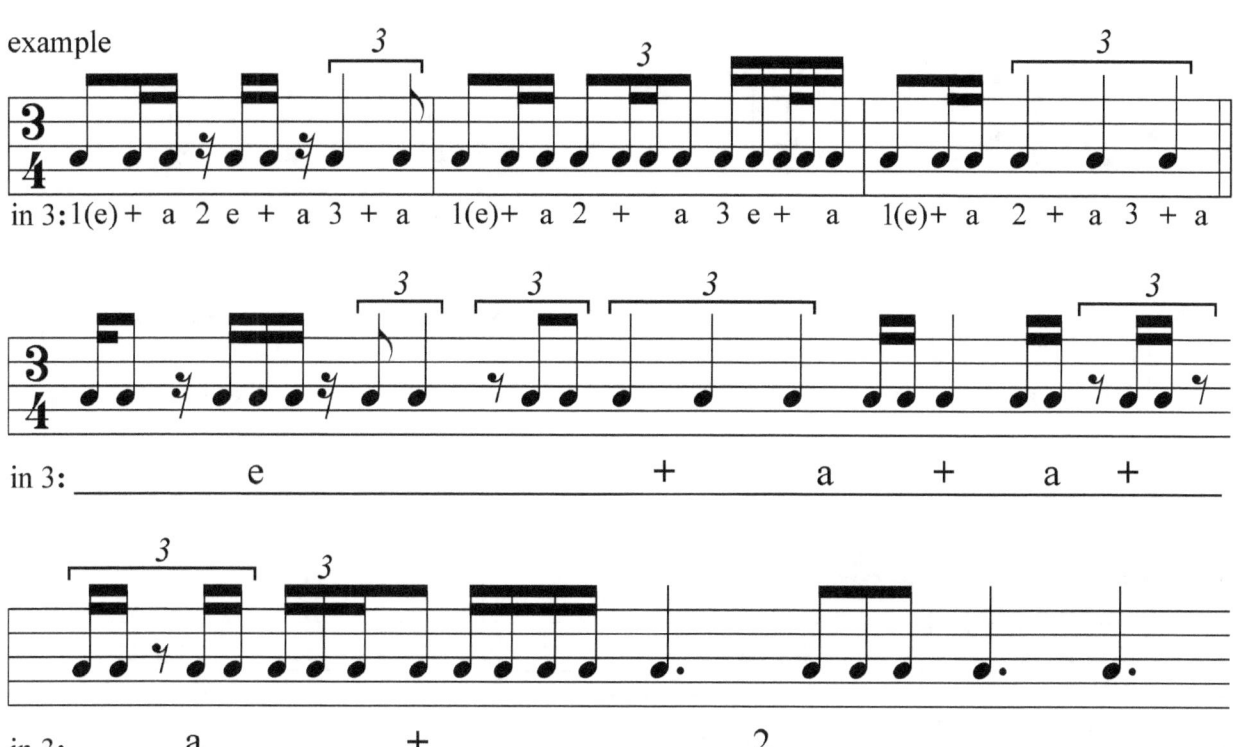

Worksheet 7–2

Name _____

Chapter 7: Advanced Concepts in Meter

Given the following meter, place bar lines in the proper places and write the counts directly under the appropriate note or rest. Do not forget to write in the bar line at the end of the final measure. Use the supplied counts to help you determine the counts not given.

Worksheet 7–3

Name _____

Chapter 7: Advanced Concepts in Meter

Given the following meter, place bar lines in the proper places and write the counts directly under the appropriate note or rest. Remember that "common time" is the equivalent of $\frac{4}{4}$ time (see Chapter 1, p. 7). Use the supplied counts to help you determine the counts not given.

Worksheet 7–4

Name _____

Chapter 7: Advanced Concepts in Meter

Given the following meter, place bar lines in the proper places and write the counts directly under the appropriate note or rest. The final measure requires the addition of a rest (and a count below it); moreover, be sure to observe any incomplete "pickup" measures at the beginning of the exercise when completing the final measure (see above, p. 15 and example 1–23d). Do not forget to write in the bar line at the end of the final measure. Use the supplied counts to help you determine the counts not given.

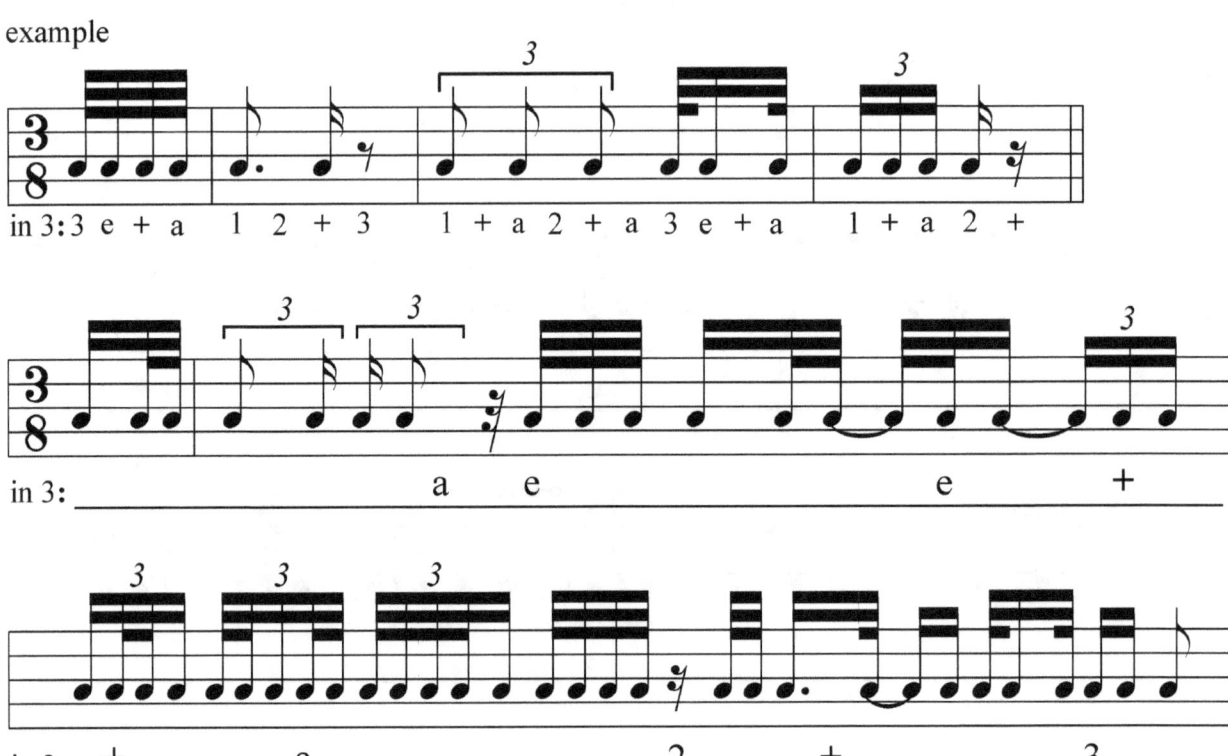

Worksheet 7–5

Name _____

Chapter 7: Advanced Concepts in Meter

Given the following meter, place bar lines in the proper places and write the counts directly under the appropriate note or rest. The final measure requires the addition of a rest (and a count below it); moreover, be sure to observe any incomplete "pickup" measures at the beginning of the exercise when completing the final measure (see above, p. 15 and example 1–23d). Do not forget to write in the bar line at the end of the final measure. Use the supplied counts to help you determine the counts not given.

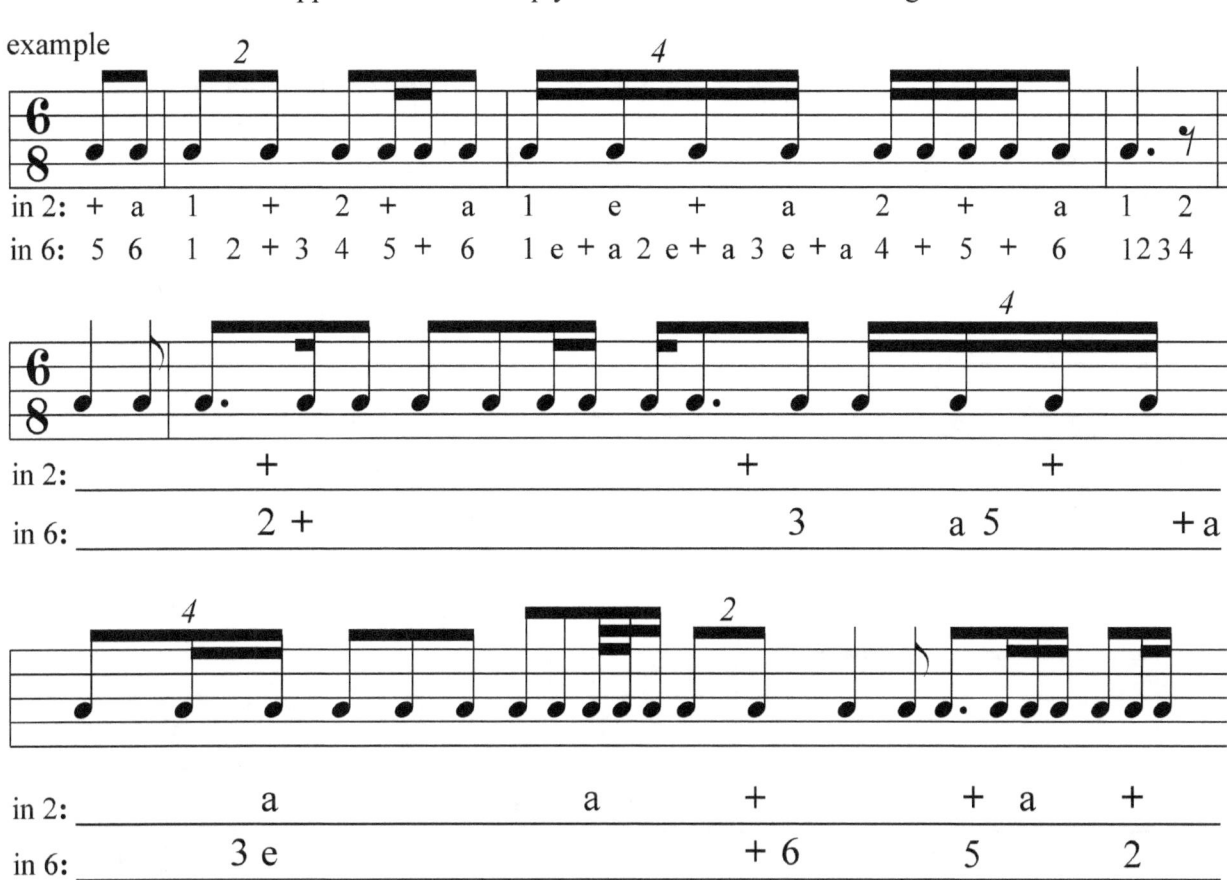

Worksheet 7–6

Name _____

Chapter 7: Advanced Concepts in Meter

Given the following meter, place bar lines in the proper places and write the counts directly under the appropriate note or rest. The final measure requires the addition of a rest (and a count below it); moreover, be sure to observe any incomplete "pickup" measures at the beginning of the exercise when completing the final measure (see above, p. 15 and example 1–23d). Do not forget to write in the bar line at the end of the final measure. Use the supplied counts to help you determine the counts not given.

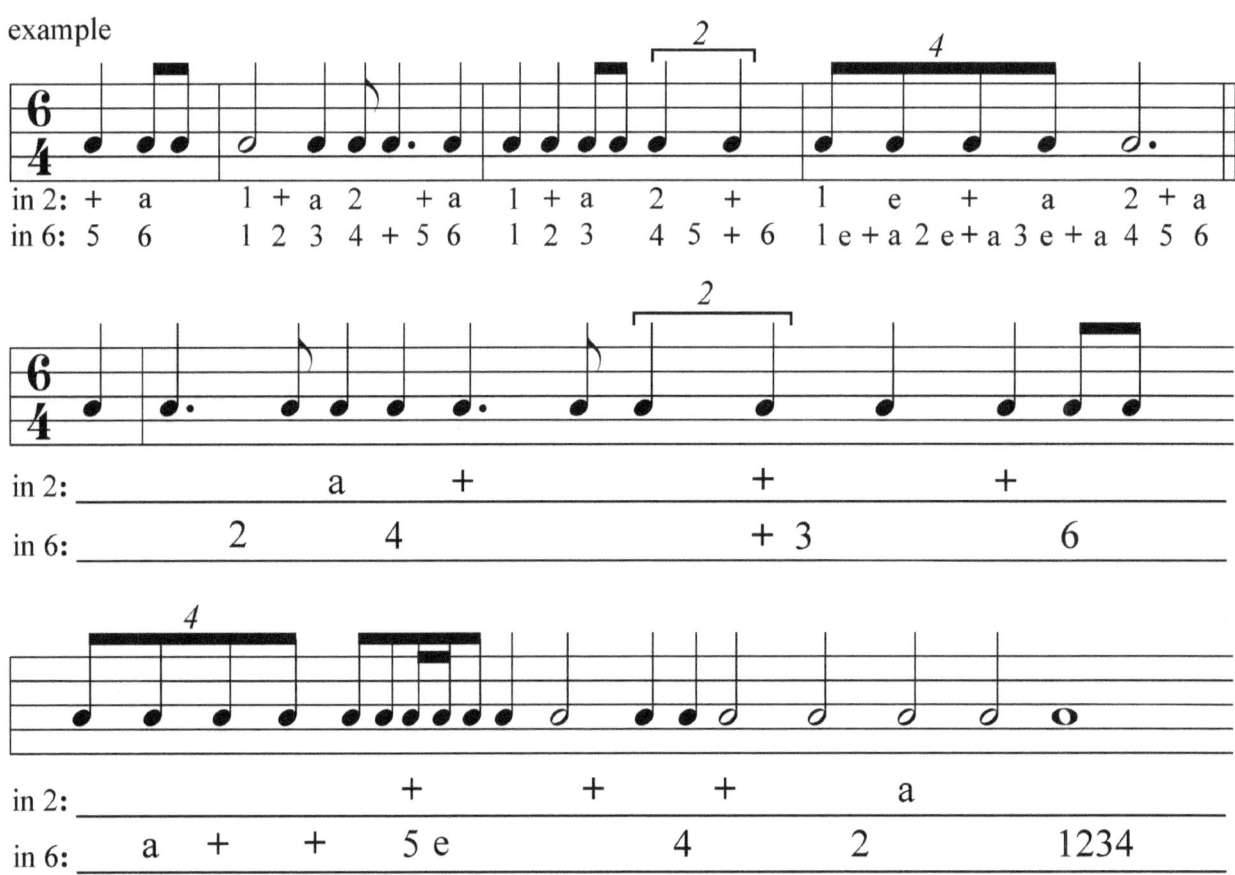

Worksheet 7–7

Name _____

Chapter 7: Advanced Concepts in Meter

Given the following meter, place bar lines in the proper places and write the counts directly under the appropriate note or rest. The final measure requires the addition of a rest (and a count below it); moreover, be sure to observe any incomplete "pickup" measures at the beginning of the exercise when completing the final measure (see above, p. 15 and example 1–23d). Do not forget to write in the bar line at the end of the final measure. Use the supplied counts to help you determine the counts not given.

Worksheet 7–8

Name _____

Chapter 7: Advanced Concepts in Meter

Given the following meter, place bar lines in the proper places and write the counts directly under the appropriate note or rest. The final measure requires the addition of a rest (and a count below it); moreover, be sure to observe any incomplete "pickup" measures at the beginning of the exercise when completing the final measure (see above, p. 15 and example 1–23d). Do not forget to write in the bar line at the end of the final measure. Use the supplied counts to help you determine the counts not given.

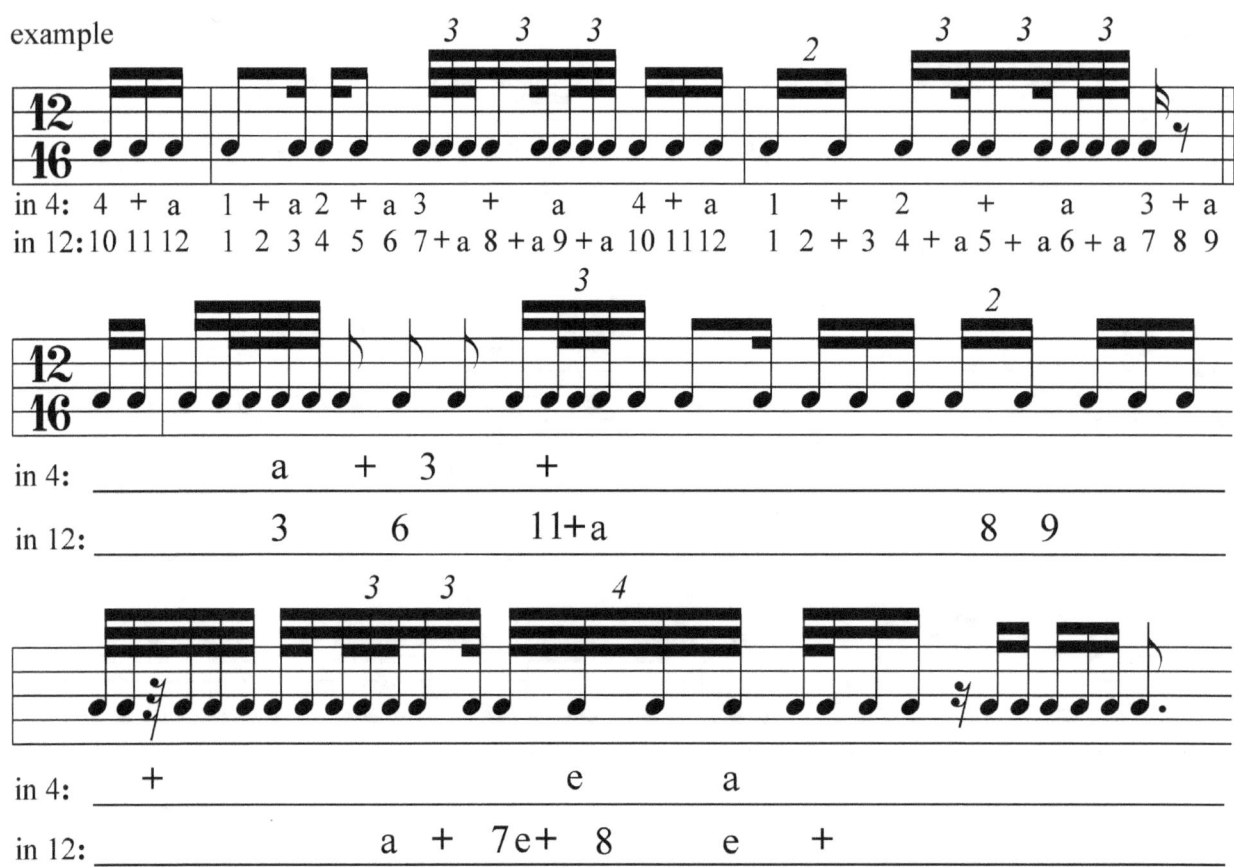

Worksheet 7–9

Name _____

Chapter 7: Advanced Concepts in Meter

Identify the meter signatures below according to general type, beats per measure, value of the beat, value of the first division, and value of the second division (use the indicated abbreviations for the category of general type):

General Type	Abbreviations
1. Simple Duple	S – D
2. Simple Quadruple	S – Q
3. Simple Triple	S – T
4. Simple Asymmetrical	S – A
5. Compound Duple	C – D
6. Compound Quadruple	C – Q
7. Compound Triple	C – T
8. Compound Asymmetrical	C – A

examples

$\frac{5}{16}$ $\frac{6}{8}$ $\frac{4}{4}$ $\frac{12}{4}$ $\frac{2}{1}$ $\frac{7}{8}$ $\frac{4}{8}$ $\frac{9}{2}$

General Type: S – A   C – D   S – Q   ____   ____   ____   ____   ____

Beats Per Measure: 5   2   4   ____   ____   ____   ____   ____

Value of the Beat: ♪   ♩.   ♩   ____   ____   ____   ____   ____

Value of the First Division: 𝅘𝅥𝅯   ♪   ♪   ____   ____   ____   ____   ____

Value of the Second Division: 𝅘𝅥𝅰   𝅘𝅥𝅯   𝅘𝅥𝅯   ____   ____   ____   ____   ____

Worksheet 7–10

Name _____

Chapter 7: Advanced Concepts in Meter

Identify the meter signatures below according to general type, beats per measure, value of the beat, value of the first division, and value of the second division (use the indicated abbreviations for the category of general type):

General Type	Abbreviations
1. Simple Duple	S – D
2. Simple Quadruple	S – Q
3. Simple Triple	S – T
4. Simple Asymmetrical	S – A
5. Compound Duple	C – D
6. Compound Quadruple	C – Q
7. Compound Triple	C – T
8. Compound Asymmetrical	C – A

examples

	15/16	6/8	3/4	12/16	15/8	4/2	9/4	6/2
General Type:	C – A	C – D	S – T	____	____	____	____	____
Beats Per Measure:	5	2	3	____	____	____	____	____
Value of the Beat:	♪.	♩.	♩	____	____	____	____	____
Value of the First Division:	♪	♪	♪	____	____	____	____	____
Value of the Second Division:	♬	♬	♬	____	____	____	____	____

Worksheet 7–11

Name _____

Chapter 7: Advanced Concepts in Meter

Identify the meter signatures below according to general type, beats per measure, value of the beat, value of the first division, and value of the second division (use the indicated abbreviations for the category of general type):

General Type	Abbreviations
1. Simple Duple	S – D
2. Simple Quadruple	S – Q
3. Simple Triple	S – T
4. Simple Asymmetrical	S – A
5. Compound Duple	C – D
6. Compound Quadruple	C – Q
7. Compound Triple	C – T
8. Compound Asymmetrical	C – A

examples

$\frac{5}{16}$ $\frac{6}{8}$ $\frac{2}{4}$ $\frac{6}{32}$ $\frac{2}{2}$ $\frac{7}{4}$ $\frac{4}{8}$ $\frac{3}{16}$

General Type: S – A C – D S – D ____ ____ ____ ____ ____

Beats Per Measure: 5 2 2 ____ ____ ____ ____ ____

Value of the Beat: ♪ ♩. ♩ ____ ____ ____ ____ ____

Value of the First Division: ♬ ♪ ♪ ____ ____ ____ ____ ____

Value of the Second Division: ♬ ♬ ♪ ____ ____ ____ ____ ____

Worksheet 8–1

Name _____

Chapter 8: Triads

Identify the quality of the following root-position triads. Since all the of the triads are in root position, it is not necessary to include the figured bass ($^5_3$).

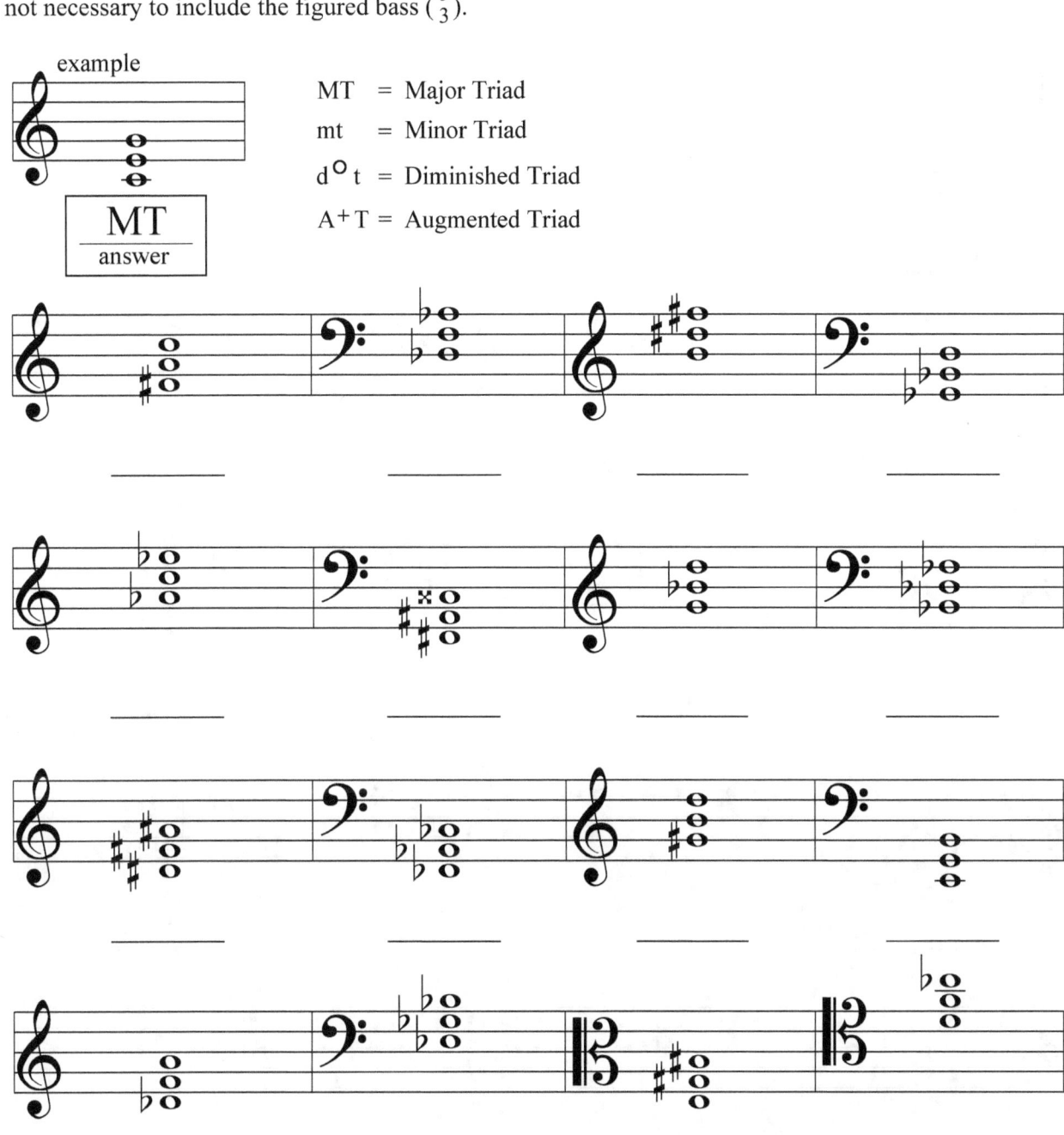

Worksheet 8–2

Name _____

Chapter 8: Triads

Identify the quality of the following root-position triads. Since all the of the triads are in root position, it is not necessary to include the figured bass ($^5_3$).

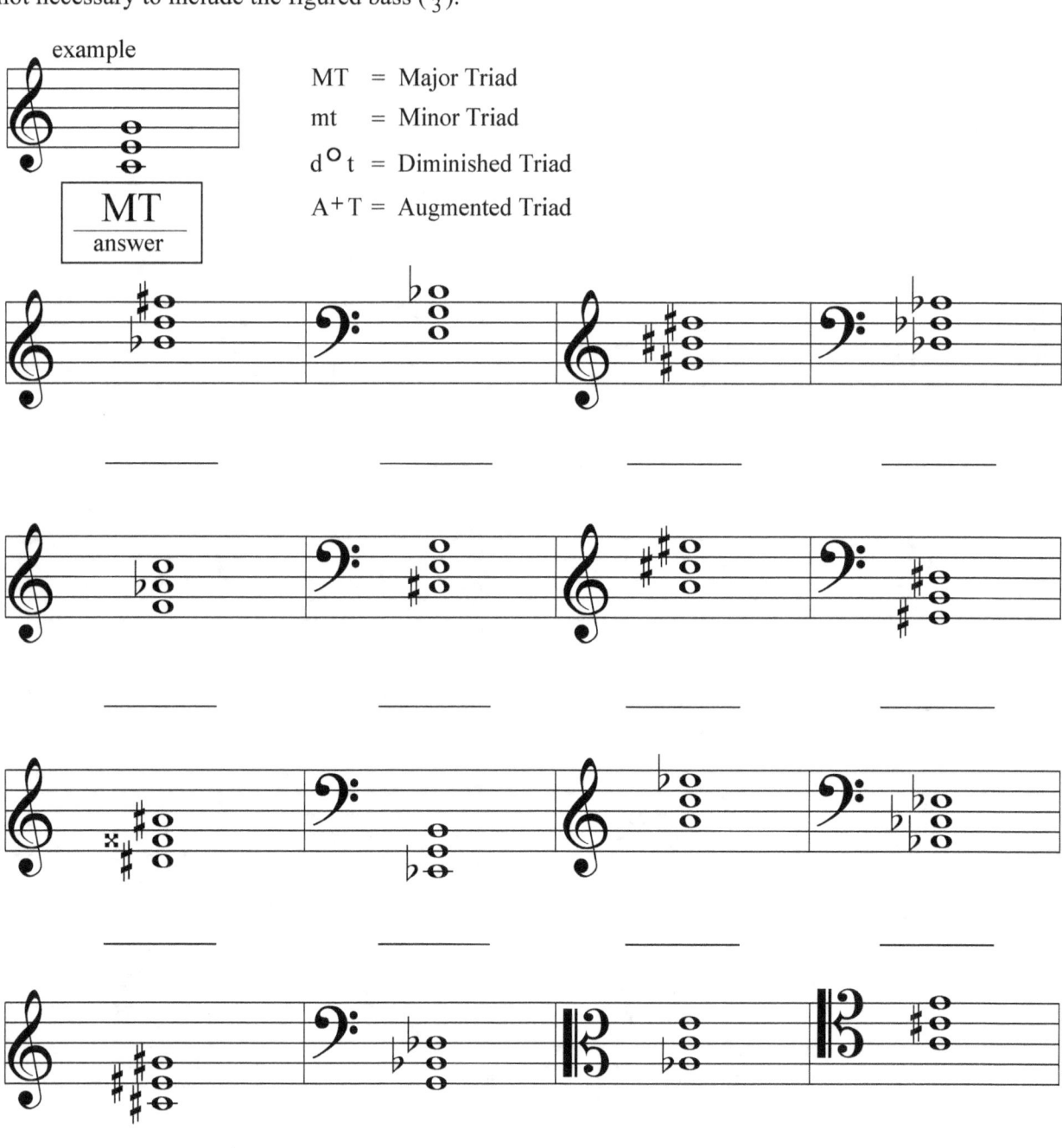

Worksheet 8–3

Name _____

Chapter 8: Triads

Identify the quality of the following root-position triads. Since all the of the triads are in root position, it is not necessary to include the figured bass ($^5_3$).

MT = Major Triad
mt = Minor Triad
d°t = Diminished Triad
A⁺T = Augmented Triad

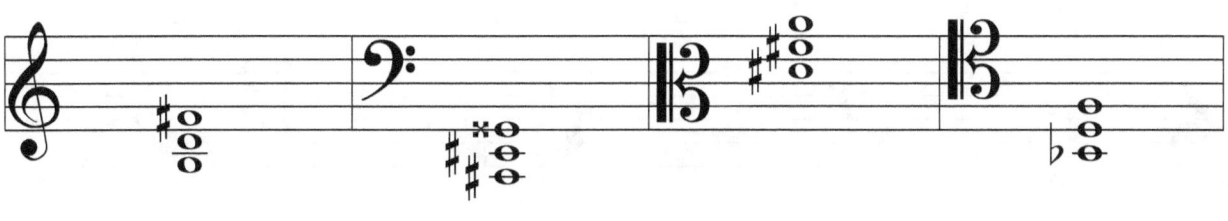

Worksheet 8–4

Name _____

Chapter 8: Triads

Identify the quality of the following inverted triads. Since all of the triads are inverted, you must include the correct figured bass ($^6_3$ or $^6_4$). Remember that for all of the inverted triad qualities, the upper note of the written 4th is the root of the chord.

MT = Major Triad
mt = Minor Triad
d°t = Diminished Triad
A+T = Augmented Triad

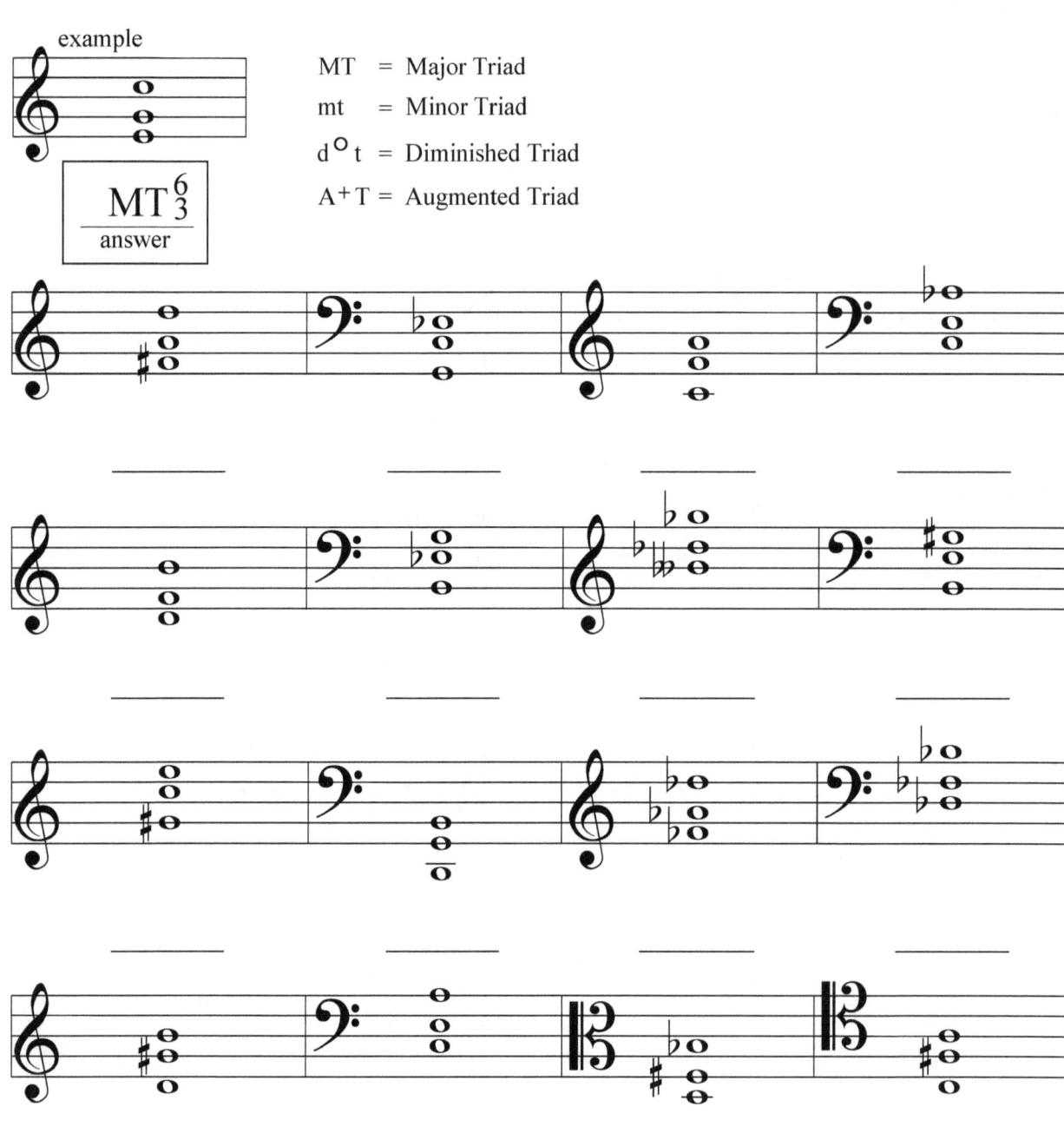

Worksheet 8–5

Name _____

Chapter 8: Triads

Identify the quality of the following inverted triads. Since all of the triads are inverted, you must include the correct figured bass ($^6_3$ or $^6_4$). Remember that for all of the inverted triad qualities, the upper note of the written 4th is the root of the chord.

Worksheet 8–6

Name _____

Chapter 8: Triads

Identify the quality of the following inverted triads. Since all of the triads are inverted, you must include the correct figured bass ($^6_3$ or $^6_4$). Remember that for all of the inverted triad qualities, the upper note of the written 4th is the root of the chord.

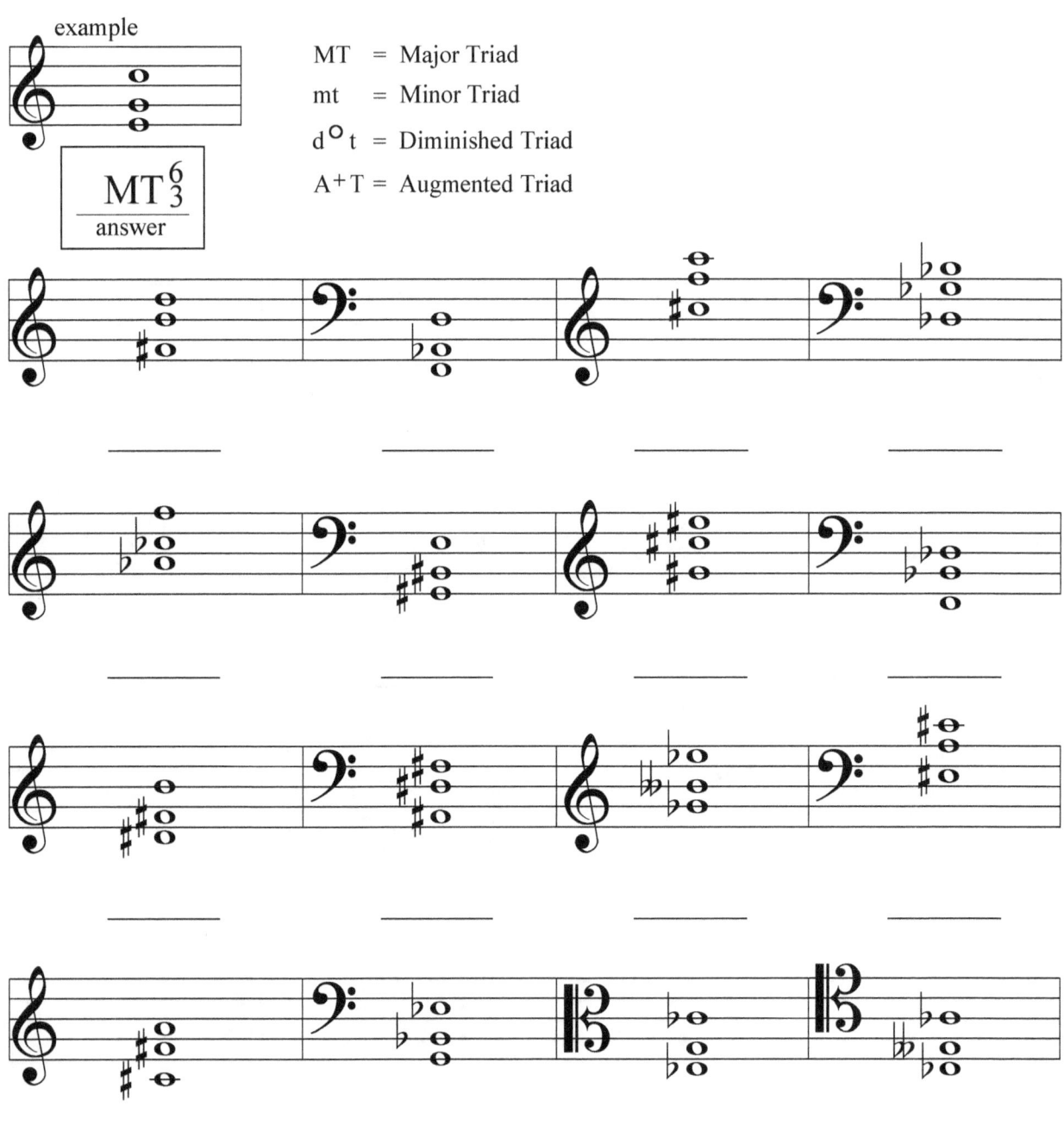

Worksheet 8–7

Name _____

Chapter 8: Triads

Using whole notes, construct above the given tone the appropriate triad quality according to the figured bass ($\frac{5}{3}$ or $\frac{6}{3}$ or $\frac{6}{4}$).

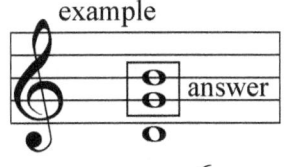

MT = Major Triad
mt = Minor Triad
d°t = Diminished Triad
A+T = Augmented Triad

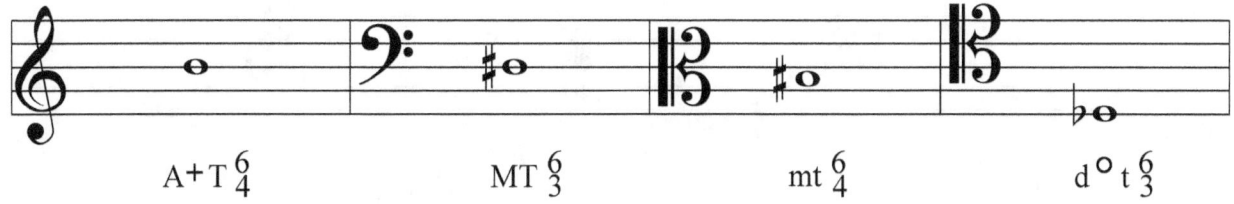

Worksheet 8–8

Name _____

Chapter 8: Triads

Using whole notes, construct above the given tone the appropriate triad quality according to the figured bass ($^6_3$ or $^6_4$).

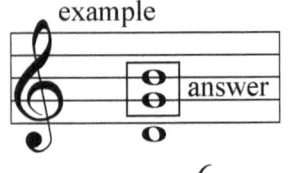

MT = Major Triad
mt = Minor Triad
d°t = Diminished Triad
A+T = Augmented Triad

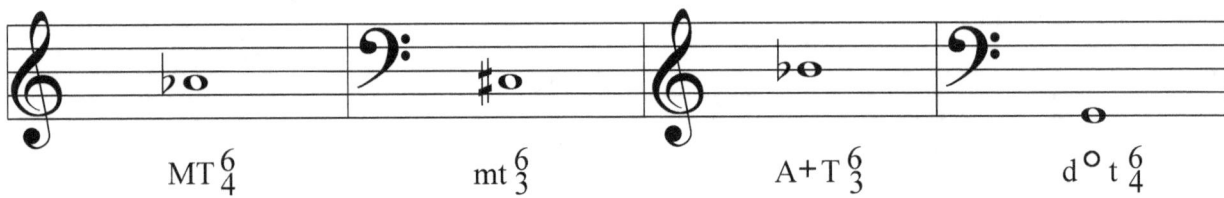

MT $^6_4$ mt $^6_3$ A+T $^6_3$ d°t $^6_4$

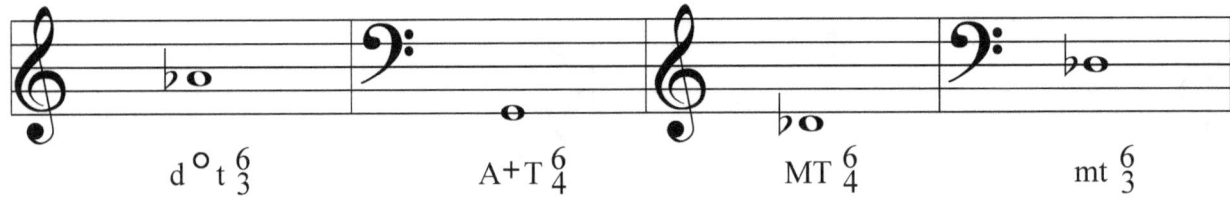

d°t $^6_3$ A+T $^6_4$ MT $^6_4$ mt $^6_3$

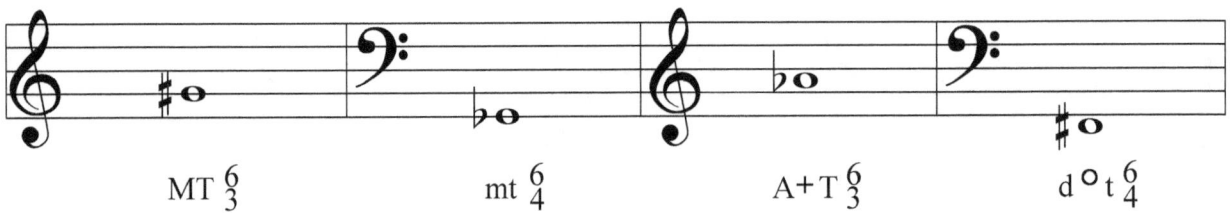

MT $^6_3$ mt $^6_4$ A+T $^6_3$ d°t $^6_4$

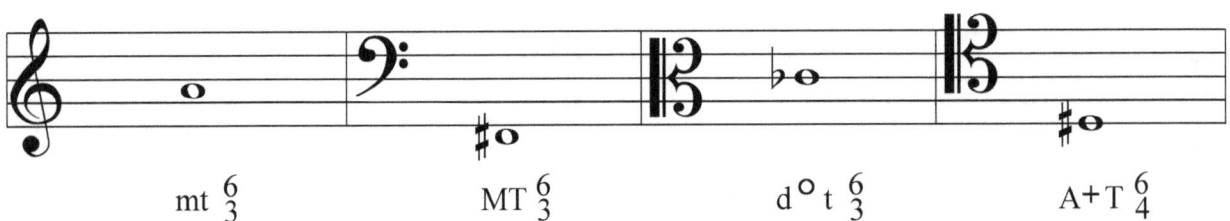

mt $^6_3$ MT $^6_3$ d°t $^6_3$ A+T $^6_4$

Worksheet 8–9

Name _____

Chapter 8: Triads

Using whole notes, construct above the given tone the appropriate triad quality according to the figured bass ($^6_3$ or $^6_4$).

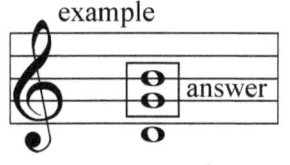

MT = Major Triad
mt = Minor Triad
d°t = Diminished Triad
A+T = Augmented Triad

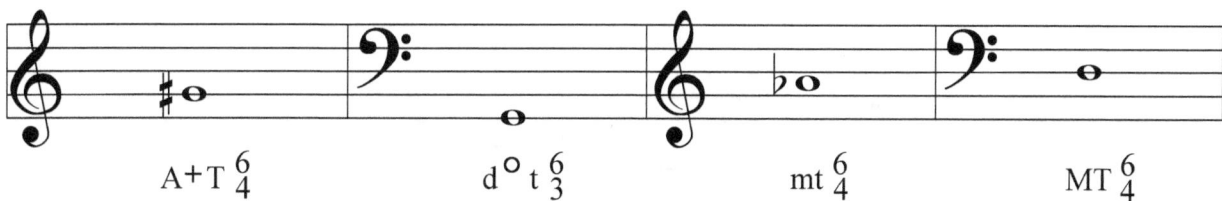

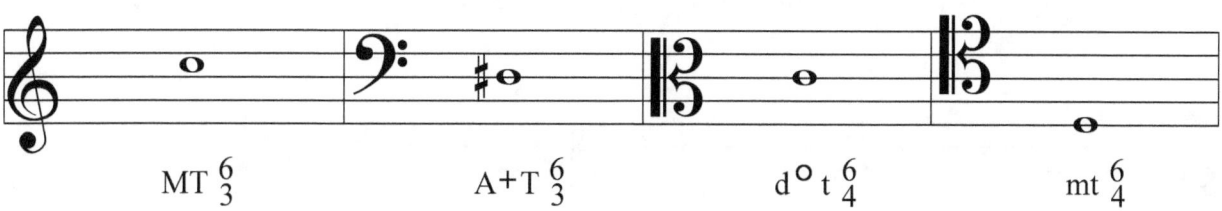

Worksheet 8–10

Name _____

Chapter 8: Triads

Given the key, mode, clef, and chord symbol, construct the appropriate triad. Use whole notes for your answers. Note carefully that if the key is presented with uppercase letters (for example, C:), then the mode is major. If, however, the key is expressed with lowercase letters (for example, c:), then the mode is minor. Since there is no figured bass following the Roman numerals in this exercise, it can be assumed that all of the chords are in root position. Remember that uppercase Roman numerals (without the plus sign) indicate major triads, while lowercase Roman numerals (without the superscript circle) signify minor triads.

Worksheet 8–11

Name _____

Chapter 8: Triads

Given the key, mode, clef, and chord symbol, construct the appropriate triad. Use whole notes for your answers. Note carefully that if the key is presented with uppercase letters (for example, C:), then the mode is major. If, however, the key is expressed with lowercase letters (for example, c:), then the mode is minor. Since there is no figured bass following the Roman numerals in this exercise, it can be assumed that all of the chords are in root position. Remember that uppercase Roman numerals (without the plus sign) indicate major triads, while lowercase Roman numerals (without the superscript circle) signify minor triads.

Worksheet 8–12

Name _____

Chapter 8: Triads

Given the key, mode, clef, and chord symbol, construct the appropriate triad. Use whole notes for your answers. Note carefully that if the key is presented with uppercase letters (for example, C:), then the mode is major. If, however, the key is expressed with lowercase letters (for example, c:), then the mode is minor. Since there is no figured bass following the Roman numerals in this exercise, it can be assumed that all of the chords are in root position. Remember that uppercase Roman numerals with the plus sign indicate augmented triads, while lowercase Roman numerals with the superscript circle signify diminished triads.

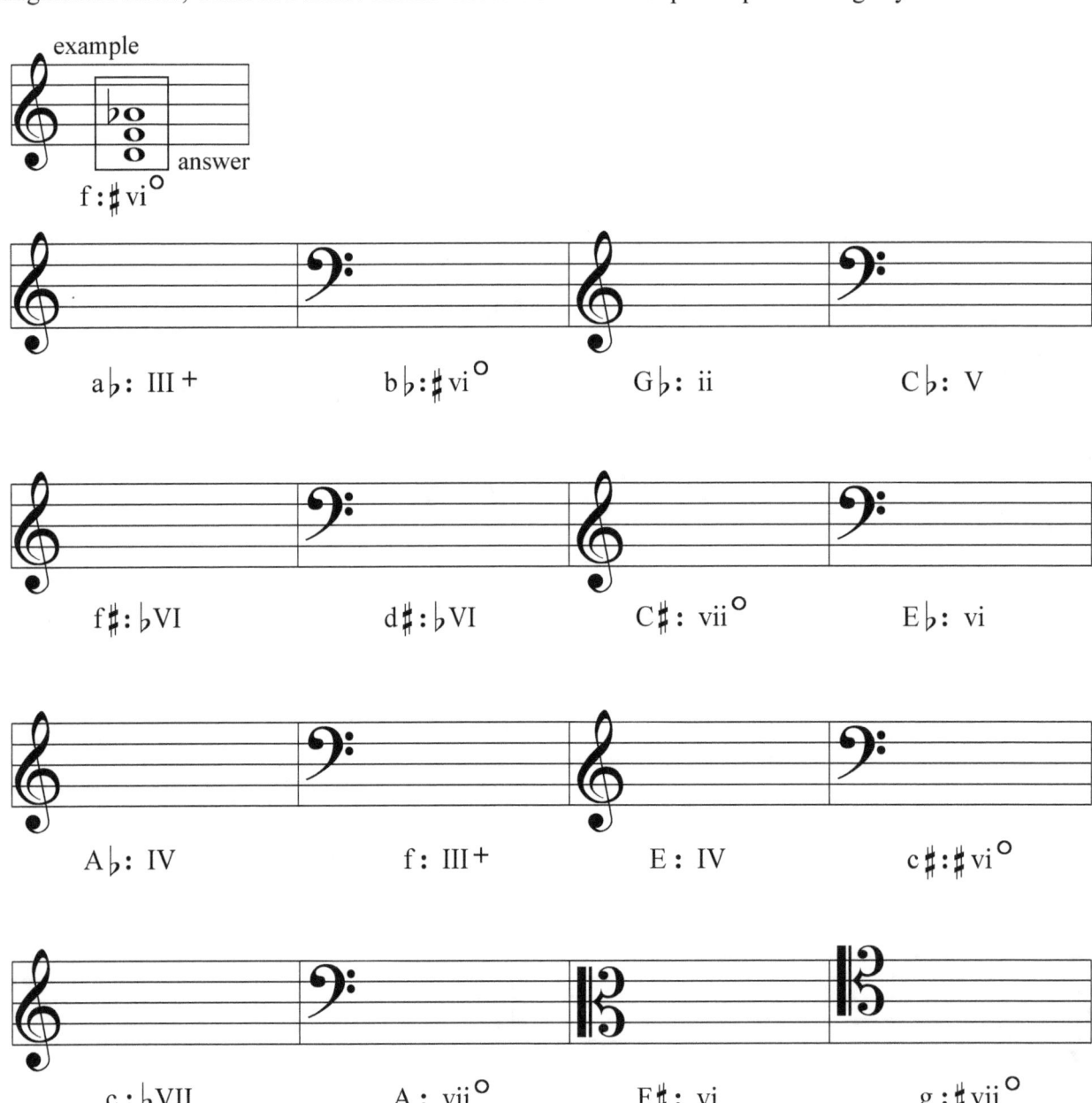

Worksheet 8–13

Name _____

Chapter 8: Triads

Given the key, mode, clef, and chord symbol, construct the appropriate triad. Use whole notes for your answers. Note carefully that if the key is presented with uppercase letters (for example, C:), then the mode is major. If, however, the key is expressed with lowercase letters (for example, c:), then the mode is minor. Since there is no figured bass following the Roman numerals in this exercise, it can be assumed that all of the chords are in root position. Remember that uppercase Roman numerals with the plus sign indicate augmented triads, while lowercase Roman numerals with the superscript circle signify diminished triads.

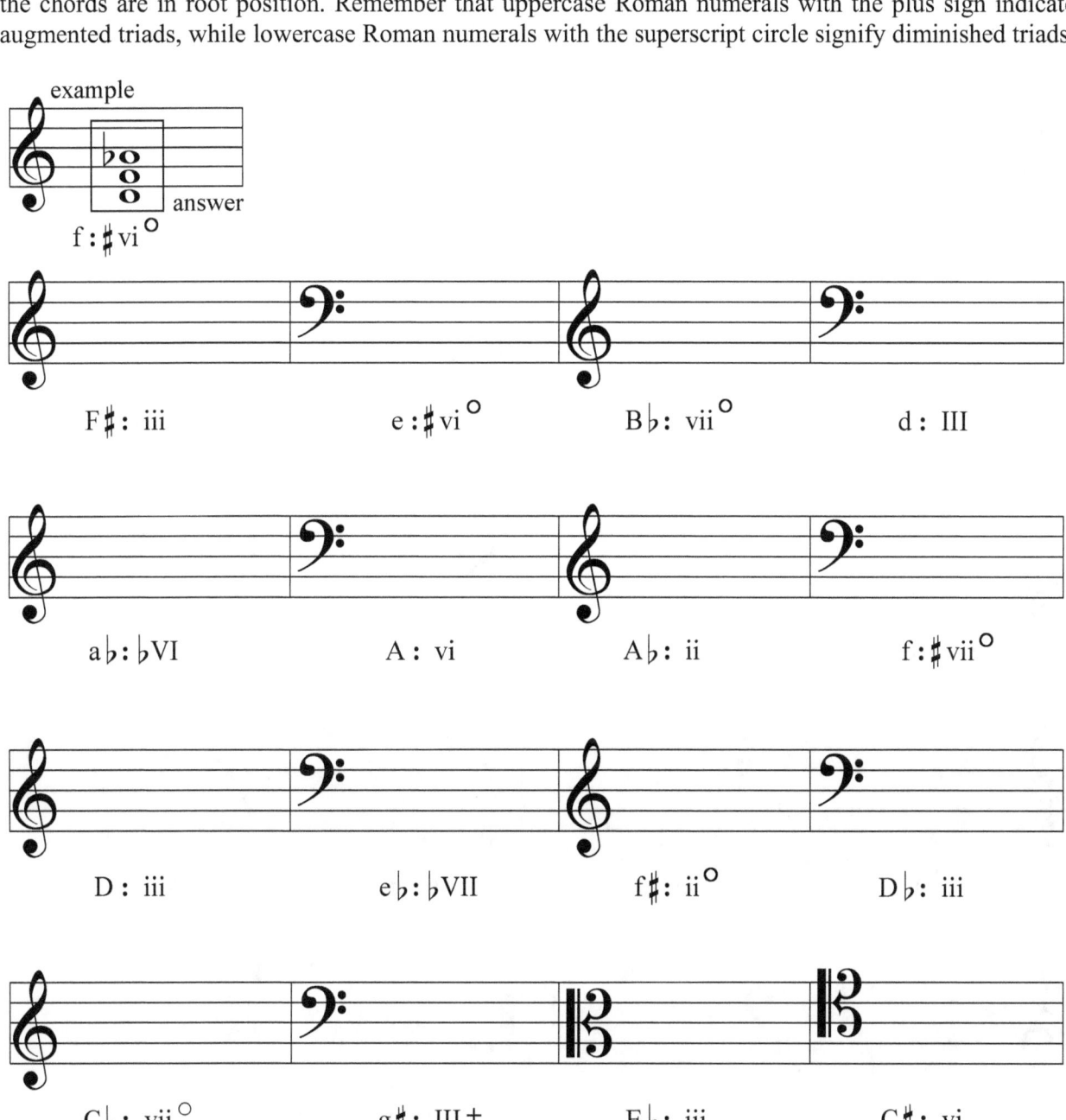

Worksheet 8–14

Name _____

Chapter 8: Triads

Given the key, mode, clef, and chord symbol, construct the appropriate triad. Use whole notes for your answers. Note carefully that if the key is presented with uppercase letters (for example, C:), then the mode is major. If, however, the key is expressed with lowercase letters (for example, c:), then the mode is minor. Since there is no figured bass following the Roman numerals in this exercise, it can be assumed that all of the chords are in root position. Remember that uppercase Roman numerals with the plus sign indicate augmented triads, while lowercase Roman numerals with the superscript circle signify diminished triads.

Worksheet 8–15

Name _____

Chapter 8: Triads

Given the key, mode, clef, chord symbol, and figured bass, construct the appropriate triad. Use whole notes for your answers. As stated in Chapter 8, whenever a Roman numeral represents a triad in root position, it is not necessary to use figured bass to indicate the chord position; for the absence of $^5_3$ implies that the chord is in root position. Whenever a Roman numeral represents a triad in $^6_3$ position, it is not necessary to include 3 under 6. With the $^6_4$ position, however, 4 below 6 cannot be omitted because then the figured bass for the first and second inversions would be indistinguishable.

Worksheet 8–16

Name _____

Chapter 8: Triads

Given the key, mode, clef, chord symbol, and figured bass, construct the appropriate triad. Use whole notes for your answers. As stated in Chapter 8, whenever a Roman numeral represents a triad in root position, it is not necessary to use figured bass to indicate the chord position; for the absence of $^5_3$ implies that the chord is in root position. Whenever a Roman numeral represents a triad in $^6_3$ position, it is not necessary to include 3 under 6. With the $^6_4$ position, however, 4 below 6 cannot be omitted because then the figured bass for the first and second inversions would be indistinguishable.

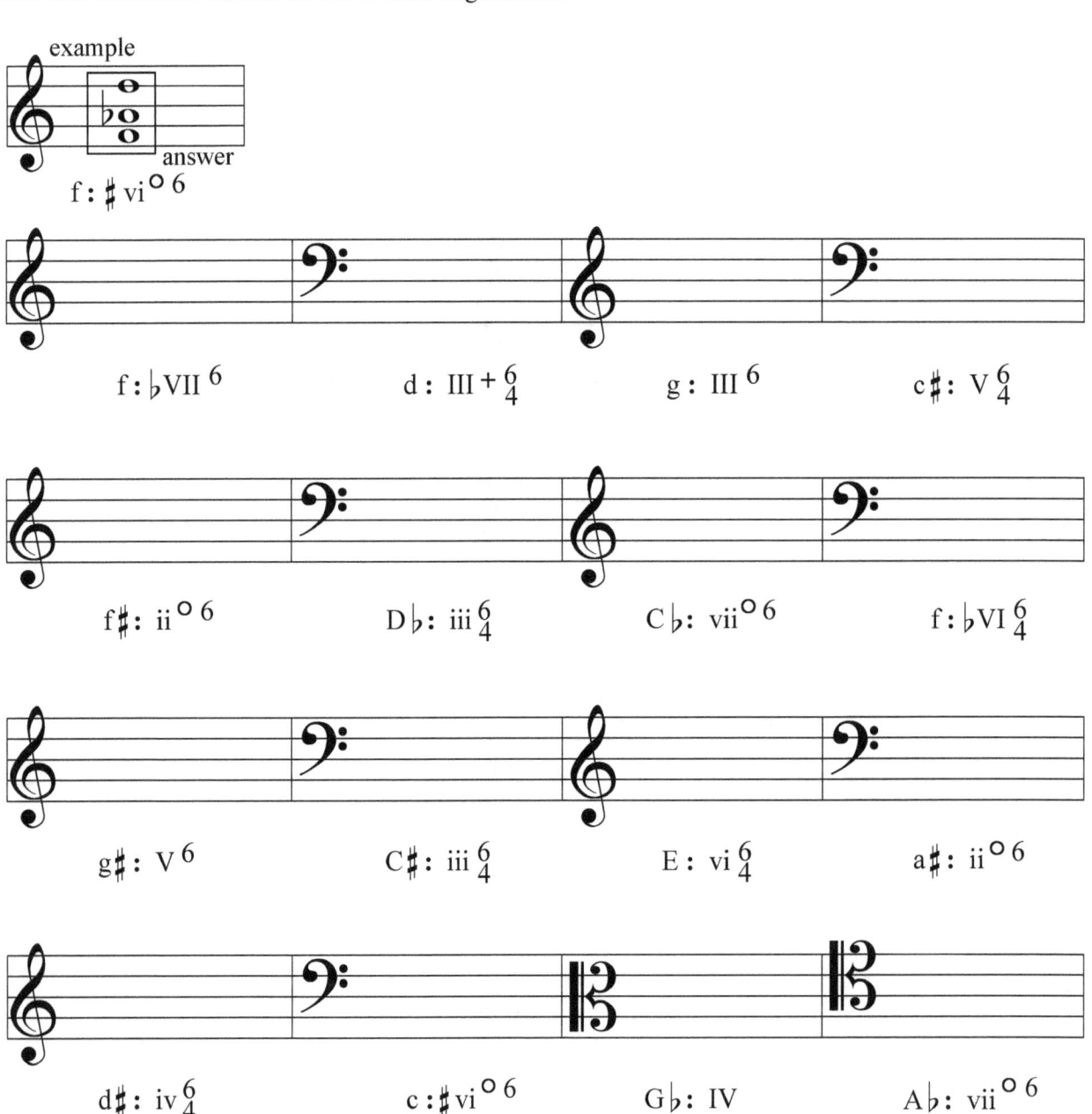

Worksheet 8–17

Name _____

Chapter 8: Triads

Given the key, mode, clef, chord symbol, and figured bass, construct the appropriate triad. Use whole notes for your answers. As stated in Chapter 8, whenever a Roman numeral represents a triad in root position, it is not necessary to use figured bass to indicate the chord position; for the absence of $^5_3$ implies that the chord is in root position. Whenever a Roman numeral represents a triad in $^6_3$ position, it is not necessary to include 3 under 6. With the $^6_4$ position, however, 4 below 6 cannot be omitted because then the figured bass for the first and second inversions would be indistinguishable.

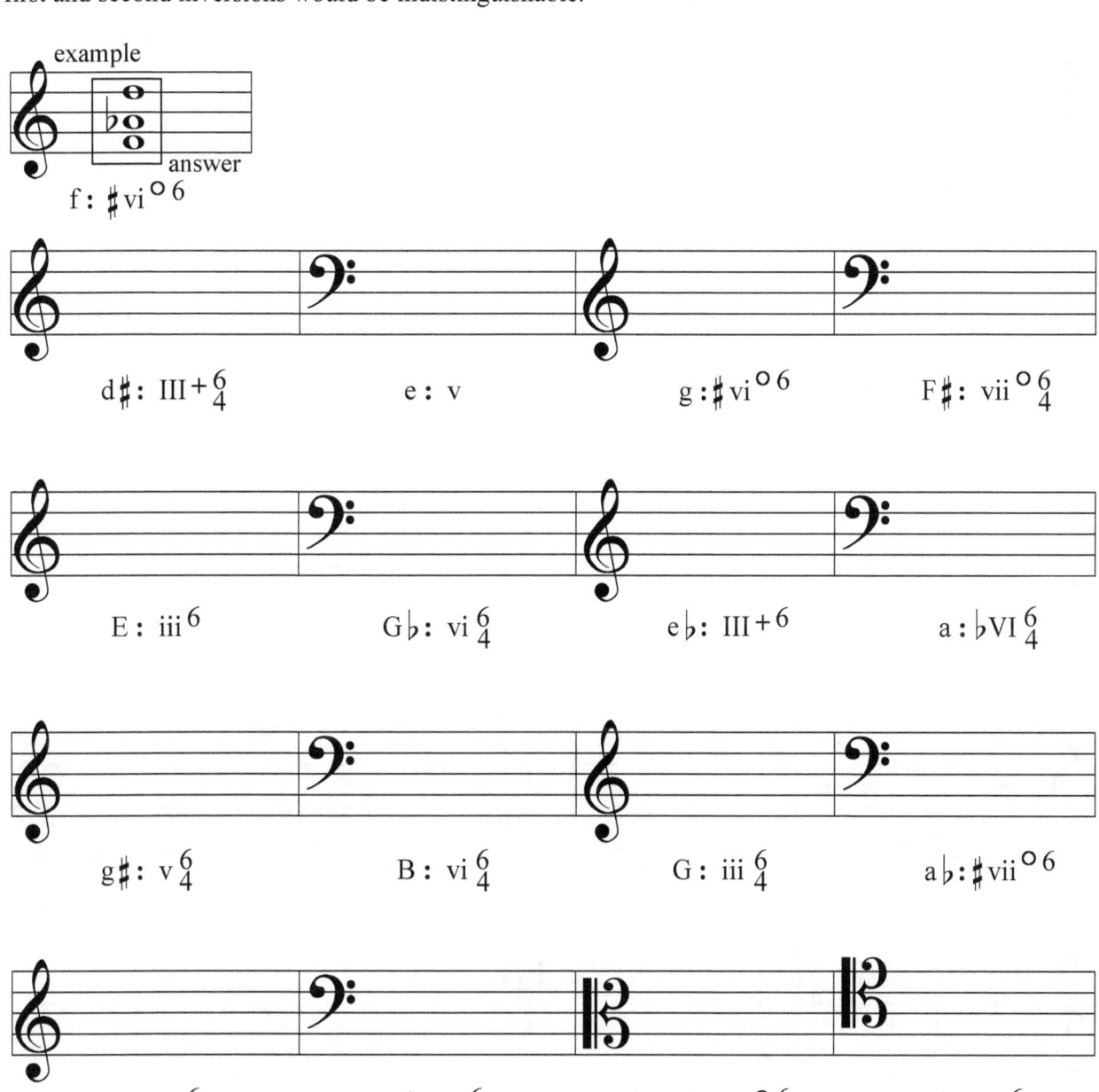

Worksheet 8–18

Name _____

Chapter 8: Triads

Given the key, mode, clef, chord symbol, and figured bass, construct the appropriate triad. Use whole notes for your answers. As stated in Chapter 8, whenever a Roman numeral represents a triad in root position, it is not necessary to use figured bass to indicate the chord position; for the absence of $^5_3$ implies that the chord is in root position. Whenever a Roman numeral represents a triad in $^6_3$ position, it is not necessary to include 3 under 6. With the $^6_4$ position, however, 4 below 6 cannot be omitted because then the figured bass for the first and second inversions would be indistinguishable.

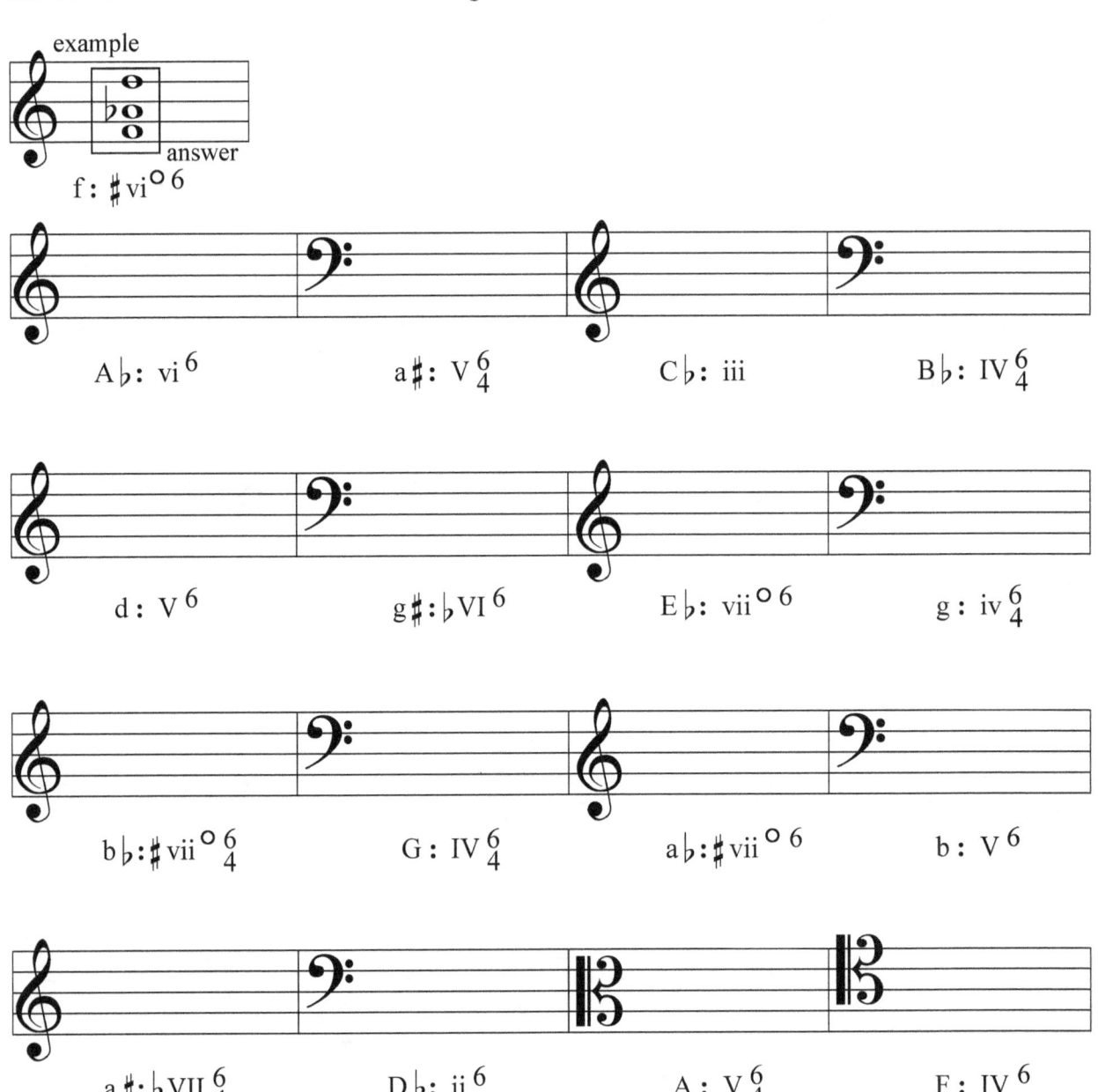

Worksheet 8–19

Name _____

Chapter 8: Triads

Identify the elements of the given open-structure triad exactly as in the example: circle the root or roots; mark the bass element as either R (root), 3 (third), or 5 (fifth); indicate the chord position with figured bass ($^5_3$ or $^6_3$ or $^6_4$); designate the chord quality using the abbreviations MT (major triad), mt (minor triad), d º t (diminished triad), or A + T (augmented triad).

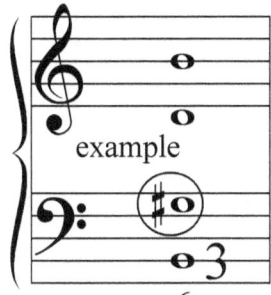

position: $^6_3$

quality: d º t

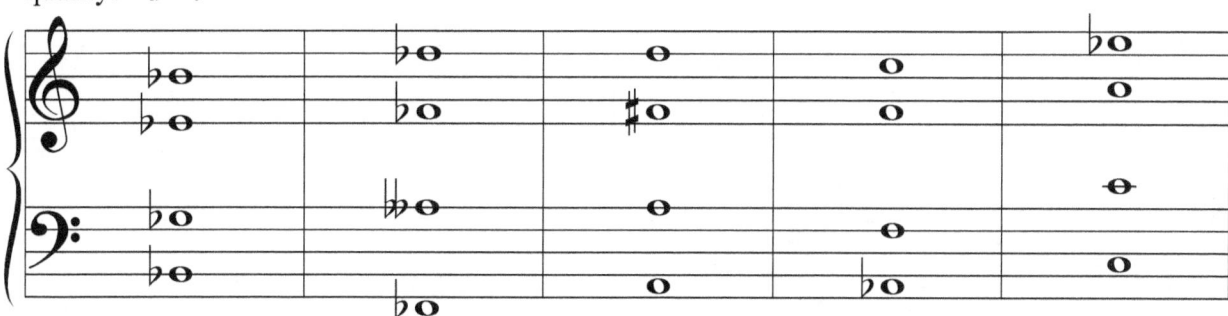

position:

quality:

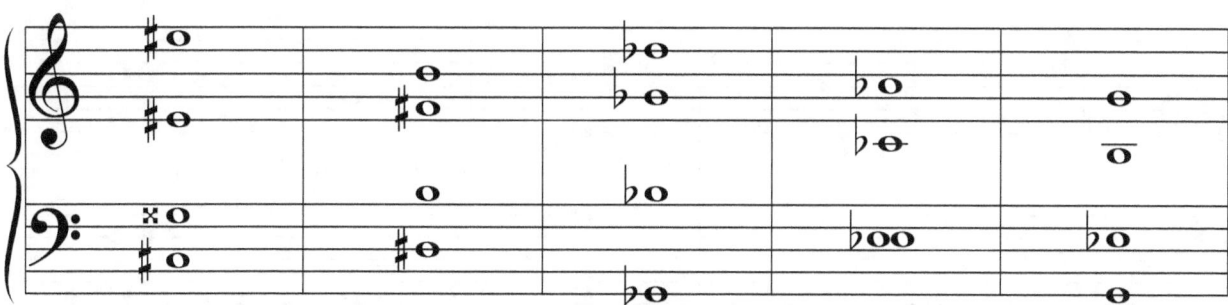

position:

quality:

Worksheet 8–20

Name _____

Chapter 8: Triads

Identify the elements of the given open-structure triad exactly as in the example: circle the root or roots; mark the bass element as either R (root), 3 (third), or 5 (fifth); indicate the chord position with figured bass ($^5_3$ or $^6_3$ or $^6_4$); designate the chord quality using the abbreviations MT (major triad), mt (minor triad), d °t (diminished triad), or A + T (augmented triad).

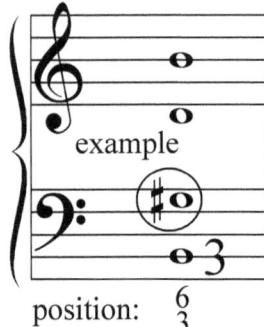

position: $^6_3$

quality: d °t

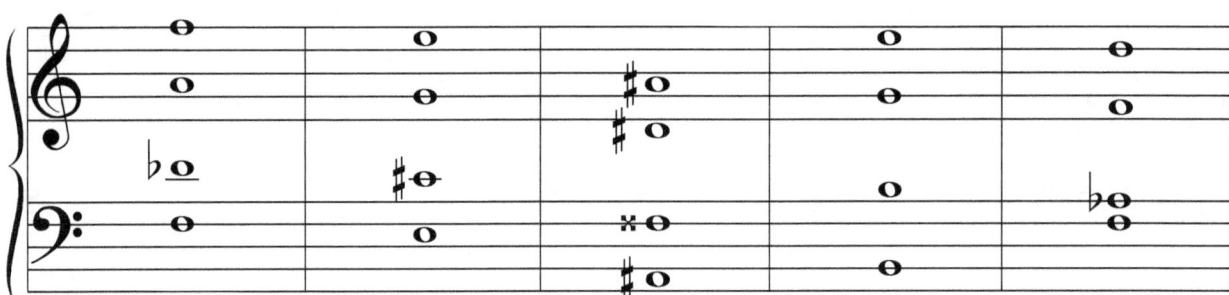

position:

quality:

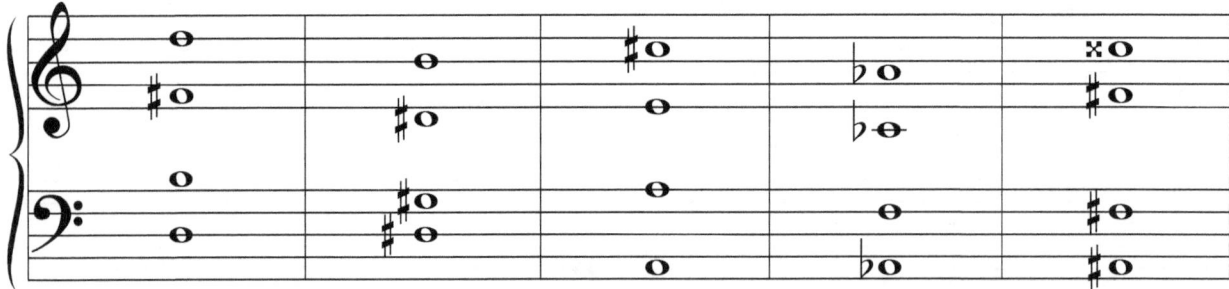

position:

quality:

Worksheet 8–21

Name _____

Chapter 8: Triads

Identify the elements of the given open-structure triad exactly as in the example: circle the root or roots; mark the bass element as either R (root), 3 (third), or 5 (fifth); indicate the chord position with figured bass ($^5_3$ or $^6_3$ or $^6_4$); designate the chord quality using the abbreviations MT (major triad), mt (minor triad), d $^\circ$ t (diminished triad), or A + T (augmented triad).

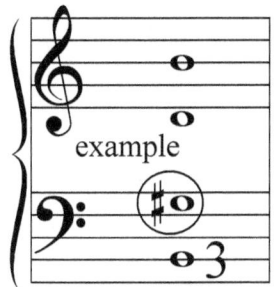

position: $^6_3$

quality: d $^\circ$ t

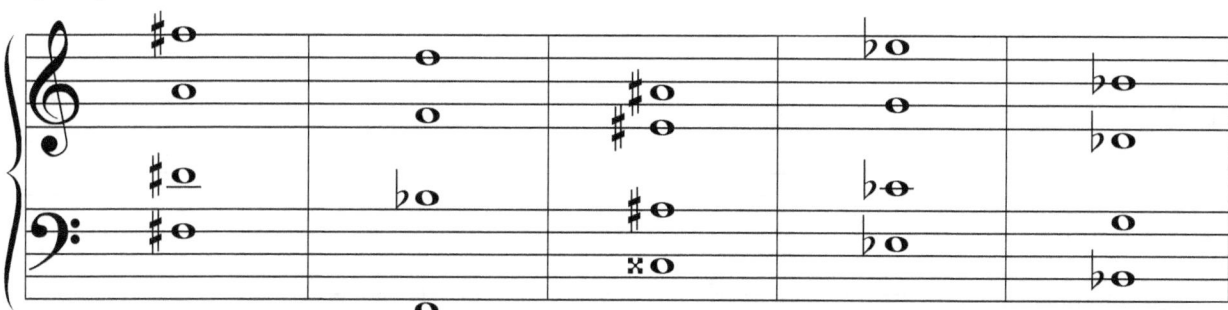

position:

quality:

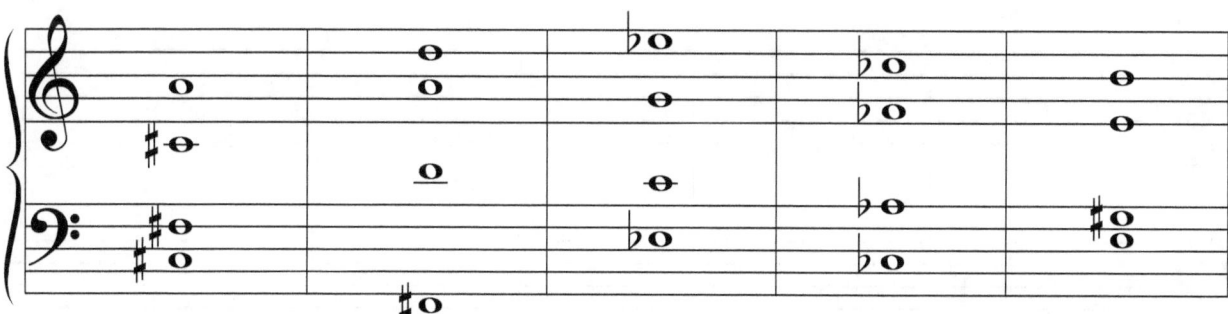

position:

quality:

Worksheet 8–22

Name _____

Chapter 8: Triads

Given the key, mode, clef, chord symbol, and figured bass, construct the appropriate triad in open structure. Use whole notes for your answers. Remember that in textures with four voices in open-structure, there should be at least one octave between the soprano and tenor voices. The soprano, alto, and tenor voices are spaced so that a chord tone can be placed between either the soprano and alto, alto and tenor, or between both pairs of voices. There should be no more than one octave between adjacent voices except between the tenor and bass. Review the doubling principles presented in Chapter 8 before attempting this exercise (see above, p. 158).

a: ♯vii°6

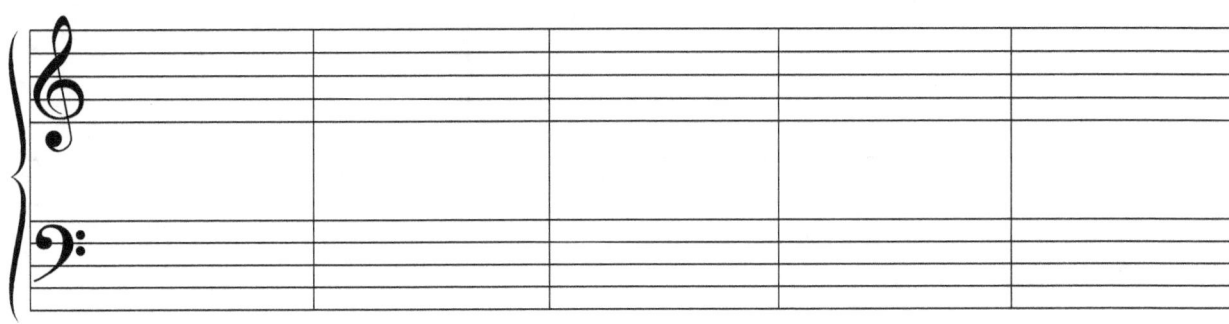

d: iv$^6_4$ B♭: iii   G♭: vii°6   c♯: ii°6   a♭: V^6

E: vi$^6_4$ a♯: ♯vii°6   d♯: V$^6_4$ A: IV   e♭: III+^{6}

Worksheet 8–23

Name _____

Chapter 8: Triads

Given the key, mode, clef, chord symbol, and figured bass, construct the appropriate triad in open structure. Use whole notes for your answers. Remember that in textures with four voices in open-structure, there should be at least one octave between the soprano and tenor voices. The soprano, alto, and tenor voices are spaced so that a chord tone can be placed between either the soprano and alto, alto and tenor, or between both pairs of voices. There should be no more than one octave between adjacent voices except between the tenor and bass. Review the doubling principles presented in Chapter 8 before attempting this exercise (see above, p. 158).

a: ♯vii°6

C♭: vi6   A♭: vii°6   d♯: III+6   f: ♭VII 6/4   c♯: IV 6/4

e: v6   F♯: ii6   g♯: V 6/4   D♭: iii6   b: ♭VI 6/4

Worksheet 8–24

Name _____

Chapter 8: Triads

Given the key, mode, clef, chord symbol, and figured bass, construct the appropriate triad in open structure. Use whole notes for your answers. Remember that in textures with four voices in open-structure, there should be at least one octave between the soprano and tenor voices. The soprano, alto, and tenor voices are spaced so that a chord tone can be placed between either the soprano and alto, alto and tenor, or between both pairs of voices. There should be no more than one octave between adjacent voices except between the tenor and bass. Review the doubling principles presented in Chapter 8 before attempting this exercise (see above, p. 158).

a : ♯vii°6

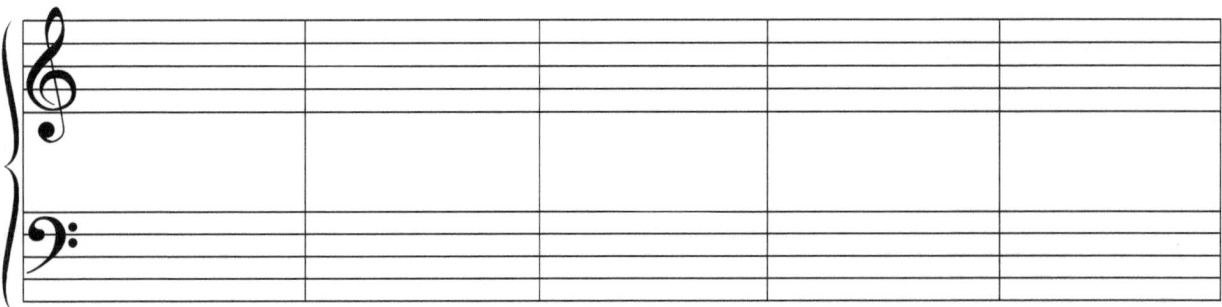

a : ♭VII 6   E♭ : ii 6/4   c♯ : ♯vii°6   F : iii 6   D♭ : I 6/4

D : vi 6   g♯ : IV 6/4   e♭ : ♭VI 6/4   C♭ : V 6   a♯ : ♯vi°6

Worksheet 8–25

Name _____

Chapter 8: Triads

Given the key, mode, clef, chord symbol, and figured bass, construct the appropriate triad in open structure. Use whole notes for your answers. Remember that in textures with four voices in open-structure, there should be at least one octave between the soprano and tenor voices. The soprano, alto, and tenor voices are spaced so that a chord tone can be placed between either the soprano and alto, alto and tenor, or between both pairs of voices. There should be no more than one octave between adjacent voices except between the tenor and bass. Review the doubling principles presented in Chapter 8 before attempting this exercise (see above, p. 158).

a : ♯vii°6

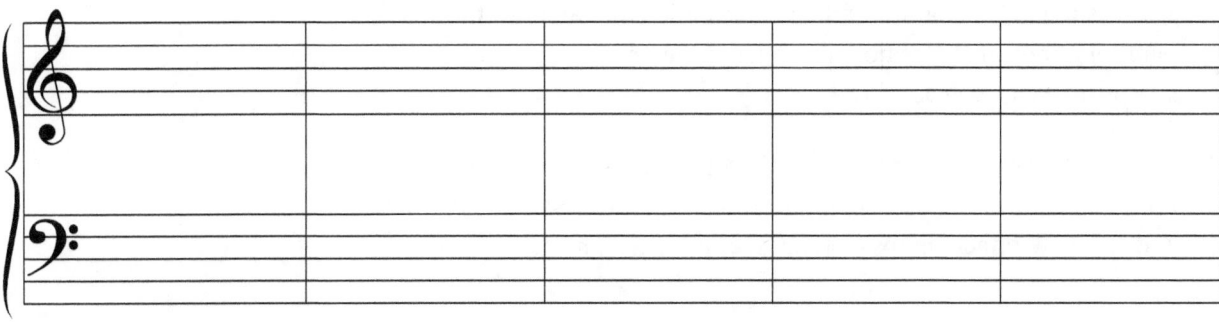

A♭: IV6   B♭: vi 6/4   d: V6   B: vii°6   g: ♯vi°6

f: ♭VI6   c♯: ♭VII 6/4   E♭: iii6   b♭: III+6   C♭: ii 6/4

Worksheet 8–26

Name _____

Chapter 8: Triads

A Minor Challenge (and Review)

1. What is the relative major of e♭ minor? (give the name of key)   1. _____

2. What is the parallel major of b minor? (give the name of key)   2. _____

3. What minor key signature has four sharps? (give the name of key)   3. _____

4. What key is the relative minor of the parallel major of 3. above? (give the name of key)   4. _____

5. What is the key signature of the parallel minor of G♯ major? (give the number and stipulate either sharps or flats, such as: 2♯, 4♭, etc.)   5. _____

6. What is the key signature of the relative minor of C♭ major? (give the number and stipulate either sharps or flats, such as: 2♯, 4♭, etc.)   6. _____

7. What is the key signature of the relative minor of the parallel Major of e♭ minor? (give the number and stipulate either sharps or flats, such as: 2♯, 4♭, etc.)   7. _____

8. What is the key signature of the relative major of the parallel minor of F♯ major? (give the number and stipulate either sharps or flats, such as 2♯, 4♭, etc.)   8. _____

9. What is the key signature of the enharmonic equivalent of the parallel minor of B♯ major? (give the number and stipulate either sharps or flats, such as: 2♯, 4♭, etc.)   9. _____

10. What is the key signature of the enharmonic equivalent of the relative major of the parallel minor of C♭ major? (give the number and stipulate either sharps or flats, such as: 2♯, 4♭, etc.)   10. _____

Worksheet 8–27

Name _____

Chapter 8: Triads

A Minor Challenge (and Review)

1. What is the relative major of f♯ minor? (give the name of key) 1. _____

2. What is the parallel major of e♭ minor? (give the name of key) 2. _____

3. What key signature a♯ minor? (give the number and stipulate either sharps or flats, such as: 2♯, 4♭, etc.) 3. _____

4. What key signature b♭ minor? (give the number and stipulate either sharps or flats, such as: 2♯, 4♭, etc.) 4. _____

5. What is the key signature of the parallel minor of F♯ major? (give the number and stipulate either sharps or flats, such as: 2♯, 4♭, etc.) 5. _____

6. What is the key signature of the relative minor of B♭ major? (give the number and stipulate either sharps or flats, such as: 2♯, 4♭, etc.) 6. _____

7. What is the key signature of the relative minor of the parallel major of a♭ minor? (give the number and stipulate either sharps or flats, such as: 2♯, 4♭, etc.) 7. _____

8. What is the key signature of the relative major of the parallel minor of C major? (give the number and stipulate either sharps or flats, such as 2♯, 4♭, etc.) 8. _____

9. What is the key signature of the relative major of the parallel minor of G major? (give the number and stipulate either sharps or flats, such as: 2♯, 4♭, etc.) 9. _____

10. What is the key signature of the enharmonic equivalent of the parallel minor of D♭ major? (give the number and stipulate either sharps or flats, such as: 2♯, 4♭, etc.) 10. _____

Worksheet 8–28

Name _____

Chapter 8: Triads

Meter and Rhythm

Given the following meter, place bar lines in the proper places and write the counts directly under the appropriate note or rest. Do not forget to write in the bar line at the end of the final measure.

example

in 5: 1 + a 2 e + a 3 e + a 4 + a 5 + a   1 e +   2 e + a 3 e + a 4(e)+a 5   +

in 5: _____

in 5: _____

in 5: _____

www.ingramcontent.com/pod-product-compliance
Lightning Source LLC
Chambersburg PA
CBHW081344230426
43667CB00017B/2719